DATABASE MACHINES AND DATABASE MANAGEMENT

Esen Ozkarahan
Arizona State University

Prentice-Hall, Inc.
Englewood Cliffs, N.J. 07632

Library of Congress Cataloging-in-Publication Data

Ozkarahan, Esen (date)
   Database machines and database management.

   Bibliography: p.
   Includes index.
   1. Database management.   2. Electronic digital
computers.   I. Title.
QA76.9.D3095 1986   005.74   85-12277
   ISBN 0-13-196031-8

Editorial/production supervision
 and interior design: Tracey L. Orbine
Cover design: Whitman Studio, Inc.
Manufacturing buyer: Gordon Osbourne

ISBN 0-13-196031-8 01

Prentice-Hall International (UK) Limited, *London*
Prentice-Hall of Australia Pty. Limited, *Sydney*
Prentice-Hall Canada Inc., *Toronto*
Prentice-Hall Hispanoamericana, S.A., *Mexico*
Prentice-Hall of India Private Limited, *New Delhi*
Prentice-Hall of Japan, Inc., *Tokyo*
Prentice-Hall of Southeast Asia Pte. Ltd., *Singapore*
Editora Prentice-Hall do Brasil, Ltda., *Rio de Janeiro*
Whitehall Books Limited, *Wellington, New Zealand*

To Irem, Aysin, Goksin, and my parents

CONTENTS

Chapter 2 *DBMS-I* 20

Chapter 3 *DBMS-II* 66

Chapter 6 *ASSOCIATIVE PROCESSORS 183*

Chapter 7 *DATABASE MACHINE SURVEY 224*

Chapter 9 **DATABASE MACHINE SOFTWARE** *367*

Chapter 10 **DISTRIBUTED DATABASES** *408*

Chapter 11 **DATABASE MACHINE PERFORMANCE** *453*

Chapter 13 **DOCUMENT (TEXT) RETRIEVAL COMPUTERS 530**

APPENDICES 573

Appendix I **RAP DBMS ASSEMBLER LANGUAGE UNIX VERSION 575**

Appendix II **RAP GDBMS SYSTEMS AND ITS HIERARCHICAL AND NETWORK DATA LANGUAGES 595**

PREFACE

Computers were first conceived to meet the needs of research groups in performing very special computational tasks, but it was not long before their usage became more widespread. Nowadays, computers are involved in all facets of everyday life—in commerce, in industry, in households, and in public services. This evolution, or rather explosion, of computer usage arose mainly from the fact that computers have found application increasingly in nonnumeric applications, that is, those applications lying beyond numerical computation, for example, in the area of document and fact storage, retrieval, and manipulation. As memory, the prime component of a stored program computer, is reducing continually in cost, following the rapid advances in integrated circuit technology, computer hardware is becoming dramatically less and less expensive. It is this fact which allows the present exponential growth of the nonnumeric applications of computers.

As nonnumeric tasks came to dominate the use of numeric computers, it became obvious that conventional computer organizations were inadequate. The typical von Neumann processor, while organizationally unsuited to nonnumeric problems, was challenged to operate at speeds which approach the ultimate limits of technology. As this disparity of tool and task became more obvious, alternatives were sought incorporating parallel, associative, and associative/parallel architectures. There have been numerous proposals, some of which have been constructed as experimental and/or full-scale prototypes for use as research tools or for very special military applications. Thus the literature of nonnumeric processors, that is, of parallel and/or associative processors, has grown to its present stage. Numerous combinations of new architectures have been explored, and each new and interesting approach to a logic or system design has resulted in large numbers of research publications.

With the evolution of nonnumeric processing, other changes have occurred. As it began to evolve naturally, the field of nonnumeric processor design was dominated at first by toolmakers, by electrical engineers, and by physicists. These designers tried their best to reach out and solve the problems of the users or the users' advocate, the computer scientist. However, while electrical engineers succeeded in introducing novel architectures and logic designs, they did not reach the heart of the matter in solving the problems of nonnumeric processing.

This was quite natural for two major reasons: first, the problem evolved in such a way as to require the interdisciplinary effort of the electrical engineer and the computer scientists; second, database management, which came to represent a major focus of nonnumeric processing, became an important part of computer science, a very young and newly developing field. In fact, it is with database management that many ad hoc techniques of early electronic data processing are now finding a theoretical basis as new disciplines evolve and as needs and guidelines are set. With the introduction of modern database management systems (DBMS), where very large volumes of integrated and/or distributed databases are shared among concurrent users each demanding consistent data, efficient performance, and real-time response, it is quite natural to observe that new concepts in data management are evolving. Several data models have been developed to describe the varying needs of different types of users. Each involves a query or data manipulation language. Each provides, for its special purpose, an efficient database management system. Each is now much in demand.

However, it has been discovered that for such systems working with high volumes of data, the structure of a von Neumann uniprocessor is a great handicap to the provision of data consistency and efficient real-time response. Because of their concern for the ultimate need for computational speed for achieving high throughput, early designers introduced parallel and/or associative architecture alternatives to the uniprocessor machine.

At this point, we can return to the argument that the field of nonnumeric processor design needs a change of perspective. To get to the heart of the matter (that is, to the roots of the problems of modern DBMS), the person on whose shoulders the problem has fallen, that is, the computer scientist, must be broadly equipped, even with electrical engineering experience if possible. Such an individual properly acquainted with the problems, can exert some control in the field originally created by designers and can tailor the architecture and processor logic to fit his or her needs exactly. In very recent studies, some parallel and/or associative processors have been designed with this new perspective. These processors are now referred to by the generally accepted term *database machines*.

Database machines support one or more data models directly and have an instruction repertoire in machine language that supports the needs of database management in general. Such needs involve data definition and storage, retrieval, manipulation, and special functions. Although the term *database machine* has acquired other shades of meaning including even a software virtual search machine or some modification or combination of conventional (e.g., von Neumann) architectures for doing database management, the most general use of the term fits the description given. By being a subdiscipline (not withstanding the possibilities of its flourishing ultimately as a discipline itself), database machines must confront a host of basic problems in computer design, implementation, and performance. Although the field is very new and although a text is most easily written after a field has thoroughly matured, the author, by being an early designer of a complete database machine, is committed to the importance of presenting a manuscript that would meet the requirements of both a reference and textbook in this young field. It is hoped that this work will assist in focusing and directing the efforts of researchers in the field, to inform those interested and, most important, to provide tools and guidance for the growing legions of future users.

TO THE READER AND INSTRUCTOR

In the preface, I have tried to emphasize the interdisciplinary nature of the field of database machines and the incompleteness of the early work especially in database machines due to lack of the prerequisite knowledge in the field. While the wide interdisciplinary nature of the field helped it to develop rather fast, there have been certain discrepancies in the process. This can be exemplified by the missing or loose ends of some published work or lack of justification of certain designs. It has been an almost established pattern to see some sort of *buck-passing* between the disciplines. That is, we either see a software-heavy (and sometimes strong) paper lacking architectural justification or, similarly, a strong architecture (a tool) design without much software background and motivation. The reason for this buck-passing, which we can best summarize with the following caricature, is the lack of proper database machine education whose definition follows. The proper database machine education must contain a well-balanced knowledge of both software and hardware in nonnumeric processing. Because nonnumeric processing entails database management, document databases,

Passing the 'buck'

deductive databases, and other relative concepts, we should be equipped with the adequate knowledge of these fields for the software background and also be equipped with the knowledge of basic and non–von Neumann–type architectures, memory technology, and digital systems. This text, albeit not perfect, is a pioneering attempt to presenting an exposure for such an education. Because of this, it can be used as a text or as a reference book in the fields of database machines/computers, database management, information (document) retrieval, and computer architecture. However, for complete assimilation, a two-semester coverage may be more appropriate (e.g., starting with a senior undergraduate course and finishing at the graduate level).

The best way to study this text is to read it completely in the order it is presented. However, those readers with adequate knowledge in database management and design can skip Chapters 2 and 3. Also, those readers who are interested only in formatted databases can skip Chapters 12 and 13. The following outlines, very briefly, the layout of the text.

Chapter 1 is an introduction that motivates the need for new hardware architectures for database management as well as nonnumeric processing in general. We contrast the well-known bottlenecks of the von Neumann architecture with the basic architectural needs of nonnumeric processing and then give basic definitions of database machines and define their expected software personalities and hardware functionalities needed to support the former. We then make an assessment of the possible developments for the future.

Chapters 2 and 3 provide the necessary database management knowledge. Chapter 2 introduces database management and related basic mathematical notions and then covers the three popular data models: hierarchies, networks, and relations. In this chapter, the data structural and related specific properties of these data models are discussed. This discussion includes some relational database theory such as relational algebra and design concepts relating to schema design, such as normalization and lossless joins. Chapter 3 carries on with the data model theory and covers operational aspects of the models discussed in the previous chapter. This includes data selection and manipulation by relating them to specific data language or languages per model. The chapter covers issues of security and integrity, which includes concurrency. Since I believe that the basic concepts of theory and software must be well knit together with the concepts in architecture, I felt that the inclusion of these chapters in the text was essential. In fact, as the reader goes through the other chapters, it will be easy to see the homogeneous dispersion of these necessary knowledge ingredients of the new computer architectures in the topics covered.

In **Chapter 4,** the emphasis is on parallelism and pipelining, with the examples of these concepts found in numeric processing. We briefly review how parallelism of computations are exploited and we also discuss the resulting speed-ups. The chapter includes discussion of implementations both in array processing and pipelining. Because similar concepts are needed in nonnumeric processing, this chapter is relevant for the rest of the text.

In **Chapter 5,** we start introducing the architectural concepts that are specific to nonnumeric processing. In that regard we devote this chapter to associative memories, their various types, and the basic search primitives executed on them.

In **Chapter 6,** we move to associative processors. Again, we categorize the types of various systems and present their basic primitives. We then discuss various system design and implementations varying from the early designs to the most recent ones. The problem of I/O bottleneck is first introduced in this chapter. Following that, the secondary memory–based associative processors and I/O interfacing are discussed.

In **Chapter 7,** we survey the majority of the database machine designs and implementations published in the international media. The survey is presented under the categories of cellular associative systems, multiprocessor-based systems, in-stream and/or pipeline processing, logic-enhanced primary memory (VLSI) systems, filters, and commercial database machines. Since a total detailed coverage would both duplicate the published literature and also make this chapter alone grow into a textbook, our emphasis was to remain at the unique features and concepts of the systems involved and provide background for the subsequent chapters.

In **Chapter 8,** we make an attempt to identify and outline fundamental problems relating to database machines in an effort to set the groundwork for future research to be called database machine theory. By doing this we hope to add to the discussion of individual implementations a new direction in fundamental research in database machine theory.

Chapter 9 discusses database machine software. The chapter is organized to cover system software, high-level language and other desirable software personalities, and multimodel DBMSs supported by database machines.

Chapter 10 covers issues of distributed databases including query execution and concurrency. The emphasis of this chapter is to relate the concepts of distributed database architectures to database machine architectures for the simple reason that the future of distributed databases will be built upon the latter.

In **Chapter 11,** we discuss the important issue of database machine performance. Our approach to this issue is not to present individual studies made for specific systems, but rather provide the basic ingredients to database machine performance modeling. And this is done in such a way as to remain time independent.

In **Chapter 12,** we cover the basic issues of document (text) retrieval. The chapter summarizes the important concepts and know-how related to unformatted databases in an effort to bring together various facets of nonnumeric processing. This looks more natural if we also consider the make up of text retrieval hardware proposed to date. It is not only that database machines and text retrieval computers have a lot in common, but that office information systems of the future will rely heavily on the integration of DBMS and IR (information (document)) retrieval.

Chapter 13 concludes the book by discussing architectures of the text retrieval computers. While various unique features of the text retrieval hardware

are discussed, such as various finite state machines, we also make an attempt to present an integrated DBMS/IR architecture with hardware support.

In the appendices, we present the syntax of various software that are available. They are the RAP assembler language, LSL and MRI language translators, and an ANSI/SPARC DBMS software that combines the previous three with the addition of a conceptual data modeling facility and the integrated context sensitive full text retrieval capability. These software are made available to interested readers so that they may have hands-on experience with DBMS, ANSI/SPARC-based DBMS, full text retrieval, and associative/parallel and tag (mark)-based database machine programming.

ACKNOWLEDGMENTS

This text came into being with the help of various individuals to whom I am grateful. Especially, I would like to thank Diane Karr (of Intel) for her assistance in editing, Ching-Min Lai for his great patience in entering the text for word processing, Pat Moss and Sheah-Jen Hu for their assistance at various stages of word processing, all students of the CSC591 Database Machines class (spring 1984–85 semester) at ASU for screening the text for technical accuracy, and Chuck Moser and Bill Moreno (of Intel) for their artwork. Thanks are also due to all my colleagues at the University of Toronto (starting with Professor K. C. Smith): METU, ASU, and Intel; and my former students who got involved in the RAP database machine project whose work is presented as one of the many covered in the text. I would also like to thank my editor, Jim Fegen, of Prentice-Hall, for his encouragement and trust in the development of this text.

Esen Ozkarahan
Arizona State University

names of employees who are younger than 35 years of age and whose salary is $40,000.

1.3 LOCATION VERSUS ASSOCIATIVE ADDRESSING

The differences in the way data entities are conceptualized and their individual members personalized have made a difference in the way we have built computers from the very beginning (and we know of no other way yet—at least not commercially). In other words, the way the memory units are built and the way that the central processing unit addresses memory contents are all determined by numeric processing. Before we proceed, consider the following examples:

Example 1.1

```
    DO 10 I= 1,10
 10 A(I) = A(I) + X * B(I)
```

Example 1.2

```
    SELECT NAME
    FROM EMPLOYEE
    WHERE AGE < 35 AND SALARY = 40,000
```

The way to address the arrays (vectors) A and B in the FORTRAN example is to determine the array address and use the value of I as an index to the individual elements, just as the program is written. Similarly, the value of variable X is retrieved by using the variable name, X, as the label (or entity address). The von Neumann computer architecture was built to suit the way that data are addressed in computer programs such as the one in Example 1.1. This meant that the memory had to be accessed by first determining the beginning location. In other words, the memory location of a data element is determined by finding out the starting address (beginning of the array or memory) and the relative offset of the individual data element and by decoding the sum of these quantities in the access mechanism.

The von Neumann computer architecture is composed of five main functional units, namely, the memory unit, the control unit, the arithmetic/logic unit (the previous two are also referred to as the central processing unit, CPU), the input unit, and the output unit. This is still the architecture of present-day-computers. Although this basic architecture has remained the same, the use of computers has shifted mainly toward nonnumeric processing. To elaborate further, let us go back to Example 1.2. Unlike the way in which Example 1.1 addresses data, Example 1.2 is requesting names of employees based on the contents of the attributes (fields) age and salary. This is different from the way in which elements (fields) of arrays A and B are addressed. The addressing scheme of Example 1.2 is referred to as *associative reference* or *associative addressing*. Thus far, we have not said anything about the way in which the memory unit should be built for this new type of addressing. We are not ready to propose a model yet. However, regardless of the type of memory, associative addressing in programs has become a fact. If we ignore the old file programs that accomplished associative addressing implicitly buried in their logic, most of the programming in computer science uses and depends upon nothing but associative addressing. This is natural both semantically (we think of personalities) and physically (how can we provide location address of every piece of data?).

1.4 PARALLEL PROCESSING

We now have established the notion of associative addressing. Let us think a bit more about nonnumeric processing. We already noted that nonnumeric processing usually involves huge amounts of data. Let us think what we may do with that data by listing some applications:

(a) We may give a salary raise to all employees of a company.
(b) A bank computes interest on balances of all the saving accounts.
(c) All inventory items are updated in a warehouse.
(d) A given abstract is searched in all the texts of a library or a bibliographic retrieval system.
(e) A given description of a contract is searched in all legal files.
(f) A given patent application is searched for a possible duplicate in the related patent files.

Besides these examples, we can also mention other set-oriented processing such as matrix operations, vector processing, or solution of simultaneous equations in numeric computing. Similar to the examples given in (a) through (f), we can see an inherent orderliness and repetition in these tasks. We can easily see that most of the time-consuming tasks in both numeric and nonnumeric processing can efficiently exploit parallelism in the sense of repeating the same operation on groups of data where groups are processed by identical processors (one or more per group) simultaneously (i.e., in parallel). Parallelism is a natural fit for set-oriented processing. What has happened up to the present, instead, is that we have tried to meet the needs of associative addressing and parallelism by the von Neumann computer, which is a uniprocessor utilizing location addressing on its memory. Let us further elaborate the limitations of the von Neumann architecture.

1.5 BOTTLENECKS OF THE VON NEUMANN ARCHITECTURE

1.5.1 Processor Bottleneck

Let us conceptualize the memory in the von Neumann architecture as a single-level entity as shown in Figure 1.1. In reality, we have a hierarchical structure

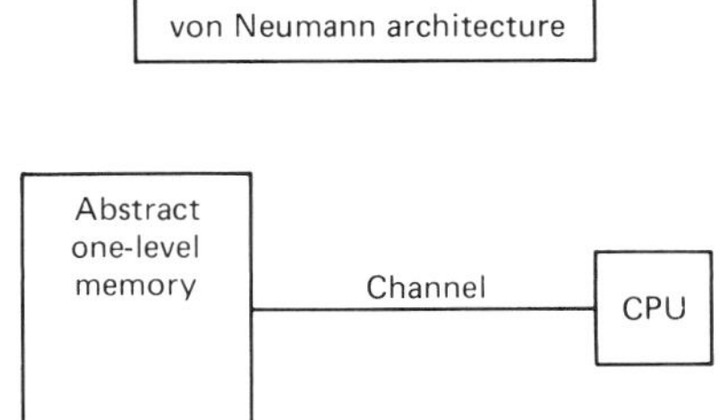

Figure 1.1 Memory versus CPU in the von Neumann architecture.

covering a span starting from the main memory down to the slow mass memories. Logically, however, they all store the instances of the data entity we want to process. As far as the processing is concerned, all the data must be brought to the CPU through a channel and searched or compared for eligibility, and if eligibility is met, the required computation is made and the result sent back via the channel either to be output or updated on their respective storage.

As can be seen, all the data, which is enormous in quantity, must be handled by a single (uni) processor. Consider the mismatch between the billions of bytes (characters) of data awaiting to be handled by a scarce, single facility called the CPU, as well as the protocols to be obeyed in entering the trip through the channel, and the same on the way back: the result is the bottleneck portrayed by Figure 1.2. In other words, we have a single hammer (CPU) against a huge

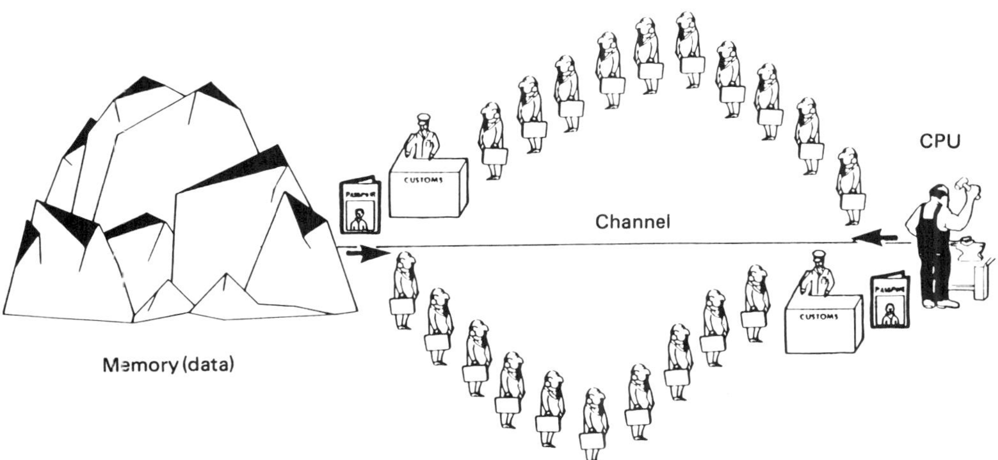

Figure 1.2 Processor bottleneck in the von Neumann architecture.

mountain (data), and the communication between the two is like a constant travel between two countries. Large delays in queues are the outcome, which is something that the real-time response to a user waiting on a terminal cannot tolerate. What is the solution then?—the concepts that have been alluded to so far! That is, we must make two changes, at this stage (more to come later):

(a) Use parallel processors (CPUs).
(b) Bring those CPUs to the mountain rather than the mountain to them, to eliminate the constant travel between the two.

Here, (a) accounts for parallelism, and (a) and (b) together form distributed logic or logic with memory. In this way, we would bring the CPU to data only once, at design time, rather than bringing data to the CPU at every program execution.

1.5.2 Memory Bottleneck

Now, let us return to the way in which the memory unit is addressed. We have seen that the von Neumann architecture's memory unit is addressed by location and that this is suitable for numeric processing. However, we also know that associative reference is the way data entities are addressed in nonnumeric processing. Because the only architecture available to run nonnumeric processing is that used for numeric processing, a way had to be found to implement associative reference. That way is to emulate associative addressing by means of the underlying location addressing. To do that, lookup tables (i.e., directories) have to be set up to translate an associative reference to its corresponding location address in the memory space. These directories are referred to as access paths since they are the means to reach memory locations. Considering the millions and billions bytes of the data mountain shown in Figure 1.2 waiting to be searched and/or processed, you can imagine the access path overhead.

In other words, to construct an access path, we have to duplicate parts of data and attach the corresponding memory addresses to it. Because access paths themselves end up being large data files for very large data mountains to be addressed, we construct directories of directories in a hierarchy until the final directory becomes manageable in size. What we end up doing then is creating another set of mountains in front of the already existing ones. The former will be called access path mountains. We picture the situation in Figure 1.3. What is seen in that picture is that the data mountain of Figure 1.2 is placed far in the background (left top of the figure). To emulate associative addressing for that mountain, an access path mountain is placed as shown in the foreground. Assuming that a user operates at the cable house (that is, places the request there), there will be a multilevel climb to the access path mountains until the final address (at the lookout point) lookup can be made. A multilevel climb

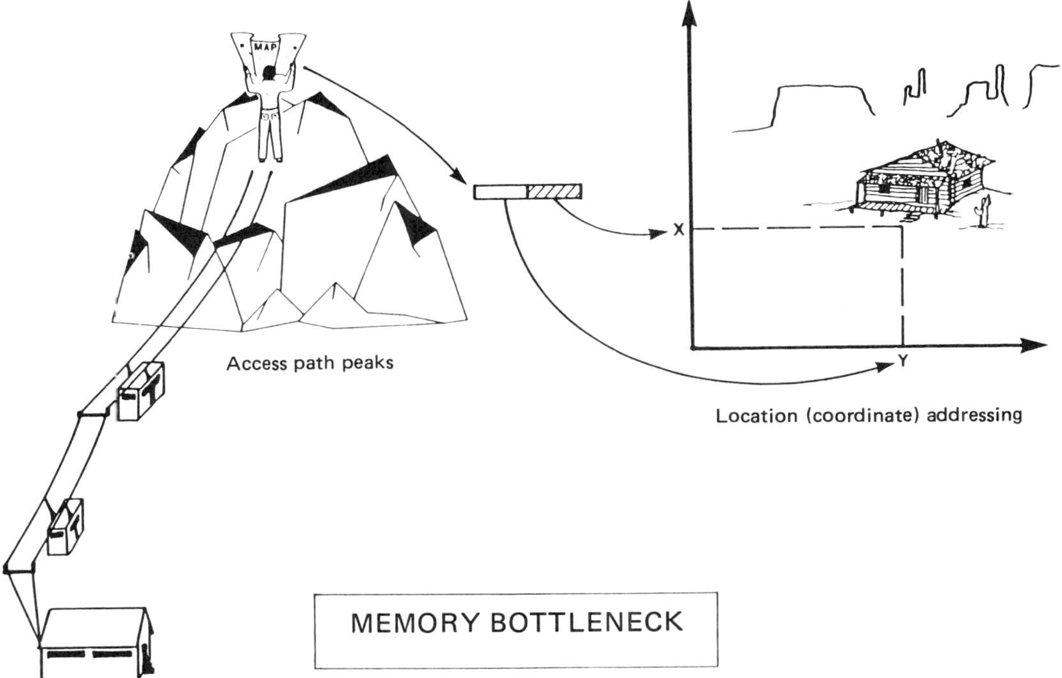

Figure 1.3 Memory bottleneck in the von Neumann architecture.

corresponds to a search of multilevel directories which we may have to set up for the very large database. Once the final address (i.e., corresponding to the location of desired data) is determined, its coordinates are decoded to determine the location in the memory. We denote this location by a little house on the prairie situated within the data mountain range. In the end, we finally arrive at our destination. However, at what cost? Can you imagine the time and space overhead involved that may translate to an obstacle for real-time operation? This is because, although we would be cutting down the search time considerably compared to a brute force scan of the data mountain, we pay dearly elsewhere. That is, in an environment where updates are frequent, we have the heavy maintenance of the access paths (as if the mountain is a constantly erupting volcano!). This is because, as the values are changed or deleted, or as new values are added in the data files, access paths will no longer point to correct locations in the memory; hence, they have to be reconstructed. Therefore, the overall performance stated as the combination of both retrieval and update performances will suffer greatly. Except for the lookup services, who can deny the existence of updates in nonnumeric processing? New facts must be added and new conclusions must be produced for survival!

1.6 ASSOCIATIVE MEMORIES

Just as we have seen in the processor bottleneck of the von Neumann architecture that the cure is parallelism with processor brought to memory, there is a cure also for the memory bottleneck. This cure is to eliminate emulation of associative addressing, hence to eliminate access paths and their associated software overhead. This can be achieved by a memory that can be accessed directly by the values stored in it, that is, a memory that can be addressed by its content rather than the location of the content. Such memories are called content-addressable or associative memories.

Figure 1.4 symbolizes the contrast between the location-based addressing of memory content, as shown in Figure 1.3, and the content-based addressing of the same using an associative memory. As opposed to the search climb overhead both in data and associated software of location-based addressing, the convenience and efficiency offered by the use of associative memories (to implement associative references of users directly) are analogous to the convenience and efficiency of a direct descent on the target by a parachute.

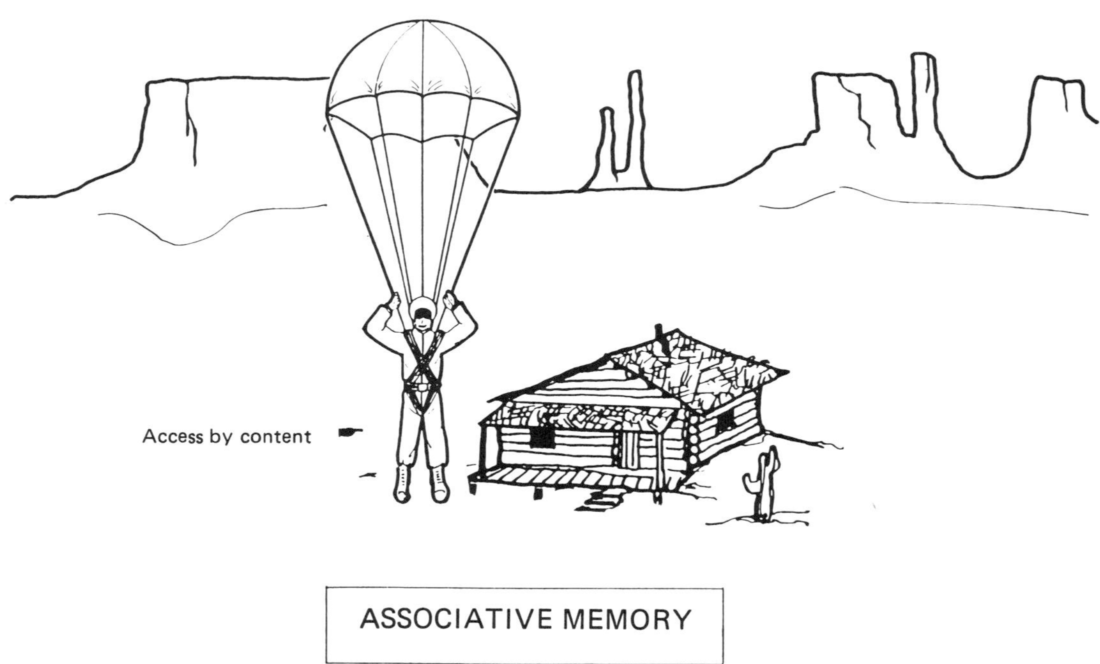

Figure 1.4 Access by content in associative memory.

1.7 NEW HARDWARE CONSTRAINTS AND THE SEMANTIC GAP

The von Neumann architecture was the right choice of its time because hardware was expensive but labor was cheap; however, nowadays, the situation is exactly the opposite. In computer design, hardware constraints play an important role since these constraints are directly determined by the manufacturing costs, technological parameters of the state of the art, and so on. With the advent of very-large-scale integration (VLSI) of hardware components (as opposed to vacuum tubes and transistors of the von Neumann era), the cost of hardware has decreased and design and packaging rules have changed. On the other hand, due to the ever-increasing software development costs (let alone the error-prone nature of software), a constant search is under way to minimize the cost of the overall system. The special-purpose new architectures promise to be the best as they offer a top-down approach to computer design, driven by the needs of dominant applications. As we have seen, the memory system becomes an integral part of a computer system in nonnumeric processing. Associative memories and high-level, specially tailored instruction sets can close the huge semantic gap that exists today between the von Neumann architecture and the requirements of modern-day applications (e.g., in data types, language constructs). Parallelism and processor within memory would be needed for efficient implementation of these features.

Aside from nonnumeric processing, the reader can refer to Myers [1983] to explore the semantic gap between a von Neumann computer and the features offered by a general-purpose programming language such as PL/I or all programming environments, for that matter. With regard to arrays of multidimensions, structures, string processing, and various data types in the user environments, one finds nothing close to these in the underlying machine (computer) architecture. All that exists is a linear memory space, index registers, byte addressability (as the lowest level of addressing) to implement arrays, and bit and character string processing. Machine data types and precision do not directly match those of the programming environment. There is no hardware counterpart of block-structured addressability and various forms of software interrupts that the present-day programming languages frequently use. These semantic gaps contribute to the high cost of software, software unreliability, excessive code, execution inefficiency, and compiler and operating system complexity. These compound the overall system ineffectiveness and inefficiency.

We can now focus on nonnumeric processing, which involves fact and document retrieval, knowledge-based question-answering systems, business transaction processing, and so on. All these applications depend on, in general, data management which has been carried out (rather primitively) by the traditional file processing systems since the earlier times. In our present time, however, we are increasingly relying on modern database management system(s) (DBMS). Let us briefly review their evolution.

1.8 CHARACTERISTICS OF MODERN DBMS

The evolution of database management systems starts with the earliest methodology of information processing. The concept of information structure and the operations of retrieval, update, insertion, and deletion were all embedded in the body of user's particular logic for a particular storage structure. This resulted in a bi-directional data-program dependency. Because changes to data and/or processes are natural in a data processing environment, each time a change on either side of the dependency was made, it resulted in a change of the program or rearrangement of data. Whatever has been said up to this point describes the traditional approaches of implementing databases, using file systems and a collection of file processing programs.

The difficulties faced with the previous DBMS methodology, in implementing complex information systems, resulted in efforts to set standards for DBMS requirements. The standards called for maximum possible data independence, which meant the separation of information structure from its physical representation. This new concept for databases implied a structured collection of integrated data that can be shared by concurrent users.

Databases are the most important facility of management information systems. To offer services to users and to administer the entire database utility, database management systems have been implemented. These systems isolate databases from the applications using them. The DBMS embody a complex integration of software and hardware that provides users with a logical view of their database, distinct from its physical implementation (i.e., the way that files are organized and manipulated). The users are provided with query languages with which they can specify retrievals and modifications. Figure 1.5 shows a comparison of user environments before and after new DBMS standards.

The requirement to make the logical view and the physical representation of data distinct from each other has created the need for several levels of indirection, for the purpose of mapping one structure into the other. The implementation of this requirement created software complexities at several levels. At the language level, a high-level query language must first be translated into some type of intermediate or procedural language with which a set of retrieval or manipulation functions are implemented. These are then compiled into machine language for execution. At the information representation level, all aspects of storage structure and the access path connections, to implement efficient access for associative references, have to be considered. Thus, pointer mechanisms for various cross-reference linkages and inverted lists (i.e., directories) for search optimizations have to be included at varying complexities. As seen earlier, these are extra data requiring extra storage, access, and maintenance. Also, mappings required

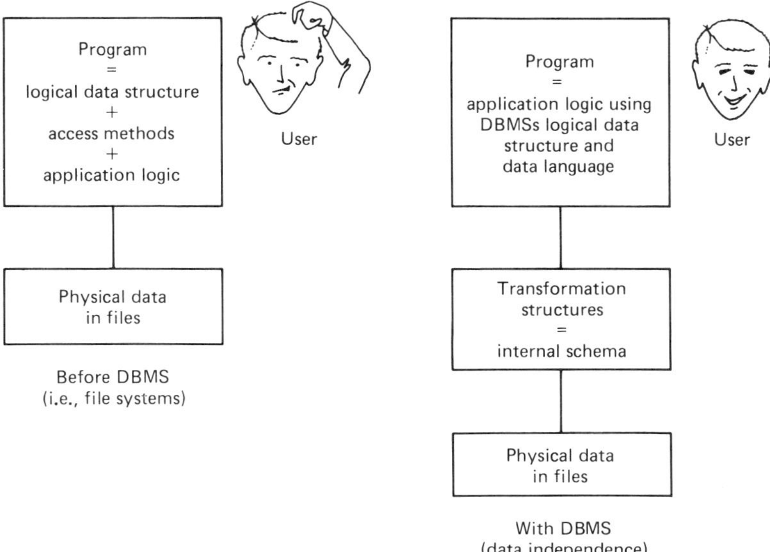

Figure 1.5   Before and after new DBMS standards.

by logical structures are error prone because software is involved. Because system software is transparent to the user, errors can only be identified by a costly operation of data confirmation. All these make it difficult to design systems that would remain efficient over a broad range of user applications with varying information structures. To overcome this, the following requirements are critical for modern database management systems:

- Data independence
- Powerful query language
- Fast response
- Reduction and/or elimination of data transformations and access paths

Data independence is a basic requirement for DBMS, and powerful query languages are important for satisfying demands of users. These languages possess associative reference and set-oriented features, which make them amenable to efficient implementation by means of the new computer architectures we portrayed in the first paragraph of Section 1.7.

1.9 PROBLEMS WITH THE CONVENTIONAL ARCHITECTURES

Now that we have had some introduction into DBMS and its requirements, we can be more explicit about the causes of the semantic gap that exists between nonnumeric processing and the conventional computer characterized by the von

Neumann architecture. The following problems exist in implementing DBMS on conventional computers:

(a) Poor overall performance. All the extra data and software, designed to achieve fast retrieval, actually degrade the update response because of the maintenance of these extra structures, thus resulting in poor overall performance.

(b) From the operating system point of view, all extra data and software are system resources that need to be managed in an operating system environment. This implies extra overhead in system software.

(c) The increased number of resources, such as data and software, both in applications and the operating system, implies a reduction in system reliability.

(d) The extra data required for access paths increase with the growing database size, and this is accompanied by the related software, both of which hamper performance. Also, software is error prone; hence, errors can easily cause the database to be inconsistent.

As indicated earlier, the excessive amount of mappings between the logical and physical structures, access path data and software, set-oriented processing based on only one record at a time input/output, and the need to transfer data to the CPU over channels are among the main causes for the foregoing problems. To cope with these problems, we are forced to make compromises such as

(a) We have to keep either static or dynamic subsets of data so that their size would make real-time operations possible. However, the following prices are paid: static subsets introduce data duplication and inconsistency of base data until the updates to subsets are reexecuted on them also. If we are keeping dynamic subsets, we have to create, manipulate, and destroy them after updates are reexecuted on the base data, every time a database operation needs to be performed on them. These extra processes add to system overhead which is critical for concurrent environments.

(b) Rather than implementing generalized systems, what happens instead is that specially tuned systems for the needs of specific environments proliferate. This creates inflexibility for future adaptation of systems to advances in both hardware and software.

1.10 NEW ARCHITECTURES FOR NONNUMERIC PROCESSING

We have established in the earlier sections that the solution to all the problems listed so far is first to eliminate the von Neumann bottlenecks and then make the new architectures such that no semantic gaps are created. Our guidelines so far have established that a new architecture for nonnumeric processing should possess

- Parallelism with processor on memory
- Associative memory coupled with set-oriented processing
- Special-purpose instruction set directly implemented in hardware
- Efficiency in concurrent user support (as called for by the definition of modern DBMS)

The past efforts of building new computer architectures have taken two directions. Those studies that aimed at overcoming the limitations of conventional architectures in numeric processing have concentrated on parallelism (i.e., array processing) and vector operations. These will be discussed in Chapter 4. Those that concentrated on nonnumeric processing used both associativity and parallelism and are generally referred to as associative processors. Because DBMS and other aspects of nonnumeric processing, which are constantly evolving, were not well understood, the concepts themselves were not sufficiently developed; and because the hardware technology was not as favorable as at present, the early proposals were inadequate and/or incomplete, in the following sense:

(a) The gap between logical and physical data structures was not sufficiently closed.
(b) Associativity could only be partially implemented.
(c) Complex context searches and storage operations for insertion/deletion were not directly implemented in hardware.
(d) Instruction sets were ad hoc and incomplete.
(e) Some designs still left considerable dependence on the outside computer for their primitive operations.
(f) Some designs did not address very large databases and restricted their structure within primary memory limits.

1.11 DATABASE MACHINES

It was only with the conceptualization of database machines that the foregoing limitations and issues have started to be considered. Database machines have been proposed to support one or more data models (i.e., logical data structure) and to directly execute their associated data languages. For example, a relational database machine supports the relational data model (see Chapters 2 and 3), and relational algebra is the associated instruction set. As proposed in the early studies, database machines have been placed as a special-purpose peripheral device (a backend processor) to offload the chores of a von Neumann general-purpose (host) computer (GPC). This is pictured in Figure 1.6. The resulting configuration is a master-slave coupling where the slave is referred to as a *hardware backend,* if the slave possesses a new architecture. Alternatively, we can delegate the backend responsibility to another (possibly mini) GPC of the conventional architecture. This is referred to as a *software backend,* meaning

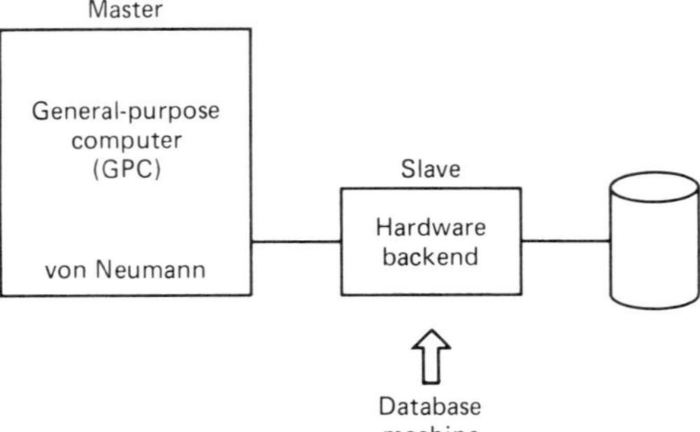

Figure 1.6 Database machine as a backend processor.

that the solution is software oriented, making the DBMS software execute on the dedicated backend computer. Whether hard or soft, these dedicated backends are referred to as *database machines* in general.

The reader should realize that this backend configuration must not be taken for granted. On the contrary, we encourage the following questions:

(a) Is the configuration of Figure 1.6 always the best?

(b) Would this configuration impose a certain cost relationship between the GPC and the hardware backend?

(c) If the answer to (b) is yes, do you think that this might have been a negative factor in the feasibility assessment (or market acceptability) of database machines?

(d) What is the level and nature of interface between the master and slave?

(e) What impact may the answer to (d) have on the overall system performance?

(f) Can we define alternative configurations for a database machine?

(g) If the answer to (f) is yes, what must be the hardware functionalities and software personalities of the new system?

At this point, we do not intend to provide answers to these questions. On the contrary, we want to plant more questions into the reader's mind to motivate reading of the entire book. In the following, we will present a description of the outlook for the new computer architectures of the future. As we have said, the main intention is to plant the seed of curiosity rather than prematurely delve into unjustifiable details—unjustifiable because we have not yet laid out the background material, which is the purpose of the entire book.

1.12 WHAT IS HIDDEN IN THE FUTURE?

The continuous research with database machines and the rapid advances in hardware technology have helped us to establish the following facts:

1. High parallelism and associativity can no longer be feasibly implemented as processor per track or processor per platter machines on electromagnetic disks. This would not mean however that the long-established basic architectural constructs of parallelism and associativity are not needed. What it implies, instead, is that we have to change horses to implement these constructs.

2. Some database operations are determined to be *hard* in complexity on devices (the so-called associative disks or associative memory arrays) that rely only on associativity and parallelism of the SIMD (Single Instruction Multiple Data) architectures. These hard operations are the binary set operations of join, difference, and union, and the unary operation of projection. Other architectural constructs need to be added with the basic ingredients of parallelism and associativity to improve the performance of these operations.

3. For business transaction processing involving simple update requests, the brute force method of driving the database machine per simple request defeats the purpose of a database machine. This is because the device is underutilized and the frontend host overhead overshadows the gains made at the backend. A better way of processing transactions must be found.

4. Technological advances and the potentials of VLSI and ULSI (U stands for ultra) have made several important breakthroughs possible, such as

   (a) Data filters capable of selection filtering at the channel speed of data can now be made into a low-cost VLSI chip. With certain attachments, they can also perform more complicated operations, such as projection on the background concurrent with the database machine (DBMS processor) operations on the foreground as shown in Figure 1.7.

   (b) Semiconductor random access memories (RAMs) are increasing in density while decreasing in cost. In a year or two from the time of writing this

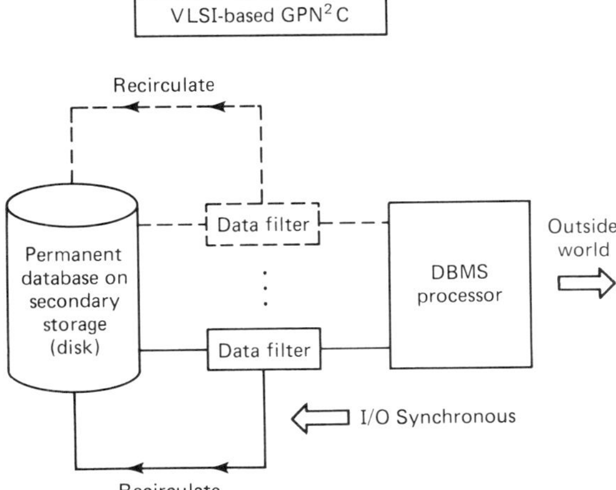

Figure 1.7 Role of VLSI data filters in new database architectures.

book, one dynamic RAM chip will have 1 megabits of storage. Currently, the OEM (original equipment manufacturer) prices of RAMs per megabit are competing with that of fixed-head disks and will match those of the low-capacity movable head disks in less than a decade.

(c) More capabilities are increasingly being expected of database machines and more applications of the nonnumeric domain are being developed such as generalized database management systems, distributed databases, information (document) retrieval, transaction processing, knowledge-based information and question-answering systems, and so on.

The term *machine* in database machine has gained the connotation of a relief processor at the backend as shown in Figure 1.6. We will use *database computer* to mean a stand-alone (autonomous) database or DBMS processor. We will also use *database architecture* to imply a hardware architecture to cover, in the broad sense, all architectures ranging from a backend to varieties of autonomous configurations.

In the article titled *Desirable Functionalities of Database Architectures* [Ozkarahan, 1983], the author stressed the need for dedicated computers to serve all the needs of nonnumeric computing in general. In that article, such computers were termed *general-purpose nonnumeric computers* (GPN^2C) that would be used as *network servers*. These servers can be used both directly as autonomous computers and/or coupled with other GPCs through high-level interfaces at the request-response level. Having postulated their existence, we would then be faced with defining the hardware functionalities as well as the software personalities for such architectures.

1.12.1 Software Personalities of GPN^2Cs

The GPN^2C must be rich in its personalities (i.e., functions, capabilities provided for the user). In its core, it must be a database processor (i.e., a more general role than a database machine) able to support

- Generalized database management systems
- Distributed databases
- Transaction processing

As mentioned earlier and as shown in Figure 1.8, GPN^2Cs should be used as network servers so that an adequate work load that utilizes their high transaction rate can be provided.

These architectures should also support text (document) retrieval and knowledge bases needed for artificial intelligence applications. A close examination of all the mentioned applications reveals the fact that they all need similar architectural capabilities. And in fact, in the fifth-generation computer project

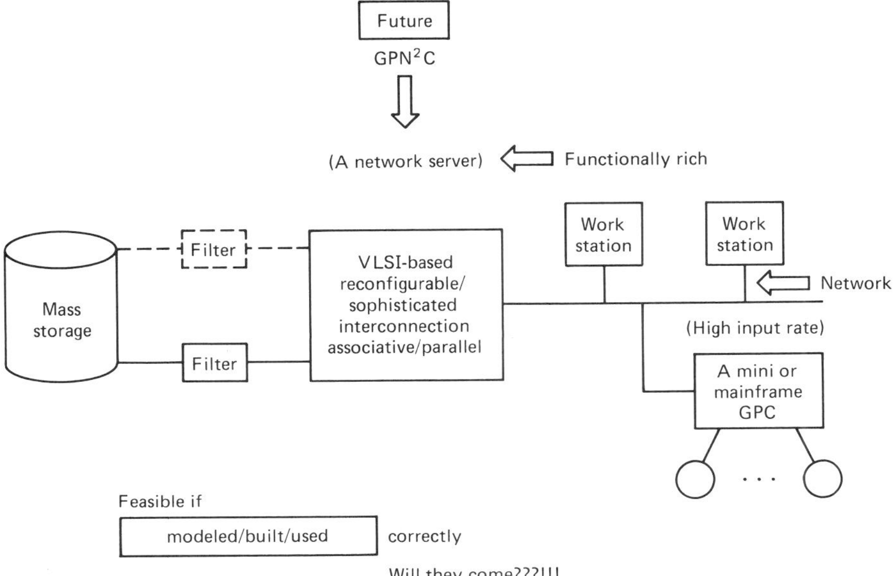

Figure 1.8   Future configuration of a GPN^{2}C.

of Japan, the main core of their proposed knowledge-based system is established with a *relational database machine* as the underlying search and manipulation engine [Moto-oka and Fuchi, 1983]. To be able to support all these personalities, the following basic capabilities should be provided at the software level:

(a) Associative reference
(b) High-level, special-purpose instruction set, which implies that the underlying architecture must be a *high-level language computer*
(c) Ability to process both formatted (structured) and unformatted (unstructured) data
(d) Ability to process predicate calculus (hence, relational algebra) and set operations efficiently using the language constructs of (b).

1.12.2 Hardware Functionalities of GPN^{2}Cs

Up to now, we have already established that the basic hardware architecture for nonnumeric processing should have the capabilities of

- Associativity
- Parallelism
- Processor on memory, all based on VLSI

These basic functionalities are what the various personalities commonly require. Such a system would also maintain a balanced performance in the dynamic environment of data updates.

In addition to these basic hardware capabilities, some personalities may require a set of high-level architectural capabilities to improve performance, such as the case with the hard database operations of join, difference, projection, and so on. As we shall see in the remainder of the book, some possible high-level architectural capabilities can be

- Reconfigurability of parallel processors as well as their memories
- Complex interconnection topologies other than the simple linear array of processors used in the early database machine proposals
- Multiprocessor organizations that augment the basic architecture with some level of functional distribution to allow data flow control, concurrency, sorting, merging, and so on.

1.12.3 Data Space Partitioning and Problem Decomposition

Instead of forcing any given architecture's physical limits with the hope of applying sheer parallelism and computing power to a problem's solution, the external (with respect to internals of a given architecture) space should be studied to design an overall cost-effective system. This means the exploitation of data space partitioning as well as the decomposition of a given task. The former avoids irrelevant parts of the data space without overloading the architecture, such as in a join operation. If we can determine compatible and incompatible data bands (value ranges) between two relations (files), then we will not have any need to send incompatible pairs of bands (from two relations) for late discovery of the incompatibility in the machine by brute force processing. Similarly, a given task may be processable by a smaller machine if there exists an efficient way of decomposing the task into finer steps.

The modern computer architecture needs a more complex selection of trade-offs in view of the increasing number of alternatives provided by the advancements in technology. For a given environment, we have to optimize both the architecture and the data/problem space to arrive at cost-effective systems.

In conclusion, we have somewhat provided an answer to questions such as: "Are database architectures feasible or will they ever come?" The answer is: Certainly, as depicted also by Figure 1.9, which indicates that on the way to the future (toward the light), the computer architecture is bound to arrive at the GPN^2C era. This will happen sooner if we make these architectures functionally rich and then model, build, and use them correctly.

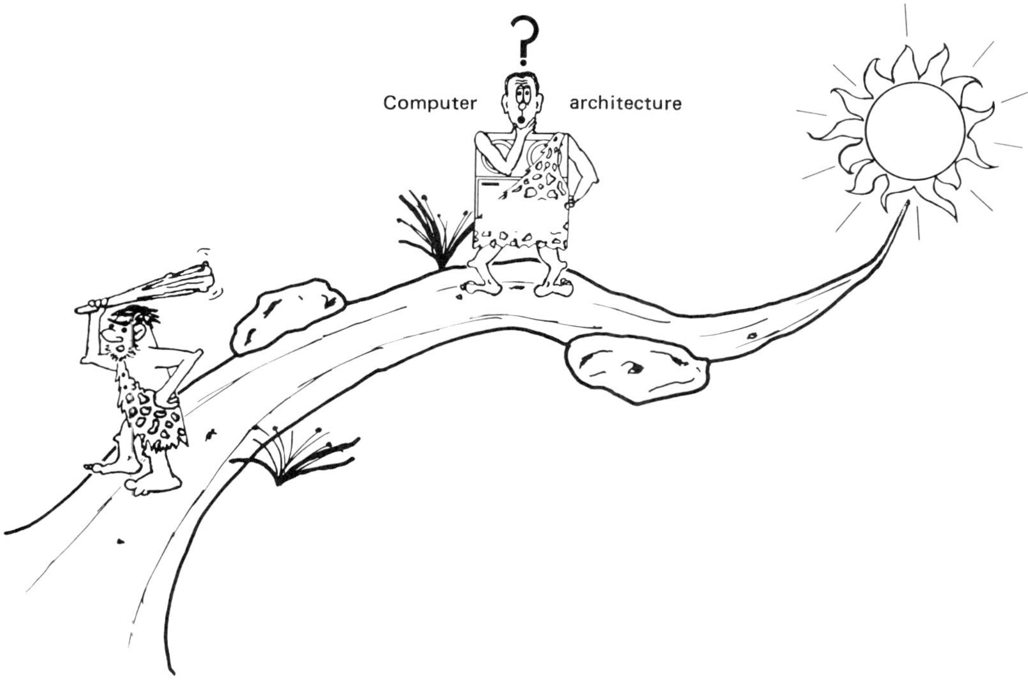

Figure 1.9   Will database architectures come? Are they feasible?

EXERCISES

1.1. Identify nonnumeric processing applications and see whether their processing demands are similar. How can you describe them?

1.2. Do you think that the architectural capabilities described in the chapter would be used effectively to meet the demands you determined in Exercise 1.1.? Describe the way each capability would be utilized and the resulting advantage and/or gain.

1.3. Give some query or programming examples to demonstrate associative reference. In addition to databases, you can consider other areas of computer science.

1.4. How do the von Neumann architecture's bottlenecks translate to everyday life as related to computers?

1.5. Can you elaborate, by giving examples, on the semantic gaps of the von Neumann architecture?

1.6. Can you provide some answers to questions (a) through (g) in Section 1.11.? If so, elaborate and revisit them after you finish reading the rest of the book.

1.7. How do you think that the computer architectures will evolve in the future? Do you see the fifth-generation computer as an extension of GPN^2C or as a subclass of the latter with an emphasized personality?

2

DBMS-I

The term *database* denotes a common base of data collection. There is a distinction, however, between the terms *document database* and *fact database*. The former implies a collection of unformatted text strings of documents; the latter implies a common pool of formatted data, storing facts of an information system. The terms *database management systems* (*DBMS*) or simply *databases* are used to mean the latter, that is, the fact retrieval systems. In the present and the following chapters, we will summarize the important concepts and theory of DBMS. The knowledge of DBMS is an integral part of this book. Chapters 12 and 13 will deal with document databases.

2.1 DEFINITIONS

Physical data.   These are data stored in the computer's storage. Typically, the volume of data is large so that secondary storage devices such as disks, tapes, and so on are used.

Logical view of data.   This indicates how a user views the physical data. The distinction between the physical data and the corresponding logical view is that in the logical view, one conceptualizes certain meaningful relationships among the physical data elements. For example, we may have sets of names and monies recorded in files. The logical view or interpretation of these sets of data can be that the names belong to (or identify) employees and that the monies recorded correspond to their salaries.

Data independence.   DBMS are used to provide flexibility between the users and the physical data. Besides the various conveniences they provide, which will be outlined shortly, DBMS provide isolation between the two extremes, namely, the user and the physical data. Changes in the organization of physical data and/or in the storage device parameters are absorbed by DBMS and therefore do not affect the user or, more accurately, the application program. Similarly, changes in user's view and/or addition of new views are also absorbed by DBMS so that physical data are not affected in the sense of forcing a costly reorganization and/or access mechanism change for data files. This flexibility of being able to live with changes in the both ends (i.e., user and physical data) is referred to as data independence. This flexibility, that is, data independence, is absent in the traditional file systems. This implies rigidity and high cost for maintenance of existing programs and developing new applications.

Although data independence is a general term, we also hear the terms *logical data independence* and *physical data independence*. These terms roughly mean the flexibility at their respective ends and are used in conjunction with the multilevel (layered) DBMS architectures which will be briefly mentioned in this chapter and in Chapter 9.

Database management system.   This is a utility responsible for

(a) Providing data definition and manipulation facilities for its users. These facilities are in terms of *data* languages of the *definition, DDL (data definition language)*, and *manipulation, DML (data manipulation language)*, type. A data language is either or both of these two languages, and the word *data* distinguishes it from the other types of languages such as COBOL, PL/I, Pascal, and so on. However, a data language can be embedded within a general-purpose language like COBOL, PL/I, Pascal. In such a facility, the general-purpose language and the data language are referred to as the *host* and the *data sublanguage (DSL)*, respectively. A stand-alone (i.e., nonhost-embedded) data language is also referred to as a *query language*.

(b) Providing *data models* for its users. A data model is a facility with which the user defines the logical view of the physical data belonging to an application.

(c) Providing software to implement the functions of DDL and DML. This software implements the definition, creation, and manipulation (i.e., retrieval, update, insertion/deletion) of logical data. It maps these operations into the respective operations on physical data.

(d) Providing security and integrity controls for the system. With these controls, only the authorized users are allowed to use the system (security) and the consistency of the stored data is preserved during the operations of users (integrity). This implies the following: DBMS are intended to support multiple users in a shared environment. Furthermore, the shared environment is made possible on the common pool of physical data. This means that the same data must be kept consistent between the operations of different users. Typical examples of inconsistency deal with mismanagement of concurrent updates. Problems such as lost updates and dirty reads will be studied later under security and integrity, as will such problems as *selling more items than the quantity on hand* or *selling more tickets to a fight than the available number of seats*. A good DBMS should provide integrity control mechanisms to prevent possible inconsistencies that may result during the course of use of a database.

Data model.   A data model has three components. They are

1. A data structure to represent user's logical view of the database.
2. Operations performable on the data structure. These constitute the data language base of the data model. It is not enough to have a good data structure. That structure must be operable on with the various primitives of the DDL and DML. A rich data structure would mean very little if the user could not manipulate its contents.
3. Constraints for integrity control. That is, a data model should be equipped with means to preserve its integrity, to protect itself. Examples are constraints such as
   (a) Every subtree must have a parent node. One cannot keep children nodes without a parent in a tree-structured (hierarchical) database.
   (b) There cannot be identical tuples in a relation meaning (analogously) that there cannot be identical records in a file.

Schema.   This is a tool with which a data model is defined. In fact, a schema contains more than a data model. It also records the semantic information pertaining to an application. In a data model, we can define the fact that our database will store the employee data along with company data. However, the fact that a given employee cannot work for more than one department in the company reflects the semantics of the application. This semantic fact should be maintained for every individual employee occurrence in the database. The enforcement of the constraints of a given data model in a database is also part of the security/integrity control function of DBMS.

2.2 FEATURES OF DBMS

2.2.1 Comparison with Traditional File Systems

File systems represent a tight coupling between physical data and user's program. They lack almost all the flexibilities offered by a DBMS. Most of the indispensable facilities of a DBMS are, therefore, forced to be absorbed by user's program. In other words, besides the logic of the application, the user has to provide logic for constructing the logical view of data, has to interpret the operations on the logical view and translate them into the primitive file operations, and has to be responsible for maintaining the files that store the physical data. In such an environment, it would be impossible to achieve data independence. The changes in either end would immediately affect the user's program which represents the software doing everything. This tight coupling and interdependence between a user's application and the physical data would not allow sharing of the same data by other applications that may need to view and manipulate them differently. This then forces the data to be duplicated among various applications. Besides inefficiency and waste of storage, one immediate consequence of this duplication is an inconsistent database, for there would be no general mechanism to reflect dynamically the updates of one application onto the same data of other applications. For example, a given item may have been shipped out or discarded from a warehouse and updated correctly in the warehouse files, yet the finance department may still be unaware of the situation (due to lack of a healthy, integrated, and dynamic information system) and may periodically request an accounting of the inventory from the various responsible departments.

File systems lack dynamism in the sense that the application programs are designed, coded, debugged, and catalogued ahead of time for the preconceived requests and applications. They will in no way be able to cope with ad hoc requests which typically demand real-time response. The following list summarizes the problems of file systems that can be overcome by DBMS:

(a) Data dependence
(b) Rigidity
(c) Staticity
(d) Lack of integration
(e) Data duplication
(f) Inconsistency
(g) Nonsharability
(h) Inefficiency
(i) Inability to handle ad hoc requests

2.2.2 DBMS Standards

Modern DBMS are introduced to eliminate the drawbacks of file systems. The Guide/Share report [1970] attempted to define some guidelines for DBMS to follow. They are

(a) Data independence.
(b) Data relatability, meaning that the DBMS should have a powerful data model capable of representing user's logical view.
(c) Compatibility, meaning that the DBMS should be able to cope with future

developments both in software and hardware. It should be able to live with changes.

(d) Data nonredundancy, meaning that, unlike file systems, the database must be a common pool of integrated data.

(e) Data security, meaning that the DBMS must protect the database against unauthorized access.

(f) Data integrity, meaning that the DBMS must protect the database against the misuse of the authorized users.

(g) Concurrency control, meaning that the DBMS must protect the database against inconsistency in the shared use. All user requests (transactions) should execute in the right order to preserve database consistency.

We have been discussing the concepts of the items (e), (f), and (g) earlier. Data independence is the most important feature since it implies the presence of all the other related concepts such as data integration, nonredundancy, sharing, and the ability to enforce security and integrity.

In addition to the Guide/Share standards, we should add the following:

(a) A DBMS must be general purpose, that is, it should be able to support multiple data models within a unified logical and physical framework. In this way, differing user needs and preferences can be easily met.

(b) A DBMS must be able to handle distributed databases besides the centralized DBMS. In our modern times, data distribution and computer networking are becoming quite common. A DBMS for a geographically dispersed, multilocational enterprise in which local autonomy of data is important has to be a *distributed database* (*DDB*) *system*. This implies the ability to handle tasks such as

  (i) Data allocation

 (ii) Distributed query execution

(iii) Concurrency control over multiple sites

(iv) Optimization of query execution to minimize the amount of data communication among the sites

We will deal with the generalized DBMS in Chapter 9 and distributed databases will be covered in Chapter 10.

2.2.3 DBMS Environment

Various people come in contact with and use a DBMS. Users may range from those who are skilled, that is, those who know the system's details and can program, to those who are unskilled and/or casual and need not know the details of the system. The latter category can be the managers or professionals of other disciplines. In the skilled user category, we have also an administrative function, which is the responsibility of the database administrator (DBA). The DBA can be a single person or group of persons equipped with a series of automated tools and utilities. The DBA is responsible for coordination between the users and the system, database creation and maintenance, database security and integrity, and system monitoring and performance tuning. In all these activities, the DBA's responsibilities range from design and implementation to control and enforcement.

As we pointed out earlier, the user's contact with the system is via data languages. We have also mentioned DDL, DML, DSL, and query language in connection with data languages. While a DDL serves to define schemas to the system, a DML is constantly used during the operations of a given application on the database. If a DML is used as a DSL in a host language, then there will be interactions among various system components. Figure 2.1 shows a simplified view of some of these interactions.

A DML, as a language, can be of varying functionalities. Those DML that are at a low level of functionality are typically procedural; those that are at a high level are more descriptive. Procedural languages require skilled users since programming in them is much like programming in an assembler language, whereas high-level languages are more suitable for casual users. In the latter case, the maneuverability is mostly transferred onto DBMS. Regardless of the level of a DML, however, the important characteristics that it should possess are

- Data independence (i.e., should not rely on system details below the schema level)
- Completeness in manipulative power (i.e., should be capable of reaching and manipulating all the existing relationships defined in the schema)

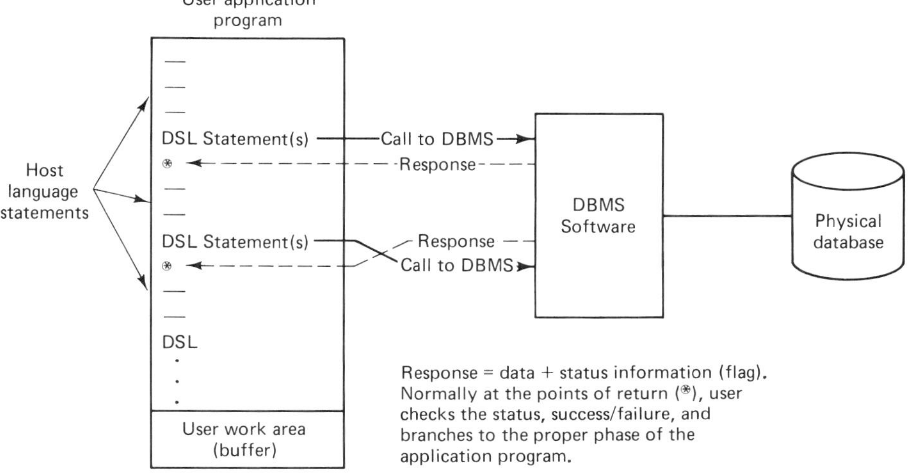

Figure 2.1   Host-embedded DML (DSL) and DBMS interaction.

- Completeness in system control as well as utility (i.e., lock/release, arithmetic updates, aggregation, and other file and I/O control capabilities should be included)

Much the same type of requirements exist for the DDL; however, this time the manipulative role of the DML is replaced by the definitional capabilities of the DDL. The language should be capable of handling schema and data dictionary definitions and any procedure definitions such as those for integrity control and various conversions and mappings that are an integral part of those definitions. For example, to define a file we must declare

- File name
- Names of its fields
- Attributes (properties) of each field
- Any synonymous names for the field names
- Names of authorized users
- Permitted range of values for certain fields
- Conversion routines between various data types and units of quantities
- Mapping procedures for transforming the file (if applicable) to different structures such as a subset structure including only a selected set of records and only the required set of fields within them.

At this stage, we will not be able to give more sophisticated examples since we are not yet equipped with the knowledge of the necessary concepts and terminology. However, with as much of the example as we can deal with at this point, we see the need for

- Name declarations
- Data attribute declarations (i.e., type, length)
- Synonym handling
- Ability to define structural entities (i.e., file, field, subsets of entities)
- Procedure definition capability for security and integrity
- Conversion routines between data attributes and values
- Mapping procedures between structural entities

In a DBMS, one may see a schema or data dictionary or both depending on the implementation. While a data dictionary usually contains more passive declarations that are useful for system analysts/designers, a schema (or active dictionary) contains the definitions and procedures that are part of the automated system and therefore utilized directly by the system software. For example, a procedure that is written to constrain the values of a given field would have to be invoked automatically by the language processor (i.e., of the DML) each time an update which modifies an existing value or inserts a new record is received in the operational environment.

2.3 DATA MODELS

2.3.1 Notation

Humans dealing with information start, in the first place, with the conceptualization of facts, beings, objects, and events of interest. This takes place in the mind. We will refer to the things conceptualized as *entities* in general. Each entity is a mental picture or set of similar things (e.g., employees, houses, enrollment in a course). An entity, in turn, has the basic features that characterize it. For an employee, the social security number, name, salary, age, and so on are examples. In data modeling, that is, in coming up with an abstract representation of our conceptualizations, we make certain formalizations to represent our logical view. In so doing, we move from the domain of conceptualization to the domain of information representation. This requires speaking in terms of a logical view by means of a data structure of a chosen data model. In data model terms, an entity is represented by a *record type*. Notice that, although we are speaking of data model, we have not pointed out which one—this is exactly the purpose of the use of the term record type, which stands for a generic use in the information representation of an entity. A record type may play different roles in different data models. For example, in the relational model, it becomes a relation, in a hierarchical model a segment or node, and in a network data model an owner or member record type. The features that characterize an entity are called *attributes* (of the record type). Finally, the physical structure corresponding to the logical representation comes into the picture. It describes the data actually stored in the computer. The terminology belonging to this form is not new for it is, or comes from, the traditional file systems. A record type is materialized as a set of record occurrences (or instances) with each occurrence representing data of an instance of the corresponding record type. For example, each employee's data represent a record occurrence (or simply a record). The entity (or entity set), therefore record type, *employee* represents a set of similar things, that is, people who are described as employees and share the same features or attributes. The term *file* is file system equivalent to the term *record type* in the logical frame of reference. A record occurrence is made up of items (or data elements) which correspond to values of attributes. (That is, social security number is an attribute and 999-40-3929 is an item, or data element, or simply an attribute value.)

2.3.2 DBMS Architecture

The following example, Figure 2.2, shows two DBMS architectures. Figure 2.2(a) shows an early-generation DBMS. It has a single data model offered to its users.

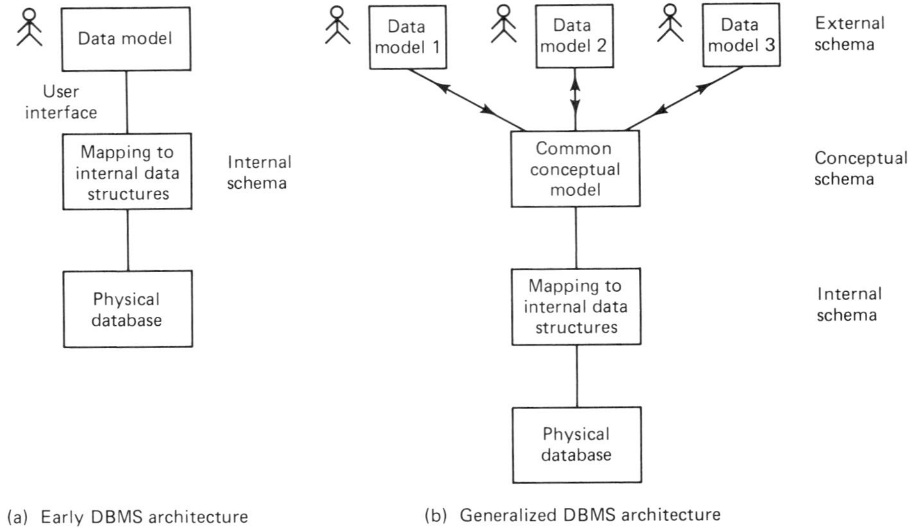

Figure 2.2   DBMS architectures.

The *mapping to internal data structure* is a transformation stage that maps the logical structure of the data model at the user interface into the corresponding structures of the physical database. In fact, this mapping facility is referred to as the internal schema.

Figure 2.2(b) shows a more general facility also known as the ANSI/SPARC GDBMS architecture [ANSI/X3/SPARC, 1975]. In this architecture, multiple models are derived from a single conceptual data model (upward-going arrows). A conceptual data model has more abstraction capability and semantic richness (this will be clear after reading Chapters 3 and 9) compared with the data models at the user interface (the external schema). The latter are also referred to as the *syntactic* or *operational* data models, meaning that they are more syntactically driven and are a vehicle of user's manipulations. One other distinction is due to Langefors [1980], who refers to conceptual data models as the *infological* models while the external schema models are referred to as the *datalogical* models. In Figure 2.2(b), user queries (operations) are expressed in the language of the datalogical models that are then mapped into the corresponding operations on the infological model (downward-going arrows).

As we have observed up to this point, there are levels of abstraction in data modeling (the extremes being conceptual and physical) that, in turn, influence the DBMS architectures. The architecture of Figure 2.2(b) has multiple levels, which is a price to be paid for flexibility. In this architecture, we can speak of *logical data independence* and *physical data independence* distinguishably. We will come back to DBMS architectures in Chapter 9.

2.3.3 Some Early Mathematical Notions

In discrete mathematics, one speaks of two *sets* A and B and their relation, which is notated as A **R** B. This simply conveys a *relationship* among the members of the individual sets, and there are types of relationships such as reflexive A **R** A (related to itself), transitive (related indirectly), and so on. In practice, we attach some interpretation or meaning to relationships and to the cardinality (i.e., count of members) of relationship instances between the sets. The sets can correspond to attributes or record types. There are also functional relationships in which relationship instances obey the constraints of a mathematical function. The cardinality of relationship instances is also referred to as the type of mapping between pairs of sets. There are one-to-one ($1:1$), one-to-many ($1:N$), and many-to-many ($M:N$) mappings.

A relationship, therefore, is a correspondence (or mapping) between the members of two or more sets. Let us clarify these concepts by going through a series of examples. Figure 2.3 shows some example entities, their properties (features), and the corresponding representations as record types and attributes.

In these examples, we see different types of sets. First is the set of similar things or entities (or entity sets) such as all the people working in an organization conceptualized and then described as employees. Similarly, Houses, Suppliers, and Parts represent sets of similar entities, all generically conceptualized by their respective entity names. Each entity is, in turn, represented by its properties. As a result, for each entity set there correspond multiple sets, each being the set of values corresponding to a given property. In more representative terms, an entity set is represented as a record type and a record type is described by its attributes. An instance or occurrence of a given record type corresponds to a single entity such as an employee, a house, a supplier, or a part (just as a *record* of an employee *file* corresponds to an individual in file systems). In the physical (data) domain, we store values corresponding to a set of attributes that make up the stored instance of a record type. The following list enumerates some relationships:

Conceptual Domain		Representation Domain
Entities	Properties	Record Types (list of attributes)
Employee	Social security number, employee number, name, salary	Employee (SSN, EMPN, NAME, SALARY)
Houses	Lot number, type, price	Houses (LOTNO, TYPE, PRICE)
Supplier	Supplier number, name, location (city of business)	Supplier (SN, SNAME, CITY)
Part	Part number, part description, quantity on hand	Part (PN, PDES, QOH)

Figure 2.3   Some example entities and properties.

(a) For each employee number value, there corresponds a unique social security number value, and vice versa.

(b) Employees (may) own houses.

(c) Some employees manage other employees.

(d) Suppliers supply (sell) parts.

(e) The type of a house that an employee lives in can be determined from its price.

We will elaborate further on these relationships. In doing so, we will use different notations for sets (e.g., a diagram, a symbol, or a mathematical notation) to best suit the concept being described. Figure 2.4 depicts various relationships among the instances of various sets in the order corresponding to the relationships (a) through (e) given in the foregoing list.

If we examine the types of relationships shown in Figure 2.4, the following characteristics can be noticed:

1. Figures 2.4(a) and (e) are relationships among attribute sets—also referred to as *attribute relationships*. These relationships are *intra-entity* types.

2. Figures 2.4(b), (c), and (d) are relationships among entities (i.e., *inter-entity* relationships). Complex relationships involving more than two entities are possible, such as the case in which "suppliers supply parts to projects and projects use the parts." Inter-entity relationships are also referred to as "associations." One exception to the inter-entity relationships shown in the figures is the case in which the "manages" relationship involves a single entity; that is, the relationship is among the members of a given entity set (i.e., entity related to itself).

3. In Figure 2.4(a), there is one-to-one correspondence between the members of respective sets, and this correspondence is bidirectional.

4. In Figure 2.4(b), we can see that not all the employees own houses and those that own houses can own more than one.

5. In Figure 2.4(c), we see that some employees manage other employees and that every employee has a manager (E_2 manages E_1 who is also a manager). One exception to this can be the president of a company who can manage himself or herself (or be managed by the board of directors!).

6. In Figure 2.4(d), we can see that all suppliers are active—that is, all of them supply parts—and that a given supplier can supply several parts and a given part can be supplied by various suppliers.

7. In Figure 2.4(e), we see that the price of a house determines its type. (For the sake of the example, we used single-point values for the prices of houses, whereas in real life a range of dollars would be applicable.)

If we examine the mapping properties of these relationships, that is, the

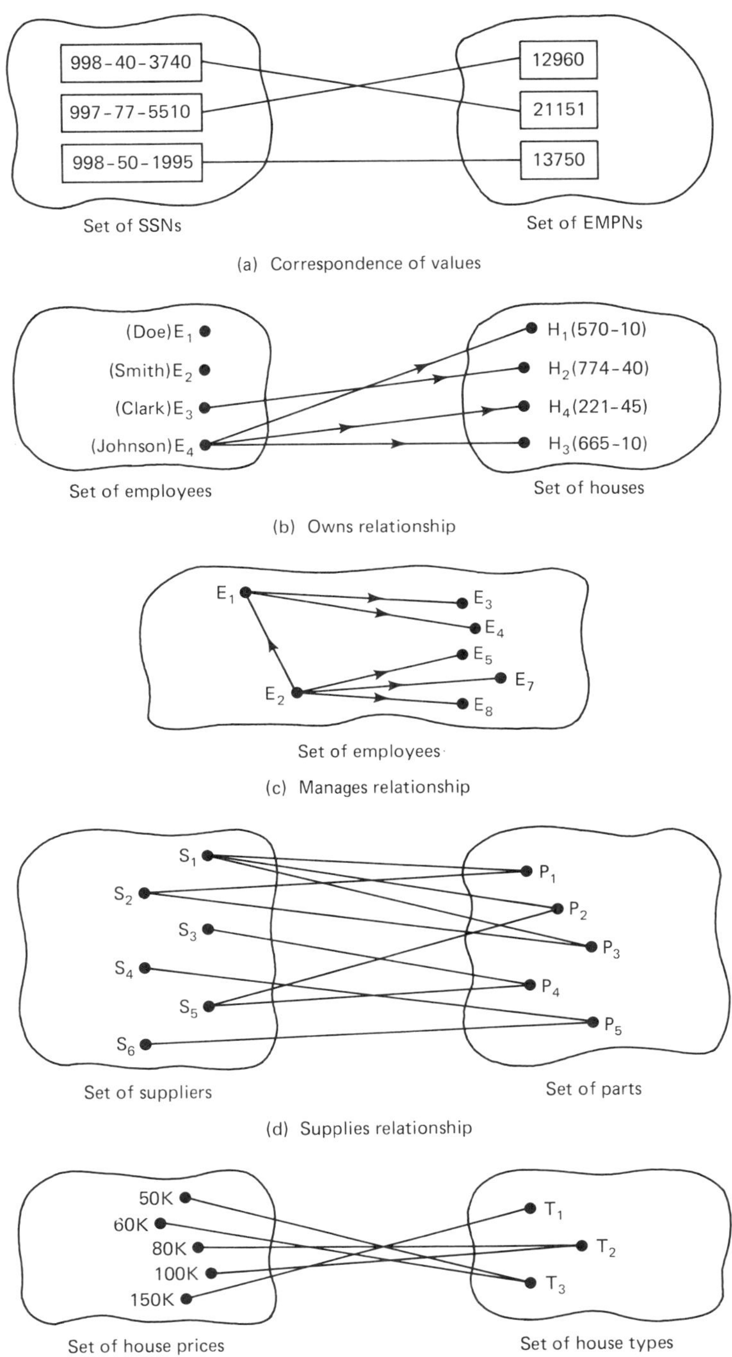

(a) Correspondence of values

(b) Owns relationship

(c) Manages relationship

(d) Supplies relationship

(e) Relationship between prices and types of houses

Figure 2.4 Relationships among set instances.

cardinalities of the relationship instances, we can abstract them as in Figure 2.5 with the corresponding set symbols.

As can be seen in Figure 2.5, sometimes a shorthand notation may be utilized to use symbols for sets and to label the relationship arcs with their semantic interpretation. A more formal approach would be to use a conceptual data model. In Figure 2.6, we show the interentity relationship of the example in Figure 2.5(b) in terms of the entity/relationship (E/R) diagram [Chen, 1976], which will be detailed in Chapter 9.

Before we proceed any farther, we can indicate the additional questions introduced by Figure 2.6. How can we represent the relationship Owns? How can we represent the Manages relationship in Figure 2.5(c)? These questions

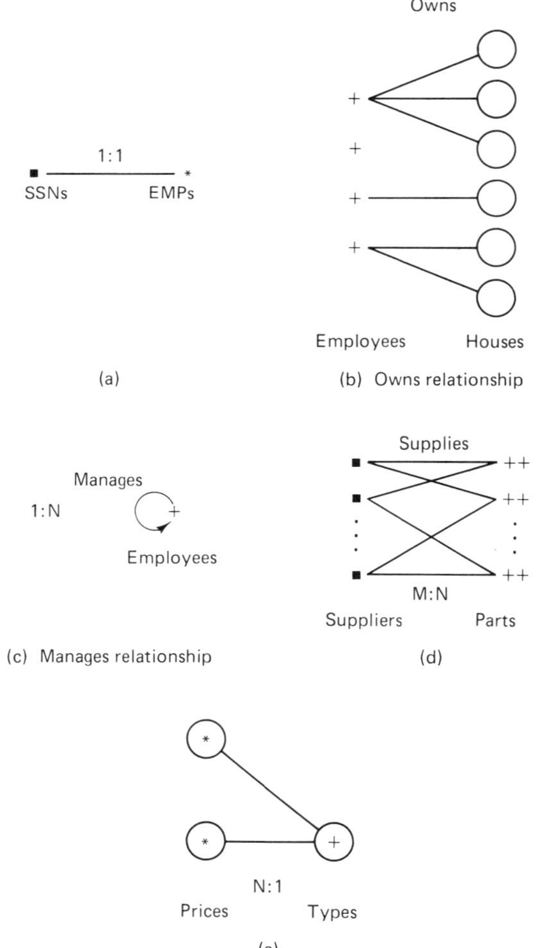

Figure 2.5 Cardinalities of relationships.

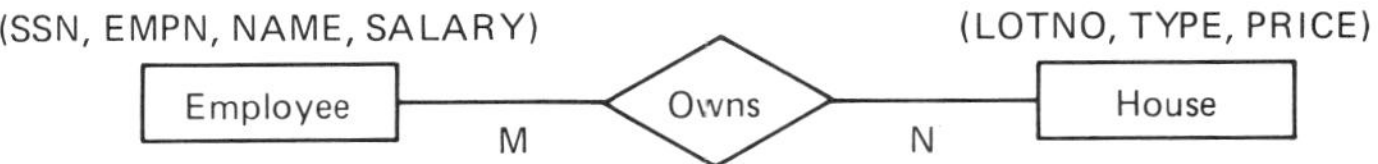

Figure 2.6   Owns relationships in the (E/R) notation.

will be clarified in Chapter 9. Let us return to the characteristics of relationships. At this point, we will interject mathematical *functions*.

A mathematical function, f, is a mapping between two sets called the domain (D) and range (R) and can be shown as

$$f : D \longrightarrow R \ (f \text{ from } D \text{ to } R)$$

A function is a subset of the Cartesian product $(D \times R)$ of sets D and R, such that if $[x,y]$ and $[x,z]$ are ordered pairs in f, then y and z must be equal to each other. That is, an element in D always maps into a unique point in R. Furthermore, a function f is *total* when $\{x|[x,y] \in f\} = D$, that is, every domain value maps into the range, and is *partial* when f is defined over a proper subset of D. Accordingly, if we examine the relationships in Figure 2.4, we can determine the following properties:

1. In Figure 2.4(a), the relationship between the attributes SSN and EMPN is functional and total. This property applies in both directions of the relationship. That is, an SSN value maps into a unique EMPN value, and vice versa. This is a consequence of the $1:1$ mapping property.

2. In Figure 2.4(b), the Owns relationship is functional since the mapping property is $N:1$; that is, each set of domain values maps into a unique range value. In this case, the type of mapping is partially functional because some employees do not own houses.

3. In Figure 2.4(c), functionality applies only to the inverse of the Manages relationship (to be interpreted as "managed by") because the mapping from employees to managers is $N:1$.

4. Figure 2.4(e) shows a totally functional mapping from the house prices to the types of houses.

In all the functional relationships, we can see that the attribute (or entity) that is the domain *uniquely determines* the attribute (or entity) in the range. (For example, "if you tell me the price of a house, I can tell you (determine) its type" is a fact in databases.) The attribute that is the domain is said to determine the attribute that is the range or the latter is said to depend on the former. This fact gives rise to *functional dependencies (FDs)* in database theory. FDs play an important role in database design. Armstrong [1974] specified some properties of functional relations and formulated them as axioms. These axioms are also referred to as *inference rules* since one can deduce/derive other valid relationships from those that are known—this is important in database research and design. The following are the inference rules:

Basic rules

1. **Reflexivity:** Given set X and $Y \subseteq X$, then $X \to X$ or $X \to Y$, which is a trivial FD, meaning that something determines itself.
2. **Transitivity:** If $X \to Y$, $Y \to Z$, then $X \to Z$.
3. **Augmentation:** If $X \to Y$ and $X \subseteq W$, then $W \to Y$.

Consequences of the basic rules

1. **Additivity (Union):** If $X \to Y$ and $W \to Z$, then $XW \to YZ$, or if $X \to Y$ and $X \to Z$, then $X \to YZ$.
2. **Projectivity (Decomposition):** If $X \to YZ$, then $X \to Y$ and $X \to Z$.
3. **Pseudotransitivity:** If $X \to Y$ and $YW \to Z$, then $XW \to Z$.

Example

If $A \to B$ and $B \to CD$, then why is $AE \to D$? (Assume $E \nsubseteq A$.)

Solution

1. By transitivity, $A \to CD$.
2. By projection (decomposition), $A \to D$.
3. By augmentation, $AE \to D$.

FDs convey the semantics (i.e., the meaning) of a database. At a given time, we may be given only the known semantics in terms of FDs that are valid and applicable. However, as we have seen in the inference rules, we can deduce other information or meaning about the database that is not explicit and/or obvious from the available information.

2.4 *HIERARCHICAL SYSTEMS*

In the hierarchical DBMS, the underlying logical structure is hierarchical or, more formally, a tree. The tree structure is defined among the relevant record types (or segments) according to an application schema or, equivalently, a definition tree. In the tree, record types are the nodes and the arcs represent the parent-child relationships between the ancestor and descendant nodes, respectively. If the level difference between the ancestor and the descendant is one, then the relationship is the closest parent-child relationship with no intervening nodes. Figure 2.7 shows a hierarchy among five record types, a shorthand version of the original schema, and an abstraction of the populated database.

In Figure 2.7(c), we observe the *hierarchical database record* (*HDR*) instances (or occurrences) in the database *forest* populated with respect to the definition tree. At a given time, a hierarchical database record need not have all of its segments present. (Notice the first record R_1 and the second from the end,

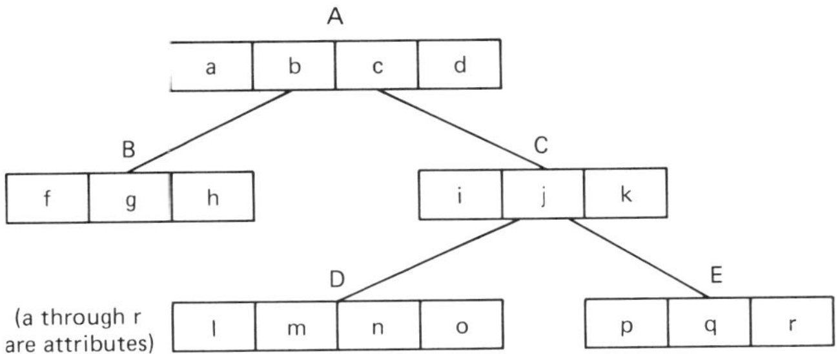

(a) A hierarchical schema among five record types

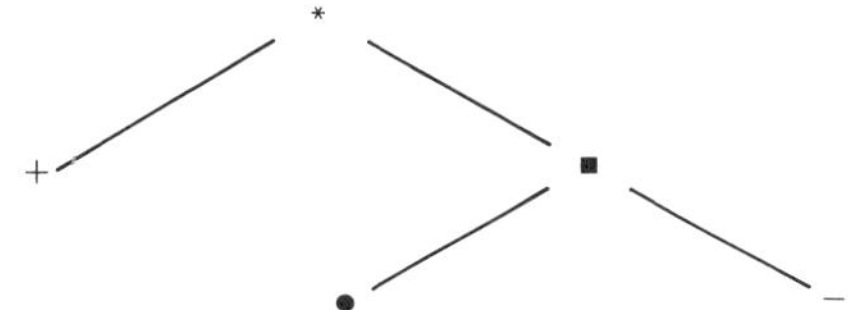

(b) A shorthand version of the definition tree

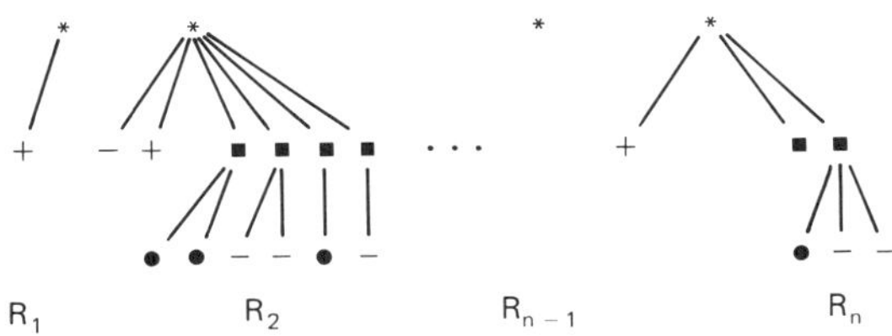

(c) A populated database

Figure 2.7 A hierarchical database.

R_{n-1}.) Also, one may add/delete as many occurrences of a record type as necessary, as dictated by the application. Suppose that we interpret the record types A, B, C, D, and E, as Course, Prerequisite, Semester, Teacher, and Student, respectively. Accordingly, a given course may have not yet been implemented (e.g., R_{n-1}), but a prerequisite may have been defined (R_1). The reader, as an exercise, can continue and see whether a sensible interpretation can be found for the rest of the HDRs stored (populated) in the physical database. (One can assume that assignment of teachers to a course at different semesters and preregistration of students to courses are carried out independently and that the decision to run the course is made at a subsequent date—if sensible at all!)

The way that HDRs are stored in the physical database depends on the specific implementation, which chooses a method to map the (logical) trees to the (physical) file structures of a given system. A straightforward way in which to *linearize* a tree is the *preorder* traversal in which the subtrees are stored consecutively in the root/left–child/right–child order of record type occurrences.

2.4.1 Some Characteristics of Hierarchical Systems

The tree structure implies an $N:1$ mapping from children to parent instances. Since we cannot have a child node without a parent node in the tree (exception is the root), this mapping is totally functional. Therefore, one-to-one and many-to-one strongly connected relationships can be represented directly by hierarchies. However, one has to duplicate trees to represent a many-to-many relationship. As an example, for the relationship of Figure 2.4(d), we have two options as shown in Figure 2.8, in the hierarchical schema design.

In hierarchical databases, search operations are implemented in a way to suit the underlying tree structure, and hence, a search starts from the root and proceeds down to the descendant nodes. If a given implementation does not add any direct access features to a given record type in addition to the natural tree traversal, then the position of a node in the tree makes a big difference with respect to ease of access. In our Supplier-Parts application, we have an $M \times N$ mapping between the record types. If we do not know the type of access most frequently executed on the database we must store both versions (i.e., Figures 2.8(b) and 2.8(c)) for general utility and flexibility—if we can afford it of course! Otherwise, we have to choose one and accept the consequences. For example, in Figure 2.8(b), it will be much easier to answer the request (query) that wants all the parts supplied by a given supplier than the request that wants all suppliers of a given part (which is easily answered, without scanning all the leaves, by the Figure 2.8(c) representation). In a hierarchical database, therefore, data duplication and/or more search effort is required to deal with complex relationships.

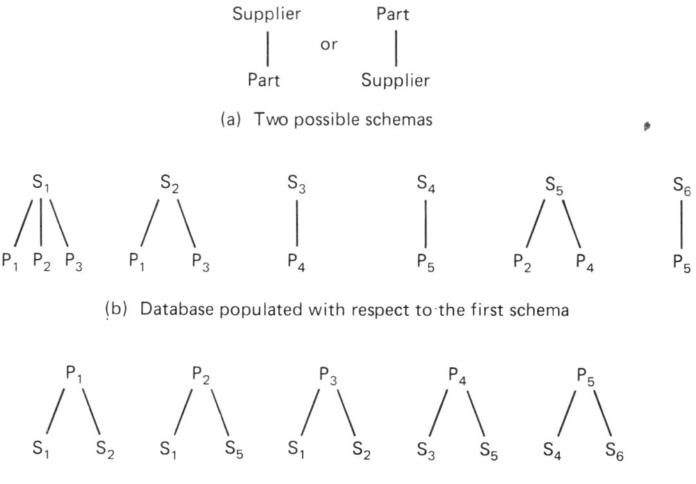

Figure 2.8   Hierarchical representations of the Supplier-Parts database.

Another problem with hierarchies is that a child instance cannot exist in the database without an associated parent instance, or else we must invent a *dummy* parent. Consequently, the deletion of a given parent instance implies the deletion of all its children instances (all subtrees) that coexist with it. These restrictions may create problems in certain applications. That is, schema design may not be straightforward in some applications.

2.4.2 Implementation Considerations

We will touch upon the implementation issues of hierarchical systems very briefly. The reasons for doing this are that the physical implementation of the other systems can be decomposed into hierarchies and that it will not be relevant for the scope of the book to delve into this problem once more in depth. In fact, the database computer hardware is a solution to this otherwise hard problem of physical database design. The following presents some thoughts on various ways of implementing hierarchies:

1. *Physical contiguity:* We can map logical tree occurrences into physical storage by linearizing subtrees in preorder (because it is suitable to serial representation) and storing the linearized data in fixed- or variable-sized blocks.

2. We can use pointers between record-type instances. A parent can point to all of its children, or to the oldest child (on the left), and then the children can be linked together. There are various trade-offs with respect to pointer space, addition/deletion, and access time to a given record type instance.

3. We can partition record type instances into various files organized differently with respect to access speed. For example, in the hierarchical DBMS of IBM [IBM, 1978] called the *information management system* (*IMS*), there can be the following options:

   a. HSAM: The entire linearized physical structure is organized as a sequential file.

   b. HISAM: The root record type instances are separated and organized as an ISAM (indexed sequential access method) file. The rest of the data is placed in a sequential file which is linked from these root occurrences. In this way, it becomes possible to randomly locate the beginning of a given HDR occurrence.

   c. HDAM: The record type instances are organized into a direct address file so that each instance can be accessed directly. The tree structure among the record type instances is indicated by means of pointers embedded in the record type instances.

   d. HIDAM: Combines the advantages of (b) HISAM and (c) HDAM. That is, the roots are stored in an ISAM file, so that they can be accessed both sequentially and randomly, and they point to the remainder of the tree stored as an HDAM file.

4. Node addressing technique: In this scheme, we will talk about *traces* [Lowenthal, 1971]. In the trace method, we assign a logical address to each node instance in HDR. Accordingly, for each node instance there corresponds a trace tuple, fixed or variable in length, which indicates the following information:

   a. Record type identifier, in terms of a type number

   b. The relative occurrence of the node instance (e.g., the third HDR's fifth descendant of a given type number)

Figure 2.9 shows a definition tree and traces of the nodes of the fifth HDR. The traces are formed as fixed-length trace tuples.

As can be seen, for Figure 2.9(b) there are four positions in a trace tuple corresponding to four possible type numbers. The trace (5, 0, 2, 2) can be read as the second − son of the second ○ son of the fifth HDR.

Traces also have the following advantages. A request for (5, 1, 2, 2) can be refused at compile time because type 3 cannot be a valid descendant of type 2, as implied in the request. We can also walk in the tree simply by manipulating digits in the trace. Truncating digits on the right would take us to ancestors, the opposite to descendants; adding/subtracting one to the rightmost digit would take us to younger/older siblings; and so on. Traces can be stored as a directory table with each trace pointing to the address of the corresponding node instance (data occurrence) stored in a file.

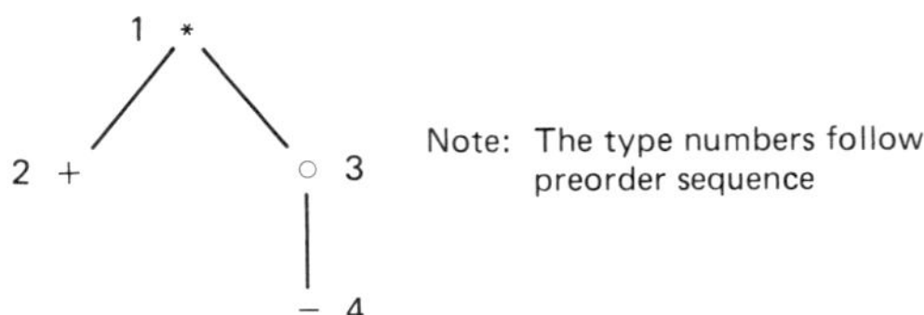

(a) Definition tree and the type numbers

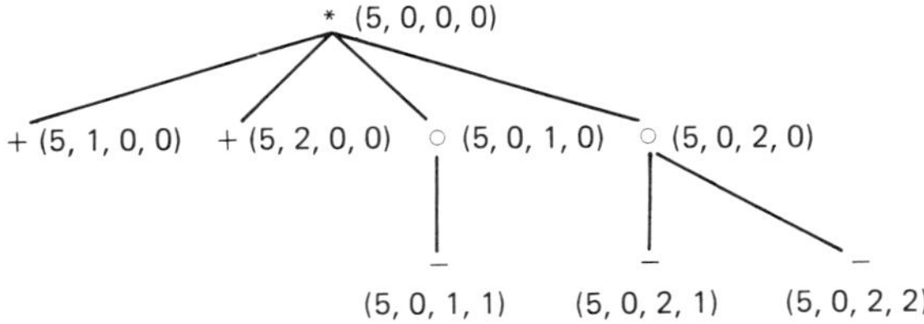

(b) Node addresses for the fifth HDR

Figure 2.9 Trace structure.

2.5 NETWORK SYSTEMS

The network data model is the data model of a network DBMS. The network data model can be described, in the graph theoretical sense, as a graph having no cycles (with the exception of self, L_{ii}, links), and a collection of record types connected by a set of links. Figure 2.10 depicts a network schema and a corresponding *network database record* (*NDR*) occurrence.

The network data model definition in Figure 2.10 is too general for implementation purposes in the sense that there is virtually no limit (except for cycles) in the way that record types can be connected in the database. The network data model introduced by the Data Base Task Group of the Conference on Data Systems Languages [CODASYL, 1971] has defined some restrictions for its DBTG network data model as can be seen in the following description.

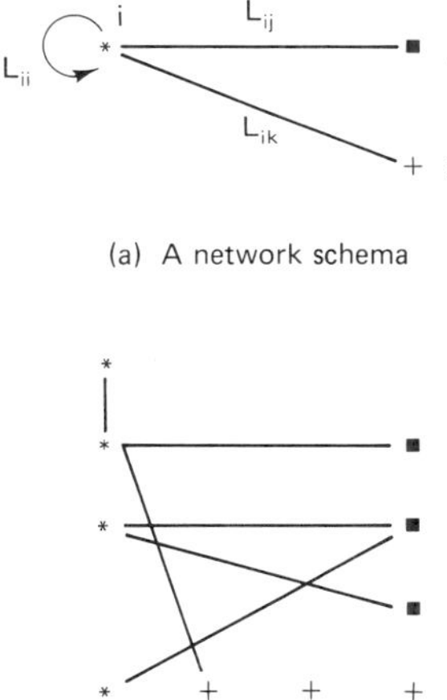

(a) A network schema

(b) An NDR instance

Figure 2.10   A network database structure.

2.5.1 CODASYL's DBTG Network Model

A DBTG network database consists of a collection of *owner* and *member* record types and *set types* defined among them. A set type defines a relationship between the owner and member record types in the following manner:

(a) There must be one-to-many relationships between an owner and the member record types. This implies that a DBTG database is built from tree structures.

(b) There must correspond a unique set of member occurrences for a given owner occurrence.

(c) A given record type cannot be both an owner and a member in a given set type.

In (a), there is one exception to the strict hierarchical structure and that is the fact that there can be a member occurrence not currently owned. This means that there can be a child without its parent existing in the tree, thus modifying the total functional mapping from members to the owner restriction of hierarchies to a partially functional one. Also, in a DBTG network, more than one set type can be defined between the owner and member record types so that there can be multiple relationships defined among them, unlike the single parent-child relationship allowed in a tree structure.

There are various ways of dealing with the restrictions of (a), (b), and (c) in the sense of converting a more general, less restrictive structure to a DBTG structure. We show these in the following:

To convert a general network schema, as exemplified by Figure 2.8(a) between Supplier and Part, we can introduce a link or buffer record type. In this way, we can convert the $M \times N$ mapping between the record types into multiple $1 \times N$ mappings (i.e., hierarchies), thus satisfying restriction (a). We can arrange the link record types in such a way that restriction (b) is also satisfied. In addition, link record types can also be made information carrying (e.g., *quantity of shipment* can be stored with the link record type). Figure 2.11 shows these conversions.

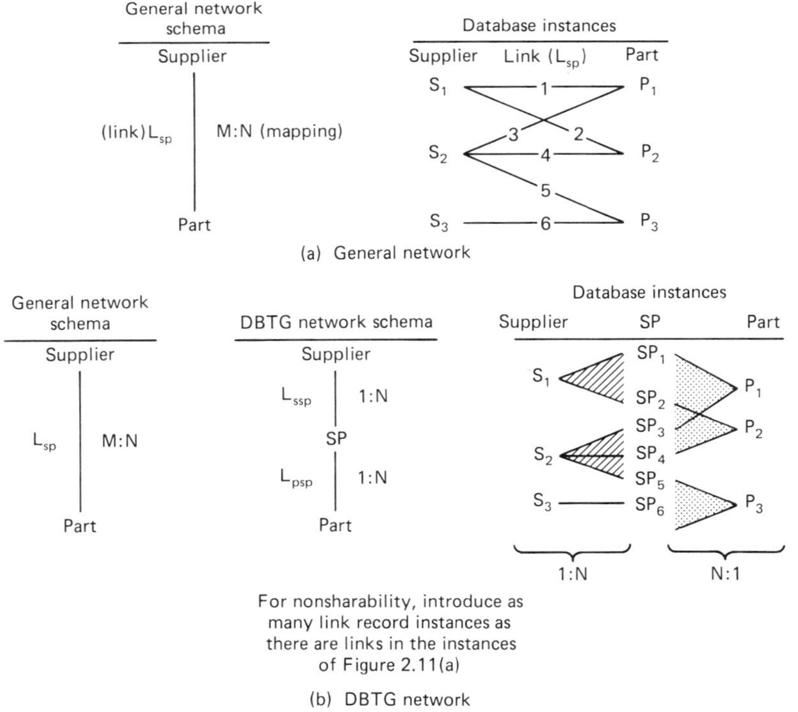

Figure 2.11   Conversion into a DBTG network database.

As can be seen from the conversion in Figure 2.11, to convert a general structure into a more restrictive structure, we must introduce more links (set types) and more record types. This is another example showing that we have to introduce duplication to represent a complex and powerful structure in terms of a relatively primitive and/or restrictive one.

To deal with the restriction (c), let us turn back to the example shown in Figures 2.4(c) and 2.5(c) for the Manages relationship. As can be seen, in DBTG terms, both the owner and the member must be the same record type, which is not allowed. In this case, similar to the previous solution for the restrictions of (a) and (b), we can represent the given relationships by introducing either different record types for the different roles of the same record type or, better yet, by adding a dummy record type between the owner and the member record types. These concepts are demonstrated in Figure 2.12.

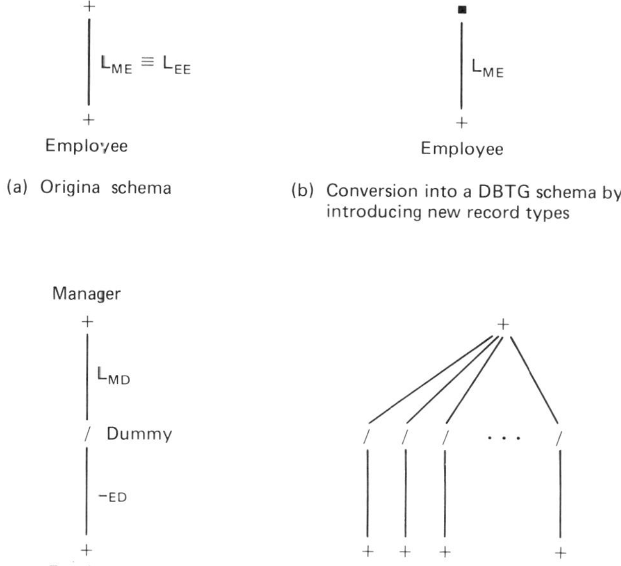

Figure 2.12 Conversion into a DBTG network database.

2.6 RELATIONAL SYSTEMS

The relational data model [Codd, 1970] is the data model for relational DBMS. In terms of the concepts we have seen up to this point, we can describe a relation as an aggregate of relationships among n attributes, that is, as an n'ary attribute relationship. Only the sensible and/or allowable combination of attribute rela-

tionships are included in the corresponding data representation. A series of
formal definitions is given in the following:

(a) A domain is a homogeneous pool of data values. Examples are the domain
of money, domain of names, domain of integers, and so on.

(b) An attribute was defined earlier as the representation of an entity's property.
Two or more attributes can draw values from a same domain. In this
respect, the domain values play different roles as different attributes to
describe the information structure that uses them. (Both the Salary and
Commission attributes for an Employee entity (relation) draw values from
the money domain.)

(c) Given n domains, D_1, D_2, . . ., D_n, not necessarily distinct, a relation **R**
is defined to be a set of ordered n-tuples such that it is a subset of the
Cartesian product of the domains, and the domain (set) D_i is represented
as the ith value in the n-tuples. The order requirement within an n-tuple
can be removed if we identify each role played by a domain with a distinct
attribute name.

The fact that a relation is a subset of the Cartesian product of the constituent
domains can be demonstrated by the following simple example. Assume that
we want to construct a binary relation (i.e., a relation with two attributes)
consisting of the attributes *name* and *age*. Suppose that we have the following
data in the respective domains:

Name Domain	Age (from domain of integers)
Doe	25
Clark	37
Johnson	43

The relation R(*NAME,AGE*)—attribute names can be listed in any order
within the parentheses—is represented as R $\subseteq$ *NAME*$\otimes$*AGE* ($\otimes$ denotes Cartesian
product), because as can be seen in the following:

$$NAME \otimes AGE \ = \ <DOE, 25>, <CLARK, 25>, <JOHNSON, 25>$$
$$<DOE, 37>, <CLARK, 37>, <JOHNSON, 37>$$
$$<DOE, 43>, <CLARK, 43>, <JOHNSON, 43>$$

which is a set of nine 2-tuples. However, in reality, only three of the age values
will apply to the three individuals. Therefore, the relation

$$R(NAME, AGE) \ = \ <DOE, 43>, <CLARK, 25>, <JOHNSON, 37>$$

will represent the real-world picture, which is a subset of the Cartesian product
just shown.

2.6.1 Properties of Relations

(a) A relation is said to be normalized if every attribute value in an *n*-tuple (or simply a tuple) is a simple, atomic value not consisting of a group of values. This prohibits replacing an attribute by another relation (which would result in a nested or a hierarchical relation).

(b) A normalized relation is a tabular structure such that the table name corresponds to the relation name, the column headers to the attribute names, and the rows of the table to the *n*-tuples.

(c) Ordering of rows is immaterial theoretically; however, it may affect the efficiency of accessing tuples.

(d) All rows (tuples) must be unique within a relation.

(e) There can be more than one single attribute or composite attributes that uniquely identify the tuples in a relation. These are called *candidate keys,* and one of them is chosen as the *primary key* for implementing tuple accesses.

(f) A relational database is a collection of time-varying, normalized relations of varying degrees that can be interrelated with each other through common domains.

A few remarks regarding item (f) are as follows. The difference between a mathematical relation and a database relation is that, in the latter, there can be addition and/or deletion of tuple instances over time so that the state of the relations can vary. The number of attributes making up a relation is called the *degree* of the relation, whereas the *cardinality* of a relation is the number of tuples in the relation. We can navigate through the relations in a database by *joining* them together through their join attributes which are defined over common or compatible domains. The join operation involves taking join attribute values of one relation (the source relation) and selecting tuples in the other relation (the target) based on an exhaustive comparison that compares all the target tuples with each of the values taken from the source tuples. The following section will demonstrate this operation.

2.6.2 Relational Algebra

In this section, we will briefly cover the operations of relational algebra by demonstrating a series of examples. For each operation we will use descriptive notation of both the algebra and calculus. The latter will follow the notation used by Codd [1972]. The first five operations, which are Projection, Union, Difference, Cartesian product, and Selection, are the basic operations. There are also the frequently used operations of Intersection, Join, and Division which can be expressed in terms of the five basic operations. The relations and their data that will be used in the examples are given in the following:

$$
\begin{array}{lll}
P(D_1, & D_2, & D_3) \\
1 & 11 & x \\
2 & 11 & y \\
3 & 11 & z \\
4 & 12 & x
\end{array}
\qquad
\begin{array}{ll}
Q(D_4, & D_5) \\
x & 1 \\
x & 2 \\
y & 1
\end{array}
\qquad
\begin{array}{llll}
R(M, & P, & Q, & T) \\
x & 101 & 5 & a \\
y & 105 & 3 & a \\
z & 500 & 9 & a \\
w & 50 & 1 & b \\
w & 10 & 2 & b \\
w & 300 & 4 & b
\end{array}
\qquad
\begin{array}{ll}
S(A, & B) \\
5 & a \\
10 & b \\
15 & c \\
2 & d \\
6 & a \\
1 & b
\end{array}
$$

As seen, the relations are described as the relation name followed by the list of attribute names written in parentheses (this definition is also referred to as the *intension*). Their tuple instance population (*extension*) is listed underneath the definitions. In the descriptions to follow, we will use the letters R and S to denote relations while A and B will each represent a list of attributes (for simplicity, the reader can assume a single attribute whenever convenient).

Projection

Algebra	**Calculus**
$R[A]$	$\{r[A] : r \in R\}$

Accordingly, the projection operation involves selecting from each tuple in the relation R only those attributes included in A and then eliminating duplicate tuples in the resulting relation. In the calculus notation, the lowercase r represents a *tuple variable* in the resulting set so that each tuple which is left with the A attributes is a member of the original relation. The process of eliminating duplicate tuples is implicit as dictated by the definition of a relation.

Example

$$
R[M, T] =
\begin{bmatrix}
x & a \\
y & a \\
z & a \\
w & b \\
\cancel{w} & \cancel{b} \\
\cancel{w} & \cancel{b}
\end{bmatrix}
=
\begin{bmatrix}
x & a \\
y & a \\
z & a \\
w & b
\end{bmatrix}
$$

Union

Algebra	**Calculus**
$R \cup S$	$\{t : t \in R \vee t \in S\}$

In order that union can be performed, the operand relations (R, S) must be union compatible; that is, their corresponding attributes should have compatible domains. Implicit in each relational algebra operation is that duplicate tuples in the result relation must be eliminated.

Example

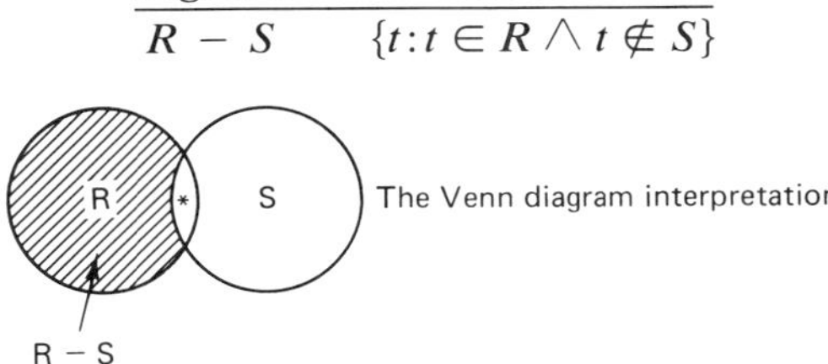

$$R[Q, T] \cup S = \begin{bmatrix} 5 & a \\ 3 & a \\ 9 & a \\ 1 & b \\ 2 & b \\ 4 & b \end{bmatrix} \cup \begin{bmatrix} 5 & a \\ 10 & b \\ 15 & c \\ 2 & d \\ 6 & a \\ 1 & b \end{bmatrix} = \begin{bmatrix} 5 & a \\ 3 & a \\ 9 & a \\ 1 & b \\ 2 & b \\ 4 & b \\ 10 & b \\ 15 & c \\ 2 & d \\ 6 & a \end{bmatrix}$$

Domain   Domain
of integers   of literals

Difference

Algebra	Calculus
$R - S$	$\{t : t \in R \wedge t \notin S\}$

The Venn diagram interpretation

R − S

Example

$$R[Q, T] - S = \begin{bmatrix} 5 & a \\ 3 & a \\ 9 & a \\ 1 & b \\ 2 & b \\ 4 & b \end{bmatrix} - \begin{bmatrix} 5 & a \\ 10 & b \\ 15 & c \\ 2 & d \\ 6 & a \\ 1 & b \end{bmatrix} = \begin{bmatrix} 3 & a \\ 9 & a \\ 2 & b \\ 4 & b \end{bmatrix}$$

Cartesian Product

Algebra	Calculus
$R \otimes S$	$\{(r\|s) : r \in R \wedge s \in S\}$

As can be seen in the calculus notation, a cross product is implied between the extensions of the operand relations and the result is the concatenation (indicated by $\|$) of the corresponding tuples. Accordingly,

$$\text{Degree } (R \otimes S) = \text{degree } (R) + \text{degree } (S)$$

$$\text{Cardinality } (R \otimes S) = \text{cardinality } (R) \times \text{cardinality } (S)$$

This implies a space explosion on the part of the result relation. In practice, a more restrictive version of this operation called *join* is used. Let

$$R_A = [M, T] \qquad \text{and} \qquad R_B = R[Q, T] \cap S$$

These were the results of the previous examples. Accordingly,

$$R_A = \begin{bmatrix} x & a \\ y & a \\ z & a \\ w & b \end{bmatrix} \quad \text{and} \quad R_B = \begin{bmatrix} 5 & a \\ 1 & b \end{bmatrix}$$

$$R_A \otimes R_B = \begin{bmatrix} x & a \\ y & a \\ z & a \\ w & b \end{bmatrix} \otimes \begin{bmatrix} 5 & a \\ 1 & b \end{bmatrix} = \begin{bmatrix} x & a & 5 & a \\ x & a & 1 & b \\ y & a & 5 & a \\ y & a & 1 & b \\ z & a & 5 & a \\ z & a & 1 & b \\ w & b & 5 & a \\ w & b & 1 & b \end{bmatrix}$$

The degree of the result is 4 (2 + 2), and the cardinality is 8 (2 × 4).

Selection (Restriction)

Algebra	Calculus
(a) $R[A\theta v]$	$\{r : r \in R \land (r[A]\theta v)\}$
(b) $R[A\theta B]$	$\{r : r \in R \land (r[A]\theta r[B])\}$

In the preceding notations, v signifies an external constant, whereas B is another attribute of the relation R. θ can be one of the comparison operators $<, \leq, =, \neq, \geq$, and $>$.

Examples

$$P[D_1 > D_2] = \phi \quad \text{(null) because in none of the tuples is}$$
$$D_1 \text{ greater than } D_2$$

$$P[D_2 = 11][D_2] = \begin{bmatrix} 1 & 11 & x \\ 2 & 11 & y \\ 3 & 11 & z \end{bmatrix} [D_2] = [11]$$

Intersection

Algebra	Calculus
$R \cap S$	$\{t : t \in R \land t \in S\}$

Also, $R \cap S = R - (R - S)$, which corresponds to the area marked by an asterisk in the Venn diagram shown in the difference operation.

Example

$$R[Q, T] \cap S = \begin{bmatrix} 5 & a \\ 3 & a \\ 9 & a \\ 1 & b \\ 2 & b \\ 4 & b \end{bmatrix} \cap \begin{bmatrix} 5 & a \\ 10 & b \\ 15 & c \\ 2 & d \\ 6 & a \\ 1 & b \end{bmatrix} = \begin{bmatrix} 5 & a \\ 1 & b \end{bmatrix}$$

Join

Algebra	Calculus
$R[A\theta B]S$	$\{(r\|s) : r \in R \wedge s \in S \wedge (r[A]\ \theta\ s[B])\}$

As can be seen from the definition, the join operation resembles the Cartesian product with the exception of introducing a *condition* so that, instead of taking a cross product of all the tuples unconditionally, only those that satisfy a condition between the join attributes (A, B) of the respective relations are included in the result. The join operation has the following variations:

(a) *Theta- and equi-join:* In this join, A and B are the compatible join attributes and the degree of the join is the sum of the degrees of the operand relations. This join is referred to as the θ-*join* (*theta-join*) and the equality case is also known as the *equi-join*.

(b) *Natural join:* In this join, the join attributes have common (identical) domains and after the join, one of these common domains is discarded leaving the relation with a degree one less than the sum of the degrees of the operand relations.

(c) *Composition:* This join is the same as the natural join with the difference that both of the join attributes are discarded from the result. Hence the degree of the result relation is two less than the sum of the degrees of the operand relations.

Examples

Theta-join

$$R[Q > A]S$$

In doing the join, for each R-tuple, we have to look at the Q value and compare it with the A value of every tuple in the S relation. The following is the result:

$$\begin{bmatrix}
x & 101 & 5 & a & 2 & d \\
x & 101 & 5 & a & 1 & b \\
y & 105 & 3 & a & 2 & d \\
y & 105 & 3 & a & 1 & b \\
z & 500 & 9 & a & 5 & a \\
z & 500 & 9 & a & 2 & d \\
z & 500 & 9 & a & 6 & a \\
z & 500 & 9 & a & 1 & b \\
w & 10 & 2 & b & 1 & b \\
w & 300 & 4 & b & 2 & d \\
w & 300 & 4 & b & 1 & b
\end{bmatrix}$$

As can be noticed, the tuple $< w\ 50\ 1\ b >$ of the R relation was not eligible in this θ-join operation.

Natural Join $P[D_3 = D_4]Q$

$$
\begin{bmatrix}
1 & 11 & x & x & 1 \\
1 & 11 & x & y & 2 \\
2 & 11 & y & y & 1 \\
4 & 12 & x & x & 1 \\
4 & 12 & x & y & 2
\end{bmatrix}
=
\begin{bmatrix}
1 & 11 & x & 1 \\
1 & 11 & x & 2 \\
2 & 11 & y & 1 \\
4 & 12 & x & 1 \\
4 & 12 & x & 2
\end{bmatrix}
$$

Division

Algebra	Calculus
$R[A \div B]S$	$\{r[\overline{A}] : r \in R \land S[B] \subseteq g_R(r[\overline{A}])\}$

A and B are compatible and/or common division attributes. For easy interpretation of the definitions, assume R is a binary relation consisting of A and the complement of A, which is $\overline{A}$ signifying all attributes other than A.

For each partition in $R[\overline{A}]$, that is, for each unique tuple $r[\overline{A}]$ do the following:

(a) Select all the corresponding tuples in $r[A]$ and call this set of tuples T, where T is equal to $g_R(r[\overline{A}])$. T is called the image set (g_R) of the partition.

(b) If there is one tuple r in T, for every tuple in $S[B]$ (i.e., $S[B] \subseteq T$), then put $r[\overline{A}]$ in the answer.

Examples

$P[D_3 \div D_4]Q = \phi$ (null) because

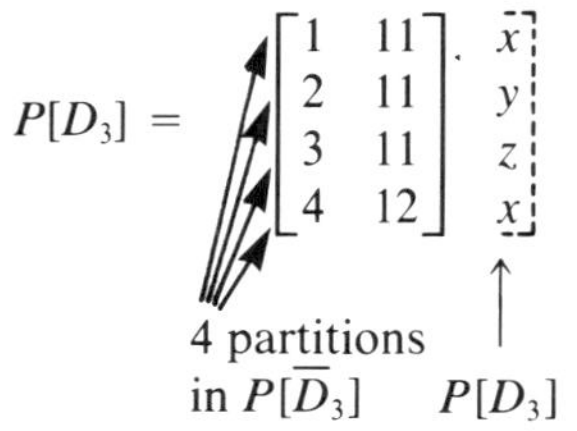

$$
P[D_3] =
\begin{bmatrix}
1 & 11 \\
2 & 11 \\
3 & 11 \\
4 & 12
\end{bmatrix}
\begin{array}{c}
x \\ y \\ z \\ x
\end{array}
\qquad \text{and} \qquad
Q = \left\{ \begin{array}{c} x \\ y \end{array} \right\}
$$

4 partitions
in $P[\overline{D}_3]$ $P[\overline{D}_3]$

$$
\{x\} \nsupseteq \left\{ \begin{array}{c} x \\ y \end{array} \right\}
$$

$$
\{y\} \nsupseteq \left\{ \begin{array}{c} x \\ y \end{array} \right\}
$$

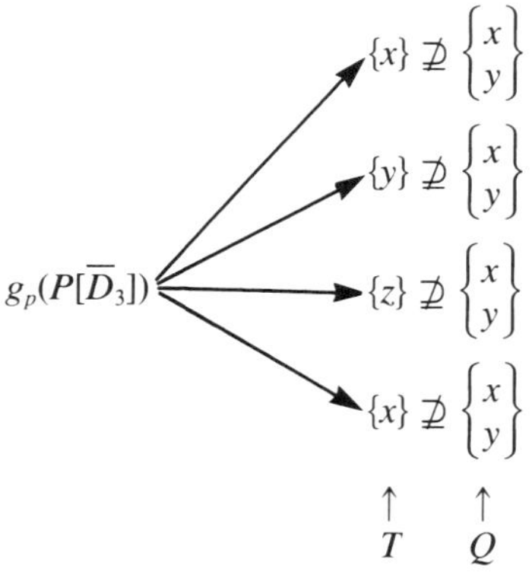

$g_p(P[\overline{D}_3]) \qquad \{z\} \nsupseteq \left\{ \begin{array}{c} x \\ y \end{array} \right\}$ Hence there is no eligible $p[\overline{D}_3]$ for output.

$$
\{x\} \nsupseteq \left\{ \begin{array}{c} x \\ y \end{array} \right\}
$$

$T \qquad Q$

If, however, we were asked to do the following division,

$$P[D_2 D_3][D_3 \div D_4]Q$$

$$P[D_2 D_3] = \begin{bmatrix} 11 & x \\ 11 & y \\ 11 & z \\ 12 & x \end{bmatrix} = PD$$

$$PD[\overline{D_3}] = \begin{bmatrix} 11 & x \\ 11 & y \\ 11 & z \\ \hline 12 & x \end{bmatrix}$$

two partitions

$$\begin{Bmatrix} x \\ y \\ z \end{Bmatrix} \supset \begin{Bmatrix} x \\ y \end{Bmatrix} \longrightarrow pd[\overline{D_3}] = \begin{bmatrix} 11 \\ 11 \\ 11 \end{bmatrix} = [11], \text{ which is the answer.}$$

$$T \longrightarrow \{x\} \not\supseteq \begin{Bmatrix} x \\ y \end{Bmatrix}$$

Division in Terms of the Basic Operations. Similar to the definition given by Ullman [1982], division of R by S is a set of $(d_r - d_s)$-tuples p such that for all d_s-tuples u in S, the tuple pu is in R—d_r and d_s indicate the degrees of the corresponding relations R, S. In terms of the previous definition, $R[\overline{A}]$ corresponds to the projection of R on the first $(d_r - d_s)$ attributes which will be called P. Accordingly, $(P \otimes S) - R$ would correspond to r-tuples that are not in R, but formed by taking the first $(d_r - d_s)$ tuples of R (i.e., $r[\overline{A}]$) and concatenating each by a tuple in S. Let V be the set of $(d_r - d_s)$-tuples p that correspond to the first $(d_r - d_s)$ attributes of R such that for some s-tuple u in S, pu is not in R. Accordingly,

$$R[A \div B]S \text{ (or } R \div B \text{ in short)} = P - V$$

Applying this to the previous example would give us the following:

$$R = \begin{bmatrix} 11 & x \\ 11 & y \\ 11 & z \\ 12 & x \end{bmatrix} \qquad S = \begin{bmatrix} x \\ y \end{bmatrix}$$

$$d_r - d_s = 1$$

$$P = \begin{bmatrix} 11 \\ 12 \end{bmatrix} \qquad P \otimes S = \begin{bmatrix} 11 & x \\ 12 & x \\ 11 & y \\ 12 & y \end{bmatrix} - R = [12 \quad y]$$

$$V = [12]$$

$$P - V = \begin{bmatrix} 11 \\ 12 \end{bmatrix} - [12] = [11]$$

2.6.3 A RAP Relation

A RAP relation R is a normalized relation augmented with a set of mark (tag) domain (bits) as $R(m_1, \ldots, m_k; A_1, \ldots, A_n)$. Accordingly, each RAP relation tuple has k one-bit mark attributes followed by n attributes in the usual sense of a normalized relation. Furthermore, a RAP relation can be a *multiset* in that there can be duplicate tuples. The true relational interface is enforced on top of this *multiset* structure. The uses of RAP relations as well as their mark bits will be clarified in the subsequent chapters.

2.6.4 Normal Form Theory

In relational databases, the schema information contains both the structural and semantic information. The former corresponds to relation declarations, and the latter is conveyed with a set of known functional dependencies among the attributes of the relations declared in the schema. Certain FDs in the relations, however, may be undesirable because of the side effects or anomalies they cause in the course of database updates. We are, therefore, confronted with the question as to whether a given schema is proper. An affirmative response to this question would imply the absence of undesirable FDs in the schema. If, however, this is not true, then we would be faced with a process called *decomposition* which replaces a given set of relations with a different set of relations (whose total number is increased) which are projections of the former with the aim of eliminating the undesirable FDs (hence, anomalies). This is exactly what is done in the normalization process. In other words, normalization is a step-by-step reversible process of replacing a given schema (or collection of relations) by successive collections in which relations have a progressively simpler and regular structure.

Normal form theory defines various normal forms in which the types of allowable FDs a relation can have are restricted. To accomplish this, as we stated, we resort to decomposition. Once we do that, then we introduce the problem of reversibility (i.e., the ability to recover original schema). What this means actually is that we must be able to preserve *equivalence* of schemas once we change a given schema into another by decomposition. To maintain equivalence of schemas, we must be able to have decompositions that are both lossless and dependency preserving. This is another way of stating that the original schema must be preserved. The lossless decomposition guarantees reversibility; that is, the obtaining of the original set of relations from a series of natural joins on their projections by which no spurious tuples are introduced as a result of *connection trap* (i.e., improper join). Dependency preservation deals with the validity of the original set of FDs on the decomposed relations of the new schema.

To be able to judge about lossless and dependency preserving decompositions, we need to know all possible FDs present in a given schema. At a given time, we may know a subset of FDs valid for a schema, but we can produce the remainder by the use of inference rules of functional relations we have presented earlier in the chapter.

An attribute that participates in a key is called *prime*; otherwise, we refer to it as *nonprime*. A *full functional dependence* means that if $A \rightarrow B$, then B must be dependent upon all of A and not a part (subset) of it. For example, if $A = A_1, A_2, \ldots, A_k$ and $A_1, A_2 \rightarrow B$, then B is said to be nonfull functionally dependent on A.

In the remainder, we will cover various normal forms from first to fifth, including Boyce-Codd normal form. These will be abbreviated as 1NF, 2NF, 3NF, BCNF, 4NF, and 5NF. The first (1NF), second (2NF), and third (3NF) normal forms restrict dependence of nonprime attributes on keys. The Boyce-Codd normal form (BCNF) also restricts dependence of prime attributes. The fourth normal form (4NF) places a restriction on the types of multivalued dependencies, which will be discussed later. The fifth normal form introduces another form of dependence, called the join dependence.

The level of normalization of a given relation is a matter of semantics and cannot be solely determined from the values stored in it at a given time. This implies that one must be given semantic information in terms of FDs.

First normal form (1NF).   A relation is said to be in first normal form (1NF) if all of its attribute values are simple (or atomic). That is, an attribute value should not consist of a set of values or repeating groups. Unnormalized relations correspond to nested tables (i.e., hierarchies) as opposed to the flat, tabular structure of a normalized relation.

Example

```
FLIGHT (FNO,ORIGIN,DESTINATION,SCHEDULE)
SCHEDULE(DAY,DEPARTURE-TIME)
```

Assuming the following flight data,

```
TW101 CHICAGO PHOENIX MON 940
                      WED 940
                      FRI 1030

TW800 PHOENIX NEWYORK MON 730
                      TUE 730
                      FRI 730
```

To convert this unnormalized relation to 1NF, we have to replace SCHED-ULE in FLIGHT with the constituent attributes as follows:

```
FLIGHT(FNO,    ORIGIN,    DESTINATION,    DAY,    DEPARTURE-TIME)
       TW101   CHICAGO    PHOENIX         MON     940
       TW101   CHICAGO    PHOENIX         WED     940
       TW101   CHICAGO    PHOENIX         FRI     1030
       TW800   PHOENIX    NEWYORK         MON     730
       TW800   PHOENIX    NEWYORK         TUE     730
       TW800   PHOENIX    NEWYORK         FRI     730
```

Second normal form (2NF).   Let us have a SUPPLY relation indicating the fact that a given supplier (identified by SNO) supplies various items at some predetermined prices; that is,

```
SUPPLY(SNO, ITEM, PRICE)
```

Assume that a supplier can supply various items and that an item can be supplied by more than one supplier. Accordingly, the key (indicated in bold) of the relation will be the SNO, ITEM composite. However, we also know that items alone determine their prices (i.e., all suppliers charge the same price). Accordingly, we have the following semantic information:

```
SNO, ITEM → PRICE   (by being the key)
ITEM → PRICE
```

As can be observed, PRICE is nonfull functionally dependent on the key because it depends on only a part of it, not the whole composite. This leads to the following anomalies:

Insertion Anomaly.   If a supplier decides to carry a new item, we cannot record the item and its price unless the supplier starts supplying it.

Deletion Anomaly.   If a given item ceases to be supplied, then we have to delete the item and its price from the database even though the supplier may stock it.

Update Anomaly.   To change the price of a given item, we must search the entire relation to locate all the suppliers of the items so that the price change is reflected on all suppliers. As can be seen, an update that affects a single item has to be made on multiple tuples; otherwise, the database would remain inconsistent.

The main reason for these anomalies is the nonfull functional dependence of PRICE on the key forcing the SUPPLY relation to carry two semantic facts in a single structure. The solution to this problem is to decompose the SUPPLY relation into two relations so that the nonfull functional dependence is eliminated. A relation is in 2NF if it is in 1NF and every nonprime attribute is full functionally dependent on the key(s). The following decomposition will be in 2NF:

```
SUPPLY(SNO, ITEM)
ITEM_PRICE(ITEM,PRICE)
```

We can still determine the price for a supply tuple by joining the two relations over ITEM. However, ITEM-PRICE relationship would now involve only the second relation so that a price update would affect a single tuple in the ITEM-PRICE relation.

Third normal form (3NF).   Let us consider the following type of transitive dependence: If $A \rightarrow B$ and $B \nrightarrow A$ (B is not a key), $B \rightarrow C$ then $A \rightarrow C$ transitively.

Let us assume a relation called STOCK(**COMPANY**, WAREHOUSE, CA-PACITY), which gives the information on which companies receive their supplies from which warehouses and the capacity of a given warehouse. The applicable FDs are

```
COMPANY  →  WAREHOUSE   (a company receives its supplies from one warehouse)
WAREHOUSE  →  CAPACITY
```

Anomalies.   If there is no company currently being supplied by the warehouse, we cannot enter the capacity information of the warehouse into the database (insertion anomaly). If the last company using the warehouse ceases to use it, then we cannot keep the warehouse and its capacity data in the relation (deletion anomaly). If the capacity of a given warehouse changes, then the entire relation must be searched and multiple tuples (for as many companies that use the warehouse) should be updated (update anomaly). As in the 2NF case, the transitive dependence (nonfull functional dependence in 2NF) causes two facts to be stored in the same relation forcing these anomalies.

The solution is to decompose the schema into a 3NF schema. A 3NF schema is a 2NF schema having no transitive dependence of nonprime attributes on key(s). The following decomposition will solve the problem:

```
STOCK(COMPANY, WAREHOUSE)
W-CAPACITY(WAREHOUSE, CAPACITY)
```

Boyce-Codd normal form (BCNF).   Let us have a relation called PROJ-ECT(**P#**, **PJ#**, S#) indicating the fact that projects use parts that are supplied to projects by suppliers. A project uses several parts, and each part of the project is supplied by only one supplier. Each supplier supplies to only one project, but projects may be supplied by different suppliers (however, not for the same part). Parts, projects, and suppliers are identified by their respective numbers, P#, PJ#, and S#. The following FDs apply:

```
P#, PJ#  →  S#   (by being a key)
S#  →  PJ#
```

This relation is 3NF since there are no nonfull functional and transitive dependence of nonprime attributes on keys; however, the following anomalies apply.

Anomalies.   The fact that a supplier supplies parts to a project cannot be recorded unless the project actually starts using those parts (insertion anomaly). If the last part supplied by a supplier and used by the project is consumed, we can no longer keep the supplier in the database (deletion anomaly). If the supplier of a set of parts used by a project changes, we must search the entire relation to update this change on all the tuples that contain those parts for the supplier (update anomaly).

The solution is to decompose the original schema into BCNF relations. A

BCNF relation is a 3NF relation having no dependence of prime attributes on nonprime attributes. An equivalent definition states that all determinants (i.e., domains in the functions of FDs) in a relation must be candidate keys. This would preclude S# → PJ# in the 3NF relation. The following decomposition will yield BCNF relations:

```
PROJ-PART(P#, PJ#)
SUPPLY(S#, PJ#)
```

Multivalued dependencies.   Up to this point, we have talked about functional dependencies. There are other dependencies in relations. One such dependence is the *multivalued dependence (MVD)* of a given attribute (B) on another attribute (A) in a relation R, which includes other attributes. In that case, we say A multidetermines B in R (or that B is multidependent on A), indicated as $A \rightarrow\rightarrow B$, if for an A value there corresponds a set of (possibly zero) values of B and these values are in no way connected to the other attributes of R. To demonstrate this, let us assume the relation called PROFESSOR(**ID#**, **CHILDREN**, **COURSES**, RANK), which signifies that a professor can have children, can teach various courses, and has a rank. Between the professor and children the relationship is one to many, and between the courses and professor the relationship can be many to many, assuming that some courses are taught by more than one instructor. Let us assume the following data for the relation:

```
   ID#      CHILDREN   COURSES      RANK
 525-111     JOHN      CS410     ASSOCIATE
 525-111     KATHY     CS412     ASSOCIATE
 525-111     JOHN      CS412     ASSOCIATE
 525-111     KATHY     CS410     ASSOCIATE
 340-055     JACK      CS410     ASSISTANT
```

If we claim multidependence of CHILDREN or COURSES on professor (ID#), then we should be able to interchange, in all possible ways, the values among the tuples of these attributes beyond the pair ID and CHILDREN or ID and COURSES, respectively. Let us take a tuple <525-111 KATHY CS412 ASSOCIATE>. The only other value for the courses attribute is CS410, and substituting it in the tuple yields <525-111 KATHY CS410 ASSOCIATE>. Similarly, substituting JOHN for KATHY yields <525-111 JOHN CS412 ASSOCIATE>. (The order of substitutions follows the order of preceding statement.) Both of these tuples exist in the relation. In other words, the other values in the tuples are not connected to the values of the multidetermined attribute in any way. Therefore, ID# $\rightarrow\rightarrow$ CHILDREN and ID# $\rightarrow\rightarrow$ COURSES holds. To have MVDs in a relation, it takes a minimum of three attributes, that is, the key and the independent MVDs, which cannot be less than two (to be independent of each other!).

Axioms (Inference Rules) for MVDs.   MVDs have introduced additional inference rules to the original set of inference rules we presented earlier. Assume that X, Y, and Z are the attributes of relation R and that U represents the set of all attributes of R. The following are the two important inference rules applicable to MVDs:

(a) *Complementation:* If $X \rightarrow\rightarrow Y$, then $X \rightarrow\rightarrow U - X - Y$. This rule has no counterpart in FDs.

(b) *Transitivity:* If $X \rightarrow\rightarrow Y$ and $Y \rightarrow\rightarrow Z$, then $X \rightarrow\rightarrow Z - Y$. This is more restrictive than the transitivity of FDs.

A more complete coverage of additional axioms and other forms of MVDs such as the *embedded MVDs* can be found in Ullman [1982]. The reader can relate the complementation rule to the example. Considering that an FD is a special case of an MVD, the relationship between ID# and RANK can be resolved.

Fourth normal form (4NF).   In practical terms, a 4NF relation is a BCNF relation in which a relation cannot have two or more independent MVDs that are not also FDs. An alternative definition states that for every nontrivial MVD (i.e., $X \rightarrow\rightarrow 0$ or $X \rightarrow\rightarrow U - X - Y$ are trivial) $X \rightarrow\rightarrow Y$ in a 4NF relation, X must include the key of the relation. The following are 4NF versions of the previous example:

```
R1(ID#,CHILDREN)
R2(ID#,COURSE)
R3(ID#,RANK)
```

A 4NF relation proves that although a relation can be in BCNF, there still may be some anomalies, especially in updates. For example, if another child was born to the professor, we must add not one tuple but as many tuples as the courses the professor teaches. (A similar argument holds for adding a new course for the professor.) These multiple updates would be needed to *preserve* the independence among all possible values stored for the attributes.

Fifth (projection/join) normal form (5NF).   The fact that a given relation can be reconstructed losslessly by joining on its *certain* projections is referred to as a *join dependency*. A relation is said to be in 5NF if and only if every join dependency in R is implied by the candidate keys of R [Date, 1981]. In other words, each projection of R contains one or more candidate keys and zero or more nonprime attributes. Let us look at an example and contrast 5NF with 4NF. Assume the following relations:

```
R1(S#, P#, DEPT)   R2(S#, P#)   R3(P#, DEPT)   R4(S#, DEPT)
    S1  P1    A         S1  P1       P1    A         S1    A
    S1  P1    B         S2  P1       P1    B         S1    B
    S2  P1    A         S2  P2       P2    A         S2    A
    S2  P2    B         S3  P1       P2    B         S2    B
    S3  P1    A         S3  P2                        S3    A
    S3  P1    B                                       S3    B
    S3  P2    A
    S3  P2    B
```

As can be seen, in the R1 relation there are no independent MVDs and the relation is all-key (i.e., all prime attributes); hence, it is in 4NF. (It is BCNF because it is all-key; it is 4NF because it is BCNF and/or there are no independent MVDs.) There is no pairwise decomposition of it that can be lossless and 4NF. However, relations R2, R3, and R4 are in 5NF because the R1 relation satisfies the join dependency of R2, R3, and R4. The advantage of a schema with R2, R3, and R4 over a schema with R1 is that the former eliminates redundancies and therefore update anomalies in the latter.

2.6.5 Lossless and Dependency Preserving Joins

Lossless joins are important because a lossy join would not enable reconstruction of an original schema from its decompositions. Therefore, among the possible decompositions, those that have the lossless join property must be used in the schemas. As we stated earlier, equivalence of schemas calls for lossless and *dependency preserving* decompositions.

Assume that relation R is a schema with a set of FDs. This schema is said to have a lossless join decomposition R_1, R_2, . . ., R_k with respect to the FDs, if for every extension r of R, r can be reconstructed from the joins of the extensions of its projections, that is, $r = r[R_1] * r[R_2] * . . . * r[R_k]$ (* denotes a natural join).

Lossless join test.   If R_1 and R_2 form a decomposition of R with respect to a set of FDs, then this decomposition has a lossless join with respect to the FDs if and only if,

$$R_1 \cap R_2 \longrightarrow (\text{or} \rightarrow\rightarrow) R_1 - R_2 \quad \text{or} \quad R_1 \cap R_2 \longrightarrow (\text{or} \rightarrow\rightarrow) R_2 - R_1$$

Intersection and differences are between attribute lists contained in the relations.

Example

Assume a schema with an employee relation and an FD that states that employees can work only in one department as

```
EMPLOYEE(EMP#,DEPT,CITY)
EMP# → DEPT and (EMP#-> CITY Key property)

    DECOMPOSITION1:        E₁(EMP#, DEPT)
                           E₂(EMP#, CITY)


    DECOMPOSITION2:        E₁(EMP#, DEPT)
                           E₂(DEPT, CITY)
```

For decomposition 1,

$$E_1 \cap E_2 = EMP\#$$

$$E_1 - E_2 = DEPT$$

$$E_2 - E_1 = CITY$$

Therefore, $E_1 \cap E_2 \rightarrow E_1 - E_2$ holds (i.e., follows from given FDs); hence, the decomposition is lossless.

For decomposition 2,

$$E_1 \cap E_2 = DEPT$$

$$E_1 - E_2 = EMP\#$$

$$E_2 - E_1 = CITY$$

Since DEPT does not determine EMP# and CITY, the decomposition is lossy. Let us verify these with the following data for the EMPLOYEE relation:

```
525-111   SHOE   PHOENIX
345-055   SHOE   LA
```

DECOMPOSITION 1:

	E_1			E_2	
525-111	SHOE	and	525-111	PHOENIX
345-055	SHOE		345-055	LA

$E_1 * E_2$ (over EMP#) =

```
525-111   SHOE   PHOENIX
345-055   SHOE   LA            therefore lossless
```

DECOMPOSITION 2:

	E_1			E_2	
525-111	SHOE	and	SHOE	PHOENIX
345-055	SHOE		SHOE	LA

$E_1 * E_2$ (over DEPT since it is the only common attribute) =

```
525-111 SHOE PHOENIX
525-111 SHOE LA          which is lossy due to the resulting connection trap.
345-055 SHOE PHOENIX
345-055 SHOE LA
```

For decompositions having more than two relations, the *tableau* method [Ullman, 1982; Aho and Ullman, 1979] can be used. Without going into much detail, we can summarize this method as follows:

Given is a schema with its decomposed relations and a set of FDs. The procedure is to construct a table whose rows are the decomposed relations and columns are the list of attributes $A_1, \ldots, A_n$ of these relations, without repeating a given attribute. The table is filled with a_j if the element at row i by column j corresponds to an A_j which is in R_i, otherwise put b_{ij}. After the table is initialized, repeatedly consider each FD ($X \rightarrow Y$). If for attribute X, there are columns whose rows agree in value for X, then equate the corresponding values under the column Y (to all a_j's for an existing a_j, if none, to all b's with respect to a chosen subscript). If at the end, some row in the table becomes all a's (at all columns), then the join is lossless; otherwise, it is lossy.

Example

Let us assume a relation $R(A, B, C, D)$ and the FDs:

$$A \to C, B \to C, CD \to B, C \to D$$

The decomposed schema is

$$R_1(A, B), R_2(B, D), R_3(A, B, C), R_4(B, C, D)$$

The table will be as follows:

	A	B	C	D
R_1	a_1	a_2	b_{13}	b_{14}
R_2	b_{21}	a_2	b_{23}	a_4
R_3	a_1	a_2	a_3	b_{34}
R_4	b_{41}	a_2	a_3	a_4

Consider

$A \to C$

a_1	a_2	(a_3)	b_{14}
b_{21}	a_2	b_{23}	a_4
a_1	a_2	a_3	b_{34}
b_{41}	a_2	a_3	a_4

(circle indicates value change)

Next

$B \to C$

a_1	a_2	a_3	b_{14}
b_{21}	a_2	(a_3)	a_4
a_1	a_2	a_3	b_{34}
b_{41}	a_2	a_3	a_4

Next $CD \to B$ no change

Next $C \to D$

a_1	a_2	a_3	(a_4)
b_{21}	a_2	a_3	a_4
a_1	a_2	a_3	(a_4)
b_{41}	a_2	a_3	a_4

There exists a row with all a's; hence, the decomposition is lossless

Some concepts of FDs.   If F is a set of given FDs, then F^+ is the *closure* of F. In other words, F^+ represents FDs in F and all those implied by F. If $F \neq F^+$, that is, if F is not the full set of FDs, then we can compute the other FDs in F^+ by using the inference rules. However, F^+ may be large even for a small F and, hence, time consuming to compute. Instead, we can compute X^+ that is the closure of X with respect to F ($X \subseteq U$, i.e., X is a subset of the set of all attributes). X^+ is the set of attributes so that an FD, $X \to A$, can be deduced from F by the inference rules. This would enable us to know whether a given dependency $X \to B$ would follow from F without computing F^+.

To compute X^+, we start with X and look for the left sides of all the FDs that are included in X and concatenate with X all the attributes on the right side of these FDs. The procedure is continued recursively until no more concatenation is possible. A set of FDs is *minimal* if every attribute on the right side of a dependency is a single attribute, no FD in F is redundant, and no attribute on the left-hand side is redundant. If F and G are FDs in R and if $F^+ = G^+$, then F and G are said to be equivalent. In this case, F covers G, and vice versa.

Dependency preserving decompositions.   The projection of a set FDs F onto a set of attributes Z is the set of FDs $X \to Y$ in F^+ such that $XY \subseteq Z$. A given decomposition preserves a set of FDs F if the union of all the FDs projected on the decomposed relations implies F.

A lossless join property of a decomposition does not necessarily guarantee that it is also dependency preserving. Similarly, not every dependency preserving decomposition has the lossless join property. The following example demonstrates this.

Example

Let us consider the schema discussed earlier in the Boyce-Codd normal form. In that, we had the dependencies

```
P#,PJ#  →  S#
S#  →  PJ#
```

If we decompose PROJECT into R_1 (P#, S#) and R_2 (PJ#, S#), we will have a lossless decomposition because $R_1 \cap R_2$ (S#) $\to R_2 - R_1$(PJ#). The projection of the above FDs on this decomposition gives S# $\to$ PJ# and the trivial dependencies such as P# $\to$ P#. These, however, do not imply P#, PJ# $\to$ S#. The following are example data for the decomposed relations:

R_1		R_2		
P1	S1	PJ1	S1	
P1	S2	PJ1	S2,	which satisfies S# $\to$ PJ#

R_1 * R_2		
P1	PJ1	S1
P1	PJ1	S2,

which is a lossless join that violates the dependency P#, PJ# $\to$ S#. (In other words, P1 can be supplied by more than one supplier but not to the same project.)

The following algorithm is proposed in Biskup et al. [1979] for a 3NF decomposition with lossless join and dependency preservation properties.

Algorithm for dependency preserving 3NF decomposition.   Given is a schema with R and F, which is a minimal cover.

Procedure.   If there are any attributes of R not involved in any FD of F, on either side of the dependencies, those attributes can form a relation by themselves. If one of the FDs in F involves all attributes of R, then R itself is the result. Otherwise, the decomposition is a schema XY for each dependency $X \to Y$ in F. However if XY_i, $1 \le i \le n$, is in F for all i, then use $XY_1 \cdots Y_n$.

Lossless and dependency preserving 3NF decomposition.   To obtain a lossless and dependency preserving 3NF decomposition, the key of R should be included in the decomposition either as an additional element or as part of a decomposed relation.

In this chapter, we covered the basic concepts of DBMS, DBMS architecture, and the popular data models. We introduced the structural properties of these models. In the following chapter, we will deal with the operational aspects of DBMS relating to the data models discussed in this chapter and also security and integrity of DBMS.

EXERCISES

2.1. What form of an access path would you propose to process qualification criteria of the disjunctive normal form? Why? *Hint: This question suggests a review of some basic data and file structure material before getting into the details of DBMS. A disjunctive normal form is a Boolean expression in the form of ORs of ANDs—* $(c_1 \wedge c_2 \wedge \cdots \wedge c_k) \vee (c_{k+1} \wedge c_{k+2} \wedge \cdots) \vee \cdots \vee (c_p \wedge c_{p+1} \wedge \cdots \wedge c_n)$, *where each c_i, $1 \leq i \leq n$, is a simple condition (see index). Inverted lists, multiattribute indices, hashing, and so on or their combination can be considered as a starting point. Each proposal must be evaluated in terms of efficiency of access, insertions, deletions, and modifications of the attribute values (of any record type) on which the simple conditions are based. A starting reference can be Teorey and Fry [1982].*

2.2. Assume the two record types called Supplier and Part. Supplier contains the supplier number and supplier information and Part contains the part number and part details. Each supplier number and the part numbers the supplier supplies are given in the following pairs of lists (only the keys are shown).

Supplier Number	Part Number
1	A
2	A, B
3	A, B, C
4	B, C

   (a) Show the foregoing database information with respect to one hierarchical, one network, and the relational model of data (show only the key populations.)

   (b) Give a procedure for each model for retrieving the suppliers supplying a specific part. *At this point, the reader is expected to write possible access algorithms with the available knowledge (possibly based on linked structures and/or file access methods). However, the reader is recommended to revisit this question after studying data selection with respect to various data models in the next chapter.*

2.3. Assuming the following definition tree (nodes are indicated as record type names followed by attribute names in parentheses), give two implementation techniques:

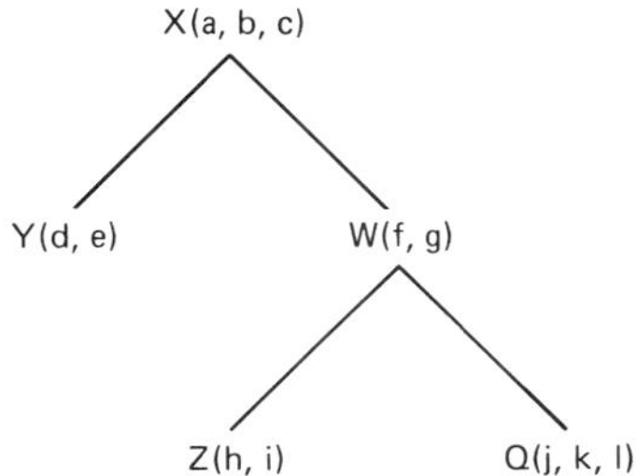

one based on relational representation (i.e., representing the nodes as tables) and the other on traces in such a way that hierarchical access can be executed on them. *Hint: You may assume keys for each record type (root keys as the key of the HDR and the descendant keys unique either within the tree or in the database).*

2.4.

    (a) Given the following tree occurrence, show an equivalent representation of it based on traces. *Hint: Draw a definition tree first.*

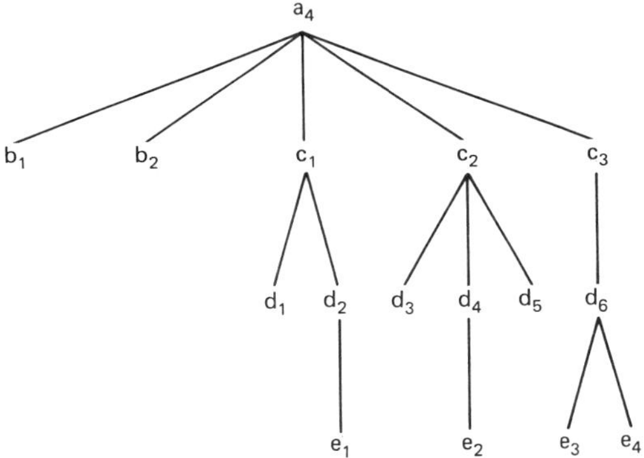

    (b) Assuming a preorder type number assignment, draw the corresponding definition tree and tree occurrence for the following sequence of traces: (5, 0, 0, 0, 0), (5, 1, 0, 0, 0), (5, 2, 0, 0, 0), (5, 3, 0, 0, 0), (5, 0, 0, 1, 0), (5, 0, 0, 2, 0), (5, 1, 1, 0, 0), (5, 1, 2, 0, 0), (5, 2, 1, 0, 0), (5, 2, 2, 0, 0), (5, 3, 1, 0, 0), (5, 0, 0, 2, 1), and (5, 0, 0, 2, 2).

2.5. Discuss the relative advantages and disadvantages of each of the following implementation strategies for mapping the trace node addressing technique into physical database.

    (a) Hashing

    (b) B-trees

    (c) Inverted lists

       Hint: You may assume a trace table as the starting point. The reference [Tsichritzis and Lochovsky, 1977] may be consulted.

2.6. Given the following relations R and S, evaluate the following relational algebra expression (from innermost to outermost sequence).

$$((R \otimes S)[A \geq C]) [B, C] = ?$$

where

$$R = \begin{bmatrix} A & B \\ 1 & a \\ 1 & b \\ 1 & c \end{bmatrix} \qquad S = \begin{bmatrix} C & D \\ 1 & y \\ 1 & w \end{bmatrix}$$

2.7. Assuming relations $R_1(N, T, O, L)$ and $R_2(A)$, whose tuples are given below. What will be the result of the following division operation (i.e., what will be in B?).

$$B = R_1[T, O, L][L \div A] R_2$$

R_1	N	T	O	L	R_2	A
	b	1	7	x		x
	a	1	3	x		y
	a	1	12	y		
	a	1	7	y		
	c	2	3	x		
	c	2	12	y		
	d	2	3	z		
	e	2	3	x		

2.8. Assuming the following database:

```
SUPPLIER (SNO, SNAME,   CITY,    STATUS)    SP (SNO, PNO, QTY)
         S1   SMITH NEW YORK     20             S1   P1   3
         S2   JONES PHOENIX      10             S1   P2   2
         S3   BLAKE TUCSON       30             S1   P5   4
         S4   CLARK MONTREAL     20             S1   P6   1
         S5   ADAMS TORONTO      30             S2   P1   3
                                                S2   P2   4
                                                S3   P5   2
                                                S4   P5   4
                                                S5   P6   5


PART (PNO, PNAME, COLOR, WEIGHT)
      P1 NUT    RED      12
      P2 BOLT   GREEN    17
      P5 CAM    BLUE     12
      P6 COG    RED      19
```

and the relational algebra expression

```
(SUPPLIER/((((PART[WEIGHT>12])[PNO])[PNO=PNO]SP)[SNO]))[SNAME,CITY]
```

Show the results of all the intermediate operations and the final answer for the preceding expression.

2.9. The Department of Computer Science at ASU employs many professors and offers different courses. A course may have multiple sections. A professor may teach different courses and possibly different sections of the same course, but a section of a given course is taught by one professor only. Therefore, a course with more than one section may be taught by different professors. A student may take different courses but cannot take different sections of the same course. A professor is assigned one office which may not be shared by another professor. The student's

STUDENTNAME and YEAR are unique. Moreover, the student's GRADE in a given course is unique.

Consider the following relations:

```
COURSES:  COURSENAME  SECTION  PROFNAME  PROFOFFICE
             A           1        EO         281
             A           2        BL         218
             A           3        EO         281
             B           1        BL         218
```

```
SG:  STUDENTNAME  YEAR  COURSENAME  SECTION  GRADE
        AB          2        A          1      3.0
        BZ          2        B          1      2.5
        AC          1        A          2      3.0
        DC          3        A          2      4.0
        AB          2        B          1      4.0
        AB          2        A          3      3.5
```

(a) Use the statement of the problem as given, without adding any more restrictions of your own, to find the functional dependencies between the attributes in relation COURSES.

(b) Same as part (a) for relation SG.

(c) Are the given occurrences (tuples) in relation COURSES consistent with the statement of the problem or with the functional dependencies as defined in part (a)? If not, delete from relation COURSES any inconsistent tuple.

(d) Same as part (c) for relation SG.

(e) Identify a primary key of COURSES.

(f) Same as (e) for SG.

(g) Identify insert, delete, and update anomalies, if any, in COURSES. If so, how do you get rid of these anomalies?

(h) Same as (g) for SG.

2.10. Consider the following relations and the functional dependencies among the attributes:

Relations	Functional Dependencies
$R_1 (A, B, C, D)$	$A \rightarrow B$
$R_2 (A, B, E)$	$AC \rightarrow D$
$R_3 (D, F)$	$A \rightarrow E$
	$B \rightarrow CD$
	$D \rightarrow F$

(a) Identify a primary key for the relations.

(b) Which of the relations are in first, second, and third normal form? What decompositions are necessary for those that are not in 2NF, 3NF?

Hint: If R is a relational schema with attributes A_1, A_2, $\cdots$, A_n and functional dependencies F, and X is a subset of A_1, A_2, $\cdots$, A_n, we say X is a key of R if

    $X \rightarrow A_1, A_2, \cdots, A_n$ *is in* F^+

    For no proper subset $Y \subseteq X$ *is* $Y \rightarrow A_1, A_2, \cdots, A_n$ *in* F^+.

2.11. If you are given an all-key relation (i.e., a relation all of whose attributes are prime), say $R(A_1, A_2, A_3)$, which one of the normal forms 1NF, 2NF, 3NF, BCNF, 4NF would this relation satisfy and why? Are there any normal forms that it may not satisfy? Why? And what must be done to the relation to make it satisfy all the normal forms?

2.12. Assume a first normal form relation called SRECORD(STUDENT#, COURSE, REPEAT-COURSES, AGE, SCHOOL-YEAR) and the following dependencies:

```
STUDENT#  →  AGE
STUDENT#  →  SCHOOL-YEAR
STUDENT#  →→  COURSES
STUDENT#  →→  REPEAT-COURSES
AGE  →  SCHOOL-YEAR
```

Convert this relation into 2NF, 3NF, BCNF, and 4NF one step at a time justifying each normal form you obtain.

2.13. Assume the relation SPP(**S#**, **P#**, QTY, STATUS, CITY) and the functional dependencies S#, P# → QTY, S# → STATUS, S# → CITY, and CITY → STATUS, where S#, P#, and QTY are the supplier number, part number, and the supplier's shipment quantity of the part, respectively:
   (a) Is the relation in 2NF? If not, what anomalies do you see? Convert it to 2NF.
   (b) Is the result you obtained in (a) in 3NF? If not, what anomalies do you see? Convert it to 3NF.

2.14. Given the relation STUDENT with the following data

```
STUDENT  (STUDENT-NAME,  COURSE-TAKEN,  COURSE-REPEATED)
             ELLIS            CS100           CS101
             ELLIS            CS100           CS200
             ELLIS            CS320           CS101
             ELLIS            CS320           CS200
             BROOKS           CS210           CS101
             BROOKS           CS210           CS200
             LEWIS            CS100           CS101
             LEWIS            CS320           CS101
             LEWIS            CS410           CS101
             LEWIS            CS410           CS310
```

   (a) Are there any independent multivalued dependencies in this relation?
   (b) Is this relation in 4NF? Why or why not?

2.15. Consider the relation SG and its tuple occurrences after you deleted any inconsistent tuple as was asked in part (d) of Exercise 2.9. There are two record types present in relation SG. The record types are

```
STUDENT (STUDENTNAME, YEAR)
COURSE (COURSENAME, SECTION, GRADE)
```

   (a) What type of relationship exists between the two record types (i.e., 1:1, 1:N, $M:N$)?
   (b) Show the record occurrences of STUDENT.
   (c) Show the record occurrences of COURSE.

(d) Assume that the STUDENT record type is the parent of COURSE record type in a hierarchical schema. Show the record occurrences in (b) and (c) in this hierarchical form.

(e) Assume now we want to use the network model to show the associations between STUDENT and COURSE. Is there a need for a third LINK record type? If so, what should be the data attributes in LINK, STUDENT, and COURSE?

(f) Show the record occurrences of the three record types in (e).

2.16. Assuming a relation $R(A, B, C)$ and a sequence of projection and join operations on it as given,

$$
\begin{array}{ccc}
 & R & \\
A & B & C \\
\hline
a & x & 1 \\
b & x & 2 \\
b & y & 3 \\
\end{array}
\qquad R[A, B, C] \leftarrow R[A, B] * R[B, C]
$$

what do you observe in the result of this operation? Is there anything undesirable? What must be done to preserve database consistency? *Hint: Would the fifth normal form solve the problem?*

2.17. Which of the following decompositions are lossless? Show your solution. Use both the tableau and short test at least once.

(a) Schema is $R(A, B, C, D)$; the functional dependencies are $A \rightarrow C$, $B \rightarrow C$, $D \rightarrow B$, $A \rightarrow D$. The decomposition is $R_1(A, B)$, $R_2(B, D)$, $R_3(A, B, C)$, $R_4(B, C, D)$.

(b) Schema is $R(A, B, C)$; the functional dependency is $AB \rightarrow C$; the decomposition is $R_1(A, B)$, $R_2(B, C)$.

3

DBMS-II

In the previous chapter, we covered the basic concepts of DBMS and the structural and theoretical aspects of the popular data models, which are the hierarchical, network, and relational data models. In this chapter, we will discuss the operational aspects of these data models. Specifically, for each data model, we will cover data selection, which is the first basic step of the retrieval, update, and aggregate operations. In the remainder of the chapter, security and integrity of DBMS will be introduced.

3.1 SELECTION IN HIERARCHICAL SYSTEMS

In discussing the hierarchical systems, we will refer to two systems that characterize hierarchies in real life. These are the information management system (IMS) we have seen in Chapter 2 and MRI's System 2000 (MRI) or (S2K) [MRI, 1974]. The former will be an example of *element at a time* or *procedural* navigation procedures used for data selection of the associated DML; the latter will characterize the *set-oriented*, or *high-level*, *definitional* data selection. The following example database will be the basis of this chapter.

3.1.1 Medical Database

The medical database we will use is a popular one that is also similar to the ones used by other authors [Kapp and Leben, 1978; Tsichritzis and Lochovsky, 1982]. Figure 3.1 shows the definition tree and Figure 3.2 shows a partially

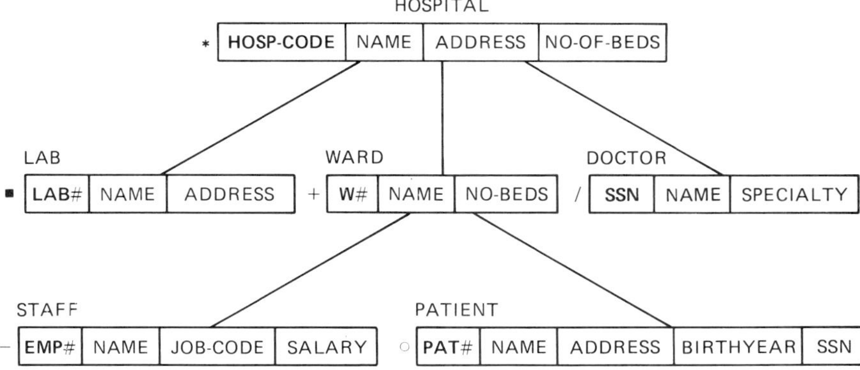

Figure 3.1   Hierarchical medical database (in bold type are the keys and segment sequence fields, i.e., keys within an HDR).

populated database. Accordingly, the medical database contains basic information for the hospitals such as their code, name, number of beds, laboratories that the hospitals use, wards and doctors in the hospital. In each ward, there are hospital staff and patients. As can be seen in Figure 3.2, the populated database reflects $1:N$ relationships between the record types. Figure 3.3 shows the full listing of the record type instances. Although the relationship between labs and hospitals can be naturally many to many, the children occurrences must be repeated under different parents to obey the tree structure. This resembles the DBTG network data model in that owners could not share a given member occurrence in a set

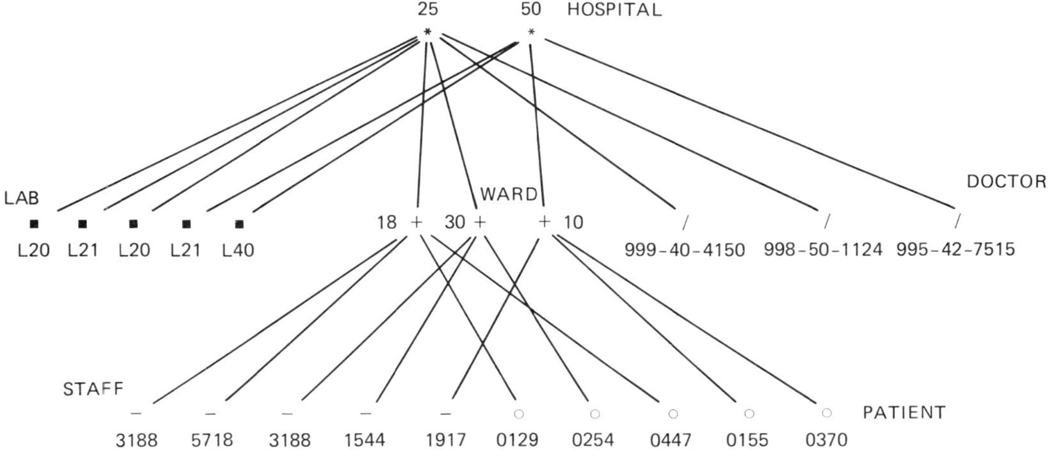

Figure 3.2   Partially populated medical database (key values of the instances are indicated).

HOSPITAL

HOSP-CODE	NAME	ADDRESS	NO-OF-BEDS
25	MEMORIAL	115 Rural	170
50	SAMARITAN	575 Mill	25

LAB

LAB#	NAME	ADDRESS
L20	Medco	50 Bell Rd
L21	LTest	340 Cactus
L40	BrownC	150 Shea

WARD

W#	NAME	NO-BEDS
18	Intensive Care	110
30	Cardiac	60
10	Pediatric	25

DOCTOR

SSN	NAME	SPECIALTY
999-40-4150	Wolfley J.	Neurology
998-50-1124	Vdhoek B.	Cardiology
995-42-7515	Miller R.	Gynecology

STAFF

EMP#	NAME	JOB-CODE	SALARY
3188	Bortman G.	Intern	19000
5718	Summers J.	Orderly	10500
1544	Hardy B.	Nurse	12500
1917	Grove J.	Nurse	13400

PATIENT

PAT#	NAME	ADDRESS	BIRTHYEAR	SSN
0129	Anderson G.	805 D. Mercurio	1937	112-99-4141
0254	Helm B.	45 Hayden	1932	104-98-7715
0447	Gibbs K.	350 Bell Rd.	1942	527-99-1819
0155	Niimy N.	29 Linda	1960	440-80-5015
0370	Zaks R.	157 Northern	1958	540-01-9949

Figure 3.3 Hierarchical record type instances.

occurrence. In the following, we will discuss access and data selection features of the two hierarchical systems.

3.1.2 Data Selection in IMS

In IMS, DSL procedures are written as calls in DL/1 (Data Language 1) from the host language. However, in the discussion that will follow, we will focus on the DSL procedures only and will ignore the syntactic details. The commands of the IMS DSL which we will consider are **GET UNIQUE (GU), GET NEXT (GN), GET NEXT WITHIN PARENT (GNP), HOLD OPTIONS (GHU, GHN, GHNP), COMMAND CODES (D, F, V), INSERT (ISRT), and REPLACE (REPL).**

The following lists their corresponding syntax:

```
GET UNIQUE record-type name [ WHERE qualification ]
GET NEXT [ record-type name [ WHERE qualification]]
```

Record type name is referred to as segment name in IMS. Qualification is a Boolean expression of *simple conditions* where a *simple condition* is a triple (*attribute name, θ, constant*), θ being one of $=$, $\neq$, $\leq$, $<$, $\geq$, $>$ and constant is either a numeric or a literal. Brackets signify optional features. The IMS terminology for qualification is *SSA* (*segment search argument*).

Retrievals involving root segments.

(a) GU *HOSPITAL*

(b) GU *HOSPITAL* **WHERE** *NO-OF-BEDS* > 30

(c) GU *HOSPITAL* **WHERE** *HOSP-CODE* = 25

(d) GU *HOSPITAL*
```
     Output NO-OF-BEDS
     Loop until end of database
          GN HOSPITAL
          Output NO-OF-BEDS
     End loop
```

The GU command establishes a position in the database. In the case of (a), the position is established at the root segment of the first HDR (hierarchical database record). An output command may follow it for the output of the desired segments and/or fields. (Answer is HOSP-CODE 25; see Figure 3.3.) In (b), the database is scanned sequentially until the first HDR with NUMBER-OF-BEDS exceeding 30 in the HOSPITAL segment is located. (Answer is Hosp-Code 50.) In the case of (c), however, because the qualification is on the key, the HDR with HOSP-CODE equal to 25 will be accessed directly rather than scanning sequentially. The retrieval in (d) lists the NO-OF-BEDS of all HDRs in the database. (Answer is 170, 25.) As can be noticed, the first GU command sets the starting position and the subsequent GN command within the loop scans the database. Although not shown, each IMS DSL command is followed by a host program instruction that tests the returned status code (e.g., end of search, not found, search is successful) to decide the next course of action in the program. (Figure 2.1 in Chapter 2 can be revisited to remember the interaction between various subsystems in a host embedded environment.)

In each of the programs (a) through (d), we could use GN instead of GU. However, the following would be the differences:

1. Different status codes are returned for different instructions after execution. Application programs must check them properly.

2. With GN, we can omit the segment name and let GN be the only command in a program loop. This will cause HDRs of the entire database to be scanned serially to the end of the database, going over all instances of all the segments in each HDR. If we qualify GN with the name HOSPITAL, however, the effect will be similar to GU with the exception of point (1) with the repeated executions in a loop. Also, the following will hold: with GN, the starting position at each new iteration is the point left by the previous iteration, causing the database to be scanned serially; with GU, however, each iteration in the loop will cause GU to be interpreted from the beginning of the database over and over thus causing multiple traces of the same segments.

Retrievals involving segments other than the root.

Query: *Find the name of the first doctor whose specialty is Cardiology.*

```
GU HOSPITAL
   DOCTOR WHERE SPECIALTY = Cardiology
```

(Answer is doctor named B. V. D. Hoek.)

In this query, the database is scanned sequentially until the first instance of the desired doctor is located. Notice that the GU command this time specifies more than one segment forming a *hierarchical path* in the tree.

Query: *Find the name of the first doctor whose specialty is cardiology in the hospital whose code is 25.*

```
GU HOSPITAL WHERE HOSP-CODE = 25
   DOCTOR WHERE SPECIALTY = Cardiology
```

(Answer is the same as the previous query.)

In this query, the HDR of the hospital whose code is 25 is located by direct access, and then from that point on the segment instances in the HDR are searched sequentially until the first instance (with respect to the direction of scan or the beginning of the database because of preorder linearization) of the desired doctor is located.

Query: *Find the names of all staff (i.e., in all hospitals) earning more than $15,000.*

```
GU HOSPITAL
Loop until end of database
   GN WARD
      STAFF WHERE SALARY > 15,000
   Output STAFF.NAME,STAFF.SALARY
End loop
```

(Answer: G. Bortman, $19,000)

Here, we have a sequential search that starts at the first HDR, but then scans only the hierarchical subpaths of *WARD-STAFF* and outputs data only from the eligible staff instances until all the database HDRs are searched.

Query: *List all the patient names of the ward whose number is 18.*

```
GU HOSPITAL
   WARD WHERE W# = 18
Loop until no more children
   GNP PATIENT
   Output PATIENT.NAME
End loop
```

(Answer: G. Anderson; K. Gibbs)

The database is scanned sequentially until the first occurrence of the desired ward is located. (To specify a unique ward, the root must be qualified first to get a unique HDR.) Immediately after, a GET NEXT WITHIN PARENT (GNP) command is used to find all the patients of the immediate parent ward with $W\# = 18$. After the last child of the parent ward is accessed, the status code reflects the end of the children segments so that the program can terminate the loop. The scope of the parentage is established by the last command accessing a segment in the hierarchical path before the GNP, and for that matter, a grandparent segment may serve as the immediate parent depending on the program; for example,

```
GU HOSPITAL WHERE HOSP-CODE = 25
Loop until no more children
   GNP PATIENT
   Output PATIENT.NAME
End loop
```

(Answer: G. Anderson; B. Helm; K. Gibbs)

In this query, we have a direct access to the hospital (with HOSP-CODE 25), followed by the output of all the patient names in all the wards, not a specific ward. This is because the parentage is set at the root and the end of children status will occur only after the last patient in the last ward under the hospital is accessed.

Command codes.   The IMS command codes cause variations in the operations of the IMS commands. There are about 10 command codes and they are used with an asterisk. We will discuss the D, F, and V command codes.

D Command Code (Path operation)

```
GU HOSPITAL *D
   DOCTOR WHERE SPECIALTY = Cardiology
```

(Answer: the first (and only) instance which qualifies is for HOSP-CODE = 25, DOCTOR.SSN = 998-50-1124)

The D command code permits us to retrieve or insert a sequence of segments in a hierarchical path using only one call instead of having to use a separate call for each segment.

Unlike its previous usage, this query will output both the HOSPITAL parent segment and the DOCTOR segment.

F Command Code (First occurrence of twin)

```
GU HOSPITAL
   WARD WHERE W# = 18
Loop until segment is found
   GNP PATIENT WHERE BIRTHYEAR < 1940
End loop
   GNP STAFF *F
   Output STAFF.NAME
```

(Answer: G. Bortman)

This query locates the first patient who is born before 1940 in the first occurrence of ward 18 and for that patient the first staff person who cared for the patient— there could be more than one staff member involved. The reason for the use of this command code is to move the position pointer backward in the linear sequence of segments within the current HDR. By the time the patient segments are searched, the staff segments are well passed over, but the query requires one of them to be output.

V Command Code (Maintain Current Position).   Instead of using the GNP command, the previous program can be equivalently processed by the use of the V command code as follows:

```
GU HOSPITAL
   WARD WHERE W# = 18
Loop until segment found
   GN WARD *V
      PATIENT WHERE BIRTHYEAR < 1940
End loop
   GN WARD *V
      STAFF *F
   Output STAFF.NAME
```

The combined effect of path specification and the V command code on the parent fixes (suppresses the pointer update) the parent between iterations so that the net effect becomes equivalent to that of GNP, of course, with a different status code to be tested.

Insertion

```
INSERT HOSPITAL
       WARD WHERE W# = 18
       PATIENT
```

This program uses the insert command (ISRT) to add a new patient to ward 18, but before this, a selection should determine the location of the insertion if the key of the patient segment is not unique. However, since each patient is identified uniquely and no insert position is specified, the patient is added to the end of the twin chain for ward 18 as default.

Deletion

```
GHU HOSPITAL WHERE HOSP-CODE = 25
    WARD WHERE W# = 18
    PATIENT WHERE PAT# = 0129
DLET
```

This program first selects the desired patient instance using the HOLD option of the GU command (here GU becomes GHU). The HOLD option reserves the segment for exclusive use until the required update (delete) is finished by the current user. This prevents other users from operating on the same segment instance or its children simultaneously.

Replacement

```
GHU HOSPITAL
    LAB WHERE LAB# = L40
Change address of the lab to new location
REPL
```

Again, the selection is made in the exclusive HOLD mode and the replace command (REPL) updates the modified information of the lab instance (LAB.ADDRESS) by copying the new value from the program area onto the database.

3.1.3 Data Selection in MRI

The MRI (hierarchical system) represents a set-oriented retrieval system as opposed to the *element-at-a-time* retrieval of IMS. MRI trees are also referred to as *inverted hierarchies* in the sense that (in addition to implementation) the user queries against the database are expressed in a manner similar to the definitional flavor of calculus expressions. The MRI selection operations have the following features:

- Downward normalization
- Upward normalization
- Flat selection
- HAS clause
- Twin selection with HAS

We will continue to refer to the medical database used in the IMS examples.

Downward normalization.   Downward normalization involves selecting the descendant occurrences under a qualified ancestor. The ancestor can be an immediate parent or a grandparent. The parent (or ancestor) should satisfy the qualification which follows the WHERE clause.

Example (referring to the hierarchical medical database of Figures 3.1, 3.2, and 3.3)

Query: *List the names of patients in ward 18.*

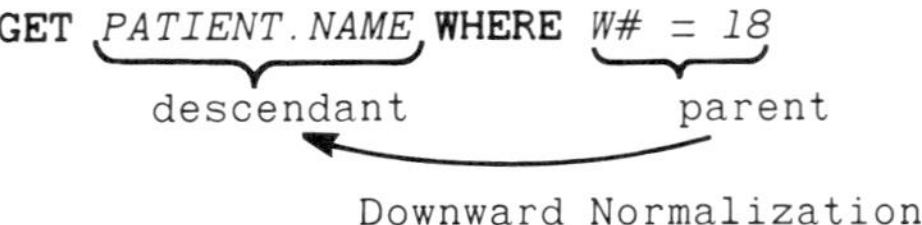

(Answer: G. Anderson; K. Gibbs)

Upward normalization.   Upward normalization is the opposite of downward normalization. This time, selection is at the descendant level and the corresponding parent (or ancestor) instance is retrieved.

Example

> **Query:** *Find the address of the hospital where staff member Joe, whose employee number is 5718, is working.*

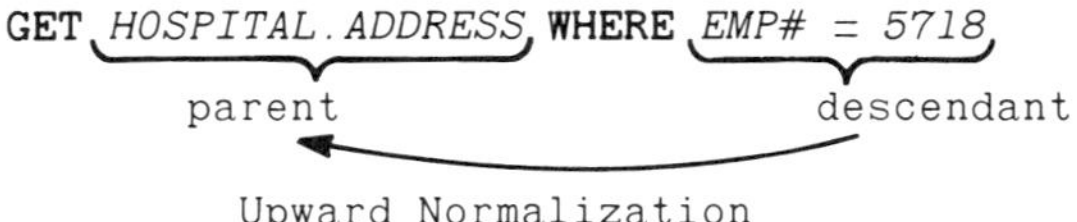

(Answer: HOSPITAL with HOSP-CODE 25)

As can be noticed, those attribute names that are unique in the schema (e.g., W#, EMP#) need not be qualified explicitly by the record type names.

Flat selection.   Flat selection is concerned with selections within a given record-type much like a retrieval from a single file.

Example

> **Query:** *List the names of staff whose job codes are either intern or nurse.*

```
GET STAFF.NAME WHERE JOB-CODE IS Intern OR JOB-CODE IS Nurse
```

(Answer: G. Bortman; B. Hardy; J. Grove)

HAS clause.   The HAS clause forces a special kind of upward normalization as can be seen from the following example.

Example

> **Query:** *List the names of wards that have both orderly and intern assigned to them.*

```
GET WARD.NAME WHERE JOB-CODE IS Orderly AND JOBCODE IS Intern
```

(Answer: none)

The reason for having no answer for this query is because the entire Boolean predicate is executed on each instance. However, no instance can satisfy more than one value at a time. To produce the correct answer, the HAS clause should be used in this type of upward normalization. The HAS clause tests each condition of the Boolean predicate separately on the record type instances and locates the common parent (if there is one) for those instances where all the conditions are satisfied. This is done by tracing (following) from the satisfying descendant instances upward toward the ancestor level and selecting those parent instances at which the traces of all the conditions coincide. The following example shows the use of the HAS feature.

```
GET WARD.NAME WHERE WARD.NAME HAS JOB-CODE EQ Orderly AND
    WARD.NAME HAS JOB-CODE EQ Intern
```

(Answer: intensive care)

Twin selection with HAS.   Twin selection using HAS can select a record instance based on a qualification of a twin under a specified common parent.

Example

Query: *List the staff salaries in the hospital where doctor Wolfley (SSN = 999-40-4150) works.*

```
GET STAFF.SALARY WHERE HOSP-CODE HAS DOCTOR.SSN = 999-40-4150
```

(Answer: 19,000, 10,500, 12,500)

The selection in this option is symmetrical; that is, we could ask for doctors working in the hospital where a certain staff member is working. The levels of the record types involved can be different as is the case with this example. As can be noticed, the user should specify the common path between the record types. In this example, it is the key of the hospital record type (i.e., HOSP-CODE) specified before HAS.

For further exposure, the reader can refer to Appendix II for an example of an MRI interface. This interface is built in the RAP GDBMS, which will be covered in Chapter 9.

3.2 SELECTION IN NETWORK SYSTEMS

In the network systems, we will discuss LSL (link and selector language) and CODASYL'S DBTG. LSL will provide an example for set-oriented network navigation; the DBTG network model will demonstrate element-at-a-time navigation similar to the cases with MRI and IMS, respectively, in the hierarchical systems.

3.2.1 Selection with LSL

The original syntax of LSL was specified in Tsichritzis [1976] as having the following basic structure:

```
SELECT record-type name
WHERE Boolean qualification
LINK WITH set (link) name TO record-type name
KEEP output list
```

where Boolean qualification includes simple conditions of the form used in IMS earlier. One exception here is that both in simple conditions and output lists, we can specify aggregates (e.g., SUM (A_i)). Figure 3.4 shows possible ways of linking record types.

In the original LSL syntax, to go from R_1 to R_2 using Figure 3.4(a), we specify

```
SELECT R₁
WHERE ---
LINK WITH L₁₂ TO R₂
SELECT R₂
```

To do the same for Figure 3.4(b) we specify:

```
SELECT R₁
WHERE ---
LINK WITH L₁ TO Rₗ
SELECT Rₗ
LINK WITH L₂ TO R₂
SELECT R₂
```

In an alternate syntax as used in the RAP GDBMS (see Appendix II for the LSL interface), the following is used for the links of Figure 3.4:

For Figure 3.4(a)	*For Figure 3.4(b)*
`SELECT R₁`	`SELECT R₁`
`WHERE ...`	`WHERE ...`
`LINK WITH R₂ TO R₂`	`LINK WITH Rₗ TO R₂`
`SELECT R₂`	`SELECT R₂`

As can be seen, the latter version of LSL uses only the record type names in specifying navigations.

Let us take a portion of the medical database used in the hierarchies section and with it define the following LSL database. For the links, we will assume that link record types, as in Figure 3.4(b), are used. These links can either be materialized and stored as physical record types or derived, as needed, from R_1 and R_2 by using the definitions. The schema of the LSL medical database is

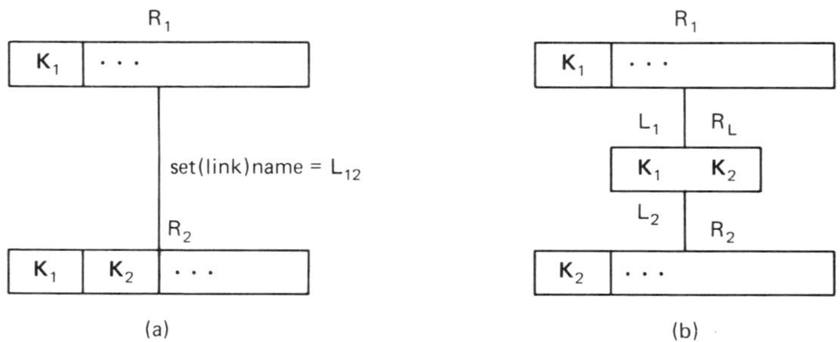

Figure 3.4 Linking record types.

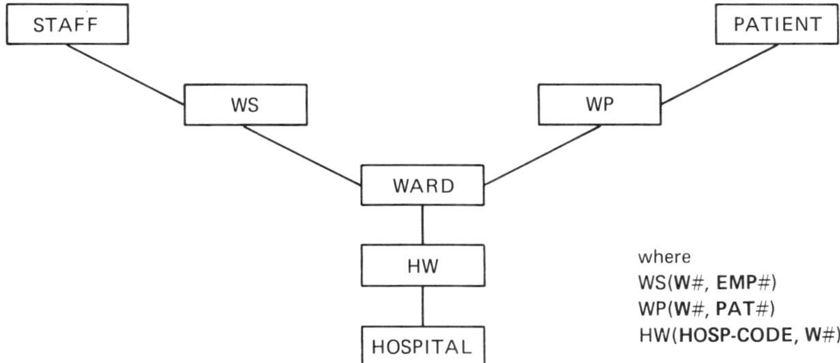

Figure 3.5   LSL medical database.

shown in Figure 3.5. Attributes of the record types are not shown (except the record-type names) since they are the same as in Figure 3.1.

Example

> **Query:** *Find the salaries and the maximum salary of the staff of the hospital where patient G. Anderson (P# 0129) is being treated.*

```
SELECT PATIENT
WHERE PAT# = 0129
LINK WITH WP TO WARD
SELECT WARD
LINK WITH HW TO HOSPITAL
SELECT HOSPITAL
LINK WITH HW TO WARD
SELECT WARD
LINK WITH WS TO STAFF
SELECT STAFF
KEEP SALARY, MAX(SALARY)
```

(Answer: 19,000, 10,500, 12,500, and 19,000)

If we did not navigate down to the hospital (hence twice through the HW link), then the answer would have been (19,000, 10,500, and 19,000), which would miss one of the salaries. This is because the query is asking for the staff salaries in the hospital of the patient, not only the staff of the ward in which the patient is being treated. The syntax of LSL presented in Appendix II includes additional features, such as value saving and update (the same holds also for MRI).

3.2.2 Selection with DBTG

The selection primitives of the DBTG network model are of the following two types:

- Record occurrence selection
- Set occurrence selection

In record occurrence selection, the following are the possible alternatives:

1. To use a *database key* which is a unique identifier (key) attached by the system to each instance of the record-type.
2. To use a user-implemented (or system supplied by default) access method. Most commonly, a direct access mechanism is implemented by the use of a hashing algorithm.

To specify these choices in DBTG, we use schema declarations such as

```
LOCATION MODE IS DIRECT      for (1)
LOCATION MODE IS CALC procedure name USING item list  for (2)
```

In other words, the location mode clause defines the file organization and the access method for a given record type. The procedure name corresponds to the name of the user-supplied access procedure, which uses the items (attributes) in the item list as the means of access.

In the selection of set types, we access either a member or owner occurrence in order to get hold of a set occurrence. Before inserting a new record occurrence into the database, we must first determine the set occurrence (or occurrences) that the new incoming member will participate in. To do that, we must have declared schema definition clauses such as

```
SET SELECTION IS THRU CURRENT OF set name SET
SET SELECTION IS THRU OWNER USING item name
```

We can have record selection tied to set selection as follows:

```
LOCATION MODE IS VIA set name SET
```

Program environment.   DBTG DML, like IMS, works as a DSL in a host language. The data and status information are placed in (or taken from), by DBTG, the user work area of the user's program. This area also contains program variables and *currency indicators (pointers)*. These indicators keep track of where the user was or what was last done in the program. This may be very necessary because at a given time, a user can navigate through multiple sets. The currency indicators are also useful in debugging a program. The following are the currency indicator types maintained by the system:

(a) *Currency of run unit:* Indicates the place of last access made in the program, regardless of the type of the structure.
(b) *Currency of record type:* Indicates the last-accessed occurrence of a record type.
(c) *Currency of set type:* Indicates the last-accessed occurrence of a set type.

These indicators are updated automatically by the system as a result of a DML operation. Occasionally, it may be necessary to override this feature by

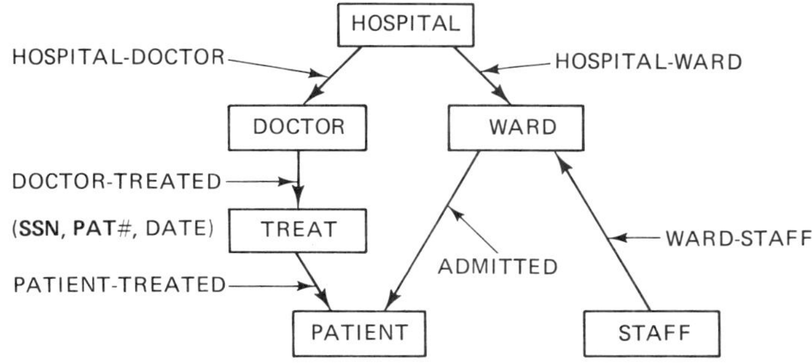

SET-TYPES	OWNER	MEMBER
HOSPITAL-WARD	HOSPITAL	WARD
HOSPITAL-DOCTOR	HOSPITAL	DOCTOR
WARD-STAFF	WARD	STAFF
ADMITTED	WARD	PATIENT
DOCTOR-TREATED	DOCTOR	TREAT
PATIENT-TREATED	PATIENT	TREAT

Figure 3.6 DBTG medical database.

a currency suppress (or retain currency) command. An example will be provided in the programs which follow.

As can be seen in Figure 3.6, we can represent nonhierarchical relationships easily in a DBTG schema. (Please refer to Figure 3.3 for the occurrences of HOSPITAL, WARD, DOCTOR, STAFF, and PATIENT.)

Figure 3.7 shows the set occurrences corresponding to the schema of Figure 3.6. Those set types that have one-to-many (or one-to-one) relationships between

HOSPITAL-WARD

(HOSP-CODE,	W#)
25	18
25	30
50	10

HOSPITAL-DOCTOR

(HOSP-CODE,	SSN)
25	999–40–4150
25	998–50–1124
50	995–42–7515

WARD-STAFF

(W#,	EMP#)
18	3188
18	5718
30	3188
30	1544
10	1917

ADMITTED

(W#,	PAT#)
18	0129
18	0447
30	0254
10	0155
10	0370

TREAT

(SSN,	PAT#,	DA)
995–42–7515	0155	10 11 1983 (m, d, y)
995–42–7515	0370	05 18 1983
998–50–1124	0254	02 22 1983
998–50–1124	0447	09 19 1982
999–40–4150	0129	07 20 1982
999–40–4150	0447	09 10 1982

Figure 3.7 Set occurrences of the medical database.

the owner and member occurrences can be represented either as derivable or materialized (stored) record types to represent linkages for the relationships.

In the case of many-to-many relationships, we must create the TREAT record type to permanently break the many-to-many relationship into two $1 \times N$ relationships represented by the PATIENT-TREATED and DOCTOR-TREATED set types. This concept was demonstrated in Chapter 2.

DBTG FIND commands

Record Selection

$$\text{FIND } record\text{-}name \text{ RECORD } \begin{Bmatrix} \text{USING} \\ \text{DB-KEY-IS} \end{Bmatrix} dbd\text{-}name$$

$$\text{FIND } \begin{Bmatrix} \text{ANY} \\ \text{NEXT DUPLICATE} \end{Bmatrix} record\text{-}name \text{ RECORD}$$

Brackets indicate options and braces are for selective use. The first find accesses a record occurrence based on an identifier placed in *dbd-name* which represents a database key. In the second find, **ANY** with the **CALC** option in the location mode of the record causes a direct access to the record occurrence. If the **NEXT DUPLICATE** option is selected with the **CALC** option, then the records whose item values are identical (for the items **CALC** is based upon) are accessed. (Actually, in DBTG, the find commands perform selection. This should be followed by a **GET** command if the selected record occurrences should be accessed [i.e., retrieved].) The uses of record selection, for at least one of the options will be included with the examples of the other **FIND** commands which follow.

Set Selection
Selection of set members

$$\text{FIND } \begin{Bmatrix} \text{NEXT} \\ \text{PRIOR} \\ \text{FIRST} \\ \text{LAST} \end{Bmatrix} \begin{bmatrix} \pm \text{ n} \end{bmatrix} record\text{-}name \text{ RECORD OF } set\text{-}name \text{ SET}$$

The value of n qualifies the selected keyword (e.g., NEXT n records of the set). If $n = 2$ with NEXT, the second record next in the order is selected. If n is negative, then the reverse direction (i.e., prior), with respect to the direction of navigation, is taken. The default value for n is $+1$. Figure 3.8 demonstrates the use of this version of the **FIND** command. This figure shows a set occurrence with an owner and six members. Sequential access of members follows the counterclockwise direction.

Selection of set-owner occurrence

$$\text{FIND OWNER RECORD OF } set\text{-}name \text{ SET}$$

This command selects the owner record occurrence of a specified set occurrence. The use of this command assumes that the set occurrence is selected first by

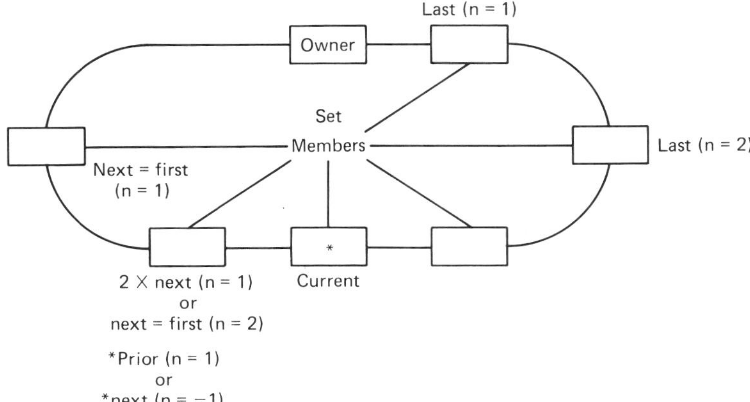

Figure 3.8 Sequential selection of record occurrences within a set occurrence (with the exception of those marked with *, every other access is with respect to the owner).

using one of the options declared in the set selection clause. This can be accomplished usually by selecting a member occurrence either directly or via membership in another set which will be the topic of the next command.

$$\text{FIND} \left[\text{OWNER IN } \textit{set-name} \text{ OF} \right] \text{CURRENT OF} \left\{ \begin{array}{c} \textit{record-name } \textbf{RECORD} \\ \textit{set-name } \textbf{SET} \\ \textbf{RUN-UNIT} \end{array} \right\}$$

If the **OWNER IN** option is excluded, then the currency status indicator specified in the command is assigned to the CURRENT OF RUN-UNIT. In other words, the currency of run-unit can be manipulated. If the **OWNER IN** option is included, then the owner record occurrence of the set is selected by using the currency status indicator specified in the command. The latter option accomplishes *set switching* between two set type occurrences.

Example

Query: *Find the birthyear of the patients treated by the doctor whose SSN is 999-40-4150.*

```
Move 999-40-4150 to SSN in DOCTOR
FIND ANY DOCTOR RECORD
FIND FIRST TREAT RECORD OF DOCTOR-TREATED SET
Repeat while there are members
    FIND OWNER IN PATIENT-TREATED OF CURRENT OF DOCTOR-TREATED SET
    GET PATIENT; BIRTHYEAR
    Print BIRTHYEAR
    FIND NEXT TREAT RECORD OF DOCTOR-TREATED SET
End
```

The first **FIND** command selects the desired doctor's record occurrence. The second **FIND** navigates to the set member in the *DOCTOR-TREATED* set. The third **FIND** selects the *PATIENT* owner in the *PATIENT-TREATED* set via set switching by navigating from the *DOCTOR-TREATED* set. The **GET** command performs the actual retrieval (i.e., moves the BIRTHYEAR value from the selected database record into the user work area) and the last **FIND** command advances to the next member record occurrence in the DOCTOR-TREATED set.

(Answer: 1937; 1942)

Qualified selection of set members

```
FIND record-name VIA [CURRENT OF] set-name [USING dbd-name-1, [ ...,
dbd-name-k]] IN record-name
```

If the **CURRENT OF** option is included, the current occurrence of the set is scanned for the first member record occurrence having the data item (attribute) values equal to those given after **USING** in the command. If the option is excluded, set selection is performed on the set type specified in the command and the owner record occurrence of the desired set occurrence is selected. Afterwards, the procedure is the same as if the **CURRENT OF** option is included. If the **USING** option is excluded, the first member record occurrence of the set occurrence is selected. The double brackets indicate multiple selection of the options.

Example

Query: *Find the date on which the patient with PAT# 0129 is treated by the doctor whose SSN is 999-40-4150.*

```
Move 999-40-4150 to SSN in DOCTOR
FIND ANY DOCTOR RECORD
Move 0129 to PAT# in TREAT
FIND TREAT VIA CURRENT OF DOCTOR-TREATED USING PAT# IN TREAT
GET TREAT; DATE
Print DATE
```

(Answer: 07 20 1982)

In the following **FIND** command, the set member selection is made for those that have identical (duplicate) values for the qualifying attribute values.

```
FIND NEXT DUPLICATE WITHIN set-name USING dbd-name-1, [..., dbd-
name-k] IN record-name
```

Example

Query: *Find the patients (PAT#'s) treated during 1982 by the doctor whose SSN is 998-50-1124.*

```
Move 998-50-1124 to SSN in DOCTOR
FIND ANY DOCTOR RECORD
Move ????1982 to DATE in TREAT
FIND TREAT VIA CURRENT OF DOCTOR-TREATED USING DATE IN TREAT
Repeat while there are members
   GET TREAT; PAT#
   Print PAT#
   FIND NEXT DUPLICATE WITHIN DOCTOR-TREATED USING DATE IN TREAT
End
```

Assuming that **date** can be searched by don't cares (i.e., ?, the wild-card character) for day and month, the last **FIND** command will execute for as many times as there are patients for the same doctor who treated them during the year 1982.

Singular Sets.   In cases where we want to select instances of a given record type independently, we can declare a set whose (implicit) owner is the system (run-unit) and whose members are the occurrences of the record type to be selected. Such sets are referred to as *singular sets*.

Suppose we declare a singular set called *ALL-DOCTORS*. The following example can then be given:

Example

Query: *Find those doctors whose specialty is gynecology.*

```
FIND FIRST DOCTOR RECORD OF ALL-DOCTORS SET
Repeat while there are members
   GET DOCTOR; SPECIALTY, NAME
   If SPECIALTY is GYNECOLOGY then
   Print NAME
   FIND NEXT DOCTOR RECORD OF ALL-DOCTORS SET
End
```

(Answer: R. Miller)

Currency Manipulation.   In certain instances, we may not want the system to update the currency indicators automatically after the current selection. This is because we may be involved in set switching followed by a sequential scan of the second set and then return to the first set (that is, to the set in which we started our selection), and continue the selection in this first set.

Example

Query: *If the birthyear for any of the patients treated by the doctor whose SSN is 998-50-1124 is greater than 1935 (i.e., younger), then output the date the patient was treated.*

```
Move 998-50-1124 to SSN# in DOCTOR
FIND ANY DOCTOR RECORD
FIND FIRST TREAT RECORD OF DOCTOR-TREATED SET
```

```
Repeat while there are owners
   FIND OWNER IN PATIENT-TREATED OF CURRENT OF DOCTOR-TREATED
   SET
   GET PATIENT; BIRTHYEAR
   If BIRTHYEAR > 1935 then
     Begin
     FIND CURRENT OF TREAT RECORD
     GET TREAT; DATE
     Print DATE
     End
   FIND NEXT TREAT RECORD OF DOCTOR-TREATED SET
End
```

(Answer: 09 19 1982)

The **FIND CURRENT OF** command in the Begin block makes the currency of run unit equal to the current of the *TREAT* record type because the **GET** command uses it. Note: Issuing the single DBTG statement **GET** without qualification causes system to move from the database buffer to the program-accessible user work area all attribute values of the record type which is current of the run unit (regardless of the record type you may have intended)! Supplying specific attribute names in the **GET** statement causes DBTG to move only those corresponding values to user work area.

Example

Query: *For each doctor who treated the patient with PAT# 0447, find the other patients treated by the same doctor and output the doctor's name and the patient's number.*

```
Move 0447 to PAT# in PATIENT
FIND ANY PATIENT RECORD
FIND NEXT TREAT RECORD OF PATIENT-TREATED SET
Repeat while there are members of PATIENT-TREATED set
   FIND OWNER RECORD OF DOCTOR-TREATED SET
   GET DOCTOR; NAME
     Repeat while there are members of DOCTOR-TREATED set
     FIND NEXT TREAT RECORD OF DOCTOR-TREATED SET RETAINING
     CURRENCY FOR PATIENT-TREATED SET
     GET TREAT; PAT#
     If PAT# ≠ 0447 then
        Print DOCTOR.NAME, PAT#
     End
   FIND NEXT TREAT RECORD OF PATIENT-TREATED SET
End
```

(Answer: B. V. D. Hoek, 0254; J. Wolfley, 0129)

Other Commands in DBTG

Updates

MODIFY *record-name; list of attribute names*

This command follows a **GET** and an update procedure in the user's program and replaces the current of run-unit with the values of the record occurrence, or only the attribute values (if the attribute list is specified), by the modified values in the user's program (user work area).

Insertion and deletion

To insert a record occurrence into a DBTG database, first, the record must be physically stored in the database, and, second, all the links with the sets that the record type is associated with must be established. Therefore, the associated **STORE** command's effect depends upon how the **MEMBERSHIP IS** clause is declared in the schema. If the membership is declared as *automatic,* all links are established automatically by the system whenever the record is inserted. If, however, the membership is declared as *manual,* then the **STORE** command cannot be used. Instead, the **INSERT** command must be used for each set type to which the record belongs. In the case of automatic membership, the system must be properly provided with the declarations of set selection.

The **REMOVE** command does the opposite of **INSERT**. It cuts the links from the associated sets, but does not physically delete the record occurrence. The use of this command also depends on the membership declaration. The command works as described if the membership of the record type in the associated set type is declared as *optional.* If the membership is declared as *mandatory* however, the **REMOVE** command has no effect. In that case, the **DELETE** command must be used. **DELETE** cuts the links and deletes the record. If the record occurrence is an owner occurrence however, **DELETE** has no effect unless it is used as **DELETE ALL**. In the latter case, care should be taken not to trigger chained deletions in the database (i.e., owner deletion causing deletion of members and members in turn causing deletions in the other sets, and so on).

3.3 SELECTION IN RELATIONAL SYSTEMS

3.3.1 Introduction to Relational Calculus

Relational calculus is used in the abstract formulation of queries, and it is an alternative to relational algebra. As compared to the latter, it is more definitional than procedural. Codd [1972] defined the following elements of the applied predicate calculus:

Tuple variables represent relations in the tuple oriented calculus. They are defined over the *ranges* of relations that define the scope of the tuple variable. Tuple variables can qualify attribute names (e.g., for $t.a$, t is the tuple variable and a is an attribute name).

Dyadic predicates are of the form $x\theta y$, where θ is one of the comparison operators $=$, $\neq$, $\leq$, $<$, $\geq$, $>$. They are also referred to as *join terms*, where

x is a tuple variable and y is either a tuple variable or an individual constant. *Monadic* predicates indicate ranges of relations. A relational calculus expression contains monadic and/or dyadic predicates.

A *well-formed formula (WFF)* is constructed from predicates, Boolean operators (*AND, OR, NOT*), and the quantifiers existential, $\exists$ (*there exists*), and universal $\forall$ (*for all*), according to the following rules:

(a) Every predicate is a WFF.

(b) If f is a WFF, then so are (f) and *NOT*(f).

(c) If f and g are WFFs, then so are $(f\ AND\ g)$ and $(f\ OR\ g)$.

(d) If f is a WFF in which t occurs as a free variable, then $\exists\ t(f)$ and $\forall\ t(f)$ are WFFs.

(e) Nothing else is a WFF.

A variable is called *free* if it is not within the scope of a quantifier; otherwise, it is a bound variable.

3.3.2 Query Examples in Relational Algebra and Calculus

As mentioned earlier, relational algebra is procedural while relational calculus is more definitional. That is, with relational algebra, it is the user's responsibility to specify operation sequences that lead to the answer. The answer (result) is placed in a new relation. In relational calculus, however, the user gives the requirement specification, and the way of obtaining the result is left open to one of the various implementation alternatives. As will be seen, most relational algebra queries are answered by the use of the popular operations of *selection*, *join*, and *projection*. We will use the following relational version of the medical database used earlier in the chapter. These relations contain the same data as the DBTG database with the exception of W# in TREAT.

```
HOSPITAL (HOSP-CODE, NAME, ADDRESS, NO-OF-BEDS)
WARD (W#, NAME, NO-BEDS)
DOCTOR (SSN, NAME, SPECIALTY)
TREAT (SSN, PAT#, W#, DATE)
STAFF (EMP#, NAME, JOB-CODE, SALARY)
PATIENT (PAT#, NAME, ADDRESS, BIRTHYEAR, PSSN)
```

Examples

Query 1: *Find the names of doctors who treat the patient with patient number 0447.*

```
RANGE TREAT X
GET W (DOCTOR.NAME): ∃ X(DOCTOR.SSN=TREAT.SSN ∧ X.PAT# = 0447)
```

(Answer: B. Vdhoek, J. Wolfley)

As can be seen, the specification (output) part of the query is to the left of the colon, whereas the qualification expression is on the right. The specification implies projection of the result. In the qualification expression, we have a selection for the patient followed by a join of the selected (restricted) TREAT relation with the DOCTOR relation. The existential quantifier implies a disjunction of the individual evaluations of the TREAT tuples. That is, the final result is the union of those TREAT tuples that qualify for the join operation with the DOCTOR relation (i.e., the result is one or more doctors).

Another quantifier is the universal quantifier, which implies a conjunctive evaluation of the individual results of the calculus expression. That is, for the result to hold, all tuples of the relation within the scope of the quantifier must successfully evaluate to true in the qualification expression. The universal quantifier generally implies a division operation, whereas the existential quantifier implies a join.

The query can be expressed in relational algebra. The following is a possible solution:

```
((( TREAT[SSN, PAT#]) * {'0047'}) [SSN] * DOCTOR) [SNAME]
```

Since the natural join between TREAT and '0447' (i.e. a unary relation) is equivalent to a division where the unary relation is the divisor, we can write the same expression as

```
((( TREAT[SSN, PAT#])/{'0447'}) * DOCTOR) [SNAME]
```

As can be noticed, the operations grow from the center to the outer nestings as indicated by the parenthesized groupings. Also, division eliminates the need for the second projection.

Query 2: *Find the names of doctors who treat at least one patient born after 1942.*

```
RANGE PATIENT X
RANGE TREAT Y
GET W(DOCTOR.NAME): ∃Y(DOCTOR.SSN = Y.SSN ∧ ∃X(TREAT.PAT# =
                        X.PAT# ∧ X.BIRTHYEAR > 1942))
```

(In pure relational calculus, we need to use range and its tuple variable, even for the unbound result relation.) This query can be read from left to right as: "There exists a doctor treating a patient and the patient treated was born after 1942." Alternatively, if we read the expression from right to left, which is usually the order of execution, we can express it as: "There exists one or more patients born after 1942, link them to the doctors who treat them."

In relational algebra, a possible solution is

$$((((PATIENT[PAT\#, \ BIRTHYEAR])/\{'1942'\})*TREAT[SSN, \ PAT\#])$$
$$[SSN]*DOCTOR)[NAME]$$

Query 3: *Find the names of doctors who do not treat the patient with patient number 0155.*

```
RANGE TREAT X
GET  W(DOCTOR.NAME):  ∀X(DOCTOR.SSN≠X.SSN ∨ X.PAT#≠0155)
```

This can be interpreted as "For all TREAT tuples, either the doctor does not treat anybody or whoever the doctor treats is not the patient whose number is 0155." An equivalent expression can be as follows.

```
GET  W(DOCTOR.NAME):  ¬ ∃X(DOCTOR.SSN = X.SSN ∧ X.PAT# = 0155)
```

which is the negation of the negated query (i.e., doctors treating patient 0155). In relational algebra,

$$DOCTOR[NAME]-((TREAT[SSN, \ PAT\#]/\{'0155'\}) \ * \ DOCTOR)[NAME]$$

Query 4: *Find the IDs of doctors who treat all the patients in the hospital.*

```
RANGE PATIENT X
RANGE TREAT Y
GET  W(DOCTOR.NAME):  ∀X ∃ Y(DOCTOR.SSN=Y.SSN ∧ Y.PAT#=X.PAT#)
```

As can be seen in the use of the universal quantifier, the overall expression must be valid for all the PATIENT tuples. That is, for a doctor to be in the answer, the doctor must have a join path to each patient in the TREAT relation. Such uses of the universal quantifier imply the use of the division operation in relational algebra, as shown in the following:

$$((TREAT[SSN, \ PAT\#]/PATIENT[PAT\#])*DOCTOR)[SSN]$$

The PATIENT relation's projection onto PAT#s will give the set of all patients. As can be remembered from Chapter 2, the division operation can be interpreted as a *match into* operation of the divisor set into each partition of the dividend relation. The partitions are formed on the remaining attributes of the dividend after the division attribute(s) are excluded, and the former is output for the eligible partitions. The abstract example in Figure 3.9 demonstrates the basic steps of division. Recall that the partitions are formed with respect to the identical SSN (i.e., DOCTOR-ID) tuples, which are also the output for the eligible partitions in the division. Eligibility in division is determined by the inclusion or equality of the set of PAT#s of the dividend to the set of PAT#s of the divisor (hence, in a sense, those partitions into which (or with which) the divisor can be matched).

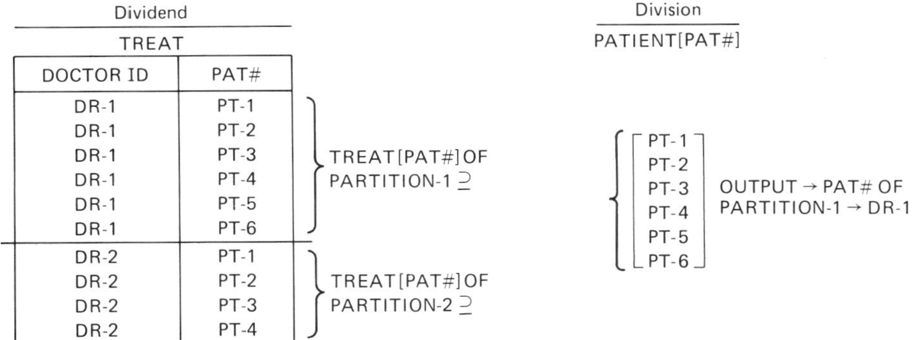

Figure 3.9   Division revisited.

3.3.3 Query Examples in SEQUEL (SQL)

In this section, we will give an example of a high-level relational query language originally called SEQUEL (Structured English Query Language) [Chamberlin and Boyce, 1974] which was the successor of the more mathematically oriented version called SQUARE [Boyce et al., 1975]. SEQUEL, which was subsequently called SQL, is offered as a data language in the IBM products and it is the DML of IBMs System R relational DBMS [Astrahan et al., 1976].

SEQUEL is a block-oriented language. A block in SEQUEL is made up of SELECT FROM WHERE expressions (the last two keywords are optional). A query may be expressed by a one block program, or several blocks may be nested in various ways. Qualifications within a block and nestings of blocks correspond to intra- and interrelation mappings, respectively (although in the latter, sometimes a single relation is involved). Depending on their type, nestings (i.e., composites) imply a join or a division.

The typical use of the *SELECT FROM WHERE* block is as follows:

- *SELECT list of attributes and/or their aggregate functions*
- *FROM relation name(s)*
- *WHERE qualification expression*

The qualification expression can be a Boolean expression of simple conditions and a condition may span other blocks.

Examples.   We will continue to use the medical database of Section 3.3.2 in the following examples:

Simple Selection

Query 1: *Find the names of patients born after 1937.*

```
SELECT NAME
FROM PATIENT
WHERE BIRTHYEAR > 1937
```

Selection Involving Join

Query 2: *Find the names of patients treated by the doctor whose SSN is 995-42-7515.*

```
SELECT NAME
FROM PATIENT
WHERE PAT# =
        SELECT PAT#
        FROM TREAT
        WHERE SSN = 995-42-7515

or  SELECT NAME
    FROM PATIENT, TREAT
    WHERE PATIENT.PAT# = TREAT.PAT#
    AND TREAT.SSN = 955-42-7515

or  SELECT NAME
    FROM PATIENT
    WHERE PAT# = ANY(SELECT PAT#
                     FROM TREAT
                     WHERE SSN = 995-42-7515)

or  SELECT NAME
    FROM PATIENT
    WHERE PAT# IN (SELECT PAT#
                   FROM TREAT
                   WHERE SSN = 995-42-7515)

or  SELECT NAME
    FROM PATIENT
    WHERE EXISTS
                (SELECT *
                 FROM TREAT
                 WHERE PAT# = PATIENT.PAT#
                 AND SSN = 995-42-7515)
```

As can be noticed from the examples, as the SEQUEL language evolved, alternative syntaxes were introduced. The choice of any given one would be the user's decision. While some of the foregoing examples have a relational algebra flavor, the others are more like relational calculus. Some are easily understood when read from bottom up while others are more suited to top-down interpretation. In all the examples, the idea is to determine an intermediate answer set from one of the relations and then join that set with the relation whose output is required. With regard to the **SELECT** keyword, * implies an entire tuple or set of tuples and **SELECT UNIQUE** forces duplicate elimination in the projection of the result.

Selection Involving Set Comparison (Division)

Query 3: *Find the names of doctors who treat all the patients born before 1935.*

```
SELECT NAME
FROM DOCTOR
WHERE SSN =
        SELECT SSN
        FROM TREAT
        WHERE PAT# = ALL
                SELECT PAT#
                FROM PATIENT
                WHERE BIRTHDAY < 1935
```

In this query, the middle nesting corresponds to the existential quantifier (i.e., join to DOCTOR), whereas the lowest level of nesting corresponds to the universal quantifier (i.e., division into TREAT). The alternate syntax for this query is

```
SELECT NAME
FROM DOCTOR
WHERE SSN =
        SELECT SSN
        FROM TREAT
        WHERE SET (PAT#) CONTAINS
                        SELECT PAT
                        FROM PATIENT
                        WHERE BIRTHDAY < 1935
```

CONTAINS can also be followed by a set of constants, instead of a **SELECT** block, if we know the values and they are few in number. For example, if we knew that the qualified patients were G. Anderson and B. Helm, we could write the last part of the query as

```
WHERE SET (PAT#) CONTAINS ('0129', '0254')
```

Selection Involving Grouping.

Grouping is a form of partitioning a relation based on the attribute specified with the **GROUP BY** clause and the qualification in **WHERE**.

Query 4: *Find the names of doctors who treat more than five patients.*

```
SELECT NAME
FROM DOCTOR
WHERE SSN =
        SELECT SSN
        FROM TREAT GROUP BY SSN
        WHERE COUNT (PAT#) > 5
```

Query 5: *Find the patient numbers for patients who are treated by more than one doctor.*

```
SELECT PAT#
FROM TREAT GROUP BY PAT#
WHERE COUNT (SSN) > 1

or      SELECT UNIQUE PAT#
        FROM TREAT, TREATX
        WHERE PAT# IN
                      (SELECT PAT#
                       FROM TREAT
                       WHERE SSN ≠ TREATX.SSN)
```

Selection Involving Correlation.   Correlation is similar to grouping in that a single relation is involved and a free variable is used as in relational calculus. In correlation, however, we have single tuples that are correlated rather than grouping so that we can envision a double cursor operation as follows: while the master (outer) cursor points to a single tuple at a time, the inner cursor scans all the tuples of the relation for correlation for each position of the former, the operation terminates whenever the master cursor finishes with all the tuples of the relation.

Query 6: *Find all pairs of doctor names such that two doctors have the same specialty.*

```
SELECT FIRST.NAME, SECOND.NAME
FROM DOCTOR FIRST, DOCTOR SECOND
WHERE FIRST.SPECIALTY=SECOND.SPECIALTY
AND FIRST.NAME < SECOND.NAME

or equivalently,

B1:  SELECT NAME, B2.NAME
     FROM DOCTOR
     WHERE SPECIALTY =
     B2:            SELECT SPECIALITY
                    FROM DOCTOR
                    WHERE NAME > B1.NAME
```

In the first version, by including the **AND** condition, we make sure that the same name and permutations of two names do not appear. The second version uses *block labeling* in much the same way as the implementation of the dual cursor operation.

Selection Involving Scalar Quantification

Query 7: *Find the names of the staff earning more than any nurse.*

```
SELECT NAME
FROM STAFF
WHERE SALARY > ALL
        SELECT SALARY
        FROM STAFF
        WHERE JOB-CODE = Nurse
```

Alternatively, we can use the following for the first **WHERE** clause in the comparison of salaries.

```
WHERE SALARY > ANY     or   WHERE SALARY >
      SELECT SALARY            SELECT MAX(SALARY)
```

If the query asked for the names of the staff earning more than some nurse, then the salary comparison could be

```
WHERE SALARY > SOME    or   WHERE SALARY >
      SELECT SALARY               SELECT MIN (SALARY)
```

Aggregate functions (i.e., SUM, COUNT, MAX, MIN, AVERAGE) can be used in the qualifications following the **WHERE** clause. In **SELECT COUNT (*)** and **SELECT COUNT UNIQUE** (*SALARY*), the nulls are countable with the former and not so with the latter.

Selection Involving (Binary) Set Operations

Query 8: *Find the names of doctors who do not treat the patient with patient number 0155.*

```
SELECT UNIQUE NAME
FROM DOCTOR
DIFFERENCE
SELECT NAME
FROM DOCTOR
WHERE SSN =
      SELECT SSN
      FROM TREAT
      WHERE PAT# = 0155

or  SELECT NAME
    FROM DOCTOR
    WHERE 0155 ≠ ALL
                  (SELECT PAT#
                   FROM TREAT
                   WHERE SSN = DOCTOR.SSN)
```

Other set operations such as UNION and INTERSECTION can also be used. The second version requires the execution of universal quantification in a negated form.

Updates.   For relation modifications and deletions, the query templates are:

For modifications,

```
UPDATE relation
SET attribute = value
WHERE any SQL query
```

For deletions,

```
DELETE relation
WHERE any SQL query
```

Insertion is same as deletion except that data for the inserted tuple must be supplied with the query.

3.3.4 Relational Completeness

Assume a relational database that consists of relations $\{R_1, R_2, \ldots, R_n\}$ and the set $C(R)$ represents the set of relations obtained from R by using relational algebra operations. The set $C(R)$ represents all the relationships present in the database. If a language can capture all the relationships representable by $C(R)$, then it is said to be relationally complete. That is, the language will have the same expressive power as relational algebra or calculus [Codd, 1972].

In language implementations, the following two operations are needed to assure relational completeness:

(a) The ability to represent assignments, that is, the ability to create new relations to store the results of relational algebra operations that are also relations. $(R_1 \leftarrow R_2 * R_3$ indicates that the join of R_2 and R_3 is created (assigned) as the new R_1 relation.)

(b) The ability to compute transitive closures which enables recursion and/or nesting of relational algebra operations to express expressions of arbitrary complexity. For example, $R_1 \leftarrow ((R_2[A, B] * R_3)[B] * R_4)[C]$ involves nested expressions and assignment, which are necessary to produce the answer.

3.4 RAP RELATIONAL LANGUAGE

The RAP relational language, which is also referred to as the RAP DBMS assembler, is the language of the RAP database machine/computer. The underlying structure is the RAP relation, which augments a normalized relation with a set of mark or tag bits (as defined in Chapter 2) and allows duplicate tuples. The RAP language, although called an assembler due to its register manipulation, branch, and control capabilities, is a high-level language that can be directly used by application programmers.

3.4.1 RAP Syntax

A RAP instruction is of the form

```
<label><opcode><specification><qualification><parameter>
```

The label is a symbolic instruction address. The opcode specifies a DBMS operation, which is also a RAP hardware primitive. A specification has the following format

```
<relation-name>[(<attribute-name-1>, ..., <attribute-name-k>)]
```

A qualification can be null or a Boolean expression of disjunctive normal form of simple conditions Q_i, where a Q_i can be one of

(a) *<attribute-name><comparator><operand>*
(b) *MKED(<t_c>)* denoting any combination of true (i.e., set or marked) mark bits
(c) *UNMKED(<t_c>)* denoting any combination of false (i.e., reset or unmarked) mark bits

where *<comparator>* is one of the comparison operators $=, \neq, \leq, <, \geq, >$ and *<operand>* is a numeric or literal constant, or another attribute-name. *<parameter>* specifies the second operand in arithmetic operations, the RAP registers, or the source relation with mark qualification as used in the binary relational operations, specifically in the implicit join (or semi-join, see the index).

The RAP instructions can be grouped as Data Definition and Storage, Select and Retrieve, Select and (Arithmetic) Update, Select and Scalar Aggregate, Data Save and Cursor, Register Instructions, Program Control, and System Instructions. Figure 3.10 lists the opcodes for each of the instruction groups.

The operations of the RAP instructions are self-iterative because of the underlying parallel and associative architecture. Each instruction affects the entire relation, selects eligible tuples, and carries out the operation on all eligible tuples simultaneously. Eligibility is determined by qualification evaluation on the tuple contents. The same qualification and operation specified in the instruction is executed on all tuples of the relation by self-iteration (which is a logical term when processed by parallel/associative hardware).

In this section, we will give an informal introduction to RAP programming by means of examples using the key instructions and the example query programs written in the RAP language. The various aspects of this language will be discussed also in the other chapters in different contexts. One interesting aspect,

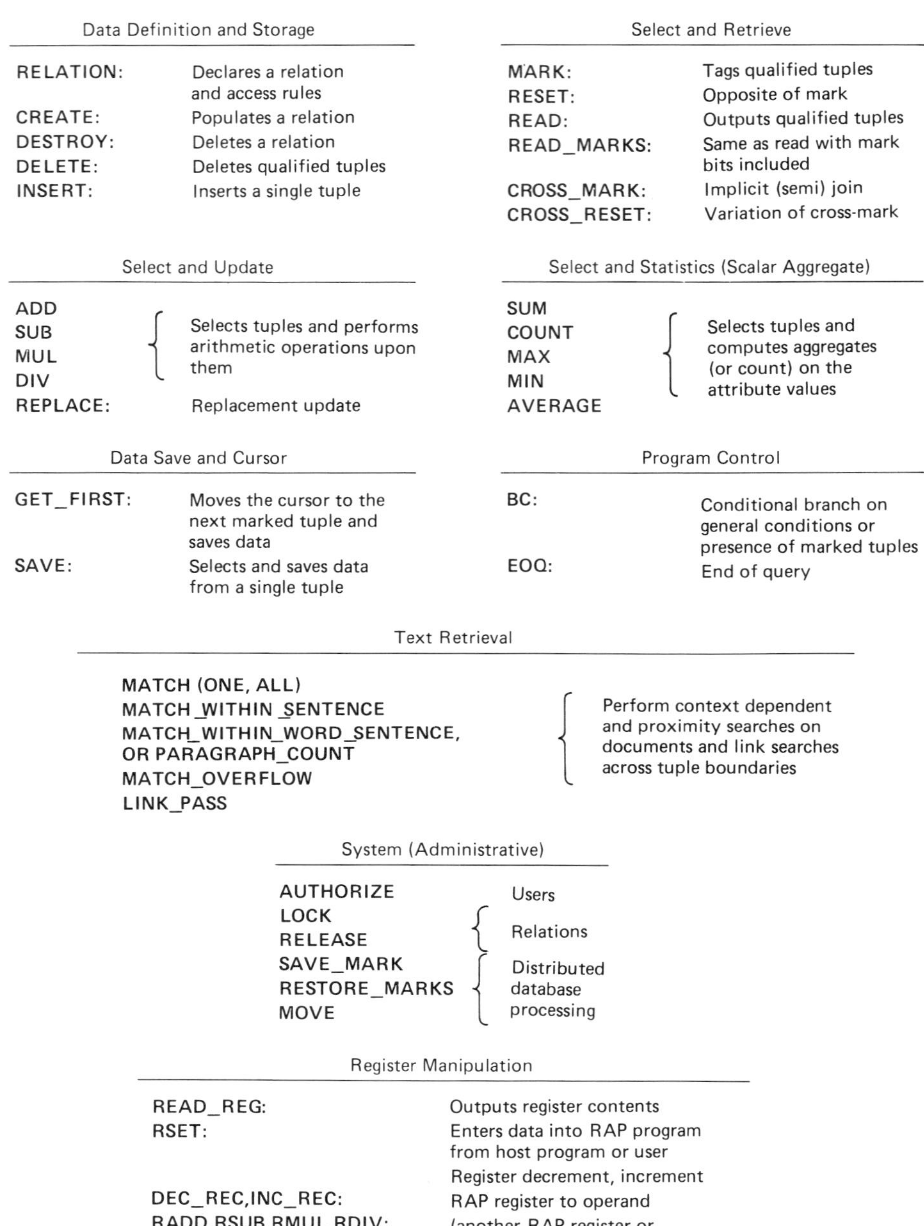

Figure 3.10 Summary of the RAP instruction set.

in addition to these discussions, is that the RAP language is implemented on various contemporary computers via its emulator software which uses efficient file processing and buffering techniques. The software emulator of RAP, called SERAP (or simply the RAP language as far as the user is concerned), is operational on several mainframes (IBM 370s, 3081; Amdahl 470), superminis (VAX 11/780-Unix), microcomputers (Intel 8086 systems, iTPS), and IBM PC/IS(XT). The language can be used as a stand-alone query language or as a DSL embedded in PL/I (IBM, Amdahl), C (VAX), or PLM/86 (Intel) host languages. Due to the time difference of SERAP versions, there may be minor syntactical differences. Also, depending on the type of the computer system, the definition of a word length varies (32 to 16 bits). Appendix I is devoted to the documentation of SERAP syntax and semantics.

3.4.2 MARK Instruction

Example

Assume a relation $R(A_1, A_2, A_3, A_4)$—mark bits are implicit—and the following instruction:

$$\textbf{MARK} \ (t_1 t_3) \ [R: A_2 > 5 \ AND \ A_3 = \text{'}bd\text{'}]$$

Relation R before the execution of the **MARK** instruction:

t_1	t_2	t_3	$\cdots$	t_{15}	A_1	A_2	A_3	A_4
0	0	0	$\cdots$	0	K_1	5	ab	50
0	0	0	$\cdots$	0	K_2	10	bd	100
0	0	0	$\cdots$	0	K_3	5	bc	200
0	0	0	$\cdots$	0	K_4	20	bd	40

Relation R after the execution of the **MARK** instruction:

t_1	t_2	t_3	$\cdots$	t_{15}	A_1	A_2	A_3	A_4	
0	0	0	$\cdots$	0	K_1	5	ab	50	
1	0	1	$\cdots$	0	K_2	10	bd	100	←
0	0	0	$\cdots$	0	K_3	5	bc	200	
1	0	1	$\cdots$	0	K_4	20	bd	40	←

Two tuples satisfied the qualification and are $(t_1 t_3)$ marked.

3.4.3 GET_FIRST Instruction

Example

```
GET_FIRST [R(A₁, A₂): MKED(t₁)]   /*cannot override implicit
register designation, i.e. do not use register names as parameter*/
```

R before execution:

t_1	t_2	t_3	$\cdots$	t_{15}	A_1	A_2	A_3	A_4
1	0	0	$\cdots$	0	K_1	5	ab	50
1	0	0	$\cdots$	0	K_2	10	bd	100
0	0	0	$\cdots$	0	K_3	5	bc	200
0	0	0	$\cdots$	0	K_4	20	bd	40

← There are two t_1 marked tuples. The first occurence will be selected.

R after first iteration:

t_1	t_2	t_3	$\cdots$	t_{15}	A_1	A_2	A_3	A_4
0	0	0	$\cdots$	0	(K_1)	(5)	ab	50
1	0	0	$\cdots$	0	K_2	10	bd	100
0	0	0	$\cdots$	0	K_3	5	bc	200
0	0	0	$\cdots$	0	K_4	20	bd	40

← t_1 bit is turned off (reset); A_1, A_2 are saved in RAP registers.

REGC registers:

1	2	3	4	
K_1	5	–	–	$\cdots$

R if iterated twice:

t_1	t_2	t_3	$\cdots$	t_{15}	A_1	A_2	A_3	A_4
0	0	0	$\cdots$	0	K_1	5	ab	50
0	0	0	$\cdots$	0	(K_2)	(10)	bd	100
0	0	0	$\cdots$	0	K_3	5	bc	200
0	0	0	$\cdots$	0	K_4	20	bd	40

← t_1 bit is reset; A_1, A_2 are saved

1	2	3	4	
K_2	10	K_1	5	$\cdots$

As can be seen, **GET_FIRST** functions like a cursor working on the first marked tuple and saving its values which can then be used in free variable operations such as projection, correlation, and grouping—examples of which will be seen in the coming RAP query program demonstrations. The values saved by **GET_FIRST** are stored in REGC_i ($1 \le i \le 9$) in a silo fashion (i.e., old values are shifted toward higher-numbered registers as in a FIFO buffer).

3.4.4 CROSS_MARK Instruction

Example

```
CROSS_MARK (t₂)[R₁: A₃ = R₂A₂][R₂.MKED(t₁)]   /*R₂.MKED(t₁) or
just MKED(t₁) * /
```

Before execution:

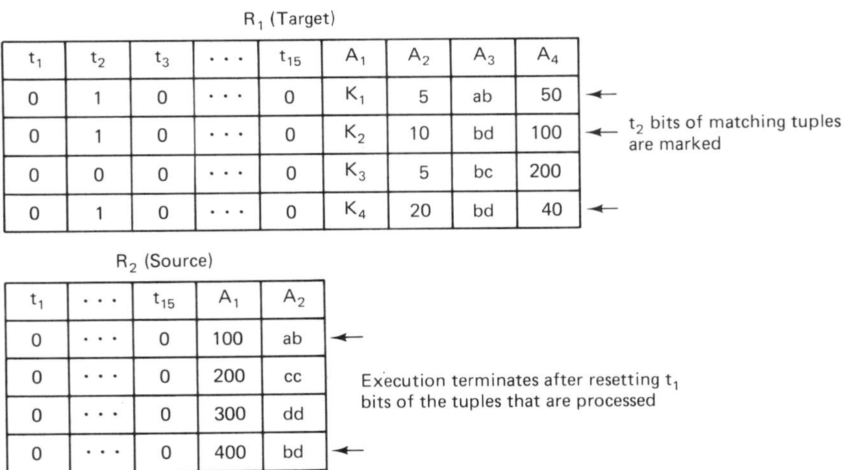

R₁ (Target)

t₁	t₂	t₃	· · ·	t₁₅	A₁	A₂	A₃	A₄
0	0	0	· · ·	0	K₁	5	(ab)	50
0	0	0	· · ·	0	K₂	10	(bd)	100
0	0	0	· · ·	0	K₃	5	bc	200
0	0	0	· · ·	0	K₄	20	(bd)	40

R₂ (Source)

t₁	· · ·	t₁₅	A₁	A₂	
1	· · ·	0	100	(ab)	←
0	· · ·	0	200	cc	
0	· · ·	0	300	dd	
1	· · ·	0	400	(bd)	←

A₂ values from the marked tuples are taken to be compared with R₁'s A₃ values

After execution:

R₁ (Target)

t₁	t₂	t₃	· · ·	t₁₅	A₁	A₂	A₃	A₄	
0	1	0	· · ·	0	K₁	5	ab	50	←
0	1	0	· · ·	0	K₂	10	bd	100	←
0	0	0	· · ·	0	K₃	5	bc	200	
0	1	0	· · ·	0	K₄	20	bd	40	←

← t₂ bits of matching tuples are marked

R₂ (Source)

t₁	· · ·	t₁₅	A₁	A₂	
0	· · ·	0	100	ab	←
0	· · ·	0	200	cc	
0	· · ·	0	300	dd	
0	· · ·	0	400	bd	←

Execution terminates after resetting t₁ bits of the tuples that are processed

As can be seen, this instruction carries out an implicit join (semi-join) in the sense that only the join attribute values are taken to be compared with the A_3 values of the R_1 relation. Instead of creating a new result relation, the same thing is accomplished by marking the specified bits of the target relation. In **CROSS_MARK**, a general θ join is executable. The difference between this type of join and the classical join of relational algebra is that (1) the result is confined to the cardinality of the target relation because a new relation is not created and (2) a marked tuple in the target could have been qualified more than once in the operation.

3.4.5 CROSS_RESET Instruction

The instruction mnemonic was CRS_COND_MARK previously.

Example

$$\text{CROSS\_RESET} \; (t_2) [R_1: \; A_3 = R_2 . A_2] [R_2 . MKED(t_1)]$$

Before execution:

R₁ (Target)

t_1	t_2	t_3	$\cdots$	t_{15}	A_1	A_2	A_3	A_4	
0	1	0	$\cdots$	0	K_1	5	ab	50	←
0	1	0	$\cdots$	0	K_2	10	bd	100	← Existing marked tuples
0	0	0	$\cdots$	0	K_3	5	bc	200	
0	1	0	$\cdots$	0	K_4	20	bd	40	←

R₂ (Source)

t_1	$\cdots$	t_{15}	A_1	A_2	
0	$\cdots$	0	100	ab	
0	$\cdots$	0	200	cc	
0	$\cdots$	0	300	dd	
1	$\cdots$	0	400	(bd)	← The only t_1 marked tuple whose A_2 value will be matched with the target

After execution:

R₁ (Target)

t_1	t_2	t_3	$\cdots$	t_{15}	A_1	A_2	A_3	A_4	
0	0	0	$\cdots$	0	K_1	5	ab	50	← Tuples that had a match remained t_2 marked whereas the first tuple had no match for its A_3 value, hence it is t_2 reset
0	1	0	$\cdots$	0	K_2	10	(bd)	100	
0	0	0	$\cdots$	0	K_3	5	bc	200	
0	1	0	$\cdots$	0	K_4	20	(bd)	40	

R₂ (Source)

t_1	$\cdots$	t_{15}	A_1	A_2	
0	$\cdots$	0	100	ab	
0	$\cdots$	0	200	cc	
0	$\cdots$	0	300	dd	
0	$\cdots$	0	400	bd	← Tuple is reset, iteration terminates

As can be visualized, this instruction can be replaced by a **CROSS_MARK** followed by a **RESET** instruction. **CROSS_RESET** may be convenient in cases where a high number of mappings between relations would be needed in a program.

3.4.6 RAP Programming Examples

The following relations of an example department store database will be used:

```
EMP (NAME, SAL, MGR, DEPT, COMM)
LOCATION (DEPT, FLOOR)
SALES (DEPT, ITEM, VOL)
SUPPLY (COMPANY, ITEM, DEPT, VOL)
CLASS (ITEM, TYPE)
NEWSALES (DEPT, ITEM, VOL)
```

where **EMP** is employee, **SAL** is salary, **MGR** is manager name, **VOL** is volume, **COMM** is commission, and **DEPT** is department.

Queries

Query 1: *Find the employee(s) whose salary is greater than that of any employee in the shoe department.*

```
MAX  [EMP(SAL):DEPT = "SHOE"][REGF_1]    /*Single quotes, 'SHOE',
         are also acceptable*/
MARK ( t₁ )[EMP:SAL > REGF_1]
READ [EMP(NAME):MKED( t₁ )]
EOQ
```

The first instruction (**MAX**) finds the maximum salary and places it in RAP register REGF_1. The second instruction (**MARK**) restricts the employee relation on the basis of salaries higher than the highest found in the shoe department. The third instruction (**READ**) reads out the name attribute values of the employee relation from the restricted tuples of the same relation which are indicated by the marked t_1 tag bits. The fourth instruction (**EOQ**) signals the end of the query.

We use the symbols (i.e., = , >, <, etc.) in the Unix and Intel versions or the mnemonics (i.e., EQ, GT, LT, etc.) in the IBM (OS/MVS) version for the comparison operators. The default (i.e., if not specified) register for storing scalar aggregates is REGF_1.

Query 2. *List the names and managers of employees in the shoe department with salaries greater than $10,000.*

```
READ [EMP(NAME, MGR):DEPT = "SHOE" & SAL > 10000]
EOQ
```

As can be seen, the qualification (DEPT is SHOE and SAL > 10000) can be used directly in the read command.

Query 3. *Move the location of the TOY department to the second floor.*

```
REPLACE [LOCATION(FLOOR):DEPT = "TOY"][2]
EOQ
```

In this in-place (on memory) update, all the toy department tuples are replaced by 2 in their floor attribute values. In other words, the update is set-oriented as are all other operations. One may think of a toy department scattered partially at various floors and, with the update, we are implying that all parts of the toy department are gathered on the second floor.

Query 4. *Delete from the EMP relation all the employees who work for Anderson's manager.*

```
SAVE   [EMP(MGR):NAME = "ANDERSON"][REGS]
DELETE [EMP:MGR = REGS]
EOQ
```

The **SAVE** instruction is useful in cases where we know that the attribute value to be saved is functionally determined (i.e., unique) by the qualifying attribute (i.e., NAME). The reason for this is because there is one RAP register, REGS, dedicated for this instruction so that we cannot save a set of values. The **DELETE** instruction deletes entire tuple(s) whose qualifications are evaluated as true.

Query 5. *Add 500 to the volume sold of the item slippers in the shoe department.*

```
ADD [SALES(VOL):DEPT = "SHOE" & ITEM = "SLIPPERS"][500]
EOQ
```

As in Query 3, the update is set oriented; that is, the volumes of all the qualified tuples are increased by 500. A semantically better example can be the following:

```
MUL [EMP(SAL):DEPT = "HARDWARE"][1.1]
```

which gives 10% raise to all employees who work in the hardware department.

Query 6. *Add the commission of salesman Clark in the shoe department to his salary.*

```
ADD (t₁)[EMP(SAL):DEPT = "SHOE" & NAME = "CLARK"][COMM]
```

This is an update that takes place between the two attribute values within the qualifying tuples in the relation. The updated tuples can optionally be marked (t_1 marked in this case) to help establish a checkpoint for the case of a possible system crash. The update takes place as *specification attribute* ← *specification attribute + parameter attribute,* which is SAL ← SAL + COMM.

Query 7. *Delete all tuples of the database relation Newsales involving employee Clark's department and the item slippers.*

```
1   SAVE  [EMP(DEPT):NAME = "CLARK"][REGS]
2   MARK  (t1) [NEWSALES:DEPT = REGS]
3   RESET (t1) [NEWSALES:MKED (t1) & ITEM <> "SLIPPERS"]
4   DELETE [NEWSALES:MKED (t1)]
5   EOQ
```

In instructions 1 and 2, once again, we see value passing between instructions via the RAP registers. In instruction 3, we see a conditional reset; that is, only those t_1 bits of the tuples whose items are not slippers are reset.

Query 8. *Find the items sold by departments on the second floor.*

```
MARK (tl) [LOCATION:FLOOR = 2]
CROSS_MARK (t2) [SALES:DEPT = LOCATION.DEPT][LOCATION.MKED
(tl)]
READ [SALES (ITEMS):MKED (t2)]
EOQ
```

Note:

  (a) If we use **READ** [SALES : MKED (t_2)] then the entire t_2-marked tuples will be read out, not only the item values.

  (b) If there are multiple occurrences of the same item, then there will be duplicate item numbers printed.

Query 8A. *In Query 8, if an item is sold by more than one department on the second floor, it will appear more than once in the output. We can prevent this by projection.*

```
      MARK (tl) [LOCATION:FLOOR = 2]
      CROSS_MARK (t2t3) [SALES:DEPT = LOCATION.DEPT][LOCATION.MKED
      (tl)]
L1:   GET_FIRST [SALES (ITEM):MKED (t2)]
      RESET (t2t3) [SALES:ITEM = REGC_1 & MKED (t2)]
      BC L1, RAIL_STAT (t2)
      /*projected item values are t3 marked. */
      READ [SALES (ITEM):MKED (t3)]
      EQQ
```

Note: On line $L1$, each time **GET_FIRST** resets the first $t2$ mark bit from the beginning of the relation.

The **RESET** instruction with multiple reset bits in the opcode works as follows: If the qualification is null, then any tuple having some or all of the tag bits is reset in those bits. If the instruction has a qualification, then only the eligible tuples are affected (i.e., reset). In the **BC** instruction, the RAIL_STAT is a register that holds the indication of marked tuples in RAP. This register is qualified by mark bit and relation name to specify the mark bit and the relation when more than one relation is marked on the same mark bit (e.g., RAIL_STAT $(t_4).R_2$). The program iteration to the instruction address ($L1$ in this case) continues until no more t_2 marked tuples are left in the relation. Figure 3.11 demonstrates a projection example on a sample of the SALES relation as a trace of the last program shown.

Steps (b) through (e) show the affected tuples as the execution of the loop between $L1$ **GET_FIRST** and **BC** instructions progresses. Latest versions of SERAP contain built-in macros for projection and division.

(a) Before projection

t_2	t_3	DEPT	ITEM	VOL
1	1	A	aa	100
1	1	A	bb	50
1	1	A	cc	200
		B	aa	500
		B	dd	150
1	1	C	bb	75
1	1	C	cc	175
1	1	C	ee	250
		D	cc	10
		D	ee	40
1	1	E	bb	90
1	1	E	cc	180

(b) After first iteration

t_2	t_3	DEPT	ITEM	VOL
	1	A	aa	100
1	1	A	bb	50
1	1	A	cc	200
		⋮		
1	1	C	bb	75
1	1	C	cc	175
1	1	C	ee	250
		⋮		
1	1	E	bb	90
1	1	E	cc	180

(c) After second iteration

t_2	t_3	DEPT	ITEM	VOL
	1	A	aa	100
	1	A	bb	50
1	1	A	cc	200
		⋮		
		C	bb	75
1	1	C	cc	175
1	1	C	ee	250
		⋮		
		E	bb	90
1	1	E	cc	180

(d) After third iteration

t_2	t_3	DEPT	ITEM	VOL
	1	A	aa	100
	1	A	bb	50
	1	A	cc	200
		⋮		
		C	bb	75
		C	cc	175
1	1	C	ee	250
		⋮		
		E	bb	90
		E	cc	180

(e) After last, fourth iteration

t_2	t_3	DEPT	ITEM	VOL
	1	A	aa	100
	1	A	bb	50
	1	A	cc	200
		⋮		
		C	bb	75
		C	cc	175
	1	C	ee	250
		⋮		
		E	bb	90
		E	cc	180

Figure 3.11 An example projection.

Query 9. *Find the total volume of items of type A sold by the departments on the second floor.*

```
1  MARK  (t1) [LOCATION:FLOOR = 2]
2  CROSS_MARK  (t2) [SALES:DEPT = LOCATION.DEPT][LOCATION.MKED
   (t1)]
```

```
3    MARK (t1) [CLASS:TYPE = "A"]
4    CROSS_MARK (t3) [SALES:ITEM = CLASS.ITEM][CLASS.MKED (t₁)]
5    SUM [SALES (VOL):MKED (t2) & MKED (t3)][REGF_1]
6    READ_REG [REGF_1]
7    EOQ
```

Alternate form for 5:

```
5    SUM [SALES (VOL):MKED(t2t3)][REGF_1]
```

Alternate form for 4 through 7:

```
4    CROSS_RESET (t2) [SALES:ITEM = CLASS.ITEM][CLASS.MKED (t1)]
5    SUM [SALES (VOL):MKED (t2)]
6    READ_REG [REGF_1]
7    EOQ
```

In this example, we see the use of the **CROSS_RESET** instruction. In both forms of the program, we are combining the two mappings made into the SALES relation. The output is in the form of a scalar readout by a register output instruction (**READ_REG**).

Query 10. *Find the names of employees who manage more than 10 employees.*

```
1        MARK (t1) [EMP]
2 L1:    GET_FIRST [EMP (MGR):MKED (t1)]
3        COUNT [EMP:MGR = REGC_1][REGF_1]
4        RESET (t1) [EMP:MGR = REGC_1]
5        BC L2,REGF_1 ≤ 10
6        READ [EMP (MGR):UNMKED (t1t2)]
7 L2:    MARK (t2) [EMP:UNMKED (t1t2)]
8        BC L1, RAIL_STAT (t1)
9        EOQ
```

Alternate form for 6, 7:

```
6        READ_REG [REGC_1]
```

Instructions 2, 3, and 4 perform grouping for each manager with respect to the free variable MGR saved by **GET_FIRST**. Instructions 5 and 6 perform output and marking of the processed tuples (managers), respectively.

Query 11. *Find the names of employees who earn more than their managers.*

```
1        MARK (t1) [EMP]
2 L1:    GET_FIRST [EMP(MGR, SAL):MKED (t1)]
3        SAVE [EMP(SAL):NAME = REGC_1][REGS]
         /*The above instruction puts the salary of the manager
         given in REGC_1 into REGS; the salary of the employee is
         placed in REGC_2 by GET_FIRST.*/
4        BC L2,REGC_2 ≤ REGS
5        READ [EMP(NAME,MGR):UNMKED(t1t2)]
```

```
6 L2:  MARK (t2) [EMP:UNMKED (t1t2)]
       /*The above instruction is used to not read the EMP tuples
       more than once, that is, processed tuples are t2 marked
       and the read instruction reads t1t2 unmarked tuples.*/
7      BC L1,RAIL_STAT (t1)
8      EOQ
```

Instructions 2, 3, and 4 perform grouping and correlation using the free variables, the employee's and manager's salaries and the manager's name. Execution continues until all the employee tuples are processed. Instruction 1 marks all the tuples unconditionally for that purpose and the **BC** command in instruction 7 skips ineligible employees. However, all the tuples whether eligible or ineligible are marked as processed by instruction 6.

Query 12. *Among all departments with total salary greater than 1 million, find those departments selling dresses.*

```
       MARK (t1t2) [EMP]
       /*Find the unique departments (marked t1)*/
L1:    GET_FIRST [EMP(DEPT):MKED (t2)]
       RESET (t1t2) [EMP:DEPT = REGC_1 & MKED (t2)]
       BC L1,RAIL_STAT (t2) /*Project by department*/
       /*Upper program segment is projection on department
       attribute. Now go through departments to compute total
       salary.*/
L2:    GET_FIRST [EMP (DEPT):MKED (t1)]
       SUM [EMP(SAL):DEPT = REGC_1][REGF_1]
       BC L3,REGF_1 ≤ 1000000
       MARK (t2) [SALES:DEPT = REGC_1 & ITEM = "DRESSES"]
L3:    BC L2,RAIL_STAT(t1)
       READ [SALES(DEPT):MKED (t2)]
       EOQ
```

In the first part of the program, we project *EMP* on the (unique) department values since department is not the key. In the second half of the program, we see a grouping of the *EMP* relation for each unique department value. The grouping operation is also referred to as a set aggregate operation. Notice that, unlike the previous two examples, here the reading takes place outside of the loop.

Query 13. *Find the companies supplying all the type A items to one or more departments on the second floor.*

```
1      MARK (t1) [LOCATION:FLOOR = 2]
2      CROSS_MARK (t2) [SUPPLY:DEPT = LOCATION.DEPT]
       [LOCATION.MKED(t1)]
3      MARK (t1) [CLASS:TYPE = "A"]
4      COUNT [CLASS:MKED(t1)][REGF_1]
5      MARK (t3) [CLASS:MKED(t1)]
6 L1:  GET_FIRST [SUPPLY (COMPANY):MKED(t2)]
7      MARK (t4) [SUPPLY : COMPANY = REGC_1]
8      CROSS_RESET (t1) [CLASS:ITEM = SUPPLY.ITEM]
       [SUPPLY.MKED(t4)]
```

```
 9        COUNT [CLASS:MKED(t1)][REGF_2]
10        BC L2,REGF_1 <> REGF_2
11        READ_REG [REGC_1]
12 L2:    RESET (t1) [CLASS]
13        MARK (t1) [CLASS:MKED(t3)]
14        RESET (t₂) [SUPPLY:COMPANY = REGC_1]
15        BC L1,RAIL_STAT(t2)
16        EOQ
```

Before explaining the program, let us give a RAP division algorithm.

RAP division algorithm

(a) Restrict divisor (if applicable), dividend (if applicable).

(b) Project divisor (if applicable).

(c) Determine divisor cardinality and save tags of divisor set in another tag bit.

(d) Partition dividend.

(e) For each partition,

    (i) Project within a partition (if applicable).

    (ii) Determine partition cardinality.

    (iii) Precheck division by comparing divisor and partition cardinalities.

    (iv) If divisible in (iii), then map divisor into partition, otherwise go to (e).

    (v) Recount partition cardinality.

    (vi) Compare cardinalities before and after the mapping of (iv).

    (vii) If the cardinalities agree in the comparison of (vi) output the answer, repeat from (e) until all the partitions are processed.

Query 13 involves division, the dividend and divisor being the SUPPLY and CLASS relations, respectively. This is because the query requires suppliers (companies) supplying *all* items of type A. This requires a division operation with each partition by company of the SUPPLY relation and the set of type A items. Accordingly, if we follow the program and the division algorithm in parallel the following trace can be described:

Instructions 1, 2, and 3 correspond to algorithm step (a). Instruction 2 identifies dividend (i.e., t_2 marked SUPPLY relation). Instructions 4 and 5 correspond to algorithm step (c). The t_1 bits of the divisor are copied into t_3 bits. The t_1 bits will be refreshed from these at each division iteration. Instructions 6 and 7 partition (by grouping at each iteration to $L1$) SUPPLY by company. In the program, algorithm step (iii) is skipped (i.e., no prechecking). Instructions 8, 9 correspond to algorithm steps (iv) and (v), respectively. ITEM is the division attribute. Instruction 12 clears partially reset (possibly) t_1 mark bits, the next instruction (13) refreshes them from the t_3 copy, and the **BC** instruction (15) repeats the loop for each partition. The idea in the mapping and checking the cardinalities afterward is that after **CROSS_RESET** (instruction 8), if the dividend did not contain or equal the divisor, some of the divisor bits (tuples) would be reset, hence, resulting in a different (lower) cardinality count. Instruction 14 clears t_2 bits to use them for another partition.

If the reader had problems in understanding some of the RAP query examples presented in this chapter, he (she) should read Appendix I and review the more basic query examples presented there with the instruction descriptions.

3.5 SECURITY AND INTEGRITY IN DBMS

3.5.1 Security

Security deals with the protection of system resources from unauthorized access and manipulation. Although the basic resources of a computer system are under the protection of an operating system, there are more specific types of protection within a DBMS. Since such specific protection needs may not be general for a computer system and its operating system, we will talk about DBMS security separately.

In DBMS security, the aim is to protect what is defined to be private data from the access and manipulation of unauthorized users. A security mechanism (subsystem) of DBMS is needed to enforce privacy. In a DBMS, users may be authorized to manipulate all or only parts of the database. The types of operations they are allowed to do vary. To define which users can do which operations on what parts of the database, an access rule tuple can be used. This tuple can be of the form (*user, data, operation, condition*). This would indicate, for each user (subject), what part of the database (object) can be accessed and manipulated by the type of the operation authorized (declared) in the tuple. Furthermore, the rule governing which object may be accessed and operated upon can be made to depend upon a condition (predicate). The simplest form of a structure used in a system is an access table or matrix. This matrix can be of the form *users by data,* and each matrix entry could store the rest of the access rule information. Figure 3.12 shows such a matrix without predicates.

D_1 through D_n can be at the record type (file, relation, segment) or attribute level. Accordingly, each row of the matrix can specify the record types or attributes (fields) of a given record type the user is authorized/unauthorized to access/manipulate. The level of control (granularity) can be brought down to individual item values (or set of values) if data are qualified by a predicate (e.g., user cannot access salaries over \$30,000). For more complex situations, a view facility can also act as a security filter. For example, in Figure 3.12, if $D_1, \ldots, D_n$ indicate attributes, then the user's view of the record type can be declared in a subschema of that record type and that information can be reflected in the access matrix. According to Figure 3.12, for example, user 2's view,

Data \ Users	D_1	D_2	$\cdots$	D_n
User 1	Read	Update		Read/update
User 2	None	Read		None
$\vdots$			$\vdots$	
User m	None	Read		Update

Figure 3.12 Access matrix.

which is also what the user is authorized for, is D_2 and nothing else. A view that may involve multiple relations can be defined as a derived record type. For example, the view *Senior citizens of ward 18* can be declared as

```
SENIORS_OF_WARD18 = (PATIENT[BIRTHYEAR > TODAYS_DATE - 65]) *
((ADMITTED[W# = 18])[PAT#])
```

*(ADMITTED(**PAT#**,**W#**,DATE)* is the relational form of the corresponding set type in Figure 3.6.) Access to users who are authorized to see only the senior citizens of ward 18 would be channeled or authorized to the *SENIORS_OF_ WARD18* relation, which would automatically protect other patients in the ward as well as the patients in the other wards.

By the use of predicates, we can also control the types of navigation in a DBMS such as IMS or DBTG. For example, set types in a DBTG-like DBMS can be declared as resources in an access matrix. To prevent an unauthorized user's access to a record type in a DBTG set, either directly or indirectly via other sets, the set types that would enable the user's access to that record type must be made unaccessible to that user. Such a measure would be in addition to the access rule that would pertain to the record type. This is because in a set occurrence a record can also be accessed via navigation through other record occurrences and/or sets.

The predicates that are used in the access rules can be of data-independent and -dependent types. In the former, the enforcement can be made during compile time without having to access the data. For example, the access rules that restrict the TIME-OF-DAY and LOCATION (Terminal#) of an access can be checked and enforced without accessing the related data (i.e., data involved in the database).

In the data-dependent predicates, enforcement can occur only at execution time with the costly operation of data access. The predicate can be a simple content dependent condition such as

```
STAFF: SALARY < 30K
```

Predicates can also be made to specify a context, that is, conditions involving more than one attribute and/or in certain relationship with each other. For example,

```
(a)   PATIENT: NOT(PAT#, ADDRESS)
(b)   PATIENT: NOT(PAT#, ADDRESS) AND NOT(SSN, ADDRESS)
```

If we do not want to disclose patients' addresses (i.e., with their access keys) a predicate as in (a) would be needed, stating that addresses cannot appear with patient numbers. However, a complete restriction can be assured only if all possible accesses via alternate keys are also blocked as in (b).

Context-dependent predicates of access control, however, cannot prevent data access via inferences. Inferences can be made by means of a series of allowable operations of aggregate type until the requested data can be singled out. Means of preventing possible inferences are the topic of *statistical databases*.

To enforce the data-dependent predicates with access rules, the user query needs to be modified. This is done by attaching to the request predicate (or qualification) of the query the additional predicates imposed by the applicable access rules. To find the applicable access rule, we must define a (set of) access rule(s) whose list of attributes in the specification (output) should minimally cover the specification attributes of the user request. By *cover* we imply set inclusion, and by *minimal* we mean nonredundant list of attributes. Once the applicable access rules are located, the user query is modified as

$$\textit{Original query: } \underbrace{S_1, ..., S_m}_{\textit{specification}} : \underbrace{Q_1, ..., Q_n}_{\textit{qualification}}$$

$$\textit{Modified query: } S_1, ..., S_m{:}(Q_1, ..., Q_n) \textit{ AND } \underbrace{(P_1 \textit{ OR } P_2, \textit{ OR } ... \textit{ OR}, P_k)}_{\textit{Access rule predicates}}$$

In the modified query, disjunction of the predicates of the applicable access rules is appended as a conjunction to the original qualification. Query modification for access control is used in the INGRES system [Stonebraker and Wong, 1974].

Example

Considering the *STAFF (EMP#, NAME, JOB-CODE, SALARY)* relation of the medical database, let us assume the existence of the following access rules:

```
Rule 1: RETRIEVE (EMP#,NAME, JOB-CODE): WHERE JOB-CODE = DOCTOR
Rule 2: RETRIEVE (NAME,SALARY): WHERE JOB-CODE = NURSE
Rule 3: RETRIEVE (SALARY): WHERE SALARY < 30K

Query 1: RETRIEVE (SALARY): WHERE NAME = SMITH
Query 2: RETRIEVE (NAME): WHERE NAME = SMITH
```

After query modification, the queries will be

```
Query 1: RETRIEVE (SALARY): WHERE NAME = SMITH AND SALARY < 30K
```

Because the specification attribute of Query 1 is *SALARY* which is covered by the specifications of rules 2 and 3, but minimally by rule 3, the predicate of rule 3 is appended as a conjunction to the qualification of the query.

> *Query 2*: `RETRIEVE (NAME): WHERE NAME = SMITH AND (JOB-CODE = DOCTOR OR JOB-CODE = NURSE)`

This happens because the specification *NAME* of the query is covered by rules 1 and 2 and their union is the minimal cover since the rules are not exactly the same.

3.5.2 *Integrity*

Integrity control is an integral part of a DBMS and aims to protect the consistency of a database in an environment where shared and concurrent manipulation of data is typical. Even in the case of a single-user system, integrity is important because each update on the database should obey and protect the structural and semantic constraints of that database. The examples of some constraints are

(a) *SALARY* should be positive integers and must be in the acceptable range of $10K < SALARY < 90K$.

(b) The same employee record should not be stored more than once, or another staff member should not be assigned the same employee number.

There are various types of integrity constraints (rules); they can be

(i) Implicit: a constraint dictated by the underlying data model such as the total functional relationship in hierarchies (i.e., there cannot be descendants without a parent) or no duplicate tuples are allowed in a relation.

(ii) Explicit: they are declared, such as the trigger procedures (or simply, triggers) supplied by user that propagate the effects of an update on a record instance to the instances of the other related records. For example, deletion of staff would necessitate deletion of the dependents kept in a dependent record type, or there cannot be a shipment of a part without the supplier existing in the supplier record type. The latter case is also referred to as *referential integrity*.

(iii) The scope (granularity) of an integrity constraint can be at the record type (relation), record instance (tuple), or a field (attribute) value level implying, respectively, low to high costs of enforcement.

(iv) The constraints can be static or transitional (e.g. balance cannot be maintained in an account file before the processing of funds transfers is completely executed).

Example

Some examples related to the list just given are as follows (integrity constraints are declared in terms of assertions):

```
ASSERT A1 ON STAFF: SALARY > 0 AND 10 K < SALARY < 90K
ASSERT A2 ON UPDATE OF STAFF.SALARY: NEW-SALARY > OLD-SALARY
```

where new and old salaries are properly addressed in the user's work space. More examples of assertions can be found in the System R literature.

As mentioned earlier in Section 3.5.1, the view mechanism is a sophisticated method of restricting a user's access to database. However, it also introduces the need for sophisticated integrity control. This is because views may cause side effects or spurious operations when they are updated. The following example demonstrates the idea:

Example

Assume the following (base) relations and the view relation defined on them:

$$R_1(A, B) \qquad R_2(C, A, D)$$
$$a_1\ b_1 \qquad\quad c_1\ a_1\ d_1$$
$$a_2\ b_2 \qquad\quad c_2\ a_2\ d_2$$
$$c_3\ a_3\ d_3$$

are the base relations. The view relation, V, is

$$V(C, A, B)$$
$$c_1\ a_1\ b_1$$
$$c_2\ a_2\ b_2$$

which is the join of R_1 and R_2.

If a new tuple $\langle c_4, a_3, b_3 \rangle$ is added to the view, this will reflect on the base relation as

(a) Insert tuple $\langle a_3, b_3 \rangle$ into R_1

(b) Insert tuple $\langle c_4, a_3, ? \rangle$ into R_2 (where ? indicates a null value)

(c) Because of (b), $\langle c_3, a_3, b_3 \rangle$ is additionally inserted into the view.

As can be seen, unless certain restrictions are placed on the definition of views, the consistency of the database may be destroyed with updates. System R simply disallows updates on views constructed by joins of relations. Some criteria were established for successful maintainability of relational views [Dayal and Bernstein, 1978].

3.5.3 Concurrency

Although concurrency control is an integral part of DBMS integrity, we will discuss it separately here. In concurrency control of DBMS, we talk about transactions and schedules. A system transaction, rather than a logical transaction, is an atomic piece of process that involves actions such as select/retrieve, modify, and rewrite on the database. A logical transaction in the application environment may be broken down to several system transactions. We will use the term transaction to refer to a logical transaction which is the topic of this section. A schedule in a concurrent environment is the relative time order in which the transactions are executed. If we denote the actions of reading and writing an item A as R-A and W-A, respectively, we can examine a series of schedules such as those given in Figure 3.13. (In the remainder we should interpret W as an update for which an input set is used.)

In Schedule 1, we cannot have an inconsistent database since the transactions, T_1, T_2, are executed serially one after the other. In Schedule 2, however, the update of T_1 is overwritten by T_2; hence, the update of T_1 is lost. Also in Schedule 3, T_2's update is lost (or unrepeatable) by the fact that subsequent to T_2's writing, T_1 is undone. The situation in Schedule 4 is referred to as *dirty read* because the base of T_2's reading is subsequently removed from the database. The two reads of Schedule 5 will see different versions of data because of T_2's intervening writing. Depending on the level of consistency required in a database, protocols must be devised that restrict the order of actions among transactions. Serial or serializable schedules lead to consistent database states. A schedule is *serial* if all actions of the transaction occur consecutively. A schedule is *serializable* if the effect of the schedule on the database is equivalent to that of a serial schedule. To determine whether a given schedule is serializable, hence consistency preserving, a graphical methodology called the *dependency graph* can be used. In that graph, the nodes correspond to transactions and an arc from a transaction T_i to transaction T_j denotes that the input of T_j depends on the output of T_i. That is, T_j uses the value produced by T_i for the item used between the transactions. If a dependency graph contains cycles, then the corresponding schedule is not serializable and, hence, is inconsistent. In Figure 3.14, three schedules and their corresponding dependency graphs are shown. According to the figure, the schedule S_1 is serial (consistent), S_2 is serializable (consistent), and S_3 is cyclic (inconsistent).

In the operational environment of DBMS, exclusive use of a given item can be enforced via locking. In such cases, no other transaction can access and use (read and write) an item until first an unlock is issued on that item. It has been shown that database consistency can be analyzed based on the precedence graphs constructed with respect to lock and unlock sequences. It will be assumed that a transaction is a LOCK-PROCESS-UNLOCK sequence. However, for simplicity, we will show only the LOCK and UNLOCK pairs. In the precedence graph, an arc from T_i to T_j is drawn if T_i starts with an UNLOCK and T_j with a LOCK for the item in question. This is because in a serial schedule, in order that T_j can start by locking, the previous transaction T_i must release its lock on the item. To test serializability of a schedule, we must construct the precedence graph as exemplified by Figure 3.15.

Schedule 1	Schedule 2	Schedule 3	Schedule 4	Schedule 5
T_1: R-A	T_1: R-A	T_1: W-A	T_1: W-A	T_2: R-A
T_1: W-A	T_2: R-A	T_2: W-A	T_2: R-A	T_1: W-A
T_2: R-A	T_1: W-A	T_1: UNDO	T_1: ABORT	T_2: R-A
T_2: W-A	T_2: W-A			

Figure 3.13 Possible schedules.

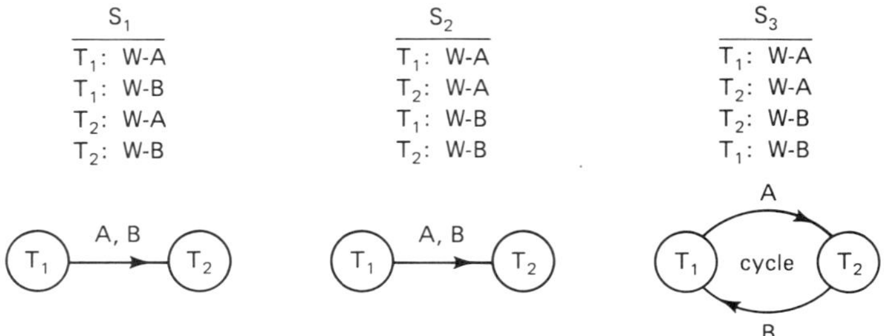

Figure 3.14 Three schedules and their dependency graphs.

In drawing the graph, the schedule is scanned to find the starting nodes that correspond to UNLOCKs and these are paired with the subsequent LOCK (which may not follow the unlock immediately in the sequence as can be seen in the last UNLOCK C and LOCK C pair). As in the dependency graph, the precedence graph must not contain cycles for consistency.

A locking protocol that guarantees serializability, hence, is integrity preserving as shown by Eswaran et al. [1976], is the *two-phase* locking protocol. The two-phase protocol has the simple rule that no lock can follow an unlock. Accordingly, a two-phase protocol has a growing phase in which all transactions acquire their locks (if they can, since there may also be a deadlock protocol and a preventive one). [Deadlock occurs in locking and it happens if two transactions are mutually locked indefinitely waiting for each other. For example, a locking schedule of (T_1: LOCK A, T_2: LOCK B, T_1: LOCK B, T_2: LOCK A) will result in an indefinite wait (deadlock) of transactions T_1 and T_2.] The growing phase is followed by a shrinking phase where all unlocks are issued whenever transactions are completed.

Up to this point, we have assumed *chained updates* between transactions in the sense that writing of a transaction T_2 depended upon the value it read for the item, which is, in turn, written by a previous transaction T_1. However, in real life, not all the requests (transactions) need to update the database; they may be the read-only type. In these cases, we can make distinction between

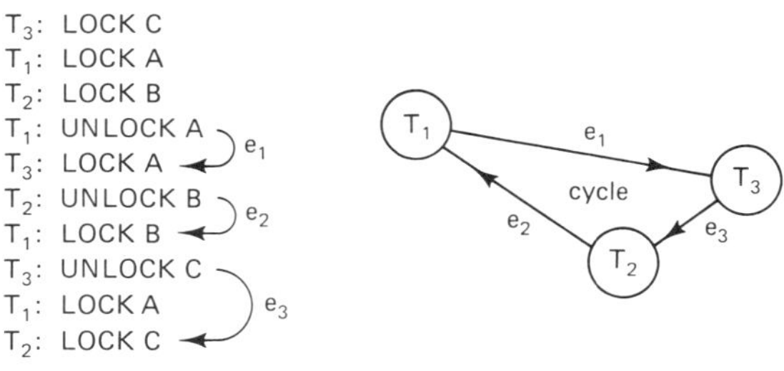

(a) A schedule   (b) Precedence graph

Figure 3.15 A schedule and its precedence graph.

read and write locks (the latter also includes reading) and that *read locks* can be *sharable* as opposed to the exclusive locking scheme discussed so far. Specifically, in our protocol, we may require

(a) When a transaction has a read lock on an item, there may be other transactions holding read locks on the same item; however, no transaction would be allowed to write lock the item while any read lock is held.

(b) When a transaction holds a write lock on an item, no other transaction can have a read or write lock on the same item.

In drawing the precedence graph of a schedule containing read and write locks, no overriding of sequences between read and write locks is allowed. That is, the dependency order between the read and write locks would be the same as if we had all write locks. However, in the schedule (T_1: UNLOCK A, T_2: RLOCK A, T_3: RLOCK A, T_4: WLOCK A), where RLOCK and WLOCK correspond to read lock and write lock, respectively, the following would hold: from transaction T_1, we would draw arcs to transactions T_2, T_3, and T_4. Our protocol would allow both T_2 and T_3 to acquire read locks concurrently, but T_4 cannot start before both T_2 and T_3 have released A; hence, the schedule should be (T_1: UNLOCK A, T_2: RLOCK A, T_3: RLOCK A, . . ., T_2: UNLOCK A, T_3: UNLOCK A, T_4: WLOCK A), where the relative order of T_2, T_3 for unlocks is immaterial and no more locks on A are assumed to be acquired before the second occurrence of T_2 in the schedule. As before, a precedence graph should be acyclic for serializability.

A two-phase locking protocol is also applicable here, so that all read and write locks must precede all unlocks. Such a schedule would guarantee database integrity, because it guarantees serializability.

As a further flexibility in the schedules, we may give up the idea that every write lock assumes a read of items and that the update writes a new value for the items read. We may rather assume that transactions read some items and write back some items and that not every item read should be rewritten, although it may be used in the computations of new values for the other items. In the precedence graphs of such schedules, we may have *useless transactions* in the sense that there is no arc propagation from them to the ending node. Such useless nodes can be removed from the graph. However, now that we can assume independent writes, the following holds: suppose we have a schedule in which T_1 writes an item and T_2 subsequently reads it (so that an arc from T_1 to T_2 can be drawn); if T_3 writes the same item, it should appear either before T_1 or after T_2, not in between. The latter results in drawing two alternate arcs in the graph so that the resulting graph is called a *polygraph* (i.e., a graph with multiple edges between pairs of nodes) [Ullman, 1982]. (Notice that according to our latest assumption, a transaction can write lock an item whose value it does not read unless it also read locks the item prior to the write lock.) After eliminating the useless nodes, the graph should be simplified, by eliminating one of the double arcs, to test for serializability. There are numerous combinations (2^n for n arc pairs) of alternatives to try before a final answer can be produced. The two-phase locking protocol is also applicable here.

Concurrency in hierarchies. Up to this point, we considered locking/ unlocking of individual items. Some protocols have been proposed specifically for hierarchical structures meaning genuine trees or hierarchical interpretation of levels of flat structures such as files or relations. In the latter, we may use levels such as a relation, a tuple, or an attribute value as the levels in a hierarchy.

In locking hierarchies, we may assume the following opposing views:

(a) Locking a parent implies locking all of its descendants.

(b) Locking a parent does not imply locking of its descendants.

In a simple tree protocol [Silberschatz and Kedem, 1980], the following LOCK and UNLOCK operations are defined:

- Except for the first lock, we cannot lock a descendant if we have not already locked the parent ((b) of foregoing is valid).
- An item is not locked twice by a transaction.

The tree protocol is proved to be serializable, and a tree protocol is not necessarily two phase because, in a tree like A(B(C)) (i.e., A is ancestor of B, B is ancestor of C), we may first lock A, then lock B, then unlock A, and then lock C. Although this schedule would not be two-phase (locking C after unlocking A), it obeys the tree protocol.

For further flexibility, warning protocols are proposed to allow locks on subtrees. According to the warning protocol, a transaction cannot lock an item before placing a warning on all of its ancestors. Once a transaction has placed a warning on a node, that node cannot be locked by another transaction. However, that transaction can also put a warning on that node and lock a descendant (of the warned node) for which no lock or warning has been issued. Warnings and locks are released by unlocks.

The warning protocols are useful to prevent conflicting locks within a tree. For example, in a tree like A(B(C(D,E))), if a transaction locks C, and therefore D and E, according to (a) of foregoing, another transaction requiring to lock only B would be in conflict with the previous transaction without the warning protocol. Similar to the simple tree protocol, the warning protocol is also serializable.

EXERCISES

3.1. (a) If you were to implement an IMS database using traces as the logical to physical address mapping, how would you implement the GU, GN, GNP, and *F commands? Assume that a definition tree is available and show the trace manipulations for executing each of these commands.

(b) Show three different access features of the MRI-2000 hierarchical language on a definition tree of your choice (make it three levels).

3.2. Given the following definition tree,

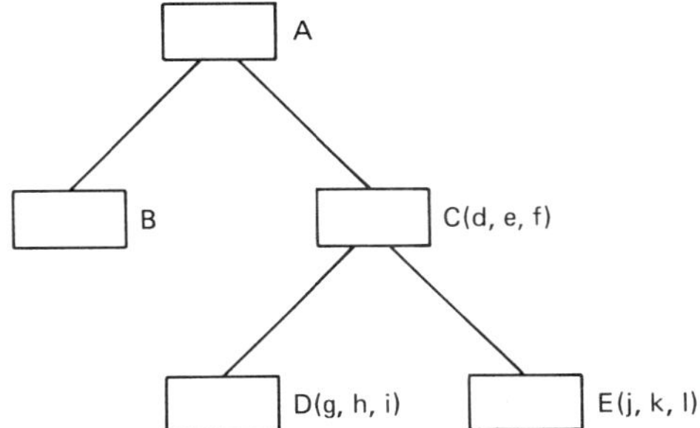

and the query, *Get all the occurrences of D with h > 1000 corresponding to all parents C with e < 2000 in the database,*

(a) Write an IMS DML procedure to answer the query.

(b) Do the same with MRI, assuming that it can be host embedded (i.e., MRI segments can be linked with program passed data). You can use any language or a pseudocode for the host.

(c) Write a query program in LSL DML to answer the request:
Give me the h of Ds corresponding to Cs whose Es have k equal to 100 and k equal to 500. Do you need a host language, or would the LSL syntax of Appendix II, which includes the SAVE feature, be sufficient? Write your answer after making this choice. You should not forget, however, that necessary links should be introduced to make this hierarchy processable by LSL.

3.3. Remembering the features of the MRI hierarchical language (e.g., upward and downward normalization, HAS clause, twin selection using HAS), simulate each feature in IMS. Your presentation should be in an algorithmic style using the IMS commands.

3.4. Assuming the following schema,

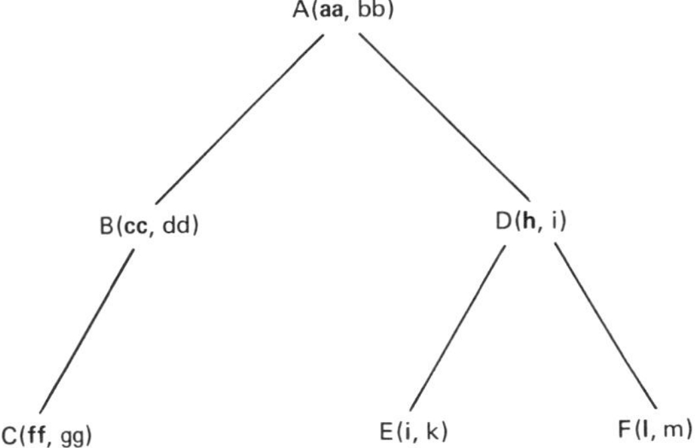

(a) Write an IMS query program (DML procedure) to answer: *Give me all Es for those As and corresponding Ds where aa > 500 and h = 100.*

(b) Write, in both the IMS and MRI languages, programs to answer: *What are the cc's of B corresponding to D where h = 'xyz'.*

3.5. This exercise is about an application of a hierarchical database designed to serve as an airlines guide.

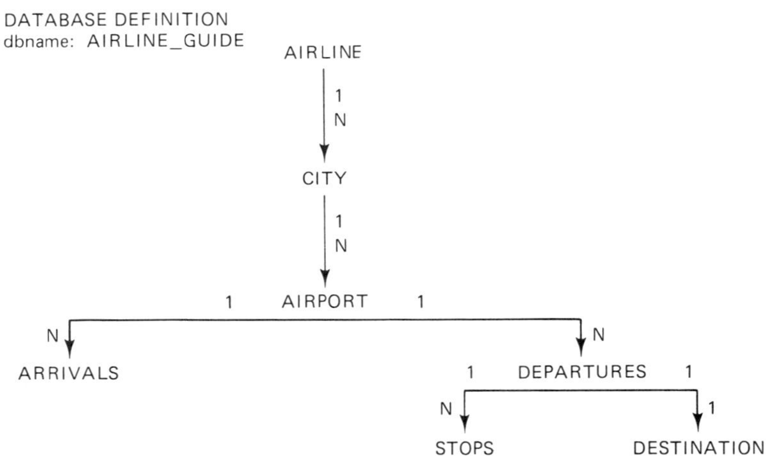

RECORD DEFINITIONS: (keys are bold)

*AIRLINE	(ANAME, **ACODE**)
ex.	ANAME: "WESTERN AIRLINES"
	ACODE: "WA"
*CITY	(CNAME, **CCODE**)
ex.	CNAME: "PHOENIX"
	CCODE: "PHX"
*AIRPORT	(PNAME, **PCODE**, TTIME)
ex.	PNAME: "SKY HARBOR INTERNATIONAL"
	PCODE: "P-PHX"
	TTIME: "20" (approximate traveling time (in mins.) to city)
*ARRIVAL	(**FLIGHTNO**, ARTIME, ARDAYS, FROMCITY)
ex.	FLIGHTNO: "WA456"
	ARTIME: "12:20A"
	ARDAYS: 1111100 (7 digits, starting from Monday, 1 if there is a flight on that day, 0 otherwise)
	FROMCITY: "LAX" city code for Los Angeles
*DEPARTURES	(**FLIGHTNO**, DPTIME, DPDAYS)
ex.	FLIGHTNO: "WA646"
	DPTIME: "9:35A"
	DPDAYS: 1001000 (same as ARDAYS of ARRIVAL)
*DESTINATION	(**FLIGHTNO**, CCODE, DTIME, DISTANCE)
ex.	CCODE: "TKY" meaning TOKYO
	DTIME: "6:30P"
	DISTANCE: 4000 miles
*STOPS	(**FLIGHTNO, CCODE**, STIME, SDURATION) intermediate stops
ex.	CCODE: "HNL" meaning HONOLULU
	STIME: "9.10P" (arrival time at the intermediate stop)
	SDURATION: 210 (minutes, stop duration)

(a) Using the schema of AIRLINES-GUIDE, program MRI queries that would be similar to each of the ones given in the MRI examples of Appendix II (which is on the DEPT, COURSE, STAFF, STUDENT, REGIST database).

(b) For all the queries you programmed in (a), write their IMS equivalents. If you have difficulties in writing the equivalents of some of the MRI queries, explain what modifications need to be made on the schema to be able to write the IMS versions.

3.6. Assume the following hierarchical HOSPITAL database,

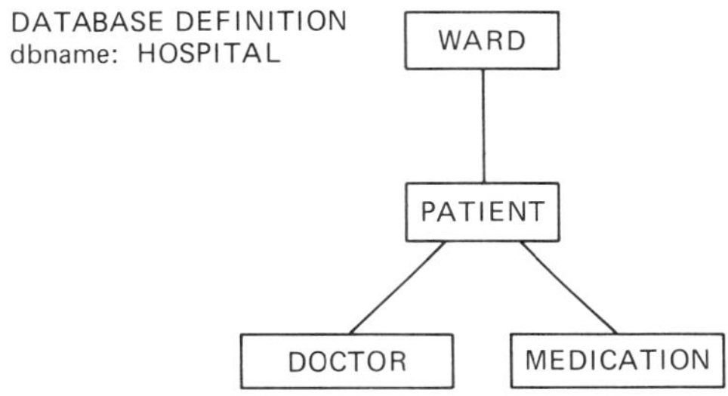

where

```
WARD(WARD-NO, WARD-TYPE, FLOOR)
PATIENT(PAT-NO, BED-NO, PNAME, SEX, DIAGNOS)
DOCTOR(DOCTOR-NO, DNAME, PHONE)
MEDICATION(MED-TYPE, SUPPLIER, EXP-DATE)
```

(a) Program the following queries on the HOSPITAL database by using the MRI language.

   (i) *Find the suppliers of medicines, which are given to the patients in wards CARDIOVASC or INTENSIVE CARE.*

   (ii) *Find the ward numbers of those patients who take medicines supplied by SQUIBB or BAYER.*

   (iii) *Find the expiration date of medicines given to the male patients with diagnosis CANCER.*

   (iv) *Find the phone numbers of doctors caring for the patients in wards on the second floor.*

   (v) *Find the medication type of the medicines that are given to patients whose doctors are BIANCA or WHITE.*

   (vi) *Find the bed numbers and diagnoses of all the female patients.*

   (vii) *Find the names of patients who have (i.e., HAS option) medicine type ASPIRIN with supplier SQUIBB.*

   (viii) *Do (vii) without using HAS, by Boolean upward selection.*

(b) Repeat (a) for IMS as asked in Exercise 3.5(b).

3.7. Assume the following network specification:

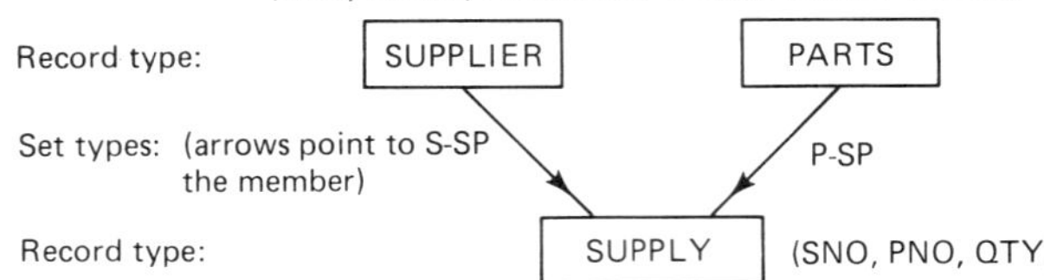

Write an LSL query program to answer the query: *Find the names of parts supplied by supplier S4 in quantities of 4.* You can assume the syntax given in Appendix II and a host language, if necessary.

3.8. The following database definition will be the network version (with slight variations) of the AIRLINES-GUIDE database given in Exercise 3.5.

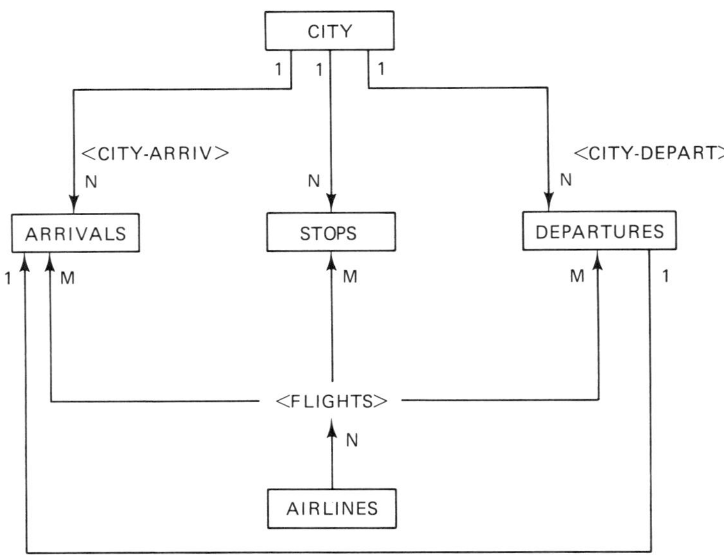

RECORD-TYPE DEFINITIONS:

CITY	(**CCODE**, CNAME)
AIRLINES	(**ACODE**, ANAME)
DEPARTURES	(**FLIGHTNO**, DPTIME, DPDAY, TOCCODE)
STOPS	(**FLIGHTNO**, STIME, SDAY, SDURATION, **SCCODE**)
ARRIVALS	(**FLIGHTNO**, ARTIME, ARDAY, FROMCCODE)

Notes:

1. According to this model, you can enter the network from two points (i.e., CITY or AIRLINES).

2. ⟨...⟩ denotes a link record type.

3. There is no link record between CITY and STOPS because a link can be established using the SCCODE field in the STOPS record. However, this is not the same for the DEPARTURES and ARRIVALS record types, because TOCCODE in the DEPARTURES record type is the city of arrival and FROMCCODE in the ARRIVALS record type is the city of departure. FROM and TO cities can also be found using the links, however, TOCCODE and FROMCCODE are added to simplify the queries.

4. A flight having no intermediate stops still has a STOP record occurrence with STIME = 0, so as to permit linkage from DEPARTURES to ARRIVALS, or vice versa.

   Example: *Find the first flight on Monday from Phoenix (PHX) to Honolulu (HNL) via Los Angeles (LAX). (It is known from a previous query that there is no direct flight from PHX to HNL.)*

```
SELECT CITY WHERE CCODE = "PHX".
    LINK WITH CITY-DEPART to DEPARTURES
SELECT DEPARTURES WHERE DPDAY > "0111111" and TOCCODE =
"LAX"
```

Bit mask positions correspond to the days of a week.

```
SELECT DEPARTURES WHERE DPTIME = MIN(DPTIME)
KEEP DEPARTURES.FLIGHTNO, DPTIME
    LINK WITH ARRIVALS TO ARRIVALS
SELECT ARRIVALS
SAVE ARTIME KEEP ARTIME
    LINK WITH CITY-ARIV TO CITY
SELECT CITY
    LINK WITH CITY-DEPART TO DEPARTURES
SELECT DEPARTURES
    WHERE DPDAY > "0111111" AND TOCITY = "HNL" AND DPTIME
> *
SELECT DEPARTURES WHERE DPTIME = MIN(DPTIME)
```

for the earliest connection.

```
KEEP DEPARTURES.FLIGHTNO, DPTIME
    LINK WITH ARRIVALS TO ARRIVALS
SELECT ARRIVALS KEEP ARTIME;
```

(a) Based on the LSL syntax and semantics information provided in the chapter and in Appendix II, write LSL equivalent of the queries you have coded for Exercise 3.5.

(b) Write the DBTG version of the queries in (a) after presenting an (almost) equivalent DBTG network schema. Use a pseudohost language.

Indicate any difficulties you may encounter.

3.9. Assume the following LSL database:

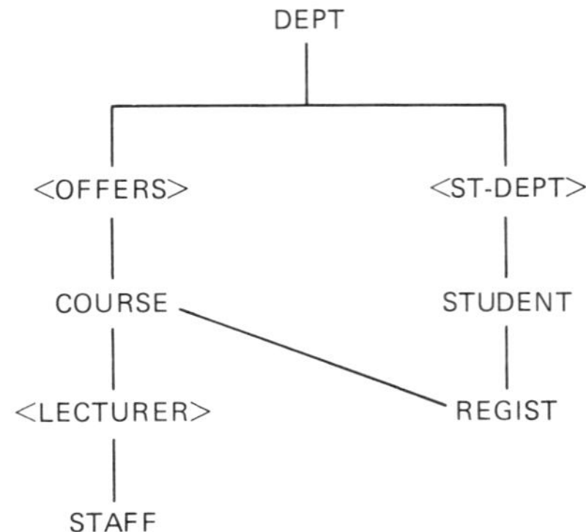

<...> denotes a link record type

DEPT:	(**DEPT-NO**, DEPT-NAME)
COURSE:	(**CRS-NO**, CRS-NAME, YEAR, CREDIT)
STAFF:	(**STF-NO**, STF-NAME, SEX, BIRTHYR)
STUDENT:	(**ST-NO**, ST-NAME, SEX, BIRTHYR, YEAR)
REGIST:	(**ST-NO**, CRS-NO, GRADE)

(a) Write LSL programs to answer the following queries:

  (i) Find the courses taken by the students of *ELECTRICAL ENG.* department.

 (ii) Find the number of students taking the courses given by the staff who are born after the year 1940.

(iii) Find the number of second-year students taking third-year courses.

 (iv) Find the departments of the students taking the courses taught by *DR. WHEELER*.

  (v) Find the names of staff teaching the courses offered by the *COMPUTER SCIENCE* department.

 (vi) Find the name of the youngest student taking a second-year course.

(vii) Find the number of the courses offered by the *ELECTRICAL ENG.* department.

(b) Show an equivalent DBTG version of this LSL database and write a DBTG DML procedure that will be identical (in the DBTG sense) to the LSL query given in the following. The items (i) through (iii) following the query provide additional information.

Query: *Find the name of the youngest fourth-year student in the department of the instructor whose name is "DOE".*

```
SELECT STAFF WHERE STF-NAME EQ "DOE"
  LINK WITH LECTURER TO COURSE
  SELECT COURSE
   LINK WITH OFFERS TO DEPT
   SELECT DEPT KEEP DEPT-NAME
    LINK WITH ST-DEPT TO STUDENT
    SELECT STUDENT WHERE STUDENT.BIRTHYR
     EQ MAX(STUDENT.BIRTHYR)
     AND STUDENT.YEAR EQ 4
    KEEP ST-NAME;
```

    (i) On the STAFF record type, the location mode is defined on the STF-NAME attribute.

    (ii) The link record types in LSL do not carry information; they include only the key pairs of the respective owners.

    (iii) A record type to link record type connection satisfies the DBTG set type rule (i.e., $1:N$ mapping between owners and members). In the REGIST to COURSE connection, assume 1 on the side of the REGIST record type, or better yet, introduce a link record type.

Hint: You may assume system owned singular sets like ALL-STAFF, ALL-STUDENTS, and ALL-DEPARTMENTS to facilitate individual and/or sequential accesses to the corresponding record types.

3.10. Assume a DBTG structure consisting of SUPPLIERS, PARTS, and SUPPLIER-PARTS. SUPPLIERS is the owner and SUPPLIER-PARTS the member of the set SP and PARTS is the owner and SUPPLIER-PARTS the member of the set PS. Furthermore, assume the following description of the record types concerned:

```
SUPPLIER(S#, SNAME, CITY)
PARTS(P#, PNAME, COLOR, WEIGHT)
SUPPLIER-PARTS(S#, P#, QTY)
```

Write DBTG programs for the following queries:

(a) Does supplier 10 supply any red parts?

(b) What quantity part 5 is sold by supplier 10 and in what city is the supplier located?

(c) What are the cities of the suppliers supplying parts heavier than 10 and in quantity (QTY) more than 5.

3.11. Using the airlines guide database of Exercise 3.5 and assuming that the respective record types are relations, write relational algebra and calculus expressions for the following two queries:

(a) Find the airlines that fly to all the cities (destination).

(b) Find the airlines that fly to only those cities flown by XYZ.

3.12. Assuming the following relational database:

```
LOCATION(DEPT, FLOOR)
```
(location of the sales department)

```
CLASS(ITEM, TYPE)
SUPPLY(COMPANY, ITEM, DEPT, VOL)
```
(suppliers supply items in volumes to sales departments)

```
SALES(DEPT, ITEM, VOL)
```
(departments sell items in volumes)

and the query, *Find the companies each of which supplies every item of type A to some department on the second floor,*

(a) Program this query both in relational algebra and relational calculus.

(b) Program the same query in the SEQUEL language.

(c) Give a relational calculus query example that would use both the existential ($\exists$) and the universal ($\forall$) quantifiers.

3.13. Assuming the EMPLOYEE (**NAME**, SALARY, BIRTHYEAR, MANAGER, DEPT) relation, write RAP assembler programs to answer the following queries:
(a) For those managers who manage more than 20 employees, output the sum of the salaries of their employees; otherwise, just output the salaries of the managers.
(b) For those employees whose salary is in the range 10,000 to 20,000 and who do not work in the TOY department, output their names and salaries if there are less than 20 of them, or else output their count and the sum of their salaries.

3.14. On a database example of your own, write an example query program for the correlation and another example for the grouping operations. Write the programs of these queries either in the SEQUEL (SQL) or the RAP (DBMS assembler) languages.

3.15. Assuming the LOCATION, CLASS, SUPPLY, and SALES relations of Exercise 3.12 and the EMPLOYEE relation of Exercise 3.13, write programs in both the SEQUEL (SQL) and RAP languages for each of the following queries:
(a) Find the number of employees in each department.
(b) Find the floors of departments selling items supplied by SANDERS or items of type A (do not output duplicate floor values).
(c) Find the total volume of items sold in the second floor departments whose total salary exceeds 1,000,000.
(d) What are the names of employees whose departments sell items of type A?

3.16. Assume the relations

```
SUPPLIER(S#, SNAME, CITY)
PARTS (P#, PNAME, SIZE)
SUPPLY (P#, S#, QTY)
```

Write query programs in SEQUEL (SQL) and RAP for the following queries:
(a) For each part supplied, get the part number and the unique names of all the cities supplying the part.
(b) What are the names of suppliers from New York whose total volume of shipments (QTY), of parts whose size is bigger than 20, is greater than 1000?

3.17. Given

```
DATABASE DEFINITION
for RAP
EMPLOYEE (ENAME, SALARY)
MANAGEMENT (ENAME, MNAME)
WORK (ENAME, DEPT)
LOCATION (DEPT, FLOOR)
SALES (DEPT, ITEM, VOLUME)
SUPPLY (DEPT, COMPANY, ITEM)
CLASS (ITEM, TYPE)

for SEQUEL

EMP (NAME, DEPT, MANAGER, SALARY)
```

(LOCATION, SALES, SUPPLY, and CLASS relations are the same as above),
(a) Write SEQUEL (SQL) programs for the following queries:

(i) Find the names and salaries of employees who work in the second floor departments and earn more than $6000.

(ii) Find the managers of employees who earn more than $5000 and work in the SHOE department.

(iii) Find the names of employees who earn more than some employee in the FURNITURE department.

(iv) Find the names of employees who work in the departments that sell items of type A or have manager CLARK.

(v) Find the suppliers who supply all the items supplied by MARTINEZ.

(b) Write RAP programs for the following queries:

(i) Find the department whose volume of sales for some item is maximum.

(ii) Find the managers of employees who work in the department described in query 1.

(iii) Find the total volume of sales of all the first floor departments.

(iv) Find the employees in the SHOE department who earn more than any employee in the TOY department.

(v) Find the items supplied by CORCI to departments on the second floor.

(vi) Find the average salary of those employees who work in the first floor departments.

(vii) Find the manager and department of employees who earn the minimum salary.

3.18. Convert the HOSPITAL database of Exercise 3.6 to a relational one that will enable you to answer the following queries. Also, write SEQUEL (SQL) and RAP programs for these queries.

(a) Find the names of doctors who look after patients in each ward that is located on the second floor.

(b) Find the names of doctors whose number of patients exceed 10 on the second floor wards.

(c) Find the names of doctors who look after all the wards (i.e., have at least one patient in each ward) that are located on the first floor.

3.19. Design a high-level, English-like user query language which is independent of any data model. Specify its semantics and syntax. Design mapping procedures for converting it into a data sublanguage of your choice for each one of the three popular (relational, hierarchical, network) data models. What additional information would you require to make such an effort effective?

3.20. Answer the following:

(a) If you need to declare a functional constraint of the form $N{:}1$ (not only $(1{:}1)$) between two attributes in your database, what sort of a SEQUEL (SQL)-like procedure should be written in your DDL declarations? Write the procedure.

(b) In (a), if the determining attribute is allowed to carry unknown values in some tuples, what sort of modification would be necessary in the procedure that you have written? Show it and explain your underlying assumption.

3.21. Assuming an E/R notation of information structuring and the following structure, (the dot indicates a *total* relationship), how and when would you enforce it, assuming that

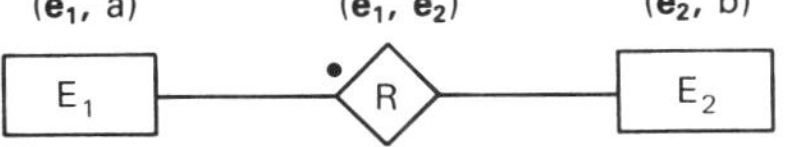

(a) Entities and relationships are represented as relations
(b) A RAP program is to be executed for enforcement?
   You should write the necessary RAP programs as the answer.

3.22. Assume the following base relations R_1, R_2 and a view called RV.

Base relations and extensions (data)		View
$R_1(A, B)$	$R_2(B, C)$	$RV(A,B,C)$
$a_1\ b$	$b\ c_1$	
$a_2\ b$	$b\ c_2$	

(a) Materialize the view.
(b) Would your integrity system allow deletion of a view tuple? Why and why not?
(c) What is the use of query modification in security enforcement? Explain briefly and clearly or show an example.

3.23. Assume that you have two programs, P1 and P2, each with two system transactions as shown below and a multiprogramming environment so that programs and their transactions can be run concurrently.

```
Pl → Tll + T12
P2 → T21 + T22
```

and

```
Tll: a ← a + 10 T12: b ← b * b
T21: b ← b + 10 T22: a ← a * 5
```

Can the schedule T11, T21, T22, T12 preserve integrity? Justify your answer by using:

A dependency graph

A precedence graph after showing the necessary UNLOCK and LOCK primitives of a locking scheme for the schedule.

3.24. Assume the following schedule among four transactions T_1 through T_4.

	T_1	T_2	T_3	T_4
1.		UNLOCK A	UNLOCK E	UNLOCK D
2.	LOCK A		UNLOCK B	LOCK E
3.	LOCK B			UNLOCK E
4.	UNLOCK C			
5.	UNLOCK A	LOCK D	LOCK E	LOCK C
6.		UNLOCK D		
7.			LOCK A	

(a) Is this schedule integrity preserving? Justify your answer.
(b) Can you change your answer to (a) if you were to modify the given schedule by differentiating between read and write locks?

4

Parallel and Pipeline Architectures

In this chapter, we want to expose the reader to the basic concepts of parallelism and parallel architectures. Parallel architectures will be the basic ingredient of various systems that will be presented in the following chapters.

At this point, let us state an observation that will lead us into the rest of the chapter. The lack of sufficient interest in commercial exploitation of new computer architectures on the part of industry and the hesitant attitude on the part of users in encouraging changes stem from the following two basic facts: (1) insufficient knowledge to exploit parallelism and (2) insufficient knowledge and experience in building cost-effective parallel systems. With respect to (1), it is sufficient to point out that the sequential line of reasoning of the human mind, and therefore, the resulting programs may be well suited to a von Neumann architecture because the latter was structured to fit the former. However, such programs or algorithms cannot be expected to drive parallel architectures effectively. We must be able to understand and/or automatically generate parallel computations that will mesh well with the underlying computing power. Problems related to (1) prevented sufficient understanding of parallel architectures and their design parameters so that with regard to (2) often supercrunchers were built which starved for data due to the mismatch between their computation speed and I/O bandwidth. The net result of these two points, when translated to real life, is the following: some powerful parallel systems are awkward to use (which is due to point (1) and the resulting lack of effective language tools) or that the systems built were not cost-effective (due to point (2), costly repetitions to provide high-I/O bandwidth were often needed to make up for the design deficiencies).

Let us turn to another finding. The performance studies made by Kuck

[1977] concluded that the speed-up achievable in programs was a linear function of the number, p, of parallel processors, contrary to some "folklore" about parallelism that states that the speed-up is of $O(\log_2 p)$. Based on the foregoing two findings, it remains for us to interpret that the $O(\log_2 p)$ limitation on speed-up of parallelism can be due to the nature of computation (e.g., sort) and/or interconnection topology (i.e., the configuration of interprocessor and/or memory connections).

The best paper of the conference on parallel processing, Rothstein [1976] talked about the ultimate limitations of parallel processing. In that paper, the bus automaton (BA), which is a cellular automaton (CA) having communication between separated cells, is taken as a theoretical vehicle to study the ultimate limitations of parallel computation. The BA is shown to have the computation universality of a Turing machine and achieves ultimate speed-ups for finite-state computations. This generalization was extended to higher dimensions of parallelism. It was stated that a large class of formal languages could benefit from parallelism (i.e., ultimate in speed-up is achievable) and that there is no inherent general limitation short of the ultimate in speed-up so that "tremendous" practical speed-up is surely possible.

4.1 PARALLELISM AND THE PROBLEM DOMAIN

We may need parallelism for various reasons. These reasons can be to decrease response time (i.e., to decrease the time to solve a given problem), to increase throughput (i.e., to solve many problems simultaneously), and to increase system utilization (i.e., to increase the time that the functional subsystems of a computing system are actually in use). Let us restrict our attention, for the sake of this chapter, to numerical computations. As we mentioned at the beginning, to be able to make use of parallelism, we must be able to derive the parallel computations properly. To do so, we must do one or more of the following:

(a) Write parallel programs. That is, by using proper constructs of a language suited for parallel computation, express parallelism explicitly.
(b) Detect parallelism automatically. By using automatic tools, a sequential program can be analyzed and
   (i) Apparent parallelism can be detected.
   (ii) Inherent parallelism can be mapped into explicit parallelism.
(c) Either manually or automatically, map the parallelism obtained in (a) or (b) into execution algorithms that will exploit the specific physical parameters of the underlying architecture.

4.1.1 Writing Parallel Programs

With regard to writing parallel programs, we will see later in the chapter, examples of parallel declarations and computations in a high-level language of Illiac IV and the vector instructions of the pipelined architectures. On the higher level, the FORK and JOIN constructs of concurrent process control can also be mentioned. In mapping parallelism to execution algorithms, usually a sequence of instructions identified as a process can be made to run concurrently with one or more other processes.

Example 4.1

Let us assume the precedence graph of Figure 4.1 among processes of a large program.

The precedence graph indicates execution order dependencies among its processes (nodes of the graph). For example, in Figure 4.1, p_5 cannot start executing before p_2 and p_3 are finished, and in turn, p_2 and p_3 cannot start executing before p_1 is finished its execution. The dependence can be due to data flow or I/O dependence. That is, a subsequent process may depend on the values written by a former process which therefore dictates the order of execution. Chapter 3 showed us similar concepts in the discussion of dependency and precedence graphs of transactions. The following procedures express parallelism depicted by Figure 4.1 at the programming language level.

<table>
<tr><td>

Solution 1

Using Algol-like constructs of
parallel "parbegin-parend" blocks

```
P₁;
PARBEGIN
  P₄;
  BEGIN
    PARBEGIN
      P₂;
      P₃;
    PAREND
    P₅
  END
PAREND
P₆;
```

</td><td>

Solution 2

Using FORK, JOIN and GO TO's

```
        P₁;
        counter1=2;
        FORK L1;
        P₄;
        go to L4;
L1:     counter2=2;
        FORK L2;
        P₂;
        go to L3;
L2:     P₃;
L3:  JOIN counter2
        P₅;
L4:  JOIN counter1
        P₆;
```

</td></tr>
</table>

In both programs, we can see that p_2 and p_3 execute in parallel, whereas p_4 can execute in parallel with the block of p_2, p_3 followed by p_5 combined. In the

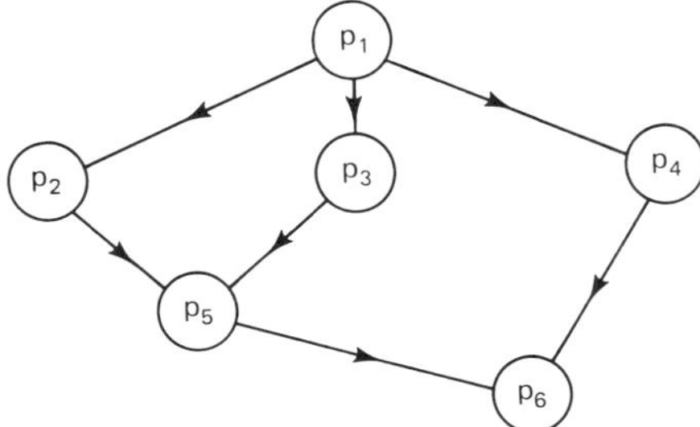

Figure 4.1 A precedence graph among six processes.

latter, p_5 is serial to the completion of p_2 and p_3 as indicated by the regular *begin-end* block. In the case of the second solution, FORK initiates parallel execution of the process following itself as well as the one at the address indicated at its operand (e.g., address L1 in the first FORK). JOIN on the other hand decrements the counter by one and passes to the next statement if the result in the counter is nonzero. If the counter is zero, the processor assigned to that process is released.

4.1.2 Automatic Detection of Parallelism

At this point, we return to the discussion of parallelism. In regards to (b), that is, the automatic detection of parallelism, we make the distinction between *apparent* and *inherent* parallelism of sequential programs. The difference between the two is that although both features of parallelism require program analysis, inherent parallelism requires a transformation procedure on the sequential code to make it parallel executable. In program analysis, a data flow graph of the program is constructed. To detect apparent parallelism among processes, read and write sets, R and W, of processes are analyzed. For any two processes i, j ($i \neq j$) to be executable in parallel, the following conditions must hold:

$$\text{(a) } R_i \cap W_j = \phi \qquad \text{(null)}$$

$$\text{(b) } W_i \cap R_j = \phi$$

$$\text{(c) } W_i \cap W_j = \phi$$

That is, input values of one process should not be modified (written) by the other and that the two processes should not modify common variables. Apparent parallelism can be detected among processes obeying the foregoing conditions. However, compilation of sequential programs for array and pipeline computers usually requires transformation of program constructs to exploit inherent parallelism. Kuck [1977] has surveyed such transformations. The survey included

(a) Height reduction of arithmetic expression trees
(b) Transformation of linear recurrence relations
(c) Statement substitution
(d) Transforming IF and DO blocks to canonical forms
(e) Loop distribution

While we refer the interested reader to the referenced survey for in-depth analysis of the subject matter, let us demonstrate the ideas of (a) and (c) in the following simple examples. Figure 4.2 shows parse trees for the arithmetic expression of $(((a + b) + c) + d)$. Figure 4.2(a) shows the minimum height tree for the original expression whose height is 3. Figure 4.2(b) shows the tree whose height is reduced to 2 by transforming the original expression to $(a + b) + (c + d)$ using associativity. Tree height reduction achieves execution speed-ups in the order $O(n/\log_2 n)$ using $O(n)$ processors for an arithmetic expression

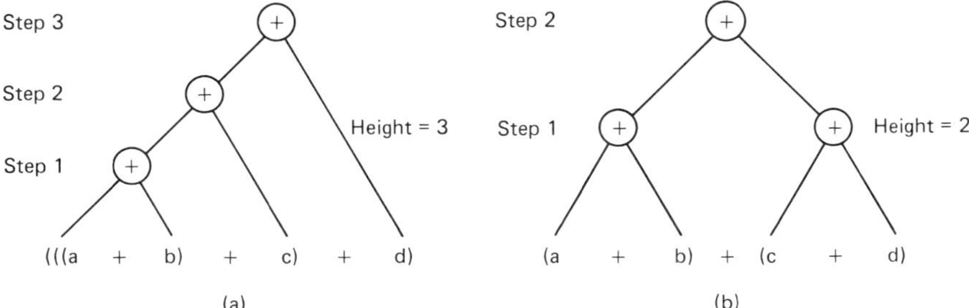

Figure 4.2 Tree height reduction. From D. J. Kuck, "A Survey of Parallel Machine Organization and Programming." *ACM Surveys*, 9, 1, © 1977 Association for Computing Machinery.

with n variables/constants. In the example of Figure 4.2, the expression is evaluated in two steps instead of three required for the original expression.

Let us consider the following block of assignment statements:

```
X = BCD + E
Y = AX
Z = X + FG
```

Using one processor, this block can be evaluated in six steps if we assume one time step per arithmetic operation. Using statement substitution, we can obtain the following:

```
X = BCD + E
Y = ABCD + AE
Z = BCD + E + FG
```

The resulting block can be executed simultaneously in three steps yielding a speed-up of $6/3 \rightarrow 2$ using $n = 5$ processors. These transformation examples showed us execution speed-ups achievable by exploiting parallelism and expression optimization.

4.1.3 Mapping Parallelism to Underlying Architecture

In regard to our discussion of mapping the parallelism of programs into execution algorithms that will exploit the specific parameters of the underlying architecture, the following brief statement and example are in order. Parallel architectures, especially new architectures such as the array processors characterized by Illiac IV, achieve high performance if parallelism is mapped to execution considering the architectural constraints. The skewed storage scheme can be given as one example of this. In order to access and operate on the elements of a matrix row and column, the row and column elements must be distributed among the processor memories so that they can be accessed and operated on in parallel. Ordinary or straightforward storage of the matrix would cause conflicts in the sense that a given processor (or processing element, PE) would store all the elements of a matrix row or column in its memory depending on the storage scheme. Skewing not only distributes matrix elements, but also provides for a predictable addressing scheme (e.g., in Figure 4.3(b) elements of a column differ by one in address among the neighboring PEs).

Figure 4.3(a) shows a 5×5 square matrix. Figure 4.3(b) shows the same matrix in skewed form where each resulting column is stored in a PE. Skewing is achieved as follows: For each $n \times n$ square matrix and α and β, each successive column (first dimension) element is stored $\alpha(\bmod n)$ PEs away from the previous element. The same holds for the row elements using β. In this skewing scheme, if n is chosen as a prime number, then the memory access conflicts can be minimized. (With Illiac IV, $n = 64$ which is not a prime number.)

While storage scheme is one consideration, memory addressing (indexing) and routing (i.e., the way in which processors and memories are connected) are among the other parameters to be considered in mapping program parallelism into execution parallelism. Some examples of this will follow in the discussion of the Illiac IV system.

As a final point on parallelism, we should not forget the fact that most programs are inherently sequential and they may present a bottleneck for overall speed-up. If a program code C is made up of sequential and parallel code C_s and C_p in code units and each unit is executable during times t_1 and t_2, respectively, then we can express potential parallelism of this code as $(C_p \cdot t_2/(C_s \cdot t_1 + C_p \cdot t_2))$. If the parallel code is assigned to some number of parallel processors, then for n processors the speed-up would be $(C_s \cdot t_1 + C_p \cdot t_2)/(C_s \cdot t_1 + C_p \cdot (t_2/n))$. If the speed-up is evaluated for various values of C_s, C_p, and n, it can be observed that C_s proves to be a bottleneck limiting speed-up even if n is made equal to C_p. This also shows that overall execution efficiency of a

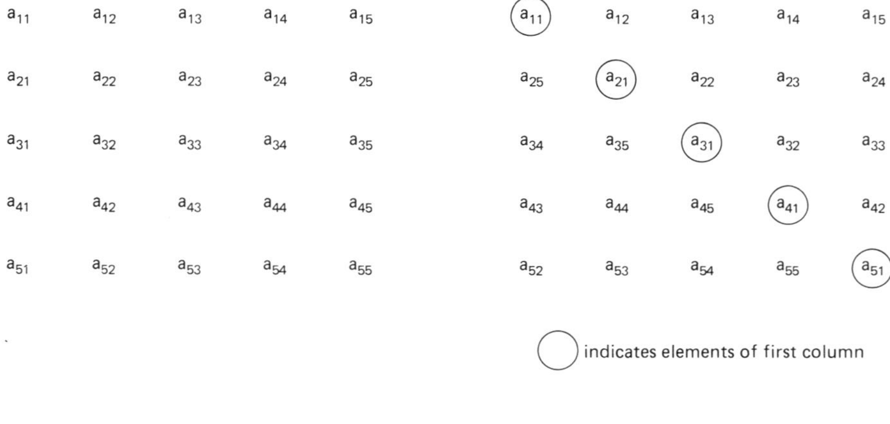

(a)   (b)

Figure 4.3 Skewed storage of a 5×5 matrix with ($\alpha = 1$, $\beta = 1$).

program also depends upon speeding up sequential code, which includes scalar computations.

4.2 PIPELINING

4.2.1 Sequential Pipes

Pipelining increases the utilization of computing resources for a given load of requests that use these resources in a predictable manner. A conveyor belt in a manufacturing organization carrying assemblies in process from one stage to another toward finished products is a good example of a pipeline organization. This is because each assembly utilizes the same resources along the way (all or some depend on the type of the pipe) and as soon as a resource is freed by one assembly, it can be immediately used by a succeeding assembly without waiting for the previous assembly to reach the end of the manufacturing line. If the line carries similar, but not identical, assemblies we have a sequential pipe, or if we have exactly identical assemblies, we have a vector pipe. Traditional examples in computer architecture are pipelined instruction execution unit (ISU) and arithmetic/logic unit (ALU) for a sequential pipe and operations among vectors for a vector pipe. In ISU, instruction fetch, decode, operand fetch, and instruction execution are defined as distinct modules corresponding to distinct operations on a pipelined processor. Similarly, ALUs having adder, multiplier, and divider as distinct entities provide pipelining within themselves, whereas multipliers and dividers can be further pipelined.

Pipelines that contain loops are called looping pipelines. Figure 4.4(a) shows pipelining of instruction execution drawn on a time-slot diagram with respect to instruction arrivals. Figure 4.4(b) shows a looping version of the same pipe assuming that, for a certain batch of multioperand instructions, we have to repeat the last two stages (i.e., operand fetch and execute) for each instruction. In Figure 4.4(b), we can see that looping can create collisions at the points indicated by the circles if certain restrictions are not obeyed. The restriction is that the interarrival time of instructions to the pipe should not be equal to the distance of two 1s in the occupancy vector of the looped stages, which is two time units (i.e., 101 in both operand fetch and execute) in Figure 4.4(b).

Pipelines can be classified as uni- versus multifunctional and static versus dynamic. A multifunctional pipe can be reconfigured between multiple tasks (i.e., roles of the stages can vary), and in a dynamic pipe this reconfiguration can be changed between individual input tasks. On the other hand, a pipelined multiplier unit that serves a single dedicated function is referred to as a unifunctional pipe with a static configuration.

The speed-up gain of pipeline is the ratio between the time taken, T_s, to process L tasks sequentially (i.e., looping through a single processing stage L times) and the time to process them through the pipe, T_p. Assuming that t_i is the time taken by the ith stage and that t_j is the time corresponding to the slowest

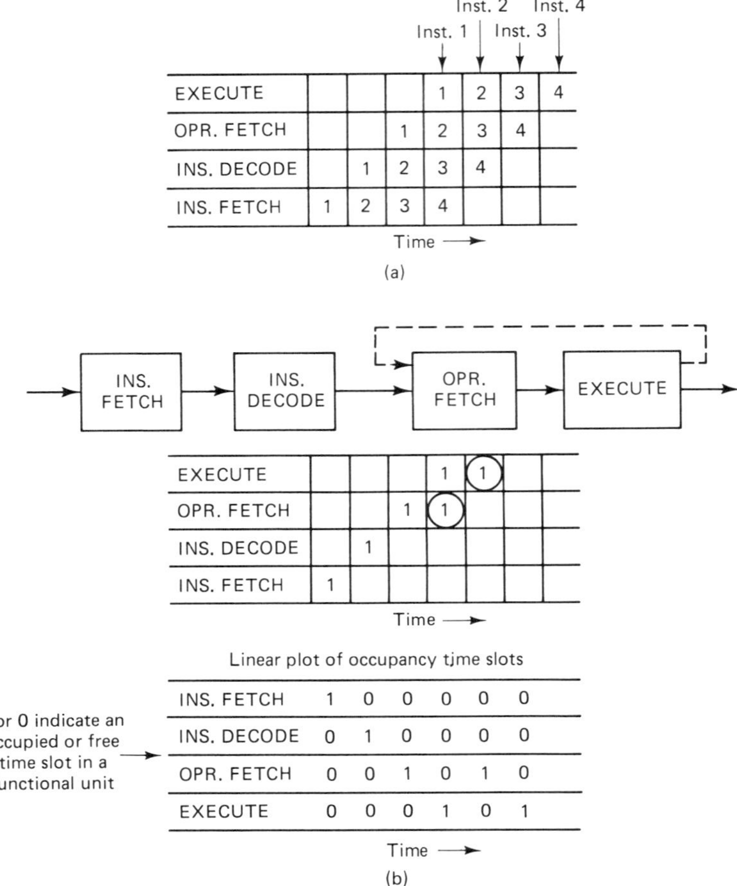

Figure 4.4 Pipeline constructs.

stage (bottleneck), if L tasks (instructions) are pumped through the pipe having n stages, then the efficiency will be

$$\frac{T_s}{T_p} = \frac{L\sum\limits_{i=1}^{n} t_i}{\sum\limits_{i=1}^{n} t_i + (L-1)t_j} \qquad \text{for } t_i = t_j \rightarrow \frac{nL}{n+L-1}$$

The following are additional considerations that are applicable to a pipeline architecture:

(a) *Buffer.* Buffering might be a necessity between stages of a pipeline in cases where there is a mismatch between the processing times of stages or when the processing time of a given stage may vary. Buffering provides for temporary storage of results between stages to smooth out timing variations.

(b) *Communication paths.* In cases where there may be data flow dependency between stages, that is, if the read set of a given stage depends upon the write set of a previous stage, the pipe may have to be paused to resolve the dependency. To resume the pipe afterward, communication paths (e.g., buses) would be necessary for status and value passing between stages.

(c) *Remedy for branching.* To prevent disruption of a pipe in case of a conditional branch, lookahead mechanisms and/or prefetching must be provided. Similar provisions and data and status-saving mechanisms should be provided against the possible disruptions due to interrupts.

4.2.2 Vector Pipes

Typical use of a vector pipe is a process between two source vectors (i.e., A, B) and a result vector, C, for an arithmetic operation such as $C \leftarrow A + B$. In this case, the pipe receives a multiplicity of identical instructions. Another vector instruction could be, for example, *SELECT A > B, ITEM COUNT TO (C)*, which would compare respective elements of vectors A and B and terminate at the first satisfaction of $A_i > B_i$ for the current *i*th element pair also giving a total count of the comparisons from the beginning in variable C. Considering the first vector instruction, that is $C \leftarrow A + B$, in which case C is also a vector, Figure 4.5 shows an example of this vector addition, which is discussed at length by Ramamoorthy and Li [1977].

In this example, the control vector is used to control the processing of the vector instruction. If the *n*th bit of the control vector is set to 1, then the result $C_n \leftarrow A_n + B_n$ is computed and stored in the result vector C. As can be seen in this example, once the addresses are computed, the operand pairs can be submitted to the arithmetic unit continuously. In this pipeline architecture, one needs registers or control vectors to hold the information needed before the instruction can be initiated. Several register load operations would take place to set up the required information for vector processing. The time taken for this preparation is referred to as the *setup time* t_s. Also, the time between the initial decoding of the vector instruction and the output of the first result element from the entire pipe is referred to as the *flush time,* t_f. Assuming that l and t_b represent the vector field length and the speed of the bottleneck stage of the pipe, then the execution time of a vector instruction through the pipe will be

$$t_{vp} = t_s + t_f + (l - 1)t_b$$

To do the same processing through a sequential pipe would require invoking the pipe l times. Unlike the vector pipes, the fetching of operands will be less efficiently performed in the sequential pipe. The equivalent of t_{vp} in a sequential pipe would be t_{sq}, which is

$$t_{sq} = t_{fs} + (l - 1)t_{bs}$$

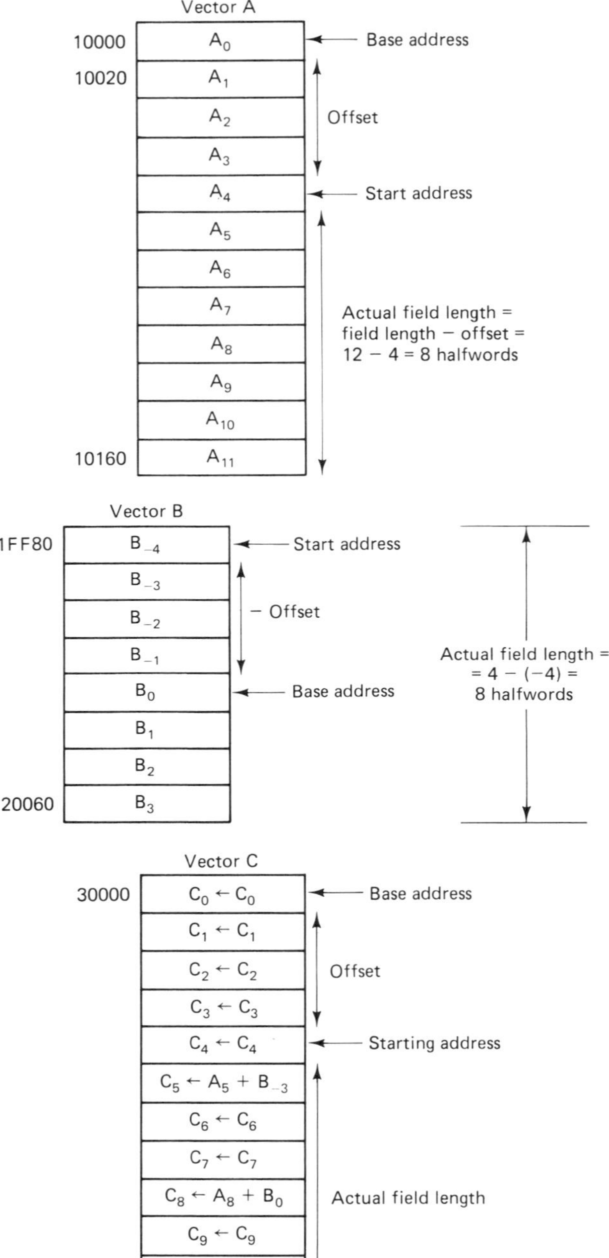

Figure 4.5 An example of a vector addition. From C. V. Ramamoorthy and H. F. Li, "Pipeline Architecture." *ACM Surveys*, 9, 1, © 1977 Association for Computing Machinery.

where t_{sq}, t_{fs}, and t_{bs} are sequential pipe processing time, sequential pipe flush time, and the speed of the bottleneck stage in the sequential pipe, respectively. If we compare t_{vf} and t_{sq},

$$t_s + t_f + (l - 1)t_b \leq t_{fs} + (l - 1)t_{bs} \qquad \text{if the following relationship holds:}$$

$$l \geq 1 + \frac{t_s + t_f - t_{fs}}{t_{bs} - t_b}$$

The foregoing relationship shows the condition under which vector pipe would be advantageous over the sequential pipe. It has been stated in Ramamoorthy and Li [1977] that the denominator is usually about one-tenth of the numerator, yielding a value of 10 or more for l.

Chaining in vector processing is the ability to overlap execution of two or more vector instructions, however, in a pipelined manner. That is, vector operations are not entirely executed in parallel since there is operand dependency. A result register of a previous operation (i.e., on a previous index) becomes the operand of a subsequent operation (i.e., on the next to previous index)

$$V_1 \leftarrow V_2 + V_3$$

$$V_4 \leftarrow V_1 * V_5$$

which should be interpreted as a chaining between the ith (previous) and $i + 1$ (current) operations:

$$V_1(i + 1) \leftarrow V_2(i + 1) + V_3(i + 1)$$

$$V_4(i) \leftarrow V_1(i) * V_5(i)$$

Therefore, in actuality, while the $i + 1$th element pair is being operated upon in the addition, the ith addition's result is passed to the ith multiplication of the second operation. As stated, the time lag is by one element addition rather than the entire vector and the two vector operations are pipelined (in a chain).

4.3 CLASSIFICATION OF COMPUTER ARCHITECTURES

After some exposure to parallelism and pipelining, we now present the popular computer architecture classification defined by Flynn [1972]. This will enable us to relate similar architectures in our subsequent discussions. The classification goes as follows:

(a) Single-instruction single data (SISD)
(b) Single-instruction multiple data (SIMD)
(c) Multiple-instruction single data (MISD)
(d) Multiple-instruction multiple data (MIMD)

The SISD category is the "contemporary" von Neumann uniprocessor architecture. In this architecture, there is a central processing unit that operates on attribute value pairs $a_i v_i$ (possibly in a loop of a numerical computation). Attribute (i.e., label) is used to locate the corresponding value in memory and the single instruction operates on the contents of the accumulator (or some register) and the value (v_i) to produce the result. At each iteration, only a single data item is taken from the input (stream).

The SIMD category entails a large class of new architectures. The main structure is a single (or central) controller driving a series of identical processors. If these processors are organized to work in parallel for a given computation initiated by the controller, then we obtain an *array processor*. If we couple each processor in the array closely with its memory and operate in an exhaustive search mode, we obtain an *associative/(array)processor*. Parallelism is the universal property of the SIMD category. In the SIMD architecture, there is a need for two types of communication: (1) the processing elements among themselves and (2) the processing elements with the memories. *Routing* and *alignment* networks are the names given in the literature for the interconnection structures that achieve the former (processor to processor) and latter (processor to memory) communication, respectively.

Depending on the capabilities of the controller, processing elements, extent of parallelism (i.e., number of processors), search mode, and the characteristics of the routing and alignment networks, the SIMD architectures can be of the following types:

(a) Array processors
(b) Associative processors
(c) Processing ensembles
(d) Pipeline architectures

Array processors are used in vector and matrix (grid) problems and generally in algorithms requiring the SIMD characteristic. Numeric computations will be restricted to this category, whereas nonnumeric computations will belong to (b). Category (c) can apply to both numeric and nonnumeric processing. Category (d), which is the pipeline and vector processors, loosely belongs to the SIMD architectures. As we will see later, they can also be grouped into the other architecture classes. The typical examples for these categories are Illiac IV for (a), Staran and database machines with associative search capability for (b), Pepe for (c), and the CRAY-1 computer for (d). We will discuss these systems later as examples of their respective topics.

The MISD category consists of multiple instructions and single data systems. The only architecture that can vaguely be considered in this category is the pipeline, and that is only if we interpret each subtask of an instruction as a separate instruction. However, the SIMD view of a pipeline is more natural than MISD. In fact, the pipe itself can be considered as an MIMD and the vector operation on a pipe makes it more like an SIMD architecture.

The MIMD category consists of multiple instructions and multiple data at the same time. The following configurations can be considered in this category although some are not as typical of the MIMD class as the others:

(a) Multiprocessor systems

(b) Multiprocessing

(c) Multiple computer systems

(d) Computer networks

In all of the systems listed, we see a multiplicity of processors. However, unlike the parallelism of array computers, what we see here is the multiplicity of a low number of processors. And what is more, rather than the processing elements of an array, we have a computer subsystem and/or system-level duplication. While (d) signifies a loose cooperation of computing systems on a network, (b) and (c) imply some sort of simultaneous execution of subtasks of a larger task by multiple processing units. The simultaneity of execution here, however, is a functional distribution; that is, each processing unit or (sub)system performs a dedicated operation (some similarity to pipelining) over the incoming requests. An example can be the sort processor, merge processor, and paging and I/O processor of a data processing system. These systems perform the same dedicated functions for all the input requests. We use the term *multiprocessing* in a rather loose sense to indicate functionally distributed simultaneous processing. Multiprocessor systems, on the other hand, are defined more formally [Enslow, 1977] as the systems having two or more processing units under integrated control. This definition is extended to imply sharing and interaction among the system components. In other words, the main memory is directly shared by all the processors and also the input/output devices are sharable by different processor and memory combinations. The entire system is controlled by a single operating system and the level of interaction among the processors is at the finest level of granularity (i.e., down to data items). We will give more details on multiprocessor organizations in the next section.

4.4 MEANS OF ACHIEVING HIGH THROUGHPUT

Let us start with a short review of the von Neumann architecture. Figure 4.6 shows the basic five units of this architecture.

In the von Neumann architecture, there is a central execution unit consisting of the ALU and the controller that operates on the attribute value pairs, stored in the memory unit, in the order directed by the stored program. Basically, a single instruction for a single program is executed at a given time. Therefore, we have a uniprocessor working in the SISD mode. In the early generations of this architecture, the entire data path including the input and output units was centered around the accumulator. (ALU register is an implied operand in the instructions.) In the following, we will discuss means of achieving speed-ups in a way somewhat parallel to the evolution of the basic architecture of Figure 4.6

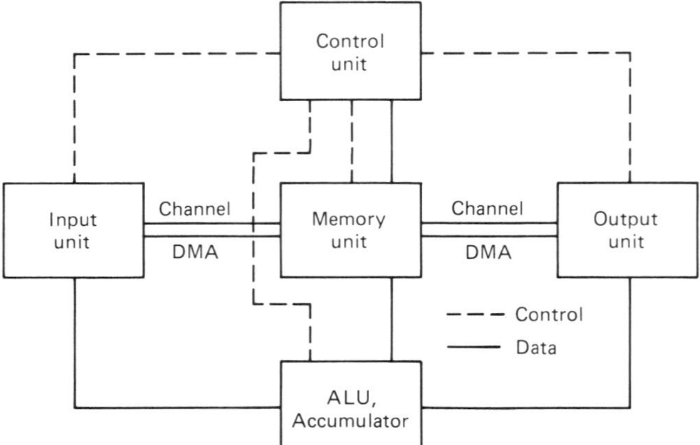

Figure 4.6 The von Neumann architecture.

to its present-day superversions. However, we will not restrict ourselves to the specifics of this architecture.

4.4.1 Speed-ups in Low-Level Hardware

In the ALU, arithmetic and logic operations were performed bit serially until parallel circuits were developed that operated on all the bits of an operand in parallel. Later, in addition to this, ALU functional units (e.g., multiplier, divider) were pipelined and the ALUs were duplicated in the systems supporting vector operations.

In controllers, horizontal microprogramming is often used for driving simultaneous operations out of the control fields of a single microinstruction as opposed to vertical microprogramming. In the latter, a microinstruction is dedicated to controlling one unit of operation. Of course, there is much more to say on the complicated issue of controller design. As in ALU, functional distribution and multiplicity are also used in controllers.

4.4.2 Speed-ups by Concurrency

The basic accumulator-oriented data path of the von Neumann architecture was later enhanced to accommodate some intelligence in the I/O operations. The direct memory access (DMA) capability of the peripherals (pictured by the double lines going to memory in Figure 4.6), overlapping of data transfers with the executions in the central processing unit (CPU), and the introduction of channel processors have been the major enhancements for the basic von Neumann architecture. Accordingly, I/O operations can start, proceed, and be chained and tested in the I/O channel while the CPU is in execution. Cycle stealing during DMA for I/O is hidden behind the memory accesses of the CPU. These overlaps in operations among the heterogeneous system units increase both the unit utilization as well as the throughput of the entire system. Such overlaps make multiprogramming possible. In a multiprogrammed system, memory is partitioned among k separate jobs. The CPU and I/O subsystems devote their attention to these jobs concurrently by overlapping an ongoing I/O operation of one job with the CPU execution of the other, according to a predetermined processor and task scheduling scheme. Priority and software interrupts add a finer level of concurrency control to co-executing jobs (programs).

Memory interleaving, instruction prefetch, multiple instruction execution units, multiple I/O channels, I/O polling, cache memories, paging or segmentation, and so on are the other means of parallelism and/or overlap possible in addition to the previous ones mentioned. More details on these can be found in the fundamental computer architecture and operating system textbooks, for example, Baer [1980] and Calingaert [1982].

4.4.3 Speed-ups by MIMD Organizations

Considering our loose classification of the MIMD class, we can view various computer organizations that incorporate multiplicity of processors as those that increase throughput, reliability, and availability. For example, CDC 6600 series contain 10 to 20 peripheral processing units (PPUs) as an integral part of the system for the efficient processing of I/O. Various commercial systems have incorporated into their products two or more processor versions of their basic models which are surveyed in Enslow, Jr. [1977]. We will conclude this section by a brief overview of multiprocessors. We will be brief for the following two reasons:

(a) The majority of the processors of the MIMD class consists of the von Neumann architecture (although highly enhanced) so that our basic building block is not a new computer architecture.
(b) The extent of parallelism is low and at a macrolevel (i.e., on a computing system level) that we purposely and categorically separated from the highly parallel new architectures.

Both (a) and (b) are in contrast to array processors which we can classify as non–von Neumann and new computer architectures. We will present a brief overview of multiprocessors and then proceed to array processors. As a final topic, we will discuss a vector computer.

Let us return to multiprocessors. Following the survey in Enslow, Jr. [1977], which will be the major source of all the related references, Figure 4.7 depicts a multiprocessor organization with its implied sharing and interaction. One classification of multiprocessors is based on the interconnection scheme between processors and memories as shown here:

- Time-shared or common bus
- Crossbar switch matrix
- Multiport memories

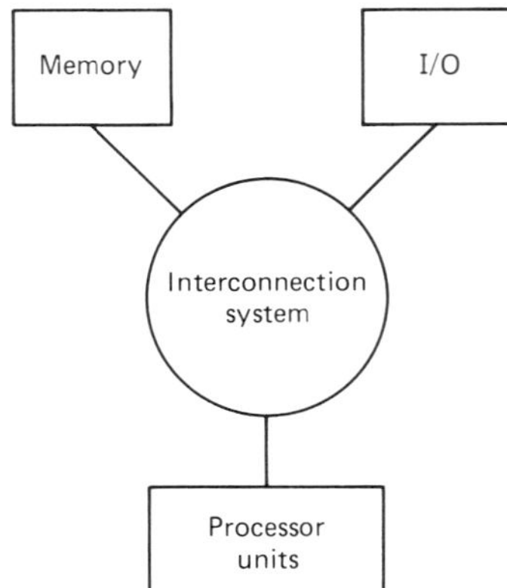

Figure 4.7 Basic model of a multiprocessor organization. From P. H. Enslow, Jr., "Multiprocessor Organization—A Survey." *ACM Surveys,* 9, 1, © 1977 Association for Computing Machinery.

Figure 4.8(a) shows a time-shared common bus system organization that employs multiple two-way buses. Figure 4.8(b) shows a crossbar switch interconnection between the processors and memories. Figure 4.8(c) is the multiport memory organization.

The multiprocessor system of Figure 4.8(a) contains a passive (nonintelligent) communication link. Sending and receiving synchronization is achieved by the communicating units. A typical communication session would possibly include the following determinations:

(a) Availability of the bus
(b) Availability of a bus to address the receiver
(c) Availability and status of the receiver
(d) Readiness of a receiver to respond to and initiate the transfer

All these actions are done by the sender. The receiver has to recognize and respond to its address as well as control signals. The PDP 11 unibus is a typical example of such a communication facility. In this multiprocessor configuration, the transfer rate and availability is limited by a single path. However, as shown in the figure, multiple two-way buses may be a partial solution to the problem at the expense of some intelligence complexity on the bus system. IBM STRETCH, UNIVAC LARC, and CDC 6600 systems are included in the time-shared bus configuration.

The crossbar organization of Figure 4.8(b) offers a dedicated communication path to each memory unit from each sender. However, the bandwidth of simultaneous transfers with a memory unit depends upon the total bandwidth of the bus structure and the ability of each switching point (i.e., each intersection) to resolve conflicting requests to the same receiver.

Burroughs' D-825 system, RCA's 215 multiprocessor, Carnegie-Mellon's C.mmp multi-mini processor, and Ramo-Wooldridge's TRW-400 polymorphic computer use variants of crossbar interconnections.

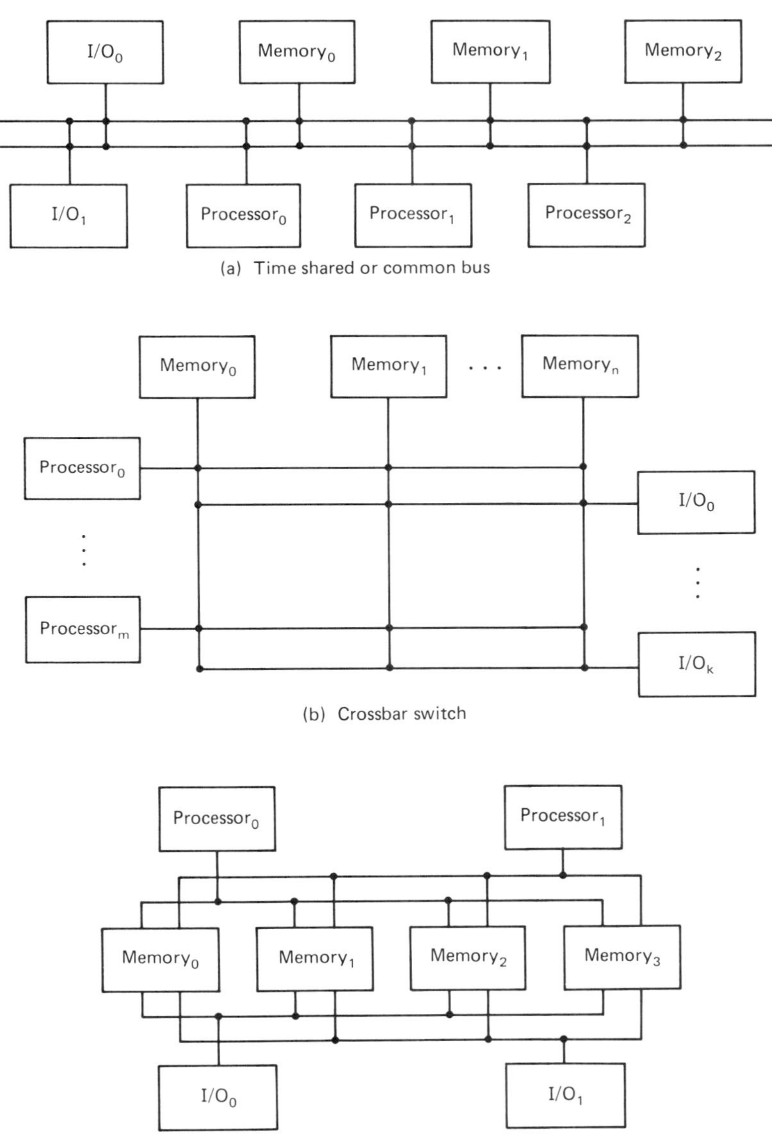

Figure 4.8 Multiprocessor system organizations. From P. H. Enslow, Jr., "Multiprocessor Organization—A Survey." *ACM Surveys*, 9, 1, © 1977 Association for Computing Machinery.

The multiport memory systems, as exemplified by Figure 4.8(c), are described as those that transferred the entire capability of the crossbar scheme to the interface of memory units. Such memory organizations are also used for memory interleaving (i.e., overlapping multiple memory accesses) by uniprocessors. However, in multiprocessors, localizing memory references may prevent memory access degradation causable by memory interleaving. Simultaneous accesses to a memory port are resolved by priority schemes. Multiport memory systems offer flexibility at low cost. Honeywell Multics and 6000 series, UNIVAC 1108, and IBM System 360/M67 use multiport memory interconnections.

A comparative analysis among these multiprocessor configurations reveals the following:

(a) The time-shared common bus can be the least complex and least costly with its simplest single-bus interconnection; however, speed and reliability would be very limited. Addition/deletion of units to the system would be straightforward. This configuration is recommended only for small systems, because simultaneous operation would degrade the system performance in larger configurations.

(b) In the crossbar organization, most of the complexity lies in the switches. This configuration offers the potential of high efficiency. Addition of units increases the cost and complexity of the switches.

(c) In the multiport memory systems, the cost of memory units is high since multiport memory and switching logic are centered on memories. There is a potential for high transfer rate for a given configuration, however these systems offer rigidity in the expansion of processor units.

According to one study mentioned in Enslow, Jr. [1977], the performances of multiprocessor systems were found to be 1.8 and 2.1 times faster than that of a uniprocessor for the two and three multiprocessor configurations, respectively. The motivation to use multiprocessors has been availability, reliability, and flexibility. The relatively low performance of these systems can be attributed to sharing, interaction, and unified control imposed upon them to achieve the main objectives (i.e., availability, reliability, and flexibility).

Pipeline and vector architectures can also be interpreted as MIMD systems. This is because simultaneous operation of multifunctional units and the structure of the pipe (i.e., its concurrently operating stages) are more similar to the nature of concurrently operating, overlapped multiprocessing units than those of highly parallel SIMD architectures. We will provide a description of a pipeline architecture toward the end of the chapter.

4.5 HIGHLY PARALLEL SYSTEMS: ARRAY PROCESSORS

In the highly parallel architectures, we have explicit parallelism among a high number of homogeneous processors. These processors are usually arranged in an array and driven by a common control unit for SIMD processing. SIMD processing implies synchronous operation of all the processors executing the same instruction at the same time (also referred to as *lock-stepped processing*) under the control of the common controller. These architectures are, therefore, referred to as SIMD (or array) architectures (processors) that are surveyed in Thurber and Wald [1975]. We will now turn our attention to the Illiac IV computer and the Goodyear's massively parallel processor. Although they are similar, the former characterizes the array processors, whereas the latter is reported as a recent effort of the VLSI era.

4.5.1 The Illiac IV System

The Illiac IV system was built by a joint project between the University of Illinois and Burroughs Corporation. The Illiac IV was the prototype realization of the earlier design called the Solomon computer [Slotnick et al., 1962]. Illiac IV followed the parallelism philosophy of the Solomon system with minor changes, such as more parallel floating-point arithmetic capability in the processors and also changes in the overall array dimensions. The entire Illiac IV array of 256 processing elements (PEs) was configured into four quadrants of 64 PEs and each quadrant was to be controlled by a control unit (CU). The entire complex of four quadrants was driven by a Burroughs 6500 mainframe as shown in Figure 4.9. Only one quadrant was built [Barnes et al., 1968].

As can be seen in Figure 4.9, the Illiac IV array computer works as a special attachment to a Burroughs 6500 general-purpose computer. B6500 provides interface to users, various peripheral equipment, computer network, and bulk memory. The general operating system, Illiac IV compilers and utilities, I/O subsystem, and application programs are all in the B6500 system with which the users communicate. The user programs are compiled into the array computer assembler code and sent, along with necessary data, to PEs. The PE programs are executed in parallel in the array. The array executions are controlled by the CU, and results are returned to the users via B6500. Since Illiac IV operates at high speed, the communication between it and the general-purpose computer (GPC) must be faster than an ordinary serial channel interface. For that purpose, a fixed-head disk system called the DFS (disk file storage) is provided between the Illiac IV array and the GPC.

The 64 PEs in a quadrant are physically contained in groups of 8 where each group is referred to as a PUC. There are two 64-bit wide data paths per cabinet, hence 16 per array, from the fixed-head disk. This explains the 1024-bit parallel connection (16 $\times$ 64 bits) to the Illiac array. Each Illiac IV fixed-head disk has a 256-bit wide data path to the array at 0.5×10^9 bits/sec data rate. The disk capacity is equivalent to 30 memory loads of the Illiac array. Considering the maximum of two such disk units initially configured for the system, we obtain a 512-bit wide data path to the I/O switch at the maximum data rate of 10^9 bits/sec. The I/O switch provides a single I/O exchange with the array at a time and establishes bulk data flow between the bit parallel data

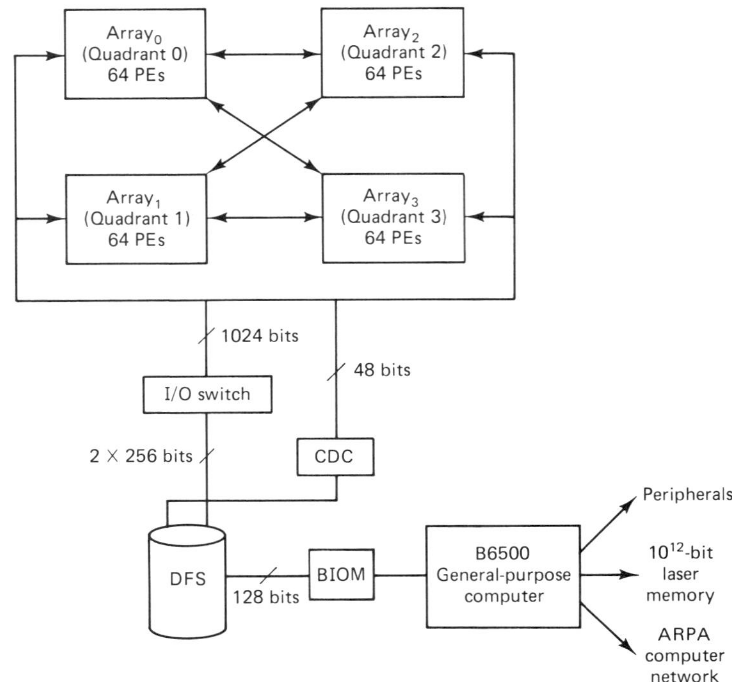

Figure 4.9   The Illiac IV system. From G. H. Barnes et al., "The ILLIAC IV Computer." *IEEE Transactions on Computers*, C-17, 8, © 1968 IEEE.

paths. The CDC (control descriptor controller) controls loading of the Illiac PE memories and activates CU at the end of a data transfer. B6500's data transfer rate is 80×10^6 bits/sec, whereas the Illiac DFS is at the rate of 500×10^6 bits/sec. For this reason, the BIOM is provided as a buffer to absorb the difference in the data rates.

Figure 4.10 shows the organization of an Illiac quadrant consisting of one CU, 64 PEs, and 64 PE memories (PEMs). Each PE has the capability of a full ALU and the control functions needed for its operations and the dedicated PE memory. Most control operations are triggered by CU and executed under the control of the resident PE microprogram. PEs can be made active (enabled) or inactive (disabled). All the active PEs operate in a lock-stepped parallel fashion for a given operation. PEs can operate concurrently with the CU. Also, some operations (such as logic and routing) can be overlapped with other operations within the PEs. Each PEM is dedicated to a PE and has a capacity of 2048 words of 64 bits and an access time of 350 nanoseconds. From each PEM, operands can be sent to the CU over a 64-bit bus. The CU has 8-word (512 bits) unidirectional communication with the PEMs. This communication is interleaved among the 8 PUCs, one word from each. Illiac IV is capable of word

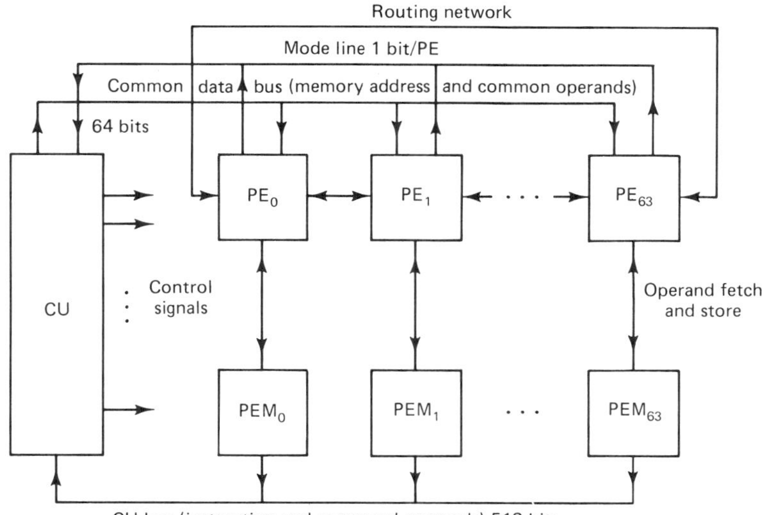

Figure 4.10   Array structure of an Illiac IV quadrant. From G. H. Barnes et al., "The ILLIAC IV Computer." *IEEE Transactions on Computers*, C-17, 8, © 1968 IEEE.

(64-bit) arithmetic; 64- and 32-bit floating-point arithmetic, 64-bit logical operations, and 64-, 32-, 24-, and 8-bit fixed-point arithmetic are supported. With the 8-bit fixed-point format, a vector of length 512 (64 $\times$ 8) bits can be added in 66 nanoseconds, which corresponds to 10^{10} MIPS (million instructions per second); 64-bit floating-point addition is performed at the equivalent of 150 MFLOPS (million floating point instructions per second).

Each PE has the following registers:

(a) A (accumulator) register, 64 bits

(b) B register, holds the second operand in binary operations, 64 bits

(c) C is the carry register, 64 bits

(d) S register, for temporary storage during programming, 64 bits

(e) R register is a routing register to transmit information from one PE to another, 64 bits

(f) X index register, to modify addresses of instructions, 16 bits

(g) M mode register, controls active/inactive status of the PE, 8 bits

Each PE can be enabled/disabled independently of the others under program control, such as the result of a register to register comparison. The M register also holds test results and program interrupts (overflow, underflow). The PE accesses its PEM with an effective address, which is computed as follows:

$$\text{Effective address} = \underbrace{\text{base} + \text{ACAR(j)}}_{\text{From CU}} + \underbrace{X}_{\text{PE}} \text{ (stored in the memory address register of PEM)}$$

Base is a 24-bit address obtained from the instruction that is modified by one of the CU accumulators (ACARS). The global address sent from the CU (the first two terms) is modified in each PE according to the contents of the index register. Considering a matrix stored in a straight way (i.e., rows across PEs and a column per PE) in a two-dimensional access, CU accesses sequentially along the rows whereas each PE accesses sequentially down the column. In the broadcast from the CU, 18 bits are sent, 12 of which indicate the row address and the remaining 6 are the starting address of the column. PEs later modify this address to access deeper elements of the column.

PEs cannot modify each other's PEM contents and do not share a primary memory. However, they can exchange information via the 64-bit wide routing network. In Illiac IV, the PEs are hardwired according to the four nearest neighbor interconnection scheme. Given a square array of n PEs, direct connections from each PE_i are available to the following PEs:

(a) $i + 1$ (cyclic interconnection)

(b) $i - 1$ (cyclic interconnection)

(c) $i + 8$

(d) $i - 8$

(a, b, c, d provide two-dimensional grid access)

Displacements of ± 8 (i.e., $\sqrt{n}$) stay within a PUC, whereas those of ± 1 can have a maximum of one PUC interdistance. Indirect routings (i.e., distances beyond ± 1, ± 8) are obtained by iterative left $(-)$ and/or right $(+)$ routings. For example, to send a word to a PE $+ 5$ distance away, a right route of 8 is followed by three left routes of 1. PEs are numbered modulo 64. Illiac IV does not provide direct connectivity for multidimensional accesses exceeding two dimensions. For example, three-dimensional access requires at least nearest six neighbor accesses.

The Illiac IV's CU organization is shown in Figure 4.11. The CU controls SIMD mode of processing. To do that, it fetches programs stored in the PEMs, decodes instructions, generates memory addresses and constants for PEMs, and initiates PE execution of decoded instructions. Besides the PE instructions, the Illiac IV instruction set also includes CU instructions, that is, the instructions to be executed in the CU alone that are needed for housekeeping, coordination, and interface tasks. Overall program flow is controlled by the CU which also handles external (from B6500) and internal interrupts (CU and PE faults).

As seen in Figure 4.11, the CU contains four accumulators called ACARs and two fast access buffers, 64 words each. One of these buffers is the instruction buffer, which is associatively addressed, and the other is the local data buffer. The ADVAST data buffer is a scratch pad area containing the accumulators.

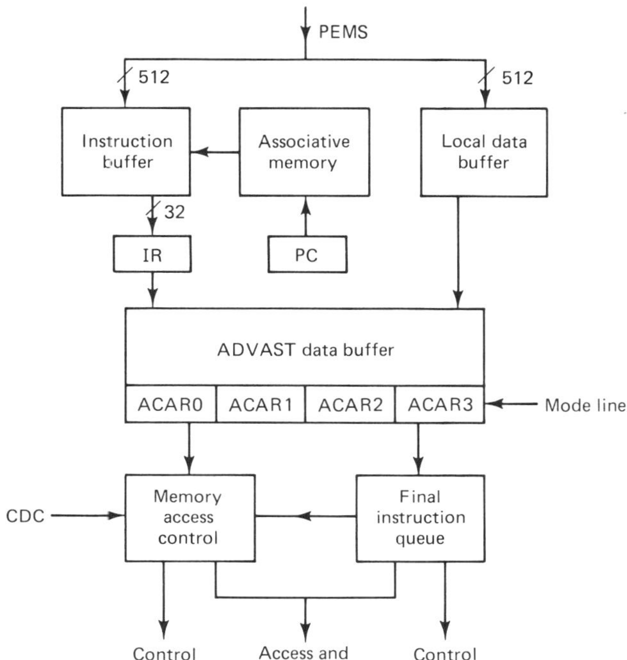

Figure 4.11 Illiac IV control unit structure. From G. H. Barnes et al., "The ILLIAC IV Computer." *IEEE Transactions on Computers*, C-17, 8, © 1968 IEEE.

The accumulators can hold data or address indices to be broadcast to PEs. As mentioned earlier, instructions are fetched eight at a time from PEMs (one from each PUC) over the 512-bit bus. Since this access incurs delay, accesses are overlapped with instruction execution whenever the instruction buffer is halfway processed. The outputs from the ADVAST buffer are the memory addresses and data operands which are stored in the final instruction queue to be executed in the PEs. The common data bus from CU to PEs broadcasts common operands to PEs. This eliminates the need for storing a common operand 64 times in all the PEs. The mode line is a 64-bit line carrying one bit from each PE into a CU accumulator. In this way, the 64-bit mode pattern can be tested in the ACAR to find out the status of the individual PEs. This information is used for program flow control (e.g., program branch in the CU).

There are several modes of partitioning in the Illiac IV array. One mode pertains to processor partitioning, which can provide speed-up in the arithmetic computations of short operands. For example, in the 64-bit precision, 64 floating-point instructions can be executed simultaneously among the PEs. If 32-bit precision is sufficient, then it is possible to execute twice as many floating-point instructions in the same amount of time (as if the number of processors were doubled). The same is true between 8 512-bit and 64 full-word (each 64-bit) integer arithmetic. In the PE array mode of partitioning, PEs can be configured to hold from a single 256-element array across four quadrants to two 128-element arrays (in two quadrants) and down to four 64-element arrays in each quadrant to fit the requirements of applications.

As we saw at the beginning of the chapter, to map a two-dimensional data structure, such as a matrix, for efficient memory access, skewed storage allocation is used. This storage allocation scheme allows equal speed of access to rows and columns. Otherwise, to do an operation on a single column in the straight storage, we would have to restrict memory accesses to a single PE at a time, down its column, idling the rest of the PEs. Note that the sum of the subscript values for any array element equals the PE number modulo $(n + 1)$. Accordingly, in the Illiac skewed storage, ith row is accessed with a row index value of i, whereas to access the jth column requires a column index value of $(i - j)$ mod 64, in the ith PE.

In the high-level language constructs tailored for the Illiac IV topology, skewed and partitioned array declarations are provided to utilize the array effectively [Kuck, 1968]. This can be demonstrated by an example drawn from the matrix examples given in Figure 4.12.

The A matrix in Figure 4.12(a) can be stored by cutting and packing. One way is to store A_{11} and follow it in the 64 PEMs of A_{11}, in a column deep manner, with the composition of A_{21}, A_{12}^T (transposed), then folding (i.e., a second layer across PEs) the remaining A_{22} in various possible ways.

Arrays can be declared partitioned. For example, if an array V is declared partitioned into 100-element partitions, then an index of 105 would be translated as:

$$V[105] = [2] \, V[5]$$

The right-hand side of this relationship shows the translation of V[105] to indicate that the addressed element is to be located in the fifth element of the second

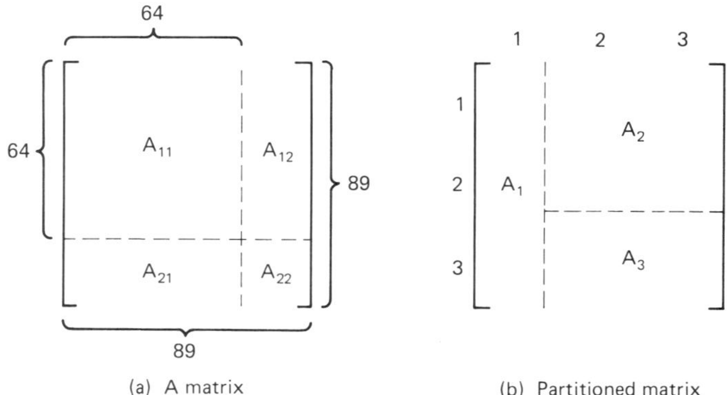

(a) A matrix   (b) Partitioned matrix

Figure 4.12 Data structure specifications. From G. H. Barnes et al., "The ILLIAC IV Computer." *IEEE Transactions on Computers*, C-17, 8, © 1968 IEEE.

partition. Similarly, the matrix partitioned according to Figure 4.12(b) can be declared as

```
PARTITION A(A1(1,1[3,1]),
           A2(1,2[2,2]),
           A3(3,2[1,2]))
```

Examining the first partition, A1, in the declaration, we see that the rows run from 1 to 3 and the column runs (remain) from 1 to 1. The first figures denote *origin*, and the second values in the brackets correspond to *array size*.

Addresses such as A(I,*) and A(*,J) refer to the *i*th row and the *j*th column, respectively. Accordingly, the following assignment statement, C ← A[*,1] + B[7,*] shows an operation, involving subsets of arrays, namely, adding the first column of A to the seventh row of B and placing the result in vector C.

Array operations.   To program Illiac IV is a difficult task because all 64 PEs must be kept busy, all executing the same instruction in parallel. As seen, special compilers and data structures are provided. In addition, as discussed at the beginning of the chapter, parallelism inherent in the programs either explicit (apparent) and/or implicit (inherent) must be transformed into parallel algorithms and mapped to the underlying array architecture. In the following, we demonstrate some operations and ways of tailoring them for array computation.

Vector Addition.   Consider addition of vectors such as the following FOR-TRAN statement:

```
    DO 100 I=1,N
100 C(I)=A(I)+B(I)
```

The three vectors can be stored across PEMs in three consecutive layers, that is, three consecutive words: one for A, one for B, and one for C. Accordingly, the entire addition will be executed 64 times faster by executing the following three operations in the PEs in parallel: *load PE accumulator with A, add B to accumulator*, and *store accumulator in C*. Parallelism replaces the iteration of the FORTRAN "do" loop. Maximum utilization of the PEs is achievable by vector dimensions, N, that are multiples of 64. While $N < 64$ underutilizes PEs, $N > 64$ may depend on the following: (1) If (N mod 64) = 0 (i.e., N is even multiple of 64), we need multiple layers of the A, B, C vectors across the PEs so that the three instruction addition must be repeated for each layer separately resulting in three times the number of layers many instructions to be executed in parallel among the PEs. (2) If, however, N is not an even multiple of 64, then the programmer is faced with either programming as in (1), which results in waste of storage and PE underutilization, or using packed storage structures that would, in turn, result in programming complications.

Log Sum Process.   Consider summing elements of a vector as in the FOR-TRAN statement:

```
     DO 100 I = 1,N
100 SUM = SUM + A(I)
```

Assuming that A is stored across the PEs, each PEM storing one element of the vector, we can think of the following parallel algorithm: continuously fold the array and add respective elements until no more folding is possible. Suppose that the following is the vector of 16 elements:

1 2 3 4 5 6 7 8 9 10 11 12 13 14 15 16

First iteration:

$$
\begin{array}{rrrrrrrr}
  & 1 & 2 & 3 & 4 & 5 & 6 & 7 & 8 \\
+ & 16 & 15 & 14 & 13 & 12 & 11 & 10 & 9 \\
\hline
  & 17 & 17 & 17 & 17 & 17 & 17 & 17 & 17
\end{array}
$$

Second iteration:

$$
\begin{array}{rrrr}
  & 17 & 17 & 17 & 17 \\
+ & 17 & 17 & 17 & 17 \\
\hline
  & 34 & 34 & 34 & 34
\end{array}
$$

Third iteration:

$$
\begin{array}{rr}
  & 34 & 34 \\
+ & 34 & 34 \\
\hline
  & 68 & 68
\end{array}
$$

Fourth iteration:

$$
\begin{array}{r}
68 \\
+ \quad 68 \\
\hline
136
\end{array} = n\,\frac{(n + 1)}{2}
$$

Since folding is equivalent to halving, the number of iterations required is $\log_2 16 = 4$; hence, the process is termed *log sum*.

We can modify this primitive procedure so that folding is equivalently achieved by gradual circular shifting, in the reverse order of folding, and that each position can keep the global sum. If we consider a PE at each position, this keeps all PEs busy and useful, especially if the end result is to be needed for a subsequent operation in all the PEs.

First iteration:

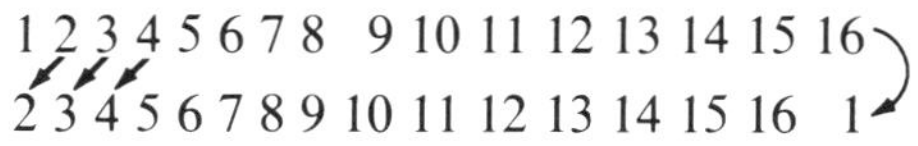

1 2 3 4 5 6 7 8 9 10 11 12 13 14 15 16

2 3 4 5 6 7 8 9 10 11 12 13 14 15 16 1

Second iteration:

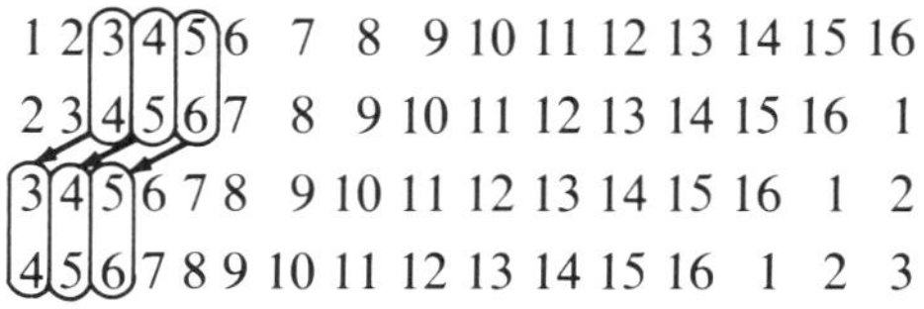

1 2 3 4 5 6 7 8 9 10 11 12 13 14 15 16

2 3 4 5 6 7 8 9 10 11 12 13 14 15 16 1

3 4 5 6 7 8 9 10 11 12 13 14 15 16 1 2

4 5 6 7 8 9 10 11 12 13 14 15 16 1 2 3

Third iteration:

```
1 2  3  4 ⎛5⎞ 6  7  8  9 10 11 12 13 14 15 16
2 3  4  5 │6│ 7  8  9 10 11 12 13 14 15 16  1
3 4  5  6 │7│ 8  9 10 11 12 13 14 15 16  1  2
4 5  6  7 ⎝8⎠ 9 10 11 12 13 14 15 16  1  2  3
⎛5⎞6  7  8  9 10 11 12 13 14 15 16  1  2  3  4
│6│7  8  9 10 11 12 13 14 15 16  1  2  3  4  5
│7│8  9 10 11 12 13 14 15 16  1  2  3  4  5  6
⎝8⎠9 10 11 12 13 14 15 16  1  2  3  4  5  6  7
```

Fourth iteration:

This iteration is carried out in the same manner as the previous ones and
an overall sum of 136 is obtained in all the PEs.

Accordingly, considering an array at the full size of Illiac IV, we would
need $\log_2 64 = 6$ additions and corresponding shifts (routings) from 2^0 to 2^5 (i.e.,
1, 2, 4, 8, 16, 32) distance. Remembering the routing scheme, the distances of
2 and 32 would be covered by two steps of $+1$ and four steps of $+8$ routings,
respectively. At each iteration, an ith PE receives the partial sum of $(i + (2 \times$
distance $- 1))$ mod 64 array elements. For example, in the case of 16 elements,
in the last shift of 8 left (during the fourth iteration), the first position received
a partial sum of $2 \times 8 - 1 = 15$ elements and 16 including itself.

This procedure can be abstracted in a high-level language, described in
Kuck [1968], suitable for Illiac IV as follows:

```
BEGIN REAL ARRAY A[0:64]; INTEGER I, J, X;
    FOR (K) SEQ(0, 1, 2, 3)DO
    BEGIN
        J←2ᵏ;
        FOR (I) SIM(0, ..., 63) DO A[I] ← A[I] + A[(I + J) mod 64]
    END;
END;
```

This program uses shift and log sum iterations. The outer "do" loop is
executed sequentially as K is assigned index values in the set {0, 1, 2, 3} element
at a time from left to right. On the other hand, the inner "begin" block indicates
simultaneous execution in all the 64 PEs, respective I's taking values of the
index set simultaneously (i.e., there will be 64 I values) so that the partial sum
in all the PEs is formed as described.

Transforming Parallelism.   Consider the following FORTRAN code:

```
     DO 100 I = 2, 64
100  A(I) = B(I) + A(I-1)
```

In the code, a sequential chaining of operations between iterations is apparent so that parallel execution is not possible. However, as discussed at the beginning of the chapter, we can transform the code by substitution as follows:

```
A(2) = B(2) + A(1)
A(3) = B(3) + A(2) = B(3) + B(2) + A(1)
      .
      .
      .
A(N) = B(N) + B(N-1) + ··· + B(2) + A(1)
```

or, equivalently,

$$A_n = A_1 + \sum_{i=2}^{N} B_i, \quad 2 \leq N \leq 64$$

The expression can be computed, using parallelism similar to the previous log sum process. The outer loop (K) will execute $\log_2 64 = 6$ times and at each iteration, we will have a right shift of 2^K and each time we disable processors 0 through J $(J = 2^K - 1)$ so that the addition is carried out in the active processors. The final result will be in PE_{63}. This would assume that the array $A_1, B_2, \ldots, B_{64}$ is stored across PEMs 0 through 63.

4.5.2 Goodyear's Massively Parallel Processor

A recent development of an array processor, called the massively parallel processor, is reported in Batcher [1980]. This array processor is developed by Goodyear Aerospace Corp. for satellite image processing under a contract from NASA. The expected work load of the application is 10^9 to 10^{10} operations per second. The array processor is capable of 6553 MIPS of 8-bit integer additions and 430 MFLOPS of 32-bit floating-point additions. Such execution rate is achieved with bit serial arithmetic in parallel among the 16,384 PEs. This parallelism is required to process millions of picture elements (pixels) at the same time. Figure 4.13 displays the organization of the massively parallel processor (MPP).

The PEs of the ARU are implemented by 2 × 4 PE custom VLSI chips. The complete ARU is an array of 128 × 128 PEs with four redundant columns added for fault tolerance. The resulting 128 × 132 array is divided into 33 groups of 128 × 4 subarrays. Each group has a disable/enable line to the array control unit (ACU). A disabled group can be bypassed by joining the groups around it together by the use of bypass gates. When a faulty PE is discovered, the entire column containing the faulty PE is disabled and replaced by a redundant column via the bypass gates.

The routing topology is essentially that of Illiac IV's four-neighbor scheme. Routing is needed to reorient data between the bit plane format of the ARU and the pixel format (spectral band resolution of 6 to 12 bits) of the outside interface. In addition, the edges of the array can be left open so that a row of zeros can

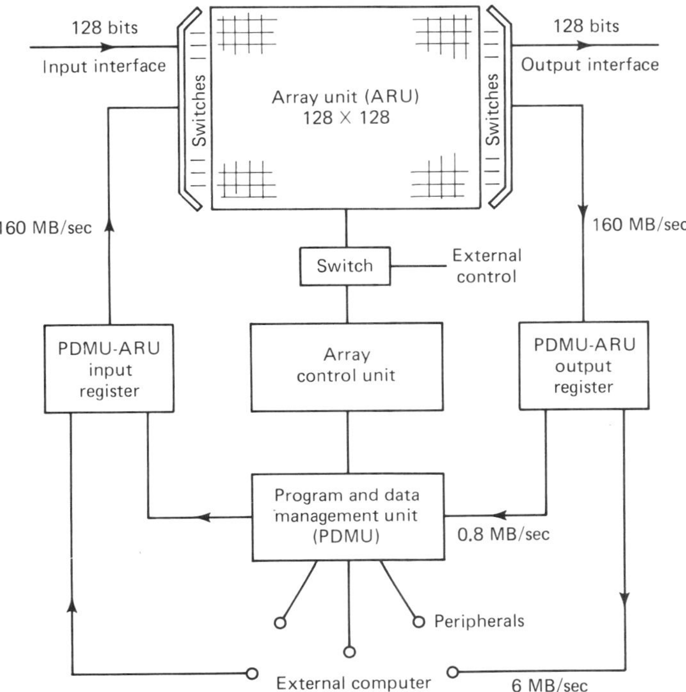

Figure 4.13 Organization of the massively parallel processor. From K. E. Batcher, "Architecture of a Massively Parallel Processor." *Proceeds of Seventh Annual Symposium on Computer Architecture,* 8, 3, © 1980 Association for Computing Machinery.

be entered or the opposite edges can be connected. The same is true for the column edges. Data can be processed both in bit-plane (row) and bit-slice mode. The latter mode is also common to Staran (see Chapter 5) and the Orthogonal Computer [Shooman, 1960].

Due to the variable-length operand requirement of the application, bit serial arithmetic is used to accommodate variable-length data. Each PE looks like a one bit version of an Illiac IV PE. Six 1-bit registers, a shift register, a 1024-bit RAM, a data bus, and a full adder are contained in each PE. The basic cycle time of PE is 100 nanoseconds (10 MHz). While the PEs are processing data in their RAMs, columns of input data are shifted into ARU (from the input interface) through the S registers, until a plane of 16,384 bits is loaded. This input plane is then stored in the PE RAMs, from the S register, in one memory cycle (100 ns) by interrupting the PEs momentarily. The reverse takes place for output and up to 160 megabytes per second can be transferred out through the ARU I/O ports.

The ACU has three control functions: PE control, I/O control, and main control. Array arithmetic in the PEs, scalar arithmetic in the ACU, and input/output can be overlapped.

The PE control contains eight 16-bit registers to hold the addresses of the bit planes of the PE memories, loop counts, and index of a bit in the common register. Horizontal microprogramming is used in the PE control. The PE control memory contains system and user-written routines including array-to-array, and array-to-scalar arithmetic operations and extraction of scalar values, such as the maximum, out of ARU.

I/O control shifts the S registers, manages flow of data, and interrupts PEs during transfers.

The main control contains a fast scalar processor and a call queue to place array arithmetic in the PE control queue. Among the registers, 3 of them control the ARU group disable lines, 13 are associated with the call queue, 12 receive scalars from the PE control, and 16 are for general purpose.

The program and data management unit (PDMU) controls overall flow of programs in the system. The control interface is via a terminal or an external computer. PDMU itself is a DEC PDP 11 with custom I/O interfaces that include wide I/O ports to ARU. The operating system is DEC's RSX-11M multiprogramming system. The PE assemblers, utilities, and the main assembler that runs in the main control, are also part of PDMU. PDMU's I/O registers for the ARU interface transfer bit columns in bit sequential order and have the capability to reorder the data to fit the requirements of the external interfaces. To do that, the registers use 2^{19}-bit multidimensional access memory. The MPP system is planned to have a DEC VAX 11/780 host as the external computer. This host will have a 6-MB/sec high-speed link and a DECNET (of Digital Equipment Corporation) control link, with the PDMU.

4.6 VECTOR PIPELINE PROCESSORS

The most advanced models of existing computers employ pipelining in various ways. The most common use of pipelining is in instruction execution and arithmetic logic units. The IBM System 360/(91 and 195), Amdahl 470 V/6, and CDC (6600, 7600, and STAR-100) are examples of instruction pipeline architectures. We will concentrate on vector processors. Some examples of these are, TI-ASC, CDC STAR-100, and CRAY-1. Although pipeline processing implies more logical parallelism than physical and, as pointed out earlier, the underlying architecture is a low-level MIMD rather than an array processor, we can classify vector processors into the category of new computer architectures. The CRAY-1 architecture is the latest vector processor. It introduced chaining, a feature not shared by CDC STAR-100 or TI-ASC. The last two are the early-generation machines and are more alike than CRAY-1. We briefly summarize the CRAY-1 architecture in the following section.

4.6.1 The CRAY-1 Architecture

Figure 4.14 is a block diagram of CRAY-1's [Cray Research, Inc., 1977; Russel 1978] functional units and major registers in the CPU. As seen along the right side of the figure, there are 12 functional units. These units are shown in groups. Grouping depends upon the type of operations performed and the registers addressed. These functional units operate only on the registers. This grouping results in speed-ups in the architecture because it allows parallelism and chaining among the functional units. Also, the functional units are pipelined and structured for vector processing. The functional units perform address calculations, logical, scalar, and vector operations of integers, floating-point scalars, and vectors. Most of the primitive operations throughout the CPU are carried out in one clock cycle (or minor cycle), which is 12.5 nanoseconds. The address arithmetic is 24 bits whereas the scalar and vector arithmetic is 64 bits.

The following are the major registers:

a) Address registers (A_0-A_7), 24 bits
b) Backup registers (B_0-B_{63}), 24 bits
c) Scalar registers (S_0-S_7), 64 bits
d) Backup registers (T_0-T_{63}), 64 bits
e) Vector registers (V_0-V_7), 64 words by 64 bits

The address (A) registers are used for addressing, indexing, shift counts, and I/O operations. B registers are backup to A registers. Transfers between A and B take one clock cycle. The scalar registers are backed up by the T registers. The scalar (S) and vector (V) registers provide operands (at every clock cycle) and receive results of the scalar and vector operations, respectively. There are 8 vector registers each containing 64 words of 64 bits. The vector length, VL, register controls the number of operations of a vector instruction.

The functional units receive their operands at every clock cycle. The transfers between A and S registers and their backup B and T registers also take one clock cycle. A memory to CPU register transfer takes 11 clock cycles. Such transfers can be pipelined at every other clock, whereas the memory to vector and backup registers can be pipelined at every clock.

The main memory consists of 16 banks that provide 16-way interleaved access to CPU. Each bank has 64K words of 64 bits (72 with error detection/ correction). The bank cycle time is 50 ns.

The instructions are 16 or 32 bits. They are fetched and executed out of the four instruction buffers. Each buffer has 64 16-bit registers. Intra- and interbuffer branching of instructions is possible. Four words are sent, at each transfer, from the memory to the instruction buffers. The P register is the program counter which also selects the appropriate instruction buffer. LIP, NIP, and CIP are instruction registers.

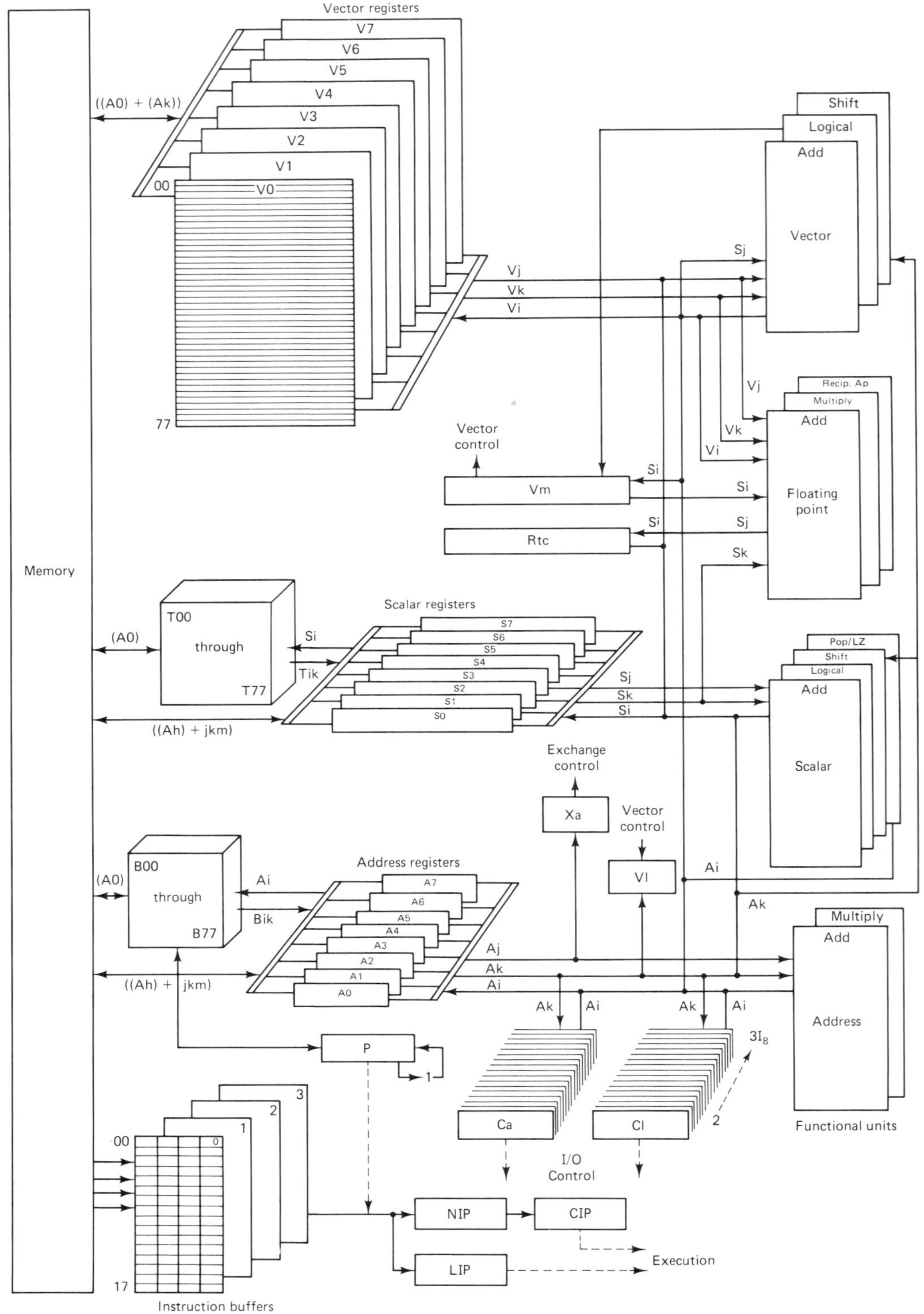

Figure 4.14 CRAY-1's functional units and registers. From R. M. Russel, "The CRAY-1 Computer System." *CACM*, 21, 1, © 1978 Association for Computing Machinery.

CRAY-1 performance has been rated as high as 100 MFLOPS. The vector operations can be (1) between two operand vectors, result is stored in a third vector; (2) between a vector and a scalar, result is stored in a second vector; (3) memory to a vector (type 3); and (4) vector to memory. The last two are needed for data transfers since the functional units operate only on registers.

A vector instruction of the first type (e.g., $V_i \leftarrow V_j + V_k$) is executed in pipeline as the corresponding bit pairs are fed through the addition pipe. During a vector instruction, the related functional unit and the operand registers are locked for the number of clock periods as determined by the type of operation and the vector length. This implies that the following operations cannot be executed concurrently:

$$V_0 \leftarrow V_1 - V_2$$
$$V_4 \leftarrow V_1 * S$$

As can be seen, both instructions require the common operand V_1. The second instruction can be executed only after the first instruction releases V_1. However, the functional units can execute instructions in parallel if they do not conflict in their resources. Also, as we have seen at the beginning of the chapter, chaining of pipeline instructions is possible, which is a concept of the CRAY-1 architecture. In addition to pipeline overlap, chaining avoids memory accesses for common data. Chaining is also performed between the type 3 vector instructions; that is, if

$$V_i \leftarrow V_j + V_k$$

needed two type 3 instructions to load the vector registers, the add can be chained with the loading of V_k (after V_j is loaded).

CRAY-1's interaction with the input/output systems takes place via 12 input and 12 output channels. The entire channel capacity is divided into four groups that communicate with the main memory through a single path. For memory accesses, a priority polling scheme is used. An arithmetic operand fetch/store has a higher priority than an I/O operation.

It has been shown that the vector arithmetic benefits from CRAY-1's architecture, especially for long vectors. The performance of CRAY-1 is better than its performance in scalar arithmetic. However, even for scalar operations it is faster than most mainframes (e.g., CDC 7600). For matrix multiplication of square matrices of dimensions greater than 64, a constant performance of 100 MFLOPS has been achieved.

Pipelining and vector processing must be properly driven by user programs. Similar to the case with array processors, parallelism in arithmetic operations must be extracted, and special vector instructions must be included in programming languages.

With regard to the overall performance of the architectures, we have surveyed in the chapter, the following holds:

(a) If user's problem is converted to a suitable parallel algorithm and the remaining sequential computation is negligible, high performance in program execution can be obtained.

(b) Whereas (a) represents a system's effectiveness in computations, one problem remains and that is the I/O bandwidth between the system and outside world. This bandwidth affects a system's efficiency.

We will defer the discussion of the I/O bandwidth problem to another chapter, where this problem will be an issue for associative processors as well. We will then generalize the so-called *I/O bottleneck* problem.

EXERCISES

4.1. Refer to Baer [1980], Hu [1961], and Kuck [1977] with regard to automatic detection of parallelism in arithmetic expressions and how to speed up program loops. Write algorithms to accomplish the following:

    (a) Minimize, using Hu's algorithm, the number of processors required to evaluate a set of expression trees in a fixed number of steps. What happens if the execution times of individual nodes in a tree are unequal?

    (b) Starting from a directed graph of a program, where a node represents a program statement and an edge represents flow of control, build a new parallel graph by

        (i) Detecting cycles and converting them to acyclic graphs

        (ii) Determining dependencies

        (iii) Combining (i) and (ii) and making modifications on the resulting graph to exploit parallelism. Your final result should be an acyclic AND/OR graph where ANDs should correspond to FORKs and JOINs and ORs should indicate program tests and loops.

4.2. Using the relationship given in Section 4.1.3 for speed-up due to potential parallelism of a program code, plot a graph of speed-up versus potential parallelism to explore various relationships among C_s, C_p, and n. You can assume that one parallel processor executes one unit of parallel code in one execution cycle.

4.3. Referring to Figure 4.4(b) in Section 4.2.1, convert the occupancy vector to a collision vector $(C_n, \ldots, C_1)$ such that $C_i = 1$ is a forbidden latency (to prevent collisions) at which initiation of another task on the pipe is not allowed. Accordingly, the collision vector for Figure 4.4(b) will be (0, 0, 1, 0) such that an initiation by a subsequent task on the pipe can be allowed after every i time unit where $C_i = 0$.

    Assuming this collision vector as the initial state, build a finite state diagram of all possible initiations where a state is a collision vector and transitions correspond to possible initiations. If an initiation occurs after i units of time, the collisions that occurred at time j, where $j > i$, will now occur at $(j - i)$. To represent this, shift the current vector i places to the right with a left fill of zeros. The new state is the OR of the previous state and the shifted vector.

4.4. Based on the t_{vp} and t_{sq} times for the vector and sequential pipes, respectively, as given in Section 4.2.2, plot a curve that would compare a sequential pipe with a vector pipe as a function of the vector length l. The comparison must be based upon the processing time of the pipes, either relative or absolute, as l is varied.

4.5. Based on the classification of computer architectures given in Section 4.3, enumerate a list of applications from real life that would be best characterized by the corresponding computing (i.e., architecture) class.

4.6. Using a given computer system and its various component timings as well as its options and expansion parameters, explore the order of various improvements achievable in increasing the throughput, as pointed out in Section 4.4.

4.7. Can you suggest other means of configuring multiprocessors than those discussed in the chapter? What advantages and disadvantages would each proposed configuration have to offer?

4.8. How far can one reach, using Illiac IV's interconnection topology, in six one-step routings? (Remember that each immediate (connected) neighbor is one step away.)

4.9. Assuming a square matrix multiplication of dimension 64, write procedures based on the Illiac IV architecture to do the multiplication using
(a) Straight storage schemes
(b) Skewed storage schemes

4.10. Using the FORTRAN code and the corresponding transformed equivalent array addition of $A_N = A_1 + \sum_{i=2}^{N} B_i$, for $2 \leqslant N \leqslant 64$, given in the chapter, write a procedure based on the following Illiac IV primitives to execute the addition on an array processor:
(a) Load accumulator, add accumulator, store accumulator, in each PE
(b) Routing (if necessary)
(c) Enable/disable PEs
(d) Log sum and necessary operations (the PEs can communicate either by routing or via CU. In the latter, broadcasting to more than one PE is possible.)

4.11. What advantages can you see of the array size and the other system parameters of the Goodyear's massively parallel processor? You can make a comparison vis-à-vis Illiac IV. Do you find any restrictions of MPP, such as in multiplying matrices or other SIMD applications of more general nature?

4.12. Assuming the following functional unit timings and the register usage of the CRAY-1 architecture,

	Register usage	Functional unit time (Clock periods)
Address function units		
Address add unit	A	2
Address multiply unit	A	6
Scalar function units		
Scalar add unit	S	3
Scalar shift unit	S	2 or 3 if double-word shift
Scalar logical unit	S	1
Population/leading		

(*continued*)		
zero count unit	S	3
Vector function units		
Vector add unit	V	3
Vector shift unit	V	4
Vector logical unit	V	2
Floating-point functional units		
Floating-point add unit	S and V	6
Floating-point multiply unit	S and V	7
Reciprocal approximation unit	S and V	14

what will be the total time to execute the following:

(**a**) Each of the four vector operation types for various arithmetic and logical operations.

(**b**) The chain of

$$V_0 \leftarrow memory$$

$$V_2 \leftarrow V_0 + V_1 \ (integer)$$

$$V_3 \leftarrow V_2 < A_3 \ (left \ shift, \ count \ in \ A_3)$$

$$V_5 \leftarrow V_3 \wedge V_4 \ (logical \ product)$$

not need associative memories. In the movie example, if we would strictly enforce maintenance and entry in all cases on Mr. Access-path's register, there would not be any time to watch the movies. This analogously explains why present-day transaction processing systems defer their updates to midnight and let things happen until then. Otherwise, there would not be any time to deal with transactions in real time, just as there would not be any time to watch movies in the theater case.

As we can see, plurality is essential for associative memory systems in the following ways:

(a) We have many memory elements (storage units) just as we had many seats in the example.

(b) The search is broadcast to every storage unit and sensed in parallel just as in the loudspeaker system.

(c) There may be more than one (as well as none or one) person with the same name responding to the loudspeaker call just as many storage units may result in content match with the sought value or search argument. We must have a way to deal with multiple responses.

Therefore, we have established that there is multiplicity in the participants as well as responders and also parallel exhaustive search in an associative memory. Let us look at Figure 5.1, which shows the structure of an associative memory system (or an associative memory array).

This search capability and structure is what is behind the alternate names of associative memory such as *parallel search memory, multiple response store, distributed logic memory, and logic in memory,* and so on. As can be realized, parallel searchability and the other necessary features of the memory system make this memory intelligent as compared to a memory accessed by location.

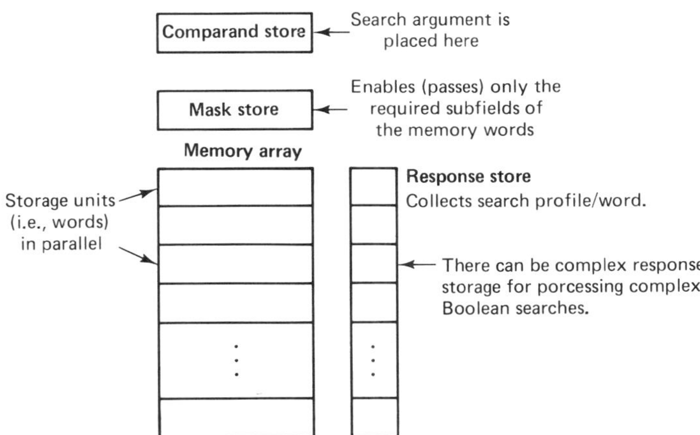

Figure 5.1   An associative memory system.

Going back to Figure 5.1, the storage area is represented by the array where there is a search element per memory unit. This unit varies from a bit, to a byte, a word, and finally a bulk memory block (e.g., a disk track). The definition of unit implies the amount of dedicated search logic associated with it. If we can have a search logic (processor) for each bit, then we would have a two-dimensional parallelism of m (number of words) $\times$ n (number of bits/word) search processors, which would make such an associative memory unaffordable in cost, because it implies that in one bit compare time, $m \times n$ processors search the entire memory in parallel. This is extremely fast but costly. Compromises diluted the number of processors from n per word to $n/8$ (i.e., per byte) and finally the most common organization, a processor per word. We should remember, however, that there are m of these processors in parallel making up a *bit slice* or bit column within the associative array, as shown in Figure 5.2.

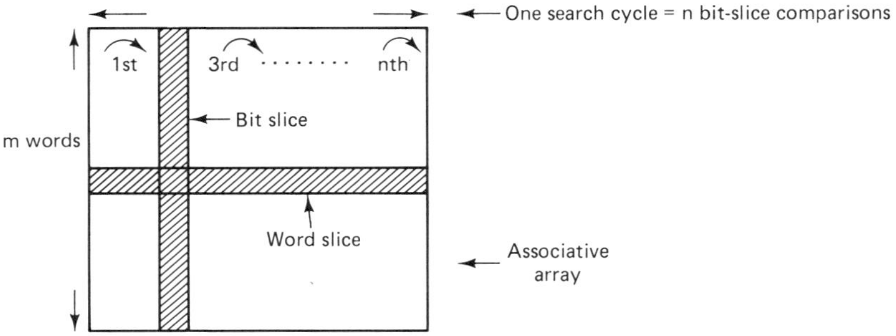

Figure 5.2 Bit and word slicing in associative memory.

Typically, bit slices are used for comparisons and arithmetic, logical operations while word slices are used for input/output (load/unload). However, writing over a bit slice, called the *multiwrite,* is another typical operation.

As can be seen in Figures 5.1 and 5.2, the memory array has data storage as well as match logic. Comparand store holds the sought value (search argument). Mask store allows passage (contact) to the desired portions of the comparand while inhibiting the other bit positions as shown in Figure 5.3.

Let us show a small example before we discuss some operations of associative memories. Suppose we have words W_1 through W_6 stored in an associative memory array. Assume that each word is five bits long and the words contain the values, in binary form, shown in Figure 5.4.

Suppose we want to find those words that match the comparand C = 11100. This means that we are interested in all the bit positions so that the mask register should provide their passage to the word array. This is done by making all the bit positions in M a binary 1. Now, the comparison will proceed as follows: we start from the leftmost bit position in all the words and activate the first bit slice comparators (i.e., bit one in W_1, through W_6). We take the corresponding C bit, which is a 1, and see if it is required in the comparison. This is determined

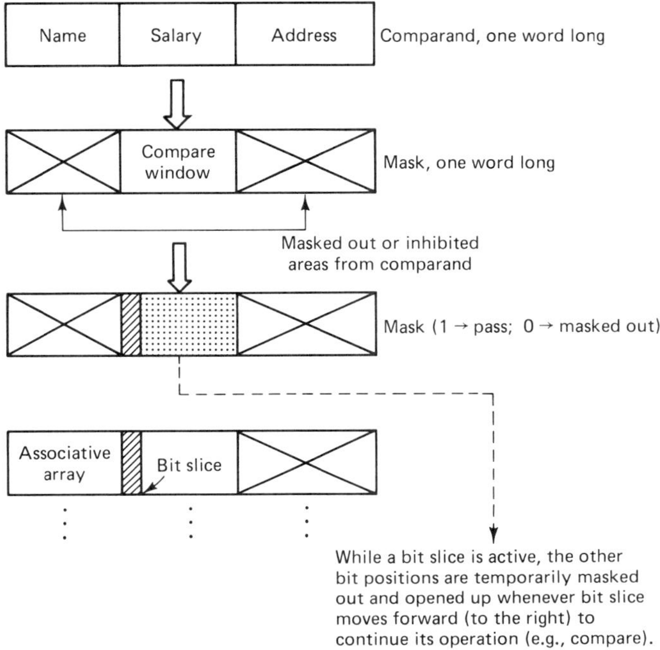

Figure 5.3   Mask store.

by looking at the corresponding bit position in the mask register M. We have a 1 at that position; therefore, at this point the bit slice processors compare simultaneously the C value with their respective values. At this point, we need a flip flop, F (i.e., a single bit) to remember the result of comparison at each word position. For our purpose here, a single bit will suffice. If a success will be indicated by a 1 in F, then we start with a 1 in F (F_0 stage) for all the words and reset those that correspond to the words that fail in the comparisons. In the end, those F positions that manage to remain as 1 will imply a match in the

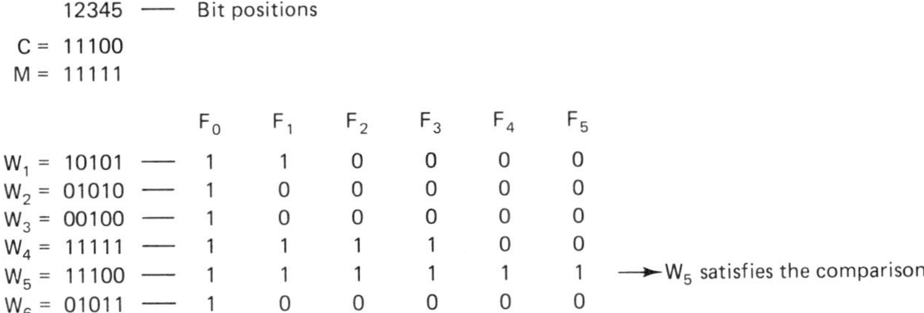

		F_0	F_1	F_2	F_3	F_4	F_5	
W_1 = 10101	——	1	1	0	0	0	0	
W_2 = 01010	——	1	0	0	0	0	0	
W_3 = 00100	——	1	0	0	0	0	0	
W_4 = 11111	——	1	1	1	1	0	0	
W_5 = 11100	——	1	1	1	1	1	1	→ W_5 satisfies the comparison
W_6 = 01011	——	1	0	0	0	0	0	

Figure 5.4   A comparison example.

corresponding word positions. Now let us start the bit slice comparisons:

(a) Bit position 1: words W_1, W_4, W_5 match; therefore, $F_1 = 100110$.

(b) Bit position 2: words W_2, W_4, W_5, W_6 match; however, W_2 and W_6 were discarded in (a); therefore, $F_2 = 000110$.

(c) Bit position 3: words W_1, W_3, W_4, W_5 match; therefore, $F_3 = 000010$.

(d) Bit position 4: words W_1, W_3, W_5 match (comparand now is 0); therefore, $F_4 = 000010$.

(e) Bit position 5: words W_2, W_3, W_5 match; therefore, $F_5 = 000010$.

The responder is W_5.

If we did not care what the second and fifth positions of the comparand contain and look for match in the remaining positions, then we specify C as

```
C = 1?10?
```

(?'s indicate *don't cares,* i.e., any value is acceptable). Then

```
M = 10110
```

because the second and fifth positions will not be compared, since they are "bona fide" success, they will be masked out. Accordingly, the following sequence of F vectors will be obtained:

$$
\begin{aligned}
F_0 &= 1\ 1\ 1\ 1\ 1\ 1 \\
F_1 &= 1\ 0\ 0\ 1\ 1\ 1 \\
F_2 &= F_1 \\
F_3 &= F_2 \\
F_4 &= 1\ 0\ 0\ 0\ 1\ 1 \\
F_5 &= 0\ 0\ 0\ 0\ 1\ 1
\end{aligned}
$$

As can be noticed, at the end of the comparison of bit position 3 we now have four responders: W_1, W_4, W_5, and W_6 instead of the previous two, W_4, W_5. Also, at the end of the comparison, we now have two responders, W_5, W_6, instead of one previously. This is because we do not now care what the second and fifth bit values are in W_1 through W_6. For example, if W_2 and W_5 were 00011 and 10101 instead of 01010 and 11100, respectively, we would have obtained the same result. This would also be true for all possible W_1 through W_6 value combinations in which each time the second and/or fifth bit position values are varied.

From what we have seen so far, we notice that in an associative memory organization of the type discussed here there is a series of *locked-step* operations among the various substructures, i.e., the associative memory array, comparand, mask, and the response store. (A locked-step operation implies a tightly coupled synchronous operation.) The essential operations among the substructures are comparison; handling one, none, or multiple responders; and bit slice operations such as compare, add, and write. The latter becomes multicompare, multiadd, or multiwrite on the entire array. There are also the usual load and unload operations that take place on word-slice basis, sometimes in parallel depending on the implementation. If we compare this organization to an ordinary location addressable random access memory (RAM), we see the following differences. At the system level, a RAM is very simple. All it has are the address decoder and read/write circuitry, one for the entire RAM. The basic operations are address decode, read, and write. Therefore, an associative memory is much more complex at the system level than a RAM and more expensive. At the bit level, there is not much difference. An associative memory bit is only 40 to 50% more complex in gate count [Foster, 1976] with respect to a RAM bit.

In Figure 5.5, we see a bit of RAM 5.5(a) and a bit of associative memory 5.5(b). In Figure 5.5(a), the select signal is assumed to be the result of various decoder, chip select, and other necessary signals external to the abstraction of the single bit of RAM. In Figure 5.5(b), selection of a memory bit is assumed

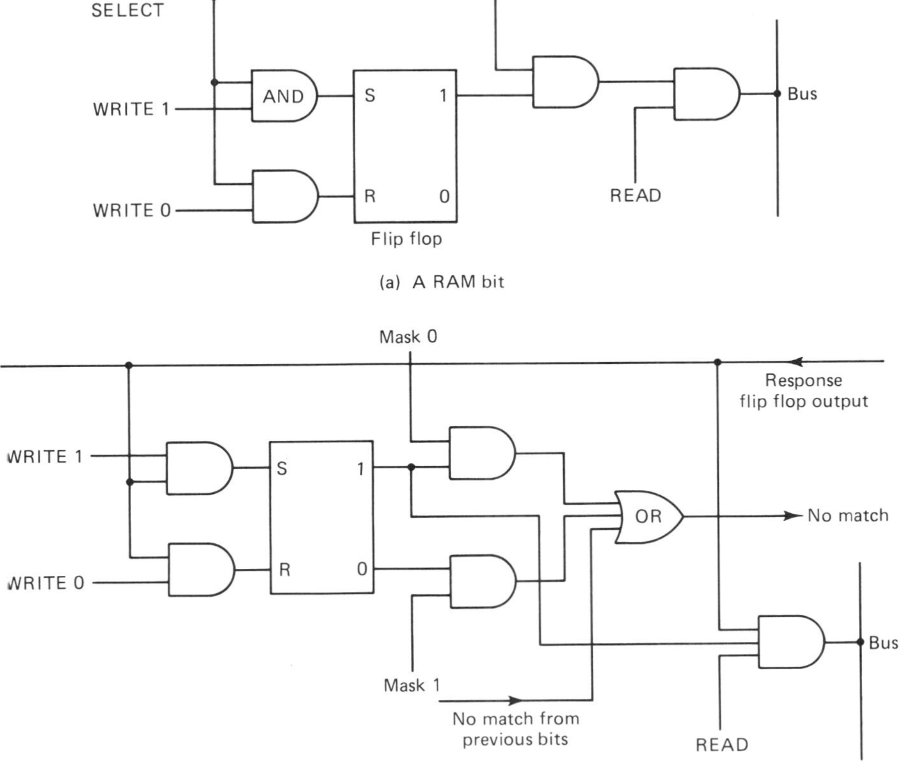

Figure 5.5 One bit of RAM and associative memory.

to be done subsequent to a necessary compare operation whose result is fed back from the corresponding response store bit. The meanings of MASK 0 and MASK 1 are as follows. Since we start with response store bit set to 1 and maintain it that way so long as success in comparison continues, we would do something (i.e., reset the response flip flop) only in the case of a mismatch. That is why we input the mask bit value (1 or 0) in the reverse order (i.e., MASK 0 to the high-bit output (1) and MASK 1 to the low output (0)) to produce a signal (a high) only in the case of a mismatch. This signal is collected into an OR gate from all the bit positions of the word to produce the signal at the word level (i.e., one bit mismatch is enough to call off the game!). In reading, we would, of course, read off only those bits of the words that were selected previously. The bit of knowledge we obtained thus far will be enough to take us into the topic of basic operations on associative memories.

5.3 BASIC OPERATIONS ON ASSOCIATIVE MEMORIES

As we have seen in the basic structure of an associative memory, there is some level of intelligence besides storage in an associative memory system. This intelligence is enough to enable us to carry out the following operations:

(a) Match (i.e., equal to)
(b) Mismatch (i.e., not equal to)
(c) Less than
(d) Less than or equal to
(e) Greater than
(f) Greater than or equal to
(g) Maximum
(h) Minimum
(i) Between limits
(k) Outside of limits
(l) Next higher
(m) Next lower
(n) Various forms of add/subtract

Other operations that can be derived from the above and/or modifications on the basic structure of an associative memory as shown here are also possible as covered in the references [Falkoff, 1962; Estrin, 1963; Foster, 1976; Slade and McMahon, 1956].

5.3.1 Match/Mismatch

Let us represent the associative memory with the configuration shown in Figure 5.6. All operations will be demonstrated with respect to the binary contents of

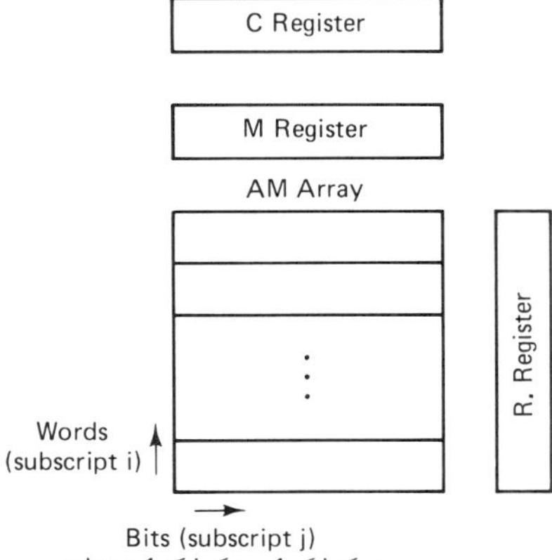

Figure 5.6 A model of an associative memory.

the registers, and furthermore, wherever applicable, their contents will be assumed positive.

Algorithm match (equal)

```
 1. C ← comparand
 2. M ← mask (a 1 at every M_j corresponding to comparand bit positions)
 3. R ← 1 (i.e., each R_i is set to one)
 4. J ← 0
 5. Do while J < n (i.e., for each bit of the comparand)
 6.     J ← J + 1
 7.     I = 0
 8.     If M_j = 1 then
 9.         Do while I < m (for every word of the memory)
10.             I ← I + 1
11.             R_i ← ¬ (C_j XOR AM_ij) ∧ R_i  (intersect comparison result
                                                with the result of previous
12.         end                                 comparisons; XOR is exclusive or
13. End                                         and ¬ is negation)
```

The operations 9 through 12 take place at each bit slice, and therefore, there is no physical (program description being logical) iteration since there is parallelism among the words.

The mismatch (not equal) can be determined from, or programmed around, the match operation.

5.3.2 Maximum

Algorithm maximum

```
 1. C ← 1 (all ones)
 2. M ← 0 (all zeros)
 3. J ← 1
```

```
 4.  M_j ← 1 (the leftmost bit is the start)
 5.  R ← 1 (all ones)
 6.  PERFORM A MATCH OPERATION FOR THE Jth SLICE
              m
 7.  If  ∑ R_i = 0 then Y ← R (i.e., no match in the Jth slice)
             i=1
 8.                    else do (indirectly copy maximum value into C)
 9.                        C_j ← 0
10.                        R ← Y
11.                        end
12.  J ← J + 1
13.  If J > n then exit
                 else M_j ← 1
14.  Repeat from 6
```

In the end, the comparand is found as transformed into the maximum value and the R register indicates the location(s) of the maximum value. We can now go ahead and compare this comparand for match to find the word (or words) that contain this maximum value.

5.3.3 Between Limits (Exclusive)

As logic and arithmetic operations get more complex, certain enhancements on our basic associative memory become necessary. For example, it is common to have three response store registers X, Y, and Z among which certain Boolean operations can be done (e.g., $Z \leftarrow X \wedge Y$). Also, for arithmetic operations we need to use the multiwrite capability in order to handle state transitions of the addition process.

To process between limits, we need to know the lower and upper bound values. In the following algorithm we will use the X and Y registers as the match response register and to ultimately identify those words that match their comparand registers. The lower- and upper-bounds are considered in turn, where during each slice, the words found not equal are included or excluded in the result and then excluded from further consideration. Words matching the boundary are finally excluded. The result from the lower-bound is saved as the initial word set for the upper-bound comparison.

Algorithm between limits (exclusive)

```
1.  C ← Lower-bound; M ← Mask
2.  R ← 1 {all words originally included}
3.  X ← 1; {used to match boundary}
4.  For each bit slice, 1 ≤ j ≤ n do in lockstep 5. thru 11.
5.  If (M_j) then      {Mask bit asserted}
6.        For each word, i = 1..m, do in parallel 7. thru 10.
7.                If (C_j XOR AM_ij) ∧ X_i then do {word does not match lower-
                      bound}
8.                    R_i ← R_i ∧ AM_ij
                        {exclude words < lower-bound, i.e., C_j = 1, AM_ij = 0}
9.                    X_i ← 0
```

```
10.                   end
11.          End parallel operation
12. End lockstep operation
13. R ← R ∧ ¬X    {exclude words matching lower-bound}
14. C ← Upper-bound;
15. Y ← R  { copy included words};
16. For each bit slice, 1 ≤ j ≤ n do in lockstep 17. thru 24.
17. If (Mⱼ) then     {Mask bit asserted}
18.      For each word, i=1..m, do in parallel 19. thru 23.
19.          If (Cⱼ XOR AMᵢⱼ) ∧ Yᵢ then do {no upper-bound match}
20.             Rᵢ ← Rᵢ ∧ Cⱼ
                   {exclude words > upper-bound, i.e., Cⱼ = 0, AMᵢⱼ =1}
21.             Yᵢ ← 0
22.          end
23.      End parallel operation
24. End lockstep operation
25. R ← R ∧ ¬ Y {exclude words matching upper-bound}
26. R register indicates words between limits (exclusive of boundaries}
```

Based on the ideas of the foregoing algorithm, one can write algorithms for *less than, greater than,* and *next higher/lower.* In the case of next higher, we first determine the words that are greater than the operand and subsequently find their minimum.

5.3.4 Add one to all words.   This addition is much simpler than adding two fields of the array to each other or adding an arbitrary constant to a field of the array. The addition in this case works like a half adder, because at any time there are not more than two quantities to add to each other, that is, 1 and the least significant bit at the beginning and carry and the AM bit for the subsequent additions until a word drops out of the addition as shown below:

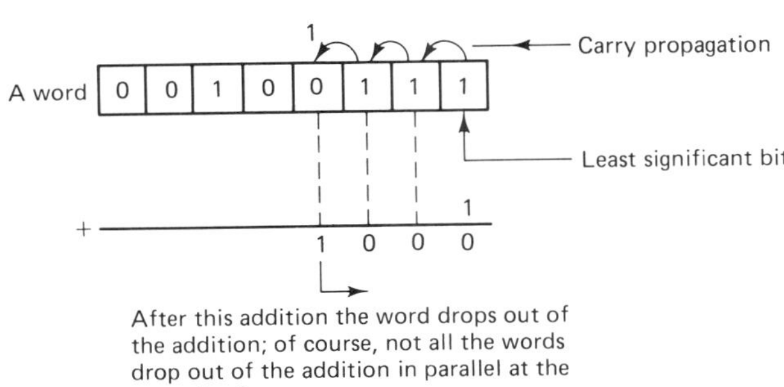

After this addition the word drops out of
the addition; of course, not all the words
drop out of the addition in parallel at the
same time!

As you remember, we assumed positive numbers throughout. Accordingly, there will be a zero bit position (the most significant bit) to hold the constant one for each word and we do not need extra storage for it.

Algorithm add one.   Since arithmetic is done from the least significant to the most significant bit direction, we will reverse our bit numbering sequence from the left to right order (i.e., the j subscript to the right to left order), and numbering will start from 0 (i.e., least significant bit).

```
 1.  M ← 0
 2.  M_31 ← 0
 3.  AM_31 ← 1 (place one into bit 31 in all the words)
 4.  J ← 0
 5.  M ← M + 2^j (make the jth bit a 1)
 6.  C ← 0
 7.  C_31 ← 1
 8.  R ← 1 (single response store will suffice here)
 9.  PERFORM A MATCH OPERATION (for the carry (=1) and the jth bit (=0))
10.  C ← 2^j
11.  WRITE C INTO AM    (from 10 and M; carry (=0) and jth bit (=1)
                             will be written).
        (Remember that the write operation is done only for the responders
         which are indicated in R.)
12.  C ← 0
13.  C ← 31
14.  C ← C + 2^j
15.  R ← 1
16.  PERFORM A MATCH OPERATION (for the carry (=1) and the jth bit (=1))
17.  C ← 0
18.  C_31 ← 1
19.  WRITE C INTO AM (carry (=1), jth bit (=0))
20.  J ← J + 1
21.  If J ≥ 31 exit else go to 5
```

5.4 SECONDARY (BULK) MEMORY–BASED ASSOCIATIVE MEMORIES

The secondary or bulk memory–based associative memory systems are also referred to as *associative drums* or *associative disks* or *quasi-associative* memories. The names reflect the concepts behind their structure. Drum or disk because they are used as the memory and quasi (seemingly) because associativity is achieved on these cheap memories by emulating the behavior of the genuine associative memories. The reason for the emergence of the associative memories of this class was because the sizes of the data to be processed were very large besides the high cost of associative memories. The latter limited their size and caused I/O bottlenecks due to excessive paging activities.

Apart from drums which were later replaced by disks, there are bulk memories made up of dynamic RAMs and magnetic bubbles. These memories can be used both as serial circulating memories to emulate disks or as random block addressable memories.

To emulate an associative memory by a bulk memory, we must emulate bit slice processing, which means a processor (comparator) per word and parallelism. This can be achieved by creating a memory cell, such as a track of a disk or a memory word and associating a dedicated processor (logic) to it. There are ways of emulating the response store, comparand, and the mask register. Depending on the design, the response store can be replaced by the concepts of tagging (i.e., marking) the memory elements (field or record) or creating result files. The comparand and mask registers are repeated in each cell processor, instead of one per entire memory, and masking can be accomplished in various ways such as counting, delimiter sensing, and so on. Now, let us look into the details of the secondary memory–based associative memory systems.

5.4.1 How to Emulate an Associative Memory (AM) Word

Using disks or drums.   As in the bit-slice structure of an AM, there must be a comparator or processor logic per cell. As indicated earlier, a cell that is typically a track corresponds to a word of AM. The bit serial iteration of the parallel AM words can be accomplished by reading in the circulating bits off the track into a processor (cell processor) and writing them back after a buffer delay. The buffer delay provides time for the cell processor to do its required functions. The associative devices using parallel cells are also referred to as cellular devices. The structure of a cell is shown in Figure 5.7.

In Figure 5.7(a), the assumption is that there must be a fixed head disk and each track must have a pair of heads, one for read and another for write, separated from each other with fine tolerances. (However, letting alone the difficulty of having pairs of heads, nowadays, fixed head disks have become a thing of the past.) Nevertheless, our discussion here is at the conceptual level. Figure 5.7(b) again assumes a fixed head disk, but this time the double head per track requirement is relaxed, and, instead, two tracks are required per cell to emulate the former. That is, while in one revolution track 1 reads and track 2 writes, in the next revolution the roles are reversed and track 2 reads and track 1 writes, and so on. In Figure 5.7(c), movable head disks with parallel readout capability are assumed. That is, in one revolution instead of a single data stream, k parallel data streams come out of the disk, one per track, k being the number of tracks per cylinder. Although in this case a cell memory is still a track, the parallelism per device is reduced from the number of tracks per disk (for (a)) or (number of tracks per disk)/2 (for (b)) to k per disk.

Using bulk RAMs or magnetic bubbles.   As the prospects of head per track disks are diminishing, the prospects of bulk RAMs or magnetic bubbles are looking bright, especially the speed of RAMs. Since these memories can be used both serially and randomly, the following modified cell structure can be constructed. Instead of circulating data, we can serially access them in blocks and bring a block into the cell processor, process it, and write it back while accessing the next block. Unlike the case with disks shown previously, we need not read and write back every bit every time. This was so with disks because of nonselectivity of data (i.e., cannot random access a disk repetitively in the

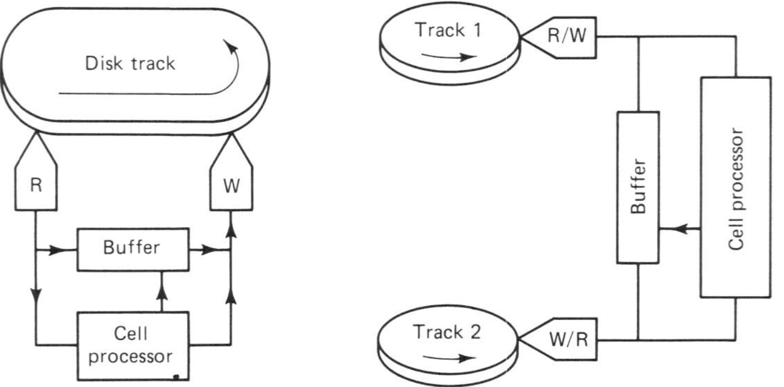

(a) A head pair per track   (b) A read/write head per track and two tracks per cell

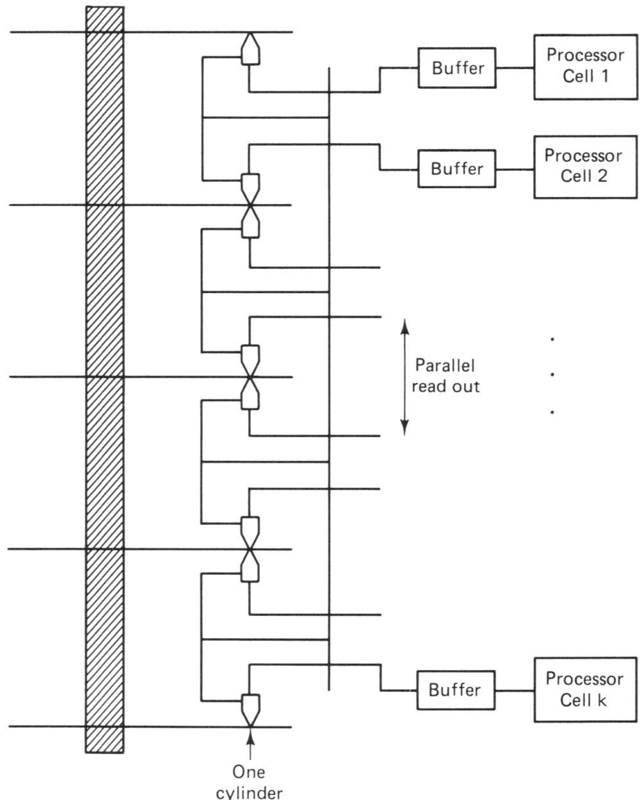

(c) Parallelism on one cylinder/disk

Figure 5.7 Disk-based cell structures.

same revolution) and because we had to write back every bit to keep in synchronization. With RAMs and bubbles, we read selective words out of memory similar to the masked portions of an AM and write back selective words or do not write at all. Figure 5.8 depicts this organization.

5.4.2 How to Structure Physical Data

Historically, data retrieval had started by the notion of providing a key or keys and retrieving those records that satisfy a predicate on the keys. This *keyed retrieval* had influenced the way in which architects designed their hardware. Figure 5.9 shows some physical storage structures that were used in the past. Figure 5.9(a) shows key data representation where keys are factored out or duplicated in front of their records as separate search blocks. Then they can be laid on tracks in the following possible ways. (1) As in Figure 5.9(c), where keys are stored separately from the data tracks. At a given angular position, all the keys are grouped for the records which are stored either at the same angular position or one after (to allow time for key processing). In this way, once the keys are evaluated the corresponding records can be immediately output. (2) Linear storage of key data streams. In this case, there must be enough gap on storage so that after key processing, the retrieval of the corresponding record will not be missed on the continuously rotating memory. As can be seen in key data organizations, the retrieval (and therefore hardware of the device) is sensitive only to the keys. That is, predicates are expected and evaluated only on the keys. In the next chapter, we will see several designs in this category. And because not 100% of data are processed but retrieved based on their portion (key), the devices of this sort are known as *partially associative* cellular devices. However, there is no reason that with the same device and hardware one could not build a device that is 100% sensitive to data and therefore fully associative. That is, speaking in terms of the old jargon, any part of data can be specified

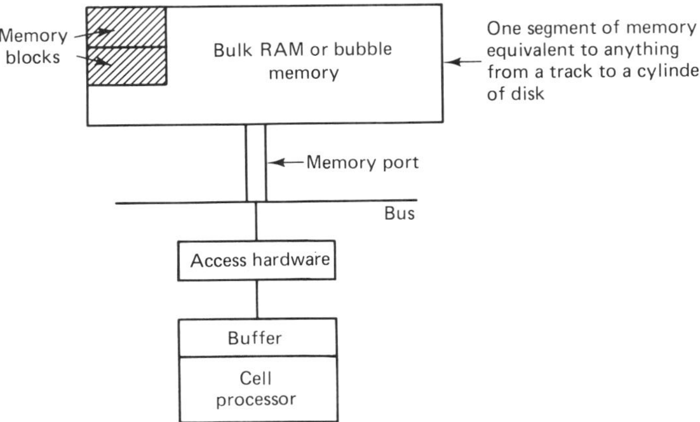

Figure 5.8 Bulk RAM or bubble-based cell structure.

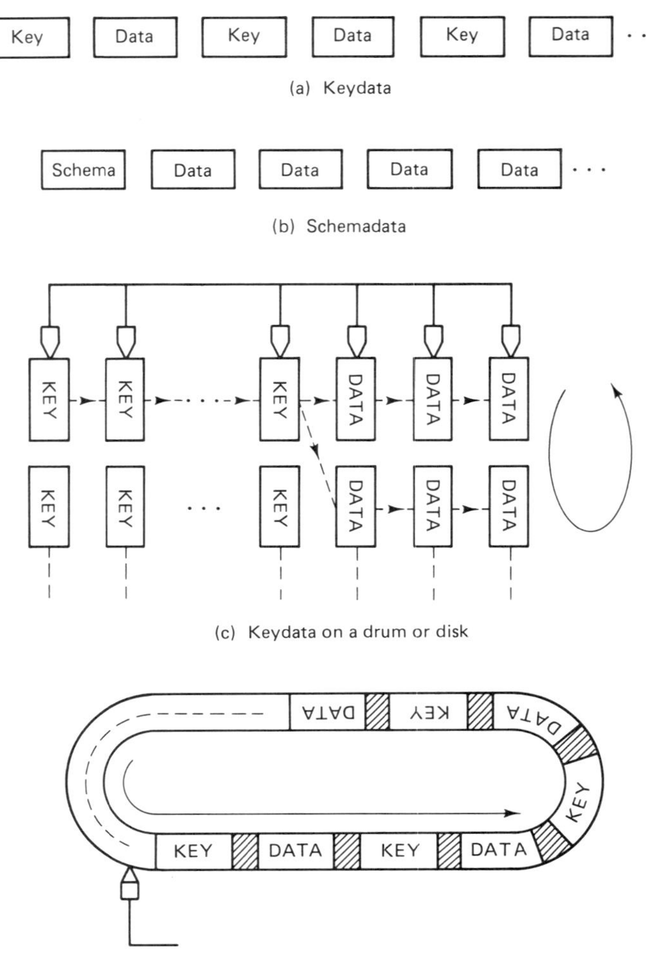

(a) Keydata

(b) Schemadata

(c) Keydata on a drum or disk

(d) Keydata on a single track of a drum or disk

Figure 5.9   Physical storage structures.

as the search key or keys. All we have to do is to use a storage structure as shown in Figure 5.9(b), which informs the cell processor, via the schema block ahead of time how the incoming data are structured. It is up to the user request at any time to specify any part of data as the search predicate. Different requests may specify different parts of data.

5.4.3 How to Process Streams of Data

In this section, we will talk about the internals of a cell. Up to now, all we knew is that several cells are used in a locked-stepped manner, as in the array processor of Chapter 4, to form a parallel (cellular) or associative/array device.

In a given cell, we will need the following basic components:

- Registers and/or buffers
- Comparators and/or adders/subtractors
- Latches and/or combinational logic to hold the results

Registers and buffers hold the query predicate and the cell memory contents while they are accessed or circulated. Comparators or subtractors compare query bit stream with the data bit stream continuously as the cell memory contents are scanned. Latches capture the result of the comparators, and combinational logic transforms the results of individual comparisons into Boolean predicate.

At this point, we need to look at the details of the physical storage structure a little more. Previously, we implicitly assumed that a data collection is stored as a file representing a record type and that record occurrences, or simply records, of the file are stored in cells for as many cells as are required. We know that the file can be searched associatively because of the parallel operation of cells and the internal structure of a cell. Before we talk about how we can process the data stream in a cell, let us indicate what we want to know about the storage structure. For a given record type, we must be provided with the following information:

- Name of the record type (file)
- Names of the attributes (fields)
- Data types of the attributes
- Length of the attributes

From this we must determine in which of the following ways we can represent this information:

(a) Encode attribute names and attribute lengths and embed them into appropriate places in the data stream. Also, use a record delimiter to indicate end of a record. This method can be briefly referred to as the delimiter approach.
(b) Factor out the common information such as the ones indicated in (a) and store it as a schema (or file template) once in the cells.

Each comparator must know when to start and how long to operate. The answer to the first question is when the attribute value is about to enter the comparator in the data stream and that of the second question is as many bit comparisons as the length of the attribute. The synchronization in these operations is established depending on the choice made for (a) or (b).

The query structures are usually represented in disjunctive normal form, that is, ORs of ANDs, which are conjunctions of simple conditions or predicates. Let us give an example based on the record type EMPLOYEE (NAME, DEPT, SALARY, AGE):

```
(DEPT = 'ENGINEERING' AND SALARY > 10K) OR (SALARY > 20K AND AGE < 35)
```

To process the query in one sweep or scan of memory, we must have at least four comparators in a cell and all the parallel cells storing the EMPLOYEE data. Generally, if k is the number of comparators in a cell and CL (criterion length) is the number of simple conditions in a query, then we need $\lceil CL/k \rceil$ many scans (revolutions) of the memory. If $k \geq CL$, then a single scan will be sufficient. Accordingly, having parallel comparators in a cell helps. However, if most of the time $k \gg CL$, then there would be waste of $(k - CL)$ comparators. They will be idle unless utilized. One possible solution is to partition k comparators into groups and assign each group to a different query. This means concurrent execution of more than one job (query) at a time. To do that, the controller and operating system of the device must be properly equipped. Figure 5.10 shows the global organization of the cell comparators.

Each comparator has a memory where the attribute value of the corresponding query predicate is stored and a bit serial comparator. As data streams through the read head, the comparator corresponding to the attribute (DEPT) is activated whenever the first bit of ENGINEERING enters the comparator bus. Activation is done by the enable line which is connected to the schema counters. No activation will take place if the attribute passing under the read head is not involved in the query Boolean predicate. As soon as a comparator is activated and data bits start entering the comparator, the attribute value (i.e., memory contents) will cause the comparator memory to circulate while the bits of it are compared with those of entering data. By the time comparison is completed, the attribute value will have been circulated back into its place as was originally found, to be ready for the same operation when the next record arrives.

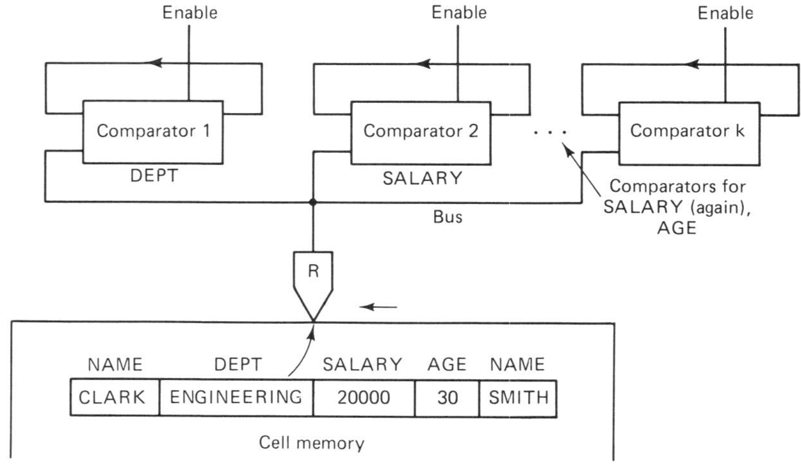

Figure 5.10 Cell comparators.

5.4.4 Potential Speed of Parallelism

To contrast the potential speed of parallelism with that of no parallelism, let us compare associative/parallel systems with a uniprocessor of the von Neumann architecture. Let us indicate the time a uniprocessor completes a comparison of an item by t_u. For an associative device, it will take time equal to t_{scan} to complete a cycle, that is, to complete the scan (revolution) of its memory. In that time, the following will happen (knowing that the following are the device parameters):

- Number of parallel cells, n
- Number of data items (records) per cell, m
- Number of comparators that are fully utilized by cell, k

Accordingly, in one scan there will be $n \times m \times k$ comparisons that have taken place by the end of the scan. From that we can find the time (effective) to make a comparison as

$$t_a = \frac{t_{scan}}{n \times m \times k}$$

Let us put some numbers into the equation:

$$\text{If } t_{scan} = 100 \text{ milliseconds}$$

$$n = 100$$

$$m = 25{,}000$$

$$k = 10$$

$$t_a = \frac{100 \times 10^{-3}}{100 \times 25000 \times 10} = \frac{1}{2.5} \times 10^{-8} = 4 \text{ nanoseconds} \rightarrow 250 \text{ MIPS}$$

which is faster than any super uniprocessor known to date. This is achieved by means of the parallelism of rather slow devices. They are slow but cheap; hence, their duplication is affordable.

At this point we conclude our brief introduction to associative memories. In the next chapter, we will see associative processors built around associative memories and survey some of the work done in that area.

EXERCISES

5.1. Write algorithms for the associative memory operations listed at the beginning of Section 5.3, excluding those whose algorithms are given in the chapter. If you need any modifications and/or additions to the basic AM structure, justify your need.

5.2. We can obtain ordered retrieval from an AM by the repeated use of the maximum or minimum operations. However, there are also sorting algorithms proposed on these memories such as the ones in references [Seeber and Lindquist, 1962; Muraszkiewicz, 1981]. Write a sorting algorithm that should be based on the simplest possible model of an AM.

5.3. Can you define cell memories other than those in the form of a disk track or cylinder? What device is your choice? Do you have any upper or lower bounds for the amount of storage a cell memory should contain, remembering the fact that for that amount of storage a cell processor must be dedicated?

5.4. As we know, not every parallel architecture is an associative architecture. What does it take, besides parallelism, for an architecture to be associative?

5.5. Discuss the relative future prospects of CAMs (i.e., AMs), RAMs, magnetic bubbles, and Bloch line memories in replacing fixed head disks to be used as bulk associative memories. What are the advantages and disadvantages of each besides the prospects for availability and marketability?

5.6. Unlike disks or drums, RAMs or magnetic bubbles can be stopped and started during their operation. What implications can this have on query processing within a cell?

5.7. As you know, the speed of cell memory impacts the overall speed of an associative device. In this regard, what types of memories offer fast speed? Can we increase that speed further by arranging memories in bit parallel fashion? What other organizations can you suggest for speed improvement?

5.8. What impact on the cell processor would the speed improvements you suggested in Exercise 5.7 have? Do you see any complications in the comparator structure? Would you rather have, as the cell processor, a microprocessor (or microprocessors) or comparand registers, latches, and comparators in your design? Discuss the relative merits of each.

6

ASSOCIATIVE PROCESSORS

6.1 INTRODUCTION

Let us first define an associative processor. An associative processor is an associative memory (AM) augmented with logic and firmware. However, as we know, there is logic in the makeup of an associative memory itself, and for this reason associative memories themselves are referred to as associative processors. Usually, however, there is more power than a simple search logic in an associative processor. As we remember from the previous chapter, parallelism for the same operation (e.g., match) is an intrinsic feature of an associative memory. This puts associative processors into the SIMD architecture class. There has been considerable amount of research on associative processors. Despite numerous proposals for large-scale associative processors, their high cost has, with a few exceptions, prevented their commercial development. Small-sized associative memories, however, have been used as subsystems in modern von Neumann machines. Associative memories are used wherever fast lookup is necessary. Cache memories, page lookup subsystems in virtual memory systems, or any other subsystem that requires fast table search can use an associative memory.

There is a classification scheme of associative processors based on their logic distribution granularity. Logic can be distributed at the bit, byte, word, or bulk memory cell level. The smaller the granularity, the higher the level of potential parallelism (if costs permit, of course). As in the previous chapter, we will group this chapter into two main sections, one dealing with systems in the AM scale and the other dealing with those associative processors in the secondary memory scale.

6.2 HIGHLY PARALLEL ASSOCIATIVE PROCESSORS

In the highly parallel associative processor category, we include the following types:

(a) Word organized AM whose parallelism is at the bit level
(b) Programmable AM systems
(c) Distributed logic memory systems

Word parallel–bit parallel associative memories belong to the first category. In such a highly parallel system, an entire memory search is completed within one bit comparison time. This amount of parallelism is very costly to implement; consequently only some earlier studies [Slade and McMahon, 1956; Yang and Yao, 1966] have considered them.

Programmable associative memory systems are exemplified by Kautz's [1971] augmented content addressed memory called ACAM. ACAM was a two-dimensional array of programmable bits having arithmetic capability. Each ACAM bit had about 40 NOR gate equivalent logic, which was about four times more crowded (and powerful!) than the previously known highly parallel systems. The bits were activated by the combination of row and column signals. In the horizontal direction, the array could be programmed for shifting, I/O, and equality search, whereas in the column direction word-level I/O and other operations were performable. ACAM required complex control and high pin count if it were to be cast in silicon.

Distributed logic memory (DLM) design by Lee [Lee and Paul, 1963] is another example of a high degree of logic distribution relative to associative memory elements. An element here is a small processor called a cell that can store and process a single character represented in the form of an *attribute name (label)-value* pair. Lee's DLM is particularly suitable for processing variable-length data since there is no restriction on the use of cells. For this reason, the proposed architecture was intended for information retrieval. In Figure 6.1 we see the DLM architecture.

The string of cells that operates in parallel under the control of common signals provides associativity. There is no limit to the length and place of text strings that can be stored in DLM. DLM cells can be loaded with data, required cells can output their data held in the S register, and they can compare data and change states and send signals to their neighbors. A cell contains a data register, S, comparison logic, and M and C registers. The M and C registers can be marked for the match indication and conditional marking, respectively, so that I/O with the cells can be localized. When the match signal comes on, the cells compare their contents with that of input. If a match occurs, the cell sends a signal to the neighboring cell and causes it to be active. When a cell is active and the propagation signal is received, the cell turns its neighbor on and then

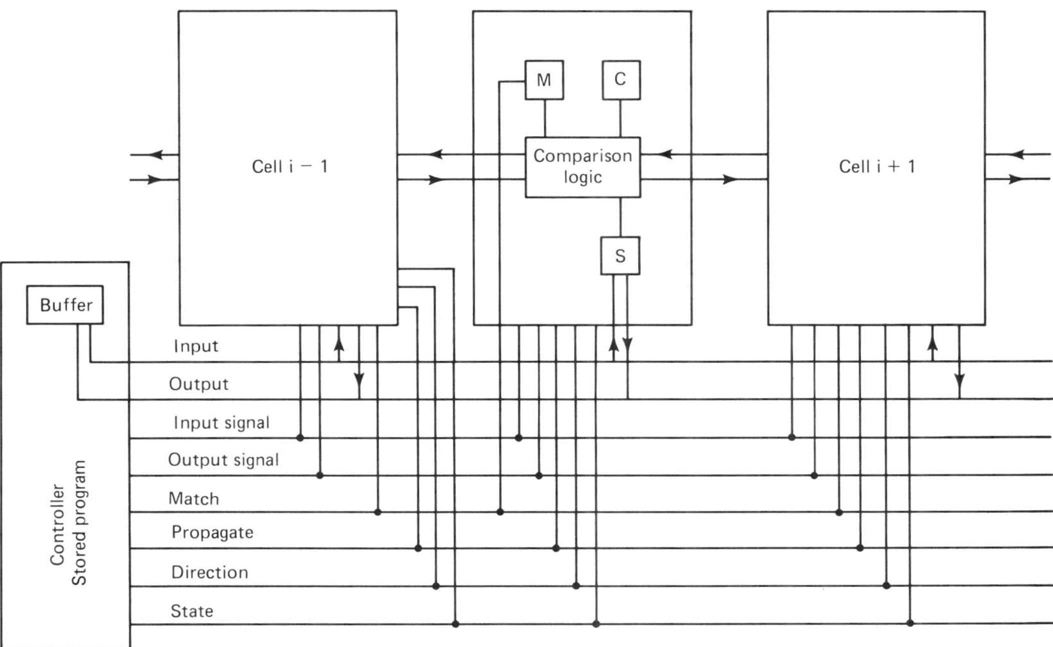

Figure 6.1   Lee and Paul's distributed logic memory.

turns itself off. The direction signal controls the direction of propagation to right or left. In a search operation, first the labels are located and then values are matched character at a time down the string of cells as comparisons continue and matching cells activate their neighbors. In searching, one can provide the label and retrieve values (parameters) corresponding to it, or vice versa. Required operations are programmed in terms of DLM instructions and stored in the controller. An instruction has *<opcode>* [*<predicate>*] format. In the optional predicate part, the settings of C and M registers are specified, as shown here:

```
MATCH A (C = 1) (sets M bit only in those cells whose C register is marked)
MATCH A (affects unconditionally all the cells)
```

A propagation step is executed as follows:

$$
\begin{cases}
\text{C} \leftarrow 0 \text{ (clear all Cs)} \\
\text{RIGHTC} \leftarrow 1 \text{ (M=1)} \text{ (marks the C register in the cell to the right of every cell whose M} \\
\qquad\qquad\qquad\qquad\qquad \text{register is marked, as a result of a match)} \\
\text{M} \leftarrow 0 \text{ (clear all Ms)}
\end{cases}
$$

If we make these three instructions a macro to be called MARKRIGHTC, the following program will show us a retrieval example.

Example 6.1

According to the data structure of DLM, the cells will be stored with consecutive label-value pairs such as #HE$300#YOU$050#HIS$120#, where # and $ are delimiters. When stored in the DLM, this string will occupy 24 cells. Let us search for the key (label) HIS and retrieve the corresponding data. Let us show the cell string and M and C registers to trace the following program written for this example:

```
                 MATCH #              /* Mark beginning of all labels; M is
                                         set */
                 MARKRIGHTC           /* Macro to clear C, then mark C = 1
                                         in those cells with M = 1 then clear
                                         M. The first character of labels is
                                         marked */
                 MATCH H (C = 1)      /* Search for H in enabled cells */
                 MARKRIGHTC           /* Enable neighbor */
                 MATCH I (C = 1)
                 MARKRIGHTC
                 MATCH S (C = 1)
                 MARKRIGHTC
                 MATCH $ (C = 1)
                 MARKRIGHTC           /* Enable beginning of data */
RETRIEVE:        READ (C = 1)         /* Read one character */
                 If # then go to END
                 M <- 1 (C = 1)       /* Set M to be able to use macro */
                 MARKRIGHT C          /* Enable next character */
                 go to RETRIEVE
END:             stop
```

In the instruction repertoire of DML, there are also WRITE counterparts of READ and LEFTC and LEFTM as counterparts of RIGHTC and RIGHTM, respectively.

DLM is a pioneering design in demonstrating the use of associative memories for applications. Considering the very large sizes of text databases, a linear associative solution such as DLM is cost and space prohibitive. Besides, its search speed would be insufficient to process very large databases. Storage garbage collection would be nontrivial, since to locate garbage and holes, some tracking mechanism must be devised. There have been several studies to enhance DLM design and/or to add arithmetic capability to cells. DLM has nevertheless inspired several systems that were built commercially (e.g., PEPE, and Hughes Aircraft Co.'s associative linear array processor, ALAP). In Chapter 13, we will survey more recent designs, some of which can be considered modern versions of DLM.

6.3 WORD-ORGANIZED ASSOCIATIVE PROCESSORS

The word-organized associative processor architecture is based on parallelism at the word level, and in the most common configuration, processing is carried

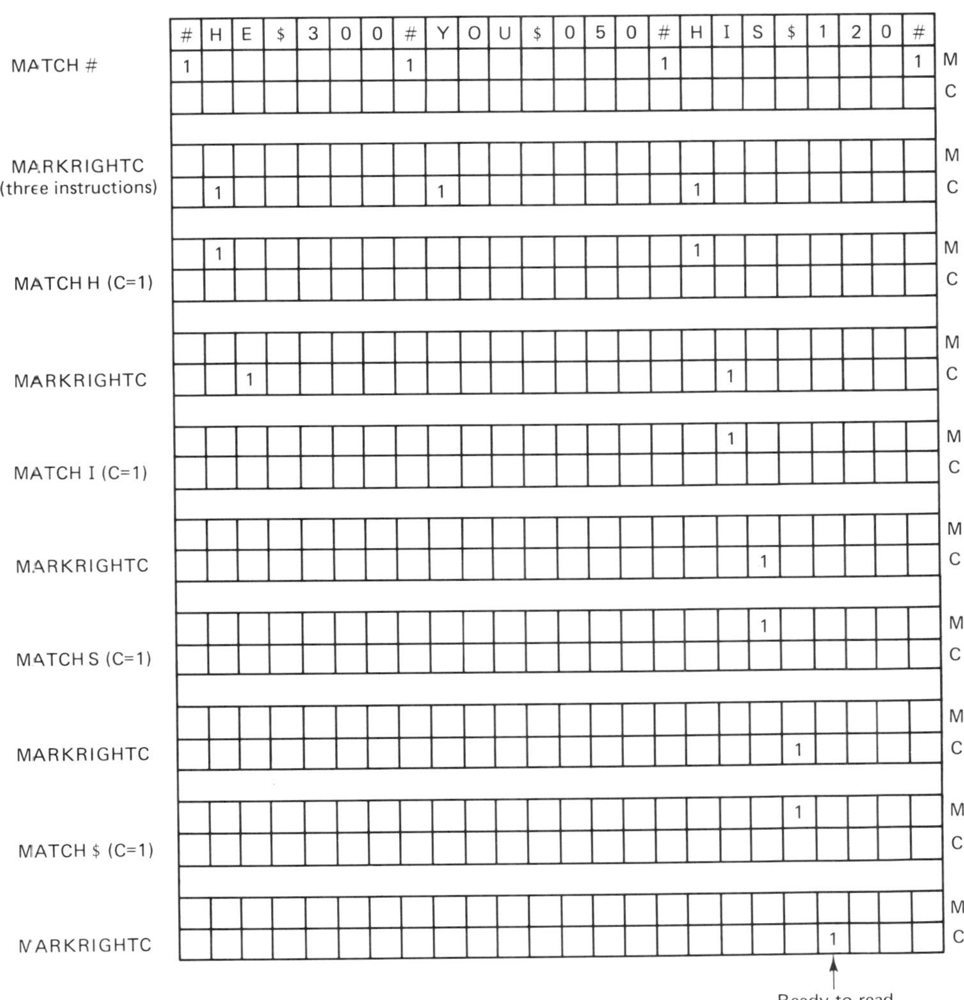

out bit serially within the words. The parallel words form the associative array or AM of the word-organized associative processor. Accordingly, there is one processing element per word so that a bit slice within the associative memory array can be operated upon in parallel. In what follows, we will first review the generic or common features of the word-organized associative processors and then describe some existing implementations of such systems.

6.3.1 Basic Structure

The basic structure of a word-organized associative processor consists of the following subsystems:

(a) AM array (associative memory array)
(b) Comparand register
(c) Mask register
(d) Response store registers
(e) Array input/output registers or buffer
(f) Word output mask/buffer
(g) Interconnection network
(h) Controller (programs and memory)

Figure 6.2 shows these components. As can be seen, this structure is similar to the basic model of an AM we discussed in the previous chapter. However, as we will see in the following, there are additional functions and facilities in the structure of an associative processor. Let us cover the items of the list (a) through (h).

Associative memory array.　　This array consists of m parallel words of n bits each. In nonnumeric processing, such a storage of an $m \times n$ matrix has

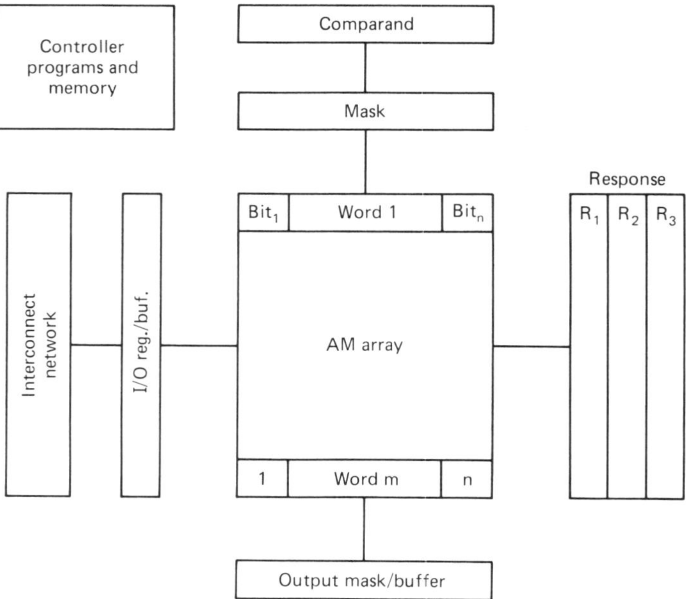

Figure 6.2　Basic structure of a word-organized associative processor.

been a suitable medium for mapping two-dimensional logical structures such as matrices, files, and relations. Each row of a matrix, each record of a file, or each tuple of a relation corresponds to a word of the array. Although overflowing of such structures into the following words is allowed, a typical characteristic of these systems is that one array word is dedicated to a single row, record, or tuple of their corresponding structures. There are several reasons for this. One is physical implementation limitations on the length of words. After a certain length, noise problems develop in hardware. Another reason is that search hardware peripheral to the AM array can handle a single search at a time unless expensive duplication is introduced. A recent exception to this, in database processing, is the Lucas system which we will see later in this chapter. In that system attributes or fields from more than one relation or file can be stored together within a word so that binary relational algebra operations can be performed on them. This may require, however, additional tuple or record construction time because the limited length of an array word may not accommodate full records. This may necessitate additional I/O from the mass storage device for providing the remainder of the tuples or records determined to be eligible in a search or database operation performed in the array.

Another characteristic of these processors is that since operations are carried out bit slice at a time serially in the words, reasonable memory access and write times are required. This in turn implies the selection of static RAMs, as opposed to slower but larger dynamic RAMs, as the storage technology. Word lengths of 256, 1024, and finally 4096 bits agree with this storage technology. (As we will see in the subsequent chapters, one cell of a RAP.3 database machine has 2 megabytes of bulk RAM storage. A cell in cellular devices corresponds to a word of these associative processors.) This order of lateral dimension in the word organized associative processors requires a vertical dimension or word parallelism directly equal to the cardinality (e.g., number of records or tuples of a file or relation) of the structure stored in them. Doing a join between two relations, each containing 100,000 tuples, would require an associative processor having 200,000 words in parallel in the AM array (100,000 in Lucas). A machine of this size has never been built or proposed until the time of writing this book!

Comparand register.   Different combinations of search operations can be done on the AM array. That is, we can compare an external value to all the AM words; we can compare two fields with each other in all the words, or we can compare a field of a selected word with the fields of all the words. In all these cases, however, the comparand must first be brought into the comparand register to make a broadcast type (or SIMD type) comparison where this one value is compared with many values in parallel. In the case of a parallel comparison of two fields in all the words, there is a parallelism of a different type and the most efficient way of doing that is to do a logical and/or subtraction operation between two fields in each word so that the end result equivalently produces the result of the comparison. In this way, although data (i.e., comparands) will be different in each word, the operation will be carried out in parallel bit slice at a time. The length of the comparand register matches that of an AM word. In the typical comparison mode the bit positions in comparand, mask, and AM words match each other. (This could be a restriction in certain old implementations.) However, this is not necessarily the case, for one can direct a certain field of the comparand to be compared with a field in different location in the AM words.

Mask register.   The mask register can be considered a simple filter or a selector of the comparand register bits. The designation of a field in the comparand register as a comparand is made via the mask register. Those bit positions outside the designated comparand are masked out (i.e., set to binary 0), whereas those in the comparand area are set to binary 1.

Response store registers.   Usually, the response store registers are a set of 1-bit flip flops resulting in one bit wide vectors along the AM array. One of these registers is referred to as the tag or response bit, which indicates or holds the result of an operation on the array. A tagged AM word, or in other words an AM word whose tag or response register is set to 1, usually indicates a success of a search or holds the result of a logic operation (such as the carry of an addition step). The second flip flop or response store bit is used as a temporary work space or scratch bit area for the operations of various data manipulation or logic functions. The third response store bit is a word select bit. It indicates whether the corresponding AM word is relevant or taking place in the operation to be performed. If, for example, we stored files A and B in the AM array, and we want to do an operation on one of the files, then we have to deselect (make 0) the word select bits corresponding to those AM words that store the other file.

Array input/output registers or buffer.   These registers play the role of a buffer while shifting data in or out of the AM array. The data activity can be localized to a single word, or it can be generalized to the entire array. The latter is usually the case when loading and unloading the AM array. The main idea in this case is to do this activity as fast as possible. This is because, owing to the relatively small size of the AM with respect to data to be processed, such activity will occur quite frequently and each time the AM array should not be idled for long periods of time waiting for the data to be paged in and out. Special I/O interfaces such as a fixed head disk or drum where each head, therefore track, of such a device is dedicated to one word of AM have been implemented. Considering an AM array of 256 words, this interface will provide an I/O path of 256 parallel bit streams, which compared to a standard byte serial I/O channel will have (256/8 =) 32 times more I/O bandwidth.

Word output mask buffer.   This buffer is used for output in word serial mode of AM contents. The masking capability will enable field selective retrieval using the same principle of the mask register.

Interconnection network.   The interconnection network in this class of associative processors is used to realize various logical proximity combinations among fields or bits of various fields in the physical medium so that the required operations can take place. Looking at it differently, we can say that the interconnection network emulates more complex processor interconnection patterns on a two-dimensional AM array. For example, in image and/or geometric processing we may be interested in operating upon grid structures where a four-neighbor connection pattern is needed. We may need a perfect shuffle network for sorting, polynomial evaluation, and so on. In the Staran system we will see in this chapter, a cubic interconnection scheme is used. In the perfect shuffle if the processors are numbered from p_0 to p_{n-1} and a processor's position corresponds to the binary pattern of $p_{n-1}p_{n-2} \cdots p_2p_1p_0$, then its perfect shuffle interconnection will be to the processor $p_{n-2} \cdots p_2p_1p_0 \; p_{n-1}$. In other words, the shuffle is equivalent to one circular left shift of the binary pattern of the processor [Batcher, 1968]. Accordingly, a pattern (0 1 2 3 4 5 6 7) corresponding to eight processors when shuffled once will correspond to (0 2 4 6 1 3 5 7), meaning that processors 2 and 4 will be connected to processors 4 and 1, respectively (because 010 and 100 became 100 and 001 after the shift).

The cubic interconnection scheme [Siegel, 1979], whose three-dimensional cube structure for eight processors is given in Figure 6.3, has capabilities to process applications such as multidimensional image processing. For example, to smooth an image the point (i, j) of an image must be replaced with the average value of the point itself and eight surrounding points, which are $(i - 1, j)$, $(i - 1, j - 1)$, $(i, j - 1)$, $(i + 1, j)$, $(i + 1, j + 1)$, $(i, j + 1)$, $(i - 1, j + 1)$, and $(i + 1, j - 1)$. For a 2^k-by-2^k image, 2^{2k} averages must be computed. It will take that many iterations of the average computation for a uniprocessor. However, if we had an associative processor of $m = 2^n$ processors, the image can be partitioned into a $\sqrt{m} \times \sqrt{m}$ array of subimages of size $2^k/\sqrt{m}$ by $2^k/\sqrt{m}$. All m subimages can be smoothed in parallel, decreasing the number of average computation iterations to $2^{2k}/m$.

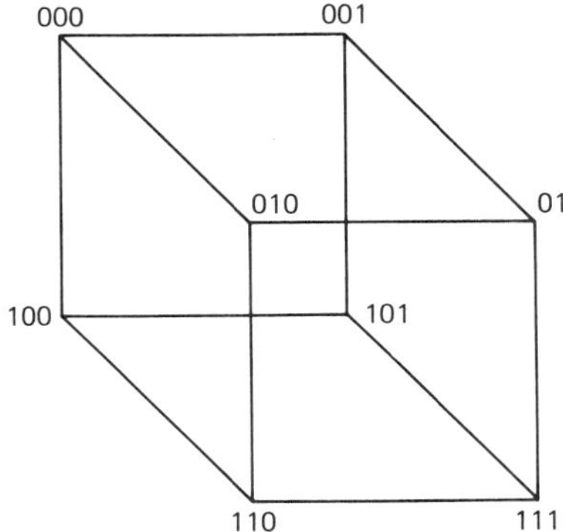

Figure 6.3 A three-dimensional cube structure of eight processors.

Controller.　　The controller is the driver of the AM array and its peripheral circuits discussed so far.　A user's request is translated into basic associative processor primitives in the host processor and sent to the controller.　The controller contains storage for the programs of the basic primitives and various registers, bus logic, interrupt mechanisms, and arithmetic/logic unit for address calculation and data shifting.　Every specific design has its special configuration of the controller, and we will defer further discussion on this functional unit to the sections dealing with those systems.

6.3.2 Basic Operations

As we have seen so far, bit slice is a basic construct in the word-organized associative processor.　There are operations that read or write a bit slice, transfer the contents of it to another bit slice location, and perform an operation on a bit slice.　At this point, we would like to borrow the operational syntax and accompanying examples from the Lucas system, which will be reviewed in the next section, for selected operations that describe the word-organized associative processors.

Load bit slice.　　This is an operation that transfers data between the response store and the AM.　Let us use the following notation:

R: word select flip flop of response store

T: tag flip flop of response store

S: source location

D: destination location

```
(a)  LOAD R        /* load R bit slice (vector) */
(b)  LOAD R [T]    /* load selected (by tag bit) R bits */
(c)  LOAD T [T]    /* load tag bits selected by previous value of the
                      tag bits */
```

Figure 6.4 presents an example for the operation of (b).

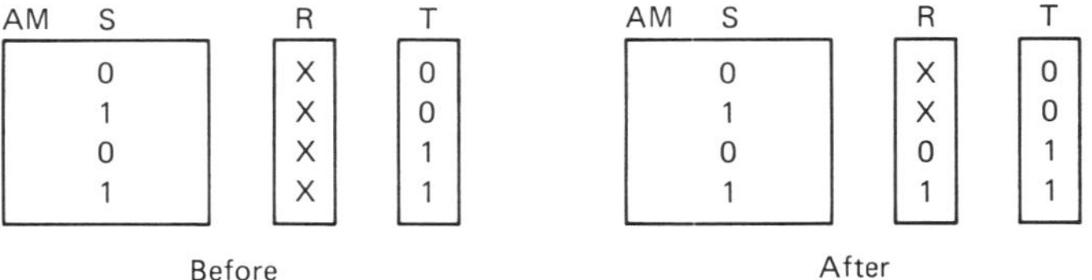

Before　　　　　　　　　　　　　　　　　After

Figure 6.4　LOAD R [T].

Store bit slice.　　This operation is the opposite of the load bit slice operation. Figure 6.5 shows an example for STORE R.

In both load bit slice and store bit slice, the location of source (S) and destination (D) are supplied by the controller.

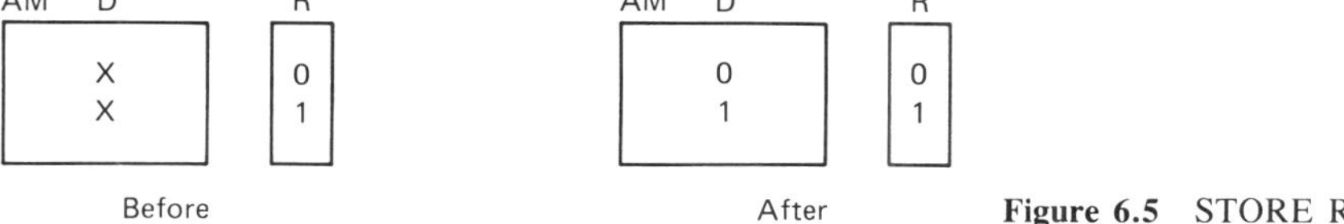

Before   After   **Figure 6.5**   STORE R.

Move bit slice.   This operation moves the contents of one bit slice to another. To do this, the word response store flip flops and therefore the load and store operations must be used. Figure 6.6 shows the effect of MOVE BITSLICE.

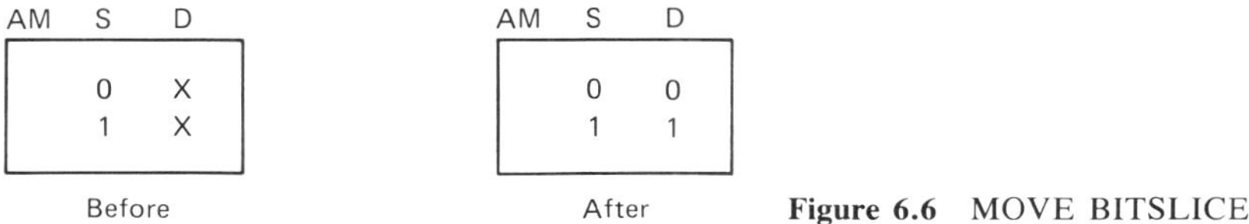

Before   After   **Figure 6.6**   MOVE BITSLICE.

Logical operations on bit slices.   In this case, two bit slices are operated upon with a logical operation, and the result is placed into another bit slice location. Again the media will be the response store flip flops so that each operation will load one of the operands in one of them, perform the logical operation between a bit slice and the response store vector, and store the result that replaced the response store vector from the vector into the result bit slice. The logical operation can be any Boolean function definable between two variables. Figure 6.7 demonstrates XOR [T].

Select first and reset.   Usually there will be more than one responder to an operation in these architectures. This is because parallelism produces a set as a result of an operation. However, certain operations of sequential nature, such as those of the cursory mode, will deal with one result at a time; they will remove the first result from the result vector and move to the next one and so on. SELECT FIRST (or GET FIRST) and RESET perform the related actions of this operation. In the tag vector, the first word with a one is located, the word address is saved, and tag bit is reset.

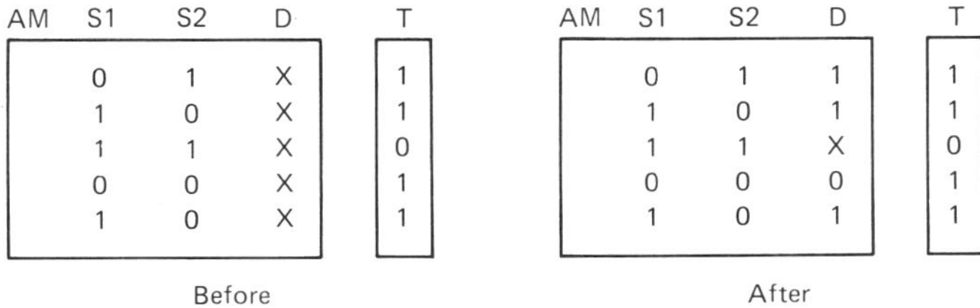

Before   After

Figure 6.7   XOR [T].

Byte operations. Byte operations are similar to the bit operations and in fact they are executed as iterations of the bit operations. In the byte operations, I/O with the I/O register and the external common register is also performed. Assuming that a one byte register corresponds to each word of AM, Figure 6.8 demonstrates the STORE and LOAD I/O operations.

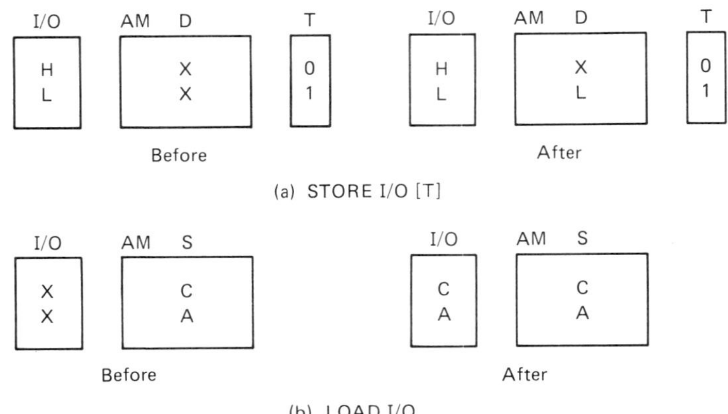

Figure 6.8 LOAD and STORE I/O operations.

Usually, the controller unit has a common register that can exchange data with the I/O registers of the AM array. Because there is only one register, the load operation on it directed from the array has the implicit select first and reset with it. Figure 6.9 demonstrates a LOAD COM operation between the AM array and the common register (COM).

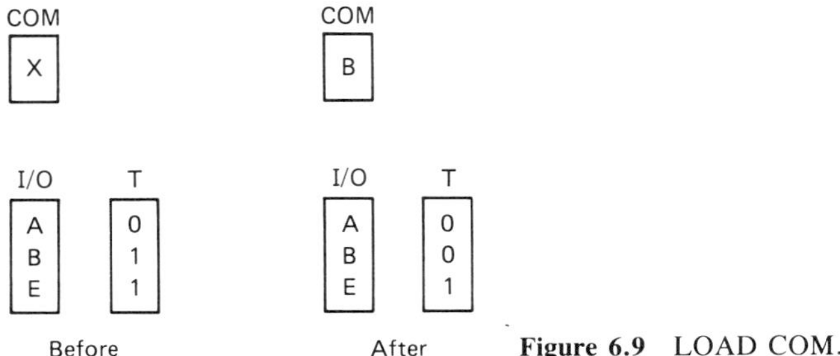

In the opposite direction of this operation, the single content of the common register is broadcast to all the I/O registers. Figure 6.10 demonstrates a SPREAD COM operation.

There are operations also to move data between comparand and mask registers and their associated I/O buffers. Figure 6.11 demonstrates a LOAD COMPARAND operation.

Also, similar to bit slice operations, a byte slice can be moved to a destination as in MOVE BYTESLICE [T].

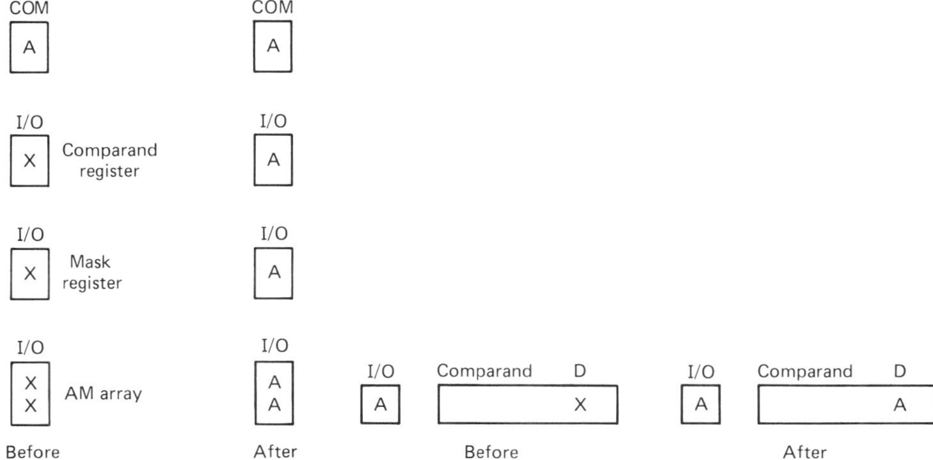

Figure 6.10 SPREAD COM.   **Figure 6.11** LOAD COMPARAND.

We can also transfer contents of the comparand register to the AM array. For example, Figure 6.12 shows a STORE CBYTE [T] operation.

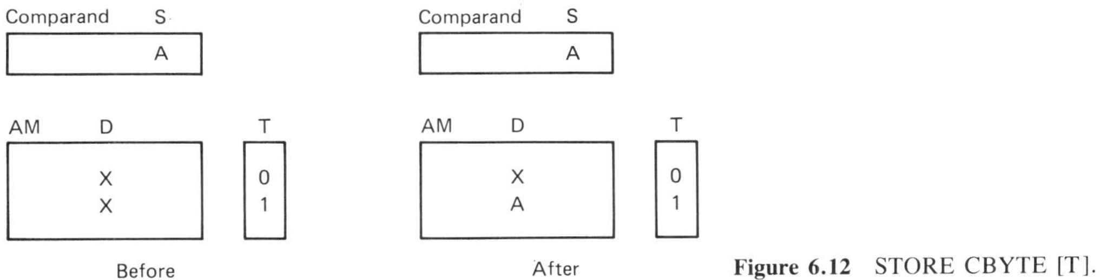

Figure 6.12 STORE CBYTE [T].

We can use the spread operation also for broadcasting a field from an AM word to all the other words. Figure 6.13 demonstrates a SPREAD BYTE operation. As can be seen, this operation is implemented in terms of the previously defined ones. (That is, LOAD I/O, LOAD COM, SPREAD COM, and STORE I/O; tag qualification comes into play during LOAD COM.)

There is also the reverse path of the data transfer between the comparand register and the AM array. Figure 6.14 demonstrates a LOAD CBYTE operation.

Field operations.   Just as byte slices can be moved, fields within AM words can also be moved. Figure 6.15 demonstrates a MOVE FIELD operation, where a bit slice in the AM array is used as the qualifier tag vector for the source and another bit slice serves as the qualifier tag vector for the destination (SM and DM bit slices, respectively).

Similar to the byte operation, fields can also be transferred between the

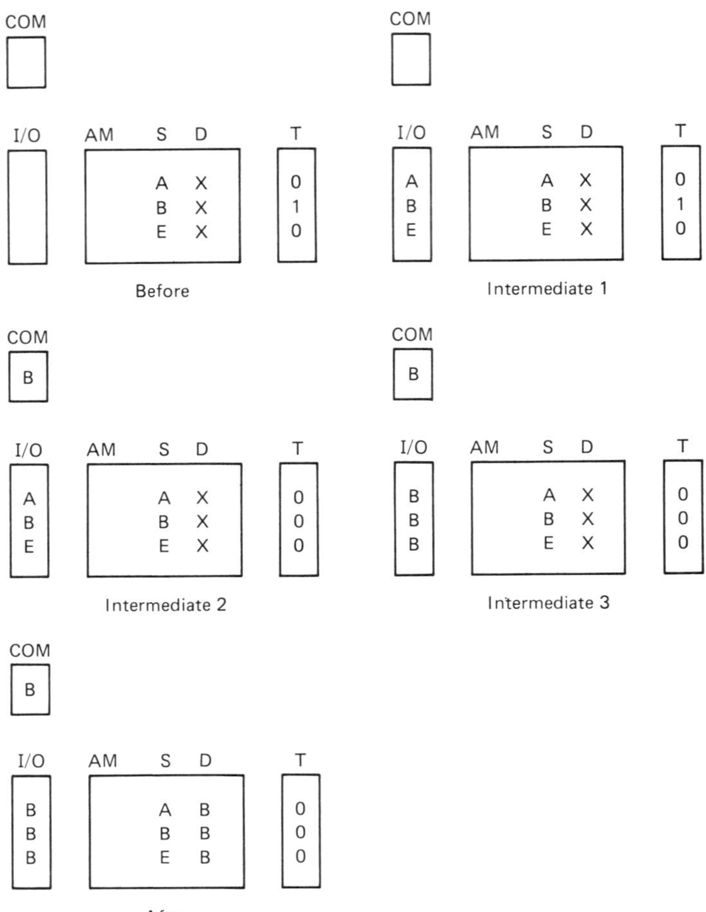

Figure 6.13   SPREAD BYTE.

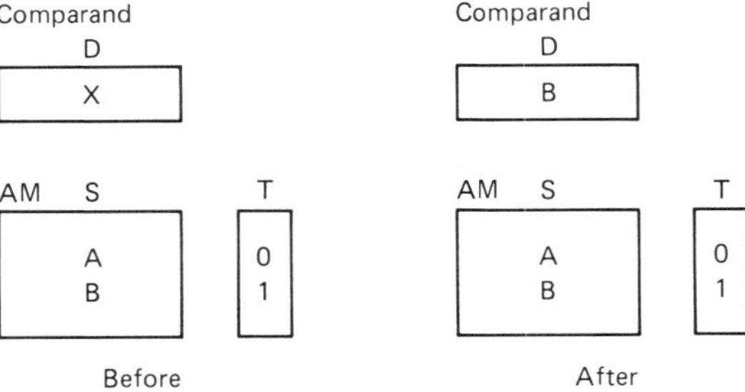

Figure 6.14   LOAD CBYTE.

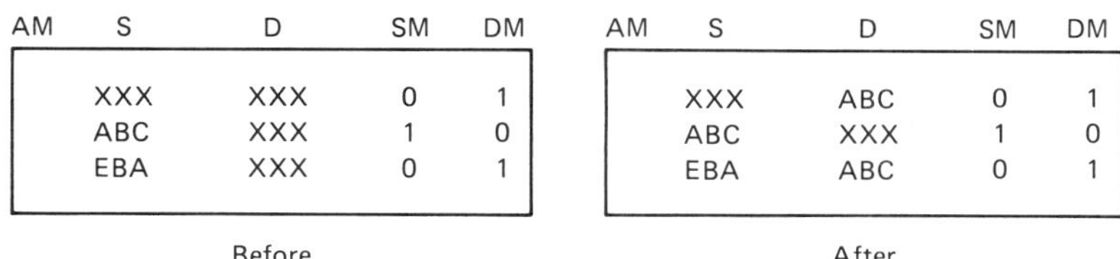

Figure 6.15   MOVE FIELD.

comparand register and the AM array. Figure 6.16 demonstrates LOAD CFIELD and STORE CFIELD operations.

In search operations that involve the AM array, the system operates like a standard AM. Either the field to be compared in the AM array can be specified by the mask register, or the controller addressing mechanism can generate sequences of bit slice addresses for the field to be compared. The results of the comparison are marked in the T vector.

6.3.3 Lucas Associative Processor

The Lucas associative processor has resulted from various research at the Lund University [Fernstrom, 1983; Kruzela, 1983; Svensson, 1983]. Because it represents a most recent word-organized processor design, we will start with the discussion of Lucas.

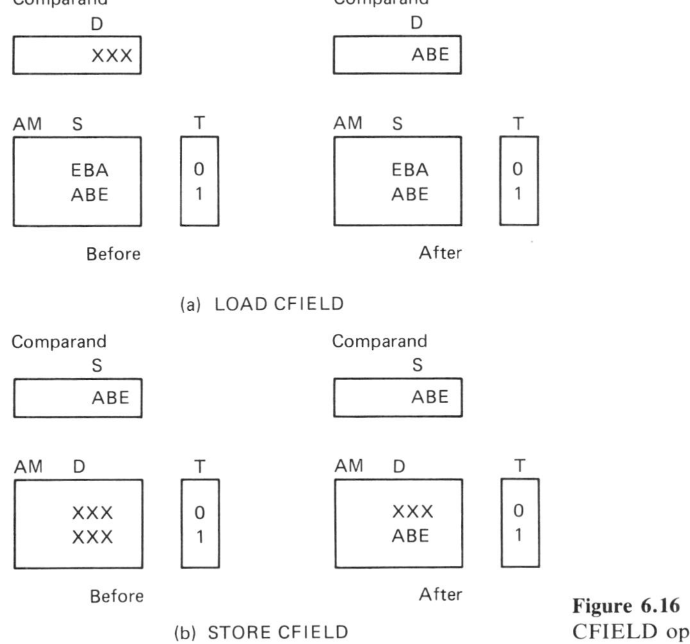

Figure 6.16   LOAD and STORE CFIELD operations.

The basic architecture of Lucas consists of a frontend host (support) computer, a control unit, and the associative array. The host computer and controller share a common memory space to speed the necessary communications. The associative array consists of 128 words (processors) of 4,096 bits each. The controller's organization is shown in Figure 6.17.

The interface in Figure 6.17 provides data, address and control signal transfer between the host computer, the controller unit, and the associative memory array.

The microprogram control unit contains microprogram memory and a microprogram control microprocessor. Microinstructions are 80-bit wide and drive horizontal microprogram execution. The microprogram memory has 4096 words and a cycle time of 55 nanoseconds. There are about 18 horizontal control fields of a microinstruction that control various operations in the system as well as the operations of the AM array.

The address processor contains an ALU and provides bit slice addresses for operations that take place on the AM array. In addition, the address processor maintains and monitors addresses, operand lengths, and loop counts, which are needed for the microprogram controller and the AM array.

The comparand and mask registers are part of the control unit. They are read and written bit serially. Their I/O is controlled by the microprogram control unit. A comparand bit drives all the AM words in the multiwrite operation. If a mask register bit contains a zero, that bit inhibits operations on the corresponding bit slice by inhibiting the test selector in the microprogram control unit.

The associative array and one processing element (PE) structure are shown

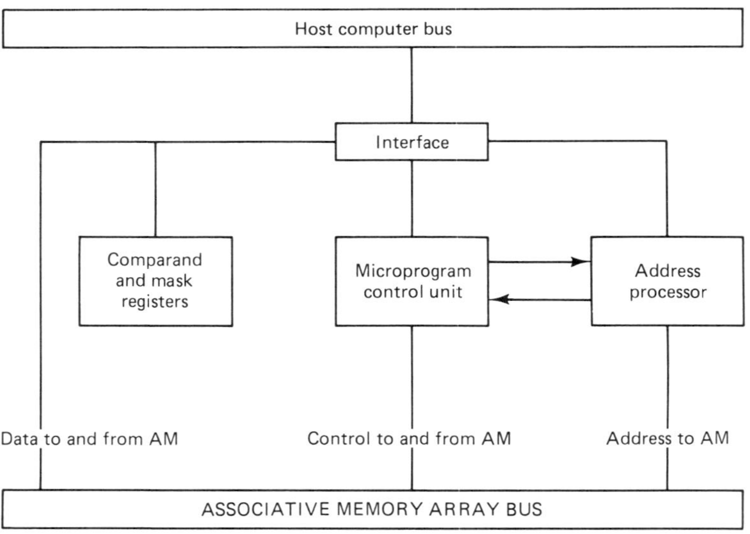

Figure 6.17 Control unit of Lucas.

in Figure 6.18. In Figure 6.18(a), we see the common I/O buffer register (IOB) and 8-bit wide I/O registers for each of comparand, mask registers, and AM words. Each AM array word has a corresponding processing element. The processing elements work bit serially and contain four flip-flops that serve such purposes as tag register, intermediate register, word select register, and so on.

The PEs are connected to the interconnection network (ICN), which provides uniform and parallel connections and exchange of information. The connection patterns of ICN are for SIMD mode of processing and controlled by the micro-program control unit. ICN sits between 128-bit wide bus (1 bit per AM word)

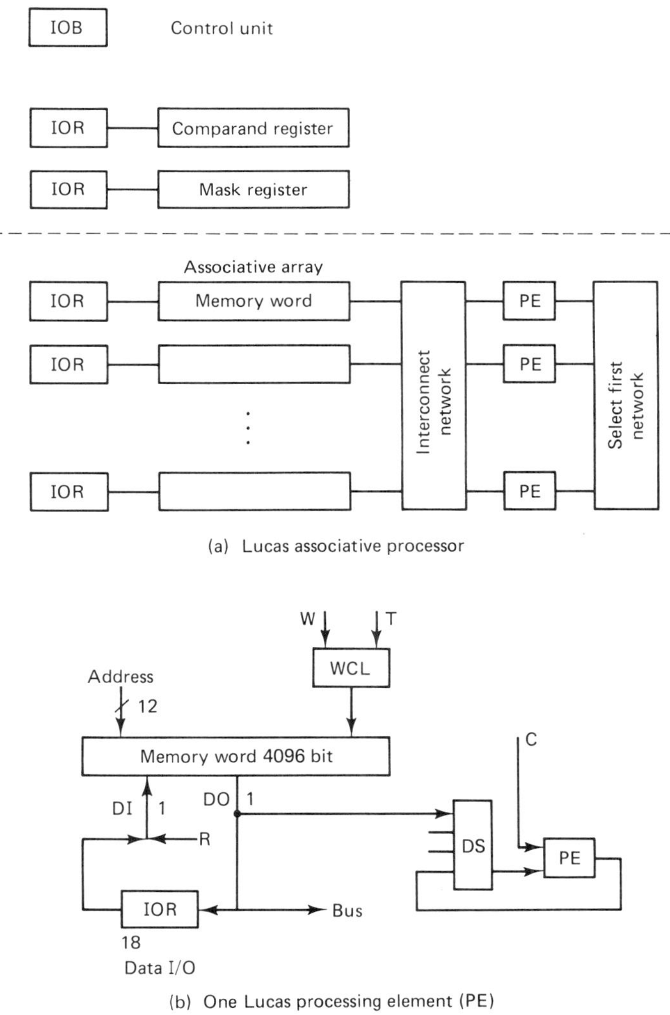

(a) Lucas associative processor

(b) One Lucas processing element (PE)

Figure 6.18 Structure of the Lucas associative processor.

and data selectors. In fact, the bus and the selectors are considered part of the ICN. The basic connection patterns of ICN are (1) with the AM word of the PE, (2) with the X flip flop of the PE, (3) with a bit from another AM word, (4) grid connection (north, south), and (5) perfect shuffle connection (not implemented).

In each PE one bit operation takes place at a time. The operation is carried out among the bit slice bit of the AM, a PE flip flop, or a bit of the comparand register. A PE contains an ALU, which is driven by a PROM. The PE also contains the T (tag) bit writing and select first logic.

The I/O registers are memory mapped directly from the host computer. The data read from an AM word can either go to the host computer or the comparand register.

According to Figure 6.18(b), the address processor supplies a 12-bit bit slice address to the AM word so that bits can be shifted (via DI) from or to the I/O register. The data paths shown with DI are also suppliable by the R flip flop of the PE, besides the I/O REGISTER. This means that we can read/write data between an AM bit slice and PE flip flops. Writing into an AM word is controlled by WCL (write control logic). The inputs to WCL are the microword fields and the tag (T) flip flop of the PE. There are two types of write operations directed into an AM word:

(a) Write all: the bit at the input is written onto the AM word independently of the T bit. This results in a multiwrite operation at a bit slice among all AM words.
(b) Write depending if T is set.

The output of data read from an AM bit slice (via DO) can go to I/O register (which can in turn go to the comparand register or the host computer), to the 128-bit bus which is part of ICN, or to the data selector which is also part of ICN.

Lucas does not possess a data language; however, it provides various arithmetic and logic function capabilities (32 of them) and also the basic primitives we have discussed in the previous section. With those basic capabilities, procedures have been defined for carrying out relational algebra operations on Lucas [Kruzela, 1983]. Before we discuss some of these operations, let us review the storage structure of Lucas. Figure 6.19 shows a storage scheme in Lucas. The Lucas associative memory supports the domain-based schema of relations. In addition to the hardware tag (T) bit in the PE, which is one per word in the array, in Lucas one can declare a soft or logical work field per file or relation and one bit slice of that 1-byte wide field is used as the mark bit slice. However, before operating on a relation, its mark bit slice must be transferred to the T vector. In Figure 6.19, we see that attributes of relations can be intermixed and that the mark bit slice corresponding to each relation indicates (by the set bits) which subset of the data stored in the AM array corresponds to a particular relation.

Relations		Attributes						
S:	SA1	SA2	SA3		SA4	SWF		
T:	TA1	TA2	TA3	TA4			TWF	
Q:	QA1	QA2	QA3		QA4			QWF
R:					RA1			RWF

AM

	S1	SMITH	20	LONDON	1	1	0	1
	S2	JONES	10	PARIS	1	1	1	1
	S3	BLAKE	30	PARIS	1	1	1	0
	S4	CLARK	20	LONDON	1	1	0	0
	S5	ADAMS	30	TUCSON	1	1	0	1

Figure 6.19   Four relations in the Lucas AM.

The TA4 attribute consists of only the first three letters of the city names. SWF, TWF, QWF, and RWF are work fields corresponding to their respective relations. The R relation is the projection of S over its fourth attribute, whereas Q is S restricted on its fourth attribute such that it is equal to PARIS. As can be seen, the address processor and the rest of the control functions need to keep track of these details of the schemas. In what follows, we will review some of the algorithms defined on Lucas for processing relational algebra operations.

Selection.   The operation here involves a typical AM array search for a match operation with respect to the argument placed in the comparand array. Some details, as can be followed from Figure 6.20, which demonstrates a selection example, are (1) the mark bit slice must first be transferred into the hardware T vector; (2) a separate work field must be reserved to indicate the result of selection in its mark bit slice; (3) for the latter to take place, the proper data path must be followed; that is, the T vector must be transferred into the R vector and then the R vector must be stored at the result mark bit slice (RWF) as indicated by the address processor.

Intersection.   In this operation, the mark bit slice of the result work field is cleared to zeros. The mark bit slice of the first relation is copied into a scratch

Comparand

LONDON

AM		A	AMF	RWF
	XXXXX	XXXXXX	0	X
	SMITH	LONDON	1	X
	JONES	PARIS	1	X
	BLAKE	PARIS	1	X
	CLARK	LONDON	1	X
	ADAMS	TUCSON	1	X

Before

Comparand

LONDON

AM		A	AWF	RWF
	XXXXX	XXXXXX	0	0
	SMITH	LONDON	1	1
	JONES	PARIS	1	0
	BLAKE	PARIS	1	0
	CLARK	LONDON	1	1
	ADAMS	TUCSON	1	0

After

Figure 6.20   Selection of tuples that have city equal LONDON.

bit in its work field. (This is done to save the mark bit slice of the first relation because the result of a select first and remove resets the top bit in the mark bit slice and leaves in T only the bit being processed as 1 and the others are cleared to zeros.) The operation is then performed in a loop where the number of iterations of this loop is equal to the number of tuples in the first relation. Each time in the loop, select first and reset is executed for the first relation which leaves in T the 1 bit corresponding to the first unprocessed tuple. This information in T is also copied into the R register. The position in R and T corresponds to the selected tuple from the first relation. This tuple is transferred into the comparand register and is compared in parallel (bit slice at a time) to all the tuples of the second relation. If, after the comparison, all tags of the second relation are reset, the loop goes on to the next tuple in the first relation; otherwise, the position of the selected tuple that was in the R vector is OR'ed with the result mark bit slice. We should notice here that before the comparison with the second relation takes place, we copy the mark bit slice of the second relation into the T vector so that the result of the tuple match can be indicated on it by resetting the bits corresponding to the mismatching tuples of the second relation. Figure 6.21 displays an intersection operation between two unary relations A and B.

AM	A	B	AWF	BWF	RWF
	LONDON	PARIS	1	1	X
	TUCSON	XXXXXX	1	0	X
	PARIS	ROME	1	1	X
	XXXXXX	LONDON	0	1	X
	MADRID	BERLIN	1	1	X
	ROME	HAAG	1	1	X

Before

AM	A	B	AWF	BWF	RWF
	LONDON	PARIS	1	1	1
	TUCSON	XXXXXX	1	0	0
	PARIS	ROME	1	1	1
	XXXXXX	LONDON	0	1	0
	MADRID	BERLIN	1	1	0
	ROME	HAAG	1	1	1

After

Figure 6.21   An intersection example.

Difference. In this operation, the marks of the first relation are copied into the result; then the rest of the algorithm is executed just as in the intersection operation. The tuples of the first relation are selected and compared with those of the second and if a match is found that tuple is deleted from the result. Figure 6.22 illustrates a difference operation.

AM	A	B	AWF	BWF	RWF
	LONDON	PARIS	1	1	X
	TUCSON	XXXXXX	1	0	X
	PARIS	ROME	1	1	X
	XXXXXX	LONDON	0	1	X
	MADRID	BERLIN	1	1	X
	ROME	HAAG	1	1	X

Before

AM	A	B	AWF	BWF	RWF
	LONDON	PARIS	1	1	0
	TUCSON	XXXXXX	1	0	1
	PARIS	ROME	1	1	0
	XXXXXX	LONDON	0	1	0
	MADRID	BERLIN	1	1	1
	ROME	HAAG	1	1	0

After

Figure 6.22   A difference example.

Semi-join.   In this operation, the procedure is similar to that of intersection, only this time the tuples of the second relation are selected and their join attributes are compared. The tuple is OR'ed into the result vector if a match is found. Figure 6.23 demonstrates a semi-join between the A relation and the B relation over the join attributes of A_2 and B, respectively.

Projection.   In projection, the mark bit slice of the result is cleared. The mark bit slice of the relation is copied into a scratch pad area in the work field so that tuples of the relation can be successively selected. The iteration of the algorithm continues for as many tuples as there are in the result. The next tuple of the relation is selected by select first and reset and transferred into the comparand register. The exact match search is performed between that tuple and the rest of the relation. All tuples that satisfy the match are deleted from the scratch pad bit slice. The first of these tuples is OR'ed with the mark bit slice of the result relation.

Division.   The division operation is executed in two phases. In the first phase, we compare for match each tuple of the divisor relation with the dividend relation. We reserve a bit slice, for each divisor tuple match, to indicate the result of the match with the dividend. This means that we would need n bit slices if the cardinality of the divisor is n.

In the second phase, we take $\overline{A}$ (i.e., complement of dividend with respect to division attribute) attribute value at a time and go to the comparand register. We group the dividend tuples on $\overline{A}$ by making a match comparison with the comparand (in other words, we partition dividend on $\overline{A}$). We then take the result bit slice and AND it with all the bit slices created in AM in phase I. If this AND operation leaves a 1 in each of these bit slices, then put $\overline{A}$ in the answer. The operation continues for all the unique $\overline{A}$ values in the dividend. Figure 6.24 demonstrates a division operation between a dividend relation with attributes A_1 and A_2 and the divisor relation B. The division attributes are A_2 and B so that $\overline{A}$ is A_1 of the dividend.

Algorithms that assemble the result

Product.   All bits of the result mark bit slice are set to one. The result mark bit slice indicates which memory words are free to receive the result tuples. The mark bit slice of the first relation is copied into its scratch pad bit slice. The algorithm iterates for as many tuples as there are in the first relation. In each iteration, one tuple from the first relation is taken and transferred to all result memory words which are not yet occupied by the tuples of the second relation. The mark bit slice of the second relation is copied into its scratch pad bit slice. A loop is entered to be executed for each tuple of the second relation. In each iteration, one tuple of the second relation is transferred into the right half of the partly filled result relation (the left halves were occupied by copies of a tuple from the first relation). Whenever a complete result tuple is assembled

Before

AM A$_1$	A$_2$	B	AWF	BWF	RWF
SMITH	LONDON	XXXXXX	1	0	X
JONES	PARIS	TUCSON	1	1	X
BLAKE	PARIS	PARIS	1	1	X
XXXXX	XXXXXX	BERLIN	0	1	X
CLARK	LONDON	XXXXXX	1	0	X
ADAMS	TUCSON	XXXXXX	1	0	X

After

AM A$_1$	A$_2$	B	AWF	BWF	RWF
SMITH	LONDON	XXXXXX	1	0	0
JONES	PARIS	TUCSON	1	1	1
BLAKE	PARIS	PARIS	1	1	1
XXXXX	XXXXXX	BERLIN	0	1	0
CLARK	LONDON	XXXXXX	1	0	0
ADAMS	TUCSON	XXXXXX	1	0	1

Figure 6.23   A semi-join example.

AM	A_1	A_2	B	AWF	BWF	RWF
	LONDON	P1	XX	1	0	X
	TUCSON	P3	P1	1	1	X
	PARIS	P2	P2	1	1	X
	XXXXXX	XX	XX	0	0	X
	LONDON	P2	XX	1	0	X
	PARIS	P1	XX	1	0	X
	BERLIN	P2	XX	1	0	X

Before

AM	A_1	A_2	I	II	B	AWF	BWF	RWF
	LONDON	P1	1	0	XX	1	0	0
	TUCSON	P3	0	0	P1	1	1	0
	PARIS	P2	0	1	P2	1	1	0
	XXXXXX	XX	0	0	XX	0	0	0
	LONDON	P2	0	1	XX	1	0	0
	PARIS	P1	1	0	XX	1	0	0
	BERLIN	P2	0	1	XX	1	0	0

After phase I

AM	A_1	A_2	B	AWF	BWF	RWF
	LONDON	P1	XX	1	0	1
	TUCSON	P3	P1	1	1	0
	PARIS	P2	P2	1	1	1
	XXXXXX	XX	XX	0	0	0
	LONDON	P2	XX	1	0	0
	PARIS	P1	XX	1	0	0
	BERLIN	P2	XX	1	0	0

After phase II

Figure 6.24   A division example.

the result mark bit slice bit is set. The operation terminates when all tuples of the first relation are processed. Figure 6.25 demonstrates an example product operation.

At this point, we will leave Lucas and go on with the discussion of other systems. At the end of the word-organized associative systems discussion, we will make some general remarks about the performance of associative processors.

6.3.4 Relacs

Relacs (relational associative computer system) was designed at Syracuse University [Oliver and Berra, 1980]. As the name implies, Relacs is a backend system constructed around a word-organized associative memory. The associative memory system is used in the dictionary/directory processor and associative query translator units. There are AM arrays to store and search relation descriptor data and Boolean query predicates. The AM array for the latter produces search addresses

AM	A	B	R1	R2	AWF	BWF	RWF
	XXXXX	XXXXXX	XXXXX	XXXXXX	0	0	X
	XXXXX	LONDON	XXXXX	XXXXXX	0	1	X
	SMITH	XXXXXX	XXXXX	XXXXXX	1	0	X
	CLARK	PARIS	XXXXX	XXXXXX	1	1	X
	BLAKE	XXXXXX	XXXXX	XXXXXX	1	0	X
	XXXXX	XXXXXX	XXXXX	XXXXXX	0	0	X

Before

AM	A	B	R1	R2	AWF	BWF	RWF
	XXXXX	XXXXXX	SMITH	LONDON	0	0	1
	XXXXX	LONDON	SMITH	PARIS	0	1	1
	SMITH	XXXXXX	CLARK	LONDON	1	0	1
	CLARK	PARIS	CLARK	PARIS	1	1	1
	BLAKE	XXXXXX	BLAKE	LONDON	1	0	1
	XXXXX	XXXXXX	BLAKE	PARIS	0	0	1

After

Figure 6.25　A product example.

for the associative unit where two large AM arrays are used to store and process database contents. Figure 6.26 shows the general structure of Relacs.

There are six main functional units of Relacs. They are a global control unit, a dictionary/directory processor, an associative query translator, the associative units, a mass storage device, and the output buffer.

Mass storage holds the database. It was envisioned that the associative units would be of the size 1000 to 10^5 words of 1000 bits each. The search speed of these units was assumed to be half of that of Staran, which we will see next.

The host computer performs syntactic checks on user queries. The dictionary processor works on user authentication and checks whether the relation and attribute names referred to in the user queries exist and that they can be related to answer the query. The necessary information is passed to the associative query translator, which translates query into a set of operations to be executed on the associative array units.

Relational operations are carried out on the associative array units. The important operation of join is executed in accordance with the nested loop algorithm where the larger relation of the two participating in the join is searched in parallel for as many times as there are tuples in the smaller relation. Relacs assumed the use of a comparand register array to speed this operation by comparing m number of tuples of the smaller relation simultaneously, where m is the number of comparand registers in the comparand array. The comparand register array concept was originated in the work of Digby [1973], which duplicated the comparand register and search hardware in the associative array. Considering the fact that the cost of a single associative array and peripheral search hardware system becomes a bottleneck in the overall system, one would not expect much of a

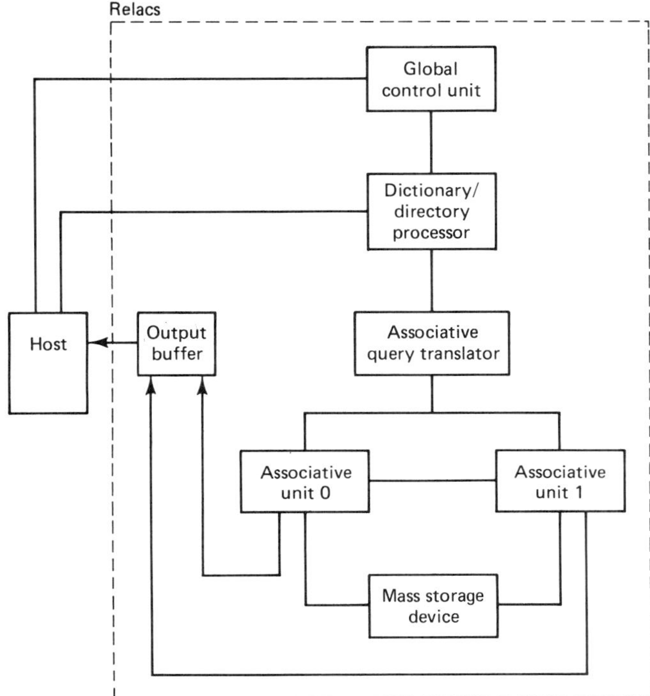

Figure 6.26 Relacs. From E. Oliver and B. P. Berra, "Relacs—A Relational Associative Computer System." *Proc. of Int'l. Workshop on Computer Architectures for Nonnumeric Processing,* © 1980 Association for Computing Machinery.

parallelism in the comparand array concept for doing a large number of many-to-many searches in parallel.

Relacs' estimated performance was compared with that of the RAP database machine, which will be seen in the following chapters, and certain advantages and/or gains of Relacs were observed. These were mainly attributable to the projected size of Relacs and, more important, the assumption of the presence of a very high bandwidth I/O between it and its mass storage system. We will have a look into one of the proposed I/O interfaces designed to provide such bandwidth.

In one of the publications of the Relacs' authors [Berra and Oliver, 1979], various ways of interfacing the AM array with the external mass storage devices have been considered. Among the three suggested configurations, Figure 6.27 shows the second configuration of the referenced study. According to the configuration shown in Figure 6.27, the interface between the associative array processor and the fast buffer memory is such that there is a dedicated I/O path to each AM word. It is assumed that there are 1024-bit serial channels operating in parallel at this interface, transferring one bit slice of 1024 bits in 450 nanoseconds. This means that if AM words have 256 bits each, the entire transfer can be completed in 115 microseconds, resulting in an equivalent I/O bandwidth of 280 megabytes per second. The transfer initiation time is 50 microseconds. Now,

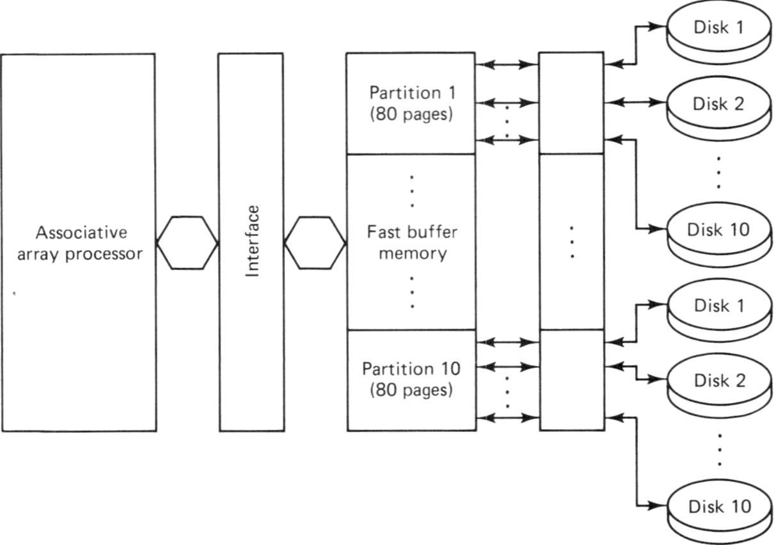

Figure 6.27 Associative array/mass storage I/O interface. From B. P. Berra and E. Oliver, "The Role of Associative Array Processors in Data Base Machine Architecture." *IEEE Computer,* 12, 3, © 1979 IEEE.

the array load is divided into eight pages where each page is 128 by 256 bits (4K bytes). To be able to operate at such speeds, the fast buffer memory must be made up of semiconductor material [Farnesworth, Hoffman, and Shutt, 1976].

According to the figures given, to search an array load (8 pages) 50 μsec setup time and 115 μsec transfer time across the interface are required. If each array load gave 10 responders that take 300 μsec to search and retrieve, then the 32K page ($>10^9$ bits) full of a database can be processed in time:

$$\frac{(50 + 115 + 300 \simeq 500\ \mu\text{sec})}{8\ \text{pages}} \times 32\text{K pages} = 2\ \text{sec}$$

In the configuration shown in Figure 6.27, the fast mass memory is envisioned as a 10-partition store where each partition would hold 80 pages of data. This fast buffer memory has dual ports and is multiplexed so that the associative array can be connected to one partition at a time. According to the capacity stated, each partition holds 10 array loads of data. Using the figures of the interface, the time to search a partition is

$$\frac{500\ \mu\text{sec}}{8\ \text{pages}} \times 80\ \text{pages} = 5\ \text{msec/partition}$$

There are 10 partitions, so that a total of 50 msec is required to search the entire buffer. However, to keep the search continuous, the interface from the fast buffer to the disk array must stage data in an overlapped manner. For this to happen, a partition must be loaded through the disk port in less than 45 msec (since it takes 5 msec to search a single partition and if we are searching the second partition, it will take us 45 msec to cycle back).

The disk side is assumed to have 100 movable head disks partitioned into 10 banks where each bank has 10 disks. It is assumed that for each partition, 10 disks operate in parallel to fill the partition. Each disk is assumed to have 20 heads and 20 surfaces and 100 tracks per surface. Each track is assumed to have one array load of data (i.e., 32K bytes). Revolution and head positioning times of 20 msec each are assumed. Assuming a full revolution to locate the data and another full revolution to read the data into the buffer, 40 msec is required if the arm mechanism does not move to another cylinder.

It was estimated that when a user query is received, it will take one revolution to search for related data and another revolution to position at its beginning ready to transfer, making a total of 40 msec. Another 20 msec will be needed to transfer it into the buffer. We know that it takes 500 μsec to search one array load hence giving a total partition search time of (10 $\times$ 500 =) 5 msec. There are 20 tracks on the cylinder; therefore, the buffer can be loaded in 20 times without incurring head movement time. This means that since there are 100 disks positioned at their cylinders and there are eight pages of data in each track 20 $\times$ 100 $\times$ 8 = 16K pages or 16K $\times$ 4K = 64 megabytes of data can be searched without moving the disk arms. The time to search this much data will be 20 loads $\times$ 50 msec per load = 1 sec. To process the entire disk capacity, 100 cylinders must be searched; hence, 100 sec plus arm move time are needed. This time corresponds to the database capacity of 64 megabytes $\times$ 100 = 6.4 $\times$ 10^9 bytes. We will have a discussion of these I/O bandwidths at the end of the section on word-organized associative processors.

6.3.5 Staran Associative Processor

The Staran associative array processor, a product of Goodyear Aerospace Corporation, is the only production-size and commercial associative processor. It has been a textbook case for several years. It evolved from 32 banks (modules) of arrays of size 256 words by 256 bits each (in Staran-B) to 9216 words of 256 bits each (in Staran-E).

Staran was originally built for radar/image processing in military applications, but its associative parallel structure lends itself to exploitation for other aspects of nonnumeric processing such as database management. In fact, a study in that direction can be found in DeFiore and Berra [1974]. Various literature on Staran is available; some of it can be found in Rudolph [1972], Moulder [1973], Davis [1974], Batcher [1974, 1977], and Lange [1976]. Figure 6.28 shows the general organization of the Staran system. Figure 6.29 shows the organization of a Staran array.

The typical and generic AM array operations we covered at the beginning of the chapter are all applicable to Staran. The Y vector (or Y_i flip flop (bit) for the ith AM word) is used for tagging. M_i is the word select bit, and X_i is used

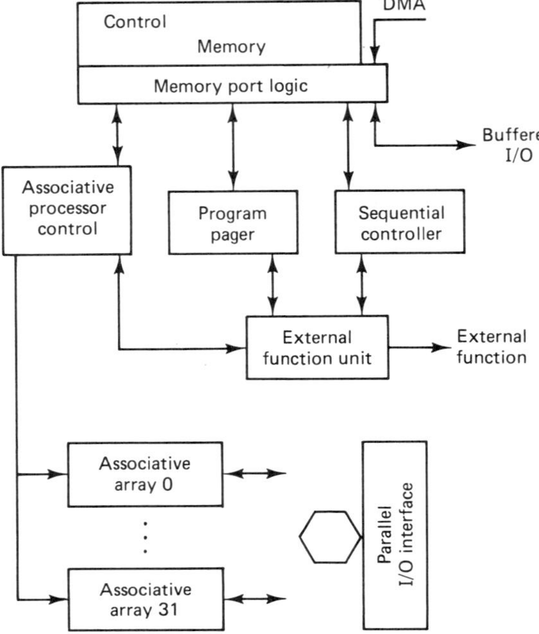

Figure 6.28 Staran system configuration. From K. E. Batcher, "STARAN Series E." *Proc. of International Conference on Parallel Processing,* © 1977 IEEE.

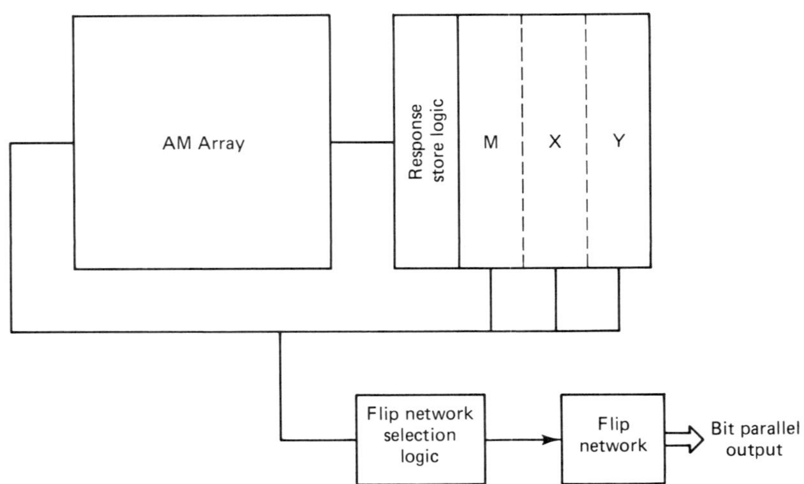

Figure 6.29 A Staran array module.

as temporary or scratch pad storage. In Staran notation, F_i represents the bit slice bit and also is used to indicate the flip network patterns. In the work reported in [Moulder, 1973], a parallel head-per-track disk interface is configured for the array I/O interface.

The associative processor (AP) control store of Staran is built in layers to accommodate various memory hierarchies and a program pager. This pager has a sequential control unit that manages program pages between various layers of the control storage without delaying operations of the AM array. At the top of the control memory hierarchy are three bipolar fast memory pages that hold the pages of program that drives the operations in the AM array. Down in the hierarchy is a high-speed buffer, a page long, that acts as a buffer in page transfers between the bipolar memory and the relatively slow core memory. The size of each page is 512 words, whereas the bulk core has 16K words. The entire AP control memory is connected to outside elements via a port switch logic that provides priority-based access. In the address range of the AP control memory hierarchy, there is a reserved address area between the top-level high-speed buffer and bipolar memories and the bottom-level core storage. At these reserved memory locations, a direct memory access (DMA) circuitry can optionally be added to access a host computer's memory so that the host and Staran can communicate directly.

The high-speed buffer and the core storage have external connections via the buffered I/O channel. The external function unit serves as coordinator/synchronizer, and all subsystems of Staran are connected to it. There is a polling circuitry in this unit that checks the status of all subsystems. All requests made to it are served in a FCFS (first-come, first-served) basis. Various system components communicate with each other via the external function unit. This unit is responsible for setting up the connections of AP control memory pages to proper devices in the system. For testing and programming purposes, some interlock flip flop settings are reserved for external use. For example, the state of the pager can be sensed and turned on or off. Interrupt testing and servicing between a subsystem and the sequential control unit as well as the host can be done via this unit.

The AP control unit includes the necessary logic and registers for controlling the operations of the AM array. The usual program counter, instruction registers, the common register, response store and array control circuitry, field pointers, length counters, and shift and bus logic constitute the internals of the AP control unit. Address computations for the AM array are done in this unit in various ways.

Staran has plenty of bit-level manipulation capabilities in addressing, external communication, logic/arithmetic, and various response store operations. Although the system does not look like the work of a database architect, it has many purposes and is powerful enough to be used for almost anything.

Some of the AM array operation codes are listed below:

(a) Load response store from the common register. This operation has various subcontrols that affect various shifting, mirroring (i.e., reverse bits end to end), and logic operations between the common register and various registers (e.g., Y, X) of the response store.

(b) Load response store directly from a register—a response store register-to-register operation.

(c) Load response store directly from the AM array.

(d) Load response store indirectly from the AM array. By the use of various field pointers, word or bit slices are selectively operated upon.

(e) Store response store in the AM array.

(f) The above operations with the mask register option.

(g) Load/store common register.

(h) Find first responder.

(i) Reset first responder.

(j) Find and reset first responder.

(k) Reset other responders.

In the flip network use, the individual stage flip control is an n-bit vector $F = f_{n-1} \ldots f_1, f_0$ which determines the way the interconnection stages will be set. If $f_i = 1$ the stage i's interchange connections are in the exchange state (toward implementing the cube topology: $N = 8$ processors require 3 (2^3) interconnection stages to produce the cubic interconnections depicted by Figure 6.3), and if 0, they are in the straight connection state.

At each stage of the total three, there are four 2-by-2 exchange switches receiving eight inputs (two per switch) and producing eight outputs. The routing of outputs to the inputs of the next stage is performed with respect to F, as explained.

Array operations. Each processor corresponding to a Staran word in Figure 6.29 contains three bits M_i, X_i, and Y_i of the respective vectors. These bits are also referred to as one-bit registers. Sixteen Boolean functions of two variables can be performed by each processor in such a way that if X_i is the state of the ith X register bit and f_i is the state of the ith flip network output, then,

$$X_i \longleftarrow \phi(X_i, f_i) \quad (i = 0, 1, \ldots, 255)$$

where ϕ is a Boolean function. Similarly, for Y_i,

$$Y_i \longleftarrow \phi(Y_i, f_i) \quad i = 0, 1, \ldots, 255$$

The programmer can operate on X alone, Y alone, or both together. If X and Y are operated on together, the same Boolean function ϕ is applied to both registers as

$$X_i \longleftarrow \phi(X_i, f_i), \quad Y_i \longleftarrow \phi(Y_i, f_i)$$

The programmer can also operate on X selectively, using Y as a mask such as

$$X_i \longleftarrow \phi(X_i, f_i) \qquad \text{where } Y_i = 1$$
$$X_i \longleftarrow X_i \qquad \text{where } Y_i = 0$$

Also, it is possible to operate on X selectively while operating on Y such as

$$X_i \longleftarrow \phi(X_i, f_i) \qquad \text{where } Y_i = 1$$
$$X_i \longleftarrow X_i \qquad \text{where } Y_i = 0$$
$$Y_i \longleftarrow \phi(Y_i, f_i)$$

In this case, the old state of Y is used as the mask of the X operation.

Example 6.2

An unmasked "add fields" operation will be demonstrated. The contents of field A will be added to the contents of field B storing the result in field S, in all the words. For n bit fields, the operation iterates n times while in each iteration, a bit slice (a) of field A and bit slice (b) of field B are read from the memory while bit slice (s) of field S is written onto memory. The operation proceeds from the least significant bit toward the most significant one. At the beginning of each iteration: $X_i = 0$, $Y_i = c_i$ that is, the carry from the previous iteration is stored in Y_i while X_i contains zeros. Each iteration has the following four steps:

Step 1: Read bit slice (a), exclusive-or ($\oplus$) it with X selectively and also Y as

$$X_i \longleftarrow X_i \oplus Y_i a_i, \quad Y_i \longleftarrow Y_i \oplus a_i \qquad \text{giving the states of X and Y as:}$$
$$X_i = a_i c_i, \qquad Y_i = a_i \oplus c_i$$

Step 2: Read bit slice (b) and do as in step 1:

$$X_i \longleftarrow X_i \oplus Y_i b_i, \quad Y_i \longleftarrow Y_i \oplus b_i \qquad \text{yielding in X and Y:}$$
$$X_i = a_i c_i \oplus a_i b_i \oplus b_i c_i = c_i', \qquad Y_i = a_i \oplus b_i \oplus c_i \oplus s_i$$

Step 3: Write the sum bit from Y into bit slice (s) and also complement X selectively.

$$S_i \longleftarrow Y_i, \quad X_i \longleftarrow X_i \oplus Y_i \qquad \text{yielding in X and Y:}$$
$$X_i = c_i' \oplus S_i, \qquad Y_i = S_i$$

Step 4: Read the X register and exclusive-or it with both X and Y as $X_i \leftarrow X_i \oplus X_i$, $Y_i \leftarrow Y_i \oplus X_i$ clearing X and storing the carry in Y to get $X_i = 0$, $Y_i = c_i'$.

The entire add operation for a 32-bit long field takes less than 22.4 μsec plus a small amount of setup time. In each array, 256 additions are performed.

System software. Staran system software consists of the following programs:

Assembler (called Apple)
Utility package
Debug package

Diagnostics

Subroutine library

All these programs are executed by the sequential controller except the subroutine library and some diagnostics which are executed by the AP control.

The instruction set consists of about 100 instructions in the following addressing groups:

Word addressing—points to AP memory

Immediate addressing

Data pointer addressing—AP memory is pointed

Array addressing—bit slice or word by either immediate addressing or field pointer addressing

With the instruction set an exact match takes 4.8×8 μsec. An addition between two fields of the same word takes 85 μsec, while between the two fields of different words it takes longer.

Apple language.   Although the programmer must define record formats via the definition statements, he or she is not required to be concerned with physical record location in the arrays. Besides the usual load, store, test, branch, and control instructions of sequential execution, Apple contains associative search and arithmetic instructions. In Staran, records of different logical files may be physically intermixed in the array as well as logically unordered. Operations may be conditional on certain field tags, hence do not require ordering of records. The program structure can be considered as a subset of PL/I with certain resemblances to FORTRAN or Algol.

Example 6.3

IF ARRAY statement,

```
DECLARE (A(200), B(200)) FIXED (15,0);
IF ARRAY A < B THEN
  A [&] = B;
ELSE
  A [&] = A * 2;
  COUNT [&] = COUNT + 1;
ENDIF;
```

The interpretation of this program is as follows. For each element of A less than the corresponding element of B, assign the latter to replace the value of the former, otherwise double the value of element A and increment its corresponding counter. The ampersand used as the subscript, in the IF ARRAY statement, means to select the subset of only those array elements corresponding to B'1' values in the nearest containing IF ARRAY <expression>. Ampersand used as the subscript in the context of the ELSE clause means to select the subset of only those array elements corresponding to B'0' values in the IF ARRAY <expression>—B'1', B'0' meaning true and false, respectively.

There are also the built-in functions such as INDEX-MIN and INTERVAL-TEST. INDEX-MIN provides the index of (one of) the minimum values of the AM array rather than the minimum value itself. This is useful in searching for unique values. INTERVAL-TEST tests ranges such as

```
IF ARRAY INTERVAL-TEST(X, previousX, delta) THEN ...
```

or, equivalently,

```
IF ARRAY ABS(X - previousX) ≤ delta THEN ...
```

6.4 I/O BOTTLENECK

We have observed in this chapter that we can obtain very effective as well as efficient computer systems from a high degree of parallelism. This potential, however, is hampered by the heavy overhead of I/O operations. These operations are needed to output the result computed in the system and to input the data into the system in the first place. This is needed because the storage requirement of the problems to be solved usually far exceeds that of the system which is our associative/parallel architecture. The result can be a fancy and expensive architecture constantly starving for data. Overall, the potential performance savings of system resident operations (i.e., once the data are loaded into the system) are overshadowed by the serial and slow paging of data into the system. This problem is referred to as the *I/O bottleneck*. To overcome this, we must match the I/O bandwidth (i.e., the number of bits transferred in unit time) to the requirement of the system and also overlap paging with processing. The I/O interface proposed for Relacs is a high-I/O bandwidth system. Historically, however, such I/O interfaces have not been commercially developed due to their high cost both in themselves and relative to the cost of the systems they would support.

To provide some quantitative measure of what we have been discussing, we quote the "rule of thumb" provided by Amdahl [1970]. The following must be satisfied:

(a) We must have as many bits of memory per processor as instructions per second performable by the processor.

(b) We must provide as many bits of I/O bandwidth to our device (processor) as instructions per second performable by the processor.

If we test these criteria on Illiac IV and Staran, the following can be observed:

Illiac IV.   Each PE has 4 MIPS (million instructions per second) power with $2048 \times 64 \simeq 128K$ bits of memory. Accordingly,

Memory: Required: $\geq 4 \times 10^6$ bits
                   Actual: 0.128×10^6 bits $\rightarrow$ the system is undermemoried
I/O bandwidth: Required: $\geq 64 \times 4 \times 10^6$ bits/sec (per quadrant)
                   Actual: 50×10^6 bits/sec $\rightarrow$ fails the test

Staran.   Assuming a bit operation rate of 6.6×10^6 (MHz) per processor,

Memory: Required: $\geq 256 \times 6.6 \times 10^6$
                   Actual: $256 \times 256 \rightarrow$ The system is undermemoried
I/O bandwidth: Required: $\geq 256 \times 6.6 \times 10^6$ bits/sec
                   Actual: Commercial systems do not provide the required
                   bandwidth $\rightarrow$ fails the test

This measure provides us the insight into designing new computer architectures. We now have an idea of where the boundary for processor memory should lie. It is now appropriate for us to investigate another class of associative processors, the topic of the next section.

6.5 SECONDARY (BULK) MEMORY–BASED ASSOCIATIVE PROCESSORS

If the reader reviews the developments that took place in the history of associative processors, he or she can observe that the secondary memory–based associative processors were the solution for the problems of high cost and I/O bottleneck experienced in the highly parallel, word-organized associative processors. However, as we will see in the coming chapters, this solution has turned out to be incomplete, although better than the others we have discussed, due to the recent developments in memory and processor technology. Let us review the developments in their logical as well as chronological order. In this section, we will concentrate on the way that secondary memory devices were utilized to exploit parallelism and also on the type of operations for which this parallelism was used.

6.5.1 Hollander's TapeDRUM

Hollander's TapeDRUM [Hollander, 1956] historically is the earliest design that aimed at providing partial associativity (Chapter 5) by the use of secondary memories. In this device, the memory medium is a tape wrapped around a drum. As the drum rotates, the tape contents resident on the drum surface, called the page, move so that data can be searched. Figure 6.30 shows the TapeDRUM.

As can be seen, there is a read/write head per track so that at each position a cylinder is accessed in parallel. Going back to Figure 5.9(c), we can see that keyed retrieval can be accomplished by providing comparators on the tracks

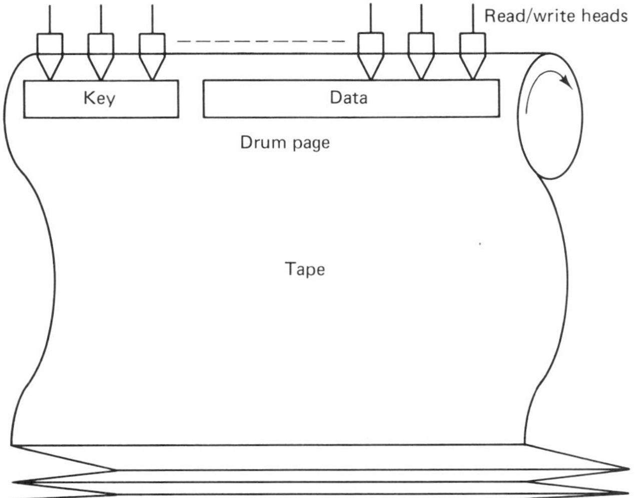

Figure 6.30   TapeDRUM device.

where keys are stored. As shown earlier, such retrieval will be partially associative. This is in fact how TapeDRUM was designed. On a cylinder, a pair of key (name) data are stored, so that the database is searched in parallel both within a cylinder and also among cylinders as the drum rotated. This design was the pioneer of secondary memory–based associative processors.

6.5.2 Minsky's Associative Disk

Minsky's design [Minsky, 1972] and those of others were developed when secondary memory–based associative processors were popular. Similar proposals were made by Slotnick [1970], Parker [1971], Healy, Lipovski, and Doty [1972], Parhami [1972], Coulouris [Coulouris, Evans, and Mitchell [1972], Love [1973], and so on.

Similar to the cylinder concept shown in Figure 5.9(c) and 6.30, Minsky's design uses disks or drums of head-per-track type. However, compared to the more ambitious designs such as those of Slotnick and Parker (which are, for that reason, discussed later), Minsky's design can be considered as a compromise for economy. This design uses the cylinder concept of the head-per-track devices, but implements partial associativity by limiting the amount of hardware to be used in associative searches.

Minsky's design is based on keyed retrieval and the physical storage structure is similar to that of Figure 5.9(c) where there is a positional delay between the angular position where keys are stored and those where data are stored. Figure 6.31 displays the basic structure of the system.

In this organization, tracks of a cylinder are divided into two regions; the *control track* and *data tracks*. While data tracks store blocks of data, the control track stores only the key portions of each data block. A key block on the control

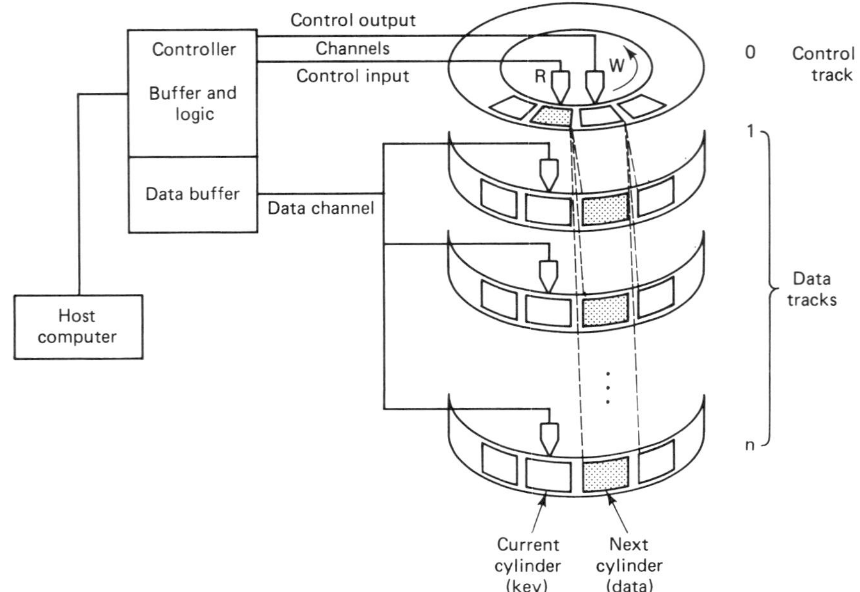

Figure 6.31   Minsky's cylinder-based associative processor.

track packs the keys of all the data blocks of a cylinder on data tracks 1 through n. As shown in Figure 5.9(c), to search the keys ahead of time, so that enough time lead (delay) would be provided for operating on the keys (i.e., compare for search, update, delete/insert), the data are stored one or more (depending on required delay) positions "later" on the tracks.

On the head-per-track disk or drum, separate read and write heads, each connecting to a dedicated control channel, are provided for the control track. The control channels are connected to a separate part in the controller where special buffers and parallel comparators/logic are provided. According to this organization, once a key block is read it is buffered, operated upon, and written back (if necessary) before the corresponding data blocks arrive, during rotation, under the read/write heads of the data tracks so that the appropriate track can be preselected. A data block is addressed by the track number and sector index combination. Accordingly, if the key sector on the control track is at the ith position, its corresponding data sector will be at the $i + c$th position while a small value of c (such as one) is preferred for less retrieval delay.

6.5.3 Slotnick's and Parker's Associative Disk

The *logic-per-track* idea to be utilized on secondary memory devices was first introduced by Slotnick [1970] and later implemented in a design by Parker [1971]. If we made every track of a head-per-track device like the control track of the

Minsky's design (i.e., having a pair of read and write heads with logic in between), we obtain the fully associative disk proposed by Slotnick and Parker. However, instead of having channels and the logic away from the memory in the controller, Parker's logic is envisioned to be simple and at close proximity to the tracks between the read and write heads. Each "track processor" is structured to include a set of registers, an operation counter, and control and processor logic. A thousand tracks with processors was the intention of the design. The storage structure of the Parker system is shown in Figure 6.32. Data are stored bit and word serially on the tracks.

Each track is divided into quadrants with special synchronization to cut down the rotational delay in locating data. The data are classified as keys, data, and holes (garbage, empty space) with each identified by a code and provided with length information. The track processors are connected to read and write heads and are controlled by signal lines connected to the outside processor. In Parker's system, a data management software layer is assumed that controls the low-level hardware operations such as search, read, count, insert/delete, search for a hole of a specified length, and search for a key or keys of a specified pattern.

When we will see the database machine architectures in the coming chapters, we will be able to say two things about this design:

(a) Although intelligence is brought onto the tracks of a memory device, the intervention of the external processor in orchestrating the operations on the tracks is not minimized.

(b) Although the device is potentially fully associative, the design has stuck with the key-data organization where all operations are directable only on the keys with the exception of doing retrieval, insert/delete on the located data. By contrast, the ideal storage structure would have been something like that of Figure 5.9(d). This implies that for full associativity in the key-data storage structure, one has to duplicate the data 100 percent in the key block that precedes it.

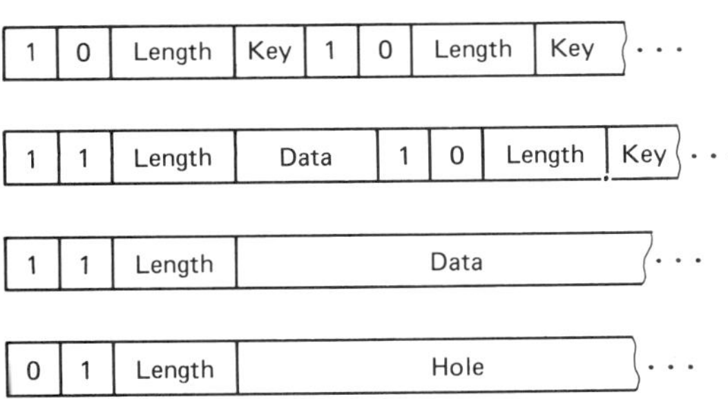

Figure 6.32 Storage structure of Parker's system.

6.5.4 *RAPID*

RAPID [Parhami, 1972] is another associative disk design. These highly parallel systems are also referred to as *cellular logic* devices, where a cell corresponds to a memory segment (such as a track) with its processor. RAPID is designed mainly for string searching, and therefore, it is character oriented. Data are stored on the memory tracks in bit parallel character serial fashion. In other words, one character is stored across $n + 1$ tracks where n is the number of bits of a character and additional one is the control bit. Logic consists of array of processors where each cell receives $n + 1$ data lines from the tracks that store character serial data. Therefore, there can be $N/(n + 1)$ cells in RAPID, where N is the total number of tracks in the memory device. Basing the physical storage structure on characters allows flexibility for string search because variable length data can be easily supported as shown in Figure 6.33.

According to this figure, λ indicates the beginning of the length field, ϕ indicates end of a field, δ is a separator between the title (name) and information (data) fields, ρ indicates end of a record, and γ is an indicator for the end of a nonempty record.

RAPID is designed for simple string search operations. It can conduct equality searches, and each character match takes one revolution. This requires much time for complex pattern searches. Each cell has separate logic to operate on the control and symbol parts of a character. When data are searched for patterns, the ends of stored records are marked if the search was successful on the information field contained in the record (or more properly, the data string).

In the instruction set of RAPID, the following are some of the operations supported:

(a) **Search for** *string:* Finds all occurrences of the string and sets the state (control bit) of the symbols that immediately follow it.

(b) **Search for marked** *string:* The same as the previous instruction with the exception that for the string to qualify, the state of its first symbol must be set.

(c) **Expand** *i:* If the state of a symbol is set, set the state of the first i (integer) symbols following it.

(d) **Expand to** *symbol:* If the state of a symbol is set, set the states of all symbols following it up to and including the first occurrence of *symbol*.

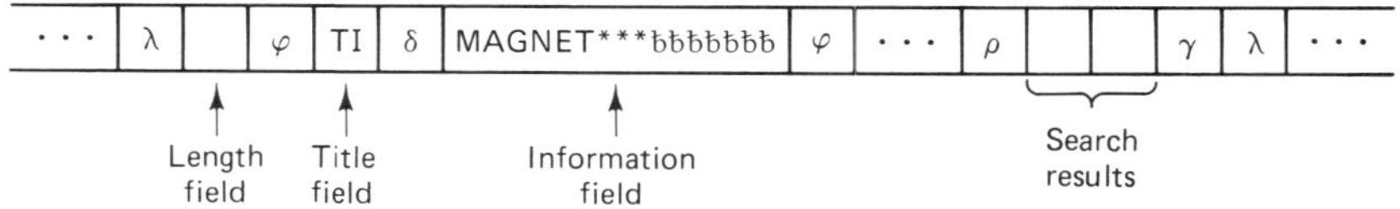

Figure 6.33 RAPID's physical storage format.

(e) **Expand *i* or to** *symbol:* If the state of a symbol is set, perform as in (d) if a *symbol* appears within the next *i* symbols, otherwise do as in (c).

(f) **Contract *i*:** If the state of a symbol is reset, reset the state of the first *i* symbols that follow it.

(g) **Propagate *i*:** If the state of a symbol is set, reset it and set the state of the *i*th symbol to its right.

(h) **Propagate to** *symbol:* If the state of a symbol is set, reset it and set the state of the first *symbol* following it.

We can now present an example search that can be demonstrated by the use of the instruction subset listed.

Example 6.4

We will mark all the nonempty records that contain in their title field (named TI) a word *magnet* as its first six characters followed by 3 to 10 nonblank characters. ♭ designates a blank character. The following presents the program listing and the trace of execution on two strings A and B.

1. **Search for** ϕTIδ /* Searches for the title field and once found marks the first character in the information field. According to Figure 6.33, we have ϕTIδMAGNET***♭♭♭♭♭♭♭*/

2. **Expand to** ϕ /* ϕTIδMAGNET***♭♭♭♭♭♭♭ϕ */

3. **Search for marked** *MAGNET*
    /* ϕTIδMAGNET***♭♭♭♭♭♭♭ϕ */

4. **Expand 10 or to** ♭   /* same as before */

5. **Contract 3**   /* ϕTIδMAGNET***♭♭♭♭♭♭♭ϕ */

6. **Propagate to** ρ /* ϕTIδMAGNET***♭♭♭♭♭♭♭ϕ...ρ */

7. **Propagate 3**   /* ϕTIδMAGNET***♭♭♭♭♭♭♭ϕ...ρ ⊐ γ */

8. **Search for marked** λ /* ϕTIδMAGNET***♭♭♭♭♭♭♭ϕ...ρ ⊐ $\gamma\lambda$ */

A title and information field combination such as ϕTIδMAGNETϕ would not satisfy the search (i.e., would not have λ marked in the end). This is because at step 5 we would start with ϕTIδMAGNETϕ and at the end of the operation, nothing would be left marked, but the search requests at least three trailing don't cares after the word MAGNET.

6.5.5 Healy's CASSS

Healy's [Healy, Lipovski, and Doty, 1972] CASSS (context-addressed segment sequential storage) is another character-oriented cellular logic device that is designed around the fixed head disk concept. The device is a logic-per-track design in which the physical storage structure is character based so that variable-length strings can be processed easily. The data are stored bit and character serially on the tracks. As the name CASSS implies, a file is mapped sequentially onto contiguous disk tracks where each track is called a segment. The cells (a cell is a track with search logic) communicate with their two nearest neighbors in a linear interconnection scheme.

At the end of each stored string in CASSS, there are four flag bits called the Start, Permanent, Match, and X bits. The Start bit is a record delimiter; the Permanent bit has different roles depending upon instruction being executed; the Match bit is used to mark strings that satisfy a search step; and the X bit is used to mark the deleted words. The following are the important operations of CASSS:

Match character S_1: Searches and marks all occurrences of S_1.

Ordered search S_2: Performs ordered search for S_2s that follow the marked S_1s.

String search S_3: Searches for S_3s that *immediately* follow (string search) the characters (e.g., S_2) marked by the previous search.

Threshold add 1,1: Adds one to the first threshold accumulator in each string where search is successful.

Programming for string search operation in this device involves a chain of ordered and string search instructions for each character of the pattern to be searched. The threshold add instruction enables processing of Boolean queries. A disjunctive normal form query such as $(SP_1 \wedge SP_2) \vee (SP_3 \wedge SP_4)$ involving search patterns SP_1, SP_2, SP_3, and SP_4 can be processed by searching for strings to match the individual patterns and using threshold add and test instructions. For this purpose, several threshold accumulators are provided. To satisfy each of the conjunctions (i.e., $SP_1 \wedge SP_2$ or $SP_3 \wedge SP_4$), the threshold accumulators must be equal to two (assuming a one is added to the accumulator for each pattern match), and for the entire expression, the accumulator (a different one) must be equal to at least one. This is because, for each successful test for equality to two in the first accumulator, we would add one to the second accumulator in processing the entire expression.

EXERCISES

6.1. Considering number of search iterations, Boolean search capability, and ability for fast template matching, how would you compare Lee's DLM, RAPID, and CASSS?

6.2. For the associative processors discussed in the chapter, assume that a prospective buyer of such systems is forced (economically and/or technologically) to use a standard, commercial I/O channel of byte serial type whose I/O transfer rate is 10 megabits per second. Using the rule of thumb for the required I/O bandwidth discussed in Section 6.4, how would these systems perform?

6.3. Considering Staran, Relacs, and Lucas, assume a database size that is a multiple of 100 in comparison to the resident capacity of each of these systems. Furthermore, assume that the entire database consists of two relations of equal size. Perform each of the relational algebra operations discussed for Lucas on these systems. Assess their performance comparatively between the following two alternatives for I/O bandwidth:

(a) High I/O bandwidth discussed with Relacs

(b) Standard I/O bandwidth used in Exercise 6.2

What order of performance degradation do you observe between (a) and (b) for each of these systems?

6.4. Considering the fact that fixed head disks are disappearing, what alternatives would you suggest for the secondary memory–based cellular devices? Would you consider RAMs, magnetic bubble memories, and Bloch line devices?

6.5. Considering RAPID and CASSS, what would you suggest in terms of architectural modification to do better than one character comparison per revolution?

6.6. In comparing Staran, Relacs, and Lucas, which are similar devices, what are the architectural differences of first order that affect their superiority with respect to each other? (The reader may have to do some research into detailed publications of these systems.) Are the differences architectural or attributable to only the technological advances?

6.7. Discuss the practicality of building a system for doing text (string) searches in very large databases. What would be the pros and cons (advantages, disadvantages) of using an architecture such as the Lee's machine and a secondary memory–based cellular device? In this respect, you can search the literature for the system called Pepe [Berg et al., 1972; Thurber and Wald, 1975; Yau and Fung, 1977], which was inspired by Lee's DLM. How does Pepe compare with the secondary memory–based devices?

6.8. Comment on the efficiency of the division algorithm of Lucas. Can you suggest a different and more efficient way of doing division on devices like Staran, Relacs, and Lucas?

6.9. Analyze the performance of doing product and join (not semi-join) on the devices referred to in Exercise 6.8. How would they compare with the case of doing these operations on the external (host) processor with and without sorting available?

7

DATABASE MACHINE SURVEY

In our previous chapters, so far, we have seen new computer architectures such as the parallel and associative processors. In each of these systems, we have the desirable features (i.e., parallelism, associativity) that a database machine should process. However, as we know from our introductory Chapter 1, a database machine must support one or more data models in data structure as well as operations (language) in addition to parallelism and associativity. Furthermore, the machine should be autonomous in these operations; that is, it should not depend on the intervention of an outside (host) computer. Also, the storage structure must be close to a logical one, hence, eliminating the need for intermediary and/or access path structures. The high-level storage structure makes the database machine operations also high level.

The systems, such as Lucas and Relacs that we discussed in Chapter 6, satisfy our definition of a database machine. However, structurally they are so representative of the distinct associative array architecture that we classified them in that architectural category which is also typified by the Staran system.

In this chapter, we will present a global survey of database machines. In doing so, we will group the systems into the following categories:

- Cellular associative systems
- Multiprocessor-based systems
- Systems with in-stream and/or pipeline processing
- Logic enhanced primary memory (VLSI) systems
- Filters
- Commercial database machines

After we review the known database machines according to this classification, we will present database machine theory in the following chapter. Database machine performance will be discussed in Chapter 11.

7.1 CELLULAR ASSOCIATIVE SYSTEMS

In this section, we will talk about CASSM, RAP, RARES, bubble memory, and EDC systems. Although there are considerable differences among some of these systems, our classification is rather broad, and our intent is not to cover details of these systems but rather to uncover their features that contribute to database machine theory. Every system will be reviewed according to the following basic features:

(a) Architecture
(b) Data structure
    (i) Logical (data model and record types)
    (ii) Physical (storage structure)
(c) Operations

7.1.1 CASSM

CASSM (context addressed segment sequential memory) system is the successor of CASSS that we have seen in the previous chapter. Unlike CASSS, however, CASSM was specialized for DBMS operations. CASSM, which is developed at the University of Florida [Copeland, Lipovsky, and Su, 1973; Copeland, 1974; Su and Lipovski, 1975; University of Florida, 1976], implements associativity by a highly parallel cellular logic system based on head-per-track disks. Each cell of CASSM consists of a memory track, a pair of read/write heads—one for read, the other for write (or equivalently by a track pair which read and write)—and processing logic to support the device operations (i.e., data search and manipulation). As in the general model of such cellular devices, the entire system also includes a controller that drives the cells and a host computer for user interaction and application support.

CASSM is designed to support the hierarchical data model. The logical data structure is that of the set-oriented view so that it can also be classified as a hierarchical relational view (i.e., unnormalized relations). In fact, for that matter, CASSM claims support of all three popular data models by its ability to process hierarchical relations. The storage structure is a direct linearized mapping of tree structures onto CASSM cell tracks, in a bit and word serial manner. The linearization is done by preorder traversal. To be able to uniquely identify each node in the serial bit stream, each node is headed by its level number (i.e., tree level) and label (i.e., node name), which are stored in a delimiter word.

In global storage structure, a physical segment is fixed and equal in length to the capacity of a disk track. A logical record may span several physical segments (i.e., track overflow condition). This situation creates the need for intercell communication during operations. In the other extreme, a CASSM segment may contain logical records of more than one record type (file).

In CASSM, segments are made up of 40-bit words. A word consists of a 32-bit value, a 3-bit tag, a 3-bit status, a 1-bit parity, and a 1-bit called the T bit. The format and meaning of various data types are shown in Figure 7.1. Accordingly, each data word in CASSM has tag bits whose values identify the data type. The status bits are categorized as the M, H, and C bits, which stand for the following:

(a) The M bit indicates that a word is marked for a match.
(b) The H bit specifies the point of insertion to be made.
(c) The C bit (for collect) specifies the word to be copied or output.

One distinct feature of CASSM is that instructions are stored in the cells with data. A program execution follows a parse tree and activates the instructions, which are then fetched into the processor for execution, or deactivates them for branching or termination. Status bits are then used for the purposes of instruction execution as indicated in Figure 7.1. For example, whether a word is an opcode or immediate operand (TP bit) or whether an instruction is active (A bit) are specified by the status bits. A delimiter word is used to mark the beginning of a record or file.

The delimiter contains the level number; the name (label); a 6-bit stack, B; a qualification, Q, bit; and a specification, S, bit. The S bit indicates the place of the search to follow and Q bit indicates the result of the search at the places (or under, in the tree context) specified by the S bit. The bit stack combines the Q searches to process Boolean search expressions. The top two bits of the stack can be AND'ed or OR'ed. Names are encoded and literal data are stored in common data pools and pointed to from the records.

Figure 7.2(a) shows a cell and 7.2(b) shows RAM addressing of data items stored on tracks. There are parallel operating modules in a cell and a track of memory. Cells can communicate with their two neighbors in their linear interconnection. The *Instruction Fetch and Operand Recall* unit prefetches activated instruction words (i.e., those with tags 100) and operands and then stores them in registers and queues to be interpreted in sequence. A prefetched instruction becomes a candidate for execution in the subsequent revolutions of the memory track. The instruction is broadcast from the lowest-numbered processor storing the relevant data to other cells for parallel execution. On-the-fly data comparisons and update take place in the *Comparison and Update* module. The *I/O Processor* handles the data transfers between the disk and the controller which was implemented on a NOVA 800 in the prototype. The data items marked previously for output can be written at the end of files to form an operand list. Input can be done in three modes; word, segment, and append. In the word mode, a word is inserted after the track word, which is H-marked. Segment mode inputs track

MNEM	NAME	T	P		TAG		STATUS			DATA/INSTRUCTION				
D	DELIMITER			0	0	0	M	H	C	NAME		LEVEL	B-STACK	S	Q
N	NAME/VALUE			0	0	1	M	H	C	NAME		VALUE			
P	POINTER			0	1	0	M	H	C	NAME or L-POINTER		R-POINTER			
S	STRING			0	1	1	M	H	C	BYTE	BYTE	BYTE	BYTE		
I	INSTRUCTION			1	0	0	A		TP						
ST	STACK/QUEUE			1	0	1	SN		F						
E	ERASE/TEMP			1	1	1	STATUS								

IDENTIFIER	Meaning
NAME	Code word
VALUE	Code word or binary number
L-POINTER	Code word or record number
R-POINTER	Record number
LEVEL	Binary number
B-STACK	Bit stack for search results
BYTE	ASCII character
TP	Type
	00 to 10 first word
	11– immediate operand
SN	Stack/queue number
STATUS	Erase status
	100 END OF FILE
	110 HOLD
	111 GARBAGE
	(all other are TEMP)
S	Specification (enables bit stack)
Q	Qualification (enables search)
M	Match (loaded by QSR search result)
H	Hold (controls some I/O)
C	Collect (collect for output)
A	Active instruction
F	Flag (marks end of stack segment)

Figure 7.1 CASSM data types, formats, and code meanings. From S. Y. W. Su et al., "The Architectural Features and Implementation Techniques of the Multicell CASSM." *IEEE Transactions on Computers*, C-28, 6, © 1979 IEEE.

size data. The append mode appends data to the end of stored files. The *Garbage Collection and Insertion and Deletion* module inserts or deletes one word on a track per revolution. CASSM garbage collection is dynamic and global on the device level. This means that to fill fragmented tracks, data are transferred across track boundaries from other tracks. The *Post Processor* completes operations that could not be performed during previous revolutions.

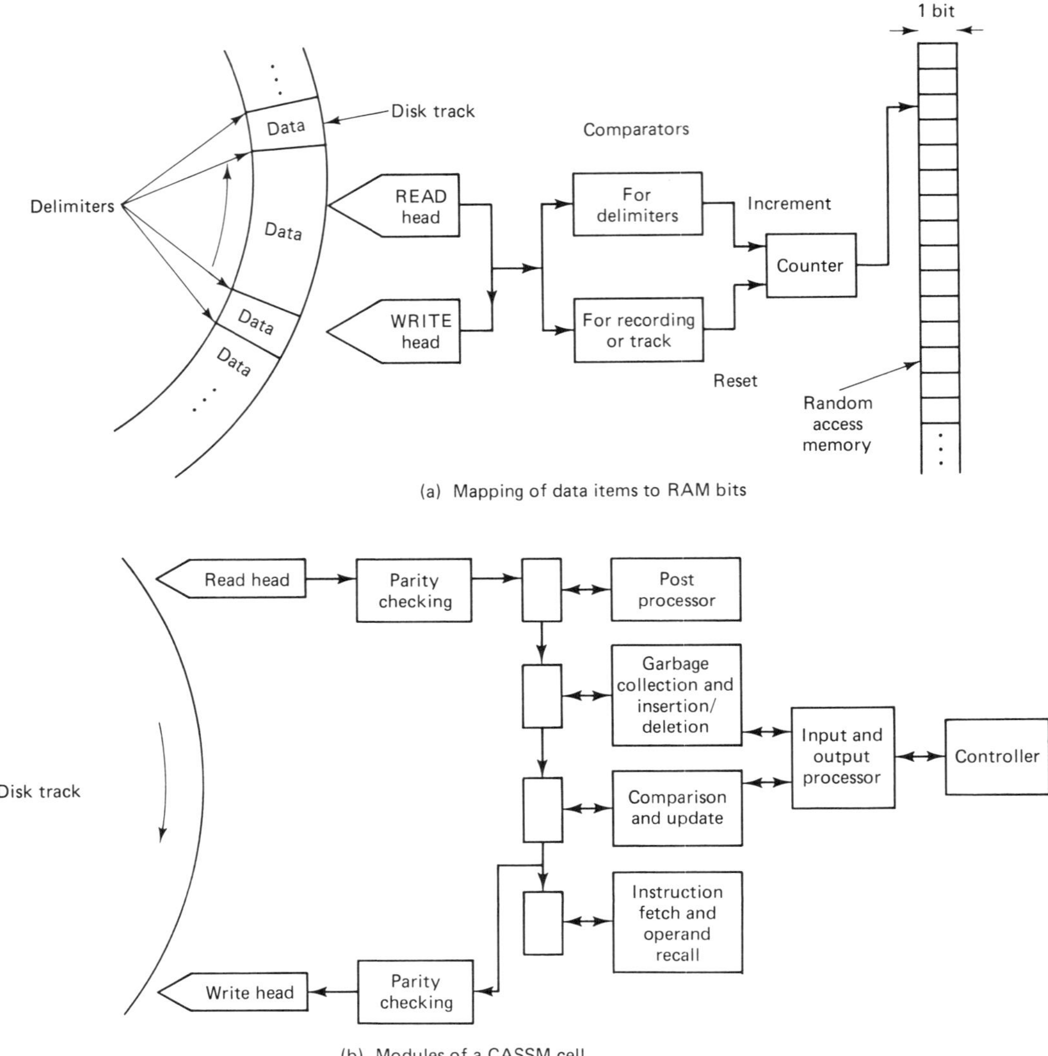

(a) Mapping of data items to RAM bits

(b) Modules of a CASSM cell

Figure 7.2 CASSM hardware units. From S. Y. W. Su et al., "The Architectural Features and Implementation Techniques of the Multicell CASSM." *IEEE Transactions on Computers,* C-28, 6, © 1979 IEEE.

Figure 7.2(a) shows the mapping hardware that recognizes data delimiters and track end and increments counters to determine the RAM bit that represents the mark position or address of a data word stored on the disk track. The individual RAMs are combined in such a way that their combined address space constitutes the global RAM (GRAM) on the device basis [Su et al., 1979].

Search operations.   A typical CASSM query involves searching and conditional marking of all occurrences of S-Q pairs throughout the database. If the occurrences overlap one another, the search takes more than one revolution. The S and Q bits can also be separated by an arbitrarily long distance with much data between them. If Q occurs before S in the memory sweep sequence (forward marking) the success of Q can be saved until S is found and conditionally marked later in the sequence. However, if S occurs first, then it cannot be marked until Q is found and satisfied later in the sequence. There must be a way to access a mark bit of S after Q is searched (backward marking). (Backward marking is somewhat analogous to the *F operation code in IMS. That is, in the search sweep, qualification comes later than the specification (output). However, in CASSM the record types can be far apart and they need not be twins.) This can be accomplished by having a set of mark bits that can be accessed independently of the circular memory segment and with a simple hardware method of mapping the mark bits to the data items on the segment. This is exactly what is accomplished by the RAM address mapping hardware shown in Figure 7.2(b). The RAM mark bit address of the specification item (i.e., ancestor in a tree) is saved for reference until the qualifying item (i.e., descendant in a tree) is reached later in the sequence. If the search is successful, then the specification mark bit is set, using the RAM address that was saved. With the tree stored in preorder along with level numbers, the algorithm simply involves remembering the RAM address of the last node at level k [a node at level k and any member of its subtree at level l ($k < l$ form an S-Q pair that does not overlap with any other pair at levels k and l].

Marking forward (down the tree) is much simpler. If a descendant item is to be marked whenever an ancestor item is successfully searched, the only thing to be remembered is whether or not the search was successful. The same hardware can be used for communication between set members of a tree node.

In forward marking across tracks, Q is remembered and when S is found on a following track, its RAM address is saved for marking it at the end of the revolution of memory. This is because Q cannot be made certain before the whole memory is searched. For backward marking, similar procedures are used; however, communication pulses are sent in the opposite direction.

Apart from searches that are carried out within a record type (i.e., selection) there are operations that perform cross-segment searches that can be used in the relational operation of join. These operations are grouped under transfer operations which are subdivided into *value matching, forward pointer transfer,* and *backward pointer transfer.* In all these, addressing via RAM or GRAM is used.

In *value matching,* a cross-segment or cross-record type matching is performed. This translates into going from one tree to another or to a relational join operation. First, a selection is performed in one record type and the qualifiers are set in their T bits (unlike the M bit, the T bit is specifically used by hardware for the transfer operation). The value parts of the T-marked words are mapped into GRAM by marking the bit at the GRAM address. Although this mapping has been illustrated as a direct value to bit address correspondence, a realistic mapping would use a hash function. After the GRAM bits are marked by the selected values of the first record type, which we can call source, they are used in the second pass to be reflected upon the second record type (i.e., target) words by a transfer RAM to data words (XRW) instruction. In other words, for each GRAM bit that was marked in the first pass, the words that correspond in value to this GRAM bit in the second record type are marked in their M bits. This concludes the value transfer. Figure 7.3(a) abstracts this operation.

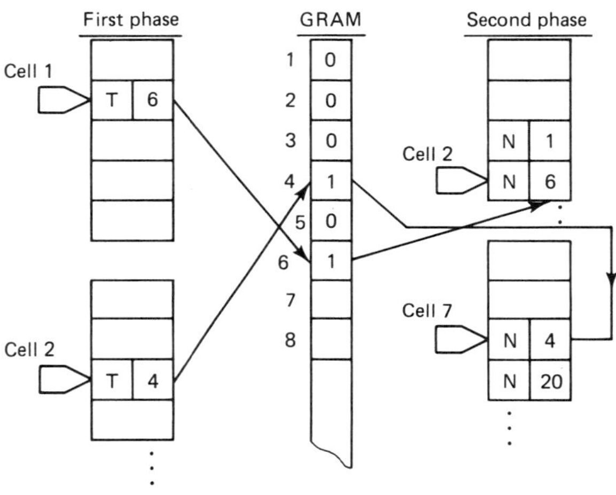

Figure 7.3 Transfer operations. From S. Y. W. Su et al., "The Architectural Features and Implementation Techniques of the Multicell CASSM." *IEEE Transactions on Computers*, C-28, 6, © 1979 IEEE.

In *forward pointer transfer,* the words of a target record type that are pointed by the pointer words in the source record type are located. Similar to value matching, the value part of pointer words, whose T bits are set, in the source record type is mapped into GRAM. The value part of the pointer words contains record numbers of the target record type. After this, the GRAM bits are transferred to the target record type by a transfer RAM to bit stack (XRB) instruction. This is done by setting the S and Q bits of the target delimiters of the records whose number match the GRAM address of the marked GRAM bits. Figure 7.3(b) abstracts this operation.

The *backward pointer transfer operation* is exactly opposite of the forward pointer transfer discussed already. In this operation, we start from the records that are selected previously and identify those pointer words that point to them in the other record type. This transfer is executed by the transfer from words to RAM (XWR) instruction, which is followed by the marking of the M bits of those pointer words whose value corresponds to the address of the marked GRAM bit.

CASSM Assembly Language.   There are seven groups of instructions in the CASSM assembly language. Each group contains one or more instructions. They are

(a) *Processor state and communication message instructions:* load and manipulate the PSW.

(b) *Delimiter mark instructions:* set S and Q bits. The Q bit is used to mark the context in which searches are conducted and the S bit marks the segment where the search result should be accumulated in the associated bit stack. The following shows the format of these instructions:

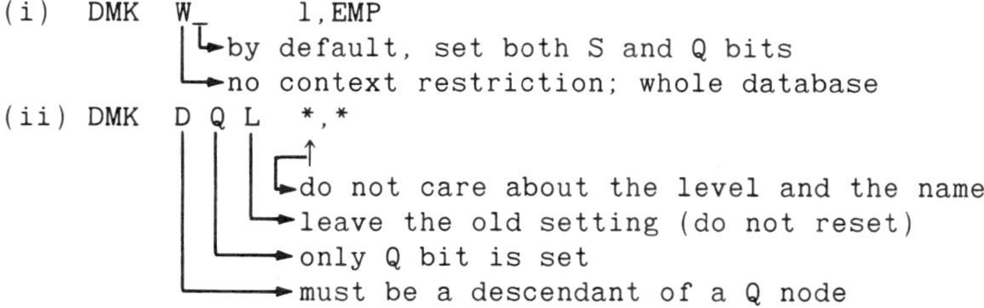

In (i), the level 1 nodes of all the EMP subtrees in the database are marked both in S and Q bits. In (ii), all nodes of the subtrees for all record types (trees) in the database are Q marked provided that their ancestors are all Q marked.

(c) *Qualified search instruction:* The qualified search instruction (QSR) searches data in the Q nodes and ORs the results within each S subtree. The result of the OR operation is then combined with the contents of the bit stack associated with the S subtree. The instruction consists of two parts. The first part deals with the search, and the second part manipulates the result. The search involves simple conditions of $=$, $\neq$, $<$, $\leq$, $\geq$, $>$ between an operand and a data word. A search context other than the Q nodes can also be specified. For example, one option is to search only those words that were successful in the most recent search. Another option would allow a search for logically consecutive words (e.g., a character string). The results of the search in individual subtrees are OR'ed together, which can then be negated and then pushed, AND'ed, or OR'ed with the top of the stack.

(d) *Find status/data (FND, FNS) instructions:* They consist of two parts. The first part locates words according to a search context (e.g., if top of a bit stack is set). The second part of the instructions can perform one of the following on the located words:

(1) Modify the word status, for example, set the C bit, load a new status to indicate that the word is to be deleted.

(2) Modify word content. This includes the capability of adding an operand to the words.

(3) Compute an aggregate function on the set of selected words.

(4) Find and mark, by setting the M bit, the top word in the set of words selected by the first part and optionally set the C bit. This allows choosing a single word from a list.

(e) *Pointer transfer instructions:* These instructions follow pointers and mark the records that are addressed by these pointers, as discussed in the previous section.

(f) *Program control instructions:* This group has four instructions: ACT, DAC, JMP, and ACS. Each instruction identifies a subtree by its delimiter containing level number and name and operates on the instructions in the subtree. If several subtrees have the same level number and name, the instructions in the subtrees will be activated or deactivated simultaneously for later execution. The instructions do the following:

ACT: It sets the activation bits of instruction words in order to include an instruction in the current list of active instructions. If the newly activated instruction precedes the previously activated ones in the sequential order, then the program flow will be interrupted and the new instruction will be given control.

DAC: It resets activation bits of instructions.

JMP: It first resets activation bits of all instructions in a record type. Afterward, it works the same as the ACT instruction. The net effect is that the instructions in a specified node to be branched are activated.

ACS: It does the same as ACT plus it pushes the value of the S bit of each delimiter in the record type onto the bit stack, hence saving the S bit pattern. In the program, a POP can be used to restore the value. The main use of this instruction is to be found in subroutine calls.

All of these instructions can operate with a qualification such as OR of M bit of data words, a CPU signal, or whether the top word of an operand list is a flag word.

(g) *Stack operation instructions:* In CASSM there are four stacks which are used to store operands or serve as queues. The instructions operate on the stacks and queues. Data can be entered into an operand buffer to be used as the next operand by LDI, ORI, ANI, and ADI instructions that load, or, and, and add immediate the addressed data to the operand buffer, respectively.

Example 7.1

Let us demonstrate a retrieval example. Our logical data structure will be the relation SALES, as shown in Figure 7.4(a), and its hierarchical representation, which is shown in Figure 7.4(b).

SALES

DEPT	VOL	ITEM
TOY	100	BALL
TOY	20	WAGON
TOY	10	GUN
SPORTS	30	FOOTBALL
SHOE	10	BOOTS

(a) The SALES relation

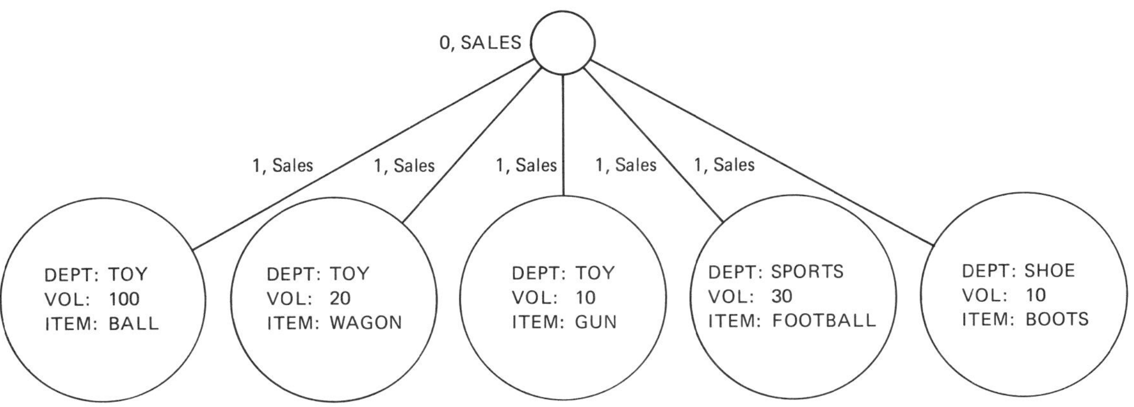

(b) Hierarchical representation of the SALES relation

Figure 7.4 Logical data structure.

As can be seen in Figure 7.4(b), the relation is transformed into a two-level tree in which root (level 0) is the relation name and all the tuples are level 1 nodes. Figure 7.5(a) shows the corresponding physical data structure.

Data Type	Contents	Bit Stack	S	Q	Bit Stack	S	Q	Bit Stack	S
D(0)	0, SALES	000000	0	0	000000	0	0	000000	0
D(1)	1, SALES	000000	1	1	000001	1	1	000001	1
P	DEPT, 7								
N	VOL, 100								
P	ITEM, 10								
D(2)	1, SALES	000000	1	1	000001	1	1	000000	1
P	DEPT, 7								
N	VOL, 20								
P	ITEM, 11								
D(3)	1, SALES	000000	1	1	000001	1	1	000001	1
P	DEPT, 7								
N	VOL, 10								
P	ITEM, 12								
D(4)	1, SALES	000000	1	1	000000	0	0	000000	0
P	DEPT, 8								
N	VOL, 30								
P	ITEM, 13								
D(5)	1, SALES	000000	1	1	000000	1	1	000000	1
P	DEPT, 9								
N	VOL, 10								
P	ITEM, 14								
D(6)	0, XREF	000000	0	0	000000	0	0	000000	0
D(7)	1, XDEPT	000001	1	1	000000	1	1	000000	1
N	SDEPT, 'TO'								
S	'Y '								
D(8)	1, XDEPT	000000	1	1	000000	1	1	000000	1
N	SDEPT, 'SP'								
S	'ORTS'								
S	' '								
D(9)	1, XDEPT	000000	1	1	000000	1	1	000000	1
N	SDEPT, 'SH'								
S	'OE '								
D(10)	1, XITEM	000000	0	0	000000	0	0	000000	0
N	SITEM, 'BA'								
S	'LL '								
D(11)	1, XITEM	000000	0	0	000000	0	0	000000	0
N	SITEM, 'WA'								
S	'GON '								
D(12)	1, XITEM	000000	0	0	000000	0	0	000000	0
N	SITEM, 'GU'								
S	'N '								
D(13)	1, XITEM	000000	0	0	000000	0	0	000000	0
N	SITEM, 'FO'								
S	'OTBA'								
S	'LL '								
D(14)	1, XITEM	000000	0	0	000000	0	0	000000	0
N	SITEM, 'BO'								
S	'OTS '								

(a) Storage structure and trace of the search operation (on the right)

Figure 7.5 A retrieval example.

```
 1. 0, BEGIN:     LDP       NOIN (Q0) (CP, WDR) AWK
 2.               DMKW      1, SALES
 3.               DMKL      1, XDEPT
 4.               QSR       N; PUB; IM SDEPT, 'TO'
 5.               QSRN      S; ANB; IM 'Ybbb'
 6.               XFR       BXSALES; PUB
 7.               DMK       1, SALES
 8.               DMKL      1, XITEM
 9.               QSR       =(N); PUB; IM SITEM, 'GU'
10.               QSRN      N; ANB; IM 'Nbbb'
11.               XFR       BXSALES; ANB, PUB
12.               LDP       NOIN (Q0) (NC) AWK
13.               FND       (N, VOL); ORS C
14.               XFR       ITEM; C
15.               LDP       NOIN (Q0) (CP, WPD) WTC
16.               DMKW      0, BEGIN
17.               DMKDL     dc, dc
18.               RPSQ      ('100---'); LDS ('111---')
```

(b) CASSM assembler program

Figure 7.5 (*continued*)

On the leftmost column, data types are indicated. The delimiters are indicated by D with their corresponding level numbers in parentheses. Integers are stored in data words indicated by N, and all the string data (i.e., literals) are stored in a cross-reference file (XREF at level 0) pointed to by pointer, P, words. In the cross-reference file, we see literal names as level 1 nodes whose first two characters are stored in data words and the remainder as character strings (i.e., S bytes).

Figure 7.5(b) shows the CASSM assembler program written for the query *find the sale volume and sale item other than Gun for the Toy department*. The following is the explanation of that program:

The first instruction is a control instruction that loads the PSW (processor state word) and specifies, among other things, that queue zero (Q_0) will be used as the operand queue. The second instruction searches for 1, SALES and marks the S and Q bits of the delimiter words D(1) through D(5). The next instruction (3) marks the S and Q bits of delimiters D(7) through D(9). The fourth instruction searches for the records, whose Q bits are set, that contain a name word (N) with name SDEPT and whose value is 'TO'. A bit is pushed (PUB) onto the bit stack of those records containing the word. In parallel to this, the M (match) bit of each matched word is set. The next instruction (5) searches for the words following the matched ones for the remaining character string 'Ybbb' and a bit (1) is AND'ed (ANB) with the top of the stack. After this instruction is executed, only the D(7) delimited record qualifies in instruction (6). A bit is pushed (PUB) onto the bit stacks of those records whose pointers have their S-bit set. The instructions (7) through (10) perform similar operations with the exception that the cross-reference table is searched for the items that are not equal to 'GUN'. The (11)th instruction transfers the pointers from records of D(10), D(11), D(13), and D(14) (i.e., $\neq$ GUN). The top bit of the bit stacks associated with the records delimited by D(1), D(2), and D(3) (i.e., TOY) are AND'ed with one. This leaves records of D(1) and D(2) with a one bit on top of their stacks. This one bit is duplicated, by the PUB option, in both stacks. This is done for the output of the marked records. The (12)th instruction changes the processor state to suppress output (NC, no collection) until the PSW is changed. The next instruction (13) searches for the item VOL and changes the status bit of the word to set the collection (C) bit. The (14)th instruction transfers pointers for items and sets the character strings of items for collection. The next instruction (15) changes the processor state to output the marked items, using the word delimited mode (WPD), to ensure that the values for VOL and ITEM will be output in pairs. The WTC option causes the processor to wait until completion of the output. The last three instructions delete the program from memory. The (16)th instruction marks the records containing the instructions. The next instruction (17) marks all of the existing subtrees and the RPSQ instruction searches for the marked records with instruction words (i.e., tag = '100') and replaces their tags with '111'; meaning erased by the LDS subinstruction. This instruction word also turns itself into a garbage word.

7.1.2 RAP

The RAP (relational associative processor) originated at the University of Toronto [Ozkarahan, 1976; Ozkarahan, Schuster, and Smith, 1975]. RAP is also a cellular associative device that was originally conceptualized on head-per-track disks. However, all of its prototypes have been built on solid-state memories in VLSI, and in fact the last RAP.3 system is designed around such memories. There have been three prototypes of the RAP database machine. While RAP.1 and RAP.2 are similar, the RAP.3 architecture has brought many new features besides eliminating various limitations of RAP.1 and RAP.2. It is for this reason that the RAP presentation will be split into two parts. In the first part, we will present RAP.1 and RAP.2 and the basic properties that are common to all RAP systems. In the second part, we will concentrate on the RAP.3 architecture. For this reason, the space we will devote to the RAP database machine will be more than that of a single system.

RAP.1 and RAP.2. The RAP architecture consists of a linear array of cells driven by a controller, which, in turn, is connected to a frontend host computer. Each cell is made up of a serial circulating memory and a specially hardwired processor. Originally, in RAP.1, the cells could communicate with their immediate neighbors; however, in RAP.2 this was removed and cells were driven solely by the controller. The controller is also responsible for polling in cell scalar aggregates to produce the global scalar aggregate result. In RAP.1, the controller was hardwired whereas in RAP.2 it was replaced by a PDP 11/10 minicomputer. Figure 7.6 shows the RAP architecture. The user interface and application program support are provided by the host computer. The controller is responsible for instruction initiation and control of program execution in the cells. It also supports the program and response I/O traffic between the frontend and the cell array.

The logical data structure supported by the RAP architecture follows the

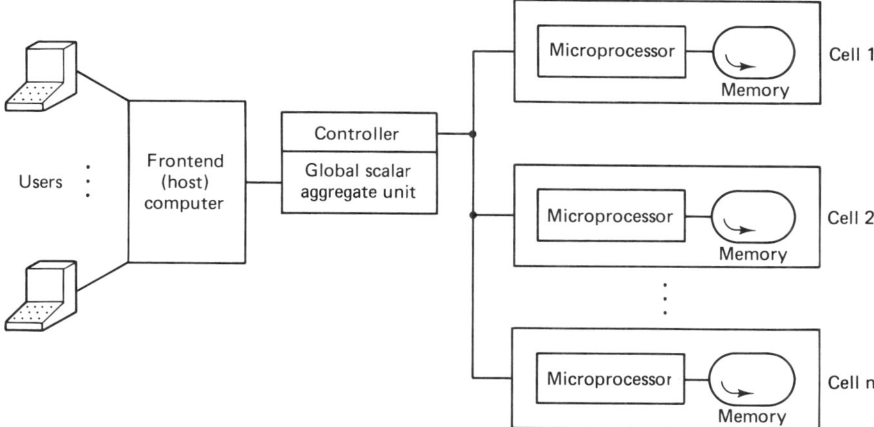

Figure 7.6 RAP architecture.

relational data model [Codd, 1970]. Although there are some designs that are restricted to binary relations, RAP does not place any restriction on the value of n, the degree of relations. Therefore, we can say that RAP supports normalized n'ary relations with some modifications, which will be outlined shortly. This free format of relational schema in RAP enables vertical fragments of relations to be stored and processed directly in the device. Vertical fragmentation [i.e., a relation split into attribute (column) clusters] may sometimes be better than the extremes such as binary or n'ary relations. However, if fragments have to be combined to reconstruct the large relations, the responsibility of directing a join operation rests with the applications or upper-level DBMS software. The modifications that RAP makes on normalized relations are as follows:

(a) To be able to implement content and context searches (i.e., associative context) without intermediate storage, RAP augments an n'ary relation with a number (16) of mark attributes and the result is called a RAP relation.

(b) The key uniqueness property of mathematical relations is not enforced at the machine level. This enforcement is delegated to the higher-level DBMS software. The advantage of this is that the RAP database machine is able to support multi-relations. Also, on-line tuple insertions to the device can be made faster while key uniqueness can be enforced at the background.

Figure 7.7(a) displays the RAP physical data structure (i.e., RAP relation format) and Figure 7.7(b) shows the mapping from a logical (relational) data structure to the RAP storage structure.

As seen in Figure 7.7, the RAP-tuples are stored in bit and word serial fashion, one after the other separated by gaps. This is the RAP.1 storage structure. In RAP.2, gaps were eliminated. The schema information consisting of relation name and list of attribute names is stored at the beginning of each cell. In RAP.1

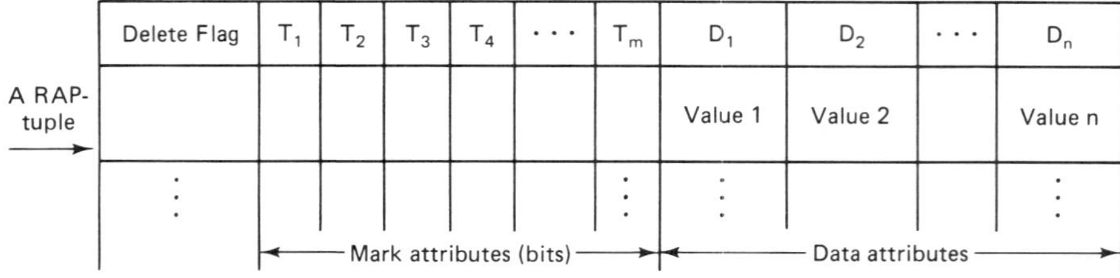

(a) RAP relation format

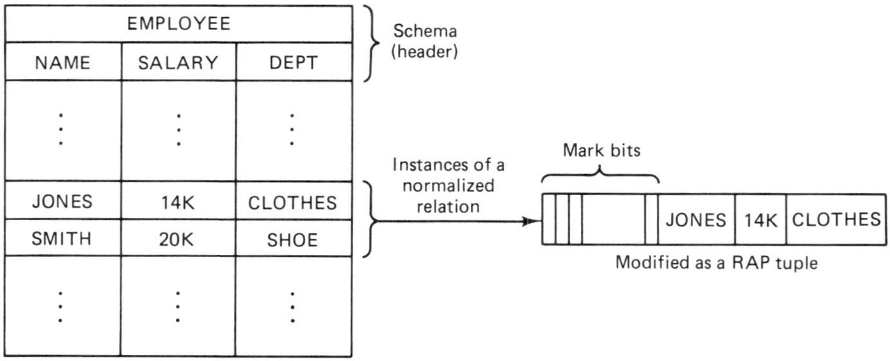

(1) Logical

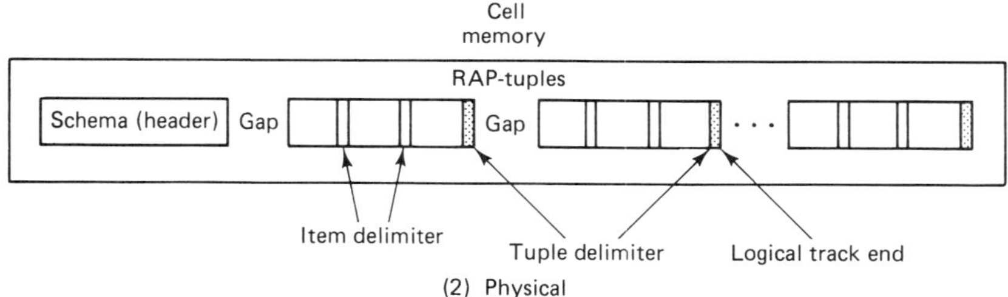

(2) Physical

(b) Mapping from a relation to RAP storage structure

Figure 7.7   RAP relation and storage structure.

and RAP.2 (RAP.1 & 2 from now on), a track could store tuples of only one relation. Tuples following the schema block contain values only. That is, attribute names are not repeated in the tuple blocks, but located by counters that are set by the schema block. Each tuple is terminated by a delimiter and data words storing attribute values are preceded by length codes. The end of relation data on a cell is indicated by a "logical track end" delimiter.

The data types supported by RAP.1 & 2 are fixed length words of full- (4 bytes), half-, and quarter-word size. The literal strings are either stored directly in consecutive words or encoded into integer values. Each RAP tuple is preceded by one delete flag and several (four in RAP.1 & 2) mark bits. By the use of mark bits, content searches can be made by setting (or resetting) mark bits of eligible tuples. Previous search results can be combined as mark qualifications into subsequent search operations for building context searches.

Each RAP.1 & 2 cell contains a specially hardwired cell processor of SSI (small scale integration) and MSI (medium scale integration) chips (around 400 in total). The cell modules work in a pipeline, as data are streamed through them, synchronous with the bit rate coming off the disk read head. Figure 7.8 shows the structure of a RAP.1 & 2 cell processor. As can be seen in the figure, the data coming from the read head are channeled into multiple paths: one to the delay buffer between the read and write heads and the other into the cell modules.

As seen from the RAP storage structure, the data format is self-driven. That is, delimiters, length codes, and the schema block contain the necessary information. To convert that information into control signals, the track format sensor module interprets the bit encodings and sends synchronization and clock signals to the rest of the cell circuitry. The data in the cell pipe go through the query analyzer, which consists of k (was 5 in the first prototype) parallel term (attribute value) comparators, and random logic, which evaluates comparator results with respect to Boolean query specifications. In the case of selection, each comparator stores a value representing a different attribute, whereas in

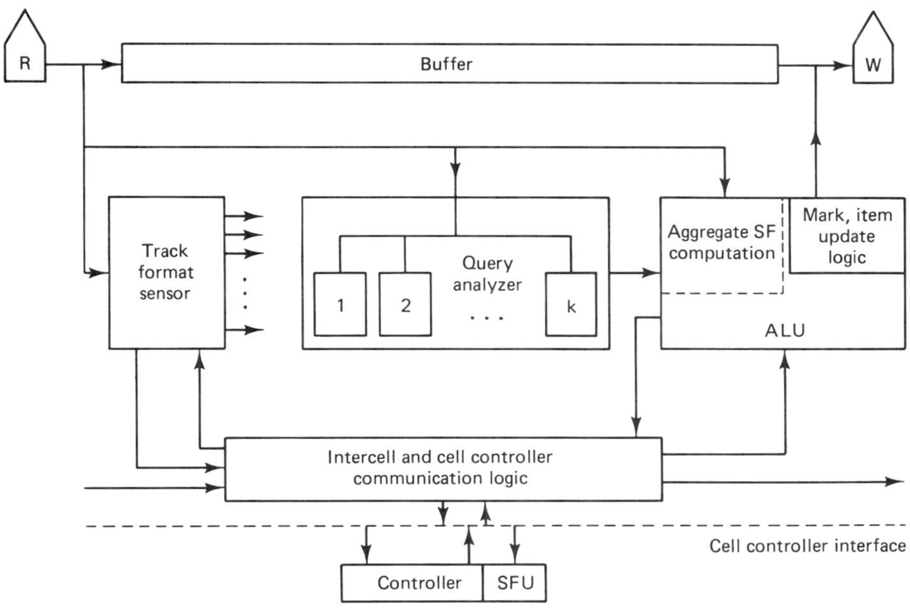

Figure 7.8   RAP.1 & 2 cell processor.

semi-join all the comparators are filled with the values of the join attribute of the source relation while the target relation join attribute values are streamed through the data bus of the comparators. To repeat the same search over and over for every tuple coming off the cell memory, the comparators work like a rotating silo as shown in Figure 5.10. In the search evaluation, the marked or unmarked status of tuples for a specified mark bit is detected in the track format sensor unit and forwarded to the query analyzer to be combined with the rest of the query evaluation. The RAP language is introduced in Section 3.4. If the reader skipped that chapter, we recommend going back to that section to cover the RAP language. At this point, we want to demonstrate qualification evaluation on a RAP tuple before the reader delves into the details of Section 3.4. A less detailed summary of the operational capabilities is also included at the end of this subsection.

Example 7.2

Assume a ternary RAP relation EMPLOYEE with attributes NAME, NCHILDREN, and SALARY, and further, assume that one of its tuples is stored with respect to the format shown below:

```
(a)   DF = 0      (delete flag)
      T1 = 1  ⎫
      T2 = 0  ⎪
              ⎬   mark bits
      T3 = 1  ⎪
      T4 = 0  ⎭
(b)   "CLARK"     (name)
(c)   3           (NCHILDREN)
(d)   9500        (SALARY)
```

0	1	0	1	0	CLARK	3	9500

Some of the qualifications that this tuple will satisfy are

```
(a)   NULL
(b)   MKED(T1)
(c)   UNMKED(T2T4)
(d)   (NAME = "CLARK") ∧ (MKED(T1T3)) (conjunction)
(e)   (NCHILDREN ≠ 5) ∨ (SALARY < 5000) ∨ (MKED(T1))
      (disjunctions)
```

In its progression, the tuple finally arrives at the ALU which contains bit serial arithmetic units, a scalar aggregate subunit that computes sum, count, and keeps track of maximum and minimum for the eligible tuples that are signaled from the query analyzer. In case of updates, the tuple items are overwritten by their updates on the way back to the write head which writes them back onto the disk memory. Part of the updating process also involves setting or resetting delete flag and/or mark bits. If tuples are going to be read they find their way to the readout unit while being written back on the memory. The SFU is the global scalar aggregate unit which collects cell aggregates from the cell array.

In RAP.1, the source join attribute values were extracted from cells and directly passed to target cells. However, cell interconnections were removed in the later versions.

In the early disk version of the RAP architecture, there was the readout contention problem. This occurred at the presence of a single serial I/O channel and when there was more than one eligible tuple to be read out in the cells and those tuples were coincident at the same angular position. This is because only one cell was given permission to output its tuple onto the serial channel and the other cells were to be delayed to subsequent revolutions of the memory. This limitation was removed when block addressable memories such as CCDs in RAP.2 and RAMs in RAP.3 were utilized.

The RAP.1 and RAP.2 systems were prototyped and tested at the University of Toronto [Schuster et al., 1979]. In the RAP.2 prototype, the system configuration was a database machine with a PDP 11/45 GPC frontend. The controller for RAP was a PDP 11/10, which was driven by the GPC. Two RAP cells utilizing CCDs for cell memories were built. In the prototype demonstration, the GPC ran SEQUEL (SQL) queries; they were translated into RAP code and executed on the cells. The cell memory had a bit and word serial format and input to the cell processor was a bit serial data stream.

Features of RAP primitives.   The RAP language was covered in Chapter 3. The language is relationally complete as well as universal (see Chapter 8). At this point we will highlight some of its features.

The backbone of the language is Boolean qualification evaluation. This is done associatively. By parallelism and data synchronous processing (a form of on-the-fly processing), while tuples are evaluated with respect to Boolean qualification, the following operations are performed on them simultaneously with qualification evaluation:

(a) Selection

(b) Arithmetic update

(c) Aggregate operations

The language also includes the mark bit–driven cursor construct of Get-first, which enables programming of all complex operations (e.g., grouping, projection, set operations). There are also registers in the language which store results of aggregates and saved data (by Get-first or other operations). These register contents can be used in the program so that, for example, a sort program can be written by iterative min(max) finding and subsequent selection. Also, with a pause statement a program execution can be temporarily interrupted and values can be externally injected into the executing program.

Semi-join, projection, and transaction processing are executed as hardware macros. The other set operations such as join, union, intersection, product, and difference can be programmed around the basic notion of tuple data saving from one relation and subsequently restricting the other relation with a construct such as

```
Loop on tag t₁
GET_FIRST [R1(A₁, A₂,  · · ·, Aₙ) : MKED( t₁)]
MARK(t₂) [R2 :  A₁ θ REGC_1 & A₂ θ REGC_2,  · · ·, Aₙ θ REGC_n]
Output or write operation
Until all tags are turned off (i.e., all R1 tuples are processed).
```

The θ is a relational (comparison) operator and REGC_i's are save registers. Chapter 3 presents an algorithm for programming division in RAP.

The RAP.3 architecture.   With the advances in VLSI and solid-state technology, it became possible to replace the specially hardwired cell processor with relatively fast and off-the-shelf microprocessors. However, since the terminal characteristics of the RAP device are rather complex, a parallel combination of microprocessors was needed to build a cell. This process was not a mere component change, but rather the entire cell structure was redesigned, without altering the terminal characteristics of the RAP database machine, by improving certain things. The result was the RAP.3 database machine [Ozkarahan and Oflazer, 1978; Oflazer, 1979; Oflazer, Ozkarahan, and Smith, 1980]. Also, at that time CCDs were being phased out and magnetic bubbles and/or RAMs were emerging for candidacy of the cell memory. These memories, besides being VLSI components, have the additional advantage of being controllable. That is, we can stop and restart them all along during the operations. This is not possible with disks and CCDs; we can slow them down, but by anticipating in advance, not dynamically without notice on a single tuple. In disks and CCDs when we slow down, we are locked up to that speed for a good many tuples on memory, therefore defeating the purpose. Memory controllability simplifies cell logic because when we need extra time to compute on a tuple, we can stop memory and continue when we are finished with computing. The alternative to this is to anticipate the worst case timing condition and design the cell processor in a complex and expensive manner for the odd moments of overload.

The restructuring of the RAP cell to use microprocessors has transformed the tightly balanced and inflexible cell operations into a firmware-based system where parallel microprocessors execute the query code on the tuples stored in their local memories from cell memory. The following are some basic changes compared to RAP.1 & 2:

(a) The storage structure is changed from the bit and word serial format to the bit parallel word serial format.

(b) In the cell memory, the schema header block, storage gaps, record delimiters, and item length codes are all removed and the necessary information is kept in the cell interface processor of each cell.

(c) Literal data type of maximum 256 characters and text data type of up to 1024 characters, which store multiple sentences, are introduced.

(d) The cell memory became universal; disks, CCDs, magnetic bubbles, or RAMs can all be accommodated.

(e) Cell chip (component) count has been reduced to one third.

(f) The readout collision contention has been eliminated.

(g) Context sensitive text operations are added to the instruction set.

(h) The limitation on criterion length (CL), that is, the number of simple conditions in the Boolean qualification (predicate) of a RAP instruction has been changed from 5 to a practically unlimited (i.e., 50 or more) value.

(i) In the instructions, attribute to attribute comparison and arithmetic have been incorporated.

(j) New hardware macros are introduced to speed the hard database operations of projection, join, and transaction processing.

(k) Tuples of more than one relation can be stored in a RAP cell and cells can be partitioned to execute more than one query in parallel. These make the RAP.3 architecture an MIMD type (Figure 7.11).

Figure 7.9 shows the RAP.3 cell structure. A RAP.3 cell consists of a multimicroprocessor structure in which k microprocessors, each of which is called a *subcell,* operate in parallel and, in addition, there is a microprocessor called the *cell interface processor (CIMPU)* responsible for overall coordination of a cell. The tuples are read in (loaded) from cell memory, word at a time (i.e., bit parallel) by the hardwired *direct memory access (DMA)* unit, and selectively written back (stored) to and from RAMs of subcells. The I/O scenario between cell memory and subcells is such that no programmed I/O is utilized. Instead, subcells are locked in a wait loop and awakened by the DMA hardware whenever a tuple is placed in their RAM from cell memory by the DMA. The reading and

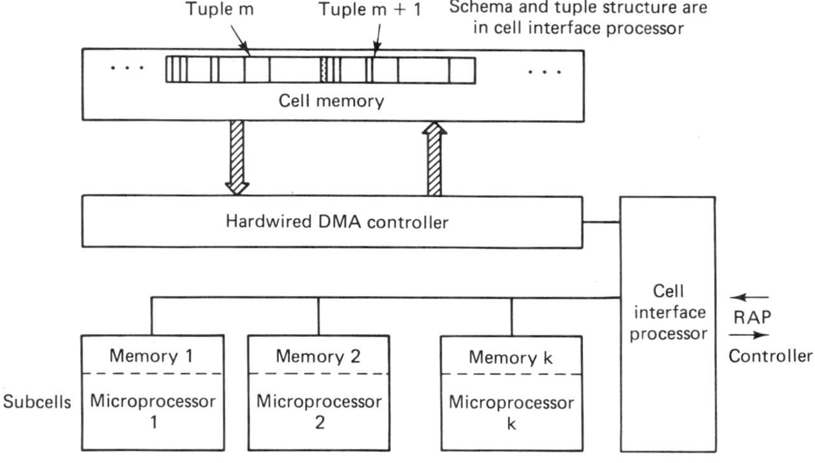

Figure 7.9 RAP.3 cell processor and storage structure.

writing of tuples on cell memory takes place concurrently (actually in split memory access cycle).

At the beginning of an instruction execution, each subcell is loaded by the microprocessor code equivalent of a RAP instruction. During the execution, each subcell repeats the execution of this code on every tuple it receives in its RAM. The coordination of subcells, such as determining the first eligible among several subcells (in a grouping operation) or consolidating mark counts or aggregates on a cell basis, control of DMA, cell memory bulk I/O, and interface with the RAP controller are among the responsibilities of the cell interface processor. Also, RAP registers are kept in its memory, and these registers are mapped into the global RAP registers in controller memory. The RAP registers are needed for the following purposes:

(a) Storing scalar aggregates.
(b) Saving values from tuples to output or use them as free variables in grouping, correlation, and so on.
(c) Injecting values into a RAP program.

RAP.3 model with universal cell memory.   Let us return to the RAP.3 cell operation. The DMA constantly fetches tuples from cell memory, while writing others back at the same time, and stores them in subcell RAMs in a cyclic fashion, the same as one deals cards in a card game. A subcell is fired to process a tuple as soon as it receives the tuple. The DMA hardware operates continuously, however. Therefore, a subcell must finish its process on the current tuple and write it back (store) on cell memory before the time arrives to start receiving (loading) another tuple. Accordingly, at a given time among the k subcells of a cell, two are constantly busy with I/O—one loads, the other stores—while the rest are processing. This implies the following relationship for the time available for a subcell to process a tuple:

$$t_{PR} = \text{time allocated to process a tuple} = \text{a function } f(k, t_{LS}) = (k - 2)t_{LS}$$

where t_{LS} is the load/store time for a tuple through DMA and is a function f of (*tuple length, memory data rate*). That is, I/O time is determined by how long (or how much) data a tuple has and how fast it can be read or written on cell memory. k is used as 4 in the RAP.3 prototype. Notice that k cannot be less than 3; otherwise, operation continuity would be lost. This is because while two subcells are performing I/O only one will be left to continue processing. The cell operation and subcell timing relationship can be observed in Figure 7.10(a). Each subcell has an Intel 8086 microprocessor and possesses the full functionality of a RAP cell (i.e., can execute all RAP instructions). The cell memory is a bulk dynamic RAM of 1 to 2 megabytes of capacity. The subcell RAM must have enough room to hold a tuple, query routine (that is the 8086 code equivalent of a RAP instruction), and comparand values. The comparand store receives 750 or 1500 values to be compared with the incoming tuples of the cell in transaction processing and semi-join operations, respectively.

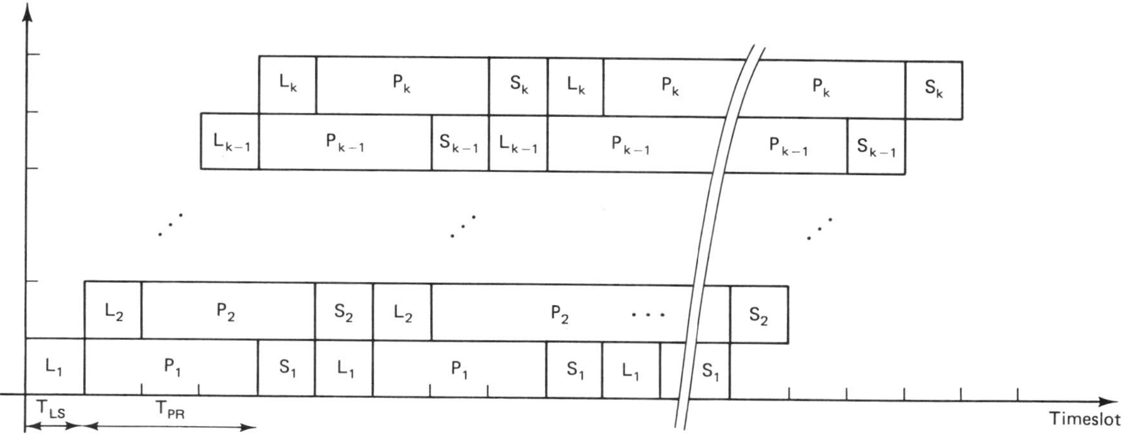

(a) Load/process/store sequences of cell operation

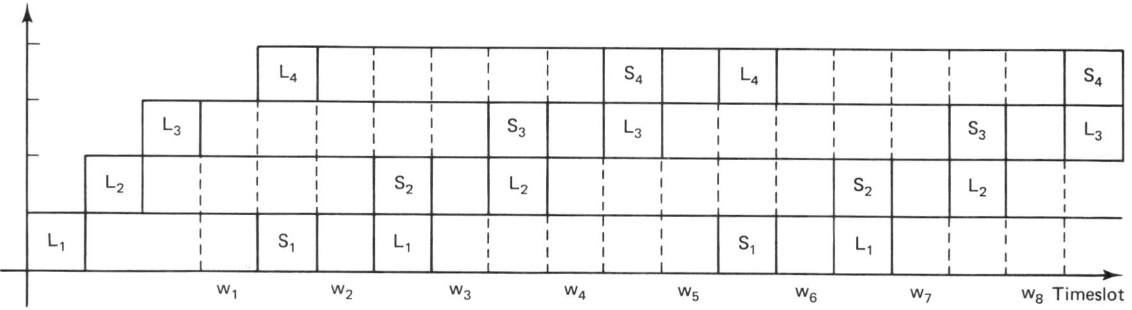

(b) Time sequences with inserted variable length waits (k = 4)

Figure 7.10   Time sequences of RAP.3 cell operations.

While the cell operation depicted in Figure 7.10(a) is good for a disk or CCD memory, RAP.3 is also tuned for controllable memories. As we mentioned earlier, the controllable memories can be dynamically stopped and restarted without prior notice. This enables RAP.3 to inject wait times into the load-process-store cycle whenever a subcell is unable to complete its processing. These wait-time slices, indicated by w, are shown on the modified cell operation diagram of Figure 7.10(b). As can be seen from this diagram, a subcell's wait request is projected upward, that is, absorbed by the other subcells working in parallel. This reduces the chance of other subcells requesting waits on their own. This picture translates into the following relationships: if we denote wait time by w, the available tuple processing time t_{PRW_i} for a subcell in the wait scheme will be

$$t_{PRW_i} = (k - 2)t_{LS} + \sum_{j=i-(k-2)}^{i-1} w_j$$

where $i = 1, \ldots, NT$; NT is the number of tuples stored in a cell; w_j is the wait time associated with the jth tuple; and $w_0 = 0$ for $j \leqslant 0$. If we define an overload factor $L \geqslant 1$, which will be multiples of tuple processing time t_{PR}, for a tuple process that will be longer than allocated due to waits, the resulting RAP.3 time t_{SCAN} will be less than L fold due to in-cell parallelism of subcells and absorption of the wait time by $(k - 2)$ previous subcell process times (as seen in the diagram). In other words, the ratio

$$\frac{t_{SCAN} \ (\text{i.e., without wait scheme})}{t_{SCAN/w} \ (\text{i.e., with waits allowed})}$$

will be less than L for $L > 1$ and is given by the relationship $(2 + L(k - 2))/k$. This relationship is demonstrated as an example in the following. The reader may skip that in the first reading.

Example 7.3

Assuming that there are NT-tuples stored in a cell, the overall time taken to search the cell memory will be shown by t_{SCAN}, which is

$$t_{SCAN} = NT.t_{LS} + t_{LAST}$$

where $t_{LAST} = (k - 1).t_{LS}$ corresponding to rewriting of the last $(k - 1)$-tuples left in the subcells at the end of a memory scan. Incorporating the wait scheme,

$$t_{SCAN/w} = NT.t_{LS} + t_{WAIT} + t_{LAST}$$

where $t_{WAIT} = \Sigma_{j=1}^{NT} w_j$ which is the total wait time incurred at the end of a memory scan. Defining the overload ratio, L, as the multiples of t_{PR} to process each tuple in the cell memory, $t_{SCAN/w}$ can be rewritten as

$$t_{SCAN/w} = (NT/k).t_{TUP} + (k - 1).t_{LS} + (L - 1).(k - 2).t_{LS}$$

where

$$t_{TUP} = L.(k - 2).t_{LS} + 2.t_{LS}, \qquad L \geqslant 1$$

with the fact that processing of tuples takes place among k subcells in parallel (to account for the first term of $t_{SCAN/w}$) and that there is an initial time for the first tuple that is not included in the allocated time (to account for the third term of $t_{SCAN/w}$). Substituting t_{TUP} into $t_{SCAN/w}$,

$$t_{SCAN/w} = ((NT/k).(2 + L.(k - 2)) + (L.(k - 2) + 1)/t_{LS}$$

neglecting the terms $(k - 1)$ and $(L.(k - 2) + 1)$ in t_{SCAN} and $t_{SCAN/w}$, respectively, the ratio $t_{SCAN}/t_{SCAN/w}$ becomes

$$((NT/k).(2 + L.(k - 2)))/NT = (2 + L.(k - 2))/k < L, \qquad \text{for } L > 1$$

By the use of the wait scheme, RAP.3 can process complex queries requiring long tuple times with the same simple hardware designed for the typical query load.

RAM tuned RAP.3 model.   In the second version of the RAP.3 architecture [Ozkarahan, 1985], the presence of controllable memories, especially RAMs, was assumed and the following suboptimizations were built into the cell structure.

These suboptimizations are listed below in a comparative manner with respect to the universal memory based RAP.3 version:

(a) Cell memory size is increased to 2 megabytes.

(b) The power of CIMPU is increased to be able to sort cell memory contents in certain cases.

(c) The DMA hardware is made more sophisticated to allow the following:
   (1) Tuple qualifications can be evaluated on the memory bus, bypassing subcells, in cases where the qualification depends only on the marked and/or unmarked tuple status.
   (2) The DMA can page in relations (for the next query) concurrently with subcell operations because the RAM tuned model became subcell processing bound (leaving idle DMA time) instead of the tuple I/O bound model of the universal cell memory based RAP.3 version.

(d) In addition to RAP instructions, new hardware macros are built in for the hard database operations of projection and join and also for transaction processing.

(e) As indicated in (c.2), cell processing has been changed from an I/O-bound model to a subcell processing bound one. In the following, this model will be described.

(f) Instead of entire tuples, selective words are accessed from tuples and ineligible tuple data are not stored back in the cell memory. This changes the cyclic synchronous cell I/O into an asynchronous I/O because at a given time a subcell with an ineligible tuple for the query leaves that tuple and requests a new one to be sent from the DMA.

In the I/O-bound cell model, the tuple processing time t_{PR} was $(k - 2)t_{LS}$. This became $t_{PR} = t_P/k$, where t_P is the time for a subcell to process a tuple. The difference between t_{PR} and t_P is that while t_P is absolute, t_{PR} is virtual or effective time. This is because to complete one memory scan, which will be indicated by t_{SCAN}, NT-tuples must be processed (serially in time $t_P.NT$). However, since k subcells do the same operation in parallel $t_{SCAN} = (t_P/k)NT$ where the first term is the effective tuple processing time. t_P falls in the range indicated by the following relationship:

$$W.t_{WLS} + \rho.W'.t_{WLS} \leqslant t_P \leqslant t_{PR\text{-}OLD}$$

where $t_{PR\text{-}OLD}$ is t_{PR} of the universal memory model, W is the number of words that are read from a tuple, and W' is the number updated back (if there is no update we need not rewrite the words we read even if the tuple is eligible, unlike the universal memory model); t_{WLS} is the word read or write time; and ρ is the proportion (i.e., selectivity) of eligible tuples. Accordingly, in this model there will not be any unused tuple I/O time. Only those words (W of them) required in the instruction specification and qualification need to be brought in subcells.

If there is an update (on W' many words) only the data of eligible tuples, whose proportion is ρ, are written back so that t_P will not be overridden by I/O as indicated by the left-hand side of the t_P relationship. Because of this relationship, DMA gains idle time to concentrate on paging activities of other relations to be input or output (paged out after an update).

As we stated earlier, the new RAP.3 design removed the early restrictions that made the device an SIMD architecture. As can be seen in Figure 7.11, multiple relations can be stored and multiple executions can be fired on the device. The DMA unit, controllable cell memory, and CIMPU eased the disk-based tight locked-step operation mode to achieve the capabilities of an MIMD device. An early simulation of the multirelation per cell idea was done also in the RAP.2 design [Sadowski, 1978].

In the disk-based old RAP model, to process a 128-byte-long tuple by evaluating a single predicate over one of its attributes it took 0.15 msec, whereas the effective tuple processing time for the same is 7 μsec in RAP.3. This is due to solid-state cell memory and in-cell parallelism (of subcells). This allowed the cell memory capacity to increase to 2 megabytes in RAP.3 from the old disk track model. In addition to these, the following factors contribute to the superiority of RAP.3 with respect to RAP.1 & 2:

(a) Ability to store a relation orthogonally across cells (Figure 7.11)
(b) Ability to store more than one relation per cell (Figure 7.11)
(c) Bit parallel, byte serial storage format
(d) Ability to process unlimited (i.e., very high) number of predicates in a qualification and/or arithmetic operations in an arithmetic update expression
(e) Random block access-based cell readout due to controllable (i.e., nondisk) cell memory

New hardware algorithms.   In the original designs of RAP systems, the limited in-cell parallelism, lack of random read/write capability of cell memory and its limited capacity, and limited capability of the hardwired query analyzer logic as opposed to the microprocessor based subcells prevented achieving high performance in the DBMS operations of projection, join, and transaction processing.

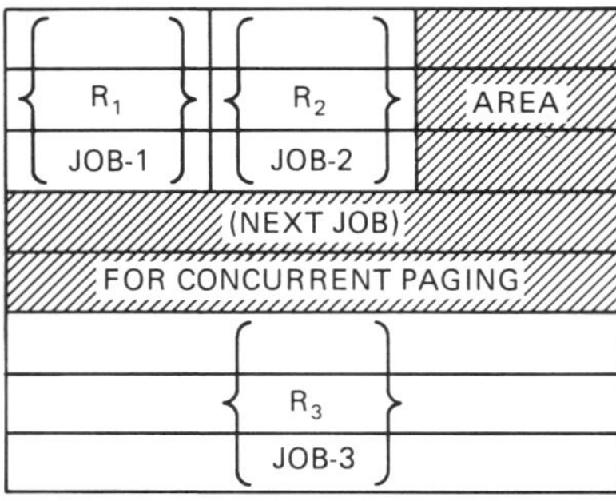

Figure 7.11   RAP.3 storage and job allocation.

In the RAP.3 architecture, with various new features, which include in-cell sorting in parallel cells, the following hardware macro operations (algorithms) are designed:

Algorithm Project

(a)

    (1) Pointer sort (i.e., without moving tuples) the tuples in cell memory with respect to the attribute to be projected. This sort is performed by the CIMPU and takes place in parallel among the cells.

    (2) Eliminate duplicates in the sorted list of (a.1) by marking the tuples with unique attribute values directly by the CIMPU in cell memory.

(b) $c \leftarrow$ Number of relation cells

Repeat:

(1) Pick the first unprocessed cell and read into the controller the sorted attribute values taken out of the marked tuples in cell memory.

(2) The controller writes these values in cell interface processor memories of all the remaining cells that store the relation, simultaneously at each iteration.

(3) By a mergelike operation between the sorted attribute values in cell memory and the sorted values in cell interface processor memory, all remaining cells compute the set difference of {*current cell values*} − {*values input by the controller*} simultaneously. This is done by resetting mark bits of the tuples containing identical values to those of the subtrahend.

(4) $c \leftarrow c - 1$

Until $c = 0$.

At the end of each iteration (1) through (4), the processed cell at step (1) contains unique attribute values within the relation. At the end, all the cells are left with marked tuples corresponding to unique attribute values.

Example 7.4

Assume three cells and their attribute values to be projected as follows (sorting is ignored):

Cell 1:   A B C D E
Cell 2:   B F G D H
Cell 3:   I A F H J

Iteration 1: A B C D E $\rightarrow$ Unique values
               B̸ F G D̸ H
               I A̸ F H J

Iteration 2: A B C D E
               B̸ F G D̸ H $\rightarrow$ Unique values (F,G,H)
               I A̸ F̸ H̸ J

No more iteration: Cell 3 $\rightarrow$ Unique values (I,J)

While the RAP.1 &2 projection model was based on a GET_FIRST–based RAP program loop, the same is achieved with a sort-based parallel hardware macro in RAP.3 as shown in the algorithm. The project time was $3.CV.t_{SCAN}$ in the RAP.1 & 2 case, CV being the number of distinct values in the attribute being projected. The new RAP.3 project timing is

$$t_{PROJECT} = t_s + t_m + c(2t_{IO} + t_m)$$

where t_s is internal sort time within a cell (Algorithm step a(1)); t_m is the time to perform, by a mergelike process within a cell, duplicate elimination (step a(2)) or set difference (step b(3)); t_{IO} is the time to transfer attribute values between cells (step b(1) or b(2)); c is the number of cells occupied by the relation being projected. Comparisons between RAP.1 & 2 and RAP.3 in projection revealed the superiority of RAP.3 by up to three orders of magnitude.

Algorithm Semi-Join

(a) Project the join attribute domain of the source relation (this step is optional and can be skipped especially in the case of key attributes).

(b) *Repeat*

    (1) Read source join attribute values into the controller.

    (2) The controller writes the values read in (1) on all subcell memories of all the target relation cells simultaneously.

    (3) All target cells execute a MARK instruction to mark qualifying target tuples that find a match with the source join attribute values stored in subcells. Each subcell performs a binary search, with the target attribute value, in the source value list that comes sorted into a subcell memory as a result of the previous project operation. A MARK instruction takes t_{SCAN} time to execute and it will take less time during subsequent iterations of this step since the hardwired bus mark logic will filter out the previously marked tuples.

Until there are no more source values to read.

The timing for the semi-join operation in RAP.3, based on the foregoing algorithm, is

$$t_{JOIN} = 2t_{IO} + (t_{p/k}) \cdot NT \cdot \frac{NS}{S}$$

where t_{IO} is same as in projection, $t_{p/k}$ is effective tuple processing time, NT is the number of target relation tuples within a cell, NS is the total number of join attribute values in the source relation, and $S = 1500$, which is the one load capacity of each subcell for holding source attribute values. Due to its fast-effective tuple processing speed and large comparand store in subcell RAMs (i.e., S values), the RAP.3 join performance has improved within two orders of magnitude compared to that of RAP.1 & 2 [Ozkarahan, Schuster, and Sevcik, 1977]. In tuple processing during join, S values are compared within each subcell with each target tuple; however, as stated in step b(3) of the join algorithm, the

S values are ordered and searched by binary search. Join terminates when all *NS* values are compared with the target relation, *S* at a time.

In regard to $O(n^2)$ complexity of the nested loop-based join (and projection) in nonresident databases, as is the case with most architectures including RAP, the DYOP partitioning strategy (to be discussed in Chapter 8) employed by the RAP.3 architecture brings this complexity down to a linear range. In that discussion we will also see the role of the VLSI filter.

Algorithm: Transaction

Repeat

(1) Page in relation R_i if not in cell memory.
(2) Obtain a batch of *n* requests from the queue of R_i (each relation, R_i, has its transaction FIFO queue polled in from the outside world).
(3) Once a batch is obtained, sort requests with respect to their keys.
(4) Dispatch the sorted batch of requests to the cells of the partition storing R_i and process the batch as an SIMD task. That is, each cell receives the same batch although there will be only one match for each key in the batch. Sorting the request batch, once removed from the queue, would not affect the semantics of the process since the entire batch will be processed in the same select and update cycle in RAP. During this select and update cycle, integrity violating requests (e.g., negative balance) are marked and all other matching tuples are updated on cell memory.
(5) Page out R_i while indicating invalid updates and/or purging their requests.
(6) Check with the operating system to select a queue $i \leftarrow j$ ($i = j$ allowed).

Until end of transaction process cycle.

Each request can be represented by a triplet $(k, v, ic)^p$, where k, v, and ic are memory words representing transaction key, operand value, and an integrity filter, respectively. For complex requests, $p > 1$, meaning composite (or power set) of triplets would be needed.

Transaction processing involves a high number of simple requests. Each transaction usually performs an update on a single tuple whose key matches the search argument in a relation. The algorithm described can be termed as a *real-time batched* transaction processing system designed to alleviate the performance problem of overhead intensive queries (i.e., transactions) when executed on database machines. The idea behind this real-time batched processing is to decrease the host overhead per transaction by executing a batch in the same database machine cycle which would otherwise be spent for a single transaction. The overhead for the batch will not be high due to the nature of the problem, for example,

(a) A batch of transactions does the same thing (i.e., same opcode) on the same relation. Therefore, instead of compiling many instructions that are all the same, a precompiled instruction can be kept in a read-only memory and only the parameters are passed to it from the batch (i.e., key and operand values) during execution.

(b) Concurrency management overhead will be overly simplified because the relation will be locked once for the entire batch instead of repeating the locks and unlocks for each member of the batch.

The performance of this batched real-time transaction processing will be identical to that of the join model shown with the following exceptions:

(a) Execution will be equal to *only one* iteration of the join.

(b) S will be half as much of that of join (i.e., 750) because here we have to input update operand along with each tuple key value which is used to search the tuples stored in the cells of the relation.

(c) In addition to join time, we must add the page out time of the updated tuples.

In the performance comparisons it has been estimated that 750 batched transactions would be executed in about 6 seconds, assuming a relation of 100,000 64-byte tuples, one standard byte serial I/O channel connecting RAP to mass memory, and a single relation update program for the transaction using the ADD instruction of the RAP language. The bottleneck in this time rests in the page out time because the remaining time can be lowered by decreasing the value of S, that is, the batch size.

RAP.3 system architecture.   The initial RAP.3 prototype [Akman, 1980; Kocagoncu, 1981] was a database machine configuration in the same way as RAP.1 & 2 prototypes were. The host computer was an Interdata 7/32 system and the controller was a custom built unit around an 8086 microprocessor as shown in Figure 7.12.

In every database machine configuration, an intermediate controller hardware (or functionality) becomes a necessity to supervise the activities of the associative array in close contact. The RAP.3 database machine configuration used a controller system based on a 8086 processor. This configuration is shown in Figure 7.12 together with its RAM and read-only memory (ROM) contents, which give an overall idea of the system operation. The major functions of the controller were

(a) Generate control signals for the cell array.

(b) Poll individual cells to compute global aggregates using the cell results.

(c) Maintain memory allocation map, that is, a cell table that indicates mapping of relations to cells and dirty bits of updated relations.

(d) Administer program scheduling.

(e) Provide for and control bidirectional buffering between the cell array and the host. Enable communication between the two ends.

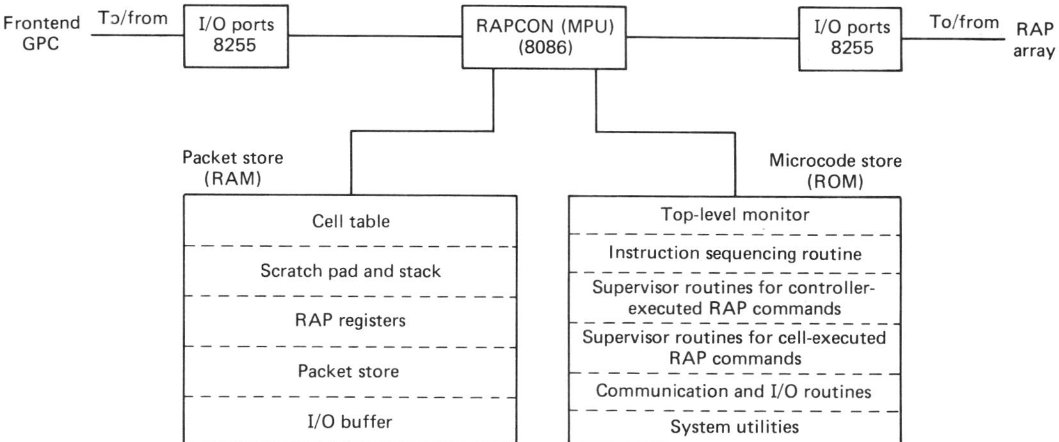

Figure 7.12   RAP.3 database machine controller.

(f) Insert free variable data saved from relations into instruction packets (IP) (see below).

(g) Execute certain RAP instructions (controller executed instructions) that need not be processed in the cells.

In the RAP.3 implementation, each RAP.3 instruction is mapped into its instruction packet which, as shown in Figure 7.13, is a data structure providing information for instruction sequencing and execution in the cells.

An IP contains cell control words (CELLCWs) that are used by the cell interface processor to control the related divisions of the cell hardware. Each IP contains microprocessor firmware and/or ROM entry addresses corresponding to a (instruction) query routine and parameter data. There is a ROM storing certain common code used to assemble a complete query routine based on the data in the IPs.

To execute a RAP program, the controller becomes the master and starts communicating with the cells. Cells that store the required relations assert their grant lines. The controller loads a sequence of CELLCWs into the CIMPU buffers and then initiates an interrupt. CIMPUs do several housekeeping chores and connect subcells to the controller buses with a DMA request. After this, the controller loads the query routines into subcell RAMs with the associated

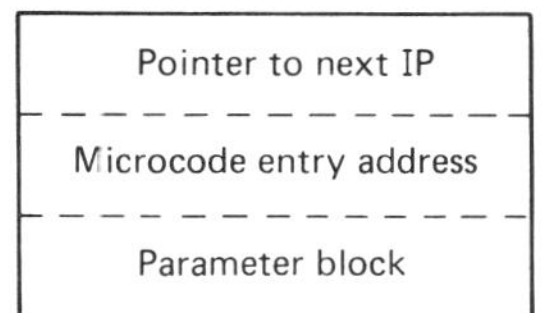

(a) Controller-executed IP structure

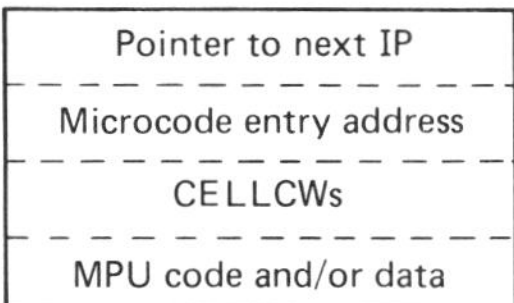

(b) Cell-executed IP structure

Figure 7.13   Instruction packets.

data. At the end of this transfer, the controller issues an interrupt for execution initiation in the subcells. At the end of an instruction execution, therefore, a memory scan, the DMA controller issues an interrupt to the CIMPU to initiate postinstruction processing. During this process, certain status and count values such as tuple and/or mark counts, aggregate subresults, saved data (e.g., free variable data) are collected from the subcells.

Operating system (OSRAP.3)   In the database machine configuration, the database machine operating system (OSRAP.3) was a software module running on top of the operating system of the host processor. In this configuration, OSRAP.3 could tap the low-level resource management facilities of the host operating system. OSRAP.3 operated via handshakes with the controller firmware routines. This resulted in signal propagation and settling delays associated with the various communication paths and protocols. Added to these were the various buffer management and buffer memory optimizations that minimized possible interruptions of executions. The major functions of OSRAP.3 were:

(a) Provide user interface.
(b) Translate a user query into IPs and send them to the controller.
(c) Receive answers from the controller and pass them to users.
(d) Keep and maintain database backups.
(e) Ensure security, detect and recover from errors.
(f) Allocate/assign/reclaim system resources.
(g) Provide facilities for database administration.

OSRAP.3 utilized a one-pass incremental, interactive compilation technique that enabled conversational utilization of the communication facilities. In this way, IPs could be generated immediately together with interactive error-handling and break-in facilities. OSRAP.3 occupied about 20K bytes of memory.

RAP.3 database computer configuration.   Lengthy communication paths, protocols, and I/O activities were bottlenecks for the system performance in the database machine configuration. In the final stage of the implementation, the overall system was integrated into a more compact and independent form, which will be referred to as *database computer,* to eliminate the constraints and overhead imposed by the database machine configuration. In this integrated system, an Intel iSBC 86/12-A single-board computer coupled with a development system via a SBC 957 monitor kit was used to accommodate the functions of the host and the controller. The functions of the controller were embedded in the functions of ROS (RAP operating system replacing OSRAP.3 and the hardwired controller). As a result of this integration, the instruction packet structure was greatly simplified. The query routines were generalized and stored in the ROMs of subcells, so that only the parameters and execution data have to be passed into subcells to assemble query routines for specific programs. This, in turn, has simplified CELLCWs down to a single-byte-long control field. ROS contained an interactive text editor and translator with the compile and go options, certain system security, integrity, and database administrator (DBA) routines. The DBA routines provided for user password and capability assignment/deassignment, system file management, database backup, and so on. Hardware diagnostics such as cell memory and subcell memory test programs and CIMPU and subcell diagnostic routines were part of the ROS functions.

As we stressed earlier, the anticipated role of a database computer configuration is that of a functionally rich special-purpose processor, more properly, a general-purpose nonnumeric computer. As shown in Figure 7.14, the best use of its functionalities can be made by a network of users through work stations and general-purpose computers as loosely attached hosts, either through a local network and/or remote networks. The interface of the database computer with any of these will be a high-level one, in the form of (Request, Response) ordered pair. This implies that the integrated system will have the DBMS software alongside of a general-purpose operating system that then would support the integrated host and replace ROS.

The other aspects of the RAP architecture, namely,

(a) Virtual memory system

(b) Concurrency and multiprogramming

(c) Data flow organization

(d) Data filtering and database partitioning

(e) Query execution in distributed databases

(f) Performance models

(g) Multimodel support

(h) Integrated support of formatted and unformatted structures

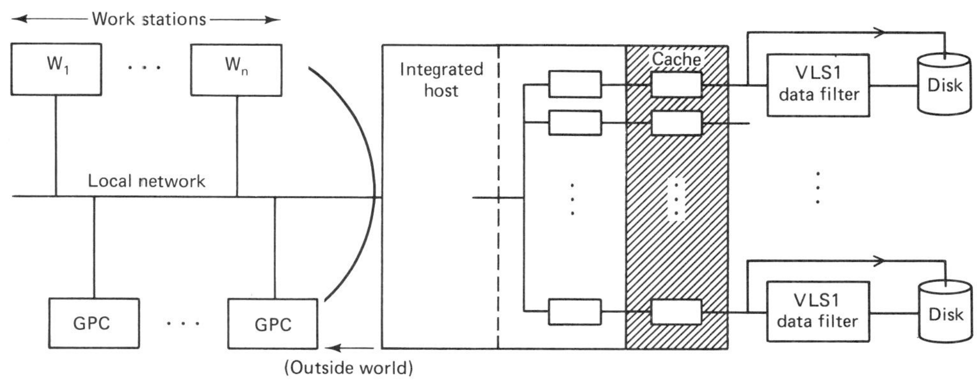

Figure 7.14 RAP.3 database computer.

will all be discussed or referenced in the subsequent chapters within their relevant contexts.

7.1.3 RARES

RARES (rotating associative relational store) was designed to support a relational database optimizer called SQUIRAL [Smith and Chang, 1975]. RARES [Lin, Smith, and Smith, 1976] was not intended to be a full functional database machine. The main purpose of RARES was to exploit its associativity and provide fast service for selection and sort operations in data management.

RARES was also oriented toward head-per-track disk usage; however, it differed from others in its storage structure. To increase I/O bandwidth of the device, tuples were stored across tracks in an arrangement called the orthogonal storage structure, as shown in Figure 7.15.

According to Figure 7.15, tuples are stored orthogonally in a band, and if a band is not large enough, tuples are folded. A relation is stored in one or more bands. Bytes within tuples are stored in parallel while bits within a byte are stored serially on a track.

As mentioned earlier, RARES hardware is tuned for only selection and sort operations and there is no semi-join capability. In fact, the reason why RARES performs sorting is to aid the external processor in the join operation.

Unlike CASSM and RAP, RARES does not have logic-per-track, but rather a logic per band is provided. Each band is processed by a search module that operates at the rate of one comparison (i.e., one simple condition) per revolution. Each search module also contains a RAM for storing marks whose positions

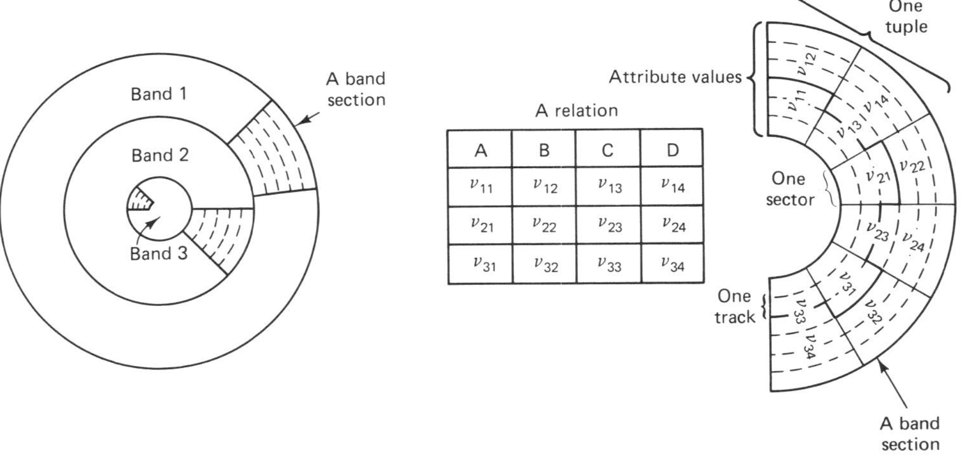

Figure 7.15 RARES storage organization.

correspond to tuple addresses. A tuple may not fit in a band width and, therefore, is folded. Each fold of a tuple takes one revolution to process and the results of intermediate revolutions are accumulated on the corresponding mark bit in RAM.

In sorting [Lin, 1977], RARES first prepares a value histogram for the domain to be sorted. This histogram is divided into bucket intervals. RARES is directed for a selection operation for each bucket interval. Once a bucket is selected, its values are sent to the external processor to be sorted. Although RARES determines buckets in order, the values within a bucket are not sorted. Because bucket size would be small compared to an entire relation, this intrabucket sorting does not take a long time. In fact, the interval selection process is a partitioning operation which will be studied in a subsequent chapter.

7.1.4 Bubble Memory—Based Query Processor

Chang [1978] proposed a query processing system based on magnetic bubble memories (MBM) for relational databases. In this system, domains of a relation are stored along minor loops and tuples are laid across major loops. If an analogy is made between a minor loop of an MBM and a disk track, this storage organization corresponds to the orthogonal storage mapping scheme of RARES. The MBM system's storage format for storing relations is similar to that of RAP and the instruction set is almost identical to the RAP language.

The MBM-based system stores a relation in one or more MBM chips and augments each MBM chip with an index chip which maintains marks in the same way CASSM utilizes its track RAM. There is also comparison logic consisting of two registers and a one bit comparator. (However, this logic needs to be modified considerably to achieve the full functionality of the RAP instruction set.) The index chip avoids redundant traversal of ineligible data on the MBM loops. Figure 7.16 abstracts the MBM-based system.

7.1.5 EDC

EDC (electronic disk–oriented database complex) [Uemura et al., 1980] is an experimental database machine with magnetic bubble memory that was developed under the PIPS project in Japan. EDC is the bubble memory equivalent of the head-per-track cellular associative systems. Similar to RAP.3, however, EDC uses controllable memories whose start/stop during the operation need not be lock-stepped among the tracks (i.e., cell memories need not be fully synchronous) and the cell memory is organized in a bit parallel fashion.

The overall structure of the EDC system is shown in Figure 7.17.

In EDC each DM can be considered as a cell. The logic associated with the cell consists of the microprogrammable microprocessor called PULCE, main memory RAM, and the microprogram (MP) memory for PULCE. The micro-program memory consists of ROM and a high-speed RAM. The cell memory consists of parallel MBM chips with a total capacity of 128K bytes (64K per

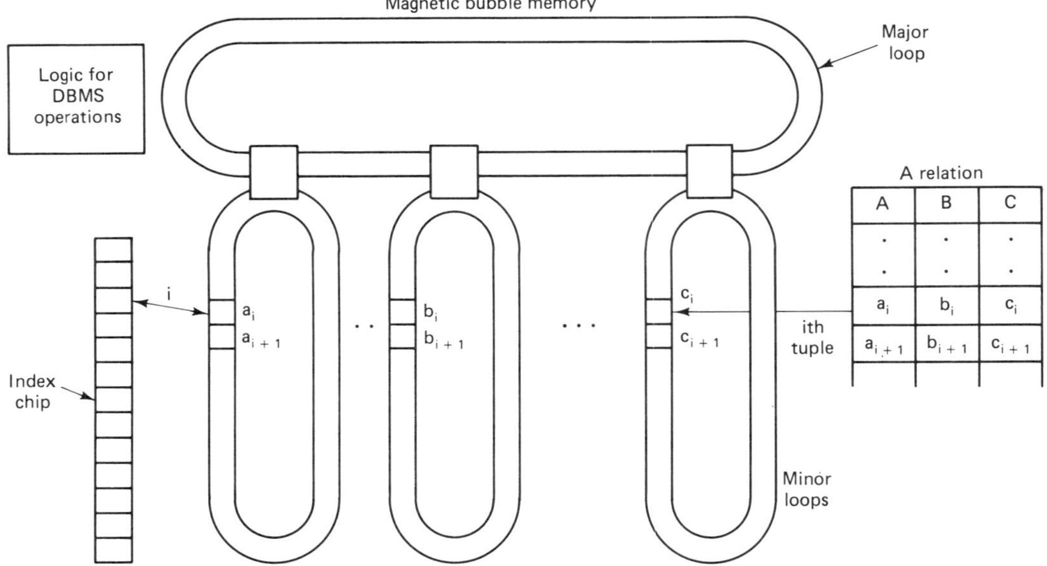

Figure 7.16 Chang's MBM-based system.

chip $\times$ 16 in parallel). This capacity was later increased to 1 megabyte (256K $\times$ 32 in parallel) with a cell data transfer rate of 1.2 megabytes per second. The first module is called the control module (CM) which controls the other parallel data modules. The CM microprocessor can share access with the main memories of DMs for easy communication. The entire (CM + DMs) array is connected to the host processor through an interface processor (IP) which also functions like a peripheral I/O controller.

The storage structure of EDC is flexible as in RAP.3. Relations can be stored across cell memories, as in RARES, or serially in cell memories. The former provides higher parallelism, whereas in the latter, less cell processors will be serving the relation. As in RARES, the orthogonal span of storage across DMs is termed a *band*.

The operational structure of EDC is as follows. At the outermost level, there is the E language layer, which is a nonprocedural relational interface. This level is mapped into the D level, which corresponds to a tuple-oriented procedural language. Either E or D level programs are accepted by the interpreter of the C level, which corresponds to EDC primitives. These primitives comprise program control, storage operations, and band manipulation instructions. The band manipulation instructions correspond to associative data management operations, an example of which is the associative read primitive whose format is

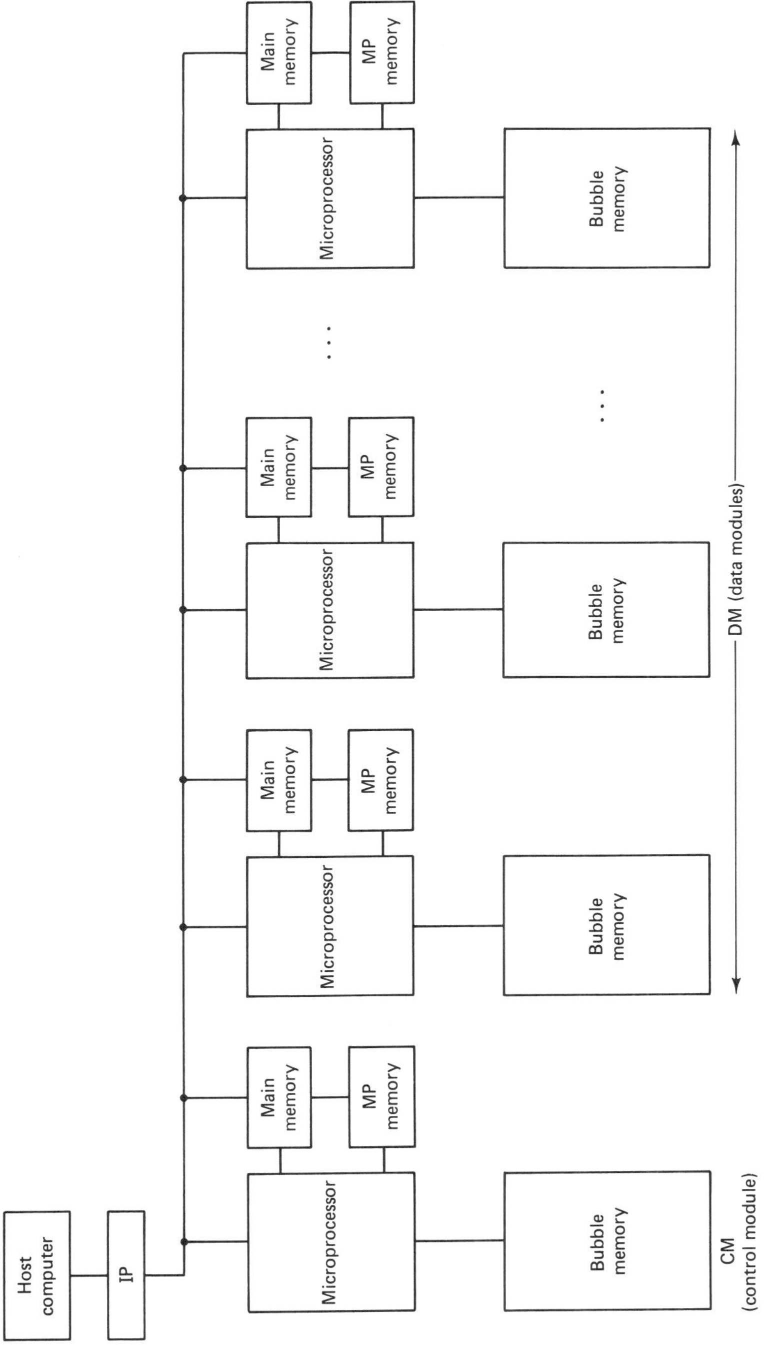

Figure 7.17 EDC system architecture. From S. Uemura et. al., "A Database Machine with Magnetic-Bubble Memory." *Computer Science and Technologies*, 1982.

```
READ-ASSOC id,<band-name>,<restriction-term>,<projection-term>,
status indicator
```

An example of this can be

```
READ-ASSOC idl,<EMP>,<JOB = CLERK>,<NAME>, stl
```

where names of employees whose job title is clerk are output from the EMP
relation. *stl* is the status indicator which indicates success or failure as in the
IMS and DBTG systems. One interesting point to note here, however, unlike
RAP and others we have seen so far, EDC does not use marking. Instead, as
in classical relational algebra, the result is stored as a separate relation in an
area declared *idl* as in the command we have seen above.

The join operation is executed in a nested loop, that is, join search and
tuple construction are executed over one of the relations for as many times as
there are tuples in the other relation.

The C interface primitives are compiled in the CM and mapped into DM
commands of the B interface. These commands are the DM version of the C
interface primitives; (i.e., if a C primitive is "*READ* the named band *ASSO-
CIATIVELY*," it is translated into "*READ* the module *ASSOCIATIVELY*").
The lowest-level A interface is the MBM control interface. It consists of simple
bubble memory control commands such as *ROTATE FIELD n TIMES*. The
PULCE processor issues these commands under the direction of the B-level
interface. PULCE sends commands and receives data via FIFO (first-in, first-
out) buffers that are placed between the processor and bubble memory. The
associative DBMS operations such as select, project, and so on are executed in
the two PULCE register files, which are 16 word by 16 bit, while data are
retrieved from the bubble memory.

7.2 MULTIPROCESSOR-BASED SYSTEMS

In this section we will review multiprocessor-based database machines. Multiprocessor-based systems can be grouped into two categories: those that use
functional distribution and those that use highly parallel configuration of homogeneous microprocessors that are interconnected with respect to some interconnection topology. Functional distribution uses a specialized processor for
each major task such as a sort, project, or index search. A multiprocessor system
using functional distribution routes its data according to the data flow requirement
of its applications through these processors. The processors implement the
concurrency of a pipeline among data flow of various tasks. When we review
the database machine architectures in the following, we will refer to them as
category A and category B to indicate whether they are of a functionally distributed
or highly parallel homogeneous type, respectively. For example, the DBC architecture belongs to category A, whereas the DIRECT architecture belongs to
category B.

7.2.1 DBC

The DBC (data base computer) was designed at the Ohio State University [Banerjee, Baum, and Hsiao, 1978; Banerjee, Hsiao, and Kannan, 1979]. DBC's design was a reaction to the infeasibility of head-per-track disks because of their disappearance as well as the high cost of database machines that are based on them. Their cost would have been high due to the high number of parallel cells that require an equal number of processors, one for each track. In the case of RAP, it was the disk track of such small capacity at the start; then it became a 1- to 2-megabyte RAM for a medium number of cells whose original high parallelism was compensated with the parallelism of subcells in each cell. In the case of DBC, it became the movable head disks with the exception of a modification that transformed them to parallel readout disks. This was achieved by assuming the capability that at a cylinder position, all the tracks of that cylinder can be read or written in parallel. To make the system work, however, DBC needed to rely quite heavily on clustering of its data. This clustering dependence can be observed from the mass memory architecture. Referring to Figure 7.18, which shows the mass memory hierarchy and processing of DBC, there can be a maximum of $m \times n$ disk drives in the system, where m is the number of disk drives in a cluster and n is the number of clusters. This means that there can be $m \times n$ cylinders positioned at their specified locations. At a given time, only one of these cylinders can be searched in parallel by the track information processors (TIP). To minimize seek time, data should be clustered such that required record types must be distributed on these $m \times n$ cylinders and their immediate vicinity. Accordingly, DBC depends upon large numbers of cylinders (enough to hold required data) that can be sought in near zero time. To make such a system work, clusters relevant to a query must be located very efficiently. This is done by the *structure loop* of the DBC system architecture. We can now go into some detail.

The DBC system consists of two major processing loops and a category A multiprocessing architecture on these loops. The major processing loops are

(a) Structure loop
(b) Data loop

The structure loop consists of the following functional units (processors):

(a) Keyword transformation unit (KXU)
(b) Structure memory (SM)
(c) Structure memory information processor (SMIP)
(d) Index translation unit (IXU)

The data loop consists of

(a) Mass memory system (MM)
(b) Security filter processor (SFP)

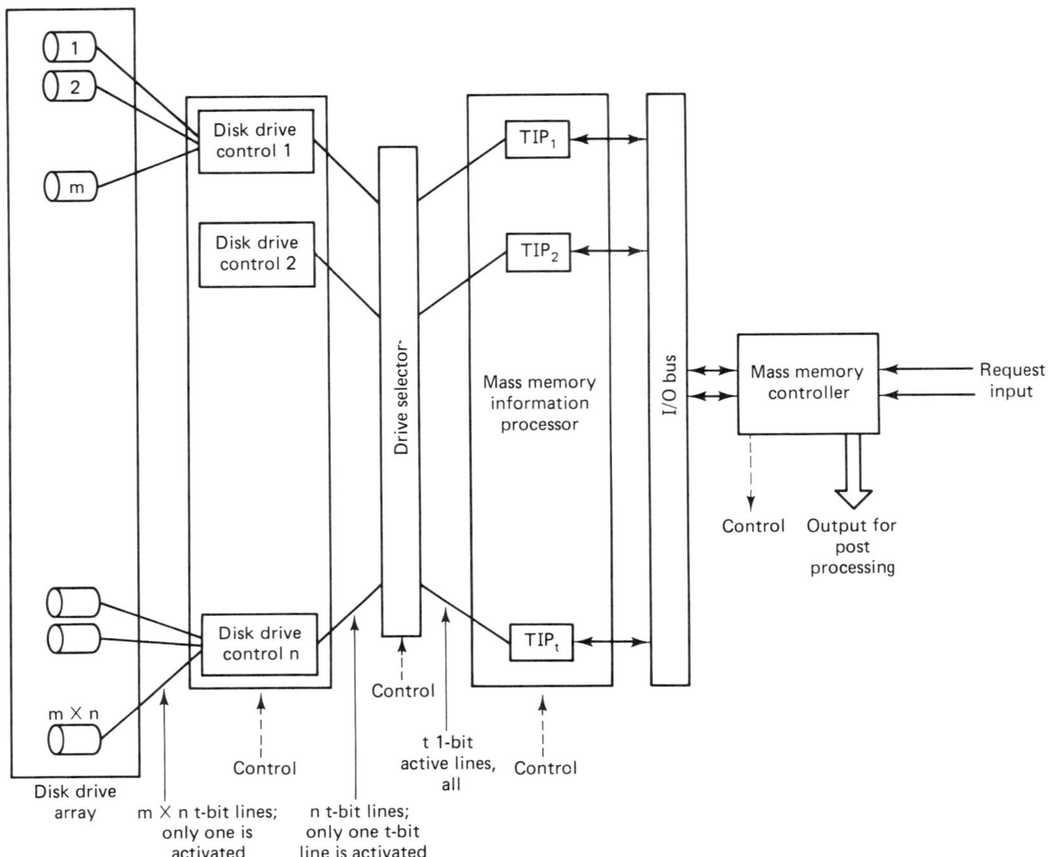

Figure 7.18 Mass memory hierarchy and processing of DBC. From J. Banerjee and D. K. Kannan, "DBC-A Database Computer for Very Large Databases." *IEEE Transactions on Computers*, C-28, 6, © 1979 IEEE.

These two major loops are connected through the database command and control processor (DBCCP).

The data stored in multiple disks are multiplexed through *n* disk drive controllers and then drive selectors (as seen in Figure 7.18) and finally arrive at the mass memory information processor. The mass memory information processor can be thought of as a cylinder of a head-per-track disk-based database machine providing a parallelism of 40 tracks (cells) which correspond to the size of content addressable data at a given time.

Storage structure. In DBC, data are stored and processed as blocks of attribute value pairs. Each block represents a data record which is preceded by a record body. Figure 7.19 displays the storage representation of an employee relation or file. Figure 7.19(a) shows the direct representation of attribute value pairs.

<RELATION, EMP>, <EMPLOYEE-NO, 10>, <EMPLOYEE-NAME, SMITH>,
<DEPT-NAME, TOY>, <SALARY, 15000>, <VACATION-EARNED, 12>

(a) Direct representation

Record template:

EMP $\boxed{1}$ EMPLOYEE-NO $\boxed{2}$ EMPLOYEE-NAME $\boxed{3}$ DEPT-NAME $\boxed{4}$ SALARY $\boxed{5}$ VACATION-EARNED

A physical record:

$\boxed{1}$ 10 $\boxed{2}$ SMITH $\boxed{3}$ TOY $\boxed{4}$ 15000 $\boxed{5}$ 12

(b) Physical record

Figure 7.19   DBC storage structure.

An attribute value pair is also called a keyword. In Figure 7.19(a), the first entry corresponds to attribute name (e.g., employee-name), and the second entry represents the value of that attribute in the record instance (e.g., Smith). In Figure 7.19(b), we see the physical record representation. According to this representation, the attribute names are encoded into unique integers. The attribute names corresponding to these encodings are stored once as a record template or schema. The record occurrences are stored as physical records as shown in Figure 7.19(b).

The query structure of DBC allows simple conditions (predicates) and their Boolean expression such as

$$(SALARY \geq 25000) \wedge (JOB \neq MGR) \wedge (RELATION = EMP) \cdots$$

The query expression is converted into a query block and is stored in the comparators of each TIP. A query block rearranges the predicates of the query expression such that the attribute encodings or identifiers involved in the predicates follow an ascending order. Accordingly, both the physical records and the query block contain n ordered pairs of attribute identifier and attribute value instances. The processing of the query block in the mass memory information processor takes place in a bit serial fashion in a similar way to the model shown in Figure 5.10 of Chapter 5. The predicates are evaluated as each record is skimmed over by comparing its attribute identifiers to those of the query block and comparing the corresponding value pairs (one for the record, one for the corresponding predicate) as soon as an attribute identifier is matched. The comparison takes place according to the relation operator (i.e., one of $=$, $\neq$, $<$, $\leq$, $>$, $\geq$) specified in the corresponding predicate.

Structure memory.   As we indicated earlier, efficiency of DBC depends upon efficient clustering of data and efficient determination of relevant clusters for a query. The clustering is accomplished such that all tuples of a relation are stored at the cylinders that result in minimum seek time, thus avoiding large sweeps over mass memory. The second issue (i.e., locating clusters for a query) is resolved by the SM processor. The SM processor stores multiattribute indices for those attributes selected as secondary keys. An SM storage space in the order of 100 megabytes is envisioned. The secondary key attributes constitute the basis for clustering. An index for a secondary key is in the form of an inverted index where the attribute value is called a keyword and the corresponding inverted list is called the list of index terms. An additional detail is that indexing is grouped with respect to value ranges of the corresponding attribute. An index term is an ordered pair (f, s) where f is the cylinder number containing keyword occurrences with matching values to that of the index keyword and s is a *security compartment*. For example, $A, 1; 16,000; (f_1, s_1) (f_2, s_2) (f_3, s_3)$ is an inverted index tuple indicating that in relation A, the keyword (1, 16,000), that is, the salary attribute with value 16,000, occurs (one or more times) in cylinders f_1, f_2, and f_3 at the security compartments s_1, s_2, and s_3, respectively.

The DBCCP provides for clustering of data, and the structure memory information processor (SMIP) provides for efficient processing of a query expression to locate all the relevant cylinders involving the keywords of the indexed attributes found in the query. To accomplish this, the SMIP must perform intersection or merging of the inverted lists of the indexed attributes found in the Boolean query expression. Considering the size of SM space, a head-per-track–based database machine subsystem (processor) is designed to execute the function of SMIP. The inverted list processing for a query in the SMIP produces a list L of index terms for the query expression. This list is screened by DBCCP with respect to the access privileges of the user and a final authorized list L' is produced to be processed associatively in the MM subsystem. The operation of the MM subsystem will now be restricted to those unique cylinder addresses contained in L'. A further elimination in those cylinders will take place for those records that do not belong to the security compartments contained in L'.

The SMIP is designed as a head-per-track–based database machine having parallel cells with each cell structured as a *memory unit, processor* pair. Each memory unit is assumed to be the collection of *memory modules* of fixed size. A cell processor can process a memory module at a time thus providing parallelism among memory modules within the entire SMIP. To fit this scheme of parallelism, an inverted index of an indexed attribute is mapped into *buckets* for a specified value range. Each bucket is in turn mapped into one or more parallel columns of memory among the SMIP cells.

The identification of relevant buckets for the keywords and their list of index terms is accomplished by the keyword transformation (KXU) subsystem. Once the bucket names are determined by KXU, their corresponding memory module locations in the SMIP are determined by a RAM directory lookup in the SMIP controller.

Join operation.   In DBC's earlier versions, the join operation was executed with respect to a nested loop algorithm. According to this algorithm, first all the source relation tuples were selected and retrieved. After this, for each retrieved source tuple a selection operation was executed over the target relation. In a subsequent study [Menon and Hsiao, 1981], a new organization in the postprocessor of the DBC architecture is proposed for speeding the join operation. The proposed organization consists of a large number of join processors connected on a ring network and controlled by a central controller. Based on certain VLSI predictions, a 200-chip network of more than 200,000 join processors has been envisioned. On the network, each join processor has access to the following memories:

(a) A memory: holds the source relation
(b) B memory: used as an I/O buffer between the mass memory and the join processor
(c) C memory: used to store the result of the join operation
(d) AM memory: a small associative memory used to speed up the join operation

First, the source relation tuples are distributed to each join processor through the B memory. Accordingly, each processor gets one-nth of the source relation tuples if there are n join processors. As soon as values are received for the source relation, each join processor extracts the join attribute value of the source tuple and consults the AM memory for a possible match. If there is no match encountered, the source join attribute value is inserted into the AM memory. (This is equivalent to projecting the source join attribute.) Then the tuple is transferred into a block of A memory which is addressed via a hash function based on the join attribute value. At the end of this phase of the join operation, all source tuples are placed in appropriate blocks of the A memories of the join processors. Next the target relation tuples are read into the B memories of the processors. Each processor removes tuples from the B memory one by one and probes its AM memory for a match on the target join attribute value. If a match is found in the AM, it is hashed to find the block number of the source tuples having the same join attribute value. All the tuples from this block plus those that were placed in the overflow area are retrieved and the join is performed between all these source tuples and the target tuple. The target tuple that is processed by the first join processor in the ring is then transmitted to the next processor in the ring and that processor repeats the same join procedure and when finished routes the target tuple to the next processor and so on. Therefore, the join processors on the ring work in a pipeline for processing the target relation tuples.

As can be seen, the new join procedure basically remains as the nested loop join algorithm; however, this time a brute force processing power that relies on VLSI and multiplicity is added to the rest of the DBC architecture. The potential cardinality of the joined relation is still in the order of the product of the cardinalities of the source and target relations. In the following chapter, we will review possible ways of reducing the join operation complexity on database architectures.

7.2.2 DIRECT

The DIRECT database machine [Dewitt, 1979; Boral et al., 1982] is a multiprocessor-based architecture of category B. The main thrust behind the design of DIRECT was to provide intra- and interquery concurrency in a multiuser environment. In other words, unlike the restrictions of RAP.1 & 2 such as storing only one relation per cell and processing one query at a time in the device (i.e., SIMD architecture), DIRECT was to be an MIMD device. However, different than the order of MIMD concurrency achieved in the RAP.3 architecture, the DIRECT machine's approach was to construct a system based on a very flexible interconnection topology among memory and processor units. In this MIMD architecture, the aim was to have an allocation scheme where the number of processors to be assigned for a query is determined dynamically based on the priority of the query, the sizes of the relations it references, and the type and number of relational algebra operations included in the query. To realize such a goal, the DIRECT architecture was designed as a backend architecture driven by a host GPC and controlled by a backend controller which is intermediary to the host connection from DIRECT. The DIRECT backend itself was configured as a complete bipartite graph in which one part consists of query processors and mass memory devices and the other part consists of a collection of CCD memory modules. To realize this bipartite graph, a crossbar switch (i.e., a matrix interconnection) was placed between the two parts as depicted in Figure 7.20. However, in the implementation of the small-sized prototype, a multiport memory-based multiprocessor topology was used. In this topology, the query processors were provided with RAM buffers and the CCD memory modules were made accessible through multiple ports.

The operation of the system is such that query processors run in parallel and search through memory modules so that the resulting architecture achieves parallelism and associativity. The associativity is that of a secondary (bulk) memory-based system rather than that of an AM array. Users submit their queries in the INGRES data language at the host GPC which is a PDP 11/40 system which also embodies the backend controller. The INGRES queries are translated into query packets and sent to DIRECT for execution. The controller is responsible for determining the number of query processors to be assigned to the query and paging in nonresident relation pages from mass memory into the memory modules.

Each query processor is an LSI 11/23 with 136K bytes of local RAM. The instruction set executable by the query processors consists of relational algebra

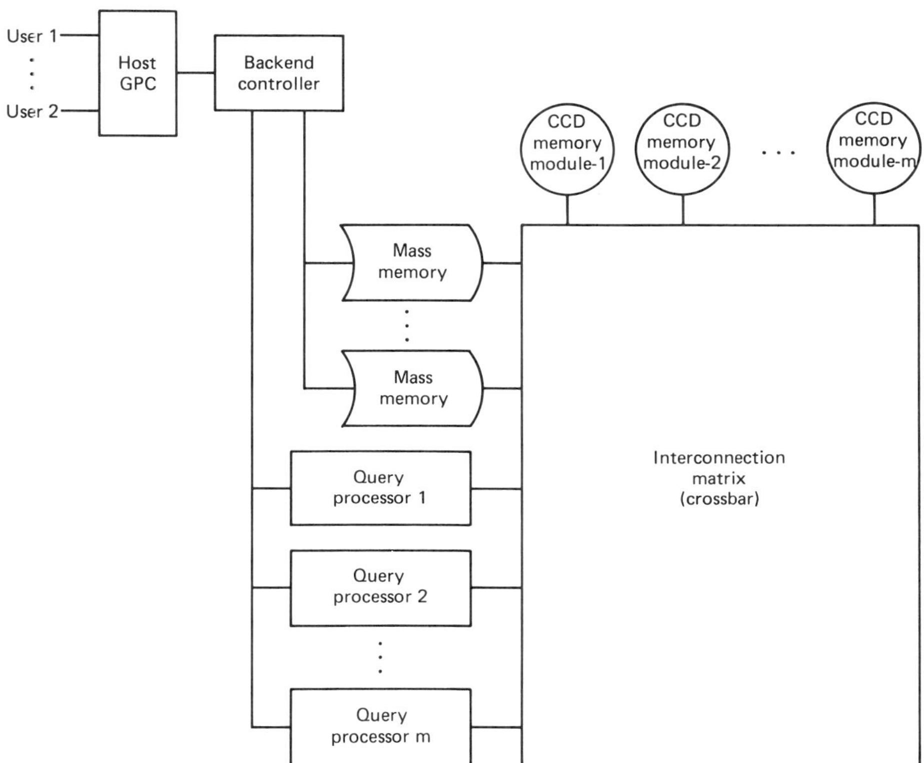

Figure 7.20   DIRECT architecture. From D. J. Dewitt, "DIRECT—A Multiprocessor Organization for Supporting Relational Database Management Systems." *IEEE Transactions on Computers,* C-28, 6, © 1979 IEEE.

operations of *RESTRICT, PROJECT, JOIN, UNION, DIFFERENCE, INTER-SECTION,* and *CROSS PRODUCT* and other operations for update (*MODIFY, INSERT*), scalar aggregates of *MAX, MIN, COUNT,* and *AVERAGE,* and the *COMPRESS* operation.

Storage structure.   Each relation in the database is divided into a number of fixed-size pages. Each page contains tuples of a relation laid in a sequential order, and there cannot be tuples of more than one relation in a page frame. The tuples are fixed length within a relation, but may vary among relations. Every page contains beginning-of-page (BOP) and end-of-page (EOP) delimiters. With these delimiters, query processors can scan a page starting at any location within the page. A page size is fixed and 16K bytes long. This corresponds to one memory module which is constructed from eight CCD chips. Each query processor assigned by the controller to execute the query packet will associatively search a subset of a relation stored in a page, and when it finishes the search of the current page it will request the next page of the relation. At a given time, several query processors may be assigned to a query and, hence, may be simultaneously requesting next pages of the relation. The controller makes sure that each query processor gets a different page to search. After receiving the address of that page from the controller, the query processor must be able to rapidly switch to that page. Also, between different queries involving the same relation, two query processors can search a common page so that redundant paging of the same data can be avoided.

Interconnection matrix. As we have seen so far, to be able to support the type of MIMD concurrency between query processors and memory modules, the DIRECT interconnection network should permit

(a) Rapid switching of a query processor between page frames of the same or different relations.
(b) Simultaneous searching of a common page by several or all query processors.
(c) A high bandwidth to allow a given byte of a page frame to be examined by all query processors rapidly. This bandwidth must be an m multiple of the byte rate of a single page frame where m is the number of query processors.
(d) The switches of the interconnection network should not introduce their own accumulated delay against the memory access bandwidth of the network.

To satisfy all these criteria, the interconnection network was selected as the crossbar switch with the difference that memory modules had to be the producers and query processors the consumers. Accordingly, each memory module continuously broadcasts its contents, and those interested query processors listen to this broadcast simultaneously.

Temporary relations. The DIRECT design preferred the temporary relation creation approach rather than the marking approach of RAP and other architectures. In this approach, as in classical relational algebra, every relational operation on a relation or pair of relations creates a new result relation stored as a temporary relation. This relation can be made permanent, used for further operations, or output to the host GPC. To provide concurrency of multiple queries on a common relation and provide flexibility in outputting results of previous operations, the temporary relation approach does not require ingenuities as would be required in the case of the marked relation approach. This, of course, occurs at the expense of page frame consumption and degree of concurrency management, which results in a net decrease in potential parallelism.

Query processing. The INGRES queries are parsed into query trees whose leaves constitute the relations referenced in the query and intermediate nodes represent relational algebra operations. A parse tree corresponds to a query packet. As we have seen before, a query packet can be assigned to any number of query processors. The query processor allocator (QAP) follows two approaches for the assignment of query processors to query packets: (1) optimal query processor allocation and (2) data flow–driven allocation. In the optimal query allocation, the assignment is made equal to the optimally needed number of query processors whose excess will not improve the performance any further. For example, for a nested join algorithm to join relation A, which is N pages long, and relation B, which is M pages long, the optimal query processor allocation would be MAX(M,N) which would take MIN(M,N) time units to compute; where a time unit is the time required to join one page of A with one page of B. A query packet table (QPKTX) is kept to indicate the optimal and current allocation quantities of query processors for those query packets taken from the queue and initiated for execution. No additional query can be initiated for execution until all query packets are optimally allocated. Accordingly, at a given time, there cannot be more than one query packet in the system, hence in the QPKTX table, whose allocation is less than the optimal. The second approach of allocation is the data flow approach in that the query processors are not assigned to whole query packets, but rather relational operations of join, project, restrict, and so on. Accordingly, the query processors are assigned to those nodes (hence relational operations) of the query where both operands become available instead of computing optimal allocations. Furthermore, if at a given time, there are no more intermediate nodes fireable for execution in a given program but there are query processors available, then allocation can be made to start executing nodes of another program. Referring to Figure 7.21, nodes 2 and 4 in program A and node 1 in program B

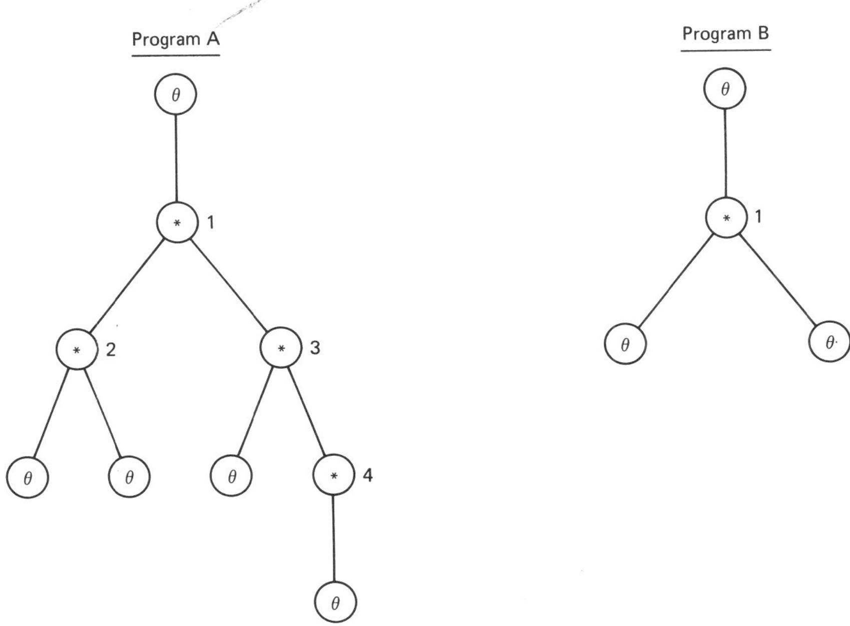

Figure 7.21   Program flow graphs.

can be fired all at once where Qs represent the same or different relations and *s represent relational algebra operations.

To keep track of memory page frame management, the DIRECT software system keeps various system tables. These include a page table for a relation which indicates presence/absence of relation page frames, their update status and address in mass memory; a QPKTX table for showing the executing query packets; and a query packet task table which keeps one entry for each entry in the QPKTX table and there is a monitor associated for each entry to control access to the query packet task table.

Accordingly, at a given time the number of query processors assigned to a query can be dynamically varied, and each of these query processors can concurrently issue *NEXT-PAGE* requests, but the monitor associated with the query packet entry in the query packet task table makes sure that each request is granted with a different page number. When a page number cannot be located in the memory modules, a page fault occurs that requires a page transfer from mass memory. With the use of these tables, anticipatory paging can be conducted by the controller to decrease the number of page faults.

The DIRECT architecture does not rely on indexing of any kind. Its concurrency control is based on a two-phase locking protocol, where the locking granularity is at the relation level.

The join operation. The DIRECT architecture, as all the previously discussed database machines, executes the join operation with respect to the nested loop algorithm. The join of relation A over attribute a with relation B over its attribute b, $JOIN (A, a, B, b, C)$ is relation C of all those t tuples such that t is a concatenation of tuple tA from A and tB from B where $tA \cdot a = tB \cdot b$. In what follows, the compiled query packet for this join operation is outlined in such a way that the entire sequence of operations can be traced from the corresponding code given below.

A and B relations are joined over a and b, respectively, and the result is saved as the C relation.

```
Create C
Do Forever
Begin
    Ask backend controller for the next page of relation A
    If end of relation is reached start executing the next query
    packet
    else
        Read page of relation A
        Set I equal to 1
        Set end of B relation to false
        While end-of-B is false
        Begin
            Get page I of relation B from the controller
```

```
              If controller returns end of relation set end-of-B to
              true
              else
                  Read page I of B
                  Join current page of A with page I of B
                  Write the resulting tuples into A buffer
                  When the buffer is full
                      Ask controller for the next page of C
                      Write output buffer into the C page
                  Increment I
          End
      End
```

7.2.3 RDBM (Relational Database Machine)

RDBM [Auer et al., 1981] is a relational database machine designed at the University of Braunschweig, West Germany, as a successor to the earlier SURE project (which will be discussed later in the chapter). RDBM uses a functionally distributed multiprocessor architecture of category A. Figure 7.22 shows the RDBM system structure.

As seen in Figure 7.22, RDBM consists of an associative memory system and a distribution of microprocessors that implement intertask parallelism as

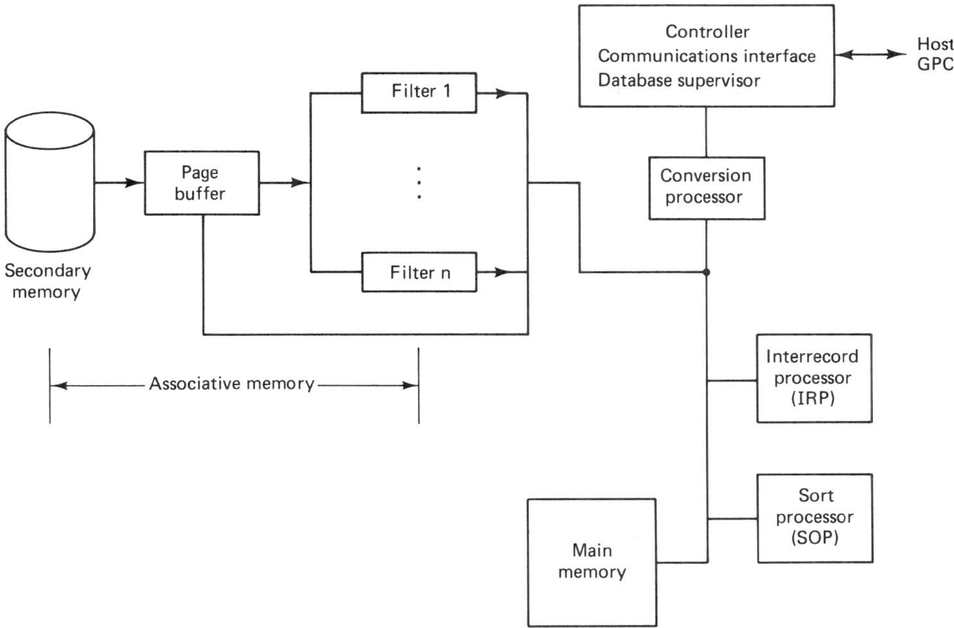

Figure 7.22 RDBM system structure. From D. K. Hsiao, *Advanced Database Machine Architecture* (Englewood Cliffs, N.J.: Prentice-Hall, Inc., 1983). Adapted by permission of Prentice-Hall, Inc.

well as intratask pipelining. The multiprocessors are connected to a bus system and communicate via a common main memory. The software processes running on these processors are synchronized by means of semaphores. The data space is virtually (logically) addressed. This is accomplished by the main memory manager and the secondary memory manager. The secondary memory system, unlike the on-the-fly filtering that was possible in the case of the SURE predecessor, has abandoned in-stream processing and adopted an I/O system that is based on address translation, paging, and buffering. The pages that are accessed from the secondary memory are buffered and individual tuples are sent to be buffered and processed in parallel by the filter processors. The filters contain a micro-programmable universal processor and input/output buffers, and they can selectively address attributes within tuples. The filters select and project tuples and store them in main memory. The filters accomplish unary relational algebra operations. However, for binary operations such as join, set operations, set quantification, and scalar aggregates, the RDBM system is also provided with an interrecord processor (IRP) and a sort processor (SOP).

The SOP performs a pointer sort on the data residing in main memory; 4,096 keys can be internally sorted. For the elimination of duplicates, a separate tag bit is employed. In external sort, each run of a merge pass contains a key list that is equal in length to the maximum number of keys that can be internally sorted. IRP works in pipeline with the filters. The join operation is carried out by means of a partial sort/merge algorithm. Assuming that both relations can be completely sorted and stored externally in buckets, the join is carried out during the merge phase by comparing minimum values of buckets for determining compatible value bands to be merged. A binary task such as join is decomposed into sort and search primitives, and these are run concurrently. For example, in joining two relations the primitive operations would be *search R1 and put result in* T_1, *sort* T_1, *search R2 and put result in* T_2, *sort* T_2, and *join* T_1 *and* T_2. Here, sorting of T_1 and searching of R2 can be performed concurrently in IRP and the filters, respectively. IRP contains two input buffers of 8K bytes each and two output buffers of 4K bytes each along with a universal processor.

The conversion processor performs buffering and format conversion of data. The physical storage format uses delimiters embedded with data in tuples of relations. Concurrency control during updates implements locking at the page level. The prototyping of RDBM is currently progressing.

7.2.4 SABRE

SABRE [Gardarin et al., 1983] is a relational database system for a multimicro-processor machine developed at INRIA, France. SABRE is a software structured system utilizing a low degree of hardware parallelism among the elements of a category A architecture. SABRE utilizes concepts and facilities such as disk cache and on-the-fly filtering. The filter processor is a virtual process which processes associative partitions of secondary memory. An associative partition is equal in size to a disk track. Figure 7.23 shows the functional architecture of SABRE.

The data space is partitioned based on a multiattribute, multilevel clustering of relations where such partitioning is referred to as the *reduced cover tree*. The conceptual modeling interface consists of a hierarchical read-only view system defined over the base and/or other view relations.

The functional architecture consists of virtual processors to support each of the processors shown in Figure 7.23. The view processor administers the data model interface. The request evaluation processor breaks a given query into primitive operations. The relation access processor determines data partitions. The join, sort, and aggregate function processors perform their respective operations on partitions of data. The concurrency control is responsible for update serialization and recovery. The cache memory processor allocates secondary and cache memories and performs page replacement. The filter processor performs selection, insertion, and deletion of tuples in a partition.

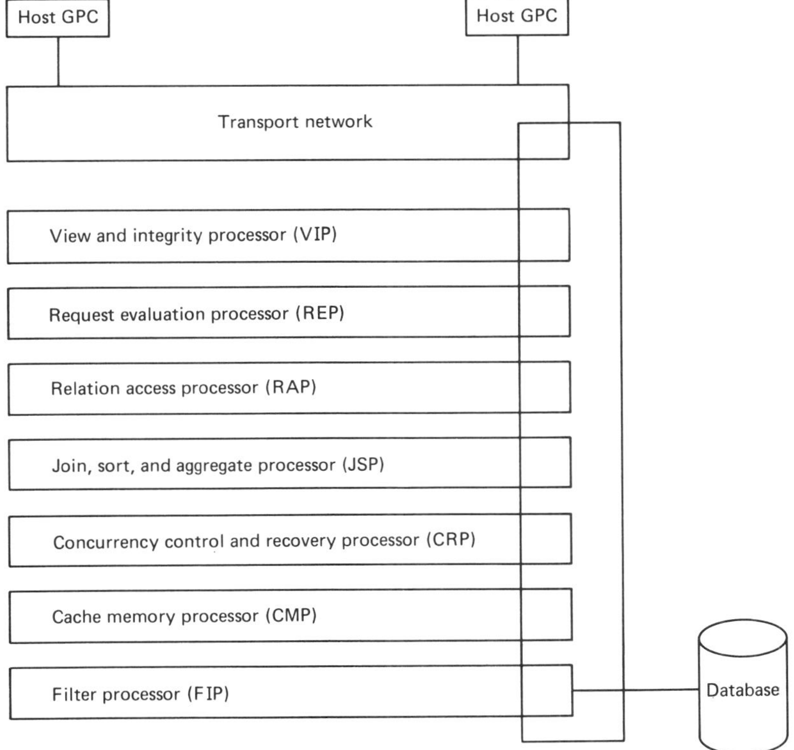

Figure 7.23 Functional architecture of SABRE. From D. K. Hsiao, *Advanced Database Machine Architecture* (Englewood Cliffs, N.J.: Prentice-Hall, Inc., 1983). Adapted by permission of Prentice-Hall, Inc.

The functional architecture of SABRE is mapped onto an operational architecture which consists of multiprocessors connected on a bus system. In the V0 and V1 versions of the SABRE prototype, the operational system consisted of a uniprocessor, the MULTICS GPC, where V0 was a single-user system and V1 was a multiuser system. In the V2 version, which is currently being developed, there will be three processors. Processor 1 will support VIP, processor 2 will support REP and RAP, and processor 3 will support JSP, CRP, CMP, and FIP.

7.2.5 DBMAC

DBMAC [Missikoff and Terranova, 1983] is a relational database machine that utilizes a multiprocessor architecture of category A and is being developed for the Italian Applied Program for Informatics. DBMAC is structured for a domain-based (vertical) relational schema. A file storing values of a domain is referred to as a *data pool*. The relational schema in the storage structure is represented as the control information for prejoins among relations. For each value in the prejoin structure, the tuples and the relations with which the value is associated are indicated. The data pool control information is structured as a multilevel hierarchy. At the first level, domain values are stored; at the second level, relations containing a given value are stored for each value node of the first level; at the third level, for each relation corresponding to a domain value the tuple identifiers (TIDs) containing that value are stored. A search of a data pool produces a list of TIDs satisfying the search predicate.

The DBMAC system is organized to include a logical architecture, which is vertically expandable (i.e., can add more functions), and a physical architecture, which is horizontally expandable (i.e., replicable). There is no backend controller in DBMAC. Its functions are accomplished by a distributed operating system which maps the logical architecture onto the physical architecture and also implements communication and synchronization primitives. The logical architecture consists of several layers. The top layer manages communications with users. The next lower level is the transaction layer, which translates transactions into internal format. The next RELMAC layer converts the transactions received in internal format into a set of operations executable on the internal schema of the database. This conversion is done according to an execution graph. The lowest layer consists of primitives that operate on data pools.

The associative search of data pools is accomplished with on-the-fly filtering. The binary relational operations are performed by searching associated data pools and outputting lists of TIDs representing relations. These pointer lists are sorted and intersected or merged. The standard result of database operations in DBMAC is the output of a list of TIDs. The basic operations at the low level of the logical architecture, therefore, consist of selection, integer intersection, and sorting.

The physical architecture consists of multiprocessors (processing units, PUs) connected on a multibus. The clusters of system data structures and system processing functions operating on them are mapped onto PUs that run in parallel.

Figure 7.24 shows the DBMAC physical architecture which is in turn broken into physical high and low systems whose interconnection is not implemented by a bus (to prevent bottleneck), but through message passing between the PUs. The PUs can be connected to any disk drive through the MM bus. Data coming off the disk are also on-the-fly filtered by IMI unit for the selection operation. The MM bus contains a single control bus which has to be arbitrated; however, there are dedicated bit serial data paths between the individual PUs and disks. These paths are established via multiplexers.

DBMAC was not intended for a high volume of update transactions. Its capabilities were tuned to handle complex queries.

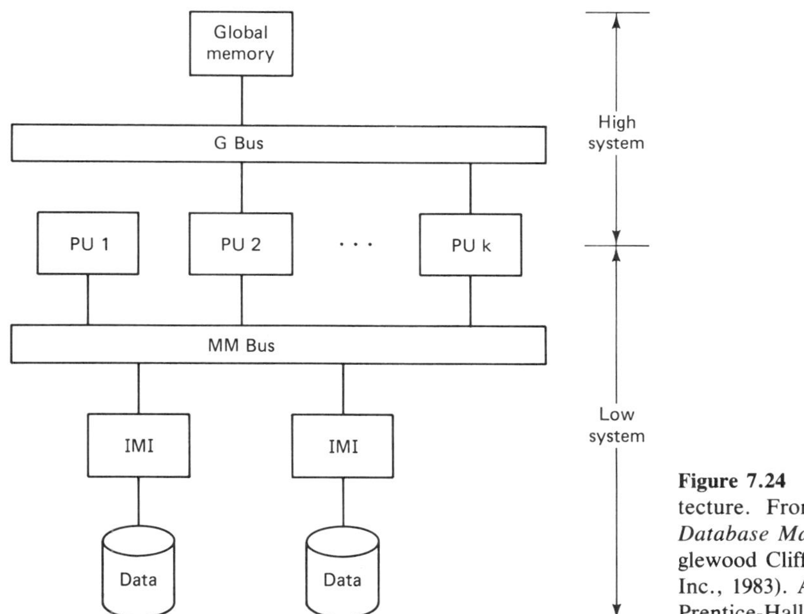

Figure 7.24 DBMAC physical architecture. From D. K. Hsiao, *Advanced Database Machine Architecture* (Englewood Cliffs, N.J.: Prentice-Hall, Inc., 1983). Adapted by permission of Prentice-Hall, Inc.

7.3 IN-STREAM AND/OR PIPELINE PROCESSING

In this group, we will discuss those designs which perform on-the-fly processing, such as pipelined search and sort, while data are streamed through functionally distributed processors. The aim of such designs is to enable processing while data are read from disk storage. For efficiency, however, a multiplicity of such systems is required sitting in serial with the data but performing parallel processing among themselves. To keep in pace with the moving data at channel speed, there must be pipelining capability among the processes of major database primitives such as search, sort, join, and project.

7.3.1 A Data Stream Database Machine
with Large Capacity

The data stream database machine is the result of several related studies by its authors [Tanaka, Nozaka, and Masuyama, 1980; Tanaka, 1983a, 1983b]. The recent study which reports the data stream database machine (DSDBM) synthesizes various concepts proven to be useful in the past. In other words, associative disks and disk cache memories are assumed to be at the low end of the memory hierarchy. Above this level, a pipelined data stream processing architecture has been developed. With the aim of obtaining a regularly modular VLSI implementation, database values are first encoded, then processed by the *kernel database machine,* and then results are output after being decoded back to their original representation. The DSDBM utilizes a network of functional units such as search engines, trie engines, and sort engines that all operate on a tree structure in a pipelined manner. In this respect, this machine also represents the features of multiprocessor-based architectures of both the A and B categories, A for the functional distribution and B for the multiplicity of homogeneous processors within a given function. Our classification, however, focuses on the major characteristic of the design which is the pipelined data stream (or in-stream) processing.

In this architecture, database is partitioned by segmenting files and the directory of segments is managed by a binary trie. Encoding of values is done by one-to-one encoding functions which are not necessarily order preserving. Ordering is achieved by a network of hardware sorters that are interconnected with the various functional units. The main thrust of this design is to overcome the quadratic complexity of the nested loop join algorithm, which has been adapted in most database machine architectures.

The storage structure of this database machine consists of a series of inverted files that store encoded attribute values and the corresponding tuple identifiers of the database relations that contain those instances.

Encoded database.   Encoding is performed for identifiers and character strings by a one-to-one function so that equality predicates can be executed on the encoded values. However, as may be expected, arithmetic operations including the aggregations of sum or average are excluded from this capability. For each data subtype (i.e., employer is a name subtype of the data type string), an encoder/decoder file is kept. The file is searched by hashing which is dynamically extendable (i.e., node splitting or merging is possible with additions/deletions to the file). The hashing is performed for the segments whose encoded data are stored in the file. The segmentation index table of the extendable hashing is accessed via a trie directory. The values in segments are not ordered. Each segment is divided into an entry portion and record portion. The search for a specified value is performed as follows. The value is hashed into a bit pattern h and the trie directory is searched with this hashed value to locate the segment containing that value. The segment is then read out of the secondary memory.

The encoding is done via hashing. Each code consists of an l bit hash value and an l_2 bit extension code which resolves synonyms. When the segment is retrieved, its entry portion is searched with the hashed value to obtain a pointer to the list which may contain the value being searched. Actually the hash functions $h(v)$ for the searched value v is formed from concatenation of two hash functions h_0 and h_1 so that for v_1 and v_2 if $v_1 > v_2$ then $h_0(v_1) > h_0(v_2)$. This structure enables value range partitioning. Figure 7.25 shows the structure of the hash (encoding) code.

The range code enables selection of the trie directory for the segments belonging to that value range. With l_0, therefore, the trie directory is located; with l_1 the trie is searched to obtain the segment address which may contain the searched value.

The encoder/decoder hardware consists of a directory processor and several file processors. This hardware performs encoding and decoding as well as insertion or deletion of codes to/from the database. When the encoder/decoder is entered with an attribute and its corresponding value (to be searched or inserted/deleted), the directory processor produces h_0 and h_1 from the range table searcher and hash code generator units. The encoder/decoder is also equipped with a *trie engine*. A trie engine is a functional unit that is responsible for

(a) Searching a trie tree T for a segment address along a path specified by a sequence of binary digits of the hash code h (see Chapter 8)
(b) Splitting a segment along a path specified by h into two segments which are entry addresses of the corresponding segment tables
(c) Merging two segments into a single segment

Each level of the trie engine contains memory and search logic. Once h_0 and h_1 are determined, they are sent to the trie engine to locate the segment address in the corresponding trie directory. In encoding, the file processor reads the segment into working memory. The entry portion of the segment is searched by the trie engine followed by the search of the list pointed to by the entry. When a match is found, the extension code is read out to form the entire code.

The decoding of a hash value h with an extension code ec is performed as follows. The hash value h is split into h_0 and h_1. The trie engine again receives these values and finds the segment which stores the code (h,ec). The file processor accesses the segment and searches the entry and record portions until h_1 addresses a cell which stores the hash part of the value (i.e., $h_0 - h_1$). The ec is then used to search a list which contains the original value corresponding to the code.

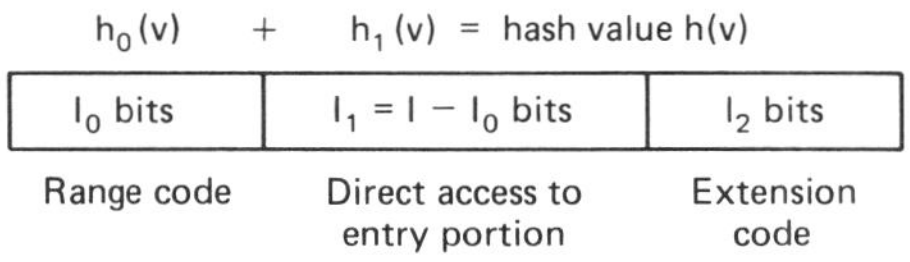

Figure 7.25 Structure of a code. From D. K. Hsiao, *Advanced Database Machine Architecture* (Englewood Cliffs, N.J.: Prentice-Hall, Inc., 1983). Adapted by permission of Prentice-Hall, Inc.

$$h_0\,(v) \quad + \quad h_1\,(v) \;=\; \text{hash value } h(v)$$

l_0 bits	$l_1 = l - l_0$ bits	l_2 bits
Range code	Direct access to entry portion	Extension code

The kernel database machine.   The kernel database machine consists of the three subsystems

- Tuple selector (TS)
- Tuple constructor (TC)
- Aggregate operator (AO)

These subsystems are connected through a sorting network along with an additional direct connection between TC and AO.

Tuple selector.   The tuple selector hardware consists of a trie engine and search and sort engines and executes selection on the encoded tuple data. Notice that tuples are partitioned into inverted files, one for each attribute. Assuming that $R(A_1, A_2, \ldots, A_n)$ is a relation, @R will represent a special attribute that corresponds to a list of tuple identifiers (i.e., a system assigned key). Accordingly, $R[\mathbf{A}, @R]$ will denote an access path (i.e., through the inverted list) for an attribute A of R. The sorter by sorting a stream S will produce a sorted list denoted by $S\uparrow$. An attribute, @ by itself, in front of a sorted stream will indicate the number of sorted elements preceding the records in the stream. The projection of relation S without duplicate removal will be indicated as S[[X]]. The capabilities of the tuple selector are as follows:

(a) Selection: $R[\mathbf{A}, @R][A = c][@R]$
(b) Linear join: $(R[\mathbf{A}, @R_1][A = B]R_2[\mathbf{B}, @R_2])[@R_1, @R_2]$
(c) Linear join: $(R[\mathbf{A}, @R][A = B][S(B, @)\uparrow])[@R, @]$
(d) Insert: $R[\mathbf{A}, @R] + S(B, @R)\uparrow$
(e) Delete: $R[\mathbf{A}, @ R] - S(B, @R)\uparrow$
(f) Generate: $S(A, @)\uparrow$

In the case of selection, A and c are used to determine the relevant segment that includes the tuples which have $A = c$. The associative disk accesses the segment and filters those tuples with $A = c$ and sends the tuple identifiers (@R) to the TS.

In the linear join of (b), the segment address generator receives the attribute codes A and B and generates a stream of paired segment numbers, one from $R_1[\mathbf{A}, @R_1]$ and the other from $R_2[\mathbf{B}, @R_2]$. These segments may contain common codes for their matching values. The associative disk controller receives the pair of segment numbers and accesses the two segments sequentially. The segment of $R_1[\mathbf{A}, @R_1]$ is sent to the sorter to be sorted on A. The sorted segment is stored in one of the free search engines. Then the segment $R_2[\mathbf{B}, @R_2]$ is sent to the searcher. The searcher searches R_1 segment with the R_2 segment and generates a pair of tuple identifiers (i.e., $@R_1$, $@R_2$) for the matching A and B values in the respective lists.

In the linear join of (c), only one of the relations is stored in TS (both R_1

and R_2 were stored in TS in (b)). Here the S relation is the sorted input stream. Each code for the attribute in the input stream determines a path in the trie directory. The trie engine converts it to a segment number. The table distributor unit in TS collects those codes with common segment numbers in the search engine. The associative disk controller accesses the segments of R and sends them sequentially to the searcher. The searcher outputs a subset of pointers [@R, @] corresponding to the matching A and B codes between the two relations.

In the operations insert (d) and delete (e), the attribute code A determines the root address of the trie directory. The sorted input stream of codes in $S(B,@R)\uparrow$ is received and for each code or code substream the corresponding segment addresses are determined by the trie engine. The associative disk controller inserts or deletes the corresponding codes in related segments.

In generation (f), a new file is generated and a trie directory is constructed for the specified attribute.

Tuple constructor.   The tuple constructor hardware is similar to that of TS. The TC translates a tuple identifier to a full tuple. To do this TC has, for each relation R, $R[@\mathbf{R}, A_1, A_2, \ldots, A_n]$. (The bold type indicates a fast access path.) The TC performs operations similar to the TS. The linear join is that of the second type in TS, that is, $(R[@\mathbf{R}, A_1, \ldots, A_n][@R = @R](S(@R, B_1, \ldots, B_m)\uparrow))[A_1, \ldots, A_n, B_1, \ldots, B_m]$.

Aggregate operator.   The aggregate operator hardware consists of an ALU, local memory, and a network of sorters. The AO performs duplicate elimination, set aggregates such as group by, and scalar aggregates which are denoted as follows:

(a) Tuple construction: $S[@,A]\uparrow, S[@,B]\uparrow, S[@,C]\uparrow = S[[A,B,C]]$
(b) Duplicate removal: $S[[A_1, A_2, \ldots, A_n]] = S[A_1, A_2, \ldots, A_n]$
(c) Group by $S[A,(B,C)/A]$; B, C are grouped with respect to A
(d) Scalar aggregate: $S[A, average(B/A)]$; Bs are grouped by A and for each group the average B is computed.

To remove duplicates the tuples must be sorted. Since the word length of the sorters is fixed, sorters must be concatenated in parallel to increase the effective width, or a nested loop must be constructed to repeat partial sorting of tuples and then link each previous sort to the next via an @ attribute. The group by operation also depends on sorting. The following examples present the selection and join operations which use the services of TS, TC, and AO.

Example 7.4

Selection of $R(A, B, C)$: $R[A = c][B, C]$:

(a) Encoder/decoder outputs $e(c)$ to TS
(b) TS executes $S_1 = (R[\mathbf{A}, @R][A = e(c)])[@R]$. That is, a list (unary relation)

of tuple identifiers of R is output to TC. If $e(c)$ is another attribute of R, then a full search over R will be necessary.

(c) TC performs a linear join (i.e., the R relation with itself) as $S_2 = (R[@R = @R](S_1 \uparrow))[[B, C]]$ and outputs it to AO.

(d) AO removes duplicates from the sorted S_2, $S_2 \uparrow$ and outputs the result back to the encoder/decoder to be decoded and sent to the user.

The linear join refers to the one-pass batch search operation between two sorted lists. We will see the batch search operation used in the search engine.
Join of $R(A, B, C)$ and $S(D, E):((R[A = c])[C = D]S)[B, C, E]$:

(a) TS carries out selection and outputs it to TC. That is, it computes $S_1 = (R[\mathbf{A},@R][A = e(c)])[@R].$

(b) TC linearly joins R onto itself as: $S_2 = (R[@\mathbf{R},C][@R = @R](S_1 \uparrow))[C,@R].$

(c) TS does the same on S: $S_3 = (S[\mathbf{D},@S][D = C]S_2 \uparrow))[@R,@S].$

(d) TC does the same on S: $S_4 = (R[@R,B,C][@R = @R](S_3 \uparrow))[@S,B,C]$

$$\text{Outputs } S_5 = S_4[@,B,C] \text{ to AO}$$

$$\text{Outputs } S_6 = S_4[@S,@] \text{ to TC}$$

(e) TC moves E along the eligible tuples of S_6 and outputs the result to AO. That is, it computes $S_7 = (S[@\mathbf{S},E][@S = @S](S_6 \uparrow))\ [@,E].$

(f) AO constructs the final result S_8, removes duplicates from S_8, and outputs the result to the encoder/decoder. The S_8 is $((S5)[@ = @](S_7 \uparrow))\ [[B,C,E]].$

The search engine (SEE).   The search engine stores a sorted table of keywords which are organized as a trie. The SEE searches a batch of input keys versus this table and for each input key it outputs the least table address whose key is greater than or equal to the input key. In the case of equality, a bit flag is also set. The table address corresponds to the storage address of the corresponding record stored separately.

Figure 7.26(a) shows the SEE sorted table of keywords and the input key stream to be processed against it. In Figure 7.26(b), we see the pipeline processing of the input key batch over the SEE key table. As soon as an input key enters the pipe represented by the sorted list of keywords (which actually form a binary trie), the search process starts on every input key entering the pipe. Every input key exits with the table address of the first table entry that is equal to or greater than the input along with a hit flag which is set to one in the case of equality. The SEE search table is organized as a binary trie which is called the *left-sided binary trie*. This is because the sorted keywords are stored in the trie in the order as indicated by the node values of Figure 7.26(c) (i.e., loading starts from node 0). Assuming for a moment that the node labels also represent the values of the sorted keys stored in them, the insertion of the next key whose value is 15 is performed as follows. Assuming that the trie is searched by labeling the arcs traversed by 0 and 1 for less than and greater than comparisons, respectively, the path for 15 will be the binary number 1011 along the insertion path which

Table address	0	1	2	3	4
Key	3	7	9	12	19

Input key stream: 5, 12, 7, 8, 3, 19, 4, 9

(a) Search engine table and input key batch

Input keys:	..	..	..	5	12	7	8	3	19	4	9	→ Pipeline
Table address:	..	0	1	2	3	4	2	0	4	1	2	processing
Table keys:	..	3	7	9	12	19	0	1	1	0	1	: Hit flags

(b) Pipeline searching of SEE

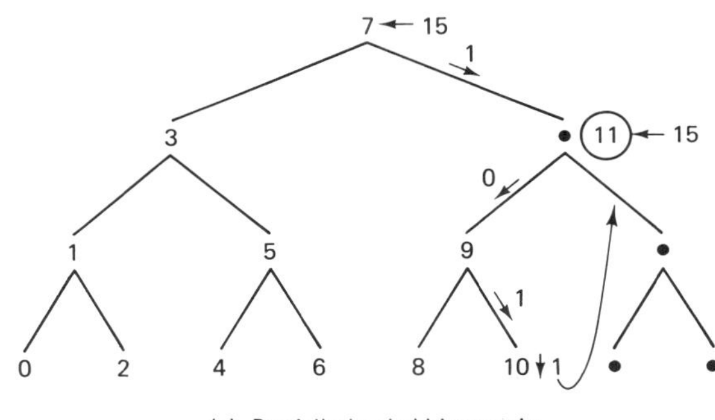

(c) Partially loaded binary trie

Figure 7.26   Search engine and its search structure. From D. K. Hsiao, *Advanced Database Machine Architecture* (Englewood Cliffs, N.J.: Prentice-Hall, Inc., 1983). Adapted by permission of Prentice-Hall, Inc.

corresponds to decimal 11. This will be the node address of the key value 15 in the trie, which is the address of the next node to be visited in the left sided trie. The trie can be concurrently (i.e., in pipeline) searched for multiple keys.

The sort engine (SOE).   The sort engine implements a pipelined heap sort. Accordingly, an SOE starts outputting its sorted list as soon as it receives the last input item to be sorted. The heap in SOE is a binary trie in which each path from its root to leaf has the node values in the sorted order. The SOE, SEE, and the trie engine all have the same structure. They have a dedicated logic and a dedicated memory bank for each level of the heap (trie). An SOE with l levels can sort $2^l - 1$ keys. A heap grows from the root of a subtree by adding nodes of the new level from left to right. Figure 7.27 shows the insertion of the next key into the heap.

During insertion, the circuits at the levels on the next path (the path of the next available node for insertion) read out their contents in parallel. Next, the key is inserted into the proper place in the retrieved list and the list is written

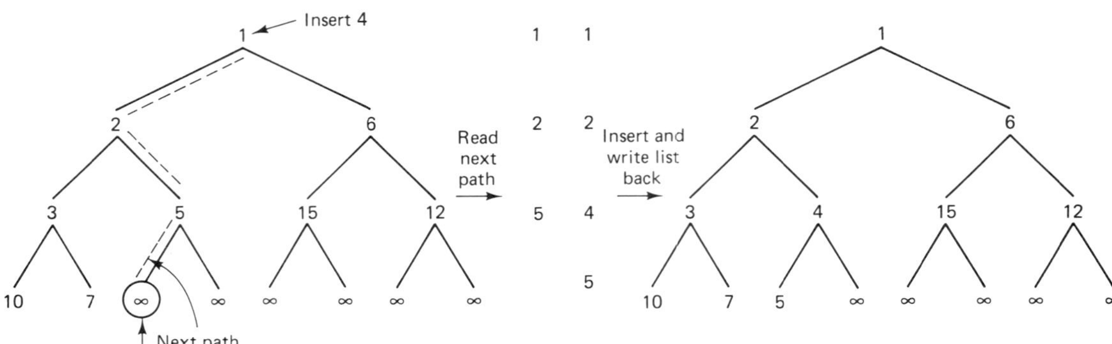

Figure 7.27   Insertion of next key into the heap. From D. K. Hsiao, *Advanced Database Machine Architecture* (Englewood Cliffs, N.J.: Prentice-Hall, Inc., 1983). Adapted by permission of Prentice-Hall, Inc.

back onto the next path. The output of sorted values from the heap is performed as in a tournament sort. First the root is output and this creates a hole. As soon as this happens, the next level circuit compares the values of the left and right nodes and sends the smaller to fill the hole in the upper level. This process continues while the holes propagate from the root to the lower levels.

The sorter needs $\log_2 n$ comparators for n keys to be sorted. The sorting time within the sorter chip is $O(n)$ while the delay between the end of input to obtaining sorted keys is zero. The sorter needs concatenation of chips if the width of data to be sorted is larger than sorter's word length. Also, for longer streams the sorters must be combined or cascaded in a totem pole arrangement where the root of a lower-level sorter is connected to the leftmost leaf of the next higher-level sorter to form a chain of sorters.

The DSDBM utilizes a network of $n \times m$ sorters which are interconnected to the functional units of the kernel database machine. n represents the order of the distribution network, that is, the number of input ports, while m is the number of destination ports. There are also equal numbers of mergers on the network. Each of the m sorters is connected to one of the output ports through mergers. Each destination processor obtains a sorted stream from the sorters in its column. The totem pole connection of sorters assumes an unlimited number of sorters. If the number is limited, the sorted strings which overflow are stored in RAMs. These overflown sorted substrings are pushed through the leftmost paths of the available sorters and the streams overflowing through the leaves are stored in RAMs. In the output, the process is reversed. Figure 7.28 shows this process. The output from Figure 7.28(c) is performed in the same way as in the case of a single sorter. Only this time, the two leftmost leaves will be replenished from the smaller of the overflown streams.

The hardware of several subsystems of the overall architecture of this

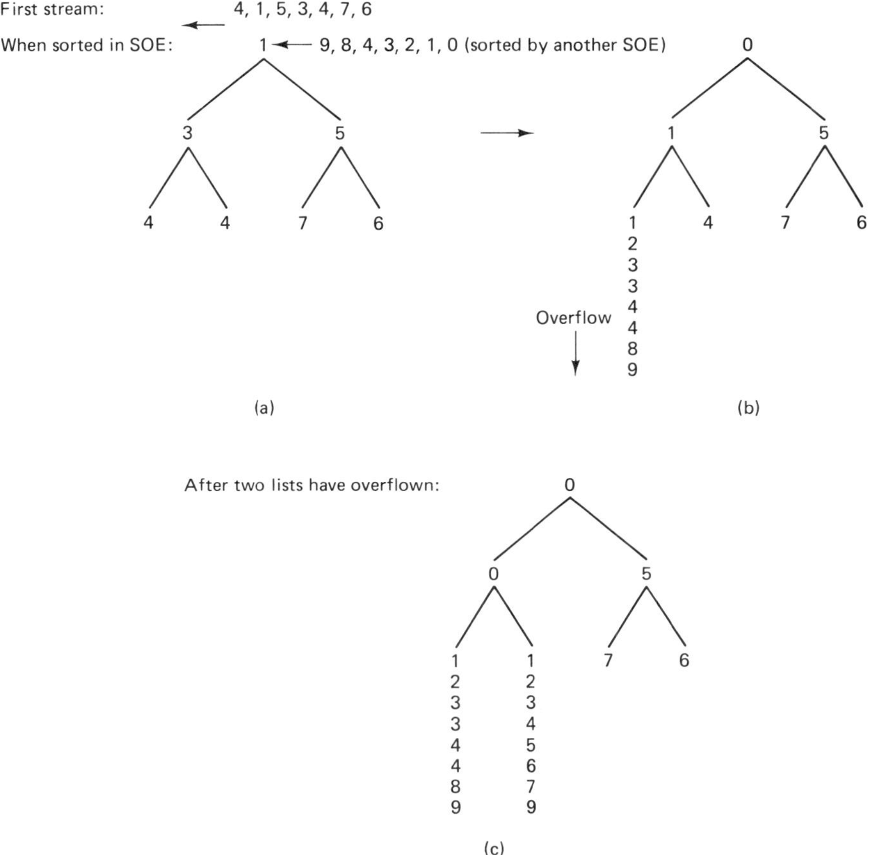

Figure 7.28   Sorting longer streams. From D. K. Hsiao, *Advanced Database Machine Architecture* (Englewood Cliffs, N.J.: Prentice-Hall, Inc., 1983). Adapted by permission of Prentice-Hall, Inc.

database machine has been prototyped at the board level. Further simulation studies have been carried out to be able to progress into detailed implementations.

7.3.2 GRACE

The GRACE relational database machine [Kitsuregawa, Tanaka, and Moto-Oka, 1983; Moto-Oka and Fuchi, 1983; Kitsuregawa, Tanaka, and Moto-Oka, 1984] is organized for join-intensive applications. It utilizes the concepts of associative disks with filtering, hash-based data partitioning, and pipeline merge sort in its processing modules. The basic premise of the architecture relies on the fact that the tuples of relations can be distributed into hash buckets determined by ranges of values of the attribute to be hashed, which is the join attribute. Accordingly, instead of the $O(M \times N)$ complexity of the brute force nested loop join algorithm, where M and N are the cardinalities of the two relations being joined, if we hashed the join attributes of these relations so that

$$N = \sum_{i=1}^{s} n_i \quad \text{and} \quad M = \sum_{i=1}^{s} m_i$$

where n_i and m_i are the sizes of the ith bucket of the respective relations and s is the number of buckets in each relation, the join complexity would be simplified. This is because we would compare only those tuples of relations which occupy compatible buckets (i.e., for $i \neq j$, we do not process n_i with m_j). Accordingly, the overall complexity would be $O(\Sigma_{i=1}^{s} n_i \times m_i)$. Figure 7.29(a) shows the complexity of the brute force nested loop algorithm whereas Figure 7.29(b) shows the reduced complexity (by the shaded areas on the diagonal) due to hash partitioning or clustering of the database.

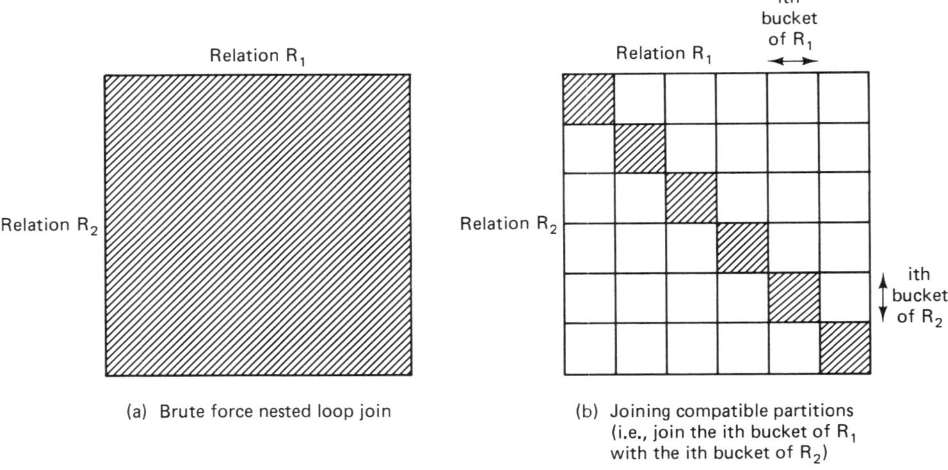

Figure 7.29   Effect of hash partitioning on the join operation. From M. Kitsuregawa, H. Tanaka, and T. Moto-Oka, "Architecture and Performance of Relational Database Machine GRACE." *Proc. of Int'l. Conference on Parallel Processing,* © 1984 IEEE.

GRACE has a pipelined parallel bucket processing architecture. Each processor is assigned to process a bucket; therefore, interprocessor communication will not be necessary. The buckets have to be determined at the low end of the memory hierarchy and then moved into the memory modules in the upper memory hierarchy which forms the staging part of the GRACE architecture. Figure 7.30 shows the overall architecture of GRACE.

As can be seen in the figure, the processing modules and memory modules are connected by a processing network while the memory modules and disk modules are connected through a staging network. The networks consist of

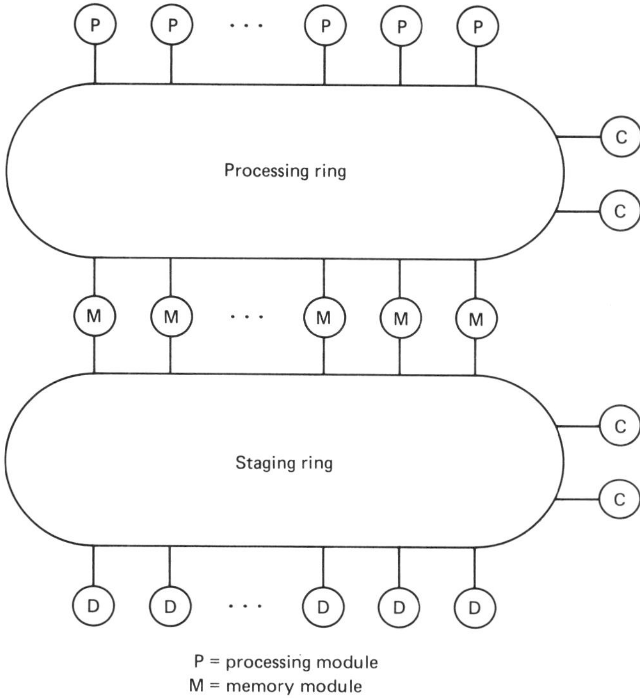

Figure 7.30   Architecture of GRACE. From M. Kitsuregawa, H. Tanaka, and T. Moto-Oka, "Architecture and Performance of Relational Database Machine GRACE." *Proc. of Int'l. Conference on Parallel Processing,* © 1984 IEEE.

multichannel ring buses. The database relations are paged into memory modules through the staging network, and then the data streams generated by memory modules flow into processing modules through the processing network. The processing modules perform pipeline sorting and processing on their respective data streams in parallel. Figure 7.31 shows a conceptual view of the staging and processing stages of GRACE.

As can be seen in the figure, the data moving from the disk modules are first filtered and then hashed on their join attribute and the resulting hash code is stored along each tuple to identify the relation bucket. Rather than dedicating a memory module to a bucket, buckets are distributed to memory modules. This results in reasonably even bucket distributions in memory modules even though buckets themselves may vary in size due to the hashing function. n number of parallel processing modules are assigned to process m number of database buckets. Normally however, $m \gg n$. In that case, bucket processing beyond n proceeds bucket serially. As can be seen in Figure 7.31, buckets are distributed to memory modules by various hashers at the low-level memory hierarchy. In the upper level, once bucket distribution is completed, the tuples of a bucket are gathered by processing modules in pipeline. That is, once processing module-1 picks its tuples from the portion of its bucket in the first memory module, it moves to

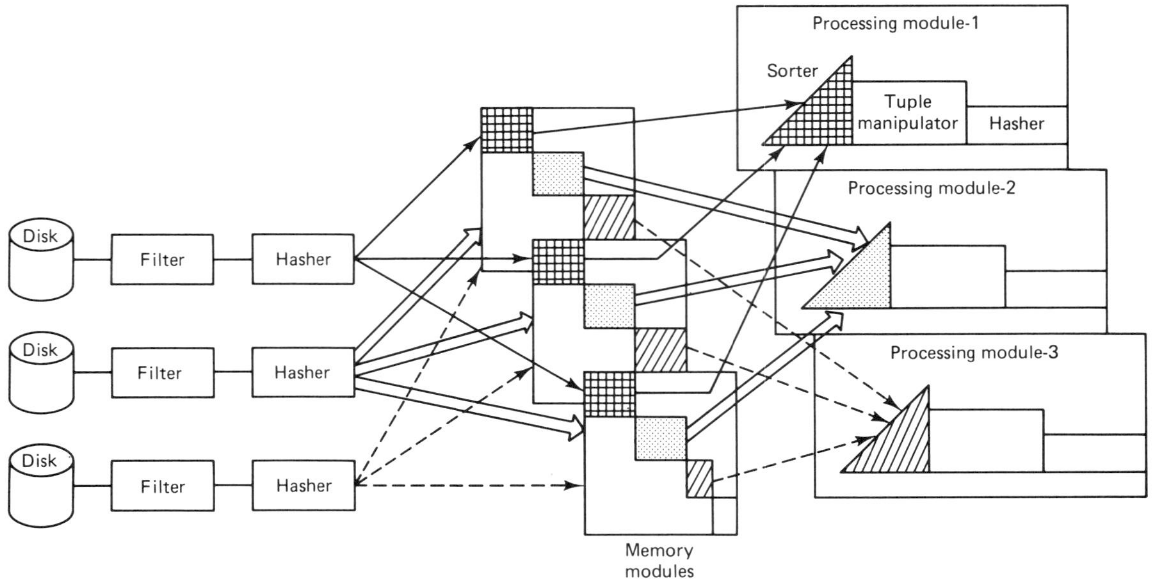

Figure 7.31   Conceptual view of staging and processing in GRACE. From M. Kitsuregawa, H. Tanaka, and T. Moto-Oka, ''Architecture and Performance of Relational Database Machine GRACE.'' *Proc. of Int'l. Conference on Parallel Processing*, © 1984 IEEE.

pick the remainder from the other memory modules. As soon as a memory module is freed of I/O with a processing module, it becomes available to the next processing module to provide its portion of the tuples in another bucket. Once tuples are received in a processing module, they are sorted by a pipeline merge sort unit. The sorter requires $\log_k N$ comparators to sort N items in $O(N)$ time where the delay between the input and output is $\log_k N$. An asynchronous data stream rate of 3 megabytes per second has been attained by the processing modules. The tuple manipulation unit performs relational algebra operations on the sorted tuples emerging from the sorter. If the query program involves further operations on the results of the tuple manipulation unit, a hasher hashes on the attribute which will be involved in the subsequent operation so that processing continues on a partitioning basis. To follow the concept of pipeline processing in this architecture, let us assume the presence of two memory modules and four processing modules for an example of GRACE. Figure 7.32 shows an overview of the pipelined bucket processing in the processing ring.

As can be seen, memory module 0, after outputting the tuples of bucket 0, starts outputting the tuples of bucket 1. And in a processing module as soon as the input and sorting of an entire bucket is finished, the processing on that bucket starts. After that, the processor is ready to receive the next bucket, which is bucket number 4 (i.e., the fifth bucket), because there are four parallel processors and memory module 0 gets the first bucket of the next load of four.

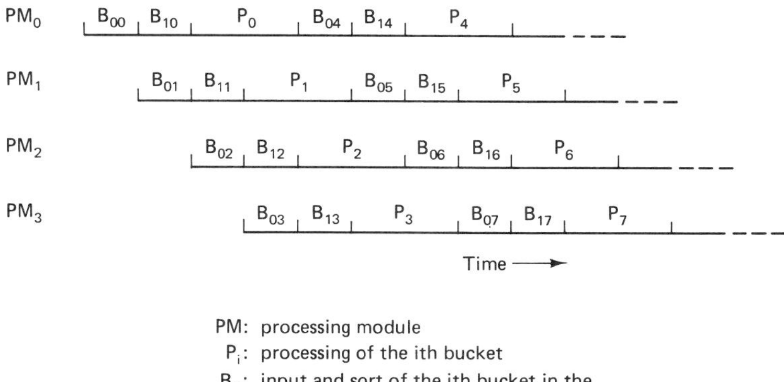

Figure 7.32 Pipelined bucket processing in the processing ring. From M. Kitsuregawa, H. Tanaka, and T. Moto-Oka, "Architecture and Performance of Relational Database Machine GRACE." *Proc. of Int'l. Conference on Parallel Processing,* © 1984 IEEE.

Returning to Figure 7.30, let us review the other functional units of the architecture. The memory unit provides the intermediate storage which generates bucket streams for the processing modules. Magnetic bubble memory technology is used in GRACE with some modification on the minor loops to provide continuous output of eligible tuples. To accomplish this the minor loops are segmented into buffer and main loops. An outside RAM is synchronized in parallel with the minor loop. The RAM stores hash codes of tuples and tag bits for them. The use of this tagging scheme and a transfer gate between the buffer and main parts of the minor loop permit ineligible tuples to be bypassed in the main loop in one bit rotation time. In this way, the buffer loop is filled with eligible tuples without redundant traversal of the loops. The current prototype uses 16 1-megabit chips in the memory module, where the sizes of the buffer and main loops are 128 and 4096 bits, respectively. Look-ahead buffering control is used in this modified magnetic bubble memory so that the tuples of the next bucket are accumulated into the buffer while the current bucket is being output.

The filter processors reduce the volume of data coming off the movable head disk drives. The hasher works on the reduced sets of data. The control module addresses the relations on disk modules and sends the Boolean predicate to the filters. The control module also provides the memory modules with the attribute being hashed so that the bubble memory operations can be controlled. The control module also informs the processing modules for the relational algebra operation, attributes to be projected, and the attributes which will be involved in subsequent operations. For a given query, the control module assigns an adequate number of processing modules for the execution of the query.

In this architecture, the performance of the processing modules is affected by the evenness (of average time between stages) in pipeline processing. For each subbucket accessed from a memory module (i.e., B_{ij} in Figure 7.31) the processor spends $O(n)$ time for sorting and another $O(n)$ time for tuple manipulation. Therefore a total of $2n$ time units is needed for n items (tuples) in the subbucket. Referring to Figure 7.31, the evenness and synchronization of overlapping operations in the pipeline would be greatly disturbed if subbuckets fluctuate in size. This fluctuation would cause the insertion of idle times into the subsequences of the pipeline. To minimize possible performance degradation due to this effect in GRACE, subbucket outputting from memory modules is performed in a sequence determined by the sizes of subbuckets. The subsequent bucket outputs are fed into the processing modules in the order of increasing subbucket size. In this way, a processing module working concurrently, on a previous subbucket of a smaller size will always be ready to input the next subbucket of larger size. The distribution of subbuckets into multiple memories reduces the chance of varying subbucket sizes; even buckets themselves vary in size. This subbucket distribution takes place at two points: one during the staging phase and the other during the postprocessing phase which prepares for the next intermediate operation.

The GRACE architecture is one of the candidate relational database machines for the Japanese fifth-generation computer project sponsored by ICOT. This project aims to construct knowledge-based information systems where an inferencing mechanism via logic programming will be built on top of the relational algebra power of a database machine. During the initial phase of the project, most functional units will be the sequential versions of the parallel units to be built subsequently. In the immediate future, a network of sequential inference machines (SIMs) will be developed which will be supported by a relational database machine called DELTA [Moto-Oka and Fuchi, 1983]. DELTA relies mostly on current technology and uses a mainframe computer as its main (processor) memory. Relational algebra processing is performed after streams of data are sorted by means of a pipeline merge/sort unit in addition to other simpler modes of processing such as filtering for selections.

7.3.3 Parallel Pipelined Relational Query Processor

The parallel pipelined relational query processor [Kim, Gajski, and Kuck, 1984] is a pipeline architecture design that is based on four processing modules which operate as iterative pipes. The processing modules are oriented toward VLSI implementation so that in each module there can be some number of chips working in parallel. The user interface and query processing capabilities of the architecture are demonstrated through the SQL language. The continuity of pipeline flow in the architecture depends upon overlap between the disk I/O and processing in the pipes. Figure 7.33 shows the overall architecture of the parallel pipelined relational query processor.

Upon receiving a query from the user, the host GPC generates a control program and stores it in the control program memory. The query processor controller uses this program to control the operation of each pipe and coordinate

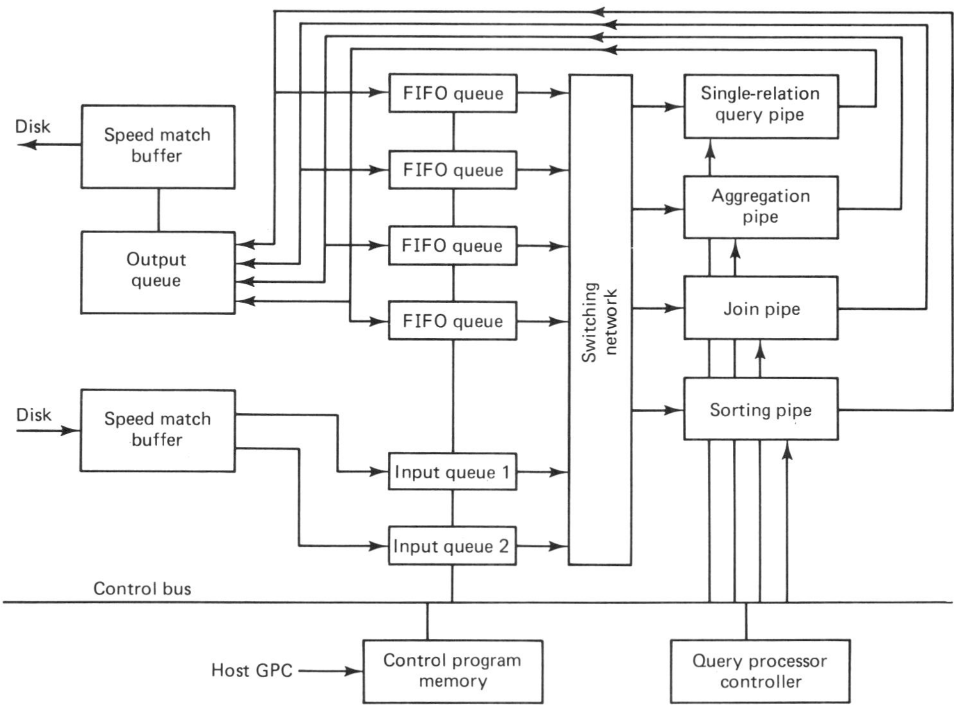

Figure 7.33 Overall architecture of the query processor. From D. Gajski, W. Kim, and F. Fushimi, "A Parallel Pipelined Relational Query Processor: An Architectural Overview." *Proc. of ACM SIGARCH Conf.*, © 1984 Association for Computing Machinery.

the flow of tuples between different pipes. Each pipe is designed to process the incoming tuples in pipeline. The tuples enter the pipes bit serially. However, the pipes are organized to receive several tuples in parallel for parallel processing within the pipe.

The single-relation query pipe evaluates the *select* and *where* clauses of a single-relation SQL query. This involves selection, projection operations, arithmetic, and attribute value permutations as required in the select clause. This pipe will be implemented with 32 chips, using 1 chip per input tuple. The aggregation pipe performs scalar aggregates (i.e., MAX, MIN, SUM, COUNT, AVERAGE), computes the *group by* clause, and separates the eligible tuples for the *where* clause from the remaining ineligible tuples. This pipe will be implemented in one chip. The join pipe performs joins between two relations and will be implemented with 32 chips. The sorting pipe will be implemented with 8 chips where each chip will be a 16×16 sorting pipe.

The FIFO queues are used to route temporary results of a pipe to the next pipe before outputting the complete result to the output queue. Each queue is a $32 \times 2K$-bit RAM implemented as one VLSI chip. The switching network switches tuples to be evaluated from any queue to any pipe. This network is a 6×6 32-bit wide crossbar switch.

Single-relation query pipe.   The single-relation query pipe consists of 32 chips where each chip processes one tuple. The chip is divided into two parts: The *where* evaluation part and the *select* evaluation part. The internal registers and the corresponding program segments of the *where* and *select* evaluation parts are loaded from the control program memory. These two parts work on the tuples independently in parallel; however, in the end a null tuple indicator flag is set by the *where* part which determines whether the output of the *select* part will be used in the answer.

Aggregation pipe.   Consider the following SQL example written on the EMP and DEPT relations:

The relations are

```
EMP(NAME, DNO, AGE, JOB, SAL, COMM, MGR)
DEPT(DNO, LOC, MGR)
```

The SQL query is

```
SELECT DNO, 0.75 * AVG(SAL + COMM)
FROM EMP
WHERE COMM > 20000 AND AGE < 30
GROUP BY DNO
```

This query is processed as follows. Using the single-relation query pipe, the *where* clause is evaluated on the EMP relation and the result is stored in a temporary relation, say, Rt_0. Rt_0 is then grouped by DNO values and the aggregation function is applied to each group. The query for the aggregation pipe is reduced to the following:

```
SELECT DNO, 0.75 * AVG(SAL + COMM)
FROM Rt_o
GROUP BY DNO
```

This query is processed by sorting the Rt_0-tuples on DNO and then passing the result through the aggregation pipe. This pipe will output one result tuple for each distinct value in the DNO attribute on which the grouping is based. The aggregation pipe includes a duplicate remover unit which takes the sorted tuples as input and reduces the repeating DNO values within each group to a single value.

Join pipe.   To follow the operation of the join pipe, let us consider the following SQL example presented by the authors:

```
SELECT DEPT.MGR, 0.75 * SAL, NAME
FROM EMP, DEPT
```

```
WHERE COMM > 30000 AND LOC = 'SAN JOSE' AND
EMP DNO = DEPT.DNO
```

As we can see both of the relations to be joined involve a restriction (selection). Because optimal query processing requires that the relations to be joined should first be reduced by their selections, two temporary relations, Rt_1 and Rt_2, are created by the single-relation query pipe after evaluating the selections (i.e., COMM > 30000; LOC = 'SAN JOSE') on relations EMP and DEPT, respectively. The join pipe now works on the following query:

```
SELECT Rt₂, C₁, 0.75 * Rt₁·C₁,Rt₁·C₂
FROM Rt₁, Rt₂
WHERE Rt₁.DNO = Rt₂.DNO
```

C_1 and C_2 are the attributes of the original relation that are projected (because they are needed in the *where* and *select* clauses) for Rt_1 and Rt_2 (i.e., $Rt_1(C_1,$ C_2, DNO) and $Rt_2(C_1$, DNO)). The join pipe forms the composite (joined) tuples and sends them to the single-relation query pipe and/or aggregation pipe for evaluating the arithmetic expressions on the *select* clause, permuting output attributes, eliminating null (ineligible) tuples, and computing scalar aggregates.

The join pipe consists of 32 chips which are identical and operate in parallel. Tuples from input queue 1 are broadcast to all 32 join chips while each of the 32-tuples from input queue 2 is sent to a different join chip. Each join chip therefore joins 32-tuples from one relation with 1-tuple from another relation (i.e., basically the nested loop join algorithm). The join attribute values from the tuples of two relations are simultaneously sent to the 32×1 comparator/switch array. Each comparator/switch indicates whether the join attribute values which intersect with it match. If there is a match, a 1 bit is generated for the switch; otherwise, a 0 bit results. This corresponds to the null-tuple indicator bit. Once this bit is known, the join chip constructs the composite tuples by letting the tuples of one relation move through the comparator switches and appends to them the tuples of the second relation. The 32 composite tuples emerging from the *i*th join chip enter a 64-tuple long duplicate remover along with the 32 composite tuples emerging from the $i + 1$th join chip. The duplicate remover sends the first group of 32 tuples to the $i - 1$th chip while it delays the sending of the second group of 32 until the next clock cycle.

Sorting pipe.   The sorting pipe is an $n \times n$ sorting chip that can sort a list of n unsorted tuples or merge a list of length $2n$ list from two n-long sorted tuple lists. The value of n is implemented as 4 in a 4×4 sorting pipe. As we know from sorting, if we must sort a list of length $N \gg n$, we will sort $\lceil N/n \rceil$ sublists, and then merge them in $\log \lceil N/n \rceil$ passes.

This database machine design was not intended to operate in high-volume update transaction environments. The system is tuned for complex query processing for decision support systems. The maximum performance of the query processor is expressed as $(n \times p)/(w \times t)$-tuples per second, where w is the tuple length,

t is delay per bit, n is the number of tuples a pipe can process in parallel, and p is the number of pipes that can be kept busy at the same time. This assumes that the bandwidth between the query processor and the external disks is balanced by completely overlapping the disk I/O with query processing in the pipelines.

7.4 LOGIC-ENHANCED PRIMARY MEMORY (VLSI) SYSTEMS

As can be noticed thus far, our classifications are based upon the main characteristics of database machines. Just as we could classify the pipeline database machine which we discussed in Section 7.3.3 as a VLSI-based database machine design, we could equally well classify the database machines under the current section as pipelined, multiprocessor, or VLSI-based systems. However, as the researchers of this class of database machines have themselves stated, the systems in this group have been originally designed for compute bound problems executed in primary memories. After some research and investigation we believe that the reader will find this classification reasonable.

7.4.1 Systolic (VLSI) Arrays

As we just mentioned, the systems of this group in general have been designed for compute bound problems. However, recently a design for using systolic arrays to execute relational algebra operations has been proposed [Kung and Lehman, 1980]. The systolic arrays have the following properties:

(a) The cells that make up the systolic array elements are homogeneous (i.e., identical) and, hence, can be modularly duplicated and used for different purposes.
(b) The systolic array's data and control flow is simple and regular so that cells can be tightly connected as a homogeneous network via regular connections.
(c) The array uses extensive pipelining and multiprocessing so that a large proportion of the cells are kept active at high data rates. (The word *systolic* has been borrowed from the physiologists. It refers to rhythmically recurrent contractions of the heart which regularly pumps blood and keeps regular flow within the body. A systolic data cell also "pumps data" and performs some brief computation before every contraction cycle.)

As can be seen in Figure 7.34, a cell has three inputs and three outputs. This type of cell is used to build a two-dimensional orthogonal systolic array (i.e., a matrix of cells). The cells can be linearly connected in a chain; only in this case a cell needs to have two inputs (one for control, one for data) and one output. Data move into a cell from the inputs. The processor performs a simple manipulation or computation on the data received and prepares it to be output through the outputs in the next pulse (i.e., systolic rhythm). It has been found that these systolic arrays can allow fast interaction among tuples of relations,

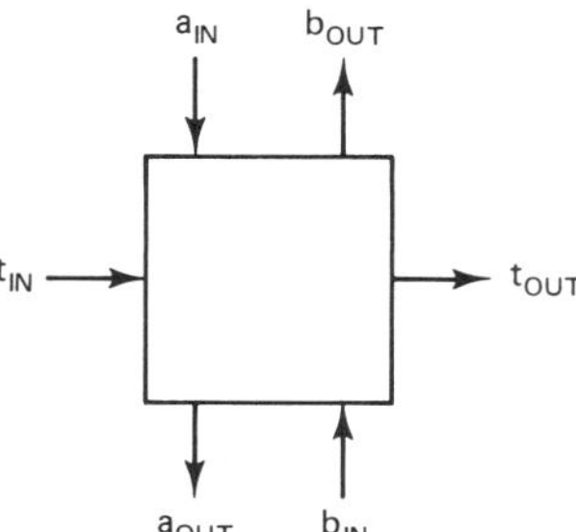

Figure 7.34 A systolic cell. From H. T. Kung and P. L. Lehman, "Systolic (VLSI) Arrays for Relational Database Operations." *Proc. of ACM SIGMOD Conf.,* © 1980 Association for Computing Machinery.

thus enabling various relational operations to be performed. Typically, the relations are pumped into the system from the top and bottom of the array (one relation from each end) and the temporary results (i.e., truth values) move from left to right. To make the whole system work properly, however, all the data and temporary results must be in the right place at the right time. Since all cells are identical and interconnections are regular, the manner in which inputs are routed and control signals timed (these correspond to the actions of an algorithm) determine the specific function an array performs. That is, we can use the same array for doing relational operations such as intersection, difference, join, and so on.

The physical data format in the systolic array system must be regular in order to benefit from the regularity of the array structure. For this reason, all data are encoded into fixed-length integers, and they are decoded back only when results are output for users. In the notation to follow, the symbol T will represent a Boolean matrix which indicates the results of systolic array operations. The element t_{ij} indicates the result of a comparison between the ith tuple of one relation and the jth tuple of another. The single subscript usage, that is, t_i, indicates the result of a logical operation (e.g., logical OR) on all the members of the ith row of T.

Arrays for tuple comparison. Comparing tuples of relations is a fundamental operation. In fact, all relational algebra operations depend upon that operation in one way or another. To build a comparison array, let us first build a systolic cell of Figure 7.34 for comparison purposes. The cell compares two of its inputs a_{IN} and b_{IN} and ANDs the Boolean result with the Boolean input t_{IN}. That is, the following will be the values of the outputs:

$$t_{OUT} = t_{IN} \wedge (a_{IN} = b_{IN}), \qquad a_{OUT} = a_{IN}, \qquad \text{and} \qquad b_{OUT} = b_{IN}$$

Using these primitive operations, a tuple comparison array can be built as shown in Figure 7.35(a). If we concatenate, in the vertical direction, multiple-tuple comparison arrays we then obtain a two-dimensional orthogonal array that can perform parallel tuple comparisons in a pipelined manner. Figure 7.35(b) shows a two-dimensional comparison array. Returning to Figure 7.35(a), to consolidate individual attribute pair comparisons into a final result, which will signal a match

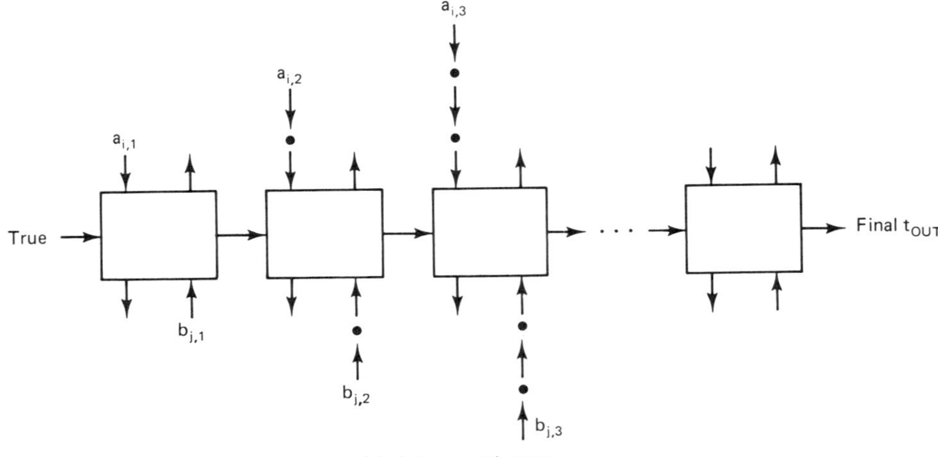

(a) A linear tuple array

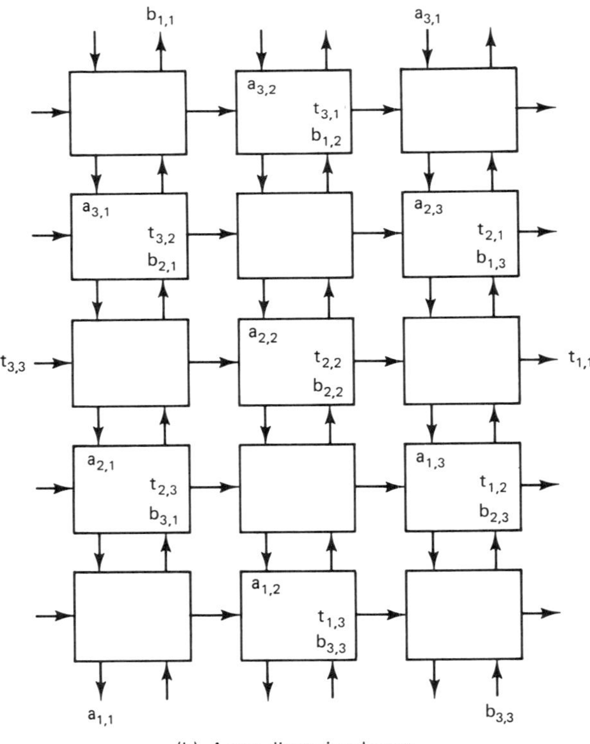

(b) A two-dimensional array

Figure 7.35   Tuple comparison arrays. From H. T. Kung and P. L. Lehman, "Systolic (VLSI) Arrays for Relational Database Operations." *Proc. of ACM SIGMOD Conf.,* © 1980 Association for Computing Machinery.

between two tuples only if all the attribute pair comparisons are successful, certain input sequences must be observed. That is, inputs to the tuple comparison array must be staggered in such a way that first the $a_{i,1}$; $b_{j,1}$ pair will enter the first comparator while the $a_{i,2}$; $b_{j,2}$ pair is delayed one cycle behind before entering the second comparator. This is done to provide the result of the first comparator as the t input to the second comparator so that comparisons can proceed by consolidating (conjunctively) the t_{OUT} truth values. Every higher-numbered attribute will be delayed by one cycle with respect to its predecessor so that a_{ik} and b_{jk} will arrive at the kth processor at the kth pulsing step. Note that the first t_{IN} is anchored at True; otherwise, we would obtain a False regardless of the outcome of subsequent comparisons. In the two-dimensional array of Figure 7.35(b), the relations are pumped from the opposite ends of the array in order to advance into the array and eventually meet at an array position to be compared. The relations are fed entering the array in the staggered fashion, as shown in Figure 7.35(b). However, subsequent tuples into the array must be spaced such that tuples will be at least two steps behind each other instead of being pumped right after one another. This method provides a buffer zone between two tuples progressing toward each other from different ends so that at the final pulse they will both enter into the same comparator (i.e., the one buffered in between) and get compared. (Otherwise they would pass each other without getting a chance to be compared.) Of course, the meeting of two tuples will occur an attribute at a time (i.e., from a_{i1}, b_{jk} to a_{ik}, b_{jk}) as shown in Figure 7.35(a) to produce the t_{OUT} output in the required way.

Looking at Figure 7.35(b) in the leftmost column, we see that $a_{1,1}$ is followed by $a_{2,1}$ and then this in turn by $a_{3,1}$ with two pulse separations. The same is true for the $b_{j,1}$ values but in opposite directions. While $t_{3,3}$ is just entering the middle, where at the next pulse it will be combined with the result of ($a_{3,1}$ = $b_{3,1}$), the $t_{1,1}$ truth value has come out of the other end of the row. Also at this time, $a_{1,1}$ and $b_{1,1}$ are leaving the array. In the meantime, $t_{2,2}$ is being produced from the comparison of $a_{2,2}$ and $b_{2,2}$.

Relational algebra operations

Intersection.   To perform intersection, we must compare every tuple of one relation with all the tuples of the other relation. This is exactly what is provided by the comparison array. By the time the last tuples of the relations exit from both ends of the array, all tuples of one relation will have been compared with all tuples of the other relation. To accumulate $t_{i,j}$ within the T matrix produced by the comparison array during intersection, an accumulation array is concatenated with the comparison array to hold $t_i = \bigvee_{i \leqslant j \leqslant n} t_{i,j}$ (a tuple will be in the answer if it matches at least one tuple in the other relation). To produce t_i the top cell of the accumulation array is anchored at False (not to impose any match) while the first $t_{i,1}$ reaches that cell as the left input and gets OR'ed with the False input. At the next time step, the result is passed to the accumulation array element below. During the same time step, $t_{i,2}$ comes from the left and gets OR'ed with True, then the ith tuple of the relation pumped from the same direction will be a member of the relation resulting from intersection. Figure 7.36 shows the truth value sequences in the comparison and accumulation arrays. As can be seen from the figure, $t_{1,1}$ and $t_{1,2}$ have already left the array and OR'ed with t_1, and $t_{1,3}$ is now ready to exit (because $b_{1,3}$ was behind $b_{1,2}$ and further behind $b_{1,1}$) at the next pulse when it will be OR'ed with t_1 coming down. If, after this, the t_1 result is True this means that a_i has matched at least one tuple of B on the way, therefore satisfying intersection.

Difference. In the difference operation ($C = A - B$), we look for t_i that is False to be a member of the answer (i.e., difference (C) relation), which means that a_i has not matched any B-tuple on the way.

Join. In doing a join, we only need an intersection between the relations, A and B, but this time instead of all tuple attributes only the join attributes of the relations are intersected. We should notice however that the T matrix is not the join but is instead the truth matrix. For each $T_{i,j}$ that is True, we need

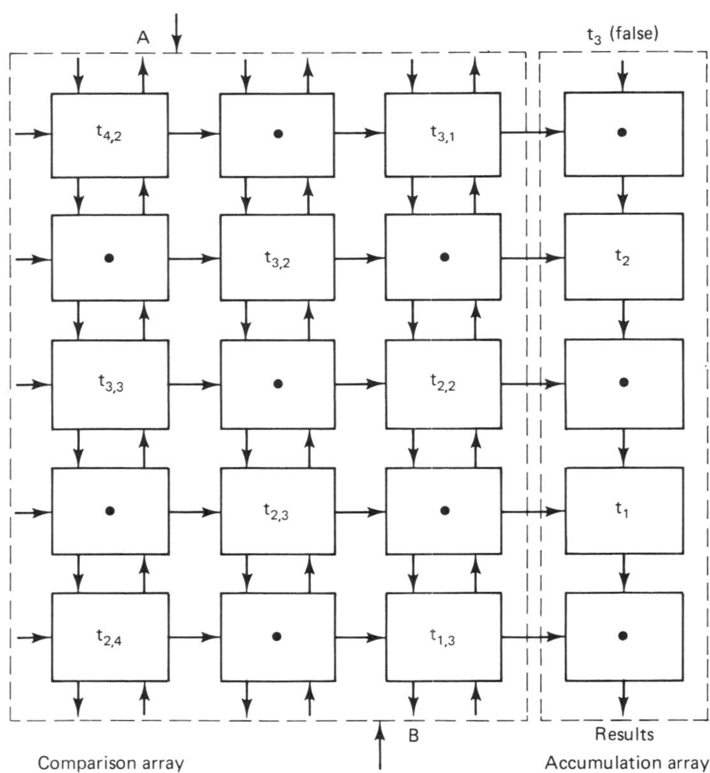

Figure 7.36 Intersection array. From H. T. Kung and P. L. Lehman, "Systolic (VLSI) Arrays for Relational Database Operations." *Proc. of ACM SIGMOD Conf.,* © 1980 Association for Computing Machinery.

to access the *i*th and *j*th tuples from relations A and B, respectively, and physically concatenate them to form the join. The structure of the join array will be slightly different from that of intersection because this time we need every match for a given tuple of a relation with multiple tuples of the other relation. In intersection, however, we obtained an accumulated OR for an a_i-tuple, hence, effectively doing projection on the way. For this reason, we need every $t_{i,j}$ exiting from the comparison array. This precludes the need for an accumulation array.

Division.   For division we need two systolic arrays: the dividend array and the divisor array. To illustrate division, let us refer to Figure 7.37(a) for a simple division operation between the binary SP (dividend) and the unary P (divisor) relations.

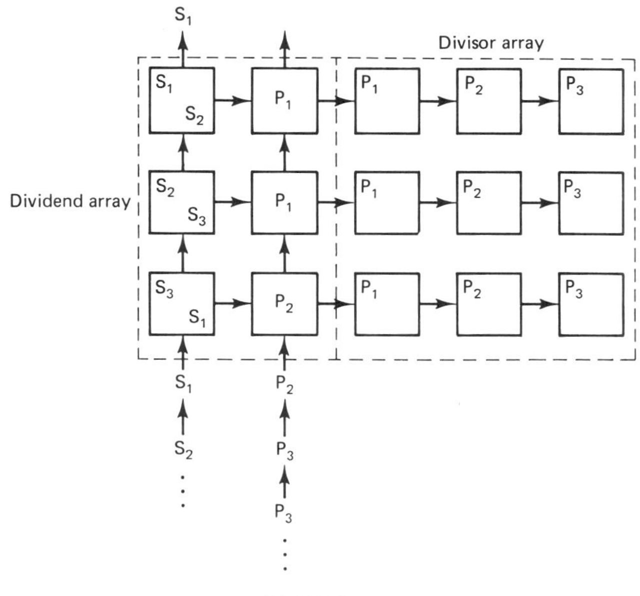

(a) A division example

(b) Division array

Figure 7.37   Operation of a division array. From H. T. Kung and P. L. Lehman, "Systolic (VLSI) Arrays for Relational Database Operations." *Proc. of ACM SIGMOD Conf.,* © 1980 Association for Computing Machinery.

The $\overline{P\#}$, which is $S\#$, in the dividend is first projected through a projection array and preloaded into the first column of the dividend array. Similarly, each row of the divisor array is preloaded with the divisor (preloaded values are shown as circled in Figure 7.37(b)). The dividend array tests for each partition in $S\#$ of SP whether the partition includes the divisor (i.e., there are three partitions as determined by unique S_1, S_2, and S_3 and the divisor set is P_1, P_2, and P_3). To make this test, we take the dividend and input it from the low end with an offset (i.e., $S\#$ enters the leftmost column before $P\#$ enters the second column). If the $S\#$s find a match with the contents of the first column, when they are moving up the column, a True is output to the neighboring cell in the second column. If a True is input to the second column cell, then the content of that cell just input from the cell below is output toward the divisor row. This is compared with the cells in the divisor row, laterally progressing toward the end of the row. If at the end of the operation a given divisor row finds match for all of its cells, then the corresponding $S\#$ value in the first dividend column is output. Referring to the example in the figure, only the first divisor row would match all the preloaded $P\#$ values (i.e., P_1, P_2, and P_3) so that S_1 would be the only dividend value output as the answer. As can be noticed, the number of systolic cells required in the division operation would be equal to

$$|DIVIDEND[\overline{A}]| \times |DIVISOR[B]| + |DIVIDEND[\overline{A}]| \times n_{DVD}$$

where vertical bars indicate cardinality and attributes correspond to the division notation of $DIVIDEND(\overline{A},A)[A \div B]DIVISOR$ and n_{DVD} corresponds to the degree of the dividend relation.

In the implementation of systolic arrays in VLSI it has been estimated that for a repetitive and regular design 1000 comparators can be cast on a chip. However, the heavy dependence of the proposed design on data encoding/decoding is apparent in the array structures.

For a complete system, a functional distribution of systolic arrays is needed, each specialized for a different operation, and with a high bandwidth of data flow among these arrays. This is because a user query program may involve various relational algebra operations to be performed on the relations involved in the query. The appropriate model needed for an integrated system to accomplish all of this has been determined as the crossbar switch as used in the DIRECT database machine. In such a configuration, there would be memory units versus systolic arrays around the switch where the memory units would be filled with data paged in from the disk mass storage system. The high I/O bandwidth of the switch ensures swift data routing among the systolic arrays via memory units.

7.4.2 Highly Concurrent Tree Machines

The attractiveness of the logarithmic communication path offered by a tree structure has been utilized in various studies. Recently, some of these studies have focused their attention on solving the problems of DBMS. Among such studies, we can mention those covered in Browning [1978], Song [1980], and Shaw [1979].

Consider the DLM of Lee that we have seen in Chapter 5. In the linear arrangement of associative cells, the following bottlenecks would result. If we had to store a very large database we would need a large number of cells linearly interconnected. Such a long connection would result in linear communication time, both in signal broadcasting and in the rippling of intermediate results, let alone the high capacitive loading of such a system in VLSI. This linear time propagation may not be tolerable in real time. In the hierarchically interconnected machines, however, processors are divided into two groups. In the first group, which constitute the leaves of the tree, the data are stored or paged in from mass storage and the processors possess associative selection capability. The other group of processors constitute the intermediate nodes through which instructions and intermediate results are bidirectionally (top and/or bottom) routed. These processors also have the capability to execute certain computations. The sublinear communication path offered by the tree structure can be exploited in database operations, especially in sorting and/or sorting based relational algebra operations such as join and projection. By designing nonbacktracking and/or single-pass algorithms, multiple operations can be executed concurrently through various paths of the tree.

Let us look at the tree machine of Song [Song, 1981] in Figure 7.38. The tree machine consists of two complete binary trees connected to each other in a mirror image fashion. There are three types of nodes in the tree which are $\bigcirc$-nodes, $\blacksquare$-nodes, and ∇-nodes. The $\blacksquare$-nodes store data and correspond to leaf processors, $\bigcirc$-nodes broadcast streams of data and instructions to the $\blacksquare$-nodes, and ∇-nodes combine and route the outputs produced by the $\blacksquare$-nodes.

The sort operation in this machine is typical of tournament and/or similar tree-based sorting algorithms. Let us refer to Figure 7.39 to follow the first, second, and the final sixth iteration of the sort of the data stored in the leaf nodes. The upper halves of the trees are omitted for simplicity. The sort proceeds as the parallel two-way merge sort starting with two $n/2$ ascending runs of n data items stored in the leaf nodes. The sort time would consist of data input time plus $O(\log n)$ sort time where the linear data input time dominates the overall timing.

If during sorting a node exchanges its data with both of its offspring when they hold equal data values, then the tree can be used for duplicate elimination, which is the hard part of the projection operation. Figure 7.40 shows the first, second, third, and the final sixth steps of a duplicate elimination example.

7.4.3 The Non-Von Database Machine

The Non-Von database machine [Shaw, 1979] has started from the idea of building a hierarchical associative architecture to execute relational algebra primitives more efficiently than the single-level associative processor designs. In the or-

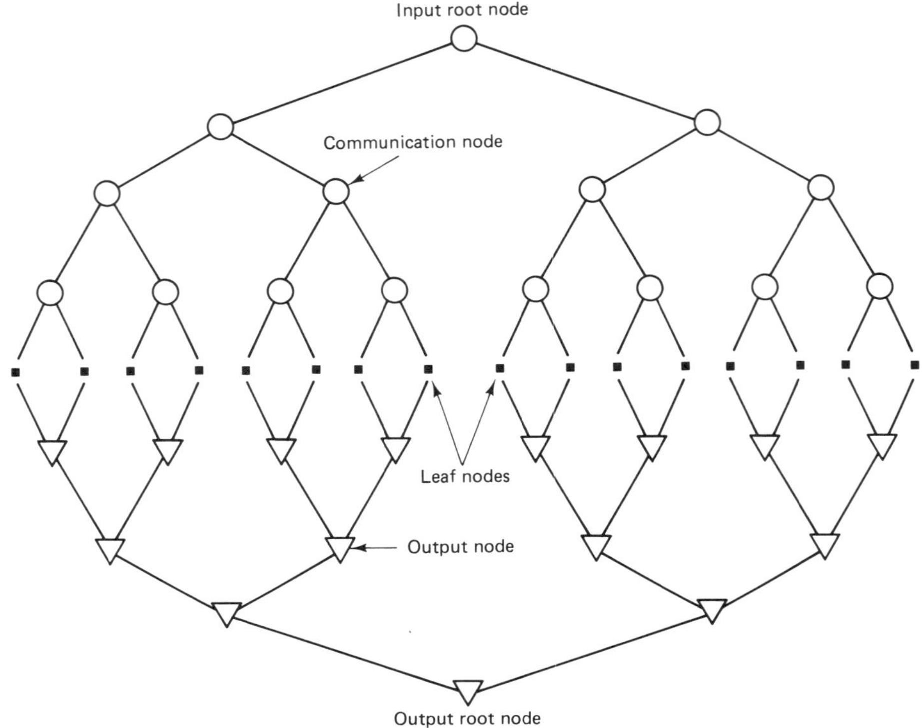

Figure 7.38   The tree machine. From Dr. Siang Wun Song, Ph.D. thesis, 1981.

ganization of the proposed hierarchy, a bottom-level secondary associative memory system (SAM) and a top-level primary associative memory (PAM) system were envisioned. The SAM was conceived as a cellular associative and/or filter device that fed the PAM with associatively selected data partitions to be further evaluated in sublinear time. In other words, PAM was organized as a tree machine of a high number of processors implementable in VLSI. In the combined architecture, SAM was to execute associative selections, whereas PAM would concentrate on binary relational operations that benefit from a logarithmic order of communications and/or operations. Later, this overall organization has started to be implemented within the Non-Von project at Columbia University. In this project, VLSI implementation of PAM is undertaken and the use of the overall system was tuned not only for relational algebra operations but also for knowledge databases [Stolfo and Shaw, 1982]. In the latter use, the DADO project implements parallel execution of production systems in PAM according to a PE (processor) per production scheme. In this scheme, the PAM is divided into three sections. The PM (production match) level contains as many PEs as there are productions to match. The upper part of the PM level handles conflict resolution, while the

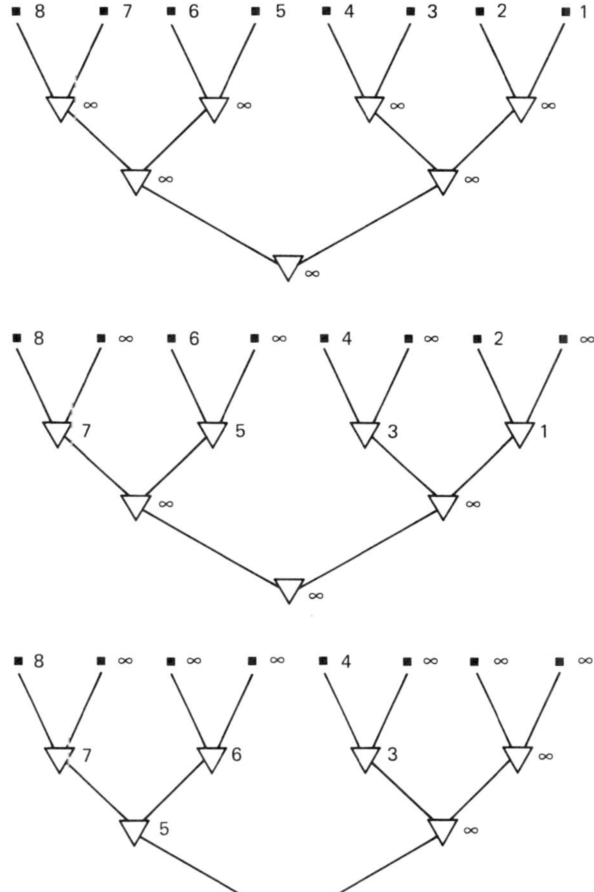

Figure 7.39 A sorting example for the tree machine. From Dr. Siang Wun Song, Ph.D. thesis, 1981.

lower part (combined with SAM) serves as the intelligent associative working memory.

Let us return to the original SAM + PAM organization. The SAM device is supposed to function like an on-the-fly filter whose main function is to extract database partitions associatively and pass them one at a time to PAM in one revolution. Since the value distributions would not be known and since usually they would not be uniform, the on-the-fly filter is not expected to make value comparisons nor to keep domain histograms (as proposed in the associative bucket sort scheme of the RARES database machine) in the cells. What is expected of SAM is rather to compute on-the-fly hash functions on the attribute(s) involved (in the case of a composite attribute combination, hash signatures can be computed as discussed briefly in Chapter 12). It is hoped (although unrealistic) that the hash codes would be nearly uniformly distributed so that SAM is expected

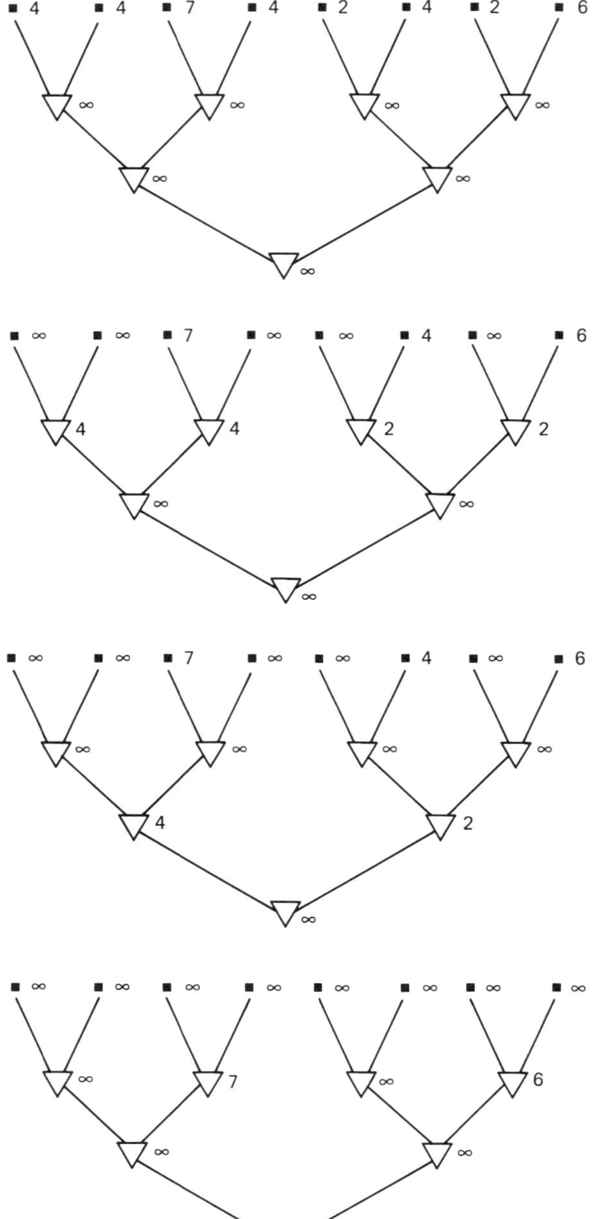

Figure 7.40 Duplicate elimination in the tree machine. From Dr. Siang Wun Song, Ph.D. thesis, 1981.

to output data whose hash codes fall into uniform ranges generated on-the-fly. Normally, the sizes of partitions generated fall within the capacity of PAM; however, occasionally PAM-overflows would occur where a partition exceeds the size of PAM, causing multiple revolutions of SAM and multiple computations in PAM.

In computing relational algebra operations in PAM, the projection operation is carried out in $O(2n)$ time, where n is the cardinality of the relation. The algorithm associatively searches duplicates within PAM for each distinct attribute value to be projected. The join operation is carried out with respect to a nested loop algorithm within PAM. In both join and project, the partitioning of relations into key disjoint buckets (i.e., a key value of a bucket is not repeated in any other bucket) is essential. In join, the key disjoint bucket partitioning is similar to that of the GRACE database machine where only the compatible tuples of the relations being joined are compared. In the case of PAM-overflows, the buckets are partitioned such that all tuple pairs can fit in PAM. The process would then involve exhaustive pairwise processing of all subpartitions in PAM.

The hash partitioning scheme and PAM-overflows were analyzed in the study of the reference. That study included an external evaluation in which the cases where partitions generated could exceed the PAM capacity were analyzed. This external evaluation, however, made a firm assumption that the entire database would be SAM resident, hence, disregarding SAM overflow situations. In the external evaluation, a nonorder preserving hash-based partitioning whose hash codes follow a uniform distribution was assumed. Accordingly, the PAM overflow was found to be independent of the size of relations and that up to a hash storage load factor of 0.90, this overflow was not expected to create an appreciable time overhead.

The VLSI implementation of PAM uses a complete binary tree, where the leaf nodes are distinct from the intermediate nodes. The chip control is handled internally by a programmable logic array, and each processor within the chip possesses a 32-byte local storage.

7.5 FILTERS

The database machine research that started with highly parallel, cellular associative database machines has reached a point where architectural limitations in the hard database operations such as project and join are well understood. This has brought the conception that a database machine system would consist of an associative selection hardware, and in addition, other hardware that would compute the hard operations efficiently would be needed. After this, we began seeing devices called *filters* which are usually (excluding certain claims) simpler than previous associative designs. With filters, on-the-fly selection is the basic operation. This makes them economical and easily implementable in VLSI. In the sections that will follow, we will begin with the earlier designs and then move toward those that concentrate on VLSI implementation. It is the latter category that makes reasonable claims for filtering functions by recognizing that they must fit within a VLSI chip. Normally, filters are used serially with disks (i.e., one chip per disk), operating in pace with I/O stream with their on-the-fly filtering. Parallelism is envisioned with multiple disk drives used through multiple channels each of which is separately filtered. In an integrated system, one can therefore have multiple data flow paths which are concurrently filtered before reaching higher levels of the database machine processing hierarchy.

7.5.1 CAFS and LEECH

The CAFS (content-addressed file store) of ICL [Babb, 1979] is a filter device which is commercially available. The CAFS filter is built between an ICL host GPC and the backend disk system. Because of the technology of its time and, therefore, cost, a realistic configuration was one such device for a disk system instead of one or more per disk. It was, therefore, necessary in the CAFS design that the device should serve a high-I/O bandwidth. This was realized by building a multiplexer between the array of disks and CAFS. A total of up to 12 I/O paths (tracks) coming from a parallel cylinder readout disk and/or different disks can be multiplexed into a single stream of data. This data stream enters the CAFS to be evaluated. Figure 7.41 shows the overall CAFS architecture.

In the CAFS architecture, there are 16 key registers each of which is stored with a label (attribute name) and a value pair. Therefore, different from the

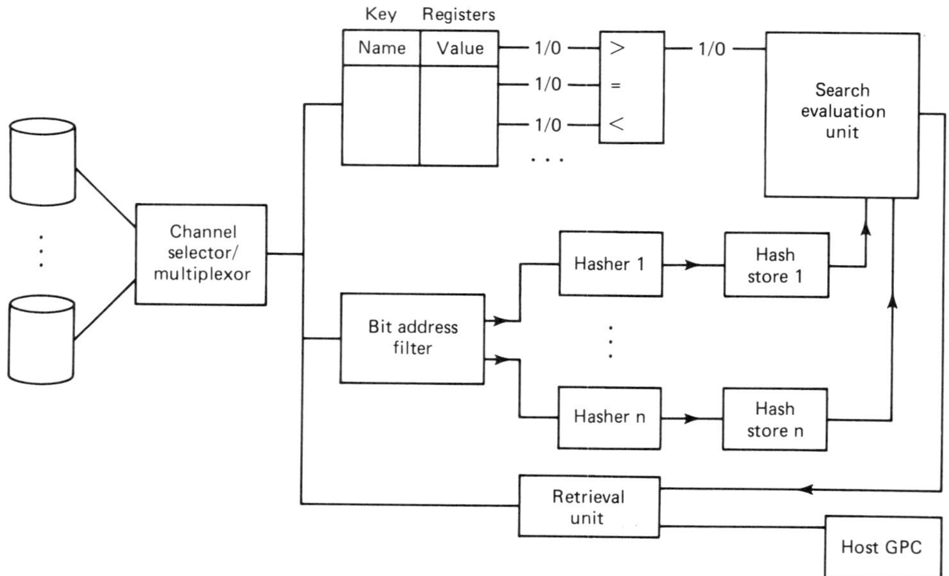

Figure 7.41 CAFS architecture. From E. Babb, "Implementing a Relational Database by Means of a Specialized Hardware." *ACM Transactions on Database Systems, 4,* 1, © 1979 Association for Computing Machinery.

associative comparator units we have seen so far, each comparator determines its attribute by comparing the attribute name with those of the data stream. Whenever the correct attribute is located in the data stream, the comparison for the value part begins. The comparator results (i.e., $>$, $=$, or $<$) are sent to latches where the comparison requested in the user query is stored and the outcome of the key register comparison is compared against it. If the comparison is successful, that is, if a 1 is received for the requested operation, the result is reported to the search evaluation unit. This unit combines individual comparisons into an overall query evaluation or to several evaluations for different queries. This can be done because the data stream is multiplexed and there are 16 parallel key registers available; hence, batching of multiple queries is possible.

Although filters, as we mentioned at the beginning, operate on-the-fly, and they are one-pass devices that can perform selections but not on-the-fly updates and hard database operations such as projection and join, every filter design also proposes some means of doing at least projection and join. CAFS does this also. Since, as we said, filters can examine a single data stream continuously and they cannot perform on-the-fly update and rewrite, their algorithms for join must be decomposed into single stream (hence, single relation) operations of the read-only type. Initially, CAFS implementations used multiple 64K-bit RAMs as bit array stores. These stores were used to encode attribute values in a one-to-one conversion so that *coupling indices* for supporting joins could be implemented. Accordingly, for each attribute value there corresponded an integer which served as an address to the bit map stored in RAM (e.g., the attribute value *transistor* was mapped to the integer, say, 5). This integer value was used as a coupling index to perform the join, which meant that these coupling indices must be computed and stored with the relation ahead of time as additional attributes.

A join using the coupling indices could be processed as follows. The first relation is selected, and for each eligible tuple satisfying the selection, the bit map filter is supplied with the coupling index value which is converted into the appropriate bit map address in one of the bit map stores (which is called a hash store in Figure 7.41). With that address, the corresponding bit is set to 1. Next, the second relation tuples are examined and for each tuple satisfying its selection (if any) the bit map store is accessed with the corresponding coupling index (the same store is accessed between the relations because the coupling index is the same index between the compatible join attributes). If the bit at the bit address contains a 1, then the current tuple is a member of the answer for the join. The projection operation using the coupling index processes a single relation and outputs only those attribute values for which there are no bits set in the corresponding bit address store; otherwise, any value with a 1 bit would be a duplicate.

The one-to-one encoding scheme and the coupling index idea had several drawbacks. First, as we pointed out earlier, the join must be preconceived, and coupling indices must be compiled ahead of time. Second, the encoding of composite attributes to be used in join and projection would be difficult. Finally, the limited size of bit (encoding) stores was a limitation for the number of distinct attribute values a relation could have. This limitation prompted the replacement of one-to-one encoding by a nonunique hashing function. The division method is used for the hashing function and composite attributes are taken just as a single continuous-bit string. Different hash functions are (effectively) obtained by rotating the bit string by a few bit positions for each hash function. The idea of using multiple independent hashing functions is to reduce the likelihood of hashing collisions by combining the hash code conjunctively among the functions. That is, for an attribute value to hash successfully to a logical bit all the corresponding bits in the individual hash code stores must be a 1. In any case, because an error is still a possibility, the final screening is left to the host GPC. To perform a join in this case a methodology similar to the one with the coupling index is used. Only this time the bit array is addressed via hash coding. At the beginning the store for the join attribute is cleared to zeros. Then the first relation is selected and hashed into the bit store. The store bit is set to 1 and the corresponding join attribute value is saved for further inspection. Then the same is done for the second relation's tuples (i.e., those that satisfy the selection and correspond to a 1 bit in the bit store). The host GPC performs the final screening by correlating the two join attribute values supplied to it and forms the actual join by accessing the corresponding tuple pairs and concatenating them.

In the subsequent research for CAFS, a storage encoding called the *joined normal form* (*JNF*) was proposed [Babb, 1982]. The idea behind this proposal was, first, to relieve the users from the burden of specifying how joins should be done between relations in a query program and, second, to eliminate the need for the join operation in the database machine. These ideas sound familiar and are what the universal relation concept is for. (A *universal relation* is a single relation that embodies all the attributes of a database. Each cluster of attributes that correspond to a 3NF relation within the universal relation is referred to as an update object [Ullman, 1982]). In simple terms, a JNF corresponds to the join path cover among database relations. In a JNF relation, all joinable relations' attributes are included. Since the entire relation begins like a universal relation, certain attribute values will have nulls (unknown values) in them. In JNF, the structure resembles that of a universal *outer join* [Date, 1983], where null values of the join attributes are also represented. However, JNF implements a compression on this representation by eliminating duplications among tuples (based on the nonnull values) and by using tag bits that indicate the relations that contain those values. Let us refer to the example provided in [Babb, 1982]. Based on the 3NF relations PS, P, and S (where PS = P * S) shown in Figure 7.42(a), the JNF will consist of J_p, J_s (which are identical to P and S, respectively), and J_{PS*P*S} (which is the entire join sequence). Figure 7.42(b) shows the J_{PS*P*S} relation, Figure 7.42(c) shows the uncompressed JNF, while Figure 7.42(d) displays the compressed JNF.

P

P#	PD
100	DIODE
101	GEAR
102	WHEEL
103	TRANSISTOR

S

COMP	COUNTRY
TEXAS	USA
ITT	USA
PLESSEY	UK

PS

P#	COMP
100	TEXAS
101	TEXAS
102	TEXAS
101	PLESSEY

(a) 3NF relations

J_{PS*P*S}

P#	COMP	COUNTRY	PD
100	TEXAS	USA	DIODE
101	TEXAS	USA	GEAR
102	TEXAS	USA	WHEEL
101	PLESSEY	UK	GEAR

(b) JNF relation J_{PS*P*S}

P#	COMP	COUNTRY	PD
100	TEXAS	USA	DIODE
101	TEXAS	USA	GEAR
102	TEXAS	USA	WHEEL
101	PLESSEY	UK	GEAR
100	—	—	DIODE
101	—	—	GEAR
102	—	—	WHEEL
103	—	—	TRANSISTOR
—	TEXAS	USA	—
—	ITT	USA	—
—	PLESSEY	UK	—

(c) Uncompressed JNF relation

P#	COMP	COUNTRY	PD	t_{PS*P*S}	t_P	t_S
100	TEXAS	USA	DIODE	1	1	1
101	TEXAS	USA	GEAR	1	1	0
102	TEXAS	USA	WHEEL	1	1	0
101	PLESSEY	UK	GEAR	1	0	1
—	ITT	USA	—	0	0	1
103	—	—	TRANSISTOR	0	1	0

(d) Compressed JNF relation using tags

Figure 7.42 JNF representation. From E. Babb, "Implementing a Relational Database by Means of a Specialized Hardware." *ACM Transactions on Database Systems, 4,* 1, © 1979 Association for Computing Machinery.

Disregarding the issues involved in interpreting user queries and updates correctly in the universal relation approach, we can see that this representation serves best for retrieval (read-only) requests. Looking at the figures, in a large database with a high transaction rate, the overhead of updating the database in real-time would be very costly because the JNF structure must be maintained for every update.

The data filter proposed by McGregor, Thompson, and Dawson [1976] of University of Strathclyde is called the LEECH machine. LEECH consists of a processor, a RAM store, and a controller all at the backend of a host. LEECH proposed to execute relational algebra operations and sort/merge besides on-the-fly selection of blocks of data rather than individual records. The binary operations (e.g., join and projection) use essentially the same hash filtering approach employed in CAFS. All hash-based algorithms are referred to as *approximates* whose *strict* evaluation are left to the host GPC.

7.5.2 SURE

SURE is the data filter built at the Technical University of Braunschweig [Leilich, Stiege, and Zeidler, 1978] as the predecessor of the RDBM project. After completion of the project, however, SURE was abandoned because of its economical infeasibility and, therefore, a paging and buffering based I/O and filtering model was incorporated into the RDBM system. The latter approach also eliminated certain restrictions of the on-the-fly filtering that was used in SURE. SURE was tuned for selection only and executing joins was not the main objective. In filtering, the search module provided the host GPC with the result vector and the tuple address of each eligible tuple so that the tuple data had to be retrieved subsequently. SURE was placed between the disk unit and control processor which was in turn connected to the host. Inside SURE's search unit there were 14 search modules working in parallel. The disk unit was a modified 60-megabyte Siemens disk with a data rate of 806K byte/sec. The modification involved converting the disk to a parallel readout design in which nine tracks are read out simultaneously. This reduced the entire disk scan down to 20 seconds, including the head movements. Figure 7.43 shows the organization of one search module.

As can be seen in the figure, the data stream and the query are compared against one another on-the-fly. The data attribute values (a_i) are separated by delimiters (F) and terminated by an end-of-record delimiter (S). The attribute name and length are not represented and close synchronization with the order in the rotating query store is assumed. Accordingly, the query store contains one search instruction (I_i) for each attribute, and the operand (o_i) corresponding to the search predicate is stored following the search instruction. Each search module contains a specially hardwired processor and a RAM called the query memory that has a 1K 20-bit word capacity and stores the instructions (I_i), operands (o_i), and the attribute values (a_i) that are passed on-the-fly from the

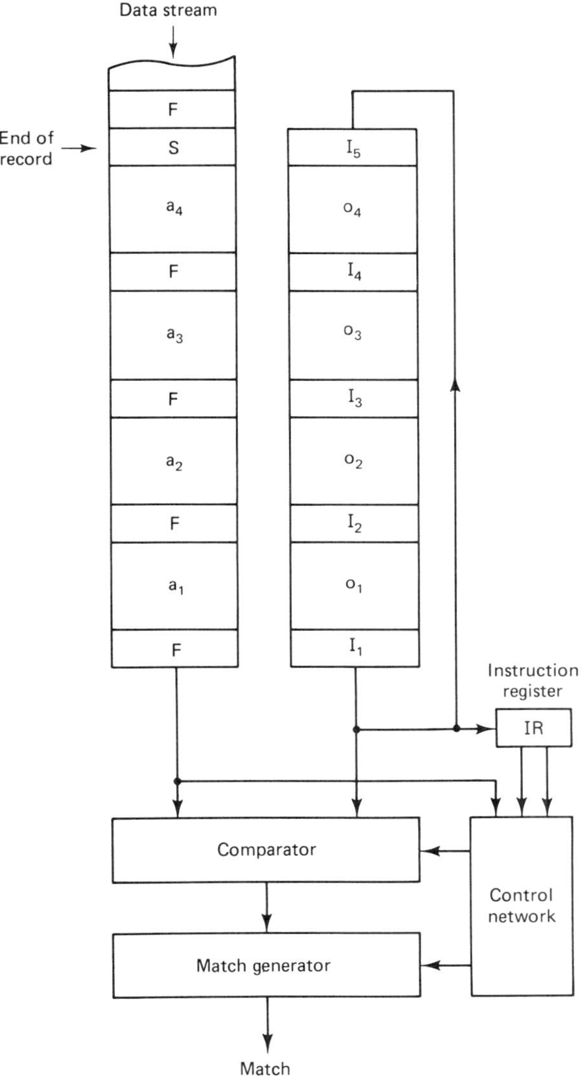

Figure 7.43   Search module organization in SURE.

data stream for attribute to attribute comparisons. The comparisons take place as in associative searching; however, since there is a close coupling between the data stream and the revolving query stream, a jump instruction will be embedded in the data stream following an attribute value that is shorter than the current query operand so that synchronization is not lost. For each passing record, the query program is reexecuted as signaled by an F delimiter following an S delimiter.

Comparisons take place a byte at a time. The comparisons must be combined to obtain a predicate result (e.g., a 32-bit comparison requires four steps). The control network handles the accumulation of comparisons into predicates and predicates into disjunctions or conjunctions and these in turn into conjunctive or disjunctive normal form Boolean expressions. The match generator produces a match signal for those records whose consolidated subresults evaluate to a success.

In SURE, as in CAFS, batching of requests can be done to utilize the parallel search modules. However, this approach should be viewed as making multicomparisons rather than having a genuine multitasking hardware. In the latter, there would not be cases where idle tasks would force idle comparators or the need for task swapping.

7.5.3 VERSO

VERSO is a filter that was implemented at INRIA in France [Bancilhon et al., 1983]. VERSO was designed for relational databases. However, the logical and physical data structures are different from most other systems. The logical interface is implemented via V relations which correspond to the universal relation or the JNF relation concept used in CAFS. These relations are mapped into nested linearized hierarchies which are partitioned into track-sized blocks and indexed on the outermost attribute.

The filter subsystem consists of a frontend microprocessor called the Pilot, which contains a M68000 microprocessor, a bus system, a memory, and an I/O controller. The Pilot provides the user interface and controls the filter subsystem. The filter subsystem contains a microprocessor, a disk controller, a bus system, I/O buffers for the filter, and the filter which has a processor coupled with its local RAM. The filter I/O buffers consist of two track-sized buffers. The filter RAM stores the 256×256 byte FSA transition matrix. (If the reader is not familiar with the FSA concept, Chapter 12 contains an introduction to finite state automata used in searching.) The filter processor scans the I/O buffer byte serially. Each entry of the state transition matrix points to a word chain that contains the next state and the output functions. The filter automaton is compiled by Pilot and loaded into the filter RAM.

For binary operations such as join, VERSO relies on sorting and uses all the buffer space for holding the relations' partitions, which creates the danger of losing on-the-fly synchronization.

The recent data filter research coupled with the ever progressing state of computer technology is resulting in reduced popularity for the implementation of a costly data filter system which must serve several disk units. The trend is for using economical VLSI filters that can be attached to individual disks or even tracks of a disk cylinder. In this way, some level of parallelism can be achieved even in the data filtering function at the low end where bulk data resides.

7.5.4 SCHUSS Filter

The SCHUSS filter is designed at the Bull research center in France [Gonzalez-Rubio, Rohmer, and Terral, 1984]. The main goal of this project is to avoid the restrictions of registers and comparators (which limited the number and type of predicates) that were used in the filters built with old technology and also to be able to support general data models and formats. This is accomplished by designing the filter function around the FSA concept (as in VERSO) and building the programmable data model and format-related options.

In the FSA for a query expression, rather than building a unique automaton for the entire query, automata are built for the individual terms of the expression and the results of individual comparisons are resolved by a Boolean evaluator logic.

The SCHUSS filter is a processor that is connected to the I/O port of a disk controller. It has two buses: one to access memory and I/O space and the other to get the data to be filtered. The processor is microprogrammable with 200 nanoseconds of microinstruction cycle time. The microinstructions are executed in the horizontal mode (i.e., several actions are driven in parallel). This makes the length of a microinstruction 112 bits. There are also two ALUs: one to compute addresses and the other for data manipulation. The comparisons are done arithmetically in the data ALU. Several basic filter instructions are programmed and the detailed ones are tuned for the needs of applications. The automaton and the results of filtering are stored in the 32K by 16 bit processor memory. For on-the-fly filtering two buffers 1K by 8 bits each, which is equal to a disk sector, are provided to overlap disk I/O with filtering.

The SCHUSS filter is interfaced with the SABRE database machine which we have seen earlier. As can be recalled, for SABRE an associative partition is a disk track. At the interface, SABRE provides the SCHUSS filter with the addresses of the tracks to be filtered. Before each filtering task an automaton is compiled and loaded into the filter's RAM. An FSA transition matrix is built for each different attribute of the selection expression.

In representing an FSA a hierarchical structure, rather than the traditional matrix representation, is used. This results in memory savings. Also, to do the same in instructions the following different types of instructions are designed:

* Linear instructions for those states which contain only one successor
* Sequential instructions for states which contain three or four successors
* Indexed instructions for states containing many successors
* Dichotomic instructions for states whose number of successors fall in the range between sequential and indexed instructions

The SCHUSS filter also attempts to tackle the join operation. First, the first relation is filtered for its selection and an automaton is built on the result set obtained. Then the second relation is filtered through this automaton. The feasibility of this approach of course depends on the size of the intermediate result set for which an automaton is constructed; otherwise, theoretically, the algorithm belongs to the nested loop category.

For very large databases, the SCHUSS filter is proposed to partition the database and select relevant partitions through partition range filtering. Once the partitions are identified they can be filtered for final selection. This approach presumes the presence of a partitioning scheme where each partition would be a disk track and also the values $Kmin(i, j)$ and $Kmax(i, j)$ which are the smallest and largest values for attribute j in the ith partition. To filter partitions, the original query must be transformed into a form expressed with respect to partition ranges. The following gives an example.

Example 7.5

Assume the original Boolean query Q is given as follows:

```
Q = (AGE > 30) AND (SALARY < 1000) OR (CLASS = 10)
```

The transformed query QT will be

```
(Kmax(i,AGE) > 30) AND (Kmin(i,SALARY) < 1000) OR (Kmin (i,
CLASS) ≤ 10) AND (Kmax (i,CLASS) ≥ 10)
```

Notice the way in which equality is expressed in terms of the range limits for $CLASS = 10$.

7.5.5 Dynamic Filtering

In a study reported by Kiessling [1983 and 1984], an intelligent I/O subsystem incorporating filtering functions is proposed. The study presumes ever-increasing disk densities and, therefore, access bottleneck at the I/O system level. The proposed filter would remedy this problem and deliver more meaningful data to the main memory hierarchy (DB cache) of a CPU. Since the size of main memories is increasing, it is expected that with the filtering subsystem most of the von Neumann bottlenecks would be eased.

In the filtering function, filtering objects are categorized as temporary relations derived from permanent relations and index sets. The following (one-pass) linear filtering tasks have been identified:

(a) Selection with respect to a Boolean predicate F
(b) Projection without duplicate elimination
(c) Scalar aggregates of MIN, MAX, SUM, AVG, and COUNT

The selection expression is canonically defined as a conjunctive normal form (ANDs of ORs). The temporary relations can be produced in two ways:

(a) $EXH_{F,\text{project–list}(R)}$

(b) $SEL_{F,\text{project–list on }(TL_R)}$

In (a), the relation R is exhaustively scanned filtering off tuples that do not satisfy the Boolean predicate F. The qualifying tuples are projected on the attributes included in the project list. In (b), the operation is same as in (a) except that instead of processing the entire relation, only the tuples retrieved with respect to tuple index set TL_R are filtered.

Dynamic filters are defined as the predicates that are derived from already computed intermediate results during the execution of a query. The motivation behind dynamic filtering is to be able to provide for dynamic query modification (i.e., adding further conjunctions to a Boolean predicate) to compute further results. The fundamental properties of dynamic filters are

(a) $F_X[r](x)$ = false $\rightarrow$ x $\notin$ X where x $\in$ dom (R, r) (i.e., x is a member of the R relation's r domain) and $F_X[r]$ is a filter for x. In other words, if we are able to produce a false out of the filter, then x is definitely not a member of X.

(b) $F_X[r](x)$ = true is interpreted as a "maybe" answer for the membership of x in X. In this case, tuples are not filtered but must be further processed by the host.

The basic filter types are defined as follows:

If $F_X[r]$ is a dynamic filter for X, then

(a) $F_X[r]$ is a *trivial filter* if $\forall$ vr $\in$ dom(R, r):$F_X[r](vr)$ is true. This corresponds to a null filtering constraint.

(b) $F_X[r]$ is a *total filter* if $F_X[r]$ = $\bigvee\limits_{vr \in X}$ (r = vr). It is within the covering range of all the specified values in X.

(c) $F_X[r]$ is a *min-max filter* if
$F_X[r]$ = MIN (vr:vr $\in$ X) $\leqslant r \leqslant$ *MAX* (vr:vr $\in$ X)
In other words a range filter is defined on an ordered domain.

(d) HA[o ... t] being a Boolean array and
H:dom(R, r) $\rightarrow$ {0, ..., t} a hash function
$F_X[r]$ is a *hash filter* if
HA[i] is true iff $\exists$ x$\in$ X : H(x) = i and
$\forall$ vr $\in$ dom (R, r) : $F_X[r](x)$ = HA [H(x)].

If $F_X^1[r]$ and $F_X^2[r]$ are two dynamic filters for X, then $F_x^2[r]$ is more selective than $F_x^1[r]$ iff $F_X^2[r] \rightarrow F_X^1[r]$.

Example 7.6[1]
Assume the following intermediate relation obtained from R:

r_1	r_2
1	10
2	17
3	3
3	9
800	6
816	8
1500	5
1502	6

Let X be the projection of this relation on r_1, that is, X = {1, 2, 3, 800, 816, 1500, 1502}.

The following are the examples of dynamic filters:

$$F_X^1[r_1] = 1 \leq r_1 \leq 1502$$
$$F_X^2[r_1] = (1 \leq r_1 \leq 3) \vee (800 \leq r_1 \leq 816) \vee (1500 \leq r_1 \leq 1502)$$
$$F_X^3[r_1] = (r_1 = 1) \vee (r_1 = 2) \vee (r_1 = 3) \vee (r_1 = 800) \vee (r_1 = 816)$$
$$\vee (r_1 = 1500) \vee (r_1 = 1502)$$

$F_X^1[r_1]$ is a min-max filter, $F_X^3[r_1]$ is a total filter, and $F_X^2[r_1]$ is an "iterated" min-max filter. $F_X^3[r_1]$ is more selective than $F_X^2[r_1]$ which is in turn more selective than $F_X^1[r_1]$.

Several algorithms for doing joins have also been defined in the referenced study. The following presents an overview of the three algorithms proposed:

Algorithm 0-JFM (zero feedback join filter method)

Step 1: Evaluate selection expression G on R ($\sigma_G(R)$).

Step 2: Project the result of step 1 on r to obtain the filter $F^0[r]$ and substitute r of R for s of S to obtain a join filter for S, JFO[s].

Step 3: Evaluate selection expression H on S conjunctively with the join filter produced in step 2 (i.e., $\sigma_{H \wedge JFO[s]}(S)$).

Step 4: Perform the join between the results of step 1 and step 3.

Example 7.7

Assuming the following relations and the SQL query:

R

r_1	r_2	tid
1	9	T_{10}
1	8	T_{11}
2	7	T_{12}
2	6	T_{13}
3	5	T_{14}
8	4	T_{15}
9	3	T_{16}
9	2	T_{17}
5	1	T_{18}

S

s_1	s_2	s_3	tid
8	1	1	T_{20}
3	2	2	T_{21}
4	3	3	T_{22}
9	4	9	T_{23}
2	5	8	T_{24}
3	6	7	T_{25}
6	7	4	T_{26}
6	8	5	T_{27}
7	9	6	T_{28}

Query: SELECT r_2, s_2, s_3
         FROM   R, S
         WHERE $(2 \leq r_1 \leq 6)$ AND $(3 \leq s_1 \leq 6)$ AND $(r_1 = s_1)$

[1] Examples 7.6–7.9 have been taken from Dr. Werner Kiessling, "Tuneable Dynamic Filter Algorithms for High Performance Database Systems." *Proceedings of the International Workshop on High-Level Computer Architecture*, 1984.

0-JFM can be evaluated as follows:

Step 1:

r_1	r_2
2	7
2	6
3	5
5	1

Step 2: $JFO[s_1] = 2 \le s_1 \le 5$

Step 3:

s_1	s_2	s_3
3	2	2
4	3	3
3	6	7

Step 4:

r_2	s_2	s_3
5	2	2
5	6	7

Algorithm 1-JFM   (1 feedback join filter method)

Step 1:   Produce an index set on R(r) by evaluating G on R.

Step 2:   Compute the join filter JF1[s] same as in step 2 of algorithm 0-JFM.

Step 3:   Select S conjunctively between H and JF1[s] same as in step 3 of algorithm 0-JFM.

Step 4:   From the result of step 3 compute JF1[r] by substituting s into the join filter obtained for S in step 3. Select R(r) again by executing the JF1[r] filter on the result of step 1 (*1st feedback*).

Step 5:   Compute G on R(r) by selecting the tuples with the use of the index set selected for R in the previous step.

Step 6:   Join R and S by using the results of steps 3 and 5.

Example 7.8

Using the same relations of Example 7.6, the following shows the example of 1-JFM evaluation:

Step 1:

r_1	tid
2	T_{12}
2	T_{13}
3	T_{14}
5	T_{18}

Step 2: $JF1[s] = 2 \le s_1 \le 5$

Step 3:

s_1	s_2	s_3
3	2	2
4	3	3
3	6	7

Step 4: $JF1[r_1] = (r_1 = 3) \lor (r_1 = 4)$

r_1	tid
3	t_{14}

Step 5:

r_1	r_2
3	5

Step 6:

r_2	s_2	s_3
5	2	2
5	6	7

Algorithm 2-JFM   (two-feedback join filter method)

Step 1:   As in algorithm 1-JFM.

Step 2:   As in algorithm 1-JFM to produce JF2[s].

Step 3:   Produce an index set on S(s) by evaluating H on S conjunctively with JF2[s].

Step 4:   As in algorithm 1-JFM but this time using the result of step 3, build a join index JF2[r] for R by substituting s for r in the join index created for S in step 3. Perform the first feedback on R same as in algorithm 1-JFM.

Step 5:   As in algorithm 1-JFM.

Step 6:   From the result of step 5 compute JF2′[s] by substituting r into the join filter obtained for R in step 5. This time apply a feedback (*second feedback*) on S in the same way as the feedback made on R in step 4.

Step 7:   Compute H on S(s) by selecting the tuples with the use of the index set selected for S in the previous step.

Step 8:   Join R and S by using the results of steps 5 and 7.

Example 7.9

Using the same relations of Example 7.6, the following shows the examples of 2-JFM evaluation.

Step 1:

r_1	tid
2	T_{12}
2	T_{13}
3	T_{14}
5	T_{18}

Step 2: JF2[s_1] = $2 \leq s_1 \leq 5$

Step 3:

s_1	tid
3	T_{21}
3	T_{25}
4	T_{22}

Step 5:

r_1	r_2
3	5

Step 4: JF2[r_1] = (r_1 = 3) V (r_1 = 4)

r_1	tid
3	T_{14}

Step 6: JF2[s_1] : s_1 = 3

s_1	tid
3	T_{21}
3	T_{25}

Step 7:

s_1	s_2	s_3
3	2	2
3	6	7

Step 8:

r_2	s_2	s_3
5	2	2
5	6	7

The efficiency of these join algorithms, as stated earlier, relies on the premise that the resulting intermediate relations will be small enough, and/or the main memory sizes will be large enough so that both relations can be main memory (or DB cache) resident at the same time.

7.6 COMMERCIAL DATABASE MACHINES

In this section we will present an overall review of database machines that have been, and are being, marketed commercially. We will not go into details and our purpose will be more of a status summary.

If we glance over Chapter 1 again, we will recall that we covered the definition of database machines, software and hardware backends, and the latest trends and developments with respect to future database machines. Because commercialization lags behind research, the most of the currently available commercial database machines mirror the earliest thinking in database machine configuration, which is the software backend idea. The transition from the software backend to the hardware backend idea has also been gradual, just as the commercial products which we began seeing in the market. In the following discussion, we will mention names of certain commercial products. Some of these products, however, may have become extinct or inactive by the time this text is published. Nevertheless, they will be useful in giving us an idea of the evolution of products.

7.6.1 Software Backend Database Machines

The first real example of a software backend project dates back to XDMS of Bell Laboratories [Canaday et al., 1974]. In XDMS, a minicomputer was attached to a GPC as backend and dedicated to run CODASYLs DBTG DBMS software. The mini was microprogrammable, and its instruction set was tuned to execute DBMS primitives efficiently. The same trend was followed in Cullinane Corporation's IDMS machine. In that system, the IDMS software, which is a variant of CODASYLs DBTG, was dedicated to run on a backend PDP 11/70. This backend was connected via a channel-to-channel adapter to either IBM or DEC host mainframes. The software was tuned for a multiplicity of backends and hosts to run concurrently. The Software AG, which is the vendor of ADABAS relational DBMS, also announced a software backend system for IBM hosts. The backend was Cambex PCM, which was claimed to improve throughput of the host by about 40%.

We can continue with the software backends by mentioning the Amperif relational data base machine. Amperif is built on the Sperry Univac 1100 series computers and executes relational query language (RQL) code [Fund, 1983]. The Datacomputer of Computer Corporation of America [Marill and Stern, 1975] was offered as a database server on ARPANET. Its DBMS was based on the CODASYL's DBTG network model and the backend processor was a DEC-10. More recently, the NEC Corporation of Japan is in the process of developing a relational software backend called information query computer

(IQC) on its computer series [Sekino et al., 1983]. IQC is also envisioned to be used as a network server.

7.6.2 Microcomputer-Based and/or Specially Built Backend Systems

In this category, we will mention Britton Lee Corporation's Intelligent Database Machine (IDM), Intel Corporation's iDBP, Teradata Corporation's Data Base Computer, and AEG-Telefunken's Synfobase.

The first two systems (i.e., IDM and iDBP) are (were) marketed as OEM products. That is, the vendor supplies only the backend, and the frontend software and interface must be developed by OEM software companies. Both backends can be classified as software backends; however, they are different than the other software backends we discussed previously. This difference results from the fact that both IDM and iDBP have synthesized hardware to implement the final product. In the case of IDM, modifications were made on a minicomputer; iDBP was an integration of microprocessor boards. Figure 7.44 shows the IDM architecture.

The IDM architecture is built around Digital Equipment Corporation's minicomputers (PDP, VAX). The added components are the database accelerator and RAM cache units. The I/O channel unit provides an interface between the frontend query processor and the backend system. The database processor is a GPC that processes commands and coordinates the entire system. The RAM cache buffers disk I/O blocks and stores program and data to process user queries. The database accelerator performs fast access path search and other DBMS primitives. The disk controller controls up to four disk drives.

A complete frontend-backend system, called the NOAH database machine of HDR Systems [Le-Viet, 1983], has been built using IDM as the backend. The frontend data language is the extended version of the relational SQL language. The frontend query processor consists of eight 16-bit Z8000 microprocessors sharing a common bus and running the Unix operating system. Various external interfaces of the query processor including a network interface are provided.

Intel's iDBP [Morgan, 1983] is a backend processor specially built from

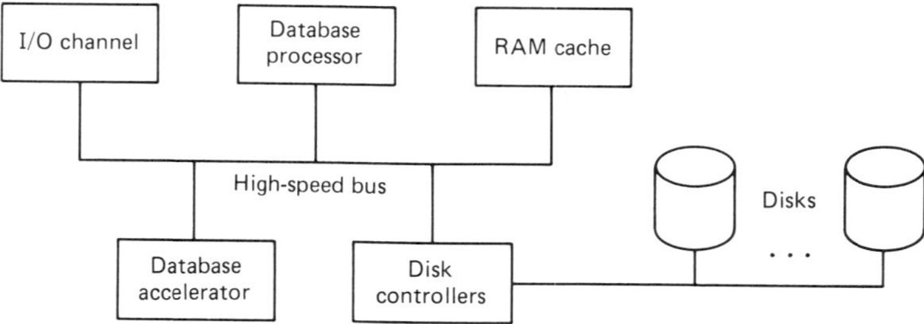

Figure 7.44 IDM architecture.

board-level products. iDBP contains memory, I/O control, communications processor, and database processor units. Each processor uses an Intel's iSBC 86/12A single-board computer. The interfaces with the outside are through asynchronous RS232 and Ethernet communications. iDBP supports relational DBMS primitives of projection, join, and selection; cursor management; view administration; and file access methods.

Another small computer product is an associative memory subsystem called Synfobase manufactured by AEG-Telefunken of Germany. Synfobase is attached to a mini- or microcomputer to perform fast associative searches (4 msec for 32 searches). Another claim to fame is that Synfobase also allows users to express their queries in a high-level language and gives them the ad hoc search specification capability [Gosch, 1982]. The associative memory unit, called REM, consists of 32 256-bit words. The processor has a Z80 microprocessor with 64K bytes of RAM, a 6-megabyte Winchester disk, and an RS232 interface which loads REM at a 150K bytes/sec rate. The 32 "superwords" of REM (i.e., 256-bit words) are simultaneously searched.

The data base computer (DBC1012) of Teradata [Ehrensberger, 1984] is a recent product geared for IBM mainframe compatibility. DBC1012 is marketed as an alternative to IBM's software DBMS products. DBC1012 can run under all IBM hosts with the MVS operating system (and a VM/CMS version will be released subsequently). DBC1012 supports its version of SQL called TEQUEL. DBC1012 claims superiority over IBM's IMS and DBase2 DBMSs. Figure 7.45 shows the Teradata DBC1012 architecture.

The interface processors provide host to backend interface and are attached to the host through block multiplexer channels. There are four AMPs built around Intel's 16-bit 8086 microprocessors. Each AMP also has its dedicated 475-megabyte Winchester disk unit. The processors are interconnected through a high-speed

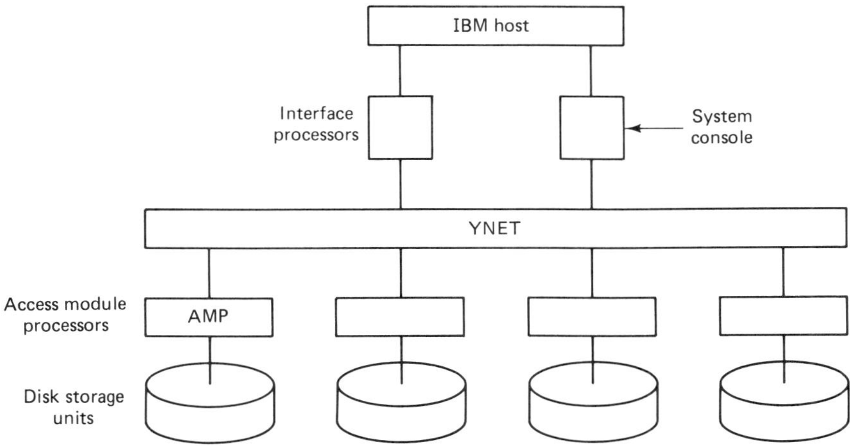

Figure 7.45   Teradata DBC1012 architecture.

logic lattice called the YNet. The system can expand up to a chain of 1024 processors on YNet. As can be seen, the DBC1012 is on the way to becoming a hardware backend with a parallel architecture. The current speed of the DBC1012 is estimated at 10 transactions (on simple keys) per second.

In this chapter, we have covered the majority of database machine-related research reported to date. Our coverage was made from a neutral viewpoint without injecting any praises and/or criticisms except for a few technical interpretations. In the following chapters, we will develop concepts and discuss performance, software, and distributed database use of database machines. Whenever needed, we will refer back to this chapter in relating certain concepts and features to the material covered. This will help make the survey covered in this chapter more analytical, at least from the reader's viewpoint.

EXERCISES

7.1. Assuming a relation EMP(EMPNO, NAME, DNO, MGR, SALARY, COMM) and the following SQL query:

```
SELECT EMPNO, NAME
    FROM EMP
    WHERE COMM =
        SELECT MAX (COMM)
            FROM EMP
            WHERE DNO > 99
            AND DNO < 200
```

Discuss how you would execute this query by CASSM, RAP.3, DBC, DIRECT, RDBM, SABRE, RDMAC, GRACE, and systolic arrays. Write the detailed query programs for at least two of these machines.

7.2. Using the same query of Exercise 7.1 discuss how you would process this query by CAFS, SCHUSS filter, and dynamic filtering. If you will program FSAs please refer to Chapters 12 and 13 for more details on FSA use in searching. In the case of dynamic filtering, what types of selections and filters can be used? Can you filter this query in one pass?

7.3. Referring to Examples 7.6 through 7.9 on dynamic filtering, compare the cardinalities of relations R and S if the join operation were to be executed in the following ways:
(a) No dynamic filtering; only the relations are selected and projected before the join.
(b) With 0-JFM in dynamic filtering.
(c) With 1-JFM in dynamic filtering.
(d) With 2-JFM in dynamic filtering.
Can you make generalizations about the superiority of one method over the others? If not, state the assumptions or conditions under which your answer would be valid.

7.4. Discuss the relative advantages and disadvantages of on-the-fly filtering versus buffered I/O systems. Remember that use of delay buffers can be possible with on-the-fly filtering.

7.5. If we do not consider the database partitioning approach used in the GRACE database machine for the moment, how would you compare the classes of database machines we have seen in the chapter with respect to performing the join operation?

7.6. How would you compare pipelined sort/merge–based join with the nested loop algorithm? Is one always superior to the other or is there a crossover point? How far is that point? (You can refer to Ozkarahan [1983] for further reading. Chapter 8 material is also relevant.)

7.7. How would you relate the degree of parallelism and the size of data clusters in the DBC architecture? Are they directly proportional with respect to each other?

7.8. Consider an MIMD architecture such as DIRECT to provide a multitasking environment. Compare the relative overhead of concurrency when multiple joins are executed concurrently with respect to the following:
(a) Temporary (or result) relation is created.
(b) No result relation is created and the result is indicated by tagging the target relation.
Hint: You may start by considering the page frame traffic.

7.9. In systems where encoding/decoding is a necessity, what additional overhead would be involved for this additional function? Can it reach a state where it can overshadow the gains achieved elsewhere? (Although the question may appear to be leading, your answer can be in either direction so long as justifying assumptions are provided.)

7.10. Compare functional distribution with data distribution in very large databases. As you will recall, the former refers to using specialized processors for different functions whereas the latter means using general-purpose database machines (i.e., those that can execute all DBMS operations) in the distributed database sense. Data must be moved constantly in the former, whereas in the latter only the nonresident data is sent from one place to the other. What are the relative advantages/disadvantages of the architectures belonging to each of these classes?

7.11. Considering the Non-Von database machine's architecture hierarchy, what modifications need to be made on the assumptions and the overall architecture if SAM could not hold the entire database and had to be externally evaluated as PAM?

7.12. Compare the uses of the following in view of updates:
(a) Order preserving dynamic hashing versus hardware sorters on a segmented (partitioned) database
(b) Dynamic partitioning via hashing versus the same with nonhash-based filtering

7.13. How would you relate database size with systolic arrays and tree machines? In the join operation, what is the ultimate complexity for these architectures?

7.14. Considering logic programming with the use of a language such as PROLOG, what logic programming constructs would benefit from parallelism and associativity, and to what degree?

7.15. In answering Exercise 7.14, if we had to use database machine power, what types of database machines would be most desirable? What architectural features would they have? Justify the need for them.

8

DATABASE MACHINE THEORY

Up to now, database machine research and development has been reported as individual cases of specific machines. There has been almost no study in developing theory for the field. Exceptions to this have been brief comparisons in the introductions of written articles and/or in justification of claims of individual designs. It is time, however, that we should identify the common basic principles and relationships of database hardware and software architectures and build a theory around them. In this chapter, we will scratch the surface in that direction by identifying certain key issues of database architectures with the hope that theoretical work can follow in the future. In our treatment of the issues, we will try to relate them to the database machines we surveyed in the previous chapter whenever possible.

8.1 DATABASE MACHINE CLASSIFICATIONS

There are various aspects of database machine classification, and each aspect has its importance. Instead of a hierarchical classification where we would force a partial order among individual classifications, we will attempt an n'ary relation approach. Accordingly, a database machine will be classified by an eight-tuple $\langle DP, A, PO, PC, PMC, ML, MS, HC \rangle$, where attributes and their values are

DP: *degree of parallelism*
    0 none (uniprocessor)
    1 low
    2 high

A: *associativity*
    0 none (access path)
    1 partial (key) associative
    2 fully associative

PO: *processor organization*
    0 filter
    1 in-stream and pipeline
    2 regular VLSI array
    3 multiprocessor
    4 cellular associative

PC: *type of processor coupling*
    0 SISD
    1 MISD
    2 SIMD
    3 MIMD

PMC: *processor-memory coupling*
    0 static (i.e., each memory has a dedicated processor)
    1 dynamic [i.e., processors are dynamically allocated (e.g., crossbar switch)]

ML: *memory level*
    0 primary
    1 secondary

MS: *memory search*
    0 direct (processor on mass memory)
    1 indirect (database machine is an outside intelligent cache system)

HC: *host coupling*
    0 tightly coupled [e.g., CODASYL machine (XDMS)]
    1 loosely coupled (e.g., relational machines)
    2 stand-alone (database computer)

Based on this classification, we can construct a classification matrix, which is shown in Figure 8.1, for the database machines we surveyed in Chapter 7. We will also include the recent designs discussed in Chapter 6. However, before we start, we should state that our classification is for nonnumeric computer architectures only. The majority of the table is for hardware backends; however, software backends are also included. The latter manifest no parallelism and no associativity, have filter simplicity and SISD, static, primary, indirect, and stand-alone characteristics, in the order of our classification tuple. To make the classification of Figure 8.1 complete, we need to add two more attributes to our classification tuple. They are

(a) Whether the database machine is a single- or a multidata model machine

(b) Whether the instruction set of the database machine is complete and universal

Classification / Database machine	DP	A	PO	PC	PMC	ML	MS	HC
CASSM	2	2	4	2	0	1	0	1
RAP3	2	2	4	3	0	1	1	1/2
RARES	2	2	4	2	0	1	0	1
EDC	2	2	4	2	0	1	1	1
DBC	1	1/2	3	2	0	1	0	1
DIRECT	2	2	3	3	1	1	1	1
RDBM	1	2	3	3	0	1	1	1
SABRE	1	1/2	3	3	0	1	1	1
DBMAC	1	1/2	3	3	1	1	1	1
DSDBM[1]	1	2	1/3	2	0	1	1	1
GRACE	1	2	1/3	2	1	1	1	1
PPRQP[2]	1	2	1/3	2	0	1	1	1
SYSTOLIC	2	2	2	3	0	0	1	1
TREE	2	2	2	3	0	0	1	1
NON-VON	2	2	2/4	3	0	0/1	0/1	1
CAFS	0	2	0	2/3	0	1	1	0
LEECH	0	2	0	2	0	1	1	0
VERSO	0	2	0	2	0	1	1	0
SCHUSS	0	2	0	2	0	1	1	0
DYNFLT[3]	0	2	0	2	0	1	1	0
RELACS	2	2	4	2	0	0/1	1	1
LUCAS	2	2	4	2	0	0/1	1	1

[1] DSDBM = data stream database machine with large capacity
[2] PPRQP = parallel pipelined relational query processor
[3] DYNFLT = dynamic filter

Figure 8.1 Database machine classification matrix.

We will leave these two attributes out because we feel that they are still not well treated in the majority of the database machine related publications. Nevertheless, we will cover them outside of the classification, in this chapter and in Chapter 9 with regard to certain concepts and/or database machine designs.

8.2 TRADE-OFFS OF PARALLELISM

In various published works, different architectures are compared with each other especially for the hard database operations such as join, projection, intersection, division, and so on. It has been well understood that algorithms that use nested loop iterations in a brute force manner become inferior to those that implement partitioning and in-stream processing where each partition can be processed on-the-fly by use of hardware sorters. We want to distinguish clearly at this point that partitioning is a storage strategy exterior to any device. In other words, partitioning is not an architectural feature. It can be incorporated in any system and used effectively. After sorting this issue out, let us, in what follows, attempt to compare cellular architecture, which represents one extreme of parallelism and associativity, with an in-stream pipeline processing–based architecture.

We will denote volume of data to be processed by N, the number of processors (cells) of a parallel architecture by c, t_u as the time to process one item of data in a serial processor, and t_{scan} as the time to execute one cycle (hence memory scan) of a parallel database machine architecture. Notice that although t_u is repeated for each data element, t_{scan} is common for all the data resident on the device.

Now, to process the entire database it will take $N \cdot t_u$ in the serial processor, and

$$\left\lceil \frac{N}{n} \right\rceil \cdot t_{scan} \text{ in the cellular (parallel) device}$$

The expression $\lceil N/n \rceil \cdot t_{scan}$ is linear if $N \leq n = c \cdot m$, where m is the number of data items stored in one cell of the parallel device. If this relationship holds, then we also have $\lceil N/n \rceil \cdot t_{scan} \ll N \cdot t_u$, which proves the high performance of cellular/associative devices in doing selections and/or other unary relational algebra operations. However, as N gets larger, then we fall into the I/O bottleneck problem we discussed in Chapter 6. In database machines, this situation gets worse in binary relational algebra operations. Consider the Cartesian product or join operation whose complexity is in the order of the product of the cardinalities of the two relations involved. Well, a brute force nested loop join algorithm (by brute force we mean without partitioning the database which corresponds to Figure 7.28 (a) as opposed to 7.28(b) of the previous chapter) runs proportionally with this complexity [Ozkarahan, 1983]. In other words, in the cellular device the number of iterations of join will asymptotically approach $O(\lceil N/n \rceil^2)$ if $N \gg c \cdot m$. Assuming that t_{IO} represents the paging time for one loading of the cellular device, then the previous relationship of overall database processing time will reverse itself to

$$O(N \cdot t_u) \leq O(t_{scan} + t_{IO}) \cdot \left\lceil \frac{N}{n} \right\rceil^2$$

At this point we should make our model more complete by considering the fact that the serial in-stream system is not swallowing data as it wishes but has to be limited by the I/O bandwidth of the channel that brings the data stream from its source, the disk system. Let us indicate bandwidth of a single I/O channel by B_{IO}. Accordingly, our relationship shown above will be

$$O\left(\frac{N}{B_{IO}} + N \cdot t_u\right) \leq O\left((t_{scan} + t_{IO}) \cdot \left\lceil \frac{N}{n} \right\rceil^2\right)$$

Considering the fact that recent in-stream devices implement pipeline searching and sorting by use of trie and heap sort engines, the foregoing relationship finally becomes

$$O\left(\frac{N}{B_{IO}} + (\log N) \cdot t_u\right) \leq O\left((t_{scan} + t_{IO}) \cdot \left\lceil \frac{N}{n} \right\rceil^2\right)$$

We should note here that no matter how well the pipeline processing can keep up with the data stream rate, which is possible due to the logarithmic order of processing, the main problem is due to $N/B_{IO} \rightarrow$ *bottleneck*. It is interesting to note that the serial, in-stream architecture should approach parallelism if the left-hand side of the timing relationship should produce a time better than a uniprocessor sort/merge–based join (or other binary operation) algorithm. Considering p parallel channels, we have to decompose N/B_{IO} into $(N/p) \cdot B_{IO}$ parallel streams. This brings up the need to replicate the in-stream sort and search processors because their claim to fame is the ability to keep up with the I/O channel speed. This means that we cannot funnel $(N/p) \cdot B_{IO}$ channels through one logarithmic path; hence, we need to introduce parallelism throughout the system. If that is done, then our relationship will be

$$O\left[\frac{\left(\frac{N}{B_{IO}} + (\log N) \cdot t_u\right)}{p}\right] \ll O\left((t_{scan} + t_{IO}) \cdot \left\lceil \frac{N}{n} \right\rceil^2\right)$$

It has been reported in a previous study [Bitton et al., 1983] that the nested loop algorithm in join performs better than that of any other method, provided that the data are resident in the database machine (i.e., $N \leq n \cdot m$) and n is large. In view of this, it may be necessary to study the trade-off between the two classes of architectures. Given fixed variables and parameters, we may want to solve for the values of n, m, p, and B_{IO} and compare the costs of resulting architectures.

8.3 COMPLETING THE ANALYSIS

Some designs in the in-stream, pipelined category, however, are not fully associative. They introduce and depend upon indices and linkages. No matter how fast these structures can be searched by tree hardware that operates in pipeline, we should not forget the bottlenecks of access paths and their maintenance that we pointed out earlier in Chapter 1.

A balanced performance assessment should not only depend upon retrievals, but also on the most costly operation of updates. We should weight the relative proportions of retrievals and updates in an environment and then come up with an overall time and/or complexity measure that would include both retrieval and updates multiplied by their normalized (both adding up to 100%) weight factors.

If we represent the I/O time involved in reading or writing a unit of data (data or pointer record) on a secondary storage device by R_{IO}, then an update operation on an access path will take $2R_{IO}$ because first the old value must be deleted and then the new value must be inserted into its proper place. If we assume that in a given operation A_t number of indices are updated for that many attributes (or less if a hierarchical indexing and/or pointer arrays are used) and that the average number of values updated for an index is represented by S, then the associated I/O overhead must be $2 \cdot S \cdot A_t \cdot R_{IO}$. If the work load of a system has W_u proportion of updates with respect to the overall transaction volume, then we should add $2 \cdot W_u \cdot S \cdot A_t \cdot R_{IO}$ to the timing expression of the database machine that uses access paths. Accordingly, we must add this expression on the side of the comparison expression we have developed in the previous section if any one or both of the database machines resort to access paths in their operations.

8.4 FURTHER ARCHITECTURAL OPTIMIZATIONS

8.4.1 Staging

As we noticed in the foregoing analysis, both the in-stream pipelined processing and the cellular/associative device depended upon I/O for data supply from the secondary storage. (As we will come to the subject matter when discussing memory technology, we conjecture that most cellular/associative devices in the future have to be based on indirect searching rather than a direct search on the entire disk system.) Any system that is based on indirect searching will depend on this I/O with the secondary storage. This brings up the architectural issue of *staging* of data between the secondary storage and the database machine. In staging, the main concern is to be able to overlap paging I/O with processing. To be more specific, by processing we mean either a complete execution of a job or its decomposition into more primitive and/or smaller job steps.

To overlap paging with each execution step that is taking place in the database machine, we would need an alternate processor memory or I/O (e.g., disk cache subsystem). The switching of processors at the completion of the current task to the one whose data are staged in the background must be accomplished electronically without delay. Accordingly, the comparison we presented between the in-stream, pipelined processor and cellular associative devices must be revised to reflect the staging scheme discussed as follows:

$$O\left[\max\left(\frac{N}{B_{IO} \cdot p}, \frac{t_u \cdot \log N}{p}\right)\right] \ll O\left[\max\left(t_{scan}\left[\frac{N}{n}\right]^2, t_{IO} \cdot \left[\frac{N}{n}\right]^2\right)\right]$$

The reason for the maximum (max) is that in an overlapped operation, the time taken will be dominated by the longer of the two concurrent operations. The maximum may however vary between the two quantities (i.e., paging or processing) from task to task depending upon the amount of paging and processing time needed for individual jobs.

8.4.2 Interconnections and Reconfigurability

In nonnumeric processing, the basic processing needs are of SIMD type. Even though we would like to have MIMD architectures to provide concurrency, this concurrency is about orchestrating multiple SIMD tasks. Up to this point, the majority of the designs we have seen implement the parallelism needed by SIMD processing with a linear processor interconnection topology (i.e., a one-dimensional array of cells or microprocessors working in parallel). Exceptions to this have been the two-dimensional crossbar switch interconnection and the tree machines.

We have also seen that the hard binary database operations require more than parallelism, especially if the sizes of the relations are larger than that of the processor memory. Among the solutions proposed for this problem, two will be discussed here.

We have seen the interconnecton topologies for Illiac IV and Staran which are among the possible SIMD interconnection topologies [Siegel, 1979]. If we consider a multiprocessor architecture, a DBMS operation involves comparisons within a processor and data transfers among processors. Assuming ordered data within a processor, a comparison will involve $\log m$ many comparisons and that many data transfers for a file of cardinality m. For unary relational algebra operations such as projection this number will be $m \log m$. A join between two sets of data of sizes n and m will require time $O(m \cdot n \log m \cdot n)$. If we also have n multiprocessors working in parallel, this time will be reduced to $O(m \cdot \log n + m \cdot \log m)$. The first term corresponds to the number of comparisons required to evenly distribute $m \cdot n$ data elements over n processors. The second term is the time to sort m data elements in a processor. As can be seen, in the multiprocessor network, there will be data transfers which depend upon synchronization, routing, and buffering. If the processor interconnection topology is not complete (i.e., every processor is connected to every other), then data transfer among the processors has to go through several bus interconnections, hence incurring a time delay. While complete interconnections can be costly for database applications where a large number of processors is required to process large files, an interconnection topology called *superimposed tree* has been proposed as a realistic interconnection topology which has reasonable interconnection time.

In comparing interconnection topologies two measures, E and G, called the interconnection extensibility [Maekawa, 1981] are used. They refer to the case of increasing the number of processors and the resulting increase in interconnection delay and the number of buses per processor. Small values of E and

G are preferable. For n processors, the superimposed tree has $O(E) = \log_m n$ and $O(G) = m^2$ where $m^m = n$ and m is the degree of the topology. Figure 8.2 shows a binary superimposed tree where $m = 2$. In this topology, every processor can reach every other processor in, at most, $\log_2 n$ communication steps as abstracted below for the ith processor:

Step 1: 2_i, 2_{i+1}

Step 2: 4_i, 4_{i+1}, 4_{i+2}, 4_{i+3}

.

.

.

Step $\log_2 n = q$, $2^q \cdot i$, $2^q \cdot i + 1$, $2^q \cdot i + 2$, ..., $2^q \cdot i + (2^q - 1)$

In this interconnection topology, the number of buses per processor is always two, and the number of processors in the network can be arbitrary. In a superimposed tree of degree m, $(m - 1)$ processors can drop out of service at a given time without stopping the operations on the entire net. To execute hard database operations such as join, however, a brute force method would yield the complexity of the nested loop algorithm (same is true for systolic arrays and tree machines in general) [Ozkarahan, 1983] if the database is not partitioned.

The other proposal [Oflazer, 1983] deals with optimizing the interconnection topology of a cellular device such as the RAP.3 database machine by employing a dynamic reconfigurability among cells. The purpose of this is to optimize the performance of the database machine in performing nested loop processing for the hard database operations of join and projection. If we notice that the interconnection topology of a cellular array is a linear one, with the cells working in parallel, the proposed reconfigurability achieves the following:

(a) *Memory reconfigure:* Cells storing a relation can cascade their memory contents in a serial fashion to build a large continuous memory.

(b) *Processor reconfigure:* All VLSI comparator arrays of individual cells are cascaded to form a long large-capacity comparator array.

In processing projections and joins associatively, values of one relation have to be compared with the values of another relation (or the same relation

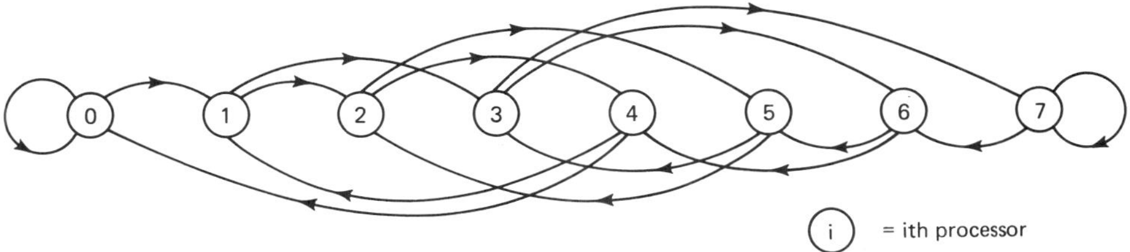

Figure 8.2 A binary superimposed tree.

in projection). The memory and processor reconfigurations transform a fragmented parallelism of the original architecture into a scheme where the overall number of iterations is decreased. This is due to the fact that, because of the cross-product nature of the operations, we would have more device cycles for each cell of the outer relation (i.e., nested loop algorithm) than the case where a comparison scheme utilizes 100% of the power of the cells storing both of the relations. In the original architecture, the cells of the outer relation remained idle (hence, the device is fragmented) while the parallel comparison took place over the cells that store the inner relation. The proposed reconfigurability solves this problem and adjusts itself over each cycle by shrinking into smaller chains of cell cascades as more and more values are completely processed and tagged. The memory reconfiguration is needed to pull in attribute values from a relation to fill in and at the same time compare with the large capacity, reconfigured VLSI comparator arrays.

8.5 DATA MODELS, OPERATIONS, AND STORAGE STRUCTURES

An ideal database machine must be general purpose in supporting data models. While one can build a database machine for each specific syntactic data model, a database machine that can support generalized DBMS will be multipurpose in data model support. The way to achieve this is not to enumerate all possible commercially available and/or published data models, but to investigate the requirements of a conceptual data model that will cover all necessary syntactic models in the sense of the ANSI/SPARC generalized DBMS (GDBMS) architecture that we have seen in Chapter 2 and will see more of in Chapter 9. If we can support the basic constructs implied by a conceptual data model in our database machine in such a way that schema and operational equivalences are maintained, then we can build a multimodel database machine. Let us elaborate on this. Figure 8.3 depicts the external and conceptual schema interfaces of an ANSI/SPARC-like GDBMS.

According to the figure, the upward-going arrows indicate a schema conversion from a conceptual schema into various external schemas. A database is *schema equivalent* to another database if there exists a schema mapping that maps schema S_2 of the second database to the schema S_1 of the first database such that all constraints in S_2 that are essential for the first database can be preserved in S_1. (We should remember that a definition of data model includes data structure, constraints necessary for its integrity, and the operations performable on the data structure.) The downward-going arrows in the figure correspond to operation conversion. This means that the operations of a data language at the external schema are converted into equivalent operations that are executed on the conceptual schema. A database is *operation equivalent* to another database if it is schema equivalent and every operation on the first database can be mapped to operations on the second database such that the consistency of the database

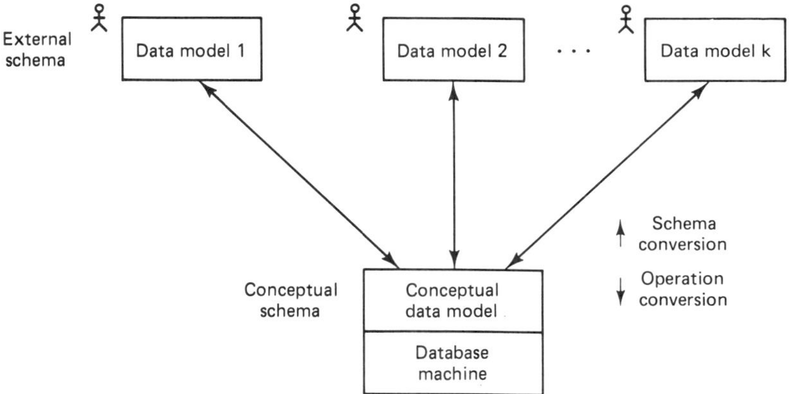

Figure 8.3   A multimodel database machine DBMS architecture.

states is preserved [Vassiliou and Lochovsky, 1980]. As can be remembered, the phrase "database state" refers to the population (extension) that a database contains at a given time. In the definitions above, we referred to two databases being equivalent to each other. In our framework of Figure 8.3, however, this is conceptual; that is, we are actually referring to the equivalence of different conceptualizations of a common database. Equivalence problems are of nontrivial nature if we try to come up with a general procedure of conversions that will be closed under all cases (e.g., complementation or set difference) [Klug, 1978].

In the database machines we have covered so far, we remember that the CASSM database machine is constructed to process hierarchies. It is also claimed that because normalized relations can be viewed as one level trees, relational algebra operations can be processed. Also, because networks are constructed from hierarchies and CASSM supports various pointer transfer operations, we can assume that CASSM can support relations, hierarchies, and networks individually.

A database machine was designed for well-connected relations (WCR) [Arora, Dumpala, and Smith, 1981]. WCRs are horizontally partitioned binary relations stored in the database machine in such a way that bidirectional reachability is associatively facilitated. With WCRs, generalized data model support is advocated because of the generality of primitive binary relations. We will come back to this architecture in the next chapter.

In the RAP.3 GDBMS architecture [Dogac and Ozkarahan, 1980; Dogac, 1980], the principles laid out by Figure 8.3 for the GDBMS architecture, mappings, and equivalence have been followed. To achieve this at the physical common denominator, which is the internal schema mapping of the conceptual schema, mappings into RAP.3 tabular structures are implemented. (As will be seen in the next chapter, RAP.3 GDBMS linearizes the bidirectional mapping scheme of Figure 8.3 to and from the conceptual schema into an always downward-going chain of mappings.) The RAP.3 tabular structures are normalized relations, and in addition, they implement multisets or multirelations by deferring the key uniqueness property of the relational model from hardware to a higher-level relational software interface. This enables support of all necessary structural constructs needed to implement a multimodel GDBMS by the RAP.3 system. We will discuss the operational aspects of multidata model support in the following.

On top of the parallel/associative structure of a database machine architecture, the following operational (i.e., language constructs) capabilities must be supported:

(a) Relational algebra operations, which, in turn, must be grouped under
   (i) Unary operations, which include Boolean selection [with externally supplied operands and/or intrarecord (tuple) values], arithmetic update directly on memory contents, scalar aggregates, and storage operations for insertion and deletion of data
   (ii) Binary operations, which include semi- and full joins and other set operations of intersection, difference, union, and projection (although projection involves a single relation, the complexity of the operation belongs to this group)
(b) Cursor operations to implement grouping, which are also known as set aggregates, correlation, or other free variable–based operations, as well as record at a time-based navigations of hierarchical and network systems.
(c) The important operation called quantification. Quantification can be grouped under value quantification and set quantification. Value quantification is expressed within predicates by *ANY* or *SOME* ⟨*attribute name*⟩ which correspond to maximum or minimum of the values in the attribute being quantified. Set quantification corresponds to existential and universal quantifiers. While the former abstracts the join (or semi-join), the universal quantifier corresponds to data language phrases such as *CONTAINS, EQUAL ALL, ONLY ALL,* and so on, which can be executed by a division operation.

All the foregoing operations must be realizable by the use of efficient set-oriented processing capability of the underlying database architecture. This is easily accomplished by a parallel/associative architecture.

While the primitive operations listed are sufficient in supporting the operations of various external schema interfaces that may correspond to different data models, there are a few more points to consider. For a high-level data language to be relationally complete, it must capture all the capabilities of the low-level primitive operations discussed. For a data language to be universal, it is not sufficient to have the personality of abstract relational algebra or calculus. The language must allow value injection during iterations; it must yield to programming of transitive closure (see Chapter 3) and "least fixed point" operators [Pirotte, 1978; Aho and Ullman, 1979; Maier, 1983].

Looking at the RAP language syntax, we can see that intra- and interprogram value input and output can be realized via RAP registers. As can be remembered, there are user registers that can input externally provided data, save registers that are loaded with tuple data during the execution of the cursor (GET_FIRST) instruction, and registers that hold results of scalar aggregate operations. These capabilities are complemented by the decision and transfer instructions. As an example of queries that will need transitive closure, or more specifically, least fixed-point operations, the following example can be investigated by the reader:

(a) In an airlines reservations system we may wish to determine the number of possible flights between two cities during a given period.

(b) Assume a relation *FLIGHTS* (*S*, *D*, *DT*, *AT*) where *S*, *D*, *DT*, and *AT* correspond to source and destination cities and departure and arrival times, respectively. If we want to compute a relation *FLIGHTS** that will include *FLIGHTS* and in addition represents all finite sequences of flights such that in each sequence:

(1) The destination of each flight (except the last) is the source of the next.

(2) The arrival time of each flight (except the last) occurs before the departure time of the next.

This relation can be expressed as the least fixed point of the equation

$$FLIGHTS* = FLIGHTS \cup ((FLIGHTS \otimes FLIGHTS*)[D = FLIGHTS* \cdot S \wedge$$
$$AT < FLIGHTS* \cdot DT])[S, FLIGHTS* \cdot D, DT, FLIGHTS* \cdot AT]$$

In storage (or physical data) structures, there have been two extremes in database machine designs. While some machines store tuples of n'ary relations, the others use the binary relation approach. That is, binary relations are not only used at the logical level but also stored at the machine level. This approach is also the same as the vertical schema approach where relations are processed on columns separately. We should not forget, however, that along with every column there needs to be a column of tuple identifiers (i.e., surrogates) that are used in n'ary tuple construction. While extra storage overhead can be the problem of the n'ary relation storage, extra update overhead, in correlating correct attribute values with respect to tuple identifiers, is the problem of the binary relation approach. It seems that the compromise lies somewhere in the middle where we would store clusters of m'ary relations such that $\sum_{i=1}^{c} m_i = n$ and c is the number of vertical clusters formed from a relation whose degree is n. As we will see in Chapter 10, a vertical cluster corresponds to a fragment of a large relation that corresponds to a semantic entity as viewed by a local site so that breaking it further would not contribute to anything.

8.6 DATABASE FILTERING

We can define a filter as a device that suppresses unwanted portions of data. Data can be anything from records in a file (or tuples in a relation), items (attributes) in a record (tuple), entries in a table, elements of an array to lines in a display or vectors in a graph (all these will be abstracted as data units). Although some filters are fixed on a given schema of one of these data units using fixed length, others have more general-purpose schema specification with variable length data units.

The memory gap between mass storage media and cache (or main memory) of computing systems has always been a problem and, coupled with the limited bandwidth of I/O channels, presents the well known problem of I/O bottleneck we have been discussing. Even though we see appreciable increases in main memory sizes, the disks, which are the popular reign of mass storage media, are here to stay and the increases in their density will maintain the memory gap. What is more, there is no appreciable speed up in sight for disk access time despite the large increases in device density. Therefore, there is a need to filter data as early as possible in the data stream by efficient and cost effective filter devices.

In Chapter 7, we discussed various filter devices. In this subsection, we will emphasize *on-the-fly* filters that can be packaged in one (or two with the FIFO output buffer) VLSI chips. It would be trivial to show that filtering hardware that does not claim full projection (i.e., with duplicate elimination) and join capability can easily be packaged in a VLSI chip with the present technology.

8.6.1 Basic Configuration of a Filter

Figure 8.4 depicts a basic filter block diagram. As can be seen, the data flow is single-pass and the delay (Δ) between input and output is zero. These correspond to the definition of on-the-fly filtering meaning that the filter can keep pace with the data stream flowing at channel speed. On-the-fly filtering can be accomplished with 1) finite state automata, 2) sequential circuits controlled by combinational logic, or 3) sequential circuits controlled by stored microprogram where usually one microprogram instruction is executed per (data) item in the data stream. The filter task in the form of automaton tables or microcode, along with data configuration (or schema), is loaded by the host computer in the filter RAM and/or registers prior to filtering.

As indicated in Figure 8.4, the basic on-the-fly filter is capable of operations that can be completed in a single pass of data. Examples of this in relational algebra are unary operations such as selection involving Boolean predicates and scalar aggregate functions such as sum, count, maximum, minimum, and average (computed from the first two previous functions). The only exception to the unary operations is projection. As can be seen between the input relation R and output relation R^1, the filter was able to perform selection and the first step of projection, that is subsetting of attributes. However, as shown in the figure, the filter could not eliminate duplicates in single pass.

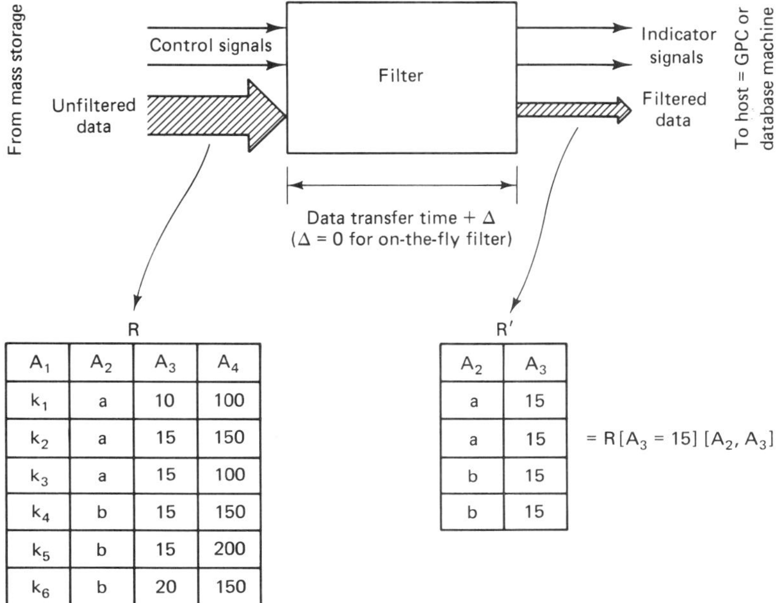

R

A_1	A_2	A_3	A_4
k_1	a	10	100
k_2	a	15	150
k_3	a	15	100
k_4	b	15	150
k_5	b	15	200
k_6	b	20	150

R′

A_2	A_3
a	15
a	15
b	15
b	15

$= R[A_3 = 15]\ [A_2, A_3]$

Figure 8.4   A basic single-pass on-the-fly filter.

8.6.2 *Filter Extensions and Recycling*

We have observed the extent of the utility of an on-the-fly filter. At this point we will discuss possible enhancements to the basic filter definition shown in Figure 8.4 and background filter recycling. Even though some filter designs claim the capability of projection with duplicate elimination and even join, given enough memory to store the intermediate results, our intention here is not to present a best case analysis to the reader. Instead, we will address the complexity level of the problems. This in turn implies that our definition of the capabilities of the single-pass on-the-fly filter presented in the foregoing is correct and that additional components and multiple-pass filtering are needed for enhancing the filtering capability.

The idea of *recycling* comes from the need to keep the overall system design cheap and its utility comes into play in background filtering. Recycling means multiple passes of data between mass storage and filter before results are sent to the front end (e.g., GPC). For maximum efficiency, such filtering should take place concurrently with the execution of other tasks in the host computer.

Duplicate elimination in projection can be accomplished without sorting by utilizing a simple FIFO buffer, an array of comparators, simple logic for tagging, and an additional RAM space in the I/O Controller that controls the mass storage devices.

The reason to use tagging (marking) with recycling is cost. As we have seen in some database machines, tagging is a technique used in associative devices to perform selection. Because tagging eliminates the need for temporary storage (or result relations) it contributes to cost effectiveness of the system. The alternative (temporary relations) would require additional storage and this would do nothing but aggravate the discrepancy in memory gap that the filter itself is introduced to remedy. We will discuss tagging in Section 8.11.

With the introduction of recycling we can redefine the utility of filtering as follows:

- Send filtered data to the host processor.
- Accomplish some of the processing in the background in instances when background recycling concurrent with host processing can be exploited. This is abstracted in Figure 8.5.

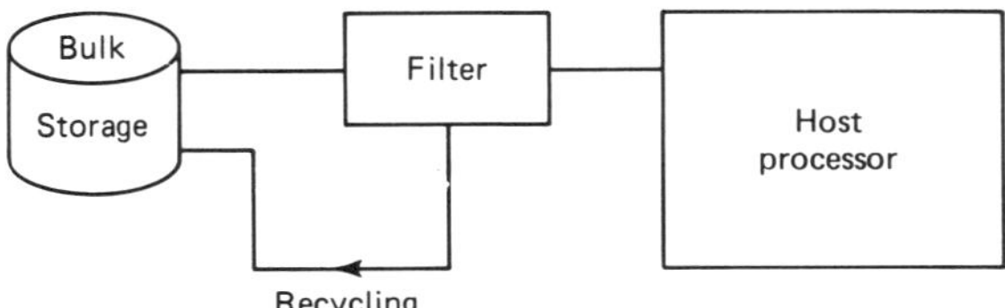

Figure 8.5   Filtering and recycling.

To elaborate on background recycling where projection can also be accomplished consider query optimization. Figure 8.6(a) is the initial query parse tree for a query involving three relations, their join, selections, and final projection. Using a query optimization technique where selections and projections are pushed

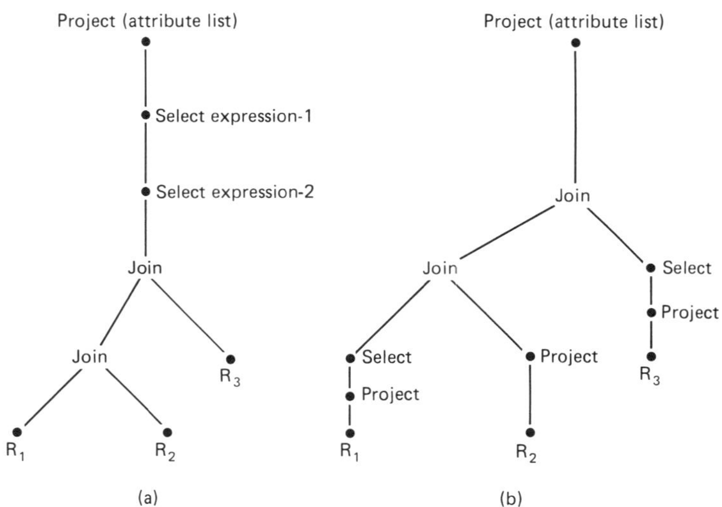

Figure 8.6   Query optimization in relational databases.

down the tree by distributing unary operations with respect to the binary operation of join and where projection is first transformed into its cascades with respect to the idempotence rule, we achieve the optimized query tree of Figure 8.6(b). (See Chapter 10 for query optimization.)

Now, the three legs of this tree, which involve selection and projection on R_1 and R_3 and projection on R_2, can be processed in the background before results are sent to the host for join and further processing. For best efficiency we would need six disk drives, one dual disk per background cycling of a leg; however, four disks would suffice if R_3 can be stored with R_1 or R_2 on a single disk. This is because recycling of R_3 can be overlapped with the join of R_1 and R_2. However, more disks increase the potential for concurrency; especially in cases where host processing is fast and/or the amount of concurrency is limited.

8.7 DATABASE PARTITIONING

As we may have noticed in the foregoing material covered for databases, the real blame for inefficiency comes from the large size of relations to be processed. Whether our architecture is in-stream, pipelined, sort based, or something else, the critical issue for success is the ability to partition the database instead of brute force processing. In the previous section on filters, we have seen that to ease the I/O bottleneck caused by the memory gap we must filter data as much as possible before processing. However, this would still leave us with brute force processing which does not completely eliminate the I/O bottleneck. To help solve this we must partition the data space and incorporate processing strategies that would exploit partitioning. Let us review the possible ways of partitioning a database by first listing the alternatives as follows:

(a) Sorting
(b) Hash-based data clustering
(c) Semantic/syntactic clustering such as the clustering methodologies discussed in Chapter 12 for document databases and vertical relation fragmentation
(d) Constructing coarse indices
(e) In-stream may-be join filtering
(f) Adaptive file segmentation
(g) Staging/paging tuned for locality of references
(h) Dynamic and order-preserving partitioning

The alternatives discussed are not all direct data partitioning strategies, but at least exploit that notion at the logical level. Also, not all of these alternatives can be overlapped in pipeline with processing. Let us review them one by one.

Sorting by definition is a natural partitioning strategy; however, unless one uses an in-stream pipeline sort-based architecture with a network of hardware sorters, sorting cannot be done on-the-fly unless it is preexisting. Dynamic and order-preserving partitioning strategy of step (h) is a recent proposal that achieves dynamic sorting–based partitioning without using much hardware.

Hash-based data clustering in step (b) computes and stores hash codes on tuples and brings the entire database into the database machine (as in GRACE). The problem with hash-based partitioning schemes is the nonuniform nature of partitions. Neither data values nor hash codes can be expected to follow a uniform distribution. If $F_X(x) = P[X \leq x]$ is a distribution function of X (i.e., of data values) such that P is the probability of $X \leq x$, then Figure 8.7(a) shows the case for uniformly distributed data values with a "close to uniform" hashing function that maps x to a uniform range in $F_x(x)$. That is, the hashing function approximates $F_x(x)$. Figure 8.7(b) shows a nonuniformly distributed $F_x(x)$ corresponding to a more typical case of nonuniformly distributed data values. Figure 8.7(c) shows a distribution function that always maps the data values to a uniform distribution. It has been shown [Weide, 1978] that such a function has the same distribution of $F_x(x)$. If Y represents its random variable, then $F_Y(y) = P[Y \leq y] = P[F_X(x) \leq y] = P[X \leq x] = y$ [Song, 1981]. While such a partitioning

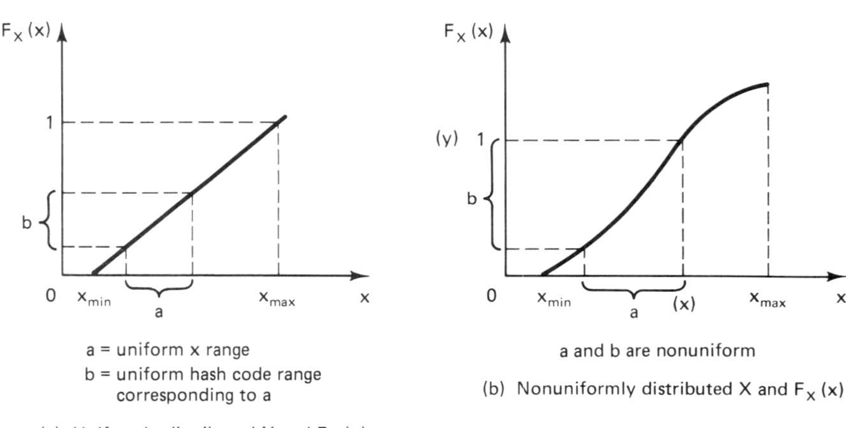

a = uniform x range
b = uniform hash code range
corresponding to a

(a) Uniformly distributed X and $F_X(x)$

a and b are nonuniform

(b) Nonuniformly distributed X and $F_X(x)$

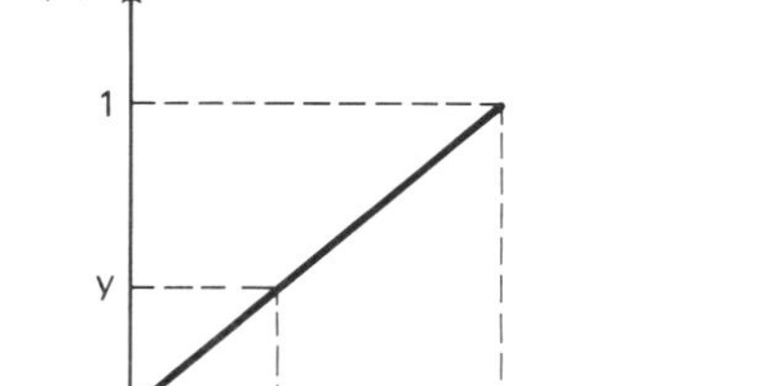

(c) A function that creates uniform data distribution

Figure 8.7   Distributions of data values.

scheme will depend on knowing the data distribution, which is hard to know ahead of time, statistical sampling techniques with small sample sizes [Weide, 1978] have been found to determine empirical distributions quite satisfactorily. The GRACE architecture takes the nonuniform data distributed as granted and tries to absorb the effect of this nonuniform distribution by further partitioning a hash partition and distributing these partitions over a large number of memory modules.

In semantic clustering mentioned in step (c), the idea is to identify data sets that are logically common to various views and/or schemas and identify them as clusters or partitions. If necessary these partitions can then be indexed based on secondary keys. This is different from physical partitioning strategies where the storage device cells of arbitrarily stored data sets are used to form hierarchies of directories based on the cell addresses and data values contained in them (e.g., building a B-tree on the contents of a storage device). We should not forget, however, that building indices does not go along with associative processing and, therefore, by "indices" here we mean coarse indices where the physical address resolution does not go lower than one or more storage cells. Therefore, coarse indexing mentioned in step (d) can be considered as a partitioning strategy by itself or in conjunction with another technique.

In the in-stream may-be join filtering mentioned in step (e), the filtering relies on knowing the join domain values of the source relation and then filtering off the definite false evaluations from the target relation during the second pass of the filter. Accordingly, we must determine the source join domain values by a first-pass filtering and resolve the strict join evaluation (by a postfiltering process in the database machine) among the values provided during the second pass. These values correspond to may-be answers (see Section 7.5.5) of the second pass. The success of this type of partitioning lies in the following factors:

(a) Enough storage to hold the results of the first pass.
(b) Exploitation of overlap between background filtering and foreground database machine processing.
(c) Enough storage in database machine to accommodate the result of the second pass.

In segmentation of files mentioned in step (f), the main concern is to avoid arbitrary segmentation that may result in accesses to most of the segments in processing queries. Most previous work on segmentation is of a static nature where an estimated probability distribution of attribute values is taken as the base. When an overflow occurred, the overflow chaining is implemented without changing the segmentation directory. In adaptive segmentation [Tanaka, 1983b], distributions are not set a priori, and when a segment overflows, the directory is rewritten by splitting the overflowing segment into two new segments by equally distributing the attribute values in them. In the following we will demonstrate the concepts used in adaptive segmentation.

While there are several segmentation schemes proposed for primary keys, only the *extended k-d tree* [Chang and Fu, 1981] is used for adaptive segmentation on secondary keys. The *k-d* tree uses values of attributes constituting the secondary key to form a path from root to leaf. A different attribute is used at each level of the tree with each internal node splitting the records (tuples) into two sets (i.e., those with higher values and those with lower values with respect to the value of the attribute node). This value can be arbitrarily chosen at each node. The resulting structure will be a binary trie, where the root of each subtree will be labeled with the attribute used as the basis of the split.

Suppose a relation is indexed by n secondary keys $(k_1, k_2, \ldots, k_n)$. If we represent each key with an m-bit hash code, we can produce an $n \times m$ long concatenated bit string $h_1(k_1)h_2(k_2) \cdots h_n(k_n)$, where h represents a hash function. In directory creation, overflowing nodes are split based on the most significant bit(s) of the attribute value. In the case of successive splitting, the unused next to most significant bits are used as the base for the split.

As an example, let us assume a relation whose tuples will contain attributes x, y, z, and others as $(x(4 \text{ bits}), y(? \text{ bits}), \text{other attributes}(? \text{ bits}))$, where ? indicates arbitrary values. Let us use attributes xz as the secondary key. At a given time, the directory may look like Figure 8.8.

To find the records for a search request, the trie is searched with respect to a node code formed by concatenating branch labels (i.e., 0, 1) on the path from the specified root to the unique node. A request may specify only a subset of the attributes of the k-d tree. For example, $X_1 = 0??$ and $X_2 = 1?$ (where ? corresponds to unspecified attributes) will return the tuple sets of {a, b, c, d} and {c, d, g, h}, respectively.

It is well known that the average height of a randomly constructed binary tree with N external nodes is $2 \ln(N - 1)$ or $1.386 \log_2 (N - 1)$. This directory scheme has the following properties:

(a) It is completely adaptive and has no restrictions on the number of segments and attributes.

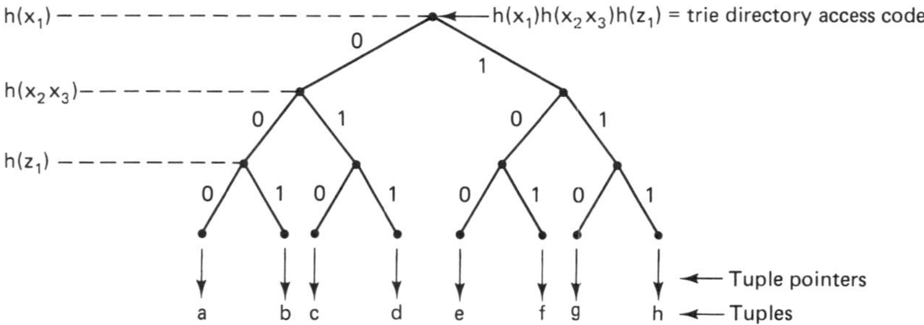

Figure 8.8   Adaptive segmentation directory.

(b) It can be arbitrarily chosen either to minimize the average number of segment accesses or to improve the worst case performance.

(c) If the values of the secondary keys are independently and uniformly distributed, a search of the directory for N segments and its local rewriting need only $O(\log_2 N)$ time for large N.

In regard to step (g), the idea is used when tuning of device operations to exploit locality of references is implementable. Although there is no partitioning performed in this case, the strategy relies on the usage pattern of the database. If this usage pattern demonstrates some locality of references, then our focus on the data space can be narrowed. Locality will be the topic of Section 8.9. We will also discuss, in a separate subsection, the dynamic and order-preserving partitioning mentioned in step (h). In Chapter 11, we will discuss the effect of partitioning on database machine performance.

8.8 DYNAMIC AND ORDER-PRESERVING PARTITIONING

The dynamic and order-preserving partitioning (DYOP partitioning in short) for database machines [Ozkarahan and Ouksel, 1985] offers significant advantages. It is essentially a dynamically maintained and order-preserving direct file organization having a data file and multi-level directories. The basic characteristics of the DYOP partitioning are:

- Search time is constant (typically two accesses, one for the directory and one for the data file).
- Directory and data file have identical structures and search characteristics.
- No overflow buckets or chaining are needed.
- Directory and data file partitions can be stored anywhere because their file addresses are kept in the directory (directories can expand into a multi-level hierarchy).
- No distributed free space needs to be kept in the directory and the data file.

We will briefly describe the DYOP partitioning by demonstrating the organization of the data file by means of repeated insertions to the file.

8.8.1 DYOP Data File

The data file can be envisioned as an n-dimensional space where each dimension corresponds to an attribute $A_i \ 0 \leq i \leq n - 1$, n being the number of attributes (fields) in a tuple (record). This means that search space corresponding to the relation (file) will be the Cartesian product of the domains underlying the attributes. For clarity we shall restrict the structure to the two-dimensional case (i.e.,

$D_0 \times D_1$, not necessarily distinct, for the attributes A_0 and A_1). A record r will correspond to a vector $r = (v_0, v_1)$ in the search space where v_0, v_1 are the values taken from the respective domains D_0 and D_1. The data file is the set of partitions (or buckets) obtained through the repeated subdivision of the search space. Again, for simplicity, we shall assume a partition size of 2 records. Let us start with a data file containing only two records hence a single partition. This is shown in Figure 8.9(a) where the number of the only partition zero is indicated in the lower left corner. In the file the partitions are numbered in the order in which they are created. In the figure the axes correspond to domains and the superscripted domain variables (D_i^0) represent the current set of possible coordinates which are later used to build the directory. The file system can be considered as a hierarchy of directories since the data file and the directory have the same structure. The data file is considered as the lowest level directory, thereby explaining the superscript zero.

Now if we insert a third record into the file an overflow will occur and the partition must be split along one of the dimensions (or interchangeably, along one axis or coordinate). We shall adopt a cyclic order policy for choosing the splitting axis (others which permit a random choice are discussed in [Ouksel, 1983]). Hence, we will split partition #0 along D_0. This split will be made by halving the ordered range of D_0 values hence maintaining the linear order within each resulting half. At this point since a single partition corresponds to the entire range of domain D_0 the split will occur at $|D_0|/2$. Accordingly, all those records whose v_0 is less than $|D_0|/2$ will remain in partition #0 while all those $v_0 \geq |D_0|/2$ will be assigned to a new partition, partition #1. Figure 8.9(b) shows the split. The partitions are numbered 0 and 1 and so are the coordinates of the partitions (i.e., while they were both 0 in Figure 8.9(a), after the split, the D_0 subranges are numbered 0 and 1). As shown in Figure 8.9(c), another insertion into partition #1 will cause it to split, but this time along D_1 according to the cyclic order of split axes. We must emphasize here that a split of a given partition along a given axis triggers the implicit splits along the same axis of all the other partitions. This type of split is termed implicit because no physical splits occur. The purpose of this strategy is to provide logical uniformity that will permit the systematic numbering of partitions presented later. That is, a unique mapping will exist between the coordinates of a partition and its assigned number. The split takes place in a linear order where all partitions are split in the order they are implicitly or explicitly created. Apart from their numbering, however, there is no other effect on the implicitly split (i.e., unconcerned) partitions. They will only be identified as implicit partitions and stored in (i.e., physically assigned to) a common explicit partition. This is referred to as the embedding of implicit partitions in explicit ones. While Figure 8.9(c) shows implicit splitting and linear numbering of implicit and explicit partitions, Figure 8.9(d) shows only the explicit partitions.

Consider adding a fifth record into partition #2. Partition #2 will still remain implicit because the insertion did not cause partition #0, in which partition #2

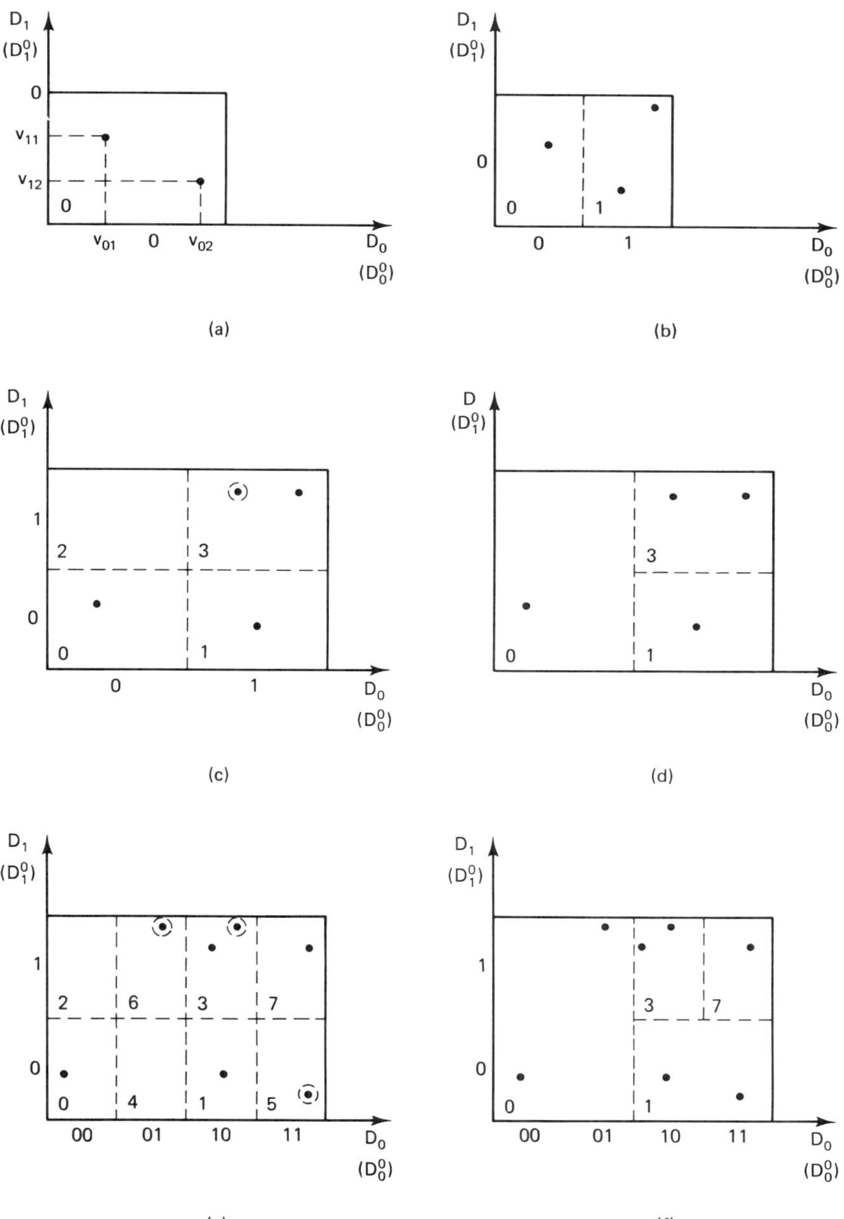

Figure 8.9 The data file.

is embedded, to split. Another insertion into the same partition region will make partition #2 explicit. And this will happen without triggering another round of splits in the search space (i.e., it will only account for a previous split). This prevents unnecessary increase in the magnitude of coordinates which in turn keeps the directory simple and smaller. If we continue with insertions some partitions will require splitting, as is the case with partition #3 in Figure 8.9(e). In the cyclic order, this time the split occurs along D_0. However, the split will occur either at $|D_0|/4$ for those records whose $v_0 < |D_0|/2$ or at $3|D_0|/4$ for those records whose $v_0 \geqslant |D_0|/2$. Figure 8.9(e) shows the linear partition splitting and numbering whereas Figure 8.9(f) shows only the explicit partitions. As can be seen in Figure 8.9(e), the split along a dimension is propagated to all the other partitions along the dimension even though only partition #3 has overflown. This creates the additional implicit partitions of 4, 5, and 6. Note also that the linear numbering of partitions starts within the split axis in the major order and then continues within the other axis in the minor order (i.e., the order of partitions is 4, 5, and then 6).

In the DYOP partition assignment scheme, we assign the lowest number to an explicit partition which may contain multiple implicit partitions (e.g., P_{i_2}, P_{i_3}, . . ., P_{i_e}) so that the assignment can be shown as $P_{i_1} \leftarrow P_{i_2}, P_{i_3}, \ldots, P_{i_e}$ where $e \leqslant m$ and m is the total number of partitions in the data file. We say that the implicit partitions P_{i_2}, P_{i_3}, . . ., P_{i_e} are embedded in the explicit partition P_{i_1}.

8.8.2 DYOP Directory

As we mentioned earlier D_0^0 and D_1^0 indicate the sets of coordinates along the axes of the data file. Accordingly, the vector $r^0 = (d_0^0, d_1^0)$ represents the coordinates, in binary form, of partitions in the data file. For example, in Figure 8.9(f) (10,1) represents the two coordinates of partition #3 while the one associated with partition #0 is (00,0). The directory is made up of records which store coordinates of the data file partitions. The length of any d_i^0 is determined by the number of splits taken place along D_i^0. In the following, we show the construction of the directory for the data file example illustrated in the foregoing. As we already know, the data and directory file structures are identical; however, since we can store more directory records in a partition (because directory records are small) the capacity of a directory partition will be large. But for clarity, we will assume it is 3. Accordingly, Figure 8.10(a) shows the initial makeup of the directory. We see four points in the directory search space corresponding to the four explicit partitions in the data file. As can be noticed, the coordinates of the directory search space are labeled D_0^1 and D_1^1, superscript 1 indicating the first level directory (one higher than the data file at level 0). These coordinates constitute the basis for the 2nd level directory in the same way the first level directory is built from the data file. We stop building higher level directories when the number of partitions in the highest level directory is

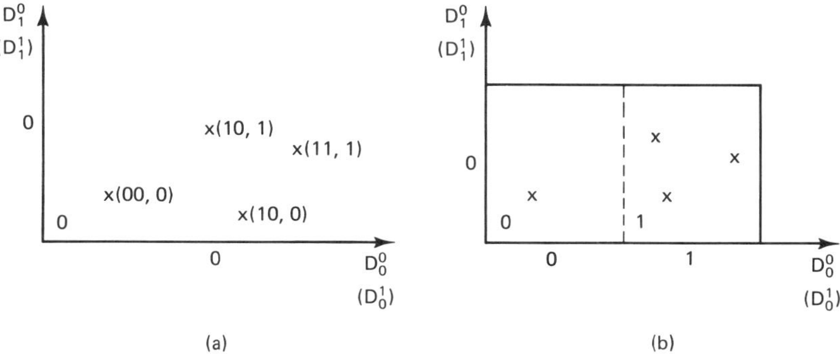

Figure 8.10 The directory.

equal to one. Looking at Figure 8.10(a) we see that the directory partition #0 needs to be split because the partition size is 3. The split starts along the D_0^0 axis. The linear order in the range of the split axis must be preserved in the same way as in the data file. Therefore, when we split along D_0^0, those records whose coordinate (i.e., D_0^1) prefixes are a 1 (i.e., 10, 11 corresponding to higher values in the range) are moved to a new partition. This is illustrated in Figure 8.10(b) where the new partition is numbered 1.

According to the DYOP directory structure, the directory record (10, 0) which represents the data file partition #1 will itself be addressed as (1,0), i.e., directory partition #1, in the higher level directory. In general $r^h = (d_0^h, d_1^h, \ldots, d_{n-1}^h)$ represents the coordinate vector of the hth level where $0 \leq h \leq maxh$ and $d_i^h = p(d_i^{h-1}, l_i^h)$ for $0 \leq i \leq n$, where n is the number of dimensions, and $1 \leq l \leq maxh$ where $p(s,l)$ denotes the prefix of length l of binary string s. Note that no records are kept in the directory for the implicit data file partitions because as we will show later we can determine the explicit partitions embedding the implicit ones without additional directory accesses.

There is another file organization, called the grid file, that is quite similar to the DYOP partitioning. In the grid file, the directory space requirement is at best a super-linear function and at worst an exponential function of the number of records. In DYOP, however, the restriction to split only overflowing partitions guarantees a linear function. The differences between the DYOP partitioning and the other related organizations we have mentioned at the beginning are more fundamental and documented in detail in [Ouksel, 1983], and [Ouksel and Scheuermann, 1983].

8.8.3 Storage Addressing of DYOP Partitions

Due to the linear order of splitting of the implicit and explicit partitions in the DYOP files, we are able to deduce a mapping which allows a unique numbering of partitions. In the data file, a record r's ($r = (v_0, v_1, \ldots, v_{n-1})$) $i+1$th component v_i will have a relative position $x_i = v_i/|D_i|$ in the corresponding ordered set D_i. As we know, this record r will be represented in the directory by the coordinate vector $d^0 = (d_0^0, d_1^0, \ldots, d_{n-1}^0)$ which gives us the coordinates of the partition storing the data record r. These coordinates are given by:

$$d_i^0 = \lfloor x_i \cdot 2^{l_i^0} \rfloor \qquad \text{for} \qquad 0 \leq i \leq n - 1$$

To compute d_i^0, it suffices to know the number of splits l_i^0, that occurred along the D_i^0 axis. This in turn can be determined as follows: Let l be the number of times the whole search space has been split. If the splitting order was cyclic then it can be expressed as $L^0 \cdot n + m$, implying that $l_i^0 = L^0 + 1$ splits occurred along axis i such that $0 \leq i \leq m$ and L^0 splits along axis j such that $m < i \leq n - 1$. That is, at a given time we may not have completed the full round of splits along all the axes involved, and some axes will remain unsplit for the current cycle. Let also d_{ij}^0 for $0 \leq j \leq l^i$ (where l^i also corresponds to the binary string length of the prefix of the ith coordinate) be the jth binary digit of d_i^0. Then the number of the partition storing the data record r can be obtained from:

$$M(r, l^0) = \sum_{i=0}^{n-1} 2^i \sum_{j=0}^{l_{i-1}^0} 2^{n(l_{i-1}^0 - j)} d_{ij}^0 \qquad \text{where} \qquad l_i^0 = \begin{cases} L^0 + 1 & \text{if} \ \ 0 \leq i \leq m \\ L^0 & \text{otherwise} \end{cases}$$

The partition number M does not differentiate between explicit and implicit partitions. Because implicit partitions are not represented directly in the directory we must have a way of mapping coordinates of implicit partitions to the same directory partition representing the explicit partition in which the given implicit one is embedded. Only in this way can the directory search be resolved by a single access. This is accomplished by the use of the same M function. This time, it is used to find the directory partition which contains the coordinates of the explicit data file partition embedding the implicit target partitions. The following relationships have been shown to hold for the DYOP partitioning:

If Π represents a partition number, then all the partition numbers for the partitions that may possibly contain partition Π is given by:

$$\Pi, \Pi - 2^\alpha, \ldots, \Pi - \sum_{s=0}^{\alpha} 2^s \Pi_s \qquad \text{where} \qquad \alpha = \left\lfloor \log \Pi \right\rfloor \ \text{and}$$

$$\Pi_\alpha \Pi_{\alpha-1} \cdots \Pi_{\alpha 0} \quad \text{is the binary representation of } \Pi$$

If we represent the coordinates of an implicit and explicit partition at the hth level directory, respectively, by r^{h_1} and r^{h_2}, then there exists an integer k such that:

$$p(r_i^{h_1}, l_i^{k+1}) = p(r_i^{h_2}, l_i^{k+i}) \qquad \text{for} \qquad h < k < maxh \text{ and } 0 \leq i \leq n - 1$$

This is a consequence of the previous relationship. The explicit partition number $M(r^{h_2}, l^h)$ is stored at the $(h + 1)$ th level directory whose partition number can also be obtained by r^{h_1}.

8.8.4 A Retrieval Example

Given a record $r = (v_0, v_1, \ldots, v_{n-1})$ and the number of times the entire search space has been split (i.e., $l = L(n - 1) + m$), we must determine the address a_0 where the record r is stored. To do that we must determine the following:

(a) Compute r_0.

(b) Compute $r^1, r^2, \ldots, r^{n-1}$; stop when you obtain a directory consisting of a single partition (i.e., $r^i = (0,0)$) which corresponds to the top directory.

(c) Search top directory partition whose number is $M(r^{maxh-1}, l^{maxh-1})$ in main memory to obtain the address a_{maxh-2} of the partition whose number is $M(r^{maxh-2}, l^{maxh-2})$ or the one it is embedded in.

(d) Search lower level directories from $k = maxh - 2$ to 1. In each search, search the partition at the address a_k for the address associated with partition $M(r^{k-1}, l^{k-1})$ or the one it is embedded in.

The number of file accesses will be $O(maxh - 1)$.

Let us assume that we want to retrieve record $r = (37500,10)$ and that $D_0 = 50000$, $D_1 = 80$, $l^0 = 3$, $l^1 = 2$, and $l^2 = 0$. Our search space is two dimensional, $maxh = 3$, and the level 2 directory will be the top directory. And since $l^2 = 0$, meaning no split has occurred, the directory consists of one partition, and it will be main memory resident. From $v_0(37500)$ and $v_1(10)$ we determine $x = (37500/50000, 10/80)$ or $(0.110, 0.001)$ in the binary form. From this, by using expression for d_i^0 we determine $r^0 = (11,0)$. That is, because the zero-th level has been split three times, then there will be two splits along D_0 and one along D_1, giving the respective powers of 2 in the expression for d_i^0. Because the first level directory has been split twice, i.e., once along each direction, we pick one digit from each of the coordinate prefixes of the lower directory to give $r' = (1,0)$ and similarly we find $r^2 = (0,0)$.

After this we determine the partition number $M(r^2, l^2)$ of the top level directory which comes out as $M(0,0) = 0$. This number corresponds to a_2 in main memory. At this address we determine a_1, the address of the partition $M(r^1, l^1)$ or the partition embedding it. $M(r^1, l^1)$ evaluates to 1. In the lower level directory we search the partition at the address a_1 for the partition whose number is calculated to be $M(r^0, l^0) = 5$, or the one it is embedded in. The address a_0 found at this point corresponds to the address of the data file partition in which the record $r = (37500,10)$ is stored. The trees shown in Figure 8.11 abstract the splits that took place along the dimensions. In Figure 8.11(a) we see the splits in the lower directory and in Figure 8.11(b) we see the splits that took place in the data file. Each level in the trees corresponds to a split along an axis. If the splits, which preserve order, are labeled with 0 and 1 along the branches of an ordered binary tree, then the binary string formed by concatenating the branches along the path from the leaf associated with a partition to the root

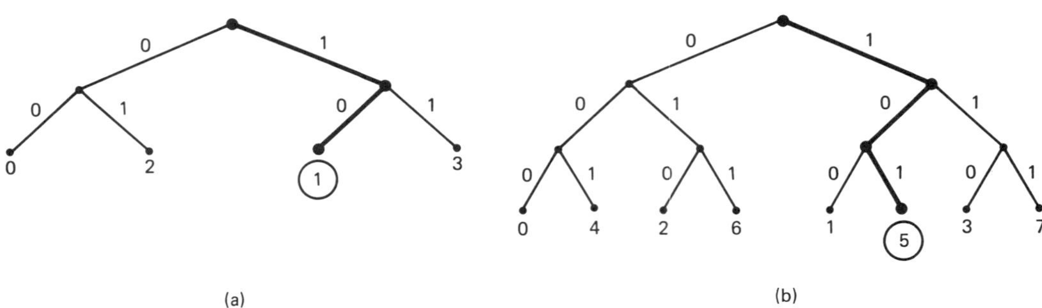

Figure 8.11   Split directions and partition numbers.

would give us partition number(s) we have determined by using the expression for M. In the figures, those partitions are circled at the leaves, and the paths are indicated in bold.

8.8.5 DYOP Partitioning For Different Database Machines

Although the DYOP partitioning is used for direct addressed files, we can adapt it for data space partitioning in database machines. The only parameter to vary will be the partition size, which will be very large in the case of database machines. To give an example, consider the RAP.3 database machine which is a cellular associative device. Each cell of the RAP.3 machine has a cell memory capacity of 1 to 2 megabytes. Therefore each load of a 16 cell RAP.3 device will require database chunks of 16 to 32 megabytes. Each chunk will be a DYOP partition.

If we consider an in-stream architecture, we need not make the partition size that large. However, a small partition size will have adverse effect on data bandwidth provided by archival storage devices (e.g., disks). In the case of a single disk drive, the larger the partition, the higher will be the bandwidth because of continuous readout from contiguous disk locations. The smaller the partition the lower is the bandwidth because of frequently intervening disk seeks between partition accesses. To overcome that we may devise an interleaving and/or multiplexing scheme by using multiple disks. Therefore, the type of database machine architecture will determine the partitioning strategy; however, multiple disks will be preferable regardless of the type of architecture.

8.8.6 Join and Projection with DYOP Partitioning

Equijoin. The join methodology we will describe here is general, i.e., can be used both for semi-join and join. The difference comes in the way partitions are processed in the database machine. If we assume two relations R and S with cardinalities N and M to be joined and if b_0 represents partition size, then it is shown in [Ouksel, 1983] that R and S will be mapped into approximately E_R and E_S pages where

$$E_R = \frac{N}{b_0}\log e \qquad \text{and} \qquad E_S = \frac{M}{b_0}\log e \qquad (e = 2.718)$$

Let us further assume that R and S were previously reduced by selection operations whose results are enclosed in the space delineated by the rectangles shown in Figure 8.12 for both R and S. The area enclosing the results of a selection is rectangular because the relations are assumed to be binary in this example and the key is composite. The area would have been a hypercube if the relations were composed of more than two attributes. In this example, both join and intersection are accomplished at once on the two attributes composing the relations. In the figure, rectangles in bold enclose the results of selections, and the second narrow rectangle in the S relation indicates region of space that is compatible with that of the selected area in R. We should only compare partitions of compatible regions between the relations to do the join operation. In the following, we enumerate the possibilities in join processing.

CASE 1: A partition is fully contained in the selected region of the relation. An example of this is partition O in relation S and its corresponding (compatible) partitions O_0, O_1, O_2, and O_3 in R. As can be noticed in the coordinates, partition O in S covers a larger region which is equivalent to the sum of the four partitions in R. The approach in join would be to:

(a) Subdivide the larger partition (here partition O in S) into smaller partitions that are equal in size to the size of partitions in the other relation with finer partition size (here R relation).

(b) Send compatible partition pairs (i.e., one from R and one from S) to the database machine to be joined. Here we assume that partition sizes are chosen such that they can both fit in the database machine memory. This

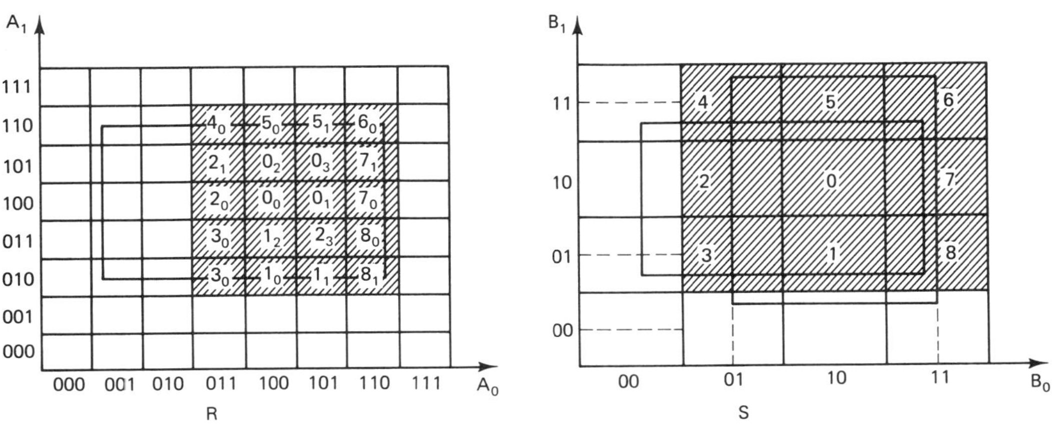

Figure 8.12 Join processing.

join will be accomplished in one pass because DYOP partitioning preserves order so that compatible tuples will not be scattered in space.

(c) Repeat the operation until all compatible partition pairs from the relations are sent to be joined in the database machine.

In (a) we mentioned subdividing partition O in S into $\{O_0^1, O_1^1, O_2^1, O_3^1\}$ to be joined with $\{O_0, O_1, O_2, O_3\}$ in R. The join will be between compatible pairs (i.e., $O_0^1 * O_0, \ldots, O_3^1 * O_3$). Here we will assume that a VLSI filter as in the RAP.3 architecture will identify O_0^1 through O_3^1 in O in the data stream during staging by looking at the high order bits of attribute values and placing them in their respective places in the cache memory prior to processing.

CASE 2: The partitions are not entirely contained in the selected regions of the relations. An example of this is partition #1 in S which corresponds to partitions 1_0, 1_1, 1_2, and 1_3 in R. Here in both relations the tuples falling out of the selected regions in the partitions must first be filtered out before they are sent for join in the database machine. Again as indicated before, during staging, the VLSI filter can both decompose the larger partition #1 from S and filter out the irrelevant tuples from the decomposed partitions on the way to the cache, giving us first the set $\{1_0^1, 1_1^1, 1_2^1, 1_3^1\}$ and then $\{1_0^{11}, 1_1^{11}, 1_2^{11}, 1_3^{11}\}$ on-the-fly. The single superscripts indicate decomposition while double superscripts indicate subsequent filtering that are both accomplished by the VLSI filter. Therefore, the join will be between the pairs: $1_0 * 1_0^{11}$, $1_1 * 1_1^{11}$, $1_2 * 1_2^{11}$, and $1_3 * 1_3^{11}$.

At the end of each join dispatch, the host processor can perform the join operation. An example of this is the execution of the RAP.3 join algorithm, given in Chapter 7, for each join dispatch involving compatible partitions of the relations being joined.

The projection operation requires a sorted relation for efficient processing. It should be noted that while DYOP partitioning preserves global order among partitions in the multidimensional search space, data within a partition are not sorted. Also in cases where implicit partitions are embedded in an explicit partition, the explicit partition will be unordered both within and among implicit partitions. Consider Figure 8.13. If we want values of A_0 ordered within A_1, then if we pull out explicit partition #0, indicated by the bold rectangle, these values will fall out of sequence because we should scan coordinate 00 of A_1 along A_0 first before we can pull coordinate 01 (i.e., implicit partitions 8 and 20). This means we need sorting within a partition whether or not it contains implicit partitions. There is no difference in the case of having implicit partitions. They are implicit, simply because an explicit partition's size is fixed (that is, the partition has not grown enough to be split).

Let us show projection by referring to Figure 8.13. Projection on A_0 of R means that the duplicates must be searched in the following groupings:

$$\{0,8,2,10\}, \{16,20,18,22\}, \ldots, \{25,29,27,31\}$$

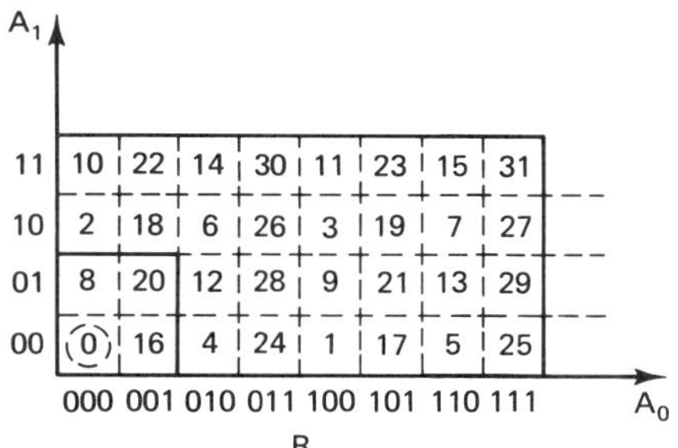

Figure 8.13   Projection of $R(A_0, A_1)$ on A_0.

The addresses in each group are computed by using the two nested loops:

* one varying along axis A_0
* the other varying along axis A_1 (within A_0)

Due to the global order (i.e., intersection of groups is empty relative to A_0) of the DYOP partitioning, projection can be processed in parallel among groups. Also, projection can be processed in parallel within a group if partitions are processed as single units. The dispatching of partitions of a group to the database machine memory (or to the cache first) will be done by the VLSI filter by examining the high order bits of the attribute values on-the-fly.

The fact that DYOP partitioning necessitates intrapartition sorting would be suitable for the RAP.3 database machine. As can be remembered in the RAP.3 projection macro, parallel sorting among cells is the first step. The processing described here for projection will also hold for general join processing. That is, if we had to join relations R and S over $A_1 = B_1$ or $A_0 = B_0$ (instead of both as in the foregoing join processing), then we would have to scan the coordinates of the join attributes (A_1, B_1; or A_0, B_0) along the other coordinates (A_0, B_0; or A_1, B_1) before incrementing the coordinates scanned in the join attributes. Having a filter on the data path (or filters on multiple paths) enables us to dispatch variable sizes of data from the compatible partitions as dictated by available processor (cell) memory in the database machine partitions. Such an MIMD architecture consisting of cell clusters or partitions each processing a join dispatch is included in the RAP.3 architecture (Figure 7.11). In Figure 7.11 we have shown the concurrent processing of the MIMD model of the RAP.3 device. For parallel join processing we must use the horizontal device partitioning [i.e., intercell partitioning as opposed to vertical (intracell) partitioning]. In this case of device (cell) partitioning, we must have parallel staging paths through filters into RAP.3 cell partitions. We can stage in variable sizes of data from compatible partitions as dictated by the memory space of cell partitions which are dynamically configured. The amount of cache memory on the staging path would also affect the system efficiency. The model of join processing discussed here enables parallel join processing both within a join and among multiple joins. It would also benefit from m-way joins because the sizes of compatible subhypercubes would conveniently be reduced to the intersection of m data spaces.

The DYOP partitioning was adapted by the RAP.3 database machine [Ozkarahan and Ouksel, 1985] to maintain the join complexity at linear order [i.e., $O(n)$ instead of $O(n^2)$ for the relations being joined, each having the cardinality of n] in nonresident databases. This is because we need not compare data from incompatible regions (i.e., as in Figure 7.29(b) as opposed to Figure 7.29(a)). Furthermore, because the DYOP partitioning preserves global order, data of a partition are not scattered in space (unlike hash-based clustering). This means that the logical picture depicted in Figure 7.29(b) is also the physical picture.

The DYOP partitioning is superior to K-D trees (or tries) or other related work such as grid files. DYOP does not use overflow areas, it does not split non-overflowing partitions because it embeds implicit partitions in the explicit ones. And furthermore, its partitioning is symmetric with respect to all attributes. That is, while the order of partitioning attributes in space would not matter in DYOP, in the case of K-D trees (or tries) a lower level index attribute cannot uniquely partition the data space hence many leaf nodes must be scanned for the desired attribute values.

As can be seen from the benefits we can obtain in efficient data space partitioning, the answer for finding better database machines cannot be based on new architecture designs alone. We should also exploit efficient and effective data space clustering and/or partitioning besides associativity, parallelism, and other desirable virtues.

8.9 *EXPLOITING LOCALITY*

In programming applications, the important property of locality of address references in a user program is used to reduce paging. One unique difference of query programs of database applications from the programs written in general-purpose programming languages is that, in the former, the address references are deterministically known ahead of execution. This is because as we compile or interpret a query program we know the relations required ahead of time. This enables us to exploit locality of query programs with more straightforward methods. Locality in databases refers to a nonrandom distribution of user references to database relations during the execution of sequences of queries over time. High locality is present when some relations in a database are referenced more often than the others. In other words, if the page frame (or relation) references are represented by a locality distribution, high locality will incur low variance. Before we carry on, let us try to justify the rationale behind having high locality in some real-life applications.

In applications where there is a constant element of time, such as reservation systems, there will be a high locality in database activities toward a deadline. In other words, when a flight departure nears in an airlines reservation system or when a convention nears in a hotel reservation system, there will be frequent references to the same relations holding reservation data.

In interactive applications, such as document retrieval, a user browses over the database and then narrows down the search by iterative query refinement through feedback. During the cycle of these operations, certain relations forming relevant clusters of data will tend to be referenced more often than others.

In batch environments, where updates against a database are accumulated over time, the requests will be ordered with respect to common data sets to optimize I/O performance. This will create a cluster of references over the same sets of data to carry out all the accumulated updates.

In executing queries involving multiple relations, therefore—join operations among them—certain association relations (such as the *SUPPLIER-PART* relation between the *SUPPLIER* and *PARTS* relations) or relations corresponding to relationships in the *E/R* model will be referenced more often by being on the join path of several relations. This situation will be more visible in a multiuser and multiquery environment.

If we look at the paging activity between a database machine and the mass storage devices storing nonresident relations, we will observe a relatively smaller number of relation pagings between successive queries (jobs) in the high-locality case than otherwise. From this, we can define a measure called *system locality* [Schuster, Ozkarahan, and Smith, 1976] as

$$SLOC = \left(\sum_{i=1}^{n} pgcom(i) \right) \Big/ \left(\sum_{i=1}^{n} pg(i) \right)$$

where *pgcom*(i) and *pg*(i) refer to the number of common resident pages and additional pages that have to be brought from mass memory between two successive jobs (i.e., $i - 1$ and i), where $i = 1, 2, \ldots, n$ consecutive jobs. In other words, if at the end of the execution of the $i - 1$th job, *pgcom* number of pages remain in the database machine because they are needed by the *i*th job and an additional *pg*(i) pages are brought in from mass memory because they were nonresident, *SLOC* is concerned with the overall relationship of these two quantities over the life of the executions of *n* jobs.

If we represent different localities by different page frame reference distributions (e.g., low, medium, high locality with uniform, exponential, and hyperexponential distributions, respectively), their effect on *SLOC* was observed [Schuster, Ozkarahan, and Smith, 1976] to display the following relationship:

```
SLOC ∝(1/log(database size))·locality      (where ∝ means
proportional to)
```

This relationship shows that the higher the locality, the better the system will perform because of less paging. It was interesting to observe in the referenced study that even a moderate locality yields appreciably better results with respect to low (or random) locality when the average time in system for a job was observed in relation to sizes of relations being processed and processing time of jobs. The processing time was also effective because in the referenced study a staging was employed where database machine processing and paging I/O were overlapped. Going back to *SLOC* relationship it can be seen that the effect of locality diminishes with ever-increasing database size where chances of reference stability also diminish statistically.

In summary, locality in databases logically partitions a database over time so that efficient staging strategies can be devised.

8.10 CONCURRENCY

By concurrency here we are impiying multiuser support by a database machine. We have seen various database machine architectures so far; some were SIMD machines and some MIMD. While multiuser support is a natural outcome of the MIMD architecture, let us review possible ways of achieving concurrency regardless of the type of an architecture. In multiuser support, each user will correspond to a job in our simple world and each job will be administered and executed by a control process. We may assign varying numbers of processors (cells) to the control process. If we implement a queuing discipline within our system for control processes we can achieve concurrency as follows. For an SIMD-type architecture, concurrency will be possible only in the multi-programming sense by priority queuing and possibly task swapping. For an MIMD architecture, concurrency will be implemented by multiprocessing; however, the solution used for SIMD can also additionally be implemented on top of multi-processing. Figure 8.14 abstracts these concurrency schemes. Figure 8.14(a) is an SIMD concurrency architecture whereas Figure 8.14(b) is an MIMD one. In Figure 8.14(a) we show a k class priority-based queuing control. Before we reached that point we could have a single queue (class) and implement various queuing disciplines such as

(a) First-come, first-served (FCFS)
(b) Nonpreemptive priority
(c) Preemptive priority, which in turn is broken into
    (1) Preemptive resume
    (2) Preemptive restart

In FCFS we would not have a concurrency scheme. This is so also with the nonpreemptive priority discipline where, although the waiting jobs are ordered by priority, once a job takes control of the system, it will seize it until completion of the job. Accordingly, concurrency can come only with task swapping or preemptive disciplines. In reality, instead of one, one has k priority classes of different priorities in the system, and every higher priority queue can preempt an executing job of lower priority. These preemptions can be stacked for a k class environment. Within each class queue the order is FCFS. In a study

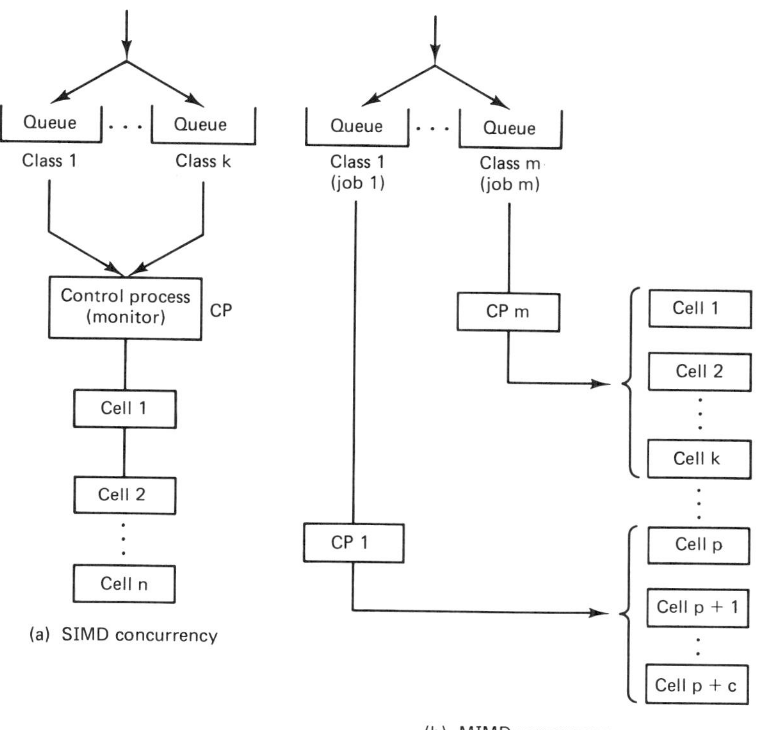

Figure 8.14   Concurrency architectures.

reported in Ozkarahan and Sevcik [1977], it has been observed that within the preemptive discipline, resume preemption (where a preempted job can continue from the point of previous interruption) achieved much better concurrency than did the restart preemptive discipline, because in the latter little productive progress was achieved over the duration of stay of a job in the system, especially at high system loads.

While concurrency of Figure 8.14(a) is more properly a multiprogramming facility over a single server (database machine), Figure 8.14(b) shows a truly concurrent environment where different jobs execute concurrently over the available multiprocessors (as in DIRECT) or multiprocessing partitions (as in RAP.3— see Figure 7.11). If there are more processors than jobs in the system, a rare case, then we can assign one control process for each job. However, a more typical case is again to define multiple-class queues in the system and administer FCFS in each queue or build the system of Figure 8.14(b) as an upper-level queuing system over each multiprocessor queue. The concurrency control issues involved in this system are typical of operating system theory and, hence, are out of the context of this text. However, one important issue, protecting the integrity of the database in concurrent updates, which limits sharing due to system enforced serialization, will be deferred to the distributed database chapter, where it will be more relevant. Before we conclude this chapter, we will discuss how to enable concurrency in database machines that do not create intermediate relations but employ tagging. This is less obvious than the same in database machines which do not use the tagging concept (e.g., DIRECT, SABRE, DBMAC, DBC, RDBM, GRACE).

Let us take the RAP.3 database machine as an example. RAP uses marking or tagging. In the previous studies of RAP, concurrency was made possible by providing multiple sets of mark bits for each job class. However, since mark bits imply associated hardware and/or firmware that, once fixed, can be hard to change, the following provision was made in the RAP.3 architecture [Ozkarahan, Tansel, and Smith, 1982]. A mark bit set saving and restoring instruction pair was introduced. By the use of the SAVE_MARKS instruction, a job can save its mark bit image in a vacant data domain of every tuple of the relation and can resume processing by first issuing a RESUME_MARKS instruction. Resumption can be by the same user at a given location or by another user at a different site in a distributed database. This scheme does not place any restriction on the number of saves that can be made within a tuple. The corresponding data domains that contain the saved mark bit values can later be identified in the system based on an association established between attribute names in a relation and job and/or user codes assigned in the system. Figure 8.15 shows the mark bit saving and restoring operations in RAP.

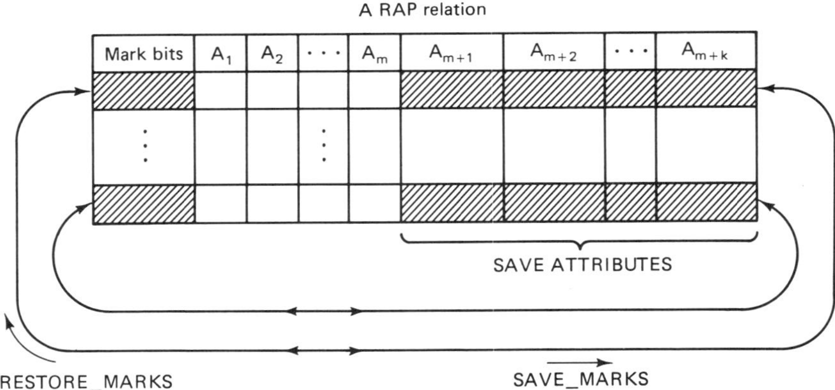

Figure 8.15   Multiple tag bit use in RAP.3.

8.11 *UTILITY OF THE TAGGING CONCEPT*

At this point we would like to present a brief discussion on the idea of the tagging (marking) concept because of its importance in database machine architectures. Up until now we have seen some machines, such as CASSM and RAP and some associative processors of the type discussed in Chapter 6 that use the tagging concept in their structure and operations. Let us review tagging here in more detail.

8.11.1 What Is a Tag?

A tag may mean many things (e.g., a delimiter, an encoding). Within the context of a database machine architecture, however, a tag is a marking in memory to indicate the result of a search or manipulation. A tag can be conceived both logically and physically. In the logical sense, a tag can be a data type associated with a data structure and an instruction set would be needed for its various manipulations. An example of this are the tag (mark) attributes in the RAP relations. In the physical sense, we would be concerned with the representation of a tag in hardware and how it is implemented.

Tagging (marking) has also been used extensively in implementing associative memories as an alternative to genuine content addressable solid-state memories. Although in the true hardware sense a tag can be implemented by a flip-flop or a similar circuit, we will be dealing with what we may call a "soft tag." Tagging/untagging would imply turning on or off, or setting/resetting (by writing in 1's or 0's) memory locations. In the majority of the past research, tagging was implemented at the character or memory word level; however, some database machine architectures (e.g., RAP) use it at the tuple level.

8.11.2 How to Use Tags

If we use tags as in the RAP machine, we can subset a relation R into 2^c horizontal fragments where c indicates any combination of m tag bits (permutations being identical). This means that without requiring any additional storage to store these 2^c possible fragments (the additional storage would have been less than or equal to $2^c \cdot MR$ where MR indicates the amount of storage needed to hold R) the same single copy of R would represent all these fragments. In other words, if we denote the unary and binary relational algebra operations, respectively, by *UOR* and *BOR* then the relational algebra operations on a tagged relation can be abstracted as:

```
R ← (UOR)R
R ← R(BOR)S  where R and S denote relations
```

The above notation resembles a two-address instruction format as opposed to a three-address one; however, there is one difference in the case of above abstractions. That is the fact that the contents of R, which hold the result, remain unchanged, whereas in the two-address instruction, R is overwritten with the result. This is because what we are actually manipulating are the tag bits, not the relation R's stored form.

By the virtue of tagging and its efficient implementation on parallel architectures we achieve associative context search operations on a bulk memory, which can be any type of memory ranging from disk storage to bulk solid-state memories such as RAM's and magnetic bubbles. We can use tags of previous operations as qualifiers of subsequent operations to accomplish powerful chains of selections and manipulations on databases.

Let us review some implications of the tagging concept in database management. Consider the following series of operations on the R relation shown below:

$$
\begin{array}{c}
R \\
A_1 \; A_2 \; A_3 \\
\begin{bmatrix} a & 1 & 10 \\ b & 1 & 10 \\ c & 1 & 15 \end{bmatrix}
\end{array}
\qquad
R_1 = R[A_1, A_2] = \begin{bmatrix} a & 1 \\ b & 1 \\ c & 1 \end{bmatrix}
\qquad
R_2 = R[A_2, A_3] = \begin{bmatrix} 1 & 10 \\ 1 & 15 \end{bmatrix}
$$

$$
R = R_1[A_2 = A_2]R_2 = \begin{bmatrix} a & 1 & 10 \\ b & 1 & 10 \\ c & 1 & 10 \\ a & 1 & 15 \\ b & 1 & 15 \\ c & 1 & 15 \end{bmatrix}
$$

which results in a lossy join. The same could be done by tagging as follows:

$$
\begin{array}{c}
R \\
t_1 \; t_2 \; t_3 \; A_1 \; A_2 \; A_3 \\
\begin{bmatrix} 0 & 0 & 0 & a & 1 & 10 \\ 0 & 0 & 0 & b & 1 & 10 \\ 0 & 0 & 0 & c & 1 & 15 \end{bmatrix}
\end{array}
\qquad
R_1(t_1) = \begin{bmatrix} 1 & 0 & 0 & a & 1 & 10 \\ 1 & 0 & 0 & b & 1 & 10 \\ 1 & 0 & 0 & c & 1 & 15 \end{bmatrix}
\qquad
R_2(t_2) = \begin{bmatrix} 0 & 0 & 0 & a & 1 & 10 \\ 0 & 1 & 0 & b & 1 & 10 \\ 0 & 1 & 0 & c & 1 & 15 \end{bmatrix}
$$

$$
R(t_3) = R_1(t_1) * R_2(t_2) = \begin{bmatrix} 1 & 0 & 1 & a & 1 & 10 \\ 1 & 1 & 1 & b & 1 & 10 \\ 1 & 1 & 1 & c & 1 & 15 \end{bmatrix}
$$

As can be seen, tagged join (or semi-join in general between two different relations) is an additional precaution to lossy joins. (The primary precaution is the lossless join test when the functional dependencies are known—we may not always guarantee enough knowledge of the semantics, however.)

The next thing we would like to point out is the handling of views. In the well known department store database example [consisting of relations LOCATION(DEPT, FLOOR), CLASS(ITEM, TYPE), SALES(DEPT, ITEM, VOL), EMPLOYEE(NAME, DEPT, SAL, MGR, COMM) and SUPPLY (COMPANY, DEPT, ITEM, VOL)] if we were asked to support a view that would represent *second floor departments that sell Toys* we can handle it with the use of tags as follows:

```
TAG t₁ IN LOCATION : FLOOR = 2
TAG t₂ IN SALES : ITEM = 'TOY'
SEMI-JOIN WITH TAG t₃ IN SALES ( t₂ ) FROM LOCATION ( t₁ ) OVER DEPT
```

In the above procedure, we selected LOCATION and SALES and indicated the results, respectively, with tags t_1 and t_2 in these relations. Then we made a semi-join from the t_1-tagged LOCATION tuples into only those SALES tuples that were t_2-tagged, and the final result is indicated by the t_3-tagged tuples in SALES. The SALES relation can be stored with its tags permanently. Later on when we access the SALES relation, we have both the entire SALES relation and the view we built on t_3 tags available for use. At this point we may be asked: What happens if the users want to use the t_3 tags for other operations on SALES? The answer for this will be in saving and restoring tags as will be shown later.

We can, therefore, use tags both for manipulations and for permanent storage. As can be remembered from the foregoing, we can store (or represent) 2^c possible different views, as materialized on the original relation, without requiring any additional storage. Let us indicate one more point before we can discuss other uses of the tagging concept.

In a relational algebra operation, each tuple of a relation is evaluated with respect to the Boolean predicate, or qualification, that is expressed in the instruction corresponding to the operation. Because tags are considered a relation's attributes, it would be conceivable to use tagged or untagged status of a tuple (on any t_c instance) as a predicate (remember the RAP instruction set). For example, in the view example given above, if we are interested in the SALES departments that sell other items besides TOY (including those that do not sell TOY as well) we can indicate it in the following predicate:

```
SALES UNTAGGED( t₂ )
```

Similarly, one can specify various intra-relation (i.e., domain) set operations such as:

```
SALES TAGGED ( t₄ ) AND UNTAGGED ( t₂ )
SALES TAGGED ( t₁ ) OR TAGGED ( t₃ ) AND TAGGED ( t₅ ), which is identical
to TAGGED( t₁ ) OR TAGGED ( t₃t₅ ) etc.
```

Having indicated these features, we can see that they can be used in query modification. In query modification, we can append a system predicate as a conjunct to a user query. Tags can be used to represent predicates and user queries can be modified to accomplish the following:

- Enforce security, e.g., control access down to a tuple level by indicating authorizations as tagged relations, or similarly, restrict a user's access to his (her) view indicated by tags on the base relation.
- Enforce integrity by indicating various assertions with tags. Also, tags can be used to implement locking down to a tuple level.

In addition to the various uses of tags we have indicated so far, we can use tagging for implementing partitioning and/or clustering of databases. This is a direct consequence of the fact that tags indicate the result of various intra-

or inter-relation mapping operations. However, to restrict the paging of database contents into database machine to only the partition or cluster indicated by tags we need to use a VLSI data filter on the I/O path (see Figure 7.14).

8.11.3 Instruction Set for Tags

In order to support tag operations in a database system there must be instructions for tag manipulation in the data language of the system. We can list the capabilities that are necessary in the instruction set as follows:

(a) Ability to specify tagged/untagged status as a qualification predicate in the instructions.

(b) Tag tuples of a relation, on t_c bits, based on a Boolean predicate that ranges over the relation.

(c) Untag tuples of a relation in the same manner as in (b).

(d) Cross tag tuples of a target relation based on the match between join attribute values of the target tuples and the tagged tuples (from a previous mapping) in the source relation, to implement a semi-join.

(e) Implement cursoring and free variable extraction on the tagged tuples of a relation.

(f) Output capability that would read tag bits together with tuple data, for each tuple output for a qualified read instruction.

(g) Tag saving/restoring operations to implement concurrency.

(h) Test instruction to check the presence of tagged tuples in a relation.

As can be seen in these capabilities, tag conditions can be used as predicates in both the unary and binary operations. In each tag operation, we need an opcode which has to be modified by a t_c to indicate the tags to be effected. The following instructions are the examples of the tag-based opcodes in the RAP database machine language:

```
1) MARK( t_c ) [Specification: Qualification] (for capability (a) above)
2) RESET ( t_c ) [Specification: Qualification] (for capability (b))
```

Example

```
MARK ( t_3 ) [SALES: MARKED ( t_1 ) & ITEM = 'TOY']
```

3) $CROSS\_MARK(t_c)$ $[R_t: D_t \; \theta \; R_s \cdot D_s][R_s \cdot \text{MARKED}(t_c)]$ (for capability (d))

Example

```
CROSS_MARK ( t_3 ) [SALES: DEPT = LOCATION.DEPT][LOCATION.MARKED( t_1 )]
This instruction is used for semi-join.
4) READ_MARKS [Specification: Qualification] (for capability(f))
5) GET_FIRST [Specification: Qualification] (for capability (e))
```

Example

This instruction is used to process tuples serially, as opposed to the self-iterative (parallel) execution of all the other RAP instructions. At each execution, it processes the first marked tuple of the relation, resetting its mark so that next time the cursor (logically speaking) moves down to the following tuple. At each execution the specified attribute values in parentheses (following the relation name) are saved in the RAP registers as free variables. The typical use of this instruction is in processing groupings or correlations. For example, "managers managing more than ten employees" will use grouping whereas "employees earning more than their managers" uses correlation.

```
6) BC Label, RAIL_STAT( t_c ) (for capability (h))
```

where RAIL_STAT is a register storing the true/false status of the presence of tc-tagged tuples in the database. If we use the same tag bit simultaneously for more than one relation, then we must add a qualification to the above instruction as:

```
    BC Label, RAIL_STAT( t_c ).R_i to check the condition only within
    relation R_i, that is, to see if there any t_c-marked tuples in R_i.
7) SAVE_MARKS [Specification: Qualification]
RESTORE_MARKS [Specification: Qualification]
```

where specification is *Relation-name* (*attribute-name*). This instruction is needed to provide concurrency on the single copy of a relation. SAVE_MARKS saves tag bits of each tuple in a specified data attribute of the tuple. RESTORE_MARKS brings a previously saved marked bits image back into the tag area (tag attributes) of the relation. We can repeatedly save tags into different attributes and thus support multiple users on the same relation concurrently. In this manner, a tuple is used like a stack (or as a queue if order is directed) to push (SAVE_MARKS) or pop (RESTORE_MARKS) tag bits between tag and data attributes as shown in Figure 8.15.

8.11.4 Advantages and Problems Related with Tagging

Advantages.   To recapitulate the advantages we have discussed:

(a) Tags save memory and execution time. This is because in a relation we can represent 2^c mappings (i.e., horizontal fragments) without requiring that many temporary relations. Less memory space and types of relations would in turn imply less resource synchronization and recovery management on the part of the operating system, therefore, indirectly contributing to the decrease in execution time. We will save time also on database operations. In the case of an update in a tagged relation, all we have to do is a rewrite on the already accessed relation. This would save a seek time at the minimum or staging/paging of an entire relation into the database machine if we had to keep various views of a relation as separate physical relations, as in the case with classical relational algebra processing.

(b) Tags contribute to a more secure and consistent database in the sense that predicates can be enforced by tags and with the associative/parallel hardware processing capability, they can be searched and manipulated very easily. Similarly, locks can be implemented efficiently and the locking granularity can be kept as low as the tuple level.

(c) Using tags to do relational algebra operations provides an additional safeguard against lossy joins.

(d) The memory space reduction indicated in (a) would have profound implications in distributed databases because the costliest thing in distributed databases is data transmissions between sites. The less the amount of data the less will be the amount of data moved, not counting the very efficient way of doing semi-join in tagged relations.

(e) Instead of requiring large memory space to build new relations, in tagging, one needs to have a simple VLSI filter on the staging path of data before the database machine so that with different filtering criteria based on tags different views (partitions) can be obtained from the single copy of a relation.

Problems.   With regard to problems, we can state the following that may concern an implementer:

(a) In cases where a high degree of concurrency is required on a relation, one may be forced to provide multiple copies of a tagged relation. This would necessitate concurrency control mechanisms that would be identical to those used in distributed databases.

(b) To protect views, and security and integrity related tags, the tag bits must be treated as critical resources and a monitor must be associated to administer the use of each bit. We may have to provide two sets of tag bits, one set for manipulative purposes for user queries and the other for view management, integrity, and security. This would minimize the amount of critical resource management we may otherwise have to be faced with.

(c) To support permanent materialization of views constructed by a generalized semi-join we would need to support the full-join operation as an additional facility.

8.11.5 Tag Implementation

Where to keep tags?   In the software emulation of the RAP data language, the tag attributes of each relation are kept separately, from the rest of tuple data, in a mark file for efficiency purposes. In the hardware implementation however, the tag word is stored together with tuple data for two purposes:

(a) A single word per tuple is not considered a big overhead considering the additional hardware/software resources one may have to provide if tags were kept separate.

(b) In addition to the memory space, we would save the additional hardware/software resources pointed out in (a) or otherwise bring back the access path problem to some degree. This is because when the tag words and tuples are kept in separate files, they must be linked and the links must be updated in cases of updates to either or both of the files. The best alternative is to establish these links as content addressable pointers to be administered by the associative database machine hardware.

There can be the added advantage of a separately kept tag file in regard to the problem stated in item (b) of the problems section. That is, it would be easier to protect view, security, and integrity-associated tags against malicious and/or unintentional tampering by users during query operations. Accordingly, it may be worthwhile to pay the additional overhead of a separately kept tag file (at least for system related tags). However, the additional overhead we are mentioning here is negligible compared to the additionally introduced whole range of complexities associated with the classical relational algebra approach (e.g., keeping temporary and/or result relations and coping with their recovery).

Tags in disk-based architectures.   In the disk-based database machine architectures, we have the following unique characteristics:

(a) Memory is serial and uncontrollable.
(b) In-memory processing takes place on-the-fly.
(c) In relational processing a tuple is dealt with once on-the-fly.

The implication of these characteristics is that we cannot easily associate entities (e.g., record occurrences, tags), which require memory controllability and fast random access at different memory locations, if we have to use disks in an efficient manner for active (i.e., direct) database machine memory. This in turn suggests that tags should be kept with tuple data so that once a tuple enters the database machine processor, it is searched, evaluated with respect to query criterion, and manipulated before the continuous data flow brings in the next tuple to be operated. Manipulation may involve arithmetic update or retrieval of data attributes and marking or resetting of tag bits as dictated by the specific data primitive being executed.

Tags in controllable memory-based architectures.   Magnetic bubbles and RAMs are controllable memories. Although whatever will be said here would be applicable to both memories of this category, we will focus our attention on RAMs.

If we use controllable memories in the database machine main memory, we gain the flexibility of selective and fast random access of data. A tuple's tags can be accessed in one RAM access cycle without serially going over the entire tuple. RAMs provide opportunity for various optimizations. The following examples can be given from the RAM-based RAP.3 implementation:

(a) Special hardware logic is built around the RAM memory bus to bypass subcells (which implement microprocessor-based firmware) for fast processing of tags. This contributes to fast cell processing especially in the case of primitives that use only tags in their search criterion as well as subsequent manipulations.

(b) The special hardware comprises a few components because all that needs to be done is to make single bit comparisons, evaluate their Boolean, and when conditions are satisfied, either mark or reset the specified bits. No general-purpose microprocessor is needed for these simple operations.

(c) An entire relation can be scanned and processed accessing only the tag word (which contains all the tag bits) in the tuples. This is accomplished rapidly because the tuples can be scanned in the page access mode of RAMs.

A few more comments are in order regarding the use of RAMs in tag manipulation. In the present conventional way that RAMs are constructed, a great deal of power is wasted within a RAM chip. If the page mode is utilized for tag word accessing from tuples, as in RAP.3, then a new RAM chip can be manufactured that can maximize the utility of the power dissipated within a chip. One possible modification is to bring the tag match logic, which resides on the external RAM memory bus, to the internals of a chip, i.e., build in the tag match logic on the internal bus of a RAM. This equality match capability can later be applied to other general attribute value comparisons on a tuple, therefore opening a way to quasi-content addressability of RAMs. (We can therefore make progress toward a CAM chip at RAM densities.)

8.12 DATABASE MACHINE MEMORY

At this point, we want to address the issue of constructing a proper memory hierarchy for a database machine architecture. We all know that the database machine architectures of the future will perform indirect searches. This is because it will be physically impossible to fit the entire database storage in a database machine searching its contents directly. Conceptually, this corresponds to building an entire disk storage as a head-per-track cellular/associative database machine. It is not only because fixed-head disks became obsolete, but also the cost of the large number of cell processors needed for such a system would be prohibitive, let alone the varieties of engineering problems one may have to face. Therefore, we need to construct a memory hierarchy and stage data efficiently between the both ends of the hierarchy, meaning mass storage and the database machine's memory space. The following factors are important for database machine memories:

(a) Access time (data rate)

(b) True random accessibility

(c) Reliability (error rate)

(d) Cost per bit

(e) Volatility (i.e., volatile or nonvolatile)

(f) Dependence on mechanical/physical restrictions

Let us consider disks, magnetic bubbles, and RAMs. In access time or data rate, magnetic bubbles are currently two orders of magnitude (e.g., 25) times slower with respect to RAMs. Disk rates stand in the middle of the two. In true random accessibility, RAMs are natural choice; magnetic bubbles provide pseudorandom accessibility through their serial operation so that additional optimizations such as the one used in the GRACE database machine would be needed. Disks would need access path structures to implement this feature. In reliability, the technologies that are relatively new and developing may have a high error rate and, hence, must be carefully investigated. Costwise, magnetic bubbles are currently two or three times more expensive than RAMs, but their cost will decrease faster in the future. Currently, bulk RAMs (dynamic RAMs) have a price decline rate of 30% over time as opposed to 15% decline in movable head disks. At this rate, there will be a crossing point between the bulk RAM and low-capacity moving head disk prices per megabyte. At present, the price situation favors disks. These predictions do not consider the future developments in both technologies. As far as volatility is concerned, we all agree that nonvolatility is a desirable feature; however, other functionalities such as data rate, random accessibility, and dependence on mechanical/physical restrictions may force us to compromise at the expense of the former. Besides, in systems performing indirect searching, this point loses its importance. Furthermore, database integrity and recovery may force us to keep before or after images of the database machine contents. This also agrees with indirect searching and reinforces the independence on nonvolatility. In the last point, that is, dependence on mechanical/physical restrictions, we mean the following. In disks, a memory unit at the track level has insufficient capacity if we need to use it as a cell memory. The next higher logical memory unit in a disk is a cylinder. However, to make instant and continuous use of that memory is not possible because we either have to wait for as many revolutions as there are tracks in a cylinder or build a parallel readout disk with a RAM or magnetic bubble buffer memory. Working with several cells in parallel would then require us to duplicate our entire database machine memory (i.e., disk plus RAM).

In building a memory hierarchy, all the points discussed, plus many more depending on the specific implementation, have to be analyzed and weighted. Another important point in this analysis will be the magnitude of I/O bandwidth and its cost between consecutive levels of the memory hierarchy. In making the final selection, the overall cost and performance of the system must be well balanced and yet remain within the expectations.

EXERCISES

8.1. Referring to our database machine classification (Figure 8.1), discuss the effect of classification attributes (with their detailed breakdown) on performance. If performance would be the first priority in database machine selection, how would you rank these attributes?

8.2. Referring to the join performance comparison at the end of Section 8.2, produce a plot of the n versus p relationship, with the rest of the variables used as fixed parameters, that would achieve equal join performance corresponding to the cases of having a resident and nonresident database on the cellular device.

8.3. Compare the superimposed tree interconnection topology of varying degrees with the crossbar switch, assuming that the number of processors is of order of four magnitude (i.e., 10^4) and the hard database operations have high priority. Your criteria can be cost, performance, setup and communication delays, and so on.

8.4. If the relational model is taken as the base, with modifications to make it support multiple data models, write conversion algorithms that would map other data models to this base. Would these algorithms guarantee schema equivalence?

8.5. Discuss how staging, disk cache, and locality would relate to each other for optimizing database machine performance.

8.6. Discuss the relative merits of hash filtering and hash clustering that are used in CAFS and GRACE systems, respectively. Can one be preferred to the other? In doing this comparison, do *not* compare CAFS and GRACE. Assume a database machine architecture that would perform the necessary operations in each case.

8.7. Identify the problems to be solved in providing a concurrent operational environment to users. Which attributes of database machine classification are important in supporting concurrency?

8.8. Define a database machine memory hierarchy together with the necessary I/O bandwidths and means of achieving them. Does your system use commercially available hardware? How does it compare in cost to anything similar (including a new numeric computer)?

8.9. Can you suggest means of achieving uniform partitioning other than the one discussed in the chapter? What needs to be known to make your system work? Can it (they) be obtained easily and accurately?

8.10. What can you predict for the newly emerging Bloch line [Konishi, 1983] memory technology if you had to include that in the memory discussion of Section 8.12? (This memory technology can be described as a similar but more dense version of magnetic bubbles.)

8.11. Discuss possible ways of exploiting the combination of the concepts such as locality of reference, partitioning, and on-the-fly and background filtering in a database machine architecture.

8.12. Show other possible ways of exploiting parallel processing of a database machine with the use of the DYOP partitioning scheme. (Consider all binary and unary relational algebra operations and develop algorithms that would exploit both the DYOP partitioning and the database machine architecture.)

8.13. Design hardware and software architectures to deal with the tag implementation issues discussed in the problems section.

9

DATABASE MACHINE SOFTWARE

In this chapter we will discuss software aspects of database machines. Our emphasis will be on system software and software that provides machine functionalities to the outside world. Our coverage will not deal with software engineering or production and/or detailed programming aspects. We will emphasize the basic properties and their application to database machines.

9.1 SYSTEM SOFTWARE

9.1.1 Database Operating Systems

The operating systems that have existed from the time computers came into use are general purpose, supporting various basic resource management needs. Because they existed long before DBMS came about, it is natural to expect shortcomings in their services for DBMS needs. The outcome was two schools of thought. One is to build new operating systems that embody DBMS specific needs; the other is to take care of those needs within the DBMS itself, which, however, results in inefficiency. What happened so far has been the latter mainly due to practical reasons. There have been some attempts [Gray, 1978; Stonebraker, 1981] to identify distinctly DBMS needs and behavior in operating systems. Before we move to database machine specific issues, let us briefly review what DBMSs expect from an operating system.

Standard operating system functions

File and I/O Management. Among the various file management options, those suitable for DBMS are based on record management because DBMSs use record types and their instances as units of data. In record management, variable-length records, access paths based on secondary keys, and multilevel file directory management are the features suitable for DBMS.

In managing buffers, the deblocking and transfer of data from the system buffer pool to user's work area must be handled with minimum overhead. The additional cost of operating system calls and memory moves must be minimized by cutting down indirect references and transfers of data between secondary storage and the user's program. Page access and replacement strategies must be flexible and not frozen at anticipatory access and/or least-recently-used replacement strategies. This is because DBMS logical access requirements may not always match time- and order-based organizations of physical storage.

The general-purpose operating systems also have scheduling facilities for multiprogrammed and/or multitasked environments, including lock management as well as crash recovery, but none of these facilities is suitable for efficient management of DBMS requirements. DBMSs need special schedules for locking and commit protocols to ensure database consistency and varying levels of locking granularity. Also, costly task-switching overhead of general-purpose operating systems is not suitable for the nature of data-scanning activities of DBMS where search and process activities are concurrently handled within the processes of a DBMS whose coordinated activity gives service to a user. This is different from the costly operating system task-switching activity among disjoint tasks.

DBMS specific requirements. The operating system responsibilities in database security, integrity, concurrency, and recovery [Gray, 1978; Fernandez, Summers, and Wood, 1981; Ullman, 1982; Date, 1983] involve various issues that have no counterparts in general-purpose operating systems and, as opposed to primitive-level functionalities of the latter, they are at a higher level. The following major activities can be identified for a DBMS operating system:

(a) Dictionary management
(b) Data communications
(c) Database management
(d) Transaction management

Before going into further detail, we should point out the debatable issue of where the dividing line between an operating system and DBMS is to be situated. At certain points, this question cannot be clearly answered, and our suggestion is to focus, in each activity, on the common core that can be utilized by different DBMSs.

Dictionary management can be paralleled to catalogue management in operating systems (OS). However, unlike an OS utility of catalogue retrieval and update, in DBMS we require the full power of a data language (e.g., to do selection) on the dictionary.

If data communications, network message management, queueing, routing, session management, and so on are to be handled, naming conventions and device independence should be established, and message recovery must be provided.

In database management, common utilities such as record type storage and access, set processing, cursor management, and view support must be handled. To do these, record, buffer, and index structures must be managed and database security and integrity must be enforced via views.

In transaction management, transaction scheduling, locking, recovery, and logging are the basic functions. Transaction scheduling must maintain database consistency by enforcing update serializability among concurrently executing transactions. Two-phase locking and two-phase commit protocols, logging, checkpoint management, and transaction undo/redo backup are among the basic chores that must be a part of transaction management which really does not have a counterpart in standard OS. Locking and compatible access modes for various types of sharing together with deadlock handling must also be integrated with the foregoing facilities.

9.1.2 Impact of Database Machines

The OS functionalities of a DBMS have certain unique characteristics when the DBMS is to be implemented on a database machine. Database machines impact OS requirements in terms of functional modifications on existing features as well as changes in the definition of certain problems. Before we delve into discussion of such issues, let us review a database machine system, including its host GPC in regard to basic functions.

Tasks of the frontend GPC.   The following are among the basic chores of a frontend GPC:

(a) Support a communication environment with the outside world (e.g., users).

(b) Compile user queries written in a high-level data language into database machine instructions.

(c) Transfer the compiled database machine program to the database machine controller (or equivalent structure) with associated data used as operands in the format required by the controller.

(d) Initiate and/or coordinate paging, and possibly overlapped staging, of non-resident data between secondary storage and database machine memory.

(e) Support a multiprogrammed and/or multitasked environment (on a SIMD, MIMD, or other types of database machine architecture) for concurrent execution of queries from multiple users.

(f) Provide a virtual database machine memory address space in conjunction with paging/staging of item (d).

(g) Maintain various system tables for schema, subschema, record types and domains, and for data encoding/decoding.

(h) Provide routines for query analysis, data encoding/decoding, mapping between logical and physical structures, and error detection and correction.

In certain systems, the frontend and the controller hardware and software are combined into one while some others are distinctly separate. For our purposes, we will not adhere to such a distinction and assume that it is a matter of implementation. Therefore, from now on when we refer to database machine software, the implication will be the entire frontend structure controlling the collection of database machine (cell) processors. In view of the above frontend functions, the database machine software will be a collection of

(a) Application software (this is not part of system software; it is included here for completeness)
(b) DBMS software (e.g., software to implement the relational data model, relational algebra, high-level query languages and data definition language, and query optimizers)
(c) Language translators that translate the languages of (b) into the database machine instruction set
(d) Database machine nucleus
(e) Data communications manager (with the outside world and the backend; manager implies a subsystem)
(f) Table and procedure protection, dictionary management subsystem
(g) Deadlock manager
(h) Database security, integrity subsystem
(i) Multiuser concurrency subsystem
(j) Transaction manager
(k) System error detection and recovery subsystem

The tasks of the frontend that are listed in (a) through (h) are what we expect from a database machine-based DBMS operating system. These tasks are implemented in the collection of software listed with the following exceptions: (1) DBMS software of item (b) is to be divided between the parts that belong to the data manager, which is to be a part of the OS as indicated in the previous section, and the part that is specific to a DBMS. (2) We identify a special nucleus which corresponds to the kernel of a database machine-based DBMS operating system. This nucleus gathers in itself those essential tasks that are necessary for the control of the backend database machine (or collection of processors (cells)). We can group the following activities under such a nucleus:

(a) Control of database machine program execution, which consists of
   (1) Loading instructions into processors' local storage
   (2) Passing necessary parameters for instruction execution
   (3) Making necessary initializations

(4) Controlling program sequencing

(5) Monitoring status information sent from the processors

(b) Data communication management at the backend for sending data relating to the activities of (a) and receiving answers from the backend

(c) Support and administer paging/staging, virtual memory, and concurrency architecture as outlined in the frontend tasks (d), (e), and (f)

(d) System error detection and recovery

All these tasks of the nucleus will differ depending on the architectural class of the database machine (e.g., those of Chapter 7). We can design and implement a general-purpose database machine-based DBMS operating system that can be ported to various systems by just changing the nucleus pertaining to the specific database machine architecture in question. Returning to the tasks of the nucleus, steps (a), (b), and (c) will be very database machine specific with the exception that for step (c) we can exploit the theory of partitioning, concurrency, locality, and overlapped staging all of which are discussed in Chapter 8 and can be benefited by any type of architecture. We want to say a few words about task (d) that we have not discussed so far in the context of database machine hardware.

We should realize that with database machine hardware, we will be introducing new types of errors to those that we have already been accustomed to in the conventional architectures. However, as opposed to the critical nature of an error (i.e., failure) on a uniprocessor, parallel/associative architectures display a fail-soft characteristic for failures. The following are possible errors that can be encountered:

(a) Bit (or burst of bits) error during memory read and/or write in the data loop of a (cell) processor. This is important in associative hardware since data scan is critical for device operations.

(b) Loss of a (cell) processor due to
   (i) Hardware breakdown
   (ii) Power failure
   (iii) Mechanical failures

Correction of both these errors can be attempted within the processor(s) by self-diagnosis and correction hardware in the processor. Failure of correction in a processor would then activate a trap/interrupt for the frontend and pass the status information, including type of the error and address of the processor. The error routines of the nucleus would then be directed to take corrective action. In most cases, a partial or complete reloading of the cells from bulk memory would be required, utilizing the facilities of the virtual memory paging/staging system. In cases where a partial correction would be sufficient, such as in the case of updates, an interrupt from the intermittent processor hardware would require the update program to be reexecuted. Similar executions or resumptions can be called for by errors like a power disturbance. In these cases, standard error routines can be provided for reading off the faulty processors and determining severity of the error from the status information recorded by the hardware trap mechanism. Due to these and other reasons, the nucleus monitor should log every piece of information about an ongoing program (e.g., current address being executed, identification of the job).

In the following, we want to stress certain differences introduced into the operating systems concept by database machines. These differences affect both the nucleus and the outer operating system in a database machine-based DBMS operating system. Some important differences are:

Buffering. The concept of buffering is totally different in database machines for the simple reason that we no longer have a central uniprocessor to which we have to carry data repeatedly through the channel to do a database operation. In a database machine, buffering would be needed for paging/staging of device memory and passing the answers to the frontend. Unlike standard buffer management, paging/staging involves the move of very large hunks of data via block moves in hardware with no intervening software procedures. In these moves and those of passing answers to the backend, shared memory addresses, memory mapped I/O, and multiport memories minimize the required indirections and explicit data transfers.

Memory Protection. In the shared environments supported by database machines, the memory penetrations via protection violation that frequently occur in conventional systems do not occur. Unlike having the parts of a database sitting in main memory along with multiple programs which use it, in a database machine system the database is separated from the frontend address space and contained in the device memory at the backend. This facilitates enforcement of database security and integrity.

Security/Integrity. In conventional systems, it is very costly to administer low granularity of access control. This is not so with database machines since any access predicate can be stored with data items and quickly checked on the contents of memory by parallel/associative hardware without any additional overhead. The same is true also for the costly data-dependent integrity constraints. For example, to enforce the constraint that *no employee can make 50% more than his or her department's average salary* would require streaming the entire database through the channel to the CPU to evaluate the aggregate in a conventional system before the constraint can be enforced—this is very costly (i.e., time consuming). In a database machine, however, aggregates are evaluated on the contents of memory directly, and the constraints are enforced by query modification. That is, the constraints are added as conjunctive predicates to query qualification and incorporated into data selection in the same machine cycle as the original query, again without incurring any additional overhead. In a similar way, database machines eliminate costly validation of operations and data by eliminating the need for streaming the database through the CPU and by performing the required operations directly on database contents (or indirectly in the indirectly searched systems, however, the magnitude of the operation is not comparable to that of a conventional system).

All the other layers of the database machine-based DBMS OS outside of the nucleus involve standard DBMS/OS functions, some of which were discussed in Chapter 3, and the concurrency issues of distributed databases will be discussed in the next chapter. At this point, we want to emphasize the impact of database machines with respect to associative tagging and database recovery since these relate to specific architectural problems.

As also indicated in the security/integrity section, the associative tagging concept greatly simplifies integrity management. With associative tagging we can easily identify those data items that (1) are not involved in an update, (2) are eligible but not yet updated (before values), and (3) are eligible and already updated (after values) without any additional overhead. A study utilizing this concept can be found in Hong and Su [1981]. The before and after value tagging can also be utilized in crash recovery by identifying the point of update resumption by just checking the after value tags of items. This checking is done simultaneously on all items by the parallel architecture.

9.1.3 Recovery

Recovery is an important issue and may be affected by the type of database machine architecture. It simply implies restoring consistency of an entire database in the case of various errors (i.e., system crash, power failure, hardware malfunction, software error). The following are the basic concepts and terminology that are needed for any recovery architecture:

Logging.   Logging involves mirroring the entire activity that takes place during the operations of a database. In other words, we shadow every movement and change that takes place. Transaction data (i.e., source, type, user ID, time, detailed logic, qualified data items), affected database values, updated version of these values, and so on—whatever needs to be known to *redo* or *undo* an operation—is recorded in a log file.

Checkpointing.   Checkpointing refers to establishing frozen states of both database and system periodically (e.g., every five minutes) so that reconstructing a consistent state of the database need not be made by a cold start that goes back to the very beginning of things. A database checkpoint is an intermediate recording of the database state which is taken when there are no ongoing updates in a system. System checkpoint refers to the similar idea with respect to the state of the system, specifically the OS. All current addresses (soft and hard), program return points, stack, buffer, and various other structure pointers must be saved to be able to replay the entire scenario if and when necessary in the future. All the necessary information for checkpointing is obtained from the combination of existing system and database values and various log files.

Redo/Undo. At a certain point in a system where recovery is required in response to an error, we must be able to backtrack and repeat the activities (transactions) that were taking place or have already taken place. Those transactions that have already reached the commit (see next paragraph) point before the error must be repeated, i.e. redone (detail of which depends on the relative position with respect to the latest checkpoint). Those transactions that were in the process of execution, however, need to be rolled back (i.e., undone). Sometimes those actions can trigger others because of possible nestings of transactions. Figure 9.1 demonstrates these concepts. In the figure, we see the beginning and ending states of an observation which contained five transactions and, at points in time, the checkpoint and system error (e.g., a crash) which triggers recovery.

At the recovery, since T_1 was completed before the checkpoint, it need not be redone. T_2 and T_3, however, must be redone in their portions after the checkpoint (which means all of T_3). T_4 and T_5 were in progress at the time of the crash, hence they must be undone.

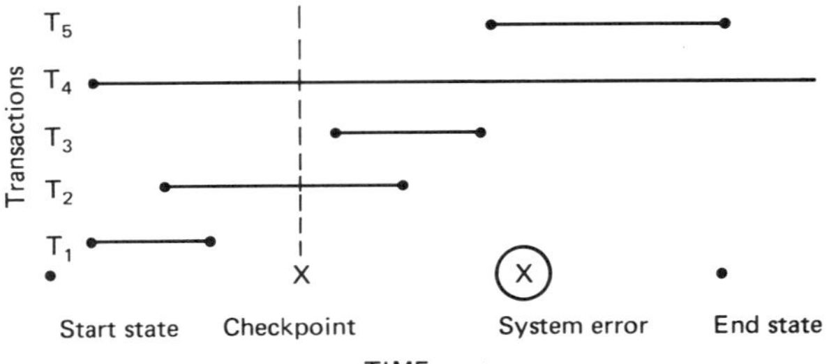

Figure 9.1 Possible transaction states.

Commit/Abort. In database updating, an update is reflected on the database after a completion point referred to as the commit point. The commit point implies that the update program has been successfully executed on all of the database (however, updates are not done directly on the database), so that whenever the commit status record and the database log are written on nonvolatile storage, the actual database update can be carried out. Contrary to this is the case where an error has occurred during the execution of the update program (or anywhere before commit has taken place) so that the transaction is aborted (canceled). A *two-phase commit* protocol is one that guarantees database consistency (as in two-phase lock) when the commit is carried out and consists of several serial message progressions. We can follow this protocol by referring to Figure 9.2. In this picture, the requestor can be interpreted as the commit manager and participants as the various resource and process managers that are involved in the chain of activities required by the update.

If there are more than two points in the process, a chain is constructed by recursively connecting requestor-participant pairs and applying the protocol to each one of them in the serial (forward and backward) progression of requests and acknowledgments. Referring to Figure 9.2(a), a success implies that all participants have agreed to commit and the process terminates after a third

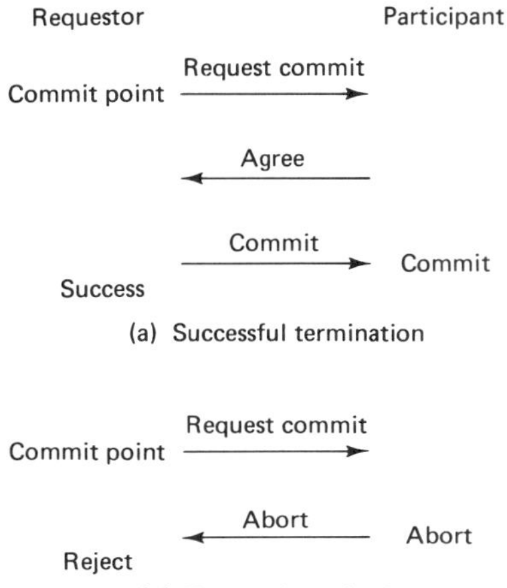

Figure 9.2 Two-phase commit protocol.

progression of *done* acknowledgments. At the point where the unanimous commit consent is received the requestor may decide to call the action off by sending an abort request instead of commit. Referring to Figure 9.2(b), the same (abort) can be caused by any one of the participants, which ends up as an abort message at the requestor.

Possible recovery strategies. As we indicated earlier, the type of a database machine's architecture affects the manner in which logs are kept, checkpoints are taken, database operations are executed, and recovery is conducted in the system. The study reported in Cardenas, Alavian, and Avizienis [1983] has introduced some terminology with respect to these activities. The study defines three scenarios with respect to update propagation

(a) Performing updates instantaneously on the qualified records that are also duplicated in a before-value (BV) file.

(b) Performing updates in a deferred fashion on a separate file that contains eligible records and merging this file, which is referred to as the after-value (AV) file, with the database at the end of the transaction.

(c) As a variant of (a), the BV file is distributed by defining three record states, which are present clean (record at the start), previous clean (duplicate copy of the former before update), and present dirty (which is the present clean after the update), and performing updates instantaneously.

In (a), insertion of records is made directly into the database, but the records become part of the database only after the transaction has successfully ended. In the case of recovery for an executing transaction, all updated records are deleted, their BV file versions are reinserted to the database, and BV is finally deleted—all these effect an undo. The BV file is also included in checkpoints to help restore or reconstruct a database.

In (b), because actions are deferred in the AV file, the AV file constitutes the part of database to which the ongoing database operations (e.g., retrieve) must be concurrently directed. At the end of a transaction, the AV file is merged with the database while the original nonupdated records are deleted. In recovery we can simply delete records in the AV file. Because there is no source for before values after the commit, a database restore would refer to the database checkpoint to obtain the before values. Once the before values are obtained, we may have to use the AV values up to the time of checkpoint (for a transaction such as T_2 in Figure 9.1) and rerun the remaining transactions.

In (c), the ongoing database operations may involve both present clean and present dirty records. In the case of modifications to these records, if the record involved is present clean it must be changed to previous clean and its duplicate must be modified at the present dirty state. As can be noticed in this operation, there are two states for a record that exist in the database: present clean and present dirty. Previous clean serves only for backup and is not kept in active database. At the end of transaction, the present dirty records are made into present clean and previous clean records are deleted. In recovery of an executing transaction, the previous cleans are changed to present clean, and present dirty records are deleted. The recovery of a terminated transaction is done as in (a) by referring to database checkpoint for the copy of before values.

As we can see from these strategies and various other similar ones we come across in the literature, the database machine architecture which employs indirect search methodology is a perfect fit for the accompanying recovery architecture based on BV or AV versions of the database. In the case of nonresident databases, however, the AV version may prove more economical, since the database operations can only be executed on the database machine holding the AV records as well as those ineligible ones in its memory. We may need additional passive memory (i.e., without processor) to store the AV values temporarily while the rest of the database is staged in for another database operation. After that the update can be resumed by reloading the database machine. In the case of the BV version, we may need an active memory (i.e., another database machine) so that both parts of the database can be processed concurrently for the concurrent operations (since the original records for the updated part would not exist in the database). If an additional database machine is not available, then the process can be iteratively executed by the use of a passive memory. However, in both the AV and BV cases, we would normally not allow another operation to interrupt an ongoing update as dictated by concurrency protocols.

9.2 DATABASE MACHINE SUPPORT OF VARIOUS PERSONALITIES

As we indicated in Chapter 1, the expectations for the role of database machines in nonnumeric processing is toward a general utility (or a general-purpose computer) in nonnumeric processing. This trend is also evident in the fifth-generation computer concept of our time. Both the low-level hardware and high-level architecture, which includes the language of the database machine/computer, should be designed to support such a general-purpose utility as the following:

(a) Formatted as well as unformatted databases: this means that both the fact retrieval (DBMS) and document retrieval must be supportable.

(b) Generalized (or multimodel) DBMS architecture: this implies support of an ANSI/SPARC-like GDBMS.

(c) Transaction processing.

(d) Distributed databases of both the homogeneous and heterogeneous type.

(e) Deductive databases: this means database machine support of knowledge-based systems.

With respect to (a), we have devoted two chapters (Chapters 12 and 13) to treating the unformatted database concept properly and developing the fundamental issues of theory as well as architecture. Item (b) will be the topic of the next major section in this chapter. In database machine support of transaction processing, we can exploit database machines in various ways. One example for this is presented in the real-time batching of transactions in the RAP.3 architecture, which was covered in Chapter 7. There we have indicated that straightforward use of database machines for processing of individual transactions resulted in overhead intensive processing with marginal benefits so that other ways of exploiting the architecture (such as real-time batching) had to be found. In regard to item (d), the next chapter will deal with distributed databases. What is left for us to discuss here is deductive databases.

9.2.1 Deductive Databases

Recently there has been a strong trend in using logic in the representation of knowledge, relational databases, and various inference mechanisms. The tool to do that would be a logic programming language and the use of logic for these roles would set a common mathematical framework. In database specific terms, it has been pointed out that there exists a "strong affinity" between relational and predicate calculi so that one can think of having a logic programming language as the common base of most nonnumeric processing activities we listed in the previous section and map this language to the language of a relational database machine. (As can be seen, the relational model—therefore, the relational database machine—has been implicitly selected not only because of the high-level and data-independent features of the relational model, but also because of the mathematical completeness and compatibility of its theory with other powerful tools such as logic.) Accordingly, a current hot research issue is how to link logic programming and the relational data model so that the power of a relational database machine can be exploited. The PROLOG [Kowalski, 1979] language has been taken as the logic programming language in most recent research. The two basic implementation problems with respect to mapping PROLOG to a relational database system are:

(a) Overriding the main memory resident internal relational database of PROLOG with a scheme where efficient, set-oriented external evaluation of that database can be made possible so that database machine use for very large database applications (and we are interested in these applications) can be introduced.

(b) Identifying a relationally complete and, at the same time, universal relational data language interface that would implement the mapping between PROLOG and this language within the context of (a).

With respect to (a), there is ongoing research, and for (b), the language-related issues we discussed in Chapter 8 are relevant. In that regard, we should remember that one needs the implementation of least fixed-point operators as well as relational completeness. In PROLOG, the least fixed-point operator concept corresponds to recursive definitions as exemplified by the following right recursive Horn clause of PROLOG [Kunifuji and Yokota, 1982]:

```
ancestor (X, Y) : parent (X, Y)
ancestor (X, Y) : parent (X, Z), ancestor (Z, Y)
parent (x₁, y₁).
      .

      .

      .

parent (xₙ, yₙ).
```

In Chapter 8 we indicated the global features for implementing the least fixed-point operations. In the remainder, we will discuss a few more language related issues.

9.2.2 High-Level Relational Language Interface

At this point we will talk about high-level query language support by database machines. One of the possible approaches to high-level language support is via logic, by using an intermediary such as the modified PROLOG [Kunifuji and Yokota, 1983]. The studies in this direction aim at natural language support via PROLOG, which is, in turn, mapped into relational database machine operations. Our emphasis here will be outside of natural language or logic. We will highlight certain concepts of building high-level relational query language interfaces and in doing so we will deal with those concepts that are not already dealt with in languages such as SQL, QBE, QUEL, and so on.

The first concept is covered by the CASDAL language [Su and Emam, 1978], which was the high-level data language of the CASSM database machine. This language had two interesting features:

(a) Formulation of queries on unnormalized relations

(b) Incorporation of general-purpose language constructs

With regard to (a), one can be within a subtable of an outer table and use a qualification predicate, which refers to "above" the subtable, or similarly, the reverse can happen and one refers to "below" the table. To demonstrate the idea assume the following unnormalized relation EMP and the two CASDAL queries that follow it:

```
EMP(NAME, SAL, BIRTHYEAR, DEPT, MGR, CHILD(NAME, BIRTHYEAR))


IN EMP: IF CHILD.NAME = 'JOE' AND CHILD.BIRTHYEAR < 1972 THEN OUTPUT
(NAME)
IN CHILD: IF NAME = 'JOE' AND BIRTHYEAR < 1972 THEN OUTPUT
(EMP.NAME)
```

In the first query, we are referring to below, CHILD subtable, and the scope takes individual attributes as separate entities so that the name JOE and the birthyear 1972 may not be referring to the same child. In the second query, however, we are within a subtable and the qualification refers to a child tuple. If we had a query *IN CHILD: IF EMP.SAL . . .* then we would be referring to above, and the priority would be on the immediate parent-child relationship. If a match cannot be found, then the entire table is used to search for the reference.

With respect to the second feature mentioned in (b), we can point out the ALGOL-like constructs of CASDAL such as

(a) Nested if-then-else

(b) Do groups

(c) Begin block

(d) Foreach (which is a variation of Repeat)

The following demonstrates some example query codes:

```
IN EMP: IF SAL >= 10000 AND SAL =< 20000 AND DEPT ≠ 'TOY'
     THEN IF COUNT < 20 THEN OUTPUT (NAME, SAL)
     ELSE (BEGIN IN LOC: IF FLOOR = 2 THEN MATCH DEPT AGAINST
     DEPT IN EMP: MARK OUTPUT (NAME) END)
```

This query outputs names and salaries of those employees whose salary is between $10,000 and $20,000 and who do not work in the Toy Department, if their count is less than 20, or otherwise outputs the name of every employee who works in a department that is located on the second floor. The second floor departments are determined by a semi-join implemented with a *MATCH* whose result marks eligible employee tuples from which the names are read out. The role of the Begin block is to isolate the scope of markings (i.e., those of outside and inside from each other). In the next query, which is

```
FOREACH (EMP.DEPT)
IN EMP: IF DEPT = X THEN OUTPUT (X, COUNT)
ENDEACH
```

the number of employees working in each department is output.

In the following, we want to mention the results of database machine supported high-level query language implementation research available for the RAP database machine. Over the years of language work on this machine, various high-level language translators were successfully implemented, which transformed the following query code to equivalent RAP code:

(a) SEQUEL to RAP translator (relational model)
(b) LSL to RAP translator (set-oriented network model)
(c) MRI to RAP translator (set-oriented hierarchical model)
(d) SYNGLISH to RAP translator (synthetic English to relational model)
(e) CASDAL to RAP translator

Among these, (e) was an interesting exercise while (d) was a pioneering research in the sense that it demonstrated the usability of the relational model and a universal language associated with it in support of natural language-based queries. Because of this, we want to demonstrate a few of the ideas of this (SYNGLISH) work. As we mentioned at the beginning, however, the proper way to go about such a work is to use artificial intelligence techniques that would utilize logic, a logic programming language, and then a relational DBMS. In passing we should point out that the experience in building the translators of (a) through (e) taught us how to build a universal relational language. Besides relational algebra operations in RAP, the use of the cursor construct, internal/ external register manipulation along with associative/parallel search and join operations enabled us to implement the least fixed-point operations.

SYNGLISH.   SYNGLISH is a very-high-level query language (and in fact a synthetic natural language) based on the semantic structure of natural English sentences. SYNGLISH was proposed for the RAP database machine [Kerschberg, Ozkarahan, and Pacheco, 1976] as a high-level language interface. In its initial form it was proposed to handle retrieval operations whose design paralleled the concepts of the Functional Data Model [Sibley and Kerschberg, 1977]. Later the language was enhanced [Ozsu and Ozkarahan, 1980] to handle updates, aggregate functions, and deletion/insertion operations. Query specification in SYNGLISH parallels the user's natural thought process and does not depend on details of the underlying logical/physical structure.

The process of analyzing the semantic structure of sentences is called predication analysis [Leech, 1974]. A predication represents a whole sentence such as an assertion, a command, or a question. Each predication may be decomposed into clusters of arguments and predicates with the provision that such predication has just one predicate. These arguments and predicates may be further analyzed into features that are the semantic description units. For example, a "woman" would have the features human, adult, and female. In the relational model, these semantic structures have relational equivalences. The predications and arguments loosely correspond to relations while the features would be attributes.

The structure of a predication is very simple. A predication consists of a predicate and zero, one, or two arguments. We can show the production rule of a predication as

$$Predication\ (PN) \longrightarrow (argument) + predicate + (argument)$$

Some examples of predication are

(a) "It is raining": has zero arguments and is called a no-place predication
(b) "John is tall": has one argument and is called a one-place predication (or attributive).
(c) "Departments supply parts": has two arguments and is called a two-place predication (or relative since it relates two arguments). The same predication can also be expressed in the passive voice, that is, *parts are supplied by departments*.

Predication analysis has a recursive structure. We can imbed predications in the sense that an argument may itself be another predication. Another way of achieving recursion is to include a predication within another in the role of a feature which is called the downgraded predication. The downgraded predications can be of qualifying or modifying type. A qualifying predication occurs within an argument and corresponds semantically to many of the adjective functions of syntax such as adjectives, relative clauses, and qualifying prepositional phrases. The modifying predication occurs within a predicate and corresponds semantically to many of the adverbial functions of syntax such as adverbs, adverbial phrases and adverbial clauses. The following are example sentences of such predications, and Figure 9.3 shows their corresponding predication structures:

A qualifying predication:
   Departments sell parts made of steel. The structure of this sentence is shown by Figure 9.3(a).

A modifying predication:
   Departments sell parts during the winter. The structure of this sentence is shown by Figure 9.3(b).

Query specification in SYNGLISH uses certain basic constructs called templates and prepositions OF, WITH (used to refer to values in the database), TO, FROM, IN, AT, ON (used in qualifying sets of values), relative pronouns WHO, THAT, WHICH, WHOSE (for linking concepts by walking from an

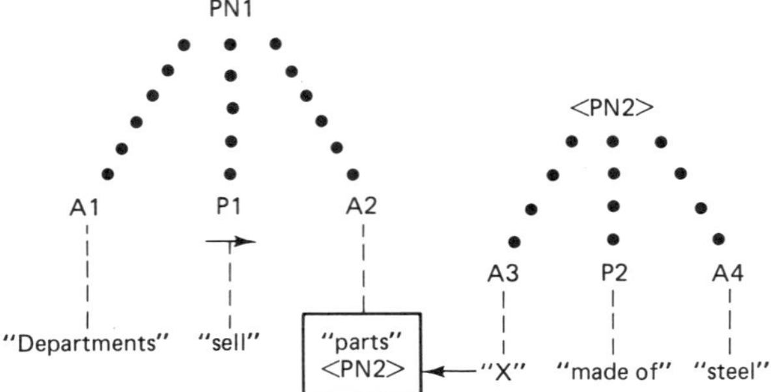

(a) Qualifying predication structure

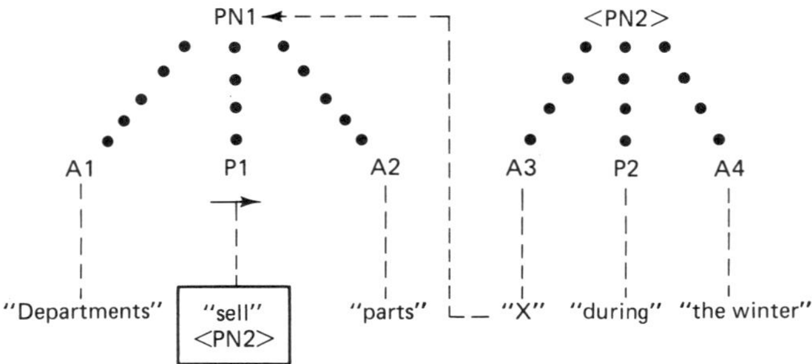

(b) Modifying predication structure

Figure 9.3 Qualifying and modifying predications.

argument set to another via a predication set), algebraic (relational) comparators, and verbal equivalents of relations. The RAP implementation of SYNGLISH was enabled because of the relational model and universal data language concepts. Every SYNGLISH template was constructed to have a SYNGLISH-to-RAP template and a few synthesis rules. The following demonstrates some example queries and corresponding SYNGLISH-to-RAP templates. The relational database used for these examples is as follows:

```
EMPLOYEE (NAME, SALARY, MGR, DEPT)
LOCATION (DEPT, FLOOR)
SALES (DEPT, ITEM, VOLUME)
SUPPLY (COMPANY, ITEM, DEPT, VOLUME)
CLASS (ITEM, TYPE)
```

The examples will start with a natural English query and will be followed by its SYNGLISH version, predication analysis, and the corresponding SYNGLISH-to-RAP templates.

Query 1. Find the names of employees in the Toy Department.

```
SYNGLISH:  WHAT ARE THE NAMES OF EMPLOYEES IN DEPARTMENT EQUAL TOY?
```

Predication analysis:

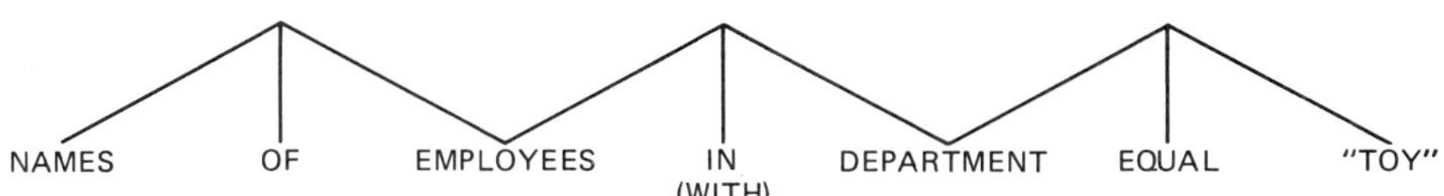

The RAP translation of this query is based on the synthesis of the SYNGLISH-to-RAP templates 1 and 2, which are

1. Attribute(s) $\rightarrow$ OF $\rightarrow$ Relation

Predication structure:

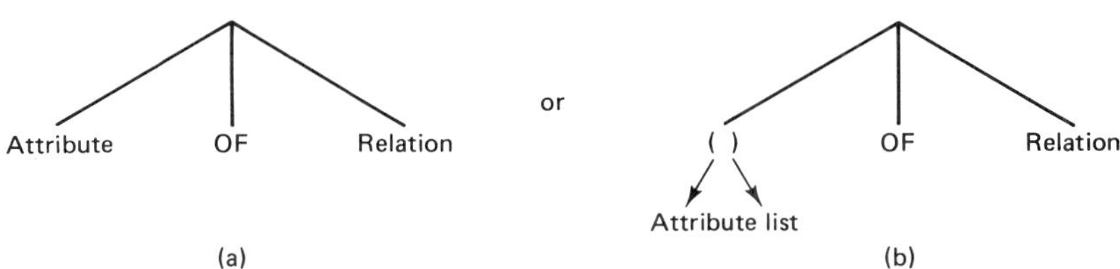

This template corresponds to a specification list in the RAP READ instruction.

2. Attribute $\rightarrow$ $\dfrac{\text{COMPARISON}}{\text{OPERATOR}}$ $\rightarrow$ value

Predication structure:

2(a). $\dfrac{\text{(SYNGLISH}}{\text{template 2)}}$ $\rightarrow$ $\dfrac{\text{AND}}{\text{(OR)}}$ $\rightarrow$ $\dfrac{\text{(SYNGLISH}}{\text{template 2)}}$ $\rightarrow$ Repeat of template 2(a)

Predication structure:

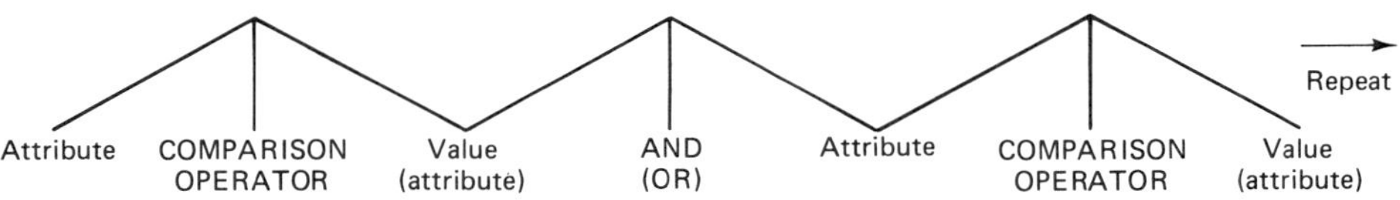

This template corresponds to a selection qualification which can be in a READ or MARK instruction.

Query 2. List the name and salary of all managers who manage more than 10 employees.

```
SYNGLISH:  WHAT ARE THE NAME ALSO SALARY OF EMPLOYEES WHO MANAGE
           MORE THAN 10 EMPLOYEES?
```

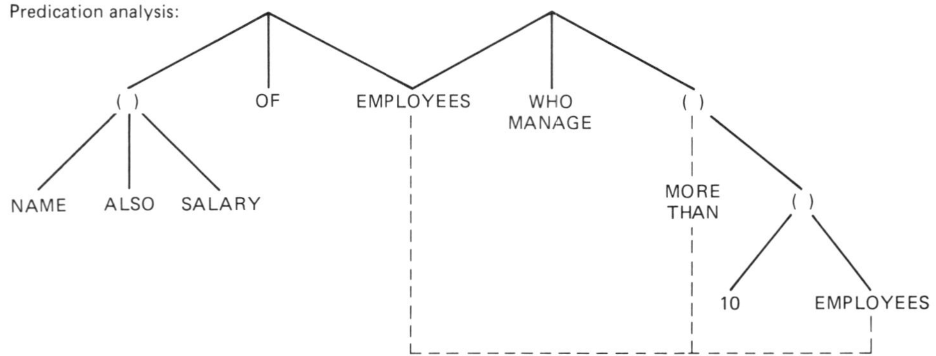

Templates 1 and 5 of the SYNGLISH-to-RAP templates (number 5 is shown below) correspond to the predication analysis. In this predication structure, the use of scalar aggregates such as SUM, COUNT, AVERAGE, MAX, MIN, and comparisons of MORE THAN, LESS THAN, and so on corresponds to a predicate. This predicate generates an implicit reference that calls for correlation operations. The keyword ALSO is used when more than one function of a set (attribute) is desired as an output. The template 5 is

$$5.\ \text{Relation 1} \rightarrow \cdots \rightarrow \text{Attribute 1} \xrightarrow[\text{(LESS THAN)}]{\text{MORE THAN}} \rightarrow \text{Value} \rightarrow \text{Relation 1}$$

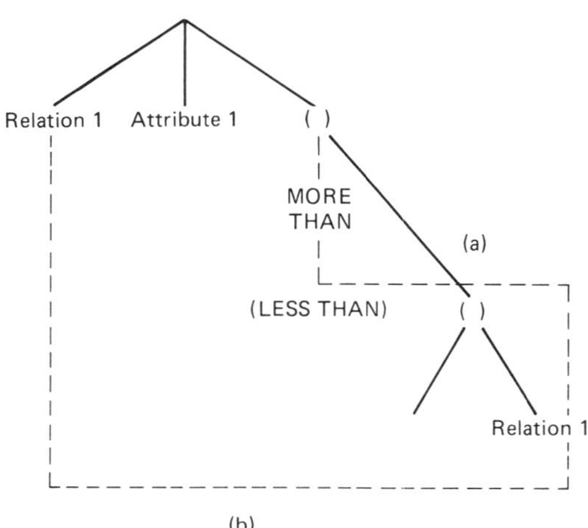

In this template pattern, (a) indicates the scalar aggregate. (a) and (b) together indicate grouping (by a free variable) operation.

Query 3. Find the names of those employees who make more than any employee in the Shoe Department.

```
SYNGLISH:  WHAT ARE THE NAMES OF EMPLOYEES WITH SALARY GREATER THAN
           ALL SALARY OF EMPLOYEES WITH DEPARTMENT EQUAL 'SHOE'?
```

Predication analysis:

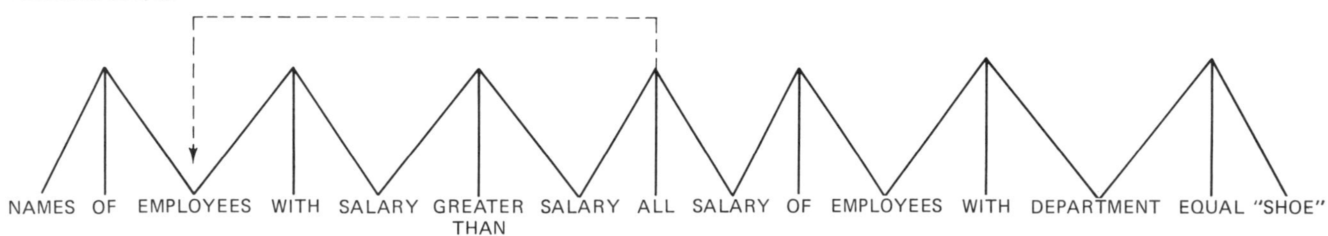

In this query, the use of quantification is introduced. Many aspects of quantification are important, since quantification is probably the most difficult facet of query languages as well as of natural English. The policy adopted in SYNGLISH is to allow a quantifier to appear immediately after a predicate (i.e., a comparison operator, a verb phrase, etc.) and immediately before a set. The type of quantification used in query 3 involves value comparison.

The corresponding SYNGLISH-to-RAP templates are the templates 1, 2, and 6 (which is shown below). As one can see from the predication analysis, the word SALARY is repeated to the left of ALL. While this allows ALL to be a predicate, it also decomposes the query into two simple subqueries. The template 6 is

$$6.\ \text{Relation} \to \cdots \to \text{Attribute 1} \to \begin{matrix} \text{COMPARISON} \\ \text{OPERATOR} \end{matrix} \to \begin{matrix} \text{ALL} \\ \text{(SOME)} \end{matrix} \to$$

$$\text{Attribute 1} \to \cdots \to \text{Relation 1}$$

Predication structure:

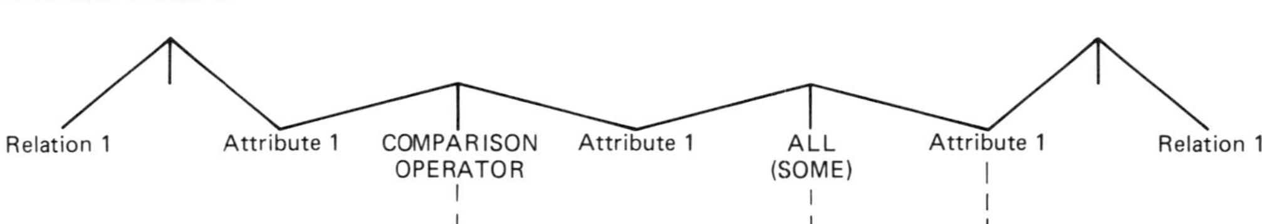

This template corresponds to the use of ALL (or SOME) in conjunction with comparison operators and makes use of aggregates. The use of this template in query specification involves quantification. The aggregate MAX or MIN is computed on Attribute 1 and the result is used in the embodying selection.

In SYNGLISH, quantification may also be used to compare sets. The quantifiers ALL, ONLY, and ONLY ALL correspond to the set operators $\supseteq$, $\subseteq$, and $=$, respectively. When strict inclusion is desired, then the keywords STRICTLY ALL and STRICTLY ONLY are used to denote $\supset$ and $\subset$, respectively. Set inequality may be denoted by NOT ONLY ALL. The following query is an example for set quantification.

Query 4. Find those companies, each of which supplies every item sold by departments on the second floor.

```
SYNGLISH:  WHAT ARE THE COMPANIES OF SUPPLY WHICH SUPPLY ALL ITEMS
           THAT ARE SOLD BY DEPARTMENTS THAT ARE LOCATED ON FLOOR
           EQUAL 2?
```

Predication analysis:

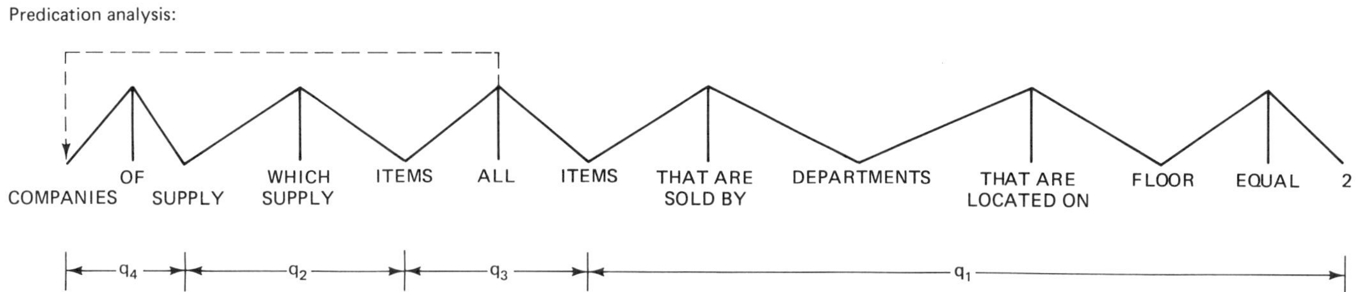

As can be seen, the query is broken into four primitive templates denoted by q_1 through q_4. Template q_1 corresponds to the join structure with a preceding selection as reflected by the SYNGLISH-to-RAP template 3. q_2 and q_3 specify quantification whose sets are the relations corresponding to the predications. In q_3, however, instead of a relation, the set is represented by the result of q_1. The corresponding SYNGLISH-to-RAP templates are 1, 2, 3, and 7 (3 and 7 are shown below).

3. Relation 1 $\rightarrow \cdots \rightarrow$ Common attribute $\rightarrow \cdots \rightarrow$ Relation 2

Predication structure:

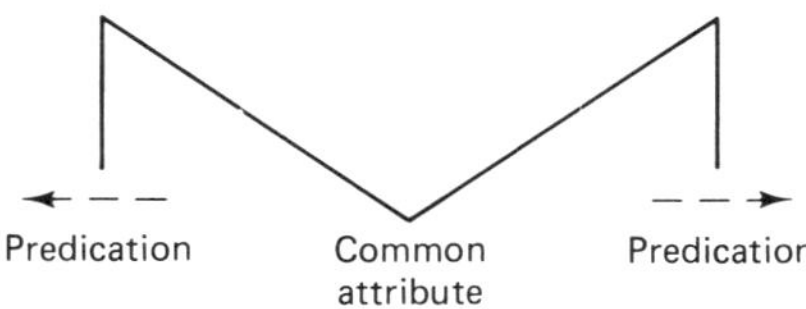

This template corresponds to an implicit join operation performed by the CROSS_MARK instruction.

7. Relation 1 $\rightarrow \dfrac{\text{ALL}}{\text{(ONLY)}} \rightarrow$ Common attribute $\rightarrow \cdots \rightarrow$ Relation 2

Predication structure:

This template involves set comparisons required by quantification. This is implemented with division and the RAP program structure for doing this was given earlier in Chapter 3. The SYNGLISH templates q_2 and q_3 establish a looping control structure for the division operation called for by the quantification. The sets compared in the division operation are those identified as a dividend partition, which is a subset of Supply tuples, and the divisor, which is the restricted subset of Sales tuples from q_1.

Query 5. Find the names of employees who work in each department that sells pens.

        SYNGLISH: WHAT ARE THE NAMES OF EMPLOYEES WITH EACH DEPARTMENT
                   THAT SELLS ITEM EQUAL PEN?

Predication analysis:

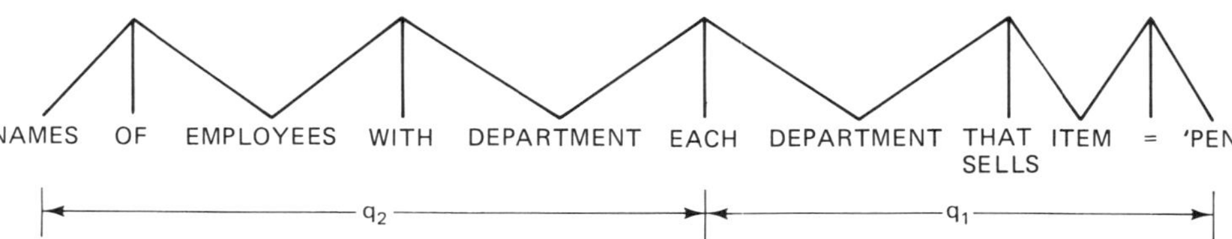

Notice that the word DEPARTMENT appears on both sides of the EACH quantifier, whose scope is the predication structure to its right (i.e., q_1). Furthermore, the quantifier EACH considers the set to its right as a set of singleton sets and creates an explicit loop. Thus each department is examined to verify if it sells pens. The corresponding SYNGLISH-to-RAP templates are 1, 2, and 8(a) (which is shown below).

8(a). Relation 1 $\rightarrow \cdots \rightarrow$ EACH $\rightarrow$ Common attribute $\rightarrow \cdots \rightarrow$ Relation 2

Predication structure:

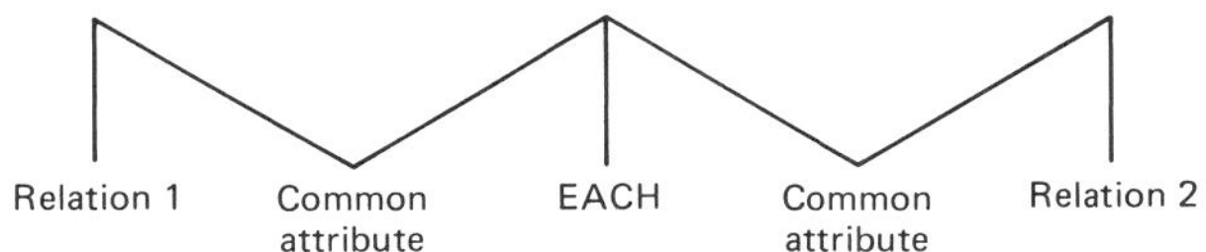

This template performs grouping without using a free variable. The quantifier EACH implies a *there exists* condition (or the existential quantifier), which is handled with the cursor operation of the GET_FIRST instruction together with a marking operation. In this way, mapping from Relation 1 into Relation 2 is realized for *each* value of the common attribute separately. This is in contrast to the cross-marking operation which maps a set between relations without further qualifying individual members of the set.

The following two example queries demonstrate the use of aggregates in query specification and qualification.

Query 6. Find the total volume of items of type A sold by the departments on the second floor.

    SYNGLISH: WHAT IS THE TOTAL VOLUME OF SALES WITH ITEM OF TYPE EQUAL
                A AND WHICH ARE SOLD BY DEPARTMENTS ON FLOOR EQUAL 2?

or

                SUM THE VOLUME OF SALES . . .

Query 7. Among all departments with total salary greater than 10^6, find those departments that sell dresses.

    SYNGLISH: WHAT ARE THE DEPARTMENTS OF SALES WITH ITEM EQUAL DRESS
                AND TOTAL SALARY MORE THAN 10^6?

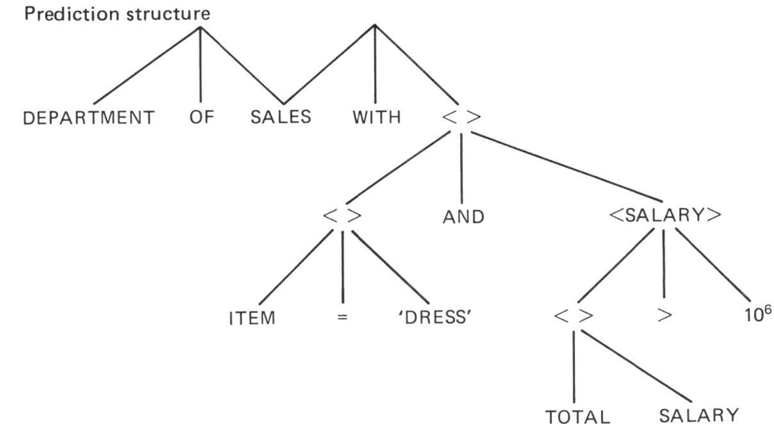

This structure involves templates 1 and 2(a) with the only exception of an aggregate as one of the terms of the latter template.

It is possible to link the context of two or more SYNGLISH queries. To do that, we use the keyword SAME, which establishes linkage, and use FIND instead of WHAT to suppress output from the inner context. Queries 8 and 9 demonstrate the concept.

Query 8. Delete from employee relation all the employees who work for Anderson's manager.

```
SYNGLISH:   FIND THE MANAGER OF EMPLOYEE WITH NAME EQUAL ANDERSON;
            DELETE FROM EMPLOYEE WITH MANAGER EQUAL SAME?
```

Query 9. Delete all tuples of the database relation Newsales involving employee Clark's department and the item Slippers.

```
SYNGLISH:   FIND DEPARTMENT OF EMPLOYEE WITH NAME EQUAL CLARK;
            DELETE FROM NEWSALES WITH DEPT EQUAL SAME AND ITEM EQUAL
            SLIPPERS?
```

9.3 MULTIMODEL DATABASE MACHINES

In this section, we will discuss two approaches, reported to date, to achieving generalized DBMS support by database machines.

9.3.1 A Database Machine for Well-Connected Relations

In Chapter 8, we mentioned a database machine for well-connected relations (WCR). A WCR is a binary relation W such that

$$(\forall x)(x \in A)(\forall y)(y \in B)(xWy)$$

That is, all elements of the first (A) and second (B) constituents of W are related (well connected). In the WCR machine, a cell track is divided into two sections and the A and B sets are stored, one set in each section. Bidirectionality is achieved by storing these A and B sets in their track sections as elementary WCRs (EWCR). An EWCR is a WCR if the first constituent has one element in it (i.e., a $1:N$ relationship between A and B, respectively). These EWCRs are doubly linked with content pointers from both track sections. Figure 9.4(a) shows a WCR, Figure 9.4(b) is an EWCR, and Figure 9.4(c) is a relation built from EWCRs.

In the network database representation the attribute relationships within a record type are the same as in n'ary relations. The relationships among record types are bidirectional through attribute relationships. The intra- and interrecord-type attribute relationships can be viewed as a collection of EWCRs whose

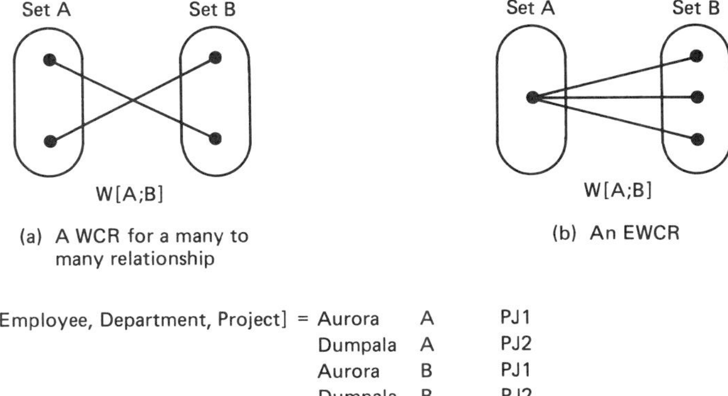

(a) A WCR for a many to
many relationship

(b) An EWCR

R[Employee, Department, Project] = Aurora   A   PJ1
                                   Dumpala   A   PJ2
                                   Aurora   B   PJ1
                                   Dumpala   B   PJ2

R[...] = W_1[Employee, Department, Project] $\cup$ W_2[Employee, Department, Project]
where W_1 and W_2 are EWCRs

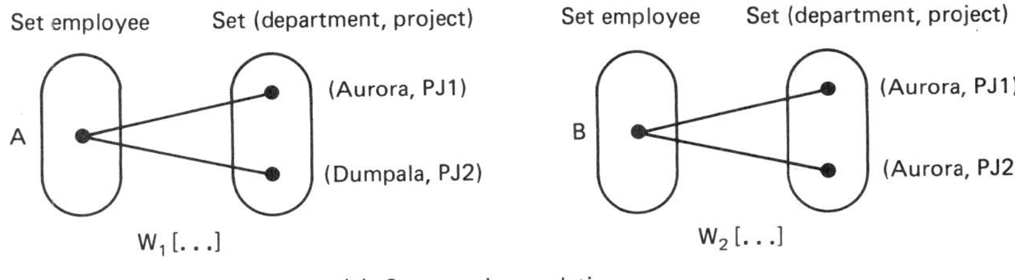

(c) Constructing a relation

Figure 9.4   WCR and EWCR constructs.

instances are formed depending on the way the attributes are partitioned (e.g., R[A,B;C,D] and R[A;B,C,D] correspond to two different partitionings).

In the WCR database machine, all three data models are supported as we just indicated for the relational and network data models above. The hierarchical data model is considered a special case of the network model.

This generalized DBMS support is demonstrated also for operations. A WCR language is designed [Aurora and Smith, 1979]. In this language, the following operations are supported: contraction (selection), projection, join, reconstitution, and set operations. The set operations are union, intersection, and difference. The join operation is divided into three types: Codd's join, brooming, and splicing. The following demonstrates the structure of the language for some selected operations:

Contraction (θ_c): $\theta_c W[A;B]$ (conditional expression) = $W_1[A;B]$.

The conditional expression is a Boolean predicate involving attributes of A and/or B. For example,

Splicing: $W[A;B](B \; \theta \; D)W_1[C;D] = W_2[A,C;B,D]$:

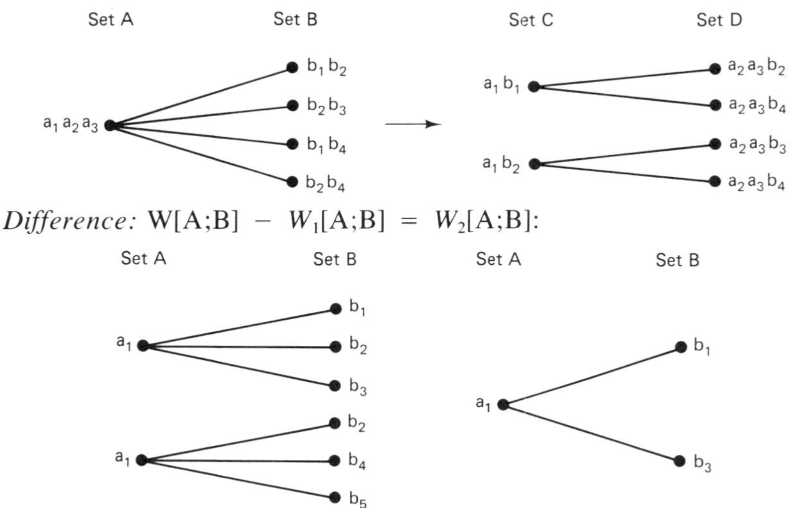

Reconstitution: $\theta_R W[A;B]$ (Attribute list) $= l[C;D] = $ A collection of EWCRs where attribute list specifies the first constituent of the collection of EWCRs, $l[C;D]$ contains the same tuples as $W[A;B]$, and $(A \cup B) = (C \cup D)$:

Difference: $W[A;B] - W_1[A;B] = W_2[A;B]$:

We can demonstrate the use of the WCR system by showing an example query and programming it on both a network database and its relational equivalent. The query states: *Find all names and SSNs of employees who earn more than their managers.* Let us assume the database whose subsection is shown in Figure 9.5.

Network query program:
Operations:

```
θ_r l₁[ ··· ](DNO, NAME, SALARY) = l₃[DNO, NAME, SSN; SALARY]
θ_r l₂[ ··· ](DNO, NAME, SALARY) = l₄[DNO, NAME, SSN; SALARY]
```

Removing managers from $l_4[\cdots]$,

```
l₄[ ··· ] − l₃[ ··· ] = l₅[DNO, NAME, SSN; SALARY]
```

Compare the salaries of employees and managers using splicing:

```
l₃[ ··· ][SALARY₃ < SALARY₅]l₅[ ··· ] =
l₆[DNO₃, NAME₃, SSN₃, DNO₅, NAME₅, SSN₅; SALARY]
```

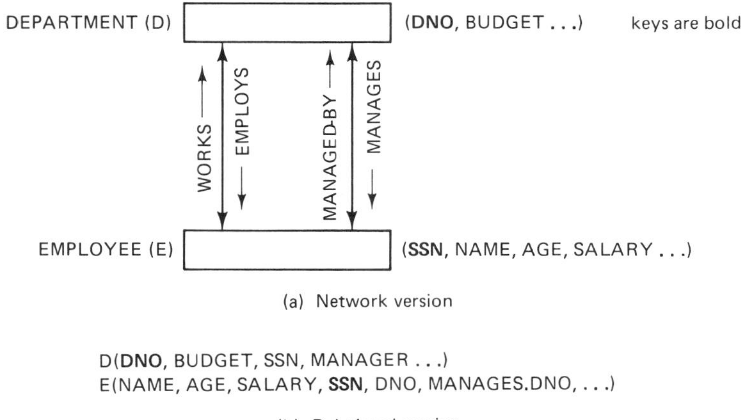

(a) Network version

D(**DNO**, BUDGET, SSN, MANAGER ...)
E(NAME, AGE, SALARY, **SSN**, DNO, MANAGES.DNO, ...)

(b) Relational version

Figure 9.5 Example database.

Select those employees whose salaries are greater than their managers' by contraction:

$$\theta_c l_6[\ \cdots\ ](DNO_3 = DNO_5) = l_7[DNO_3, NAME_3, SSN_3, DNO_5, NAME_5, SSN_5; SALARY]$$

Output employee name and SSN by projection:

$$\theta_p l_7[\ \cdots\ ](NAME_5, SALARY_5) = l_8[NAME, SSN; null]$$

Relational query program:

$$\theta_p D[MANAGER;\ \cdots](MANAGER, SSN) = l_1[D.MANAGER; D.SSN]$$
$$\theta_p E[SSN;\ \cdots\ ](SSN, NAME, SALARY) = l_2[SSN; NAME, SALARY]$$
$$l_1[D.MANAGER; D.SSN][D.SSN = SSN]l_2[SSN; NAME, SALARY] =$$
$$l_3[D.MANAGER, D.SSN; NAME, SALARY]$$
$$\theta_c l_3[\ \cdots\ ][D.MANAGER, D.SSN; NAME, SALARY](D.MANAGER = D.SSN) =$$
$$l_4[D.MANAGER; NAME, SALARY]$$
$$Q_R l_3[\ \cdots\ ](D.MANAGER, D.SSN, NAME) = l_5[D.MANAGER, D.SSN, NAME; SALARY]$$
$$\theta_R l_4[\ \cdots\ ](D.MANAGER, NAME) = l_5[D.MANAGER, NAME; SALARY]$$
$$l_5\ [\ \cdots\ ][SALARY > SALARY]\ [\ \cdots\ ] = l_7[D.MANAGER_5, D.SSN, D.MANAGER_6,$$
$NAME_5, NAME_6; SALARY]$ = employees whose salary is greater than some manager's.
$$\theta_c l_7[\ \cdots\ ](D.MANAGER_5 = D.MANAGER_6) = l_8[D.MANAGER_5, D.SSN, NAME_5,$$
$NAME_6; SALARY]$ = employees whose salary is greater than their own manager's.
$$\theta_p l_8[\ \cdots\ ](D.SNO, NAME_5) = l_9[D.SSN, NAME; null].$$

9.3.2 A Database Machine with an ANSI/SPARC GDBMS

At this point we return to the GDBMS architecture that was shown by Figure 2.2 in Chapter 2. In Chapter 8, Figure 8.3 depicted the necessary schema and operation conversions on the same architecture. This GDBMS architecture is referred to as the ANSI/SPARC model. In Section 8.5 we pointed out the necessary equivalences that must be preserved in such an architecture. Also we described the implementation version of this ANSI/SPARC model, which is an abstraction, for the RAP database machine. This implementation gave RAP the multimodel capability. The resulting RAP GDBMS architecture is shown in Figure 9.6.

As can be seen in RAP GDBMS, there is logical (at the conceptual schema) and physical (at the physical common denominator) unification within a multimodel environment so that both logical and physical data independence can be preserved, eliminating the possibility of inconsistencies at both levels.

Let us review this architecture from top to bottom. First, the operational models could not be used as the conceptual model because of the following restrictions:

(a) In the case of the relational model, there is no explicit information about the associations between relations and their mapping characteristics so that there is no guidance for navigation. Also, there are several theories as to how relations should be formed; however, rather than providing a consensus, they are wide apart in their approach and theory and, hence, confusing the designer.

(b) In the case of the hierarchical model, the total functional child-parent relationship is very restrictive for general-purpose modeling.

(c) In the case of DBTG networks, the basic structure is hierarchies, and there is the restriction of the fact that a record type cannot be both the owner and member within a set type. Therefore, both in the hierarchical and network sense, the model is restrictive for general-purpose modeling.

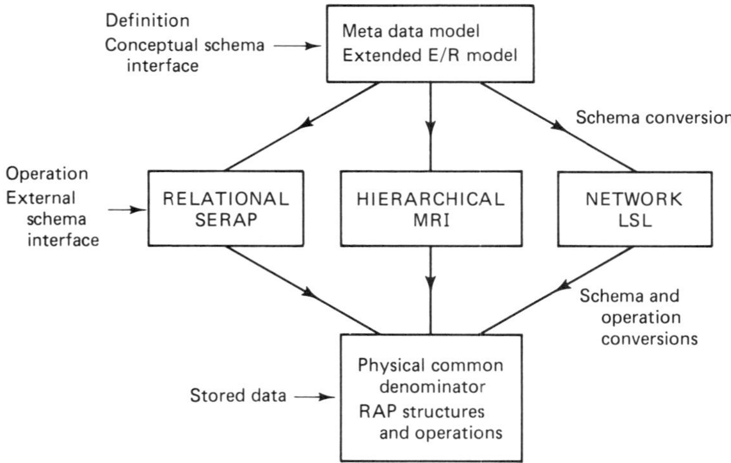

Figure 9.6   RAP GDBMS architecture.

The entity/relationship (E/R) model, which is used as the conceptual model in RAP GDBMS, explicitly indicates entities, their relationships, and the mapping properties of these relationships. Hence relationships are clearly distinguished from entities. Furthermore, relationships can be unary or k'ary ($k \geq 2$), and weak (i.e., hierarchical) relationships can be represented. Attributes of entities and relationships are defined as functions mapping entity and relationship sets to value sets. This feature clarifies certain normal form issues with respect to the relational model. The relationships and their mappings in the E/R model are easily mapped to navigational models such as hierarchies and networks.

The E/R model in RAP GDBMS has been extended with proper DDL representation to incorporate the following features:

(a) Higher-level abstractions such as aggregations and generalizations [Smith and Smith, 1977] are included in the model. (An aggregation views a relationship, such as a teaches relationship between a course entity and teacher entity as a higher-level entity (i.e., an aggregate), called class. A generalization combines the generic features of similar entities such as engineer, secretary, technician, and the like into a common entity such as employee.)

(b) Strongly connected relationships as well as functional relationships can be explicitly represented with the added DDL features.

(c) Unformatted document entities can be integrated with a conceptual schema of formatted entities, and both entity types can be interrelated via relationships. (An example of such an integrated application is given in Section 13.6.9 of Chapter 13.)

E/R to external schema transformations. The transformations from the E/R schema to each of the external interface schemas are quite straightforward and can be summarized as follows:

In conversion to relational schema, entities and information carrying and/or many-to-many relationships are made relations in a one-to-one manner (i.e., an entity or a relationship of the said type is made a relation). In the case of other (i.e., one-to-one or one-to-many noninformation carrying) relationships, explicit relation creation is not necessary since they are constructed by concatenating the keys of the related entities. Such information can be supplied to language processors of the related data languages instead of redundantly storing the data. In the relational conversion, the basic ingredients of aggregations and generalizations are converted to relations as described above; however, they are additionally identified in terms of the DDL of the external schema involved. We should remember, however, that if we related an aggregate with another aggregate or entity, the key structure of this relationship will be a key cascade; for example, if we have an aggregate related with an entity then there will be keys coming from each side, one from each entity of the aggregate if it represents a binary

($k = 2$) relationship and another key for the entity outside of the aggregate, hence a total of three keys.

In conversion to networks, since RAP GDBMS has a set-oriented network model called LSL, the conversion is exactly the same as that of the relational model with the following exceptions: each relationship is made a set type which corresponds to the link structure of LSL. If the relationship is not made an explicit relation then the link information is passed to the language translator. If, however, the relationship is made an explicit relation (i.e., information carrying or many-to-many relationship), the link structure will be straight forward, but the difference will be in the physical schema. If the network model was DBTG, however, we could not do this, because it would not allow us a set type within a many-to-many relationship without breaking it into multiple one-to-many relationships.

In the hierarchical conversion, all one-to-one or one-to-many relationships are made into one-level trees directly in such a way that the root becomes the dominant entity (i.e., the one on the one's side in the mapping). If later a leaf of one tree is a root in the other, the trees are combined to form a higher tree. This is exemplified in Figure 9.7(a).

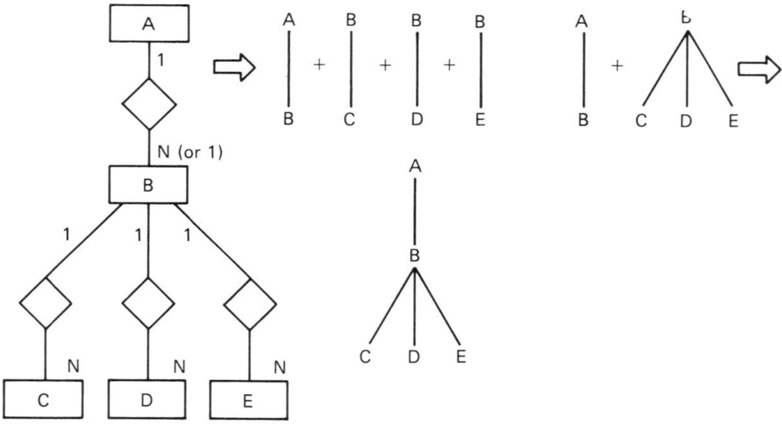

(a) Forming trees from one-to-one or one-to-many relationships

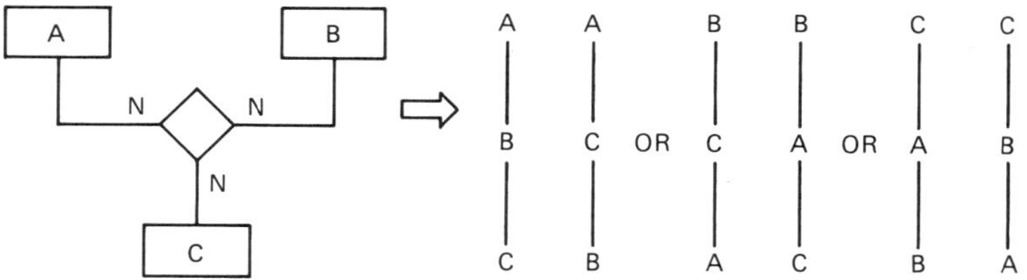

(b) Forming trees from many-to-many relationships

Figure 9.7   E/R to hierarchical model conversion.

In the case of a many-to-many relationship, we can have multiple trees by making each entity the root in turn. In the case of a k'ary many-to-many relationship we obtain a k-level tree, but it has to be duplicated several times. This is shown in Figure 9.7(b) where for a ternary relationship we had six possible tree combinations. In RAP GDBMS, the hierarchical transformation process interactively asks the user's preference and designation of the root at each level.

As we can see from the hierarchical conversion process, an E/R conceptual schema may map into a series of trees. RAP GDBMS keeps a schema relation of all the trees at the hierarchical external schema to aid in the navigation process. In GDBMS, a user can select a specific tree for proper binding with a SELECT command and then write the query on the specified tree at the external schema interface.

In conversion, all hierarchical relationships (i.e., parent-child connections) are treated as noninformation carrying links, and the necessary information is passed to the language processor without redundantly storing the concatenated keys of a child and parent.

External schema to PCS conversion.   The external schema to physical common denominator (PCS) conversion is again straightforward because the conversion is made into RAP structures which constitute the PCS. As discussed in Chapter 8, the RAP relations are actually multirelations, and the key uniqueness property of the relational model is enforced at the relational interface of external schema. This allows representation of all nodes in the hierarchical and network models as RAP relations at the PCS. Also, all link structures are explicitly stored as RAP relations. However, it is also possible to imbed the key of a node in another node as a link. In that case, the key is called a foreign key. This representation may reduce the number of joins to be executed. The mapping of the relational interface to PCS is one-to-one. The SERAP (software emulator for RAP) internally completes the mapping of PCS to stored relation files in the system of implementation (see the appendices).

The operational mappings to PCS are also straightforward. The reasons are (1) for the relational interface the RAP language is the relational data language, (2) for the hierarchical and network interfaces the MRI and LSL are set-oriented data languages which map to RAP code easily, and (3) the RAP language meets the requirements of a universal data language described in Chapter 8.

Equivalence problems.   Because E/R to PCS schema conversions have a continuous relational path and because E/R to relational mapping is one-to-one convertible per structure basis, the schema equivalence problem within RAP GDBMS reduces to the equivalences between relational and hierarchical and network systems both in schema and operations. The equivalence of relational schema and operations to those of hierarchical and network has been shown by Vassiliou and Lochovsky [1980].

Demonstration of RAP GDBMS architecture.   The RAP GDBMS software is operational on the VAX 11/780 running under the Unix operating system. Figure 9.8 shows the implemented software architecture.

According to the figure, at the user interface there is an E/R conceptual data modeling DDL facility. In addition, there is a GDBMS command set which works together with the Shell interpreter of Unix for allowing and administering all possible definition, creation, and transaction (query) running activities of an application from conceptual modeling to database creation, and use of the database at the external schema interfaces. On-line conceptual schema definition and alteration, schema transformation, database population, query editing, dictionary display, and database backup facilities are provided. Security declaration and enforcement are handled within GDBMS. Triggers, assertions, and views can be declared and stored in the data dictionary and enforced during query operations. All functions are carried out with the help of interactive editing and escape facilities to Unix. After an E/R schema is created and stored, user can request, with a transform instruction, automatic conversion of that schema to one of an equivalent hierarchical (MRI), or network (LSL) schema with a resulting display of the transformed schema in the associated DDL. Conversion into relational schema is automatic and nonoptional.

The data dictionary is itself a relational database containing relations called

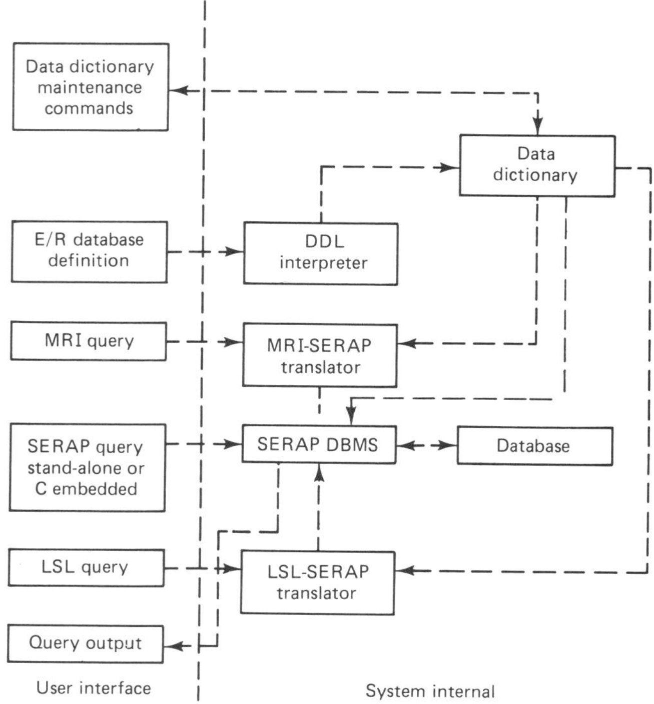

Figure 9.8 RAP GDBMS software architecture.

Schema, Node, Domain, Attribute, Member, Association, User, Access, Record type, Hierarchical tree, Tree root, View table, and View attribute.

After a database is defined and created and the schemas are refined, the user can enter queries in three languages or run precompiled application programs (which can also be imbedded in the C language at the relational interface) during the operation of the system. In what follows, we will demonstrate a subset of GDBMS usage to give an idea of generalized GDBMS to the reader.

Let us first list the syntax description of the extended E/R notation as follows:

```
DOMAIN domain_name domain_type ( domain_size )
    [ (lower_range : upper_range ) ];
ENTITY entity_name ( tuple_no ) ([*] atr_name [ :
    domain_name], . . . );
```

where

    tuple_no: estimated number of entities in the entity set.

    * :   key attribute indicator.

    domain_name: domain into which the attribute is mapped. If omitted, domain with the same name as the attribute is assumed.

```
AGGREGATE [agr_name] rel_name;
```

where

    agr_name: the relationship with *rel_name* is declared as an aggregate entity and optionally assigned an aggregate name.

```
RELATIONSHIP [*] rel_name ( tuple_no ) ([*] entity_name
    [ / rolename ] : mapping: functionality, . . .
    [ ; atr_name [ : domain_name ] , . . . ] );
```

where

    * :   weak relationship if specified before rel_name.

    * :   weak entity if specified before entity_name.

    rolename: declares the role played by the entity especially in a unary relationship. If omitted, the corresponding key attribute of the related entity will be used.

    mapping: either ONE or any string to indicate 'many' mapping.

    functionality: either TOTAL or PARTIAL. TOTAL means every key attribute of the related entity must exist in the relationship. (In the case of a nonfunctional mapping the keyword TOTAL signifies strong connectivity.)

    atr_name: attribute of the relationship itself; it must not be a key attribute.

```
GENERIC generic_name ( tuple_no )
      ( member_name, . . . ;
      [*] atr_name [ : domain_name ], . . . );
```

where

generic_name :   generic entity name.

tuple_no: estimated number of entities.

member_name :   member entity name.

* :   key attribute indicator.

domain_name: If omitted, the domain with the same name as the attribute
will be the default.

```
DOCUMENT document_name (tuple_no)
      ([*][*] atr_name [ : domain_name ], . . . );
```

where

document_name: document entity name.

tuple_no: estimated number of tuples for the document entity (relation).

*:   key attribute.

**:   document attribute indicator.

domain_name: If omitted, the domain with the same name as the attribute
will be the default.

In the foregoing notation, role name refers to a unary relationship, that is, a relationship involving a single entity playing different roles, such as part being subpart or superpart or employee being manager or subordinate. The complete syntax description of the GDBMS command set as well as BNF definition of E/R DDL are given in Appendix II.

The E/R diagram of Figure 9.9(a) conveys the conceptual model of an application. In the diagram, attributes are listed by the entities and relationships and keys are in bold type. In the figure we see a *class* aggregate which defines the *teach* relationship as a higher-level entity which can then be involved in other relationships such as *enroll*. We also see that every student must be admitted, as indicated by its strong connectivity to the *admit* relationship. A student may have a spouse whose existence in the database depends upon student, that is, via a weak relationship (or spouse is a weak entity). As can be seen, the student entity is represented as a generalization of different types of students (in_state, foreign, etc.). Figure 9.9(b) shows the E/R declaration DDL for creating the conceptual schema of the *test* GDBMS.

In Figure 9.10(a), we see the commands that create and save the test database (the E/R schema was edited in the regist.sch file). The following two DB commands show the loading of the data for entities and relationships into the database. Figure 9.10(b) shows a snapshot for creating the relational external

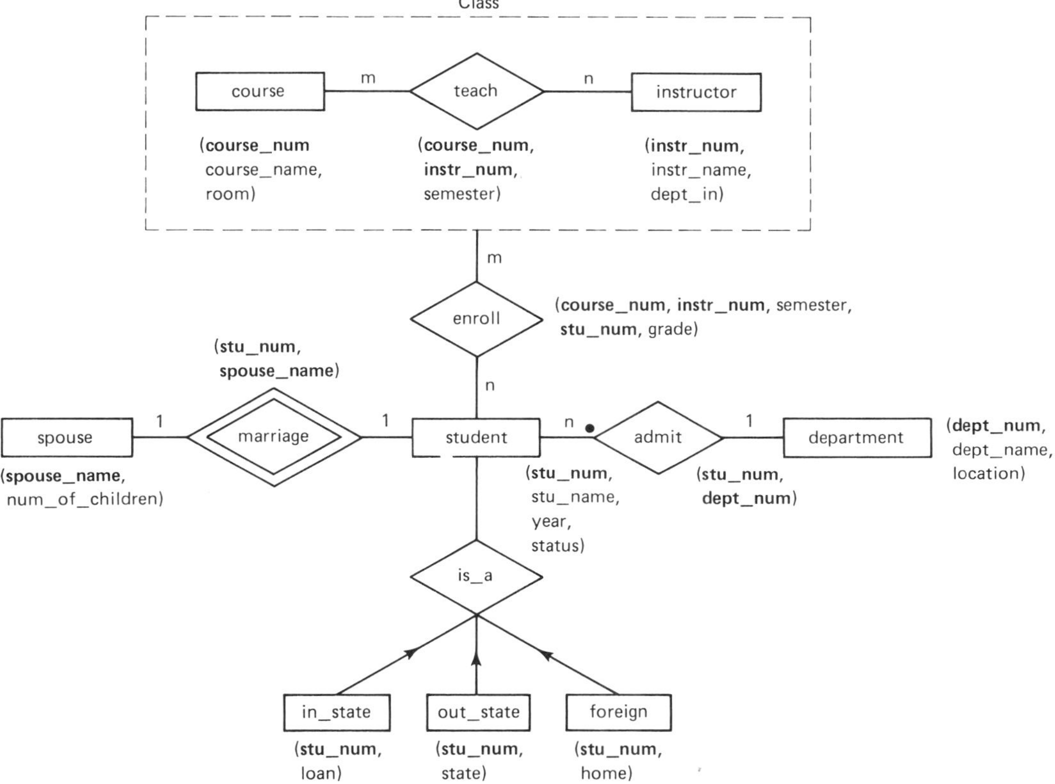

(a) E/R diagram of the test database

Figure 9.9   An example conceptual schema.

schema in terms of RAP relations. Figure 9.10(c) shows a snapshot for creating the network external schema in terms of the LSL model. Figure 9.10(d) shows the snapshot for the hierarchical external schema conversion in terms of the MRI structures. The multidimensionality of the relationships around STUDENT and its many-to-many relationship with the CLASS aggregate brings alternatives to the types of trees that can be formed. Even though the dialogue is not shown, the user requested both ways of the structure (i.e., STUDENT being both the root and the leaf). The associated DDL listing following that dialogue shows the result of the schema conversions.

In Figure 9.11, we see some example transaction executions at the three available interfaces. In the hierarchical and network interfaces, the operational mappings that are expressed in terms of the equivalent RAP codes of PCS are also shown. Figure 9.11(a) is a relational query, Figure 9.11(b) is an LSL query, and Figure 9.11(c) shows an MRI query.

```
/*DOMAIN definition*/

DOMAIN      number        INTEGER (5) (0 : 99999);
DOMAIN      name          LITERAL (30);
DOMAIN      char_array    LITERAL (10);
DOMAIN      id_num        LITERAL (9);
DOMAIN      grades        LITERAL (1);


/*ENTITY definition*/

ENTITY      course (10)            (*course_num    : number,
                                     course_name   : name,
                                     room          : char_array);

ENTITY      instructor (5)         (*instr_num     : id_num,
                                     instr_name    : name,
                                     dept_in       : name);

ENTITY      department (5)         (*dept_num      : number,
                                     dept_name     : name,
                                     location      : char_array);

ENTITY      spouse (5)             (*spouse_name      : name,
                                     num_of_children  : number);

ENTITY      in_state (4)           (*stu_num   : id_num,
                                     loan       : number);

ENTITY      out_state (3)          (*stu_num   : id_num,
                                     state      : char_array);

ENTITY      foreign (3)            (*stu_num   : id_num,
                                     home       : char_array);


/*GENERALIZATION definition*/

GENERIC     student (10)           (in_state, out_state, foreign;
                                    *stu_num   : id_num,
                                     stu_name  : name,
                                     year      : char_array,
                                     status    : char_array);


/*RELATIONSHIP definition*/

RELATIONSHIP                 teach (15)    (course : many : partial,
                                            instructor : many : partial;
                                            semester : char_array);

RELATIONSHIP                 enroll (20)   (student : many : partial,
                                            teach : many : partial;
                                            grade : grades);

RELATIONSHIP                 admit (10)    (student : many : total,
                                            department : one : partial);

RELATIONSHIP                 *marriage (5) (student : one : partial,
                                            *spouse : one : partial);


/*AGGREGATION definition*/

AGGREGATE                    class teach;
```

(b) E/R DDL declaration for the test database

Figure 9.9   (continued)

Generalized DBMS — Unix/C version

gdbms>**create** test regist.sch
gdbms>**save** test
gdbms>**db a** admit admit.dat
gdbms>**db a** course course.dat

(a) Conceptual schema and database creation

gdbms>**display serap**
relation [**course** (10)

	course_num	: integer, 4, KEY
	course_name	: literal, 30
	room	: literal, 10]

relation [**in_state** (4)

| | stu_num | : literal, 9, KEY |
| | loan | : integer, 4] |

relation [**student** (10)

	stu_num	: literal, 9, KEY
	stu_name	: literal, 30
	year	: literal, 10
	status	: literal, 10]

relation [**teach** (15)

	course_num	: integer, 4, KEY
	instr_num	: literal, 9, KEY
	semester	: literal, 10]

(b) Relational interface

gdbms>**transform**
gdbms>**display lsl**
    Define Record **spouse**
        Attribute spouse_name literal 30
        Attribute num_of_children integer 5
    Define Record **in_state**
        Attribute stu_num literal 9
        Attribute loan integer 5
    Define Record **student**
        Attribute stu_num literal 9
        Attribute stu_name literal 30
        Attribute year literal 10
        Attribute status literal 10
    Define Link **marriage**
        Owner Record student
        Member Record spouse

(c) Network interface (partial listing)

gdbms>**display** mri
    Define Tree tree1
        Record **student** Root
           Attribute stu_num literal 9 KEY
           Attribute stu_name literal 30
           Attribute year literal 10
           Attribute status literal 10
        Record **spouse** Parent = student
           Attribute spouse_name literal 30 KEY
           Attribute num_of_children integer 5
        Record **in_state** Parent = student
           Attribute stu_num literal 9 KEY
           Attribute loan integer 5
        Record **out_state** Parent = student
           Attribute stu_num literal 9 KEY
           Attribute status literal 10
        Record **foreign** Parent = student
           Attribute stu_num literal 9 KEY
           Attribute home literal 10
    Define Tree enroll1
        Record **student** Root
           Attribute stu_num literal 9 KEY
           Attribute stu_name literal 30
           Attribute year literal 10
           Attribute status literal 10
        Record **teach** Parent = student
           Attribute course_num integer 5 KEY
           Attribute instr_num literal 9 KEY
           Attribute semester literal 10
    Define Tree enroll 2
        Record **teach** Root
           Attribute course_num integer 5 KEY
           Attribute instr_num literal 9 KEY
           Attribute semester literal 10
        Record **student** Parent = teach
           Attribute stu_num literal 9 KEY
           Attribute stu_name literal 30
           Attribute year literal 10
           Attribute status literal 10

(d) Hierarchical interface (partial listing)

Figure 9.10 Creation of database and schema transformations.

```
% cat serap.q
/*Find the names of students who do not come from 'ohio'*/

mark (t1) [ out_state    : state <> 'ohio' ]
cross_mark (t2) [ student    : stu_num = out_state.stu_num ] [ mked (t1) ]
read [ student (stu_name)    : mked (t2) ]
reset (t1) [ out_state ]
reset (t2) [ student ]
% gdbms

Generalized DBMS — Unix/C  version

gdbms>use test
gdbms>serap

SERAP STANDALONE MONITOR unix version 2

serap>$input serap.q
serap>$go
(followed by output from database)
```

(a) Relational transaction execution

```
gdbms>lsl
Lsl>input lsl.q;
Lsl>continue or quit file input (type y/n) ? y
Lsl>

/*Find the course names of classes completed with grade "A" by
   the student whose id is "987654321"*/

select student
where student.stu_num = '987654321'
link with enroll to enroll
select enroll
where enroll.grade = 'A'
link with teach to course
select course
keep course.course_name;

/*RAP Translation*/

mark (t1) [ student    : stu_num = '987654321' ]
cross_mark (t2) [ enroll    : stu_num = student.stu_num ] [ mked (t1) ]
mark (t3) [ enroll    : grade = 'A' & mked (t2) ]
cross_mark (t4) [ teach    : course_num = enroll.course_num ] [ mked (t3) ]
cross_mark (t5) [ course    : course_num = teach.course_num ] [ mked (t4) ]
read [ course (course_name)    : mked (t5) ]
reset (t5) [ course ]
reset (t1) [ student ]
reset (t4) [ teach ]
reset (t2t3) [ enroll ]
```

(b) Transaction execution at the network interface

Figure 9.11   Transaction executions at the external schemas.

```
gdbms>mri
Mri>SELECT tree 1;
Mri>input mri.q;
Mri>continue or quit file  input (type y/n) ? y

/*Find the ids of students who have a loan more than 600*/

get student.stu_num
where in_state.loan>= 600;

/*RAP Translation:*/

mark (t1) [ in_state    : loan>= 600 ]
cross_mark (t2) [ student    : stu_num = in_state.stu_num ] [ mked (t1) ]
read [ student (stu_num)    : mked (t2) ]
reset (t1) [ in_state ]
reset (t2) [ student ]
```

(c) Transaction execution at the hierarchical interface

Figure 9.11   (*continued*)

The reader can find more material and examples of the RAP, LSL, and MRI languages in Chapter 3, Appendix I, and Appendix II. Appendix II also contains syntaxes of the GDBMS commands and the E/R data definition language.

EXERCISES

9.1. In the chapter, we pointed out that a general-purpose database machine operating system can be built provided that the nucleus is made variable for each database machine. Define the functions that should remain outside of the nucleus for such a general-purpose OS. In doing this you should target a sophisticated OS.

9.2. Define the details of the nucleus functions for each database machine category exemplified by the machines in Figure 8.1.

9.3. What relationship is there, if any, between a fail-soft database machine and each of the following:
(a) Degree of parallellism
(b) Type of concurrent architecture (e.g., MISD, MIMD)

9.4. Discuss the fail-softness of an in-stream pipeline architecture relative to a cellular associative system which does support MIMD processing.

9.5. Considering the ANSI/SPARC GDBMS architecture, can you suggest a different implementation architecture than that of RAP GDBMS? If you have, how did you relate it to the structures and operations of the physical database?

9.6. Write SYNGLISH queries for the following requests (assume the same database used in the chapter):
(a) What are the names of employees who work in departments which sell items of type A?
(b) Find the items of type A sold by departments on the second floor.

9.7. Show the predication analysis for each of the queries of Exercise 9.6. Also, determine the corresponding SYNGLISH-to-RAP templates for each of these queries. You can complete the question by writing the full RAP program code for the queries.

9.8. Based on the following conceptual schema, in E/R notation, of the database called BASEOPS and the associated domain definitions, write a GDBMS definition using the E/R DDL given in the chapter and Appendix II.

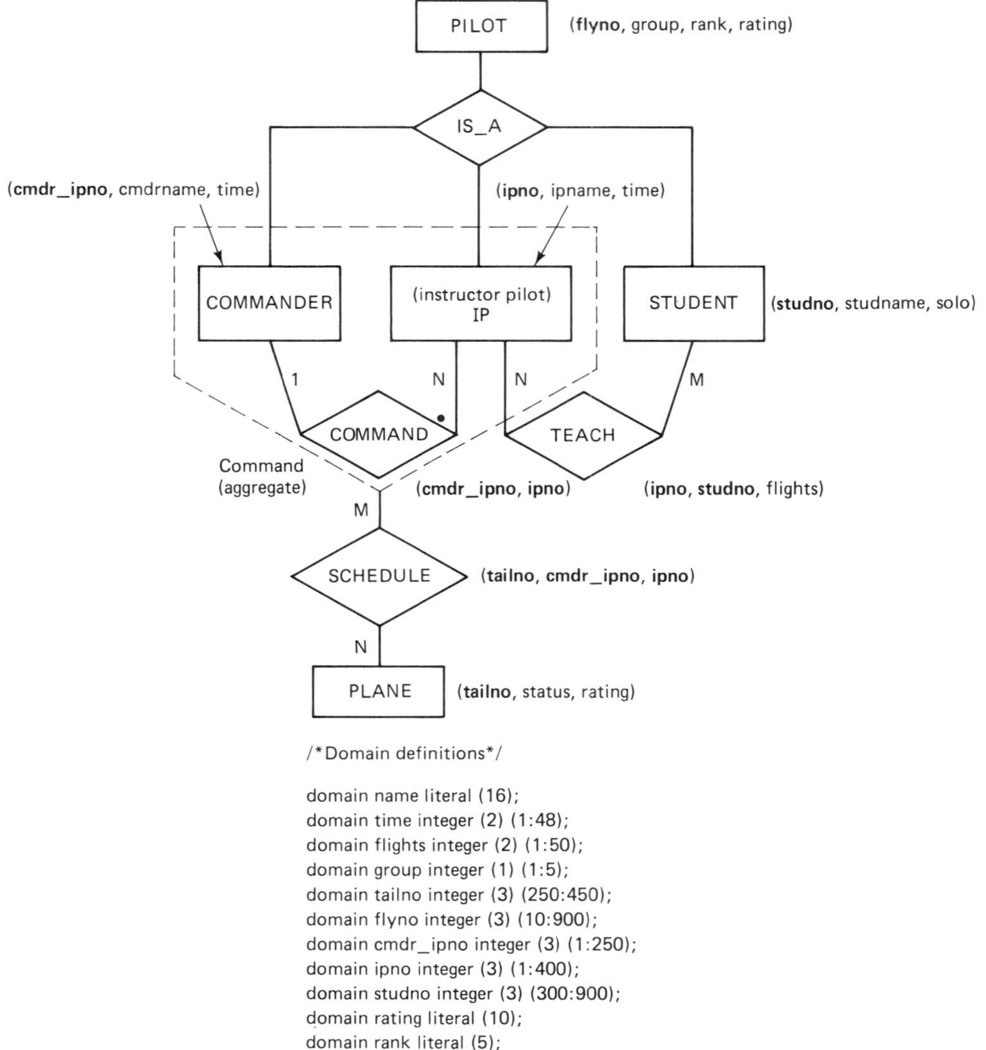


```
/*Domain definitions*/

domain name literal (16);
domain time integer (2) (1:48);
domain flights integer (2) (1:50);
domain group integer (1) (1:5);
domain tailno integer (3) (250:450);
domain flyno integer (3) (10:900);
domain cmdr_ipno integer (3) (1:250);
domain ipno integer (3) (1:400);
domain studno integer (3) (300:900);
domain rating literal (10);
domain rank literal (5);
```

All names take values from the name domain, and the domains of the attributes "status" and "solo" are rating and flights, respectively. In the generic entities, all keys come from the flyno domain.

9.9. Using the conceptual schema of Exercise 9.8 in the E/R model, transform (manually) this schema into each of the external schemas [i.e., relational (RAP), network (LSL), and hierarchical (MRI)].

9.10. Based on the external schemas you obtained in Exercise 9.9, write query programs (in their respective languages) for each external interface for the following transactions:

For the relational interface: "Find the ips who have less than the average experience of group 3."

For the hierarchical interface:

(a) "Find the students who have flown 20 or more flights."

(b) With the pilot tree "find the students who have flown 30 or more flights."

For the network interface:

(a) "Find the students who have flown less than 15 flights."

(b) "Find the ips in group 3 whose experience is less than the average."

(c) "Find the ip and student names in group 4."

(d) "Find the names of the ips and students in group 2."

(e) "Find the names of the ips assigned to group 2."

10

DISTRIBUTED DATABASES

In this chapter we will first review some important concepts of distributed databases. These concepts are centered around providing various forms of transparencies, query execution, and concurrency with updates. We will then discuss homogeneous and heterogeneous distributed database systems.

10.1 CENTRALIZED VERSUS DECENTRALIZED DBMS

DBMSs came into existence with their advantage and superiority which were due to their centralization as opposed to unrelatability, disjointedness, inconsistency, and duplication of traditional file systems. As databases grew large in size, especially in the case of multilocational organizations, economies of scale started introducing new design considerations. If we consider a centralized DBMS kept at a node of a communication network where different branches of an organization access the database, the resulting picture when database size and transaction volume grow will be

- High network traffic
- Poor fault tolerance (less reliability)
- Poor performance
- Costly development

Although in a centralized database enforcing security/integrity and maintaining consistency in updates are easier, the problems just listed pose serious concerns.

In view of these problems, we can consider decentralization as an alternative. Decentralization will introduce and/or enable the following:

- Higher degree of sharing due to higher availability through load distribution
- Better local usage and autonomy while remote access requests are accommodated
- Less cost
- Easy manageability

Small computers at the nodes of a network will be less costly, both to acquire and to build a system on (by connecting small pieces) than a gigantic effort on a gigantic mainframe.

Figure 10.1 displays the logical basis of a distributed database (DDB).

As seen in the figure, if we assume a banking system on a network, a person's activity with the local bank at CITY-A constitutes the geographical locality of reference. If that person travels to CITY-B and needs to withdraw funds at a branch of the person's bank at that city, then there will be a remote access to the bank of the customer at CITY-A to verify the account. On the other hand, the majority of the headquarter's accesses will be remote, on the global network level, for MIS (management information system) reporting. There can also be clusters of activity among the banks of a region for the purpose of a mission, such as a special credit line for the farmers of the region, which constitute a functional locality of reference among the sites of the "clique."

The DDB network we see in Figure 10.1 is a user resource network. Underneath this network there is another network, called the communications subnetwork, which provides the communication facility among the nodes of the user resource network. In the user resource network, a distributed database is a

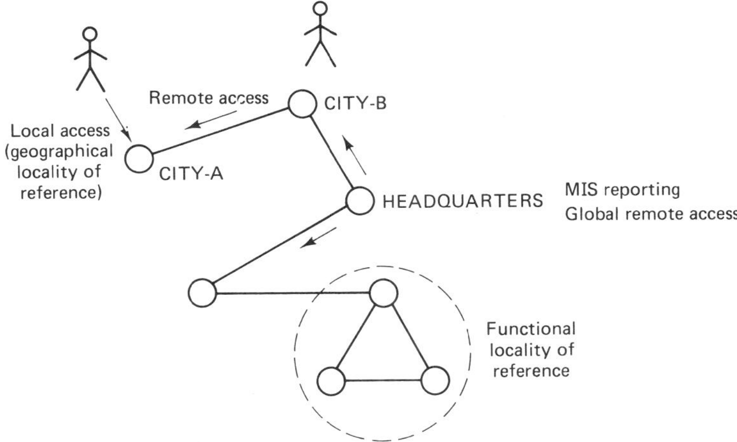

Figure 10.1   Access patterns of a distributed database.

logical whole of the locally and/or remotely (i.e., distributed) stored data. We can make the following definition: a distributed database is a set of files (relations) stored in different nodes of an information network which are logically related either by functional relations or by being multiple copies of the same file in such a way as to constitute a unique collection of data.

10.2 PROBLEMS TO BE SOLVED IN A DDB

The first task in a DDB is how to allocate (or distribute) data on the network. The following data allocation strategies are possible:

(a) Every site keeps and uses its own data but makes it available for remote accesses. This is called a *partitioned* allocation.
(b) Some data that are frequently needed also by remote sites (the terms node and site will be used interchangeably) may be duplicated at those sites. This will result in a *partially duplicated* allocation.
(c) All data can be duplicated at every site resulting in a *fully duplicated* allocation.
(d) Some files can be split (fragmented) horizontally (i.e., subset of records) and/or vertically [i.e., subset of fields (attributes)] and stored at different sites resulting in a *fragmented* allocation together with unfragmented data which can be in any form of (a) through (c).
(e) The fragments can also be duplicated as in (b) or (c).

Having left the allocation issue behind us, we can now elaborate on the problems of DDB. The problems of a DDB include the problems of a centralized DBMS; however, new problems are introduced due to decentralization. These problems include

(a) How to model networkwide data? That is, we must have a network conceptual schema to provide a global unified view of networkwide data. This will provide *logical transparency* to the users of a DDB so that when writing their queries at a terminal they will think that the entire database is under their fingertips (as if centralized).
(b) A scheme to locate the required data on the network, without the user directing the query to the site where data are actually stored, is needed to provide *location transparency* of data.
(c) A DDB can be of a homogeneous or heterogeneous type in two respects: (i) computer hardware and (ii) DBMS software. It is relatively easy to deal with (i) if the sites run the same (i.e., homogeneous) DBMS; however, in the case of (ii), we need bidirectional transformations between different data structures and languages of a heterogeneous DBMS. This will need a *local mapping transparency* in a DDB.

(d) Directory management. To provide all the transparencies outlined, a DDB should have multiple directories or dictionaries with appropriate management software.

(e) A DDB needs a different query execution methodology from a centralized DBMS, because parts of a query must be executed where data reside and subresults must be passed between sites in a coordinated fashion.

(f) A DDB needs a complicated concurrency control mechanism which would also provide update synchronization for data consistency.

(g) A data distribution and allocation, including fragmentation, strategy and methodology must be one of the basic facilities in a DDB.

Example 10.1

Assume a DDB that is stored across three sites and has the following network schema consisting of the following three relations:

```
EMPLOYEE (EMPNO, DEPTNO, NAME, SALARY, MGR)
DEPT (DIVISION#, DEPTNO, PROJECT#)
LOCATION (DIVISION#,CITY)
```

Distribution strategy 1.   Assume site #1 processes payroll and taxes and, therefore, needs EMPNO, NAME, and SALARY. Site #2 is headquarters and keeps a full copy of the EMPLOYEE, DEPT, and LOCATION relations. Site #3 is a manufacturing location and keeps only those employee records (tuples) that correspond to employees earning less than $45,000 in full and only the department and manager numbers of the other employees. We can show the allocation pictorially as in Figure 10.2.

As can be seen, while EMP1 is obtained by projection, EMP3 is obtained by selection followed by projection. Whether wanted or not, every relation contains the key, EMPNO, in order to reconstruct the full tuples correctly (that is, EMP3 is added with EMPNO besides DEPTNO and MGR). While site #2 stores relations in full, site #1 stores a vertical fragment of EMPLOYEE and site #3 stores both the horizontal and mixed fragments of EMPLOYEE. The mixed fragment corresponds to the first horizontal and then vertical splitting of EMPLOYEE.

Distribution strategy 2.   Assume this time that the schema of site #1 holds the same EMP1 fragment, but only those fragmented EMPLOYEE tuples of the employees who work in division #5. Accordingly the modified schema predicate of site #1 will be

```
EMP1 ← (EMPLOYEE * (DEPT[DIVISION# = 5][DEPTNO]))[EMPNO, NAME,
SALARY]
```

The effects of an update in both distribution strategies will be *dramatic* when the update involves those attributes that are the basis of the schema predicate. The system must then perform data migration to preserve schema consistency. This is done by inserting new tuples (fragments) into the proper places and deleting the old tuples (fragments) in all the affected parts of the database.

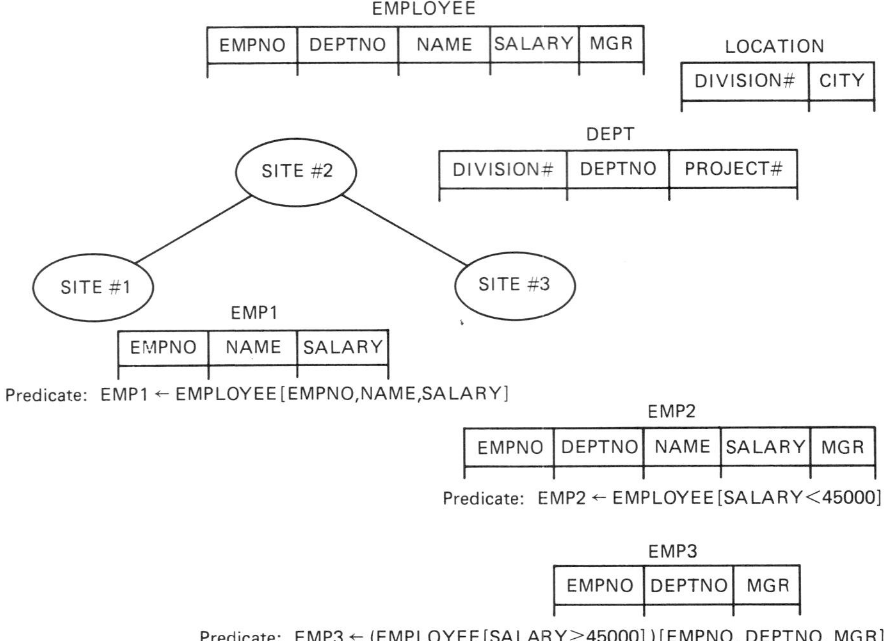

Predicate: EMP1 ← EMPLOYEE[EMPNO,NAME,SALARY]

Predicate: EMP2 ← EMPLOYEE[SALARY<45000]

Predicate: EMP3 ← (EMPLOYEE[SALARY≥45000])[EMPNO, DEPTNO, MGR]

Figure 10.2 An example data fragmentation and allocation.

In the following, we will first deal with the problems (e) and (f) of the preceding list. The other issues such as data modeling and heterogeneous DDBs will be seen within the context of studies made for a database machine.

10.3 *QUERY EXECUTION IN DDBs*

There are several issues to be covered in query execution in a DDB. Because data are distributed and may also be fragmented, the queries written by users who see the global (network) view (i.e., as if the database is centralized) would have to be converted into a form which considers data distribution as well as fragmentation. Distribution and fragmentation call for query decomposition because an entire query program cannot be executed at a single site if that site does not store all the needed data. In addition, because we need to move full relations (files) and/or results of intermediate operations to complete the execution of a program, we need optimizations of the following to minimize the costly operation of data transmission:

(a) Optimize, first of all, a given query expression (program).

(b) Given an optimized query, optimize its execution strategy by considering the required data moves.

Although (a) and (b) may be interrelated and sometimes handled together, we will take them one step at a time to deal with the concepts individually.

10.3.1 Query Decomposition

Let us assume that we are given the query: *what are the names of employees who work in the departments of the division located at New York?* which is based on the database of Example 10.1. Assuming that each relation is stored at a different site, a brute force execution strategy would be to move all the relations to the query site and process the query as a centralized database query. However, such an approach would be costly and not use the methodology of DDB query execution. In what follows, we will uncover some important concepts of DDB query execution methodology.

Let us write the relational calculus expression for this query in the following:

```
RANGE OF (E, D, L) IS (EMPLOYEE, DEPT, LOCATION)
RETRIEVE W(E.NAME)          WHERE  (L. CITY = 'NEW YORK')
                            AND    (L.DIVISION# = D.DIVISION#)
                            AND    (D.DEPTNO = E.DEPTNO)
```

As can be seen there are three (tuple) variables in this multivariable query. To simplify this query, we have to "peel off" or detach single-variable queries from this query until all queries are simple or single-variable queries. To do this, we start with a handle which corresponds to a reduction, which is most typically represented by a selection, to do the following detachment:

```
Q → original query

   ┌──► Q₁     RANGE OF L IS LOCATION
   │           RETRIEVE TEMP (L.DIVISION#) WHERE L.CITY = 'NEW YORK'
   │
   └──► Q₂     RANGE OF (E, D, L) IS (EMPLOYEE, DEPT, TEMP)
   ┊           RETRIEVE W(E.NAME)      WHERE  (L.DIVISION# =
   └──► Q₃                             D.DIVISION#)
                                       AND    (D. DEPTNO = E.DEPTNO)
```

In a similar way, we can detach another single-variable query from Q_2 until what remains is a single-variable query. What makes these detachments possible is the fact that we are breaking a join operation into multiple selections (as many as there are tuples in the source relation, i.e., the relation being detached) by substituting join attribute values from the tuples, selected by the initial reduction operation, into the join predicate. This process is referred to as *tuple substitution*. The process is recursively repeated for all source tuples and the new target is the union of individual reductions obtained from substituted tuples. The use of this process in a DDB is that each relation can be reduced at its site, and selected attribute values (or tuples if a full join is required) are sent to the site of the target for the next join in the chain. (Actually, we have not come to the move decisions yet; for simplicity let us assume that the reduced size of the source relation is less than the size of the target relation.)

10.3.2 Query Optimization

We will now discuss the "before" aspects of the query processing methodology of DDBs. This means: How does one come up with a query in the first place? Coming up with a query will be understood as a finalized query expression after optimization. Query optimization, especially in terms of relational algebra, has been extensively discussed in the literature. The reader is referred to the text [Ullman, 1982]. The idea behind query optimization lies in permuting order of operations within a query, identifying common subexpressions and executing them only once, and translating and optimizing the query with respect to fragments. Suppose we have the query discussed in the previous section. There are various ways of executing that query. Among them, let us consider the top-down order (i.e., Q_1 executed first, then Q_2, Q_3) and the bottom-up order (i.e., Q_3 then Q_2 and then Q_1). Both these executions will yield the desired result; however, the order of the top-down approach in this example will be less costly in terms of both execution time and amount of data moved. This is because we start with a reducer (i.e., a selection) and we can then use a semi-join which needs to transmit only the join attribute values between relations. In the latter order of execution, however, we need to carry EMPLOYEE·NAME all the way in the process of joins.

In query optimization, we start by drawing the query (parse) tree for the query expression. In this tree, leaves correspond to relations and internal nodes (including the root) correspond to relational algebra operations. Let us assume the query whose parse tree is shown in Figure 10.3—What are the names of employees who work in project #5—and furthermore assume that the corresponding relational algebra expression is programmed as

```
((EMPLOYEE * DEPT)[PROJECT#  =  5])  [NAME]
```

As we know from Chapter 2, the order of operations in this expression is from left to right. If parenthesized, this corresponds to innermost to outermost nesting

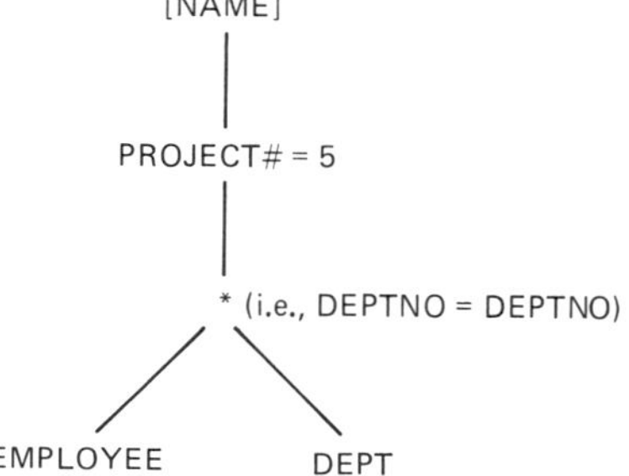

Figure 10.3 Query parse tree.

of subexpressions. The given order, which corresponds to the bottom-up execution of the query tree, is not necessarily the best in terms of cost of local processing (i.e., carrying out node operations) and data moves. Data moves correspond to branches of outdegree of more than one in the query tree for relations that are not stored at the same site. This query can be optimized by considering the following two equivalence relationships:

Idempotence (or cascading) of unary operations shows that a given unary operation can be decomposed and the executions of the decomposed pieces can be cascaded. For example,

$$R[A_1 \theta c_1 \ AND \ A_2 \theta c_2] \equiv (R[A_1 \theta c_1])[A_2 \theta c_2]$$

Distributivity of unary operations with respect to binary operations can be commuted over the operands of the binary operation. For example,

$$(R*S)[A\theta c] \equiv (R[A\theta c])*(S[A\theta c])$$

where R and S are relations, As are attributes, cs are operands, and θ is a comparison operator.

As we said earlier, performing reductions as soon as possible would lead to optimum query execution. This corresponds to pushing the unary operations in the tree toward the leaves. (Unary operations are the selection and projection operations that reduce data (relation) horizontally and vertically, respectively.) The foregoing stated equivalences would enable us to do that in our example. That is, we can distribute selection with respect to natural join (*) and cascade projection into the needed components and then distribute it as done in selection. The projection, because it will now start from the bottom, should carry the join attribute from the respective relations along with the attribute to be output which is NAME. The resulting query tree is shown in Figure 10.4.

We can include the fragmentation shown in Figure 10.2 for the EMPLOYEE relation in the example tree of Figure 10.4. To do that, we have to replace the EMPLOYEE node in the tree with the reconstruction schema of EMPLOYEE from its fragments. This corresponds to a subtree where vertical fragments are

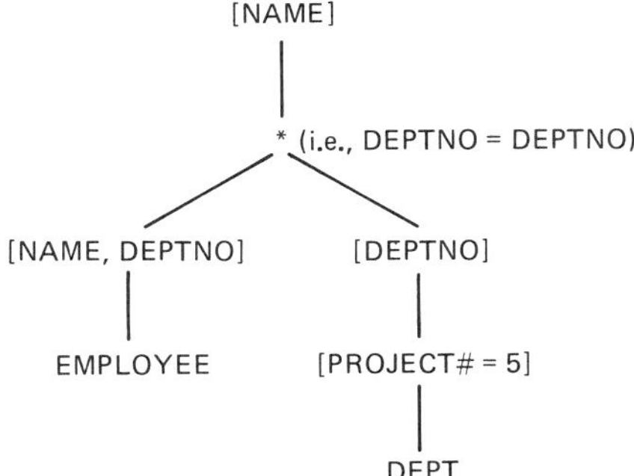

Figure 10.4 Manipulated query parse tree.

combined via join, and horizontal fragments are constructed via union. The leaves are indicated by fragments themselves in the form of their fragmentation predicates. Before we do this, let us simplify the picture somewhat as follows. (1) Let us assume that EMPLOYEE does not exist at site #2 so that EMP_1, EMP_2, and EMP_3 constitute its fragments. (2) Further, assume that the query is modified to retrieve the names of employees working in project# = 5 and earning greater than or equal to 45,000. Figure 10.5(a) shows the corresponding query tree while Figure 10.5(b) shows its optimized version. In Figure 10.5(c), we replaced EMPLOYEE with its reconstruction schema. We can now distribute

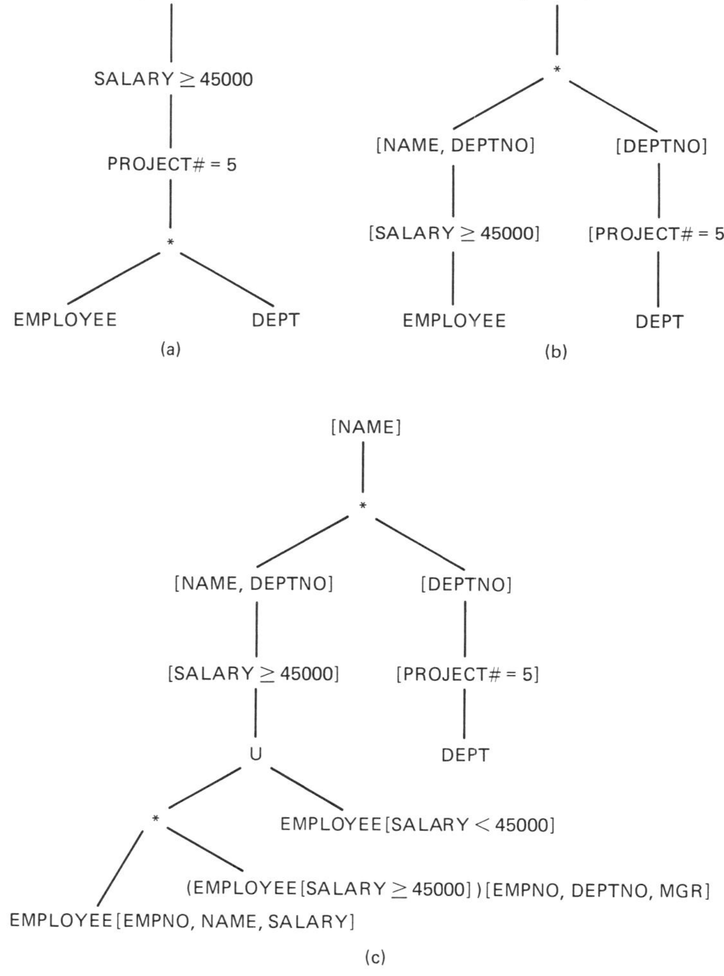

Figure 10.5   Including fragments in the query tree.

the projection and selection on the EMPLOYEE subtree with respect to union in Figure 10.5(c).

   Figure 10.6(a) shows the result. The selection can be further distributed with respect to join. Figure 10.6(b) is the simplified (optimized) version of the query tree of Figure 10.6(a). This is done by eliminating the empty set of the union. This empty set is the right subtree of the union and corresponds to a contradiction (i.e., SALARY $\geq$ 45000 AND SALARY $<$ 45000). Also, the selection on the right subtree of the lower join has a common selection (i.e., SALARY $\geq$ 45000) that need not be executed twice.

10.3.3 Semi-Joins

Semi-joins [Bernstein and Chiu, 1981] are generally a more efficient way of doing joins. Before we go any farther, let us review the equivalence between join and semi-join. If R[AθB]S is a join of R and S over A and B, respectively, with respect to a θ comparison operator, then it can be equivalently processed by semi-join as follows,

$$R[A\theta B]S \equiv ((S[B])[[B\theta A]]R)[A\theta B]S$$

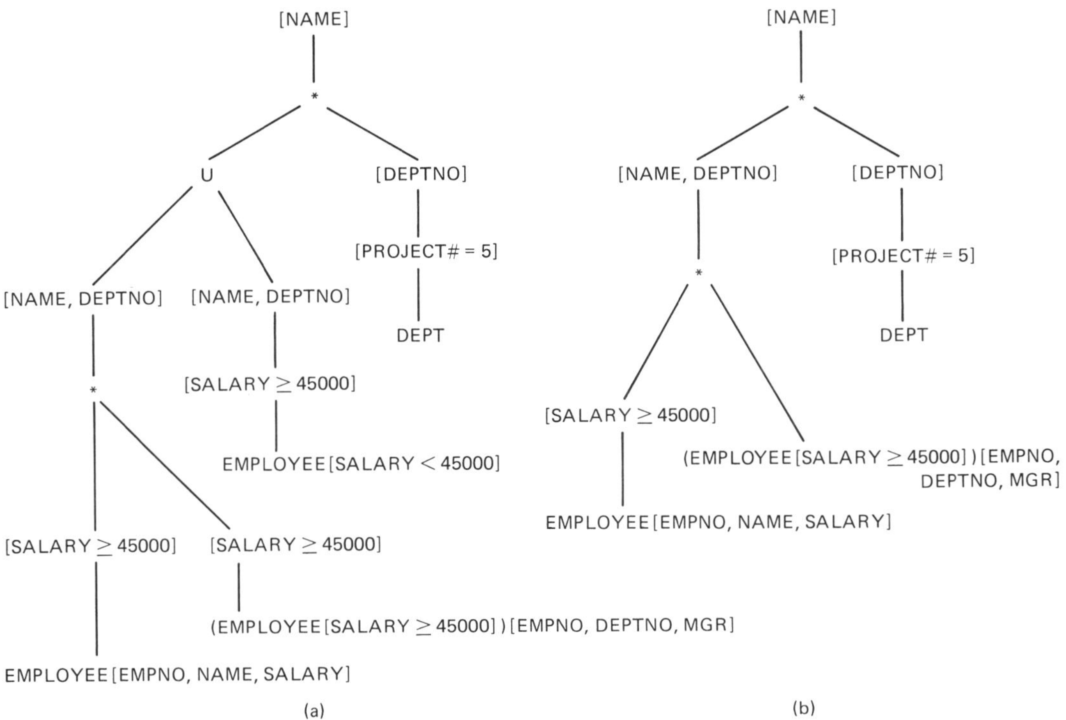

Figure 10.6 Simplifying the query tree.

where double brackets signify semi-join. According to this expression, join is equivalent to the projection of S on the join attribute and the semi-join of the result with R over A and the join of the result back with the S relation. The point of all this is that we have broken join into primitive operations (i.e., projection and semi-join) so that the project and semi-join operations provide reduction at an earlier stage. In fact, most queries are answerable via semi-join so that a full join after the semi-join is not necessary. It has been proven that for any query whose join graph is acyclic there will be at least one way to reduce any relation in the graph (this is not necessarily true for cyclic graphs (queries)) [Bernstein and Chiu, 1981; Ozsoyoglu and Yu, 1980]. (A join graph is a graph whose nodes are relations and whose edges represent joins between the relations.)

The sequence of joins (we can use the term semi-join from now on) becomes very important in distributed databases when selectivities of join operations and sizes, and locations of relations are taken into account. A query program must be optimized with respect to both reductions at the sites and data moves between the sites.

There have been several studies in the direction of finding better join strategies for DDB processing. In the study made for SDD-1 [Wong, 1977], all local processing is performed first, and an initial distribution strategy (i.e., move combination) is obtained by moving all relations to a single site. Then by a standard hill-climbing optimization technique, better solutions are sought. Each move decision in the initial feasible solution is examined and replaced by two move decisions, with local processing in between, whenever the total cost of these two move decisions is smaller than the cost of the original move decision. This algorithm is a "greedy" one, because it finds local minimums and does not guarantee to find the global optimum solution.

In the study of Chu and Hurley [1982], a cost model of query processing is developed. The optimum processing strategy is found by calculating the total cost of processing the query for each possible operation sequence. After this, the distribution strategy with minimum cost is selected.

In the studies of Hevner and Yao [1979] and Aper, Hevner, and Yao [1983], an algorithm is developed for finding optimum distribution strategies for simple queries in which the relations referred to contain only a single-join attribute. After performing all possible local processes, the relations are ordered from smallest to largest in size. An initial feasible solution is obtained by moving all the relations to the query site. This initial distribution strategy is improved by examining the relations starting from the smallest in size. For a relation, each of the preceding relations is examined to see whether moving it to the site of the concerned relation leads to a reduction in the total move cost. If the move decision results in a reduction in the total move cost, that move decision is incorporated in the distribution strategy. The study also finds "improved" dis-tribution strategies in the case of general (as opposed to simple query described above) queries.

The work done by Chiu and Ho [1980] presents optimization techniques specific to semi-join queries. The study addresses the problem of finding the least costly semi-join expression to solve a tree query. A dynamic programming-based optimization algorithm is used. A mathematical equation represents the set of all intermediate relations that can be reached from the original semi-join. The algorithm then recursively calculates the minimum cost on the basis of the dynamic optimization algorithm.

In the work of Epstein, Stonebraker, and Wong [1978], a query is first broken into its irreducible components. The best processing strategy is then searched for each irreducible component. In the next step, the sites which will participate in the process and the relations to be left fragmented are determined. Portions of the fragmented relations are moved to balance processing during the execution of the component queries. This process is called "equalizing." As this algorithm tries to optimize each step individually and does not find the overall optimum, it is a greedy algorithm.

Another study reported in Yu and Chang [1983] considers fragmented relations in a DDB and semi-joins. A query processing algorithm is optimized by the use of redundant relations to reduce communication costs by avoiding unnecessary processing, by discarding "useless" semi-joins, and by replacing poor semi-joins with better ones, or negative (anti) semi-joins. In the remainder, we will discuss execution time optimizations of a predetermined operation sequence.

10.3.4 Move Decisions

In this section, we will assume a determined operation sequence, and based on the query execution graph, an optimum overall semi-join move strategy will be determined. The query execution graph will show the execution steps (i.e., subqueries) and the join sequences in a data flow pattern.

In the move decisions, for each subquery there are two alternatives: either move the source relation to the target relation's site, or vice versa. If all the relations are at different sites, moving the smallest relation for each subquery minimizes the data movement. However, if some of the required relations for a query are at the same site, this decision may have to be modified. The move decisions should be made by considering their effect on later decisions for the succeeding subqueries. An heuristic developed [Tansel, 1981] for such move decisions draws a family of decision trees based on the explicit enumeration of all possible move decisions. A tree is drawn for each entering node of the query graph and for each critical node. All possible distribution strategies are considered and their total move costs are calculated. Among these, the distribution strategy with the lowest total move cost is selected and execution locations of the subqueries are determined accordingly.

In the decision tree construction, a binary tree is prepared for an entering or a critical node. A critical node is the junction of smaller decision trees. The binary decision involves either moving the source or target relation to the place of the other. When a subquery (an entering or a critical node) is picked, it is made the root of the tree and the decision branches are drawn from it. The total move cost is calculated. This includes the cost of all previous move decisions on the path leading to this subquery and the cost of move decisions made for the subquery itself. If there is more than one move decision on the path leading to this subquery, a total move cost is calculated for each alternative. Let us consider the query execution graph of Figure 10.7. In this graph, each node is a subquery of the original undecomposed (global) query. The numbers in parentheses indicate the sizes of the relations. The size of a target relation includes the join and output attributes whereas that of the source includes the size of only the join attribute. As can be seen on the graph, the sizes of the target relations are reduced by the incoming selectivity of the source relations after the semi-join.

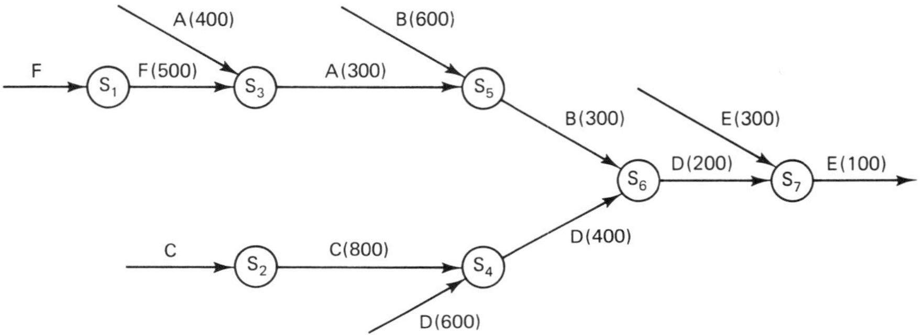

Figure 10.7 Query execution graph.

Let us assume that the relations are located as follows:

Relation	Location
F	1
A,B	2
C	3
D,E	4

The decision trees are given in Figure 10.8. The node labels correspond to subquery numbers. The notation A → B means that relation A is moved to the site of relation B. The numbers in parentheses next to a move decision indicate the total move cost up to and including that move decision. The notation A–B means no move decision because both of the relations A and B are at the same location.

According to Figure 10.8(a), when the policy of moving the smallest relation is used, relation A should be moved to the site of relation F. However, when the locations of the relations are considered, moving relation F to the site of A

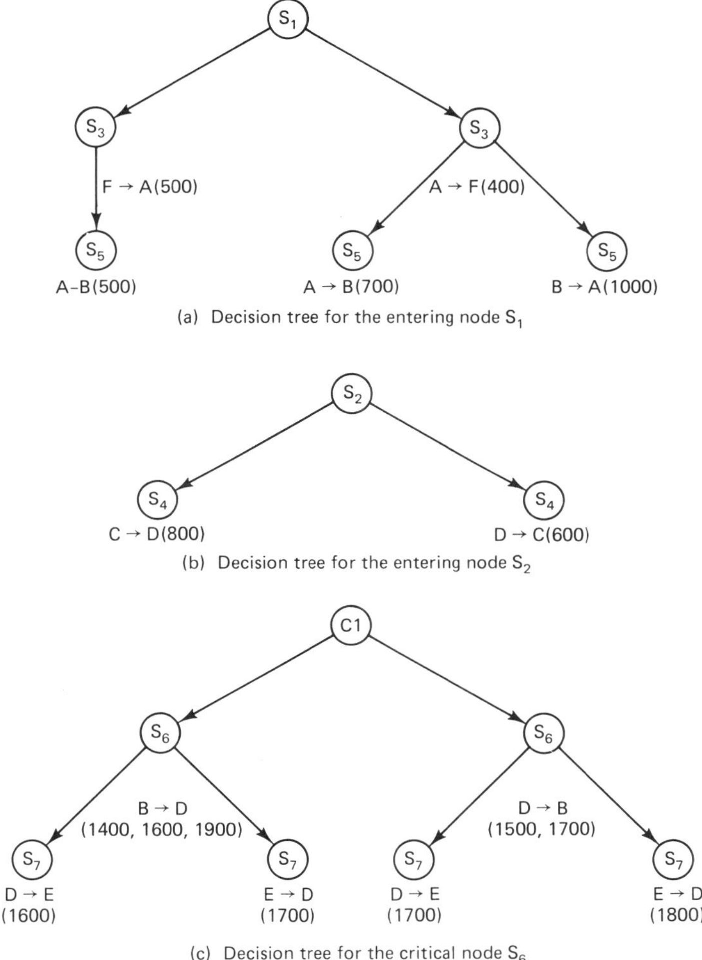

(a) Decision tree for the entering node S_1

(b) Decision tree for the entering node S_2

(c) Decision tree for the critical node S_6

Figure 10.8   Move decision trees for the example query graph.

turns out to be better because it eliminates a subsequent move decision, since both A and B are at the same location (i.e., site #2). This can be seen at the right decision subtree for S_3 which corresponds to moving A to F, hence, a subsequent need for a move between A and B. Figure 10.8(b) shows a move decision for subquery S_2, which involves a move between relations C and D. Figure 10.8(c) shows a move decision for the critical node S_6. The first decision involves the move between relations B and D. However, several move decisions were already made for relations B and D and move costs calculated. For the decision B → D in Figure 10.8(c), 300 is added to the move costs involving B (i.e., 500, 700, 1000 in Figure 10.8(a)) and also the minimum move cost involving

D, which is 600 in Figure 10.8(b). This gives the costs of 1400, 1600, and 1900 for B $\rightarrow$ D. Accordingly, 1400 is the minimum move cost up to and including subquery S_6. The costs for D $\rightarrow$ B are obtained by adding 400 to the minimum move cost for B (500) and each of the move costs for D (i.e., 600 and 800 in Figure 10.8 (b)). This gives the total move costs of 1500 and 1700. Next is the move decision between D and E. Both the left and right subtrees involve the move between D and E since D was moved to C (left) or B (right) earlier. Therefore, 200 or 300 are added onto 1400 (left) and 1500 (right) to produce the total minimum move costs of 1600 and 1700. Accordingly, the final overall move decision will be

- Move relation F to the site of relation A for processing subquery S_3.
- Move relation D to the site of relation C for processing subquery S_4.
- Move relation B to the site of relation D for processing subquery S_6.
- Move relation D to the site of relation E for processing subquery S_7.

For executing subquery S_5 no relation will be moved. This is because relations A and B are both stored at site #2. The move decision results in a total move cost of 1600.

10.4 CONCURRENCY AND UPDATES

In distributed databases, there may be more than one transaction executing at a time; furthermore, they may be using the same data possibly duplicated at various sites. In reading, one copy would suffice to provide the required information if the system assured that all copies are consistent. In updates, however, to keep all copies consistent, the update must be directed to all of them. As we know from concurrency of databases in Chapter 3, updates must be serialized or be equivalent to a serial schedule. Considering concurrent transactions executing on multiple copies, update serialization requires considerable synchronization overhead. This may lead to some compromises with respect to administering updates in a DDB. For example, in the *primary site* (or primary copy) scheme, one site for each relation is designated as the primary site to which updates are directed. After an update is successfully and consistently executed at the primary site, it is directed to the secondary copies to complete the update. In this case, it becomes a problem for a transaction to maintain consistency when operating between data already updated and those yet to be updated. Furthermore, the primary site, by being the centralized update point, imposes a threat to the reliability of the system. Alternate sites must be selected in case of failures. Also, *snapshots,* which are derived relations from the base relations of a DDB, are a way of providing "cheap" concurrency to read-only requests on the database. They may be duplicated wherever needed. These snapshots are taken (i.e., their data are saved) as of some point in time when updates could be conveniently done on the database (e.g., during off peak hours). Until the next update refresh operation, these snapshots continue providing service to users (although with old data) without being affected by the updates taking place on the base relations. We could continue on compromises; however, our main point here is to discuss methodologies for transaction synchronization, which comes next.

10.4.1 Locking in Distributed Databases

In the locking-based approach, as we said, a read transaction needs to lock one copy of data, whereas an update transaction needs to lock all copies. A transaction can read a data item if it has a read (shared) lock on any one copy of the item and it can update it if it has write locks (exclusive lock) on all copies of the data item. A read lock can be granted as long as another transaction does not have a write lock on the item. In other words, no two transactions can hold a read and a write lock on the same data item at the same time.

As we discussed in Chapter 3, the two-phase protocol in locking guarantees serializability. All locks must be exercised first before any unlock can be issued or more specifically,

- Before executing a read, obtain a read lock to prohibit a write lock.
- Before executing an update, obtain a write lock on every copy of the data item.
- Once a lock is obtained, do not release it until the transaction commit time.

Locking brings message traffic in a DDB. Requests must be sent to all sites, then acknowledgments are returned, and after the operation is accomplished, unlock requests must be sent to all the sites where data are stored.

In the primary site scheme, the responsibility of granting and releasing locks to all transactions rests with the primary site. When a lock request is received, the primary site checks to see if the requested item is already locked by another transaction; otherwise, the lock is granted. In this scheme, precedence or wait-for graphs for detecting deadlocks can be kept centrally. Also, locking message traffic is considerably reduced because only the central (primary) site is involved in lock and unlock request and acknowledgments.

In distributed databases, therefore, locking can be requested on a single site, in the primary site, or multiple sites in the distributed update synchronization. In the last case, the wait-for graphs must be maintained at the network level. (In the wait-for graph, nodes are transactions and edges are resources—data. A directed edge is drawn from a node requesting a lock on an item toward a node that is currently holding a lock on the same item. A cycle in such a graph indicates a deadlock.) Each site keeps its own local wait-for graph and represents the rest of the network with a special node [Obermack, 1980]. In this scheme, there may be a global deadlock even though none of the local graphs has a cycle. To detect this, sites link their graphs in a pairwise fashion via their special external nodes until the deadlock is detected. In the distributed update synchronization based on locking, the global wait-for graph can also be monitored by a central site. In this case, all nodes send their lock/unlock requests to the central site.

10.4.2 Timestamping

In timestamping, the deadlock danger of locking is avoided. In this method, the concurrent execution is equivalent to a specific serial execution, the one defined by timestamps, of transactions. Although deadlock is prevented in timestamping, excessive restarts and/or aborts may result.

In timestamping, every transaction is assigned a unique timestamp upon arrival at the network. This can be a global network clock time appended with the site ID. Every data item in the database carries the timestamp of the transaction that last read it and the timestamp of the transaction that last updated it. These are called read and write timestamps, respectively. If a transaction T_1 requests a database operation that conflicts with some other database operation already executed on behalf of a younger (i.e., later in time) transaction T_2, then T_1 is restarted. T_1 and T_2 are in conflict if an operation of T_1 (a) is a read operation, but the object is already written by T_2, or (b) is a write, but the object has already been read or written by T_2. If a transaction is restarted, it is assigned a new timestamp. In summary, if t is the timestamp of a transaction and t_r and t_w are the read and write times of a data item, then

(a) Execute the transaction if $t \geq t_w$ for a read or if $t \geq t_r$ and $t \geq t_w$ for a write. In the former, set the read time to t if $t > t_r$. In the latter, set the write time to t if $t > t_w$.

(b) Do nothing if the transaction is for a write and $t_r < t < t_w$.

(c) Abort the transaction if the transaction is for a read and $t < t_w$ or if transaction is for a write and $t < t_r$.

Although timestamping has its advantages, it may cause excessive restarts and aborts [Ullman, 1982]. *Conservative timestamping* is used to reduce this by forcing events to take place as well as nodes to send requests to each other in strict time sequence.

10.4.3 Voting-Based Systems

Synchronization in updates can also be administered by letting each involved site in the network vote for an update transaction. In the study reported in Ellis [1977], an update can be performed only if all the contacted sites vote positive for the request. The system is known as the unanimous vote-based synchronization. In the majority consensus voting scheme proposed in Thomas [1979], it is necessary only for the majority of the sites to accept an update. This voting system is based on the principle that no site votes to accept both of the two conflicting transactions. One of the following can happen at a site when it is considering an update request:

(a) It can vote OK to accept it.
(b) It can vote REJ to reject it.
(c) It can vote PASS indicating a possible deadlock condition exists.
(d) It can defer voting on that request.

If the request conflicts with a request that has already obtained a majority, the site must vote reject. If the request does not conflict with any other request at that site, then the site votes accept. The site may also find out that the request is conflicting with a previous request for which it has voted OK (i.e., a pending request). A request is pending if it is voted OK but has not yet been accepted by the system. If the priority of the request is lower than that of the pending request, then the site votes PASS; otherwise, it defers voting but remembers the request later on. A PASS vote indicates that a deadlock possibility exists. In order to obtain a majority consensus on a request, it is not sufficient to get OK votes from more than half of the sites. It is necessary that no site votes reject for the request while its votes are accumulated. This system is somewhat robust because failure of a site would not impact the operation much since only a majority of the sites is sufficient to carry out the operation.

There are also other schemes such as preanalyzing [Bernstein and Goodman, 1981] transaction behavior for different classes of transactions and determining conflict graphs beforehand so that runtime synchronization efforts can be minimized. However, such a system would be static because the runtime analysis of transactions for sorting them into classes and determining conflict graphs may be computationally costly.

Concurrency in distributed databases has been a popular research topic. The reader may gain more insight by reading the studies reported in Hsiao and Ozsu [1981], Garcia-Molina [1979], and Rosenkratz, Stearns, and Lewis [1979] in addition to the references cited earlier.

In all the synchronization schemes, once the synchronization is established and the update can proceed, the transaction reaches the commit point. As stated in Chapter 9, the commit process requires a protocol too. The two-phase commit protocol discussed in Chapter 9 is also applicable for DDBs. The requests and acknowledgments are propagated through the sites in a pairwise communication, and the update takes place only if all the sites can commit and if the query site terminates successfully after receiving acknowledgments from all sites for their commit.

10.5 DATABASE MACHINE-BASED DDB ARCHITECTURES

In this section we will discuss issues related to network data modeling, DDB system architecture, and query execution. We will do this by covering the basic concepts of the DDB system architectures that have been published on the RAP database machine. However, the principles applied and methodologies developed deal with problems and solutions of generic nature so that they can be generalized to most of the database machines. We will start our coverage with a homogeneous DDB system architecture and then extend it to a heterogeneous architecture.

10.5.1 A Homogeneous DDB Architecture

In this section we will discuss the RAP homogeneous DDB architecture [Ozkarahan, Tansel, and Smith, 1982]. The RAP homogeneous DDB architecture is shown in Figure 10.9. This architecture is simply the network version of the RAP GDBMS architecture shown in Figure 9.6 of Chapter 9. The following are the features specific to a DDB:

(a) The conceptual data model interface is made to model the entire network information structure. It is called the network meta data model (NMDM). Therefore, it can also be called the global network conceptual schema.

(b) The external schema interface, now called the network external schema

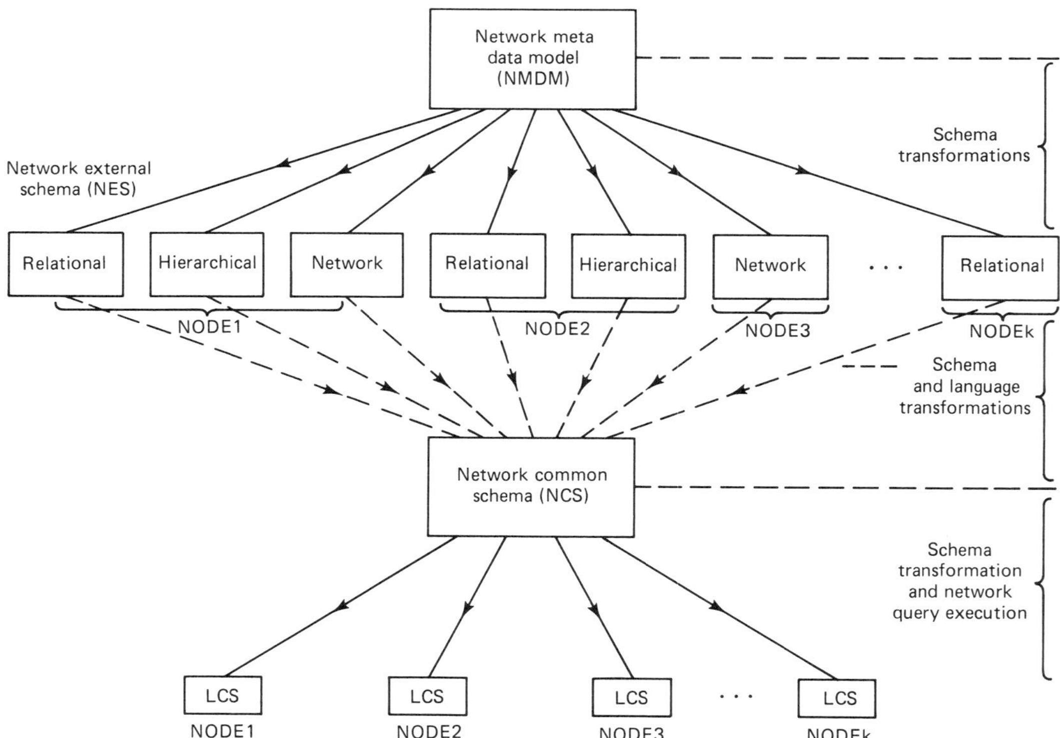

Figure 10.9 RAP homogeneous DDB architecture.

(NES), is a transformation of the NMDM to one, some, or all of relational, hierarchical, or network data models as needed by each specific site (node) in the network. This is the point where users view the network and write their queries without being concerned with the actual distribution of data in the network.

(c) Similar to RAP GDBMS, all external schema structures and programs of different external schema interfaces are transformed into a network common schema (NCS) which corresponds to the network version of the PCS in RAP GDBMS. In both cases (i.e., NCS or PCS), this layer is supported by the RAP structures and language.

(d) Below the NCS is a set of LCSs (local common schema), one for each site. Different from a centralized GDBMS, this layer is a network specific addition to the GDBMS architecture. Each LCS defines the common schema for all the external views supported at a node. The LCS for a node will contain the definitions for both the data stored locally and the data stored at the other nodes, but used at the local site. In this regard, the LCS at each node partially duplicates the NCS.

(e) The NCS in the homogeneous architecture is a virtual layer which represents the RAP translated version of a global network query. (In the heterogeneous architecture, its role is much different.) The NCS is a conceptual stage after which a data distribution–dependent query execution mechanism takes over. We will see network query execution in the following section.

A database machine at a site keeps the data local to itself and executes database operations at its site. The processor at the site consists of two components, a local database processor (LDBP) and a distributed database processor (DDBP). The LDBP contains the local data and performs retrieval and update requests of DDBPs. While LDBPs are local and unaware of data distribution, the DDBPs are responsible for handling data distribution and communication with each other in satisfying a user's request, both in sending related portions of a user's request to the related DDBPs and also in assembling the results obtained from them. Figure 10.10 shows the structure of a DDBP. As can be seen from the figure, a DDBP has four subsystems: the query decomposition subsystem, the query execution monitor, the integrity subsystem, and the reliability subsystem. The query decomposition subsystem accepts the RAP code equivalent of user queries written at the NES interfaces. The query decomposer in this subsystem performs query decomposition to construct a query graph while the query optimizer performs the global move decisions for the subqueries in the manner explained with decision trees earlier. Once subqueries and their move decisions are determined, the query execution monitor subsystem orchestrates the network wide execution, passing each local component of the query graph to the related LDBPs.

The integrity subsystem is responsible for concurrency control, locking, update synchronization, and transaction commit protocols. The reliability sub-system continuously monitors system components. In the event of a failure, it

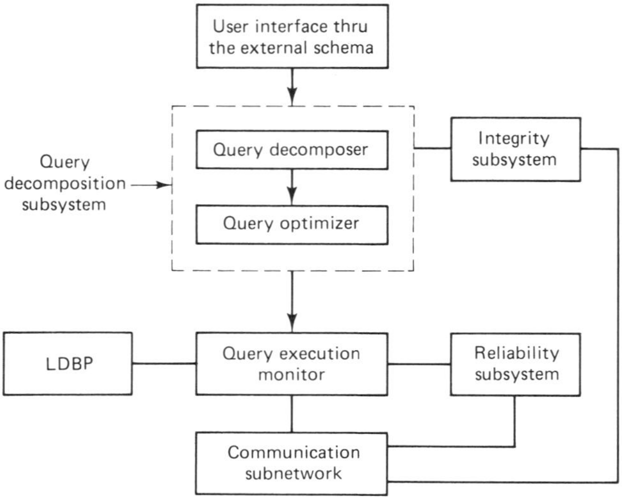

Figure 10.10 Structure of a DDBP.

broadcasts the necessary control information and/or activates the necessary recovery procedures.

Abstract model of the RAP language. We can represent a RAP relation as $R(m_1, m_2, \ldots, m_p, a_1, a_2, \ldots, a_n)$, where m_i and a_j ($1 \leq i \leq p$; $1 \leq j \leq n$) are the mark (tag) and data attributes, respectively. Let m_c indicate a mark bit combination of c bits, where $1 \leq c \leq p$ (permutations being identical) whose values are a one (i.e., set bit). As we know, a marking operation performs a selection on a relation and hence subsets it. If rc represents relation cardinality, then for any relation we can create $I = 2^{rc}$ subsets (as each tuple can or cannot participate in each subset). The use of the term "subset" here is equivalent to what some people call "horizontal fragment." Let $r_i(m_c)$ indicate the ith subset of relation R; that is, $r_i(m_c) \subset R$, where $i \in I$ and $m_c \in M^p$ (where M is the set of all mark bits m_1 through m_p). As in relational algebra, we can group the RAP instructions as the unary and binary instructions. Examples of binary instructions are CROSS_MARK and CROSS_RESET while the rest are unary instructions. The set operations of union, intersection, difference, and so on can be programmed in terms of the existing instructions.

A unary RAP instruction, u, operating on a relation is a mapping of the form

$$u{:}\{r_i(m_c), g\} \longrightarrow \{r_i'(m_c'), g'\}$$

where $i, i' \in I$; $g, g' \in G$; and $m_c, m_c' \in M^p$. That is, a unary RAP instruction may transform a given subset of a relation into another subset, a given register ($g \in G$) contents to another, and a given mark bit combination into another. The input, I^u, and output, O^u, sets of a unary instruction are

$$I^u = \{r_i(m_c), g\}, \qquad O^u = \{r_i'(m_c'), g'\}$$

A binary RAP instruction, b, of the semi-join type is a mapping on two relation subsets, r_i and s_j, as shown:

$$b : \{r_i(m_c), s_j(m_d)\} \longrightarrow \{s_j'(m_d')\}$$

where $i, j, j' \in I$; $m_c, m_d, m_d' \in M^p$. The input, I^b, and output, O^b, sets of b are

$$I^b = \{r_i(m_c), s_j(m_d)\}, \qquad O^b = \{s_j'(m_d')\}$$

Accordingly, a RAP program Q for a query is an ordered set of instructions, where $Q = \{ \langle q_1, q_2, \ldots, q_m \rangle \}$, $q_i \in U$ or $q_i \in B$, where U and B are sets of RAP unary and binary instructions and $1 \leq i \leq m$.

Query decomposition.   A RAP program Q can be decomposed into subqueries such that the execution of the subqueries in serial and, whenever possible, in parallel would produce the same result as if Q were processed as a single program. The decomposition process is based on the distinction between the unary and binary instructions. The query decomposition process maps a given program ordering into another ordering in which intraprogram parallelism is exploited while the serial dependencies are preserved. This is made possible by the data flow–driven execution methodology of the decomposed RAP program. The decomposition process of a RAP program has the following four stages:

- Determine loops
- Decompose loop free program into subqueries
- Subquery analysis
- Construction of query graph

In the decomposition process, program loops are treated as exceptions. A program loop in RAP code is needed only for certain database operations. A loop can be treated as a separate program and executed first by either moving all its remote data to a single site or by going through the query decomposition and execution process recursively. In any case, we can represent a program loop as a virtual instruction, with input and output sets, in the larger RAP program and substitute execution data into the virtual instruction during the execution of the larger program.

In a RAP program, in addition to loops (if any), there may also be unary and binary instructions. While each binary instruction is itself made a subquery, the unary instructions are treated as follows: there may be one or more unary instructions manipulating a relation. The group of unary instructions that manipulates the source relation of a binary instruction immediately before the binary instruction is made a subquery. Similar treatment is made for the group of instructions (if any) manipulating the target relation before the related binary instruction. Any other cluster of unary instructions is grouped and made a subquery on a per relation basis (i.e., each group manipulates only one relation). The following query decomposition algorithm is based on these fundamentals.

Algorithm Query Decomposition

Start all instructions tagged as unprocessed, set subquery counter to one, $SC \leftarrow 1$.

Repeat

1. Take the first unprocessed binary instruction from the beginning of the program. Let it be the kth instruction. Define a subquery qs based on the source relation (plus target relation for CROSS_RESET) as $qs = \{\langle q_1, q_2, \ldots, q_j \rangle \mid q_i \in Q, q_i$ is unprocessed, $i \in L_k$, and $j < k\}$

```
SC ← SC + 1
```

Indicate all the instructions in qs as processed (i.e., reset their tags). (Where k is the kth binary instruction, L_k is the set of instruction sequence numbers for the unary instruction group manipulating the source or target relation of the kth binary instruction, and $j < k$; that is, the group must precede the binary instruction.)

2. Make the binary instruction itself a subquery: $qs = \{q_k \mid q_k \in Q\}$

```
SC ← SC + 1
```

Indicate the instruction as processed.

Until no more unprocessed binary instructions

Group each of the remaining instruction clusters by relation and make each group a subquery.

After the query decomposition process, the input and output sets of subqueries are determined by a process called subquery analysis. The result will be a list of data flow dependencies, each of which is of the form $\langle input\ set\ [subquery\ \#]$ $output\ set \rangle$. These dependencies are used to construct a query (execution) graph.

Example 10.2

Assume the following database relations (whose meanings we already know):

```
LOCATION (DEPT, FLOOR)
CLASS (ITEM, TYPE)
SALES (DEPT, ITEM, VOLUME)
```

and the query *find the total volume of items of type A sold by the departments on the second floor.* The following is the corresponding RAP program for this query:

```
1. MARK (t₁) [ LOCATION : FLOOR = 2]
2. CROSS_MARK (t₂) [ SALES : DEPT = LOCATION.DEPT][LOCATION.MKED(t₁)]
3. MARK (t₁) [ CLASS : TYPE = "A"]
4. CROSS_RESET (t₂) [ SALES: ITEM = CLASS.ITEM][CLASS.MKED(t₁)]
5. SUM [SALES(VOLUME) : MKED(t₂)][REGF_1]
6. READ_REG [REGF_1]
7. RESET (t₂) [SALES]
8. EOQ
```

The program first selects LOCATION then joins (semi-join) the result with SALES. After, CLASS is selected and its result is also joined to SALES to reset those tags that are not selected by both joins. The volumes in the resulting tuples are totaled, the result is output from the aggregate result register, and finally the tags in SALES are cleared before ending the query. Applying the query decomposition algorithm yields the following:

Subquery	Instruction sequence number
S_1	1
S_2	2
S_3	3
S_4	4
S_5	5,6,7,8

As can be seen, most subqueries are single instructions, because the program is relatively simple as is typical of real life applications.

The subquery analysis is performed next and the following result is produced:

```
LOCATION                  [S₁] LOCATION (t₁)
SALES, LOCATION(t₁)       [S₂] SALES(t₂)
CLASS                     [S₃] CLASS(t₁)
CLASS(t₁), SALES (t₂)     [S₄] SALES (t₂)
SALES(t₂)                 [S₅] REGF_1
```

As can be seen, in the input set we can have an entire relation or a subset of it as indicated by its mark bit. The output set can be a register, a tagged relation either on a different or the same mark bit as used for input (e.g., t_2 of SALES), however not necessarily with the same relation cardinality, as some tuples may be reset by the CROSS_RESET instruction.

The next step is the construction of a query graph with the use of the results of the previous processes.

Algorithm Query Graph

Tag all subqueries as unprocessed.

(1) Take the first subquery, make it a node and indicate the subquery as processed.

Repeat

Begin

(2) Take the next subquery and let it be the lth subquery. Add it to the graph as the lth node. For its source (target) relation r_i (m_c),

(a) For each element m_j of m_c, determine the subquery k such that its output relation is input to the lth subquery. That is, $r_h (m_j) \subseteq O^k$ for the largest k, $k < l$. r_h is the subset determined by m_j. Subquery k precedes subquery l and an edge labeled $r_h (m_j)$ is drawn from node k to node l.

(b) For each register g used in subquery l determine the subquery such that the contents of g (i.e., (g)), $(g) \in O^k$ for the largest k, $k < l$. The subquery k should precede subquery l in the graph and the edge labeled g should be added between the subquery nodes.

(c) Indicate this subquery as processed even if (a) and (b) do not apply (i.e., an entering node).

End

Until there are no more unprocessed subqueries.

Example 10.3

Let us continue from Example 10.2 and construct the query graph for the example query. Figure 10.11 shows the query graph constructed with respect to the foregoing algorithm.

The graph represented in the precedence matrix form will be

$$S_j \text{ (subquery)}$$

$$
\begin{array}{c}
S_i \\
\text{(subquery)}
\end{array}
\begin{array}{c}
\begin{array}{ccccc} 1 & 2 & 3 & 4 & 5 \end{array} \\
\begin{array}{c} 1 \\ 2 \\ 3 \\ 4 \\ 5 \end{array}
\begin{bmatrix}
0 & 1 & 0 & 0 & 0 \\
0 & 0 & 0 & 1 & 0 \\
0 & 0 & 0 & 1 & 0 \\
0 & 0 & 0 & 0 & 1 \\
0 & 0 & 0 & 0 & 0
\end{bmatrix}
\end{array}
$$

In the execution of a query graph, the query execution monitor (QEM) takes the responsibility. This responsibility can be exercised either centrally, from the query site, or in a distributed manner. In the latter case, each site contains a copy of the QEM and the one in the query site is the initiator. The query graph is passed to all QEMs, which monitor their respective part of the query graph to control their part of the program execution.

In addition to the query graph, the location of each relation must be known for the move decisions. Looking at the precedence matrix or query graph of

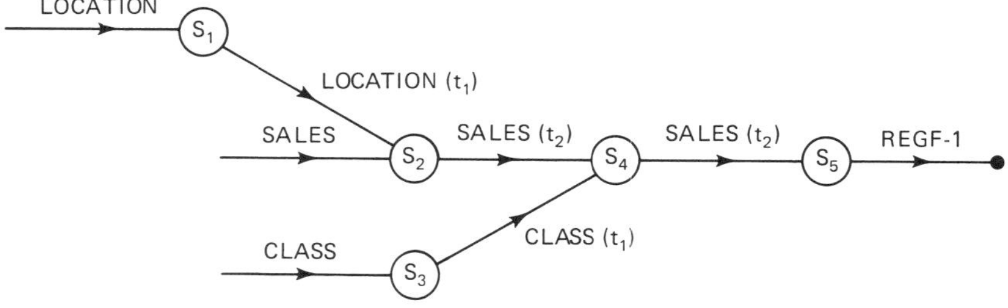

Figure 10.11   Query graph.

the foregoing example, we can see that a subquery cannot be fired for execution unless all of its inputs are received. In the matrix, each subquery looking from the row (i.e., S_i) sends input and/or acknowledgment to the subquery whose entry in the column position (i.e., S_j) is a 1. Conversely looking from the S_j column, the subquery S_j expects input from every subquery S_i whose entry in the column is a 1. Looking from column 4, we see two 1s for subqueries S_2 and S_3 which are supposed to send input to S_4, as can be verified by the graph. Looking from rows 2 and 3 we see a 1 at the fourth column for each, meaning that they have to send their output to subquery S_4. Any $S_{ij} = 0$ means that subqueries i and j can execute concurrently if there is no path of length greater than one between them. This is true between subqueries S_2 and S_3 which means that they can execute in parallel within the single program, as can also be seen in the query graph. Also, any j for which $S_{ij} = 0$ ($i = 1, \ldots, 5$) means that it is an entering node which can start execution immediately—which is the case with subqueries S_1 and S_3. For any i for which $S_{ij} = 0$ ($j = 1, \ldots, 5$) means that it is an ending node, which indicates that the end is reached and result must be sent to the user—as is the case with subquery S_5.

10.5.2 A Heterogeneous DDB Architecture

Heterogeneous DDB architectures are those distributed systems whose nodes may have DBMSs or GDBMSs of various kinds so that the response to a user's query may reside in a database with a view of data different from that of the model on which the query is formulated. As organizations and institutions that possess diverse database applications strive to integrate their database and applications into a unified framework, heterogeneous DDBs are becoming more and more important. Homogeneous DDBs can only be designed for systems which start implementation from scratch and follow a top-down implementation strategy. Because such cases do not occur very often, a heterogeneous DDB is a more typical architecture with which we may be confronted in real life.

The early solutions to supporting heterogeneous DDBs restructured (or converted) each DBMS in a DDB into a common structure under a given "standard" DBMS by forcing migration of the entire database from each remote DBMS into the standard DBMS. An alternative solution, however (such solutions came later), is to maintain the original databases and provide an effective information interchange among different systems without incurring mass migration of data. This is made possible by implementing a network architecture in which different DBMS software can communicate effectively by mapping into certain standard templates in conceptual data modeling and internal schema implementation as proposed in the RAP heterogeneous DDB architecture [Ozkarahan and Kerschberg, 1982]. There have been other studies [Cardenas and Pirahesh, 1980; Smith et al., 1981] to avoid the early solutions based on mass migration. They proposed pairwise schema and operation mappings among an arbitrary number of data models. The RAP heterogeneous architecture tries to minimize the number of mappings, especially the operational mappings, proposes standardization, and addresses both the managerial and technical problems associated with the integration of applications into the DDB system.

Overall system architecture of the RAP heterogeneous DDB. The overall architecture of the RAP heterogeneous DDB system is built by applying a membership protocol for the new members entering the system. Figure 10.12 shows the architecture of the system. The global network conceptual schema cannot be as simple as that of the homogeneous architecture because members may have different conceptual data models. The user population is assumed to use DBMS software of different generations. If we assume the first generation to correspond to traditional file system software, the second-generation database software (identified as DBMS) will be the currently commercialized systems. These systems use a single data model and both the conceptual and operational modeling use this same model—DBMS software that are called hierarchical, network, or relational systems are of this type. The third-generation systems are multimodel systems of ANSI/SPARC architecture type that are called GDBMS. Therefore, looking at Figure 10.12 we see a mixture of DBMSs and GDBMSs.

In particular, the second site from the left is RAP GDBMS-based while the second to the rightmost is an ANSI/SPARC architecture. As we can see, the members (sites) can come with different conceptual schema interfaces, including the rudimentary facility of second-generation DBMSs. Accordingly, as we stated, the global network conceptual schema which is supposed to represent the "universe of discourse" that is the integrated, sharable applications of the enterprise will not be as easily constructible as that of the homogeneous DDB. If we explain the structure in a top-down manner, the entire network is represented by a global network (conceptual) schema which is represented by the functional data model (FDM) [Sibley and Kerschberg, 1977]. In this schema, member conceptual schemas are integrated into a cohesive overall information structure.

Any DBMS or GDBMS applying for membership has decided on what portion of its (the candidate's) data will be made available to network sharing (any data that has to be disjoint and managed strictly locally is not included). This is usually negotiated between the candidate's data administrators and the network data administrators. At this time, access rights and authorizations of the member are also determined and incorporated into the system security/integrity filter. The network then, after passing the global network schema through this security/integrity filter, produces the global network subschema which is still modeled in the FDM. This subschema represents the member's view of the entire network, including its contribution to the network. Therefore, the global network subschema can be an exact copy or a subset of the global network schema. Actually, the network provides the new member with software tools and possibly consultants to construct the necessary target schemas (i.e., global network subschema and the relational internal schema as will be covered in the following). The same procedures described are also valid in the case of updates

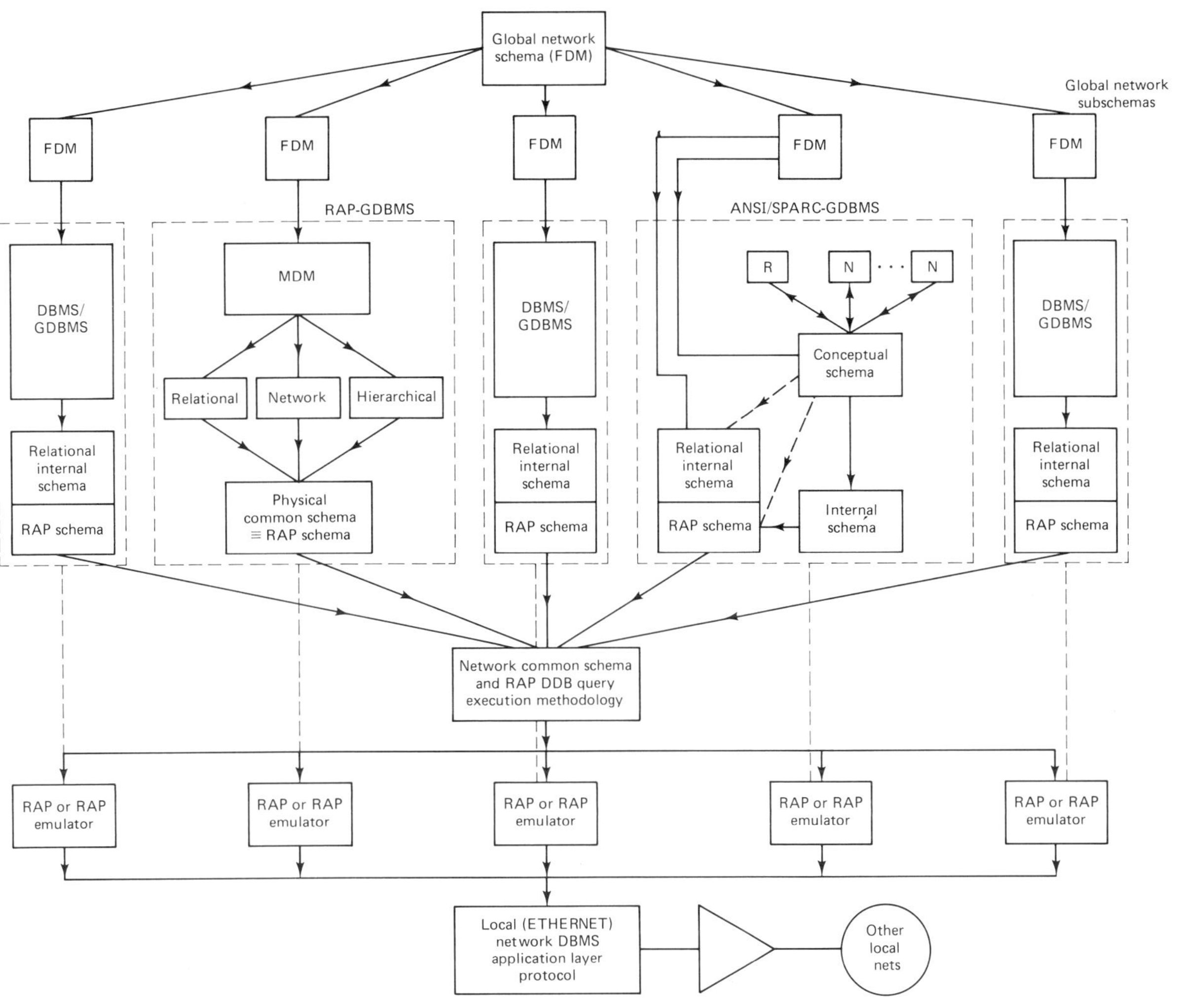

Figure 10.12 Overall architecture of the heterogeneous DDB.

by existing members to modify the information structure modeled in the global network schema.

As pointed out, the network provides the accepted member with the global network subschema translation in the FDM. The member can or cannot use this directly, depending on the type of the conceptual model utilized by the member. Therefore, the system also provides the following to the member:

(a) Semantic templates in the form of structure and semantic correspondences between the FDM and the member's local conceptual schema. Since both sides would have already agreed on what to model for the network, these templates will aid the member in making a translation of the global network schema into the local conceptual schema of the member in a consistent manner. This is necessary if the member's conceptual data model is different from the FDM so that the global network FDM subschema generated by the system cannot be directly used.

(b) The system also provides the member with the relational model version of the templates provided in (a). This is needed to help the member in creating the relational internal schema required from each member as shown in Figure 10.12. That is, according to this system architecture, all member DBMSs or GDBMSs will be required to interface with the network via their relational internal schemas that are stored as RAP relations. If a member already has a relational internal schema, such as RAP GDBMS, these templates can be used for consistency checking on the existing internal schema.

Therefore, for a membership application to be accepted, the incoming candidate must

- match its local conceptual schema with the FDM subschema and/or the semantic templates provided by the system
- match with or create, depending on the candidate's available internal schema, an internal schema interface having the schema and operational constructs of the relational data model

These procedures imply dictionary creation and reconciliation of integrity constraints both on the part of the system and the incoming member. That is, the system provides the templates and the prospective member matches them, reconciles differences, and creates the relational internal schema, if necessary.

In the initial construction of a member's global network FDM subschema, one must decide whether updates to the global network schema and global network subschemas will be permitted in addition to retrievals and database instance updates at the external schemas. If so, then the global network subschema should be designed to reflect the update semantics of the underlying local conceptual model.

This is an important point because of the way a local site will be integrated into the network. The global network subschema will be expressed in the FDM while its internal schema will be relational. Thus there are three translation mappings which must *commute*, as depicted in Figure 10.13.

In Figure 10.13, an update against the global network FDM subschema will be translated by FL to an update against the local conceptual schema, while LR will propagate the effects to the relational internal schema. This two-step process (FL then LR) should "commute," that is, have the same effect as applying FR.

By providing the global network schema, global network subschema, relational internal schema, and the necessary mapping definitions among them, this heterogeneous DDB architecture is providing conceptual and operational mapping data models in such a way as to minimize the number of levels and dimensions of mappings that would be needed in the overall system. Although, structurally, there will be two schema mappings for any prospective member, there will only be one operational mapping, and this mapping, more importantly, will be unidirectional between the respective external schema levels of the members and the internal schema interface. In simpler terms, this is equivalent to asking members to have a relational internal schema interface or to provide it as an alternate interface for entrance to the system.

Equivalence problems.   In the architecture of the overall system, several types of schema and operational mappings are involved. These involve, in the schema mappings, the following:

(a) Global network schema in the FDM to global network subschema, which can be in
    (1) the FDM
    (2) a conceptual data model other than the FDM
    (3) any data model of the operational type in the second-generation DBMS
(b) A conceptual data model, FDM or other, to any of the operational models at the external schema

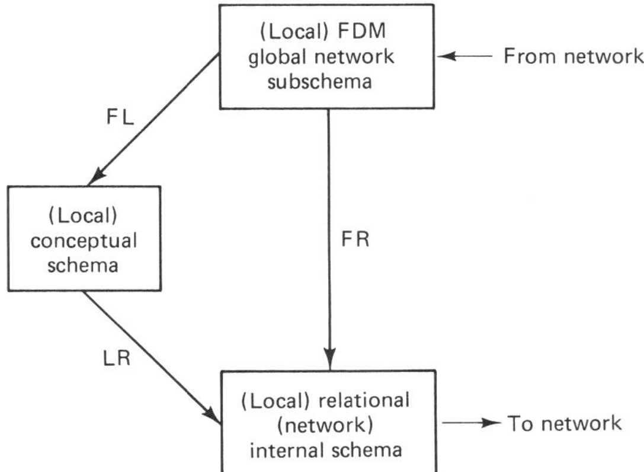

Figure 10.13 Mapping between network and local schemas.

(c) Global network subschema to the relational schema which is FDM to relational

(d) Any operational data model at the external schema to the relational internal schema

The majority of these mapping combinations fall into the realm of ANSI/SPARC GDBMS schema mappings, which were discussed in Chapter 9. In addition, any mappings involving FDM to DBTG and relational systems are discussed in Sibley and Kerschberg [1977] and Ozkarahan and Kerschberg [1982], respectively. Any additional mapping in this DDB system architecture is between the FDM and other conceptual data models.

Although conceptual data models may differ in their constructs, operations, and naming conventions, they are similar in that they support the notions of entity, property, and associations among entities via aggregation and generalization. Although strict equivalence between models is quite difficult, their similarities help us to map them into one another by the use of the semantic templates provided in the RAP heterogeneous DDB architecture.

Consider, for example, the mapping of an FDM schema to an Entity/Relationship schema or an RM/T [Codd, 1979] schema. In the case of the FDM to E/R mappings, we have the following correspondences:

FDM construct	E/R construct
Value set	Value set
Basic entity set	Entity set
Set-valued function plus converse	Weak entity set
Association entity set	Relationship set → Aggregations and
Generalization hierarchy	Not supported → generalizations are supported in the extended E/R model used in Chapter 9.

For the FDM to RM/T mappings, we have the following correspondences:

FDM construct	RM/T construct
Entity	Surrogate
Basic entity set	Kernel entity type
Association entity set	Associative entity type
Single-valued functions	P-relations
Set-valued function (COVER)	Characteristic entity type
Generalization	Generalization

Referring to the system architecture of Figure 10.12, we see that the part of the architecture below the relational internal schemas is identical to that of the homogeneous DDB architecture. That is, we have network common schema

(NCS) and local components (i.e., LCSs) under NCS all implemented in RAP constructs. This provides certain advantages in the operational mappings that involve the operations of internal schemas that are reflected upon NCS. The following elaborates on this. The RAP approach to tagged semi-join prevents certain equivalence problems. This is because the semi-join is realized within the target relation without creating temporary relations. Since only the eligible target tuples are tagged, connection problems in the form of spurious tuples are prevented. The second aspect that simplifies equivalence problems is that within RAP GDBMS, the operations of navigational data models, such as networks and hierarchies, are exactly mimicked by RAP semi-joins instead of a transformation of the former into the relational model in structure and operations (i.e., relational algebra). To clarify this point, let us refer to Figure 10.14. In Figure 10.14(a), a hierarchical schema is shown. In Figure 10.14(b) are the relational schema

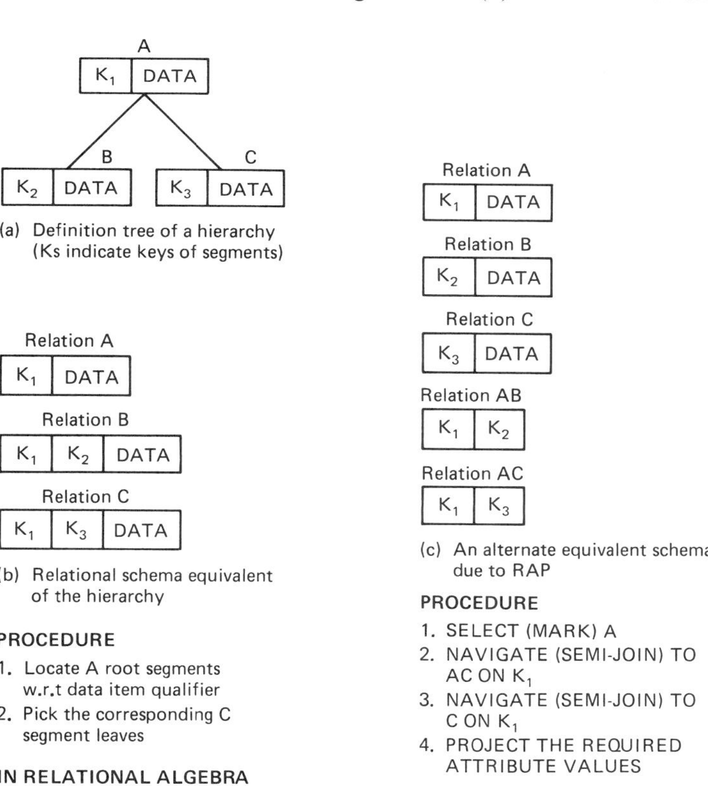

Figure 10.14 Processing a hierarchy on alternate equivalent schemas.

equivalent of the hierarchy, a hierarchical navigation procedure, and its relational equivalent in terms of the relations and relational algebra operations including a full join. In Figure 10.14(c), we see record types, which correspond to the original segments of the hierarchy and link structures which are implemented as RAP relations and the corresponding RAP navigation via tagged semi-joins. Such an operational equivalence is almost direct and one-to-one with the hierarchical operation. Similar arguments apply to network systems. Various compatibility issues between an existing relational internal schema and the relational internal schema created from the FDM global network subschema are covered in Ozkarahan and Kerschberg [1982].

Dictionary management. In the heterogeneous DDB architecture, we need several dictionaries among which the following are important:

(a) The dictionary of global network schema. This will contain mapping information pertaining to each member in the database. This dictionary can be kept centrally or partially distributed.

(b) The dictionary of global network subschema. This dictionary will be kept by each member and contain the mapping information for the relational internal schema.

(c) The dictionary of the relational internal schema. This will contain mapping information for obtaining the RAP equivalent structures.

(d) The LCS dictionary of the RAP DDB systems. This contains information on both the data stored locally as well as the remote data used locally.

10.5.3 Query Execution in the Heterogeneous DDB

In this section, we will demonstrate a two-site heterogeneous DDB that involves databases of a department store and a warehouse. It is assumed that each database is stored at a site different than the other and managed by different software (i.e., the department database is managed by the RAP GDBMS whereas the warehouse database is managed by the FDM GDBMS). It is further assumed that the global network subschemas are identical to the global network schema. This makes the conceptual schema mapping straightforward. Also, the FDM to relational external schema mapping will be identical to that of the FDM to relational internal schema, which in turn will be one-to-one with its RAP equivalent needed for the DDB architecture.

Department store semantics

(a) The department store consists of a collection of departments, locations, items, and classes.

(b) A department is uniquely identified by its D_NAME, has possibly several locations, and stocks items in a particular quantity (QTY_ON_HAND). The department sells items in specific volume (VOLUME).

(c) Items may be sold in several departments and are characterized by name (I_NAME), which is unique, WEIGHT, and SIZE. Every item may have several classes.

(d) Every class has a type (TYPE) that is unique.

(e) Every location has a unique floor (FLOOR).

Warehouse semantics

(a) The warehouse is in charge of ordering items from suppliers.

(b) A collection of suppliers supply items to the warehouse, and for each item a supplier has a maximum that it can supply (MAX_QTY_SUPPLIABLE). Every supplier is characterized by a unique number (S#), name (SNAME), CITY, and rating.

(c) The warehouse requests that items be supplied in a certain quantity (QTY_ REQUESTED) and records the date of the request.

Global semantics.   Let us assume that the foregoing descriptions apply to the distinct department store and warehouse databases. The global network schema should allow the department store to verify warehouse on hand amounts of a certain item and to obtain information about outstanding requests. Conversely, warehouse purchasers can monitor department store sales to determine reorder points for a particular item.

FDM global network schema.   In the global network schema, which is represented in terms of the functional data model, we have two types of items: department store items and warehouse items. The integration is achieved by means of the ISA-hierarchy (generalization). Figure 10.15 shows the global network schema in terms of the FDM DDL. Figure 10.16 shows the corresponding FDM diagram of the global network schema. The reader can refer to Date [1983] for an introduction to the FDM. More detailed and specific coverage to aid in understanding Figures 10.15 and 10.16 can be found in Sibley and Kerschberg [1977] and Ozkarahan and Kerschberg [1982].

In the FDM, functions model relationships among entity sets. A function between two sets is defined in the mathematical sense with various forms and mapping properties (e.g., a one-to-one and total function is a candidate key). Set-valued functions (i.e., multivalued functional mappings) are allowed. The sets in FDM are categorized as value sets, entity sets, and higher-level sets such as aggregations and generalizations. In Figure 10.15 we see the attributes of entity sets defined as functions that map into value sets in the range. Aggregations are defined as association entity sets with component entity sets defined after the keyword AS. The label attached to a function indicates that it is total; an arrow of $\nrightarrow$ (with cross) indicates a key function (with an arc for composite keys); and a domain set is defined as the inverse (superscript 1) function. A generalization (hierarchy) is defined by a set of IS_A clauses.

Global generalization on ITEM
        entityset (G_ITEM; /*GLOBAL ITEM*/
            key (G_ITEM) = {INAME}
            I_NAME : G_ITEM → character
            WEIGHT : G_ITEM → integer
            SIZE   : G_ITEM → dimension
        entityset ITEM isa G_ITEM per ILOC;
                /*DEPARTMENT ITEM*/
        entityset WITEM isa G_ITEM per ILOC;
                /*WAREHOUSE ITEM*/

Department store section
        entityset DEPARTMENT;
            key (DEPARTMENT) = {D_NAME}
            D_NAME : DEPARTMENT → character
        entityset LOCATION;
            key (LOCATION) = {FLOOR}
            FLOOR : DEPARTMENT → integer
        entityset CLASS;
            key (CLASS) = {TYPE}
            TYPE : CLASS → integer
        association ITEM-SOLD /*SALES*/
            (ITEM as object, DEPARTMENT as seller);
            key (ITEM_SOLD) = {object, seller}
            VOLUME : ITEM_SOLD → integer
        association DEPT_LOC
            (DEPARTMENT as dept, LOCATION as place);
            key (DEPT_LOC) = {dept, place}
        association DEPT_ITEM
            (DEPARTMENT as dept, ITEM as item);
            key (DEPT_ITEM) = {dept, item}
            QTY_ON_HAND : DEPT_ITEM → integer
        association ITEM_CLASS
            (G_ITEM as item, CLASS as class);
            key (ITEM_CLASS) = {item}

Warehouse section
        entityset SUPPLIER;
            key (SUPPLIER) = {S#}
            S#   : SUPPLIER → integer
            SNAME   : SUPPLIER → character
            CITY   : SUPPLIER → character
            RATING : SUPPLIER → integer
        association SUPPLY
            (WITEM as supplied, SUPPLIER as supplier);
            key (SUPPLY) = {supplied, supplier}
            MAX_QTY_SUPPLIABLE : SUPPLY → integer
        association REQUEST
            (WITEM as supplied, SUPPLIER as supplier);
            key (REQUEST) = {ordered, source}
            QTY_REQUEST : REQUEST → integer
            DATE   : REQUEST → date

Figure 10.15 Global network schema in the FDM DDL.

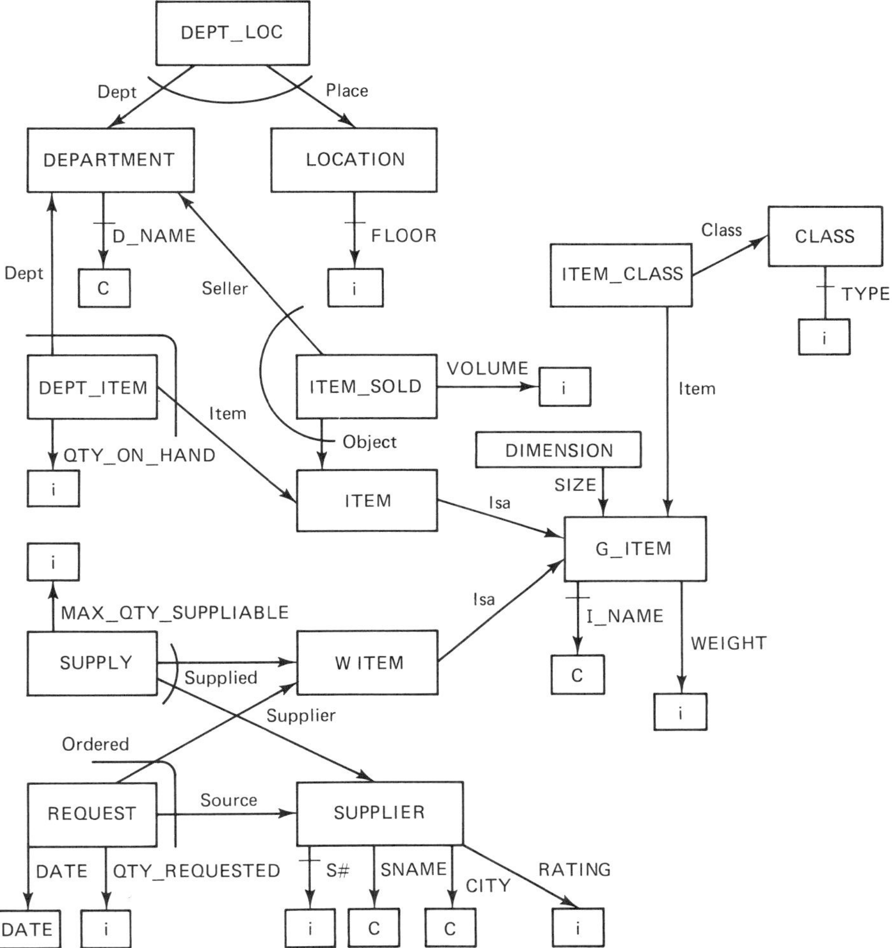

Figure 10.16   FDM diagram of the global network schema.

Conversion to global network subschema.   Since the warehouse database site uses a GDBMS with FDM as the conceptual model, the global network subschema at this site, according to the assumption made at the beginning, is the same as the global network schema. The latter will be copied into the global network subschema pertaining to this site.

With respect to the RAP GDBMS site, a conversion from the FDM to E/R semantic data models will take place by using their semantic correspondences shown earlier. Thus in E/R, entity sets map to entity sets and associations to relationship sets, and all arcs are functional. The generalization G_ITEM is handled as shown in Figure 10.17 with the member entities being ITEM and W_ITEM.

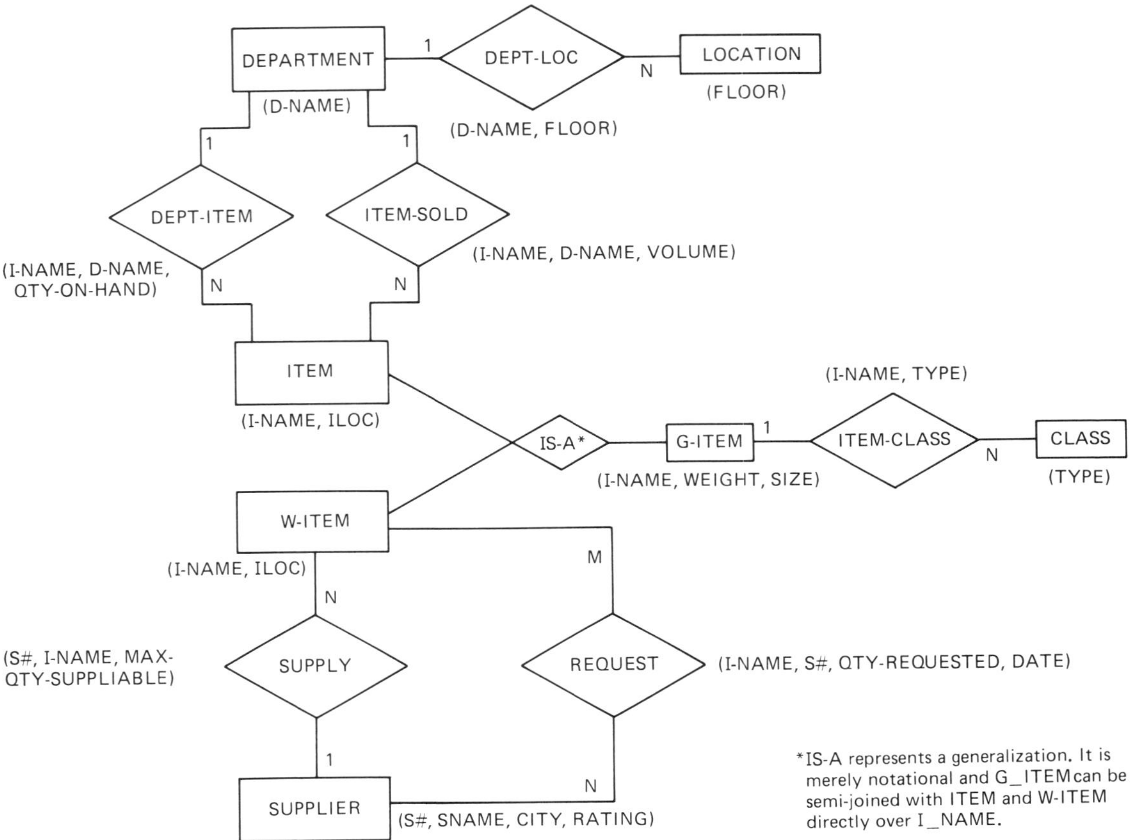

Figure 10.17   The E/R global network subschema diagram.

Network external schema (NES) relations at the RAP GDBMS.   Based on the conversion algorithms given in Chapter 9, the following network external schema interface relations would be created at the RAP GDBMS site:

G_ITEM, ITEM, DEPT_ITEM, ITEM_SOLD, ITEM_CLASS, DEPT_LOC, SUPPLY, SUPPLIER and REQUEST.

As can be seen, the relational view at the RAP GDBMS site sees its entities and relationships and also the relationships and entities modeled for the warehouse database site which may be locally or remotely stored.

The NES relations of the RAP GDBMS are mapped, on a one-to-one basis for simplicity, into RAP relations at the network common schema so that the following shows the relations at NCS including their location information which is stored at LCS.

Network common schema relations at the RAP GDBMS.   The following are the resulting RAP relations:

```
G_ITEM          Local
ITEM            Local
DEPT_ITEM       Local
ITEM_SOLD       Local
ITEM_CLASS      Local
DEPT_LOC        Local
SUPPLIER        Remote (i.e., at the warehouse site)
SUPPLY          Remote
REQUEST         Remote
```

Network external schema relations at the warehouse GDBMS.   At this point, we will present FDM to relational mapping and the relations seen at the network external schema as well as any constraints that are relevant. As mentioned earlier, this same mapping will be used for the relational internal schema interface.

In the mapping from FDM structures to relational structures, basic and association entity sets map to relations. In the global network FDM schema, the generalization G_ITEM allows a distinction between the store and warehouse items.

Let us assume that the sets ITEM and W_ITEM "cover" G_ITEM; that is, every G_ITEM is either from ITEM or W_ITEM. In fact, a "generic" item in G_ITEM may be present at the store and also be requested by the warehouse.

Thus, the generalization will be represented as the relation

```
GEN_G_ITEM (I_NAME, GEN, ROLE)
```

where the composite key is the entire collection of attributes. Thus, the item whose I_NAME is *TOY HELICOPTER* might have two tuples in GEN_G_ITEM.

The entire collection of relations and their attributes plus synonyms for the warehouse GDBMS are

```
W_ITEM (I_NAME, WEIGHT, SIZE) — Local
SUPPLIER (S#, SNAME, CITY, RATING) — Local
REQUEST (I_NAME, S#, QTY_REQUESTED, DATE) — Local
```

where

I_NAME is synonym for *ordered.I_NAME*
S# is synonym for *source.S#*

namely,

```
t1 = <TOY HELICOPTER, ILOC, store> and
t2 = <TOY HELICOPTER, ILOC, warehouse>
SUPPLY (S#, I_NAME, MAX_QTY_SUPPLIABLE) — Local
```

where

> $S\#$ is synonym for *supplier.S#*
> *I_NAME* is synonym for *supplied.I_NAME*

```
G_ITEM (I_NAME, WEIGHT, SIZE) - Local
GEN_G_ITEM (I_NAME, GEN, ROLE) - Local
ITEM (I_NAME, WEIGHT, SIZE) - Remote
DEPT_ITEM (I_NAME, D_NAME, QTY_ON_HAND)_Remote
ITEM_SOLD (I_NAME, D_NAME, VOLUME) - Remote
DEPT_LOC (D_NAME, FLOOR) - Remote
DEPARTMENT (D_NAME) - Remote
LOCATION (FLOOR) - Remote
```

Note that the last two relations are redundant because they are unary. They are formally correct but not necessary unless other properties are present.

Relational internal schema and RAP equivalent.   The relational internal schema will be identical to the relational external schema described. Also, in this application, it is assumed that the mapping from the internal schema relations to their RAP equivalent is one-to-one.

Query execution.   As a reminder, the following graph depicts the operational mappings involved:

```
                                            ,LOCAL Subqueries
(QUERY at NES)  →  (QUERY at NCS)<
                                            `REMOTE Subqueries
```

Assume that at NES the following query is presented: *what are the names of suppliers which supply items classified as type A having the sizes greater than 120 with weight 2 and whose quantity on hand is larger than the quantity requested as of August 1, to the departments located on the second floor?* The corresponding RAP program generated at the NCS will be as follows:

```
1. MARK (t₁) [G_ITEM:SIZE > 120 & WEIGHT = 2]
      /*restrict item as required*/
2. CROSS_MARK(t₁) [ITEM:I_NAME = G_ITEM.I_NAME][G_ITEM.MKED(t₁)]
3. CROSS_MARK(t₂) [DEPT_ITEM: I_NAME = ITEM.I_NAME][ITEM.MKED((t₁)]
      /*map item restriction into store items and then to DEPT_ITEM*/
4. MARK(t₃) [ITEM_CLASS : TYPE = "A"]
      /*restrict items for type A*/
5. CROSS_RESET(t₂) [DEPT_ITEM : I_NAME = ITEM_CLASS.I_NAME][ITEM_
CLASS.MKED(t₃)]
         /*combine the previous mapping on DEPT_ITEM conjunctively on
            each tuple with the restriction of type A*/
6. MARK(t₄) [DEPT_LOC : FLOOR = 2]
      /*restrict departments on the second floor*/
7. CROSS_RESET(t₂) [DEPT_ITEM: D_NAME = DEPT_LOC.DNAME][DEPT_
LOC.MKED(t₄)]
```

```
        /*combine mapping of step (5) on DEPT_ITEM conjunctively
          on each tuple with the 2nd floor restriction*/
8.  MARK(t₅t₆) [REQUEST : DATE = "AUGUST 1"]
        /*restrict by date*/
9.  CROSS_RESET(t₂) [DEPT_ITEM : I_NAME = REQUEST.I_NAME]
      [REQUEST.MKED(t₅)]
        /*combine mapping of step (7) on DEPT_ITEM on each tuple
          conjunctively with the restriction of date*/
10. L1 GET_FIRST [REQUEST(I_NAME, QTY_REQUESTED) : MKED(t₆)]
        RESET (t₂) [DEPT_ITEM : I_NAME = REGC_1 & QTY_ON_HAND = REGC_
        2]
        BC L1, RAIL_STAT(t₆)
        /*modify the mapping of step(9) on DEPT_ITEM on each tuple
          conjunctively in such a way as to reflect only those cases
          where the quantity on hand is greater than quantity
          requested*/
11. CROSS_MARK(t₇) [SUPPLY : I_NAME = DEPT_ITEM.I_NAME][DEPT_
        ITEM.MKED(t₂)]
        /*find the SUPPLY items corresponding to the overall DEPT_ITEM
          restriction through interrelational mapping*/
12. CROSS_MARK(t₈) [SUPPLIER : S# = SUPPLY.S#][SUPPLY.MKED(t₇)]
        /*find the corresponding suppliers for the restriction
          of (11) through interrelational mapping*/
13. READ [SUPPLIER(S_NAME) : MKED(t₈)]
        /*output the answer, supplier names*/
14. EOQ
```

At this point we can apply the query decomposition steps to produce the query graph. The same procedures covered in the homogeneous DDB are applied. After query decomposition, every instruction becomes a subquery. (We have restricted program loops only to relations that are stored at the same site so that they can be easily handled.) Accordingly, the next process is subquery analysis, which produces the following list:

```
G_ITEM                          [S₁] G_ITEM(t₁)
G_ITEM(t₁),ITEM                 [S₂] ITEM(t₁)
ITEM(t₁),DEPT_ITEM              [S₃] DEPT_ITEM(t₂)
ITEM_CLASS                      [S₄] ITEM_CLASS(t₃)
DEPT_ITEM(t₂),ITEM_CLASS(t₃)    [S₅] DEPT_ITEM(t₂)
DEPT_LOC                        [S₆] DEPT_LOC((t₄)
DEPT_ITEM(t₂),DEPT_LOC(t₄)      [S₇] DEPT_ITEM(t₂)
REQUEST                         [S₈] REQUEST(t₅),REQUEST(t₆)
DEPT_ITEM(t₂),REQUEST(t₅)       [S₉] DEPT_ITEM(t₂)
DEPT_ITEM(t₂),REQUEST(t₆)       [S₁₀] DEPT_ITEM(t₂)
SUPPLY,DEPT_ITEM(t₂)            [S₁₁] SUPPLY(t₇)
SUPPLIER,SUPPLY(t₇)             [S₁₂] SUPPLIER(t₈)
SUPPLIER(t₈)                    [S₁₃] SUPPLIER(t₈)
```

Using this query analysis and the locations of relations as determined from the directories at the LCS, the query graph as shown in Figure 10.18 is constructed. At this point, the query execution on the network is performed by the network

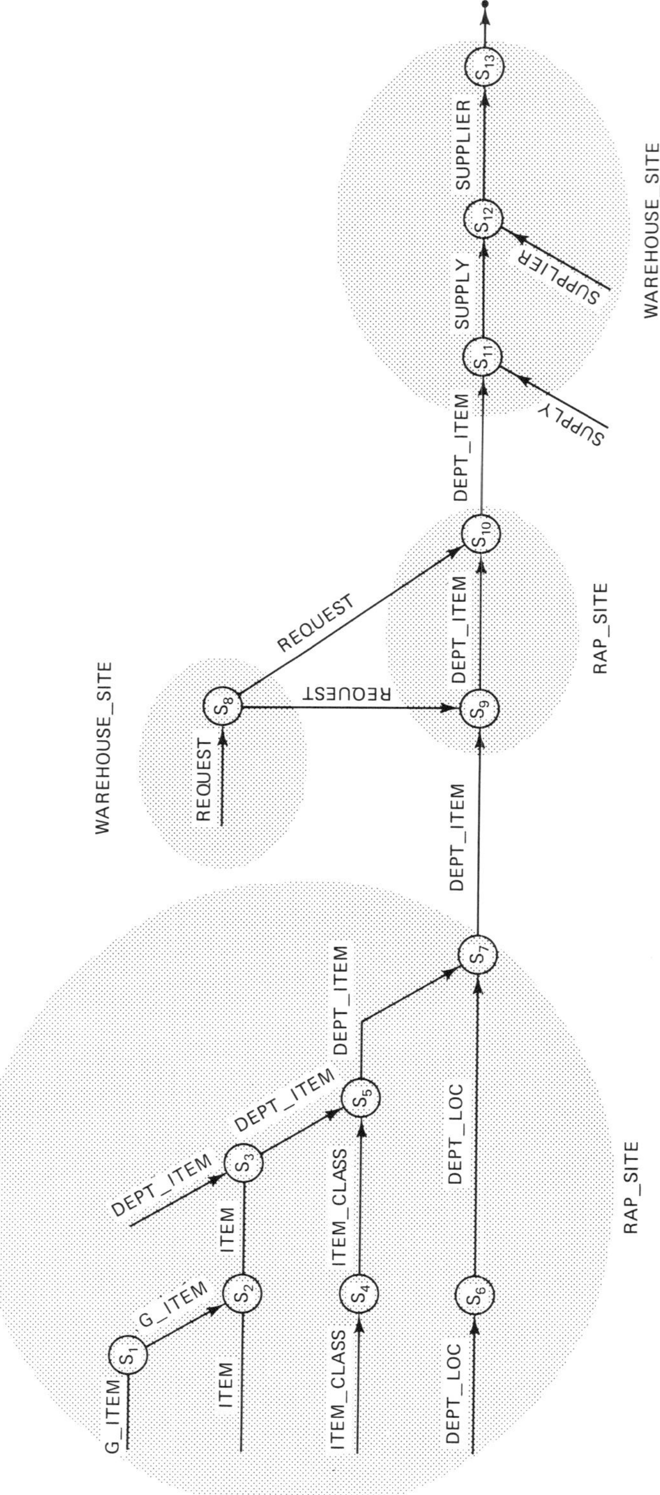

Figure 10.18 The query graph of the example query.

query execution monitor (QEM), which is part of the heterogeneous DDB interface. As can be seen in the query graph, the subqueries S_1, S_2, S_3, S_4, S_5, S_6, and S_7 are locally executed at the RAP site. The restriction on the REQUEST relation is performed at the warehouse site; however, the results are passed to the RAP site along the heterogeneous DDB interface. That is, the subquery S_8 which is received from the RAP site as

```
MARK( t₅t₆ )[REQUEST : DATE = "AUGUST 1"]
```

is modified by the QEM as

```
MARK( t₅t₆ )[REQUEST : DATE = "AUGUST 1"]
MOVE [REQUEST : MKED( t₅ ) | MKED( t₆ )] to [RAP-site]
```

Whenever S_{10} is to be processed at the RAP site, the QEM appends it with the following instruction:

```
MOVE [DEPT_ITEM : MKED( t₂ )] to [warehouse-site]
```

(The MOVE instruction transmits data from one site to another on the network.)

The warehouse site processes subqueries S_{11}, S_{12}, and S_{13} with the use of mappings that exist between the relational internal schema and the equivalent RAP schema after it receives them from the RAP site along with the results passed in the move instructions shown. Finally, the warehouse site passes the result to the RAP site with the following move statement:

```
MOVE [SUPPLIER : MKED( t₈ )] TO [RAP-site]
```

In this case, the SUPPLIER intermediate relation contains the only attribute of interest, which is S_NAME. The RAP site terminates the program with the EOQ statement.

EXERCISES

10.1. Assuming the fragmented database schema of Example 10.1 in the chapter, optimize the following query with respect to the distribution strategy used for Figure 10.5. The query is

```
SELECT DEPTNO, SUM(SALARY)
FROM EMPLOYEE
GROUP BY DEPTNO
WHERE SALARY ≥ 45000
```

Show all your optimization steps by query trees. (Note: You can distribute group by and aggregate operations with respect to binary operations so long as any given group is entirely contained in a fragment.)

10.2. Given the following query graph, draw the overall move decision tree by assuming that relations R_1 and R_3 are at the same site while R_2 is located elsewhere and that the sizes of R_1, R_2, and R_3 are, after local processing, 500, 600, and 300, respectively. Assume an incoming selectivity of 0.90 for every join.

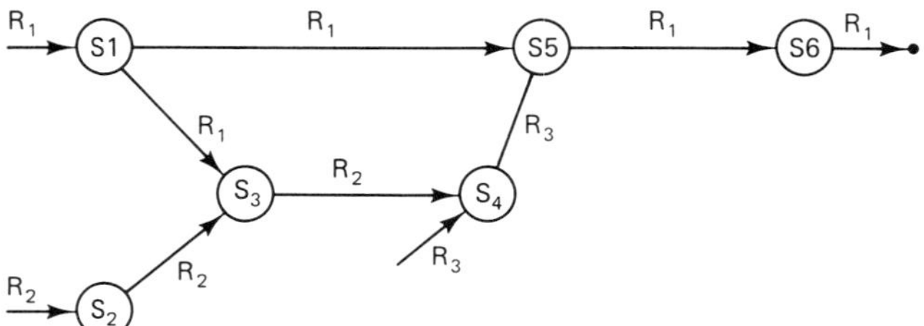

10.3. Compare the message traffic overhead for update synchronization in a distributed database having n sites among the following strategies:
   (a) Locking with
      (i) Centralized,
      (ii) Decentralized global deadlock control
   (b) Timestamping
   (c) Voting with majority consensus

10.4. Identify the differences and similarities between the RAP heterogeneous DDB architecture and those of Cardenas and Pirahesh [1980] and Smith et al. [1981] for the same.

10.5. Given the following RAP query program to be executed in a DDB, do all the steps necessary up to and including the construction of the query graph. Also, identify the subqueries in that graph that can be executed in parallel.

```
 1.  MARK (t1t2) [C : LEVEL = "ADV"]
 2.  MARK (t3) [TC : ROOM = 103]
 3.  MARK (t7) [C]
 4.  L1 : GET_FIRST [C(C#) : MKED(t₇)]
 5.  READ_REG[REGC_1]
 6.  BC L1, RAIL_STAT (t₇)
 7.  CROSS_RESET (t₃) [TC : C# = C.C#][C.MKED(t₁)]
 8.  CROSS_MARK (t₅) [SC : E# = TC.E#][TC.MKED(t₃)]
 9.  CROSS_RESET (t₂) [C : C# = SC.C#][SC.MKED(t₅)]
10.  READ [C(NAME) : MKED(t₂)]
11.  EOQ
```

10.6. Referring to the E/R conceptual schema diagram of Figure 10.17, convert that diagram into E/R DDL declarations using the syntax of Chapter 9 or Appendix II for the extended E/R model.

10.7. Based on the department store–warehouse heterogeneous DDB example given in the chapter, replace the local conceptual schema of the warehouse site with another conceptual data model of your choice and repeat the entire example from the beginning. (If you need a suggestion, how about using the RM/T model?)

10.8. Assume a RAP DDB and the query: What are the DRs of R_2 such that GR of R_3 is 500 in those tuples corresponding to the tuples of R_1 whose CR is greater than 10,000? Also assume that this query is given at site B.

(a) Program this query with RAP instructions (or any other database machine language that has semi-join) and insert move statements (whenever necessary) based on the move strategy of your choice.

(b) Compute the network cost of your program assuming that the sites A, B, and C are connected in a triangle and that network cost = total cost of messages + total cost of file (relation) transfers. Do not forget to reduce relations with their selectivities (incoming selectivity in the case of join, i.e., that of source) whenever applicable. The following are the other necessary details:

Relation	Location	No. of Tuples	Bytes/Tuple
R_1(**AR**,BR,CR)	A	10,000	99 (33 per attribute)
R_2(**BR**,DR)	B,C	5,000	50-25 per attribute- (relation is horizontally split equally between the nodes)
R_3(**ER**,BR,FR,GR)	C	20,000	24 (6 per attribute)

You can transmit messages (i.e., marking subresults obtained from a restriction) and/or entire relations between the sites. The cost of a byte transfer between two sites for files (i.e., relations) is 1, whereas the cost of every five messages sent in a message block is 9 (a block may contain fewer messages at the same cost). Use MOVE *relation name* TO *node name* and MOVE-MES TO *node name* commands in your program to send relations or results (immediately after the last instruction producing the result), respectively. Assume a buffer space at the receiving node is large enough to contain another relation or equivalent number of messages. Assume 0.01 and 0.5 to be the selectivities of equality and inequality, respectively, both in restriction and join. Also, use the equality selectivity for figuring out domain cardinalities.

10.9. Consider the following distributed database:

Number of sites = 5

Relations per site:

S#1	S#2	S#3	S#4	S#5
R	S	R	R	R,S

The following query is requested at site S#1:

$$1 - \text{Read S and R}$$

$$2 - \text{Update R}$$

Compare the following concurrency control strategies by calculating the total number of messages required for the execution of the above query (i.e., operations 1 and 2) including the centralized commit which should be included in the update:

(a) Distributed locking

(b) Primary copy locking (assume S#1 for R and S#5 for S are the primary sites)

(c) Majority consensus based voting. Assume that all sites accept the update. Show your message sequences before you give the total count.

10.10. Compare timestamping with the majority consensus voting scheme. Which one would be preferable to the other and why? Would this be valid under any circumstances? Why or why not?

10.11. Given the following two relations R and S and their data:

$R(A_1\ A_2\ A_3)$			$S(A_4\ A_5\ A_6)$		
1	a	100	2	25	aa
2	a	50	3	35	aa
3	b	50	5	35	bb
4	b	100	8	45	cc

Assume that R and S are stored at different places in a network. If we need to connect R and S with a natural join over A_1 and A_4 and moving each value in the relations corresponds to one item transfer, how many items will be transferred:
(a) If R and S are joined by a (full) join?
(b) If R and S are joined by an equivalent decomposition of the join in terms of the semi-join.

11

DATABASE MACHINE PERFORMANCE

11.1 INTRODUCTION

Database machine performance is a nontrivial topic. Although the research on database machines has continued for the past decade, we have not yet come to their industrial exploitation. This means that we cannot compare a database machine with a von Neumann GPC (from here on, it will be referred to as the conventional system) or another database machine by simply monitoring, measuring benchmark performances, and so on, on the respective systems. The only alternative we have is to use analytical models and/or simulation to assess hypothetical database machine performance. In making assessments, there are the following points to consider.

A comparative assessment will require a comparison among database machines and a conventional system. However, this may be a tricky issue. In order not to compare apples with oranges, we may be tempted to normalize different systems by changing their design parameters in an effort to make them compatible. We may change their cell memory capacity or number of processors (cells) or impose generalized algorithms that are derived out of our interpretation of the systems (different from those designed for the specific machines, partly because of our incomplete knowledge of these machines), and so on. Unfortunately, this will not solve the problem, because we will still be comparing apples with apple-size oranges. The definition of computer architecture is that of defining boundaries. An architect when designing a system optimizes the design parameters, makes certain choices based on certain knowledge and expectation of average behavior. It is not up to us to change these with a stroke of a pen. Besides we cannot be fair in doing this because not all features of one machine will be shared by others simply because there are different architectural classes. What choice can we have then in making sensible comparisons? The answer to this is twofold. First, take representative job classes with specific parameters and measure total work (or time in system) of different database machines in executing these jobs to completion. This would be a basis of comparison. The second approach is to identify architectural properties that have first-order impact on system performance and compare database machines with respect to the extent of their possession of these properties. In certain operations where spot comparisons would not be meaningful, analyze the complexity of systems in performing these operations under extreme (including worst case) conditions. Our coverage of this chapter will be more along the lines of the second approach.

11.2 BASIC RESULTS OF PREVIOUS PERFORMANCE STUDIES

The performance study reported in Ozkarahan, Schuster, and Sevcik [1977] clearly proved the superiority of database machine systems with respect to parallelism, associativity, and powerful machine primitives. Recall that, at the end of Chapter 5, we made a case for potential gain of parallelism where a secondary memory–based parallel/associative device achieved a 250-MIPS equivalent computing speed. This device did not depend upon access paths and location-based addressing with the associated retrieval and update overhead. This basic fact will be the thrust behind the superiority of database machines possessing parallel/associative structures in the basic database operations of selection and updates. A powerful set of database machine primitives would include, as shown in Ozkarahan, Schuster, and Sevcik [1977], an on-the-fly scalar aggregate computation capability (which would need a simple ALU besides the already present selection logic). This capability would then extend the superiority in selection and updates of database machines into those involving scalar aggregate criteria in selections. In the coming sections, we will present important elements of performance comparisons for these operations.

In the performance studies reported in Hawthorn and Dewitt [1981] and Dewitt and Hawthorn [1981] database machine performances were compared based on three major query types. These types comprise *short query* involving single-relation, *multirelation query* and *set aggregate* query. The first study compared specific database machines with each other after each design was normalized. However, instead of following the data language constructs of those machines, global algorithms were imposed upon them, for example, in doing set aggregates. The conclusions of this study were that

(a) Database machines did not prove feasible for overhead intensive short queries. That is, if a retrieval was to find and retrieve a few records, the overhead involved in the host GPC for the related DBMS and operating system chores, as well as the communication overhead between the GPC and the database machine, overtook the gains of the backend system.

(b) There did not seem to be an overwhelming superiority of one machine over the others.

(c) Associative disks and filters did not perform as well as the others in aggregate functions and joins.

In the second study by the same authors, database machine architectures were classified with respect to the following disk-oriented parallelism categories:

- Processor-per-track (PPT) systems (i.e., fixed-head disk–based)
- Processor-per-head (PPH) systems (i.e., based on movable-head disk with parallel readout)
- Processor-per-disk (PPD) systems (i.e., filters)
- DIRECT-like multiprocessor systems
- A conventional von Neumann uniprocessor (a VAX 11/780) running a relational DBMS called fast INGRES

The same query types as in the first study were used; however, within each query type, two more variables were included which are the selectivity factor of selections and joins and the presence/absence of indexing on the selection and join attributes. Again, each architectural category was normalized to contain an equal number of processors with equal cell memory capacities. Also, the algorithms for doing operations were globally imposed rather than adhering to specific database machine designs. The following were the conclusions of the study:

(a) Although PPT designs did well in read-only selections (simple query), when the presence of indices was assumed, the other machines did equally well.

(b) DIRECT machine did better than others in joins and aggregate functions.

(c) Even the DIRECT machine suffered from the I/O bottleneck in performing join with the nested loop algorithm so that the improvement over the uniprocessor was marginal.

The result of (a) would not be surprising because, as can be remembered from Chapter 1, we pointed out that access paths sharpen the retrieval performance in return for heavy overhead for updates which require maintenance of the access paths. The result is excellent read-only response in return for poor overall performance. In today's dynamic business and knowledge databases, transaction processing, as well as survivability, depends upon heavy updates. For example, in knowledge databases, new facts and deductions must be entered into the database via instant updates. We, therefore, suggest overall system performance as the measure which proportionally combines performances of retrievals and updates into one. However, if an application is intensely specialized, such as directory assistance, then less general machines can be built for that specific use that would rely on read-only requests.

In regard to findings (b) and (c), we have been talking about the I/O bottleneck and hard database operations throughout the text and will do so more in this chapter in terms of identifying impacts of architectural properties on such operations. It is relevant at this point, however, that we should stress the differences between associative disks and database machines whose original parallelism and associativity were based on concepts similar to that of the associative disks. As the said performance study indicates, the associative disks or PPT designs in general cannot do well in the following operations due to lack of functionality and therefore require intervention of the host GPC:

- *Joins:* The GPC has to substitute tuples of the source relation repeatedly by sending them to the backend for selection.
- *Aggregates:* PPTs do not have the capability to perform on-the-fly arithmetic to compute scalar aggregates.
- *Set aggregate functions:* The GPC has to sort and project the relation externally and send each unique attribute value to the backend to perform further selection and/or required operation on the grouped data (tuples) identified by the unique attribute value.

We can now contrast an associative disk with a database machine like RAP to explain the reason why database machines were designed in the first place.

Joins are performed as semi-joins by *CROSS_MARK* (Chapters 3 and 7) in RAP by built-in cross-segmenting hardware whose recent algorithm was explained in the RAP.3 architecture. With respect to scalar aggregates, powerful cell processors such as those used by RAP carry out arithmetic updates of four operations by an on-the-fly operating ALU whose other function is to compute scalar aggregates. With respect to set aggregate functions, the internal grouping and correlation constructs via *GET_FIRST* do not require GPC intervention. This occasion is another chance to stress the importance of the universality of a database machine language (Chapter 8), which includes relational completeness, in system performance. The GPC to backend coupling should not go beyond the request (from GPC) response (from backend) pair in all operations.

11.3 HOW TO LOOK AT PERFORMANCE

Database machine performance should be studied by a careful analysis of the variables involved. In doing so, we should differentiate among the following:

(a) Internal evaluation: How is the database machine structured? How well and completely does it perform the required operations once the data are brought into the device memory?

(b) How efficient are the supporting operations such as readout of selected data and communication with the outside world (GPC, and/or else on a network).

(c) Does the machine lend itself to multiprocessing for query operations of multiple users?

(d) Does the machine have a virtual address space? How well is the machine protected from the I/O bottleneck?

(e) Does the machine blend with higher-level system architectures? That is, does the machine lend itself logically and physically to support GDBMS and distributed databases?

All these questions and others should be answered correctly by making a stage-by-stage performance study that would follow the performance hierarchy of Figure 11.1(a) within which the lateral breakdown is also divided into progressive stages (progress is from left to right) as shown in Figure 11.1(b).

In the overall layout of Figure 11.1, we see areas that concern a database architect as well as a general computer architect so that a complete performance study would involve database machines as well as general computer systems-related performance studies. Our concentration will be on database machine specific aspects, and, in that, the coverage will be on the basic issues at varying levels of detail depending on the nature of the problem.

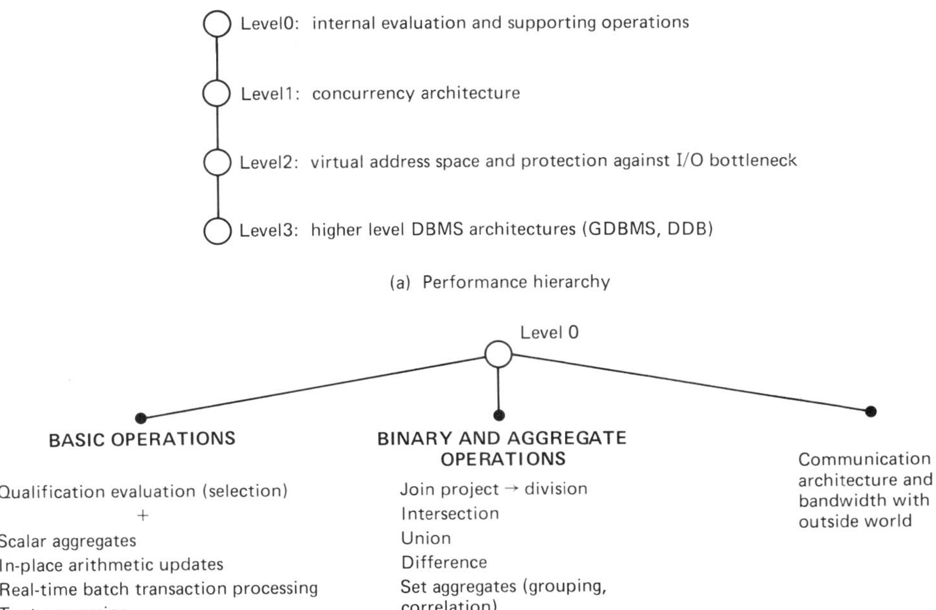

Figure 11.1   Levels and stages of database machine performance.

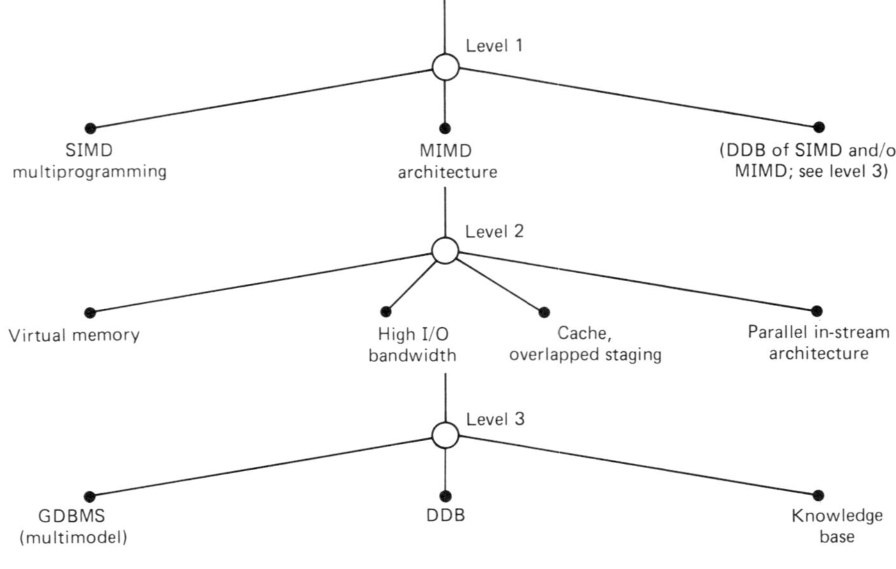

(b) Lateral breakdown

Figure 11.1 (*continued*)

11.4 BASIC OPERATIONS

The basic operations constitute the core of DBMS processing and are encountered in day-to-day operations of real life. In fact, most existing systems in DBMS architectures (software and/or hardware) concentrate solely on these functionalities. We will cover the performance aspects of these basic functionalities. In doing so, we will also contrast database machine functionalities with that of a von Neumann GPC running conventional DBMS software to give an idea of database machine performance improvements.

The basic DMBS primitive structure is of the form *<opcode> <specification> <qualification>*, where opcode signifies the database operation (e.g., select, update), specification indicates the affected attributes to be output and/or operated upon, and qualification specifies the condition (it can be a Boolean predicate) for the desired operations to take place. In what follows, we will explain qualification structure. We will avoid the term query structure because a query can correspond to a program written by use of various DBMS primitives. While we can have a query consisting of a single primitive (e.g., selection), there can be queries involving a series of complex operations.

11.4.1 Qualification Structure

Qualification evaluation is the backbone of all DBMS operations. The basic operations such as scalar aggregates, arithmetic updates, batch transaction processing, and text processing are all carried out on-the-fly on data records (tuples) that are determined to be eligible during qualification evaluation. In most machines, qualification itself takes place on-the-fly with some machines implementing more liberal buffering to be able to synchronize operations.

A qualification, in general, is a Boolean predicate. Each predicate corresponds to a simple condition, c_i of the form:

$$\langle attribute\text{-}name_i \rangle \ \theta \ \langle operand \rangle \ or \ a \ tag(mark) \ status \ of \ \begin{cases} MARKED(t_c) \\ UNMARKED(t_c) \end{cases}$$

where θ corresponds to relational operators of $=$, $\neq$, $\geq$, $>$, $\leq$, $<$ and operand can be a literal or numeric constant, a register, or another attribute name, while t_c corresponds to a combination of tag bits.

Furthermore, we can assume that the Boolean predicate can be structured and/or interpreted as either disjunctive normal form or conjunctive normal form:

- $(c_{11} \wedge c_{12} \wedge \cdots \wedge c_{1k}) \vee (c_{21} \wedge c_{22} \wedge \cdots \wedge c_{2l}) \vee \cdots \vee (c_{n1} \wedge c_{n2} \wedge \cdots \wedge c_{nm})$

which is a disjunctive normal form

- $(c_{11} \vee c_{12} \vee \cdots \vee c_{1k}) \wedge (c_{21} \vee c_{22} \vee \cdots \vee c_{2l}) \wedge \cdots \wedge (c_{n1} \vee c_{n2} \vee \cdots \vee c_{nm})$

which is a conjunctive normal form.

Example 11.1

Consider the following two single instruction queries:

$$\langle opcode \rangle \ \langle specification \rangle \ \langle a_1 \leq v_1 \wedge a_2 > v_2 \wedge a_3 < v_3 \rangle$$
$$\langle opcode \rangle \langle specification \rangle \langle (a_1 = v_1 \wedge a_2 \neq v_2) \vee (a_3 = v_3 \wedge a_4 = v_4 \wedge a_5 = v_5) \rangle$$

The first query consists of

(a) Simple conjunctions (can be interpreted as both normal forms)
(b) The qualification length of 3; that is, there are three predicates in the Boolean form
(c) All θ are for nonequality tests

The second query consists of

(a) A disjunctive normal form
(b) Qualification length of 5
(c) All predicates are for equality tests

In both the qualification Boolean forms shown above, the expression (or sub-Boolean) within a pair of parentheses is referred to as a *qualification clause*.

Assume an EMPLOYEE relation example which we have seen earlier in the chapters and the following SQL query:

```
SELECT NAME
    FROM EMPLOYEE
        WHERE SAL  =  1500
        AND    AGE  =  30
        AND    STATUS  =  2
```

where we have a qualification of simple conjunctions with qualification length of 3 and all predicates are tests for equality.

11.4.2 Database Machine Model

Let t_p correspond to time needed to evaluate a predicate on each record or tuple. Assuming that a database machine has enough logic to evaluate a clause and form the disjunction/conjunction of clauses as predicates are evaluated on the record, then it will take time $l_q \cdot t_p$ to evaluate the entire record where l_q corresponds to qualification length, that is, the number of predicates involved in the Boolean expression. This time is, of course, the upper bound since qualification can be determined earlier in taking conjunctions which apply to both forms of qualification expression. From here on, we will use the terms file or relation and record or tuple interchangeably.

If the file contained N records the overall evaluation time will be $N \cdot l_q \cdot t_p$. If the database machine has p parallel processors each working on n records serially (that is examining them one after the other in the memory module, or cell memory), then this time will be reduced to $(N \cdot l_q \cdot t_p)/p$, where, assuming uniform distribution of records in memory modules, $n = N/p$. Going back to classifications made in Dewitt and Hawthorn [1981], p will be 1 for a PPD device, 19 for a PPH device, 19 (*number-of-cylinders*) for a PPT device, and 16 for a multiprocessor architecture such as DIRECT. Assuming for the worst case that basic operations are carried out serially with the qualification evaluation and that qualification evaluation selects σ, where σ is the selectivity ($\sigma \leq 1$), the proportion of the records to be operated, then the overall time will be

$$\frac{(N \cdot l_q \cdot t_p)}{p} + \sigma \cdot \frac{N}{p} \cdot t_o$$

where t_o indicates the time to perform the basic operation on a record (i.e., computing an aggregate of an attribute, arithmetically updating an attribute, and so on). (We should point out here that in text processing, where pattern matching over the records storing long literal text attributes—see Chapter 13 for the RAP.3 approach to text retrieval computer—is involved, t_p will be long while l_q may or may not be greater than one. In other words, if qualification involves only the string search, then l_q will be one. However, if qualification will involve other criteria on the formatted attributes besides pattern search, then l_q will be greater than one.)

To complete this timing, we should consider two more variables. They are the host (or frontend) overhead and communication delays. The host overhead involves compiling, integrity checking, and operating system chores, details of each depend upon an individual system. The communication delay, which corresponds to the rightmost subtree of level 0 of Figure 11.1, involves I/O communication protocols (or initiation/termination) and data transfer delay for the following:

(a) Output of selected data to the host from the backend (we assume that host communication for sending the query code to the backend is negligible)

(b) Paging out updated data to mass or backup storage (so far, our discussion is at level 0 where it is assumed that entire database is database machine resident or alternatively, we are restricting ourselves to the internal evaluation)

The time for host overhead is comparable to the rest in the overall expression for overhead-intensive queries as pointed out in Hawthorn and Dewitt [1981]. An overhead-intensive query is a simple query involving a single relation and a simple operation, such as selection, where very few records are output. We should clarify a point here. We may have a complex query program involving several selections and joins which finally ends up with an output of a few records. This is not an overhead-intensive query in the sense that host overhead does not dominate the overall timing. What is an overhead-intensive query then? It is a query of transaction processing type where a few keys are provided for retrieval and the same number of records is output taking one match for each key in the file. While a database machine will make a comprehensive search regardless, a conventional system could do equally well or better by a simple hash-based retrieval. In Chapter 7, we discussed real-time batch processing of transactions. Batching of queries to be processed on-the-fly over a file is common in nonnumeric architectures in general. Making a safe assumption of query batching for overhead-intensive queries, where the host overhead is well amortized, can then bring us to the following assumption. This assumption is the fact that we can construct an I/O model to study first-order effects on system performance (this I/O model includes backend operations) and safely neglect CPU processing as second-order effects. (Any reader objecting to this view can easily add the host overhead to the general timing formula we will present in the following.)

The general timing formula, including the I/O indicated at items (a) and (b), will be

$$\frac{N \cdot l_q \cdot t_p}{p} + \sigma \left(\frac{N}{p} \cdot t_o + \frac{N}{B_{IO}} \right)$$

where B_{IO} signifies the bandwidth of I/O involved in the operations of (a) and (b) by making a simplifying assumption that the I/O bandwidth between database machine and the host and database machine and the secondary memory is the same. Before we produce final expressions which can be used to compare database machines with each other and also to compare database machines with a conventional system, we will now look into conventional systems and see how we can accomplish the same operations in them.

11.4.3 Conventional System Model

We will assume a two-file system for the von Neumann GPC running DBMS software. The two files will store the access path and the data, respectively. For the access path, we will assume inverted list files for the indexed attributes. Each index will be a binary relation consisting of the domains corresponding to the values of the indexed attribute for one and the record identifiers of the records having the indexed attribute value for the other. Accordingly, a tuple of the index relation will carry one unique value of the indexed attribute and the corresponding inverted list consisting of a series of record identifiers. The other file will store the data records and will be directly addressed, once the record ID is known, either by relative addressing or hashing. Furthermore, going back to the inverted index, we will assume a multilevel index organization for it (such as an ISAM or VSAM file in IBM terminology) where the upper-level indices will be stored in main memory so that only the track index and index data will be disk resident.

The following operations on these two files will be defined: to retrieve a record from the data file we need to have the following steps of access activity; (1) arm movement to the required cylinder (TAC), (2) average rotational delay (TRD), and (3) data transfer (DTR). The record retrieval time (RRT) will then be

$$RRT = TAC + TRD + DTR = TAC + 0.5ROT + DTR$$

where ROT is the disk rotation time.

To update a record on disk, we need first to access it, modify it in the host (CPU processing is neglected) and write it back. Accordingly, once the record is accessed, we cannot rewrite it sooner than a full revolution to come back to the record's position. The record update time (RUT) will then be

$$RUT = TAC + 1.5ROT + 2DTR$$

Similarly, to retrieve a record from the inverted index the following will apply. Assuming that the upper-level indices of the inverted file are main memory resident and searched at CPU speed, the index record access will include a track index search which will take ($TAC + TRD$), neglecting the small index data transfer, and subsequent access of the record with an additional TRD neglecting overflow chaining. Therefore, the index record retrieval time (IRT) will be

$$IRT = TAC + ROT + DTR$$

To update an index record, which means that a record's attribute value has changed, we must first delete the entry from the old index record and then insert the new value into the index. The index record update time (IUT) will therefore be

$$IUT = 2(IRT + ROT + DTR) = 2TAC + 4ROT + 4DTR$$

With these operations, we can derive qualification evaluation expressions that will parallel the methodology used for database machines. The predicate evaluation time t_{pc}, where subscript c stands for conventional, will be the following:

(a) For equality and inequality ($\neq$) predicates all we need to access is one index record corresponding to the operand value in the attribute index. This is because even for inequality we can access the index record as if the test is for equality, look for the sought value and take the complement of the record IDs as the answer (i.e., the set difference which excludes the record IDs in the index record). The required time will then be:

$$t_{pc} = IRT$$

(b) In the case of nonequality, we have to retrieve half of the index records on the average. Alternatively, we can do the following:
  (i) Scan the data file directly
  (ii) Use range indices and take the union of the indices falling in the range of the predicate
  (iii) Use a hashing function on the data file and successively hash on the lower or higher (whichever is applicable) attribute values within the file's range

At this point, we can see the advantage of associative processing, which does not differentiate between equality and nonequality predicates. We will assume the use of simple inverted indices, that is, inverted indices that are constructed for equality. Accordingly, in the case of a nonequality predicate, half the inverted file will be retrieved on the average (first half or last half depending upon the direction of comparison). This will take $t_{pc} = ISRT = SEQR(IT/2)$, where $SEQR$ is the sequential retrieval time of the inverted file whose total number of tracks is IT and occupied space is CY cylinders. Therefore, $SEQR(IT/2) = TAC + (CY-1)TACS + (IT/2)ROT$, TACS indicating seek time for adjacent cylinders. Inverted list retrieval may be necessary to use pointers to evaluate the rest of the Boolean predicate. However, in cases where σ is high, it may be more advantageous to scan the data file directly and check qualification predicate while the data records are retrieved. This will take $SEQR(T)$, where T is the number of tracks of the data file.

Based on the predicate evaluation timings above, we can then construct expressions for qualification evaluation for an entire file. The qualification evaluation of a Boolean predicate of length l_q will be

$$l_q \cdot t_{pc} = \begin{cases} l_q \cdot IRT & \text{(for the best case with all equalities} \\ l_q \cdot \left(TAC + (CY - 1)\, TACS + \left(\dfrac{IT}{2}\right) ROT \right) & \text{for the worst case} \\ \text{with all nonequalities (i.e., excluding tests for } = \text{ and } \neq) \end{cases}$$

11.4.4 Comparisons for Basic Operations

In this section, we will summarize the performance models of database machines and the conventional system (which is a uniprocessor GPC) we have been working on so far. The basic operations to be considered are

- Select (qualification evaluation)
- Select and retrieve
- Select and update
- Select and scalar aggregate compute

Select

Database Machine.   We have developed the timing for this operation as

$$\frac{N \cdot l_q \cdot t_p}{p}$$

Conventional System.   The time for this operation is developed in the previous section as

$$l_q \cdot t_{pc}$$

Select and retrieve

Database Machine

$$\frac{N \cdot l_q \cdot t_p}{p} + \sigma\left(\frac{N}{B_{IO}}\right)$$

Conventional System

$$l_q \cdot t_{pc} + \sigma \cdot N \cdot RRT$$

Select and update

Database Machine

$$\frac{N \cdot l_q \cdot t_p}{p} + \sigma\left(\frac{N}{p} t_0 + \frac{N}{B_{IO}}\right)$$

where t_0 corresponds to time to perform the required update on a tuple in database machine memory.

Conventional System.   If A_I indicates the number of indexed attributes that are updated (in practice, this is usually one), then

$$l_q \cdot t_{pc} + \sigma \cdot N(IUT + RUT) \cdot A_I$$

Select and scalar aggregate compute

Database Machine

$$\frac{N \cdot l_q \cdot t_p}{p} + \sigma\left(\frac{N}{p} t_0\right)$$

where t_0 is the time to compute the cumulative scalar aggregate with the value taken from a tuple.

Conventional System

$$l_q \cdot t_{pc} + \sigma \cdot N \cdot RRT$$

As we pointed out earlier, we have ignored on-the-fly overlapping of the second term with qualification evaluation in the database machine timings to produce a more general model. In the case of the conventional system, it is possible to separate the comparisons as the *best case* and *worst case* if it makes a significant difference between evaluating equality and nonequality predicates. In the model developed for l_q at the end of the previous section, this difference has been accounted for. We leave to the reader the detail of substituting values for the foregoing expressions to produce various comparison plots. However, the following results reported in Ozkarahan, Schuster, and Sevcik [1977] are applicable:

(a) In all operations where σ is relatively large (e.g., 1 to 3% of N) the database machine performance is superior to a uniprocessor by two orders of magnitude where p is also in this order.

(b) Based on the same σ values the database machine superiority in updates is clearly visible, and the gain is in the range of three orders of magnitude in favor of the database machine. The explanation for this is apparent from the absence of access path maintenance in database machines (assuming parallelism and associativity). Although it would be cheaper to scan the data file sequentially and carry out updates, one cannot leave the access paths without maintenance because otherwise they would be useless after the update. It is quite important to add at this point the fact that the select and update model must be modified for those database machines that rely on access paths such as the DBC system. Accordingly, the select and update model for such database machines becomes

$$\frac{N \cdot l_q \cdot t_p}{p} + \sigma \cdot N \cdot IUT$$

where the assumption here is that the qualification evaluation and data record updates are performed as in a database machine. We should remind at this point that in database machine architectures, where coarse indexing is maintained for nonresident databases (see next section), a certain amount of access path maintenance must be incorporated into the model.

(c) The case of real-time batch processing can be approximated with the select and update model in the database machine. For the conventional system, we can assume selection based on key and update of a nonkey attribute so that the overall time will be $t_{pc} + \sigma \cdot N \cdot RUT$. If σ is not too small, which can be controlled by the batch size, then the gain by database machine will be the same as select and retrieve. It should be remembered at this point that the response time for a transaction will not be less than the response time for the entire batch. Although the batch response time will be within on-line response limits, it can be varied by varying the batch size.

(d) In scalar aggregate operations, database machines have a distinct superiority because the conventional system must bring attribute values to the CPU to compute the aggregate after selecting the records in the first place.

Example 11.2

Based on the database used in Example 11.1, the following are examples of queries that demonstrate some basic operations:

(a) The SQL query of Example 11.1 demonstrates a select and retrieve operation whose qualification structure is discussed in the previous example.

(b) The query which asks *names of employees whose earnings are equal to the maximum salary earned in the sales department* in the corresponding SQL code is

```
SELECT NAME
   FROM EMPLOYEE
      WHERE SAL =
         SELECT MAX (SAL)
            FROM EMPLOYEE
               WHERE DEPT =  'SALES'
```

In this query, the inner block corresponds to scalar aggregate computation with the qualification structure having $l_q = 1$. The number of tuples retrieved to compute the aggregate would be equal to the number of people working in the sales department, for a conventional system. The outer select and retrieve block would then have $l_q = 1$ with the operand being the aggregate computed in the inner block.

(c) The query which asks *give $500 raise to those people who are one of the following: (4,000 $\leq$ SAL $\leq$ 8000 OR 12,000 $\leq$ SAL 15,000 OR 17,000 $<$ SAL $<$ 19,000) AND status below 6* in the corresponding SQL code is

```
UPDATE EMPLOYEE
   SET SAL = SAL + 500
      WHERE  SAL ≥ 4000
      AND    SAL ≤ 8000
      OR     SAL ≥ 12000
      AND    SAL ≤ 15000
      OR     SAL > 17000
      AND    SAL < 19000
      AND STATUS < 6
```

In this update query, $l_q = 7$, with a disjunctive normal form Boolean predicate. The Boolean predicate corresponds to a worst case because all of the predicates involve nonequality tests.

(d) The SQL code

```
DELETE EMPLOYEE
   WHERE STATUS > 6
```

is an update query that affects more than one employee. The selected people's records must be deleted from the data file, and all the inverted file records whose status value is greater than 6 must also be deleted. However, the order of processing is such that inverted file processing must be performed first to select the records to be deleted from the data file and then followed by inverted list deletions. If query were to ask to modify the status codes of people such that $(status)_{new} = (status)_{old} + 2$, where $(status)_{old} > 6$, then we would have both inverted list additions/modifications as well as deletions apart from the updates of records in the data file.

11.4.5 *Nonresident Model*

At this point, we want to extend the database machine model developed previously to consider the case with nonresident databases. The phrase nonresident databases applies to cases where database machine memory is not large enough to contain an entire database. In this case, the architectural classification of various database machines converges upon the indirect search category.

In terms of our performance breakdown depicted by Figure 11.1, so far we have studied basic operations at level 0; with these operations, we will descend lower on the hierarchy. Maintaining a single-task model which can be approximated by an SIMD architecture, we will pass through level 1 and descend to level 2, where a virtual memory addressing scheme must be supported to be able to process queries for large databases. The simple model, including a virtual memory support, will include file paging activity to bring parts of database to database machine memory for processing. Accordingly, the models developed in previous sections will be modified as follows:

(a) The conventional system model remains unchanged since at the beginning its model was constructed to do processing on data retrieved off the disks.

(b) To every database machine model we should add

$$r\left(\frac{N}{B_{IO}} + k \cdot (TAC + (CY_k - 1)TACS)\right)$$

where the meanings of N, B_{IO}, TAC, and $TACS$ are as before; k is the number of sequential file partitions on secondary storage where each partition occupies CY_k number of contiguous tracks; and r is the number of times the data must be paged in the database machine. If the database is larger than the database machine memory but the file to be processed can fit entirely into the database machine memory, once it is brought in, then $r = 1$; otherwise, $r > 1$ meaning the file must be brought in and processed in pieces. In the case with $r > 1$ the database machine model must also be modified; for example, in select and update the entire expression will be

$$r\left[\frac{N' \cdot l_q \cdot t_p}{p} + \sigma\left(\frac{N'}{p}t_0 + \frac{N'}{B_{IO}}\right) + \frac{N'}{B_{IO}} + k \cdot (TAC + (CY_k - 1)TACS)\right]$$

where N' is the number of records paged in the database machine memory at each iteration. Here the interpretation of k and CY_k must be modified to indicate the part of the data file that is loaded in the database machine at each iteration. The expression with $r = 1$ becomes

$$\frac{N \cdot l_q \cdot t_p}{p} + \sigma\left(\frac{N}{p}t_0 + \frac{N}{B_{IO}}\right) + \frac{N}{B_{IO}} + k \cdot (TAC + (CY_k - 1)TACS)$$

where in most cases $k = 1$; that is, the file is stored in one contiguous area on disk. The difference between the two expressions is that when $r > 1$, we must repeat database machine processing for every subset of the file that is brought in while paging out its updated records.

The comparisons between conventional systems and database machines will hurt database machines, although their gain would still be maintained for small r, because of nonresidence. The bandwidth in paging, B_{IO}, will be a critical design parameter for database machines. While B_{IO} is being optimized (going toward the right at level 2 in Figure 11.1), we may consider cache memories with overlapped staging and processing, exploitation of locality, and so on. At one point we may also consider parallel in-stream architectures; however, we will defer our discussion on that to nonlinear processes because we are dealing with the basic operations which are linear in complexity.

11.5 BINARY AND AGGREGATE FUNCTION OPERATIONS

The binary and aggregate function operations are those operations whose complexity is high for nonresident databases. We remember that for a nonresident relation in doing basic operations, we need r iterations of processing and paging. In processing a join with respect to the nested loop algorithm, if we assume that none of the relations can fit in the database machine memory, then we will have $r_1 \times r_2$ many iterations of nested loop processing where r_1 and r_2 refer, respectively, to the number of times the partitions of the first and second relations are paged in the database machine. Assuming relations are of equal size, then we have a quadratic function of paging I/O and processing for the join operation. This results in I/O bottleneck and diminishes performance gains of a database machine. And in fact, at some point, a sort/merge–based join algorithm executing on a uniprocessor becomes more profitable [Ozkarahan, 1983] with respect to executing join on a database machine.

11.5.1 Basic Primitives Needed for Hard Operations

Because of their complexity, as indicated, the binary and aggregate function operations are referred to as "hard" database operations. These operations are

Join	Division
Intersection	Projection
Difference	Grouping
Union	Correlation
Product	

Join is a special case of the (Cartesian) product operation. Difference uses the idea of intersection. Union needs projection, and division can be accomplished by means of projection and join or intersection. The operations of projection, grouping, and correlation involve a single relation; however, their algorithms have $O(n^2)$ complexity (for n attribute values) if executed as a nested loop algorithm. All three of these operations are essentially based on grouping with respect to a free variable provided from within the relation being processed. Accordingly, all the operations listed converge upon the following capabilities:

Joining

Intersecting pairs of relations

Grouping a relation

The basic database machine processes that have been utilized for these operations are

(a) The nested loop algorithm with varying degrees of parallelism and associativity for join and intersection.
(b) Associative cursoring for grouping and intersection (nonkey attributes) (e.g., GET_FIRST in a loop in the RAP machine).
(c) Partitioned nested loop algorithm.
(d) Pipelined sort/merge–based in-stream processing.
(e) Nested loop algorithm in a tree-connected network.
(f) Maybe join filtering.

Among the database machine designs we have seen in Chapter 7, almost all designs use a form of nested loop algorithm with varying degrees of success. The partitioned nested loop algorithm has been mentioned in the GRACE and RAP.3 machines. The pipelined in-stream processing with sort/merge has been proposed in Tanaka, Nozaka, and Masuyama [1980]. Although this design linearizes the join process, it relies on database partitioning and duplication of hardware for parallelism to achieve high performance. The GRACE architecture also uses pipelined sort/merge with database partitioning based on hash encoding. The nested loop algorithm in a tree network of machines essentially belongs to the group of architectures of item (a). Maybe join filtering is performed by some filter designs including the CAFS and LEECH machines.

11.5.2 Performance in Hard Operations

As we have indicated in the previous section, the basic capabilities for performing binary and aggregate function processing rest with the ability of performing join, intersection, and grouping. The last operation will also need the capability of basic operations we have seen earlier in order to carry out the subsequently needed operations on a group including duplicate elimination.

Just as we have generalized basic capabilities, we can also generalize the architectural features that are needed to be able to perform these capabilities. To do that, we will first outline these features and then relate them to types of architectures (e.g., a uniprocessor GPC or a database machine). The following are the architectural features that are important for executing join, intersection, and grouping:

Sort/merge

Partitioning

Uniprocessing, in-stream processing, or parallel/associative processing

A uniprocessor GPC (i.e., a conventional system) would rely on sort/merge–based processing since all three operations basically depend on sorting and merging. In Blasgen and Eswaran [1976, 1977], various alternatives (ten different methods) of doing join are comparatively evaluated. The methods differ in using the following constructs in different ways:

Sorting

Indexes that are binary relations each of which is in the form of <attribute, tuple id(TID)>

Links that implement connections between relations whose join attributes are related with one-to-many (parent-to-child) relationships

The ten different join methodologies evaluated were:

Use indices on join attributes

Use join indices and sort TIDs

Build join indices

Sort both relations

Make multiple passes

Execute a simple TID algorithm

Execute a complex TID algorithm

This comparison does not assume partitioning. In the case of partitioning, we would have observed continued superiority by database machines so long as the partitions themselves are not large enough to cause I/O bottleneck. As discussed in the GRACE architecture and DYOP partitioning of Chapter 8, there are various ways of controlling the sizes of partitions.

The following are some details of the architectures used in the comparison:

The time to execute a join on the binary superimposed tree connected network of processors is

$$t_{JOIN} = 2 \cdot k \cdot t_1 + 2 \cdot k \cdot t_2 \cdot \log_2 k + k \cdot t_3 \cdot \log_2 p$$

where we assume that there are p processors on the network each having a RAM of 256K bytes; this memory space per processor is divided equally between the tuples of two relations so that there will be k tuples from each relation per processor; t_1 is the processor time to compare two attribute values; t_2 is the processor time for one pass of the internal sort operation; and t_3 is the interprocessor communication time. Accordingly, the first term represents comparisons of sorted attribute values (merge), the second term is the time for sorting the two relation fragments stored in each processor RAM, and the third term represents the interprocessor communication for broadcasting tuples among the processors. Notice that the operations that are involved in this timing formula are executed in parallel among the processors on the network. The join is executed by sorting tuples of two relations in parallel in the processors on the network after tuples are distributed to them and then executing join between the two sorted relation fragments in each processor, in parallel among the processors. The sorting here presumes a mapping of relation tuples to processors so that tuples can be distributed in the tree network (which is accounted by the communication time) and sorted internally in the processors, in parallel on the network.

In the other nested loop architecture of c(1), the new hardware join algorithm of the RAP.3 architecture (as covered in Chapter 7) was used.

As a final note in this section, we can look at the grouping or projection operation. While the sort/merge–based model is known for the uniprocessor GPC, and the database architectures of in-stream and certain multiprocessor-based systems, we should clarify the model for the other parallel associative architectures. The following are the steps used in the RAP.3 architecture:

(a) Partition the database to machine resident fragments.

(b) Process each partition to project as follows:
   (i) Sort the relation stored in the cell memories in parallel.
   (ii) Compute the set difference among the values stored in the first cell (first operand) and those stored in the rest of the cells (second operand) in parallel. Repeat this by making every cell storing the relation the first cell in sequence.

The details of this algorithm were given in Chapter 7 under the RAP.3 architecture. The performance improvement for this operation over the models that associatively search the relation for each unique value in join, therefore needing $N_u \cdot t_{SCAN}$ passes over the associative device, is in the order of the ratio N_u/c. In other words, the model described above takes $c \cdot t_{SCAN}$ time to execute where c is the number of parallel cells so that since c will be much less than N_u, which is the number of unique values in the attribute being projected, the performance will be affected by the reduction factor of N_u/c in favor of the algorithm.

11.6 CONCURRENCY AND LOCALITY

We have discussed the issues of concurrency and locality in Chapter 8 at some level of detail. There are two studies that can be referenced in this respect which are Ozkarahan and Sevcik [1977] and Schuster, Ozkarahan, and Smith [1976]. However, because they deal with a specific database machine we will not repeat their details here. In concurrency, there are several overheads to be considered. These are

- Communication overhead among software processes that govern hardware counterparts
- Queuing delays
- Synchronization and blocking delays
- Synchronization and arbitration delays at the hardware level

While in an SIMD architecture that supports multiprogramming, the queuing system is the major element, in an MIMD architecture, we have all the four items to consider with equal importance. One important problem is to ensure consistency of a database where concurrent update requests are involved. In Chapter 3, we have seen ways of dealing with that problem in centralized databases, and in Chapter 10 the same was considered for distributed databases. The performance studies involving concurrency and locality need a careful analysis of the variables involved. While analytical modeling is preferable so long as we are not forced into making too many simplifying assumptions, the simulation model–driven performance studies usually prove to be useful in these cases.

11.7 PERFORMANCE OF GDBMS AND DDB ARCHITECTURES

According to our performance hierarchy of Figure 11.1, at level 3 we see that we can build multimodel database machines in a generalized DBMS architecture and further build distributed databases utilizing the basic and/or multimodel database machines in a network. A preliminary performance study to see the effects of a GDBMS and DDB were made in Ozkarahan and Kayakutlu [1979]. The GDBMS architecture which was constructed for the RAP machine (as outlined in Chapter 9) was studied. It was found that the RAP-based physical common denominator, which corresponds to the conceptual to internal schema mapping in an ANSI/SPARC architecture, performed better in query execution over the model which used disjoint DBMS software whose data models were mapped to RAP relations separately. In other words, the comparisons were based on query execution in the three DBMS architectures, each of which was of the type shown in Figure 2.2(a), versus the same queries executed in a GDBMS of the type shown in Figure 2.2(b) (or more specifically, the RAP GDBMS of Chapter 9). In all the architectures, both the data model and data language were supported by RAP, below the external schema interfaces. The findings were as follows:

(a) There were more relations at the PCS level of the GDBMS for the same information structure as compared to that of the individual (disjoint) DBMSs.

(b) The query execution times in GDBMS were shorter, however, compared to DBMSs. This was because of the fact that due to the more structured and unified approach of GDBMS in creating external schemas from the conceptual schema, higher normal forms were achieved by GDBMS instead of the large first normal form n'ary relations in the case of DBMSs. These higher normal forms result in lower relation cardinalities therefore winning over join operations. This is because several joins with small cardinalities win over less joins with larger cardinalities because the join operation is multiplicative in cardinalities.

The same performance study with respect to DDB architectures revealed the following:

(a) The database machines whose languages yield to query decomposition and data flow–driven execution are suitable for distributed databases.

(b) In database machines where semi-join is executed in hardware, the cost of data communication, which is the bottleneck in a DDB architecture, is reduced.

(c) In systems where tagging (marking) is used for semi-joins, as opposed to creating temporary relations, the performance was even better.

EXERCISES

11.1. Considering the following search and/or search aiding (i.e., access path) structures, construct a timing model for retrieving (sequential and random), modifying, adding, and deleting values on these structures.
(a) Hashing
(b) Order-preserving hashing
(c) Range indexing
(d) B-trees (one per attribute)
(e) A combined multiattribute index

11.2. Continuing on Exercise 11.1 construct models of conventional systems each of which uses one of the structures listed in Exercise 11.1 to evaluate various forms of Boolean qualification.

11.3. Using the results of the previous exercises, construct models of conventional systems corresponding to each of the models of Exercise 11.2 to model the basic operations in a way similar to the method used in the chapter. Your model should have two versions: one with resident database and the other with a nonresident database.

11.4. Compare the models of Exercise 11.3 with each other by assuming a file size, tuple (record) size, and other necessary parameter values. Your comparisons should vary selectivity and plot the total required work (or time in system) against it for each of the systems. This comparison must assume a resident database.

11.5. Repeat Exercise 11.4, this time by assuming a nonresident database. Your plots should vary file (relation) size and measure total work or time in system for a given selectivity. You should produce a family of curves by taking different selectivity values and I/O bandwidth as parameters.

11.6. Take a database machine from each of at least three categories of Chapter 7 and construct models for them to model qualification evaluation and basic operations that would parallel your work in Exercises 11.2 and 11.3. As in those exercises, your models should be twofold, that is, for resident and nonresident databases.

11.7. Compare each of the three database machines you modeled in Exercise 11.6 with each of the conventional system models you developed in Exercise 11.3 for resident databases. Your variables and parameters should be the same as that of Exercise 11.4.

11.8. Repeat Exercise 11.7 for nonresident databases in the same way you repeated Exercise 11.5 for Exercise 11.4.

11.9. Repeat Exercises 11.5 and 11.8, this time by assuming a database partitioning strategy (e.g., maybe filtering by hashing or other sorts of dynamic filters, or hash clustering as in the GRACE database machine).

11.10. How would you interpret your results of Exercise 11.9 with respect to the comparisons you made for both the resident and nonresident databases?

11.11. In your comparisons of database machines with conventional system models, how would you compare the different search and search aiding structures with respect to a database machine in update (modify, insert, delete) performance? How does this comparison look when your qualification Boolean predicate does not contain any equality or inequality (i.e., all nonequality) predicate?

11.12. For the four database machines to be chosen from the following specification, construct models for the operations of projection, set aggregate, join, and division. It would be preferable to have one database machine from each of

> Associative disk (i.e., a system that can do only selection)
> A RAP.3–like database machine
> A multiprocessor-based system
> A uniprocessor-based on sort/merge

Your models for each of these systems must be twofold, that is, for resident and nonresident databases. Do not normalize the architectures of these systems, but take one representative design from each category.

11.13. How do the systems of Exercise 11.12 compare with each other in the resident database? Your parameters and variables should be the same as in previous exercises. In the case of binary operations, you can presume a selection on the first relation, based on a specified selectivity and then use the same selectivity as the interrelation (e.g., join) selectivity. Your plots can be based on the percentage of responders from the result relation. In the case of division and aggregation, you can assume that the number of partitions and groups, respectively, are determined with respect to the number of distinct values in the respective domains.

11.14. Repeat Exercise 11.13 for nonresident databases by using the same variables and parameters you used for similar comparisons in the previous exercises. Your comparisons should be based on

  Nonresident database

  Nonresident database using a partitioning strategy

How do the systems compare with each other? How does the sort/merge–based uniprocessor compare with the other systems? What features of the models you have constructed contribute to the linearity/nonlinearity of the algorithms? How does partitioning affect them?

11.15. How do you find the performance breakdown shown in Figure 11.1? Do you have any suggestions for modification of it? If so, justify your answer.

12
DOCUMENT RETRIEVAL

Document retrieval is also known as text retrieval or information retrieval (IR). The term IR has gained wider acceptance and it also identifies the research community special interest group and related activities. In this chapter, we will identify IR and present the important concepts used in retrieval systems. In the next chapter, we will discuss the hardware means of implementing efficient retrieval systems.

12.1 DBMS VERSUS IR

DBMS and IR deal with retrieval and manipulation of facts and documents (texts), respectively. Facts and figures are structured data whose logical and physical representations obey the formats specified by the corresponding data models, mappings, and underlying formatted files. Information can be logically modeled as, for example, relations and stored in the physical database as flat files whose records can be of fixed or varying length. Texts or documents are the written versions of natural language whose formatting or encoding is extremely difficult. Newspapers, medical and legal systems, libraries, automated offices, and so on store massive amounts of text on computers. With the advances in storage technology, storage costs are constantly falling and the volumes of stored information are increasing exponentially. This presents a problem with the underlying von Neumann architecture, where the manner in which data are processed causes processor bottleneck (Chapter 1). Texts are usually stored as continuous strings which are mapped into physical storage blocks that can be as large as a page used in input/output. At this point, let us make the following distinctions in terminology: a text will be understood as unstructured, unformatted data consisting of strings that make up a document or a computer program. Although computer software (i.e., texts) would be relevant to our subject matter in terms of string searching and manipulation, and, therefore, text editing, we will restrict ourselves to documents specifically. However, all the techniques we will discuss, especially the hardware solutions of the next chapter, can be applied to texts in general. From this point on, we will use the terms *document* and *IR* corresponding to texts of natural language and the retrieval systems, respectively.

As detailed in van Rijsbergen [1979], there are other contrasting features between a DBMS and an IR system. We can summarize them as follows. In DBMS, we formulate a query (e.g., in relational calculus or relational algebra operations) and retrieve the qualifying set of tuples from one or more relations (or record instances from record types). In IR, however, we would search for a set of related or relevant documents for our topic of interest. The match is a partial one, based on a relationship called *similarity* and iteratively refined toward the desired goal. While in DBMS we would have an exact match between the attributes of a query and those of the record type occurrences, in IR a retrieved document may partially agree with the attributes of a request. Let us see the following example.

Example 12.1

```
SELECT NAME, AGE
FROM EMPLOYEE
WHERE SALARY > 30K
·AND DEPT = ENGINEERING
```

Give me the documents that contain the keywords DOCUMENT and (CLUSTERING or CLASSIFICATION) within the same sentence

For relation:

```
EMPLOYEE(NAME,AGE,SALARY,DEPT)
```

  (a) A DBMS query   (b) An IR request

In (a), the EMPLOYEE relation and the attributes of the query are in one-to-one correspondence and the EMPLOYEE tuples returned in the answer satisfy the request exactly, that is, tuples of those who work in the ENGINEERING department and earn over $30,000. In (b), however, the result may be a series of documents containing the sentences that may range, for example, between . . . *single-pass document clustering algorithms* . . . for one document and . . *true classification of projects was documented elsewhere* . . . for another.

Also, as opposed to the completeness of a relational algebra expression, the request in IR is incomplete in the sense of describing exactly which documents should be returned, and in a system the documents themselves are modeled or represented by statistical or probabilistic means. This sets a contrast with the completeness of the relational schema for the EMPLOYEE relation.

In our treatment of the topics of IR, we will restrict our attention to the retrieval systems, and the document representation models based on statistical

techniques. The interested reader can refer to the textbooks referenced from this
chapter for a thorough coverage of the IR field. We can, in passing, mention that
there is considerable current research on the probabilistic, linguistic, and natural
language understanding–based document modeling and retrieval systems. However,
they are still very much in their infancy.

12.2 WHAT IS OUR FRAME OF REFERENCE?

In IR, documents can be represented (modeled) either directly or indirectly.
Direct representation means storing the documents as they are in the storage
medium whereas indirect representation refers to various indexing schemes. An
index may provide us with the address or ID of the document(s), which may or
may not be stored in the computer. In both the direct or indirect representations,
the documents can be either in their full text (as they are) or in partial form
such as with stop words (fluff words) removed and the remaining words combined,
if possible, in their stems (roots).

Searching of documents can be based on the exact match of keywords with
the direct or indirect representations using string searches or various index
processing techniques, respectively. Alternatively, searching can be based on
computing similarities between requests and documents or selected clusters of
them.

String searching can be based on various comparison schemes including a
finite state automaton driven matcher operating on the data stream. Similarity
measures can use a multitude of calculations and an acceptable value of similarity
(i.e., a threshold).

Retrieval requests can be in simple keyword match form, or they may
combine the former in a Boolean expression and/or specify context such as a
sentence or a paragraph with or without relative distance between the keywords.

In the indirect representations and clustering (classification) of documents,
we use keywords or terms that are selected with respect to an automatic (or
semiautomatic) indexing scheme.

Keywords and documents can be clustered. The former is used for thesaurus
(synonym or keyword dictionary) creation whereas the latter is needed for efficiency
to partition very large document databases.

We will cover automatic indexing, clustering, and cluster search. The
chapter will conclude with a brief review of retrieval refinement and evaluation.

12.3 WHY IS IR IMPORTANT?

Document databases encompass the largest storage dimensions and can defy any
limits if users can discover efficient and effective means of making use of them.
Our scope of nonnumeric processing should include IR as well as efficient hardware
architectures to process it. The utility of efficient IR systems can be very
important considering the applications such as intelligence gathering, legal and

medical data retrieval and dissemination, library automation, office automation, and so on. This utility can be maximized if, as suggested in this text, DBMS, IR, and other nonnumeric processing such as knowledge-based retrieval can be integrated and handed over to a computer of their own—the GPN^2C. Let us first briefly understand what IR is all about before we talk about hardware solutions for it in the next chapter.

12.4 STORAGE STRUCTURES FOR IR SYSTEMS

Let us review our terminology. We can represent documents either as they are in full (or partial) text directly, or indirectly by an indexing scheme. Retrievals can be based on either string search of full (partial) text or on exact match or similarity between a request and document indices. Document indices can vary from a simple inverted file system of keywords to inversion of full text.

As we know from the knowledge of data structures and file processing, data in computer storage can be stored as linear lists or in nonlinear form. The search strategies for the former depend upon whether the lists are kept as ordered or unordered. A search of an unordered list is of complexity $O(n)$, for n items in the list. In the ordered case, a block search would be $O(2\sqrt{n})$ whereas a binary search would be as low as $O(\log_2 n)$. However, for files that exceed main (primary) memory capacity, nonlinear structures are preferred due to efficiency in list updates (i.e., in adding or deleting items in the list). In these structures, binary trees or m-way trees are used. The latter is generally preferred to the former because it results in less tree depth. Consequently, in the m-way trees, one can store more values at a given node and a node can have m descendants as opposed to the limit of two in a binary tree. Less depth implies fewer storage device accesses. A B-tree is a special kind of m-way tree in which order is also preserved.

12.4.1 Index Structure

A simple index is a binary relation $I(v, a)$, where v represents an attribute value and a represents the list of address(es) of the storage items (i.e., records—tuples—or documents) bearing that value. The extension (population) of this relation contains tuples, one for each distinct value of the attribute being indexed, with the corresponding list of addresses of the storage items bearing the same attribute value.

In DBMS, a storage entity can be a record type in physical storage which corresponds to a file. In IR, a storage entity is a document, as big as a file and m of these amount to a very large database. Therefore, linear lists are unthinkable for database implementation and efficient nonlinear structures have to be found. In practice, most software-based systems are indirect (indexed) representations of documents with efficient implementation of nonlinear index structures.

The index definition of $I(v, a)$ is also referred to as an inverted index or file in the sense that the values of the attributes in the stored items are brought up to the surface (inverted) in the index. Each instance (tuple) of the inverted index is called an inverted list. Accordingly, one may fully invert a storage entity (a file) by building an index for each attribute of that entity. The term *attribute* pertains to formatted structures of DBMS. In IR, if we are going to invert a full text completely, every word of that document must be inverted with the addition of context and proximity information. In partially inverted systems, only certain keywords (terms) that best represent the documents are selected as the *attributes* of inversion. Some systems simply stay at this level of indexing and yet some others include the context (sentence, paragraph, zone, i.e., title, abstract, body) and proximity (adjacency) information.

As an index partly duplicates the storage content, large databases end up having large indices or index files that must be accessed efficiently themselves. Usually, we build indices of indices in a multilevel hierarchy until the root becomes manageable in size. For example, we can think of inverted indices made into multilevel indexed sequential files or, equivalently on the whole, an inverted file with directories. (An inverted file is the union of inverted indices of its attributes.) One possible way of implementing such index structures with efficient dynamic maintenance is by using B-trees having address pointers to documents at the leaves. Let us show an example of a single-level partially inverted document file.

Example 12.2

Document-ID
Zone 1 (Author)
Zone 2 (Title)
Zone 3 (Abstract)
Zone 4 (Body of text)

A document format

$$\text{Document database} = \sum_{i=1}^{5} D_i, \ 1 \le i \le 5 \text{ (i.e., a five document database)}$$

Indexing base: Zone 3 only.

Storage structure consists of a document file of five full documents and a partial inversion of the file with an inverted file of keywords selected from zone 3.

Automatic indexing of documents selected the following keywords:

```
DATA, MODEL(S), LANGUAGE(S), DISTRIBUTED, DATABASE(S),
MACHINE(S), DBMS
```

Document file contains (partial contents are shown)

```
DOC-1
  -

  -
```

Zone 3: generalized database management systems with ANSI/SPARC architecture using a conceptual and three operational data models

```
–
–
DOC–2
–
–
```

Zone 3: A network data model must be available in distributed databases

```
–
–
DOC–3
–
–
```

Zone 3: A database machine is a hardware solution to von Neumann bottlenecks in nonnumeric processing

```
–
–
DOC–4
–
–
```

Zone 3: Powerful data languages are needed in DBMS

```
–
–
DOC–5
–
–
```

Zone 3: . . . a data definition language as an integral part of a DBMS . . . query processing in distributed DBMS using database machines

The inverted index

Keywords & Phrases	Document Address
DATA	: DOC-1, DOC-2, DOC-4, DOC-5
DATABASE(S)	: DOC-1, DOC-2, DOC-3, DOC-5
DBMS	: DOC-4, DOC-5
DISTRIBUTED	: DOC-2, DOC-5
LANGUAGE(S)	: DOC-4, DOC-5
MACHINE(S)	: DOC-3, DOC-5
MODEL(S)	: DOC-1, DOC-2

For efficiency in searching values and merging/intersecting a's, both the v and a values of an inverted index are kept in sorted order. The a's in a document database are considerably larger than those in a DBMS. It is therefore customary in IR to keep an inverted file of documents as three distinct files linked with pointers, as shown in Figure 12.1. This organization requires less storage for the index file, and it can be searched more efficiently. As will be discussed later, usually, more information is added to the contents of these files to satisfy user requests (search structures) of various kinds.

An alternative to indirect text representation via indices is the signature techniques proposed recently. The signature techniques transform a full text into bit strings on storage. These bit strings represent the transformation of the text with respect to a hash encoding. Two approaches have been suggested for the signature technique. The first one [Tsichritzis and Christodoulakis, 1983] hashes each word W of a text into a bit string $S(W)$, which constitutes the signature for W. Signatures (which may be stored in two, or more, bytes) of the individual words of a text are concatenated to represent the text and stored in a signature file. The signature file, however, does not store recurrences of the text words; it contains the word signatures of noncommon words. The search of the text for a query pattern, P, involves searching the signature file for $S(P)$.

In the other signature technique [Christodoulakis and Faloutsos, 1984], a text is divided into blocks, B, and their signature $S(B)$ is created using superimposed coding. The length of the $S(B)$ blocks is kept fixed. In creation, the $S(B)$ block is cleared to zeros. The signature is created by taking each noncommon word in the text and splitting it into overlapping triplets (i.e., the word RETRIEVAL generates RET, TRI, IEV, VAL). Then each triplet is hashed into a bit position in the $S(B)$ block (i.e., the bit is set to 1). If the word is short, additional bit

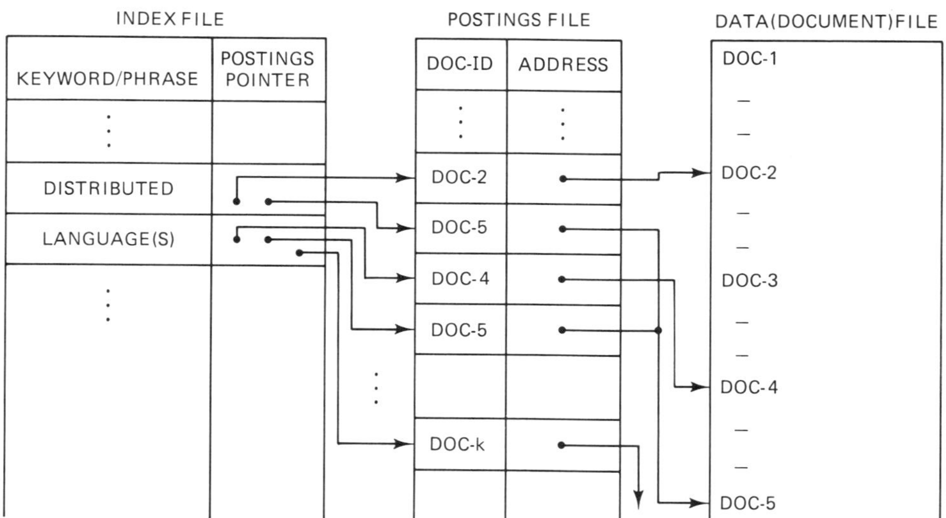

Figure 12.1 Multifile organization of an inverted index.

positions are set to 1 by a random process. Querying the text for a pattern involves the same procedure used in the first signature method.

An advantage of signature technique, besides its compactness, is the ability to handle on-line updates easily as compared to the index-based systems. On the other hand, due to the nature of hashing, there is the problem of dealing with false hits (i.e., retrieving wrong documents) that result due to synonyms. The signature technique is an alternative to indexing in indirect search. It would not be trivial to use this technique in full text search that would involve context sensitive requests whose examples will be seen in Section 12.5.4.

12.5 SEARCH STRUCTURES

In IR, the following query capabilities are frequently needed:

- Term matching
- Boolean expressions
- Numeric value and range comparisons
- Context searches
- Similarity-based searches

12.5.1 Term Matching

In this process, exact and/or partial match of terms (keywords) is specified and the identifiers of the documents containing these terms are located. For example, if we were interested in those documents that contain the term MODEL, the exact match looks for the documents that contain one or more occurrences of the term. In this search, however, those documents that contain only the occurrence of MODELS will be excluded. To include these also, the user can specify a partial match by using a *don't care character*. A ? is generally used to represent a don't care character in user queries. That is, at the position of ?, any character would be acceptable for the match. Actually no search needs to be done at that position. Therefore, MODEL? would qualify documents containing the terms MODEL and/or MODELS.

Don't care characters can be leading, trailing, or embedded. Each of these can be fixed or variable length, to correspond to a specified number of don't cares or any number of them, respectively.

M?N, WOM?N are examples of embedded don't cares to specify the retrieval of both singular and plural occurrences of the words MAN and WOMAN.

There are various ways of indicating fixed-length don't care characters (FLDCs) and variable-length don't care characters (VLDCs). (These abbreviations are used frequently and EFLDC and EVLDC stand for their embedded forms.) However, common to almost all, different symbols are used to differentiate the two. The following are some examples:

```
L??SE              for LOOSE, LEASE, etc. (EFLDC)
L*SE               for LSE, LESE, LOSE, LOOSE, LEASE, LICENSE, etc.
                   (EVLDC)
DISTRIBUT*         DISTRIBUTE, DISTRIBUTED, DISTRIBUTION,
                   DISTRIBUTIONS, DISTRIBUTIVE etc. (trailing VLDC)
DISTRIBUT??        DISTRIBUTE, DISTRIBUTES, DISTRIBUTED, but none of the
                   DISTRIBUTION, DISTRIBUTIONS, DISTRIBUTIVE, etc.
                   (trailing FLDC)
?IVE               GIVE (leading FLDC)
*IVE               GIVE, FORGIVE, MISGIVE, DISTRIBUTIVE, etc. (leading
                   VLDC)
```

In some systems, the same symbol can serve multiple purposes, such as
DISTRIBUTE? to imply DISTRIBUT (or DISTRIBUT $) (also called truncation)
DISTRIBUT??? to imply DISTRIBUT?? (or DISTRIBUT $2).*

Therefore, the query capability in term matching involves the following
search structures: (1) exact match and (2) partial match with various forms of
don't cares.

12.5.2 Boolean Expressions

Continuing along the query capabilities, next we include the capability of constructing Boolean expressions of search terms. A Boolean expression includes
search terms (i.e., term match) and logical connectives (operations) of AND,
OR, XOR, and NOT before individual search subexpressions (a recursive definition),
each of which can typically be a search term. For example, the following are
examples of Boolean search structures:

```
1. DATA AND MODEL           documents containing both DATA and
                            MODEL together (conjunction)
2. DATA OR DATABASE         documents containing DATA and/or DATABASE
                            (inclusive OR, disjunction)
3. DATA XOR DATABASE        documents containing DATA or DATABASE but
                            not their conjunction (exclusive OR)
4. DATABASE NOT MACHINES    documents containing DATABASE but not
                            together with MACHINES (such as a request
                            interested in only the software aspects of
                            databases)
```

Referring to Example 12.2, we can process these Boolean requests by the
use of the inverted file. All we have to do is to perform set operations between
the inverted lists corresponding to the search terms. The following shows the
necessary steps:

For conjunction, intersect the inverted lists—operation symbol $\cap$.

For disjunction, take the union of the inverted lists—operation symbol $\cup$.

For negation, take the set difference of the inverted lists—operation symbol $-$.

Therefore, for (1),

```
(DOC-1,DOC-2,DOC-4,DOC-5) ∩ (DOC-1, DOC-2) = DOC-1, DOC-2
```

that is, documents 1 and 2 contain both the terms DATA and MODEL.
For (2),

```
(DOC-1,DOC-2,DOC-4,DOC-5) ∪ (DOC-1,DOC-2,DOC-3,DOC-5) = DOC-1,
DOC-2, DOC-3, DOC-4, DOC-5
```

that is, all the documents in the database contain either or both of the terms
DATA and DATABASE.
For (3),

```
Result of (2) − Result of (DATA AND DATABASE) = (DOC-1, DOC-2,
[DOC-3, DOC-4, DOC-5) − ((DOC-1, DOC-2, DOC-4, DOC-5) ∩ (DOC-1, DOC-2,
DOC-3, DOC-5)) = (DOC-1, DOC-2, DOC-3, DOC-4, DOC-5) − (DOC-1,
DOC-2, DOC-5) = DOC-3, DOC-4
```

that is, documents 3 and 4 contain the terms DATA or DATABASE, but not
together.
For (4),

```
(DOC-1, DOC-2, DOC-3, DOC-5) − (DOC-3, DOC-5) = DOC-1, DOC-2
```

that is, documents 1 and 2 contain the term DATABASE and not the term
MACHINE.

12.5.3 Value and Range Comparisons

Value and range comparisons are the numeric processing capabilities required
in document retrieval. These qualifications are usually on data that can be
formatted and searched with a DBMS. However, in systems where an IR is the
only available facility, the ability to compare values and ranges is a necessity,
for example, to be able to retrieve the documents published at a specific date
or published during a period between two dates.

12.5.4 Context Searches

Context searches specify content (e.g., paragraph, sentence) and proximity (adjacency) between search terms to qualify the search request and reflect user
needs more accurately. In other words, in addition to the general context which
specifies relationships between search terms in the sense that the required terms
should appear together in the Boolean sense of coexistence, there are other
aspects that are peculiar to natural languages. In other words, in addition to
coexistence, certain natural language constructs (such as two terms should appear
in the same sentence and in certain proximity disposition) should also be obeyed
to retrieve the relevant documents. Strict Boolean search may mislead us as in

the following. Suppose we want to retrieve documents that deal with clustering (classification) of documents. Referring back to the discussion of Example 12.1, the following two documents will be retrieved:

Search request: (CLUSTER* **OR** CLASSIFICATION) **AND** DOCUMENT*
Retrieval set
   DOC-1: the single-pass document clustering algorithms
   DOC-2: true classification of projects was documented elsewhere

Although DOC-2 will also be retrieved, it does not have anything to do with the clustering of documents. A context search with a strict proximity constraint would have filtered out DOC-2. Context search operations therefore constitute an important class of search structures. The following is a list of some typical context search operations:

AB (a contiguous word phrase)	Finds the documents that contain term *A* immediately followed by term *B*.
A.n.B (directed proximity)	Finds the documents that contain term *A* followed by term *B* within *n* words of the former.
<A,B>n (undirected proximity	Finds the documents that contain terms *A* and *B* within *n* words of each other.
<A,B>ws	Finds any document that contains the terms *A* and *B* in the same sentence.
(A,B,C,D)%n (threshold or)	Finds any document that contains at least *n* of the terms *A*, *B*, *C*, or *D*. That is, for *n* = 1, this operation is an ordinary OR.
A??B (FLDC)	Finds any document that matches the character string *A*, followed by two arbitrary characters, and then the character string *B*.
*A*B* (VLDC)	Finds any document that matches the character string *A*, followed by an arbitrary number of characters, and then by string *B*.
Zone sensitive *A* **AND** *B (TI)*	Finds the documents that match the search expression only at the specified locations (zones) of the documents. As for the example, the terms *A* and *B* must both occur in the titles.

12.5.5 Similarity-Based Searches

We will defer the discussion of similarity to a latter part of the chapter. However, in passing, we can point out that similarity-based searches are system driven rather than user specified.

12.6 FULL TEXT INVERSION

If the documents in the database are represented indirectly by means of indices, the following variations in indexing can be found:

(a) *Partial inversion*. In this, as shown in Example 12.2, the postings list contains only the document addresses corresponding to terms in the index.

(b) *Full inversion*. The entire vocabulary of the documents is preserved, and all the words including the stop words are included in the index. In addition, each postings entry contains position information for each occurrence of the term in a document, for all the documents that contain the term.

(c) *Incomplete inversion*. This is a special form of (b) in which the stop words are removed and words combined in their stems when documents are stored in the database.

There are existing implementations, including the commercial ones, of the systems using partial or incomplete inversion, but none is known for (b). Although there is no implementation of (b), based on indirect representation, due to the required horrendous storage overhead, it is conceivable to have full text databases stored in direct representation.

In the inverted files implementing some form of full text, the following additional data are kept in the index and/or posting files:

(a) Content data for the term: that is, for each occurrence of the term in a document the zone, paragraph, sentence, and the word number of the term. Each subsequent value is included in the previous item in the list (e.g., fifth word of the sixth sentence). These data are repeated for each occurrence of the term in a document, for all the documents containing the term. For example, MACHINE(DOC-3, 2, 1, 3) would be returned by the system, meaning that the term MACHINE appears in document 3, in the second paragraph, in the first sentence of the paragraph, and as the third word of the sentence.

(b) Frequency information: Term and document frequencies are also kept in the index representations. Term frequency is the count of the number of occurrences of a term in a document. Document frequency is the count of documents containing the term.

(c) Synonym pointer: For each term, a pointer to the index entry of each other term that is synonymous to the former is included.

As can be seen, an inverted full text can easily amount to several fold storage that would be taken by the document itself, if it were stored in direct form.

Content data including word positions can be used to implement some of the context searches such as contiguous word phrases (CWP), directed and/or undirected proximity. For example, if the inverted document has the following entries, DATABASE (DOC-3, 2, 1, 2) and MACHINE (DOC-3, 2, 1, 3), then the following requests must be processed using the content and proximity information:

```
(a)   DATABASE? ADJ MACHINE?
(b)   <DATABASE? .1. MACHINE?>
(c)   <DATABASE?, MACHINE?> 1
(d)   <DATABASE?, MACHINE?> WS
```

In (a), depending upon a given implementation, adjacency can be interpreted as a CWP with immediate adjacency (ADJ) that is within $+1$ word distance of each other. This would be identical to (b). According to the index entries of the terms, we can see that both terms appear in the same document, paragraph, and sentence. Furthermore, they are in the consecutive word locations. In some other systems, adjacency can be interpreted as $\pm n$, where n is the distance between the terms. In this case, the interpretation would equal that of (c). This example would also satisfy (d).

With respect to don't cares, FLDCs can be handled (the same is not true for VLDCs, however) by inverted list processing. For example, the documents containing *??PAR* can be handled as follows. First, the inverted lists of all those terms matching *PAR* in the last three characters will be located. *??PAR* would then be located in those documents covered by the set union of all the inverted lists determined in the first step.

The frequency information can be used in various term, document, and query weighting and/or ranking schemes, which will be discussed later in the chapter.

Synonym pointers can be used to automatically link inverted lists of those terms that are synonymous to the user-specified term. This can improve *recall*. *Recall* is the term used to express the fraction of those documents that are relevant (i.e., satisfy the user request) and retrieved with respect to all the relevant documents in the database, some of which may not be retrieved. Similarly, *precision* is the fraction of those relevant documents that are retrieved with respect to the total number of retrieved documents. Relevance reflects another difference between DBMS and IR. In IR, although a given document may be retrieved because it contained a requested term, the user, after examining it in detail may find it irrelevant or relatively less relevant among those retrieved. In DBMS, however, the records or tuples returned by the system in response to a query predicate are those that make the predicate logically true—for example, employees who work in engineering and earn more than \$30,000.

There are various existing systems in IR that use various levels of indexing. Most systems implement proximity with indexing. DIALOG, STAIRS, BRS, MEDLARS/MEDLINE, ORBIT, The Information Bank, LEXIS, WESTLAW, JURIS (and others) [Salton and McGill, 1983] are examples. Among these, some systems use full text (however, with incomplete inversion) such as LEXIS, WESTLAW, and JURIS.

12.7 SEARCHING

Searching in IR implies the process of locating relevant documents based on the query terms of a user's request. There are two main approaches to this:

- Searching based on exact match of terms.
- Searching based on similarity (dissimilarity) measures

Searching based on exact match can in turn be classified as

- Inversion (indexing)-based systems
- Full text search with string pattern matching
- Full text search with finite state automaton (FSA)

We have already seen inversion-based document searching. In the remainder of this section, we will summarize the other search methods.

12.7.1 Full Text Search with String Pattern Matching

Various pattern matching algorithms have been proposed in the literature. Knuth, Morris, and Pratt [1977] and Boyer and Moore [1977] deal with similar algorithms. In the former, the process is of the order $O(m + n)$, whereas in the latter the complexity is $O(m)$ for a text and search patterns of m and n characters, respectively.

Let us review the latter algorithm. In the search process, we have the pattern to be matched, the text string to be searched, and a string pointer indicating the position of the string that is compared. We position the pattern from the beginning of the text string so that the leftmost characters are coincident, but start the search at the rightmost character of the pattern. The rightmost character of the pattern is compared with the text string character of the same position. If a match is detected, the comparison continues toward the left in both strings to consider the other characters of the pattern. Once a mismatch is detected, however, the shift reverses toward the right to continue the search by skipping the text string characters. To reach the end of a text as soon as possible, two delta shifts, Δ_1 and Δ_2, are proposed based on the following criteria:

(a) When a mismatch occurs, an attempt is made to locate the string character in the remaining (toward the left) portion of the pattern. If a match is found, the pattern is shifted right by Δ_1 positions to align the matching pattern character with that of the string. If no match is found shift the pattern, by Δ_1 shift, with the leftmost pattern character past the string character. The largest Δ_1 shift equals the length of the pattern.

(b) When a portion of the pattern matches the text string, a search is made toward the left to find possible recurrences of this match in the rest of the pattern. Whenever such a match is found, the pattern is shifted right, by Δ_2 shift, to align the matching pattern substring with that of the text.

Let us refer to the following example of Boyer and Moore [1977] to demonstrate the operations discussed up to this point:

```
pattern:
          AT-THAT
text:  ... WHICH-FINALLY-HALTS.-AT-THAT-POINT ...
            ↑
```

F does not occur anywhere in the pattern, hence, shift the pattern to the right by $\Delta_1 = 7$ (pattern length)

```
pattern:
                AT-THAT
text:  ... WHICH-FINALLY-HALTS.-AT-THAT-POINT ...
                   ↑
```

A match for hyphen is found in the pattern; hence, shift pattern to the right by $\Delta_1 = 4$ to coincide with the hyphen of the text.

```
pattern:
                    AT-THAT
text:  ... WHICH-FINALLY-HALTS.-AT-THAT-POINT ...
```

T matches, but L does not occur in the pattern, then there are two possibilities: Δ_2 shift of 3 to align the Ts or, since L does not occur in the pattern, Δ_1 shift of 6. Make the larger shift.

```
pattern:
                        AT-THAT
text:  ... WHICH-FINALLY-HALTS.-AT-THAT-POINT ...
                          ↑ ↑
                          | |
```

ATs match, but a mismatch occurs at the hyphen. Again, there are two possibilities: $\Delta_1 = 2$ to align the hyphens or $\Delta_2 = 5$ to align substrings AT. The larger shift is selected.

```
pattern:
                          AT-THAT
text:  ... WHICH-FINALLY-HALTS.-AT-THAT-POINT ...
                            ↑
```

At this stage, the complete match of the pattern; the text string terminates the search.

In the two algorithms we have referenced for pattern matching, preprocessing of the pattern is necessary to determine the relative positions of the pattern characters so that all possible Δ_1 and Δ_2 shifts can be calculated during the search. In the next chapter, we will refer to a modified version of the foregoing algorithm to point out an heuristic with regard to the Δ_1 and Δ_2 shifts.

12.7.2 *Pattern Matching with Finite State Automaton*

The finite state automaton (FSA) is used as a conceptual tool in modeling computational processes of a computer. The model is based on discrete, sequential processing which can be used to describe computable processes. Pattern matching is such a process. We can construct an FSA model for a pattern matching program based on the following:

- An alphabet, A, consisting of input symbols, excluding the null character
- A set of states, S
- M is a mapping $A \times S \rightarrow S$
- Starting and ending states

In pattern matching, the alphabet consists of all the symbols of the text string and that of the pattern, and we construct an FSA for the pattern showing states and all possible mappings. In the search, we stream the text through the FSA and cause the FSA to go through various transitions. If in this process, the final state can be entered, we say that the FSA recognizes (or accepts) the string that matches the pattern. Figure 12.2 shows various FSA. Figure 12.2(a) accepts USA, Figure 12.2(b) accepts *USA*, Figure 12.2(c) accepts both SMACK and SMART, and Figure 12.2(d) accepts *ISSIP*F. In these figures, # represents any character other than those shown on the transition arcs of an FSA and ■ represents the word delimiter character (e.g., a blank).

In these FSA, a node with its incoming and outgoing arcs represents the mapping $A \times S \rightarrow S$. That is, the node itself corresponds to the current state the FSA is in; the outgoing arc corresponds to the input symbol of the alphabet so that once it is received from the input text, while in the current state, the FSA changes its state to the new state (the state to the right of the arrow). This transition is shown with an arc connecting the states and the arc is labeled with the symbol causing the transition. For a node, an incoming arc shows the transition that created the current state.

In the panels of Figure 12.2, 12.2(a) shows an FSA that accepts the word USA, which is delimited by word delimiters. In 12.2(b), however, we are looking for a substring USA, which, besides that of (a), accepts such strings as USAGE, USABLE, and ACCUSABLE. In 12.2(c), we see an FSA that processes the common substrings of the words SMACK and SMART and branches into two possible states, states 6 and 9. However, at a given time, the FSA enters into only one of these states, depending upon the input character. At this point, we can see that state 5 has four possible transitions, by #, ■, C, and R. As can be seen, the first of these is common to most other nodes signifying a so-called default state, so that the FSA will enter it if the input character is not the one that causes an expectable transition toward the recognition of the pattern, with the exception of the word delimiter ■, which is recognized separately. In 12.2(d), we see transitions other than the default so that the substrings that recur in the

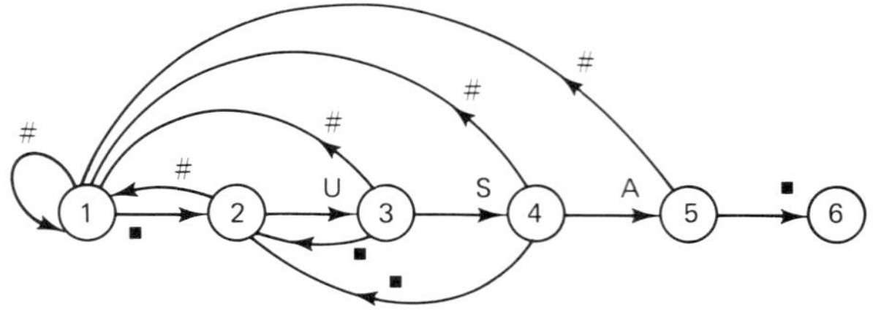

(a) FSA to accept USA

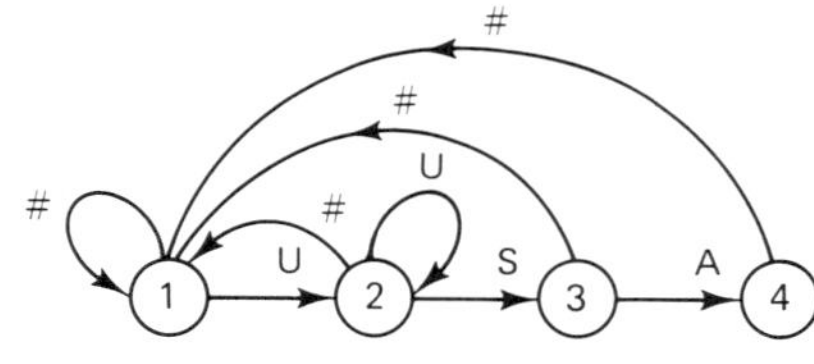

(b) FSA to accept *USA*

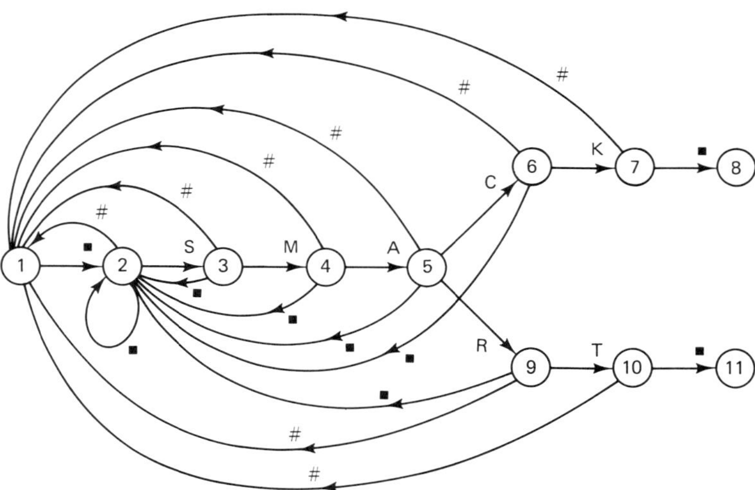

(c) FSA to accept SMACK or SMART

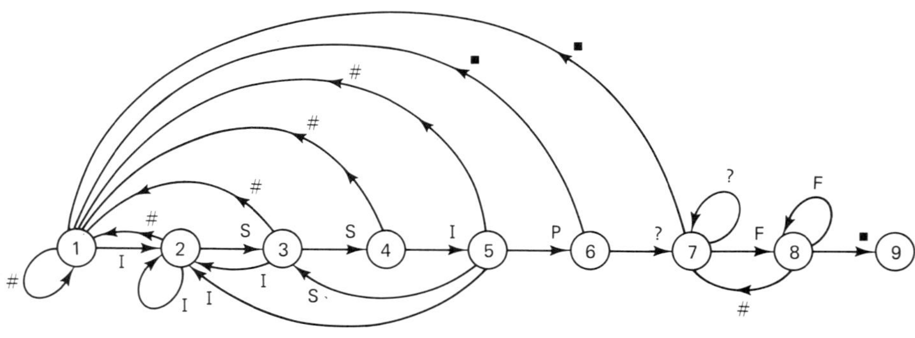

(d) FSA to accept *ISSIP*F

Figure 12.2 Finite state automata for pattern matching.

input string cannot be missed. At states 6 and 7, we subdivide a # into ? and ■ since the don't cares, except the word delimiter, become acceptable in the EVLDC that terminates with F.

Implementation of an FSA is straightforward. For each FSA, we need to create a state matrix or table which has a state block for each state in the FSA. Each state block would in turn have an array of entries indexable or addressable by each input character (e.g., 256 entries for an 8-bit character). Each entry would contain the block address of the next state to be entered. However, this straightforward implementation of an FSA would be very inefficient in memory usage. For example, 256K memory entries, each a word or more long, would be required to handle 1000 states. It is quite typical to encounter that many states in real-life applications. We will see efficient ways of implementing an FSA in the next chapter.

12.7.3 *Similarity-Based Searching*

In the exact sense of the term similarity, we see one important characteristic of IR that differentiates it from DBMS. That is, as mentioned earlier, in IR, we try to retrieve relevant documents, and relevance is a relative measure. In that sense, all methods of searching in IR fall, in the broad sense, under the definition of similarity. Although what we have discussed so far determined a relevant document based on the searches for exact match, in this section, we will deal with similarity in the more explicit sense of the word.

Similarity can be interpreted as the distance between two entities; the more similar the entities are, the closer they will be to each other. Another interpretation views similarity as the angle between two vectors representing entities in the vector space. The compared entities can be terms versus terms, documents versus documents, or query versus documents. The entities take the form of a vector rather than point values, as seen in the following. As mentioned, the entities compared are representations rather than the entities themselves. For example, in document retrieval, it is customary to represent a document by the terms (keywords) used as an index arranged in a document vector. Accordingly, a document vector D_i for the ith document will be in the form $D_i = (t_{i1}, t_{i2}, \ldots, t_{in})$ for n keywords. Each t_{ij}, $1 \leq i \leq m$ (for an m document database), $1 \leq j \leq n$, can be one of the following:

1 or 0, indicating presence or absence, respectively, of term j in D_i, if a binary representation is employed.

A constant representing the weight of term j in D_i; a zero would imply absence of the term in the document, when a weighting scheme is used.

Accordingly, we can represent our database in terms of a document by term matrix of m by n as shown:

```
TERM
D t₁₁ t₁₂ t₁₃  .  .  .  t₁ₙ
O t₂₁ t₂₂ t₂₃  .  .  .  t₂ₙ
C  .
U  .
M  .
E  .
N  .
T t_{m1} t_{m2} t_{m3}  .  .  .  t_{mn}
```

As can be seen in this matrix form, each document can be represented as a vector (i.e., rows in the matrix), and each term takes the form of a vector (i.e., columns in the matrix) showing the assignment of the term to the documents in the database. Similarly, we can also represent a query as a vector: $Q_i = (t_{i1}, t_{i2}, \ldots, t_{in})$ showing the presence or absence (or weight) of the database terms in the ith query. Once the representation is decided, we can compute similarity between the terms in the matrix. This can provide us with term classification or term clustering that can be used to construct synonym dictionaries (thesauruses). Similarly, document similarities can be computed between the rows of the matrix to provide us with document classification or clustering so that retrievals can be made efficiently. In terms of searching, we can compute the similarity between the query vector and each of the document vectors and retrieve those documents whose similarity exceeds a threshold value of T, controlled by the user. In databases where there are large numbers of documents, clustering of documents becomes a necessity. In such cases, instead of computing similarity of the query vector with each of the large number of document vectors, we compute the similarity of the query only with the cluster representatives, called *centroids*. A centroid vector, G (for gravity), can be represented simply as

$$G_i = (g_{i1}, g_{i2}, \ldots, g_{in})$$ for the centroid of the ith document cluster and n database terms, that is, $1 \leq j \leq n$, where

$$g_{ij} = \frac{1}{m} \sum_{i=1}^{m} t_{ij}$$ for m documents, g_{ij} is simply the average weight

The converse of similarity is dissimilarity and sometimes can be conveniently used in the mathematical treatment of the concept. As stated in van Rijsbergen [1979], any dissimilarity function can be converted into a similarity function by $similarity = (1 + dissimilarity)^{-1}$; however, the reverse does not always hold.

There are various similarity measures and, depending on the way they are used, they are also referred to as matching functions. Assuming that we want to measure the similarity of a document, D_i, and query Q_j, the following shows some known similarity functions, S, that can be used:

Dice's coefficient:

$$S(D_i, Q_j) = \frac{2 \left(\sum_{k=1}^{n} t_{ik} \cdot t_{jk} \right)}{\sum_{k=1}^{n} t_{ik} + \sum_{k=1}^{n} t_{jk}}$$

Jaccard's coefficient:

$$S(D_i, Q_j) = \frac{\sum_{k=1}^{n} t_{ik} \cdot t_{jk}}{\sum_{k=1}^{n} t_{ik} + \sum_{k=1}^{n} t_{jk} - \sum_{k=1}^{n} t_{ik} \cdot t_{jk}}$$

Cosine coefficient:

$$S(D_i, Q_j) = \frac{\sum_{k=1}^{n} t_{ik} \cdot t_{jk}}{\sqrt{\sum_{k=1}^{n} t_{ik}^2 \cdot \sum_{k=1}^{n} t_{jk}^2}}$$

Overlap coefficient:

$$S(D_i, Q_j) = \frac{\sum_{k=1}^{n} t_{ik} \cdot t_{jk}}{\text{minimum} \left(\sum_{k=1}^{n} t_{ik}, \sum_{k=1}^{n} t_{jk} \right)}$$

Example 12.3

Assuming the following document and query vectors, let us compute the similarity coefficients.

$$D_i = (0, 3, 4, 0, 1, 3, 2)$$

$$Q_j = (1, 1, 2, 1, 0, 0, 4) \quad \text{the weights on the query vector are supplied by the user.}$$

$$\text{Dice's coefficient} = \frac{38}{22} = 1.73$$

$$\text{Jaccard's coefficient} = \frac{19}{3} = 6.33$$

$$\text{Cosine coefficient} = \frac{19}{\sqrt{897}} = 0.63$$

$$\text{Overlap coefficient} = \frac{19}{9} = 2.11$$

As can be seen, the numerators select the matching terms, due to the products of terms, whereas denominators provide various forms of normalization. For example, in the cosine function, the normalization scales down the measure to a value between 0 and 1, by dividing the numerator with the product of the vectors' lengths. In the others, the normalization is used to prevent generating false similarities. That is, if two different document vectors agree with a query vector in equal number of terms, yet have a differing number of unmatching terms, we would be tempted to believe that the two documents match the query identically had we not provided the normalization on the denominator.

12.8 TEXT ANALYSIS, INDEXING

When we deal with the indirect representation of documents by various forms of indexing and when we classify documents into clusters for efficient retrieval, we do not use full texts of documents. What we deal with are the representatives of documents in terms of terms, phrases, and simple concepts. These correspond to statistical techniques as opposed to natural language understanding. The latter is at a quite premature state in IR. Our concern here is how one generates or assigns representatives to documents. This process is vital to IR, and without it, practically, there would not be an IR system unless we have a 100% directly represented full text system. Even then, as we have seen in database architectures, we may need coarse indexing to partition very large databases. The indexed IR systems, on the other hand, need document representatives (i.e., terms), and everything is based on them. For example, as we have seen in the discussion of similarity, one constructs document and query vectors by using terms. This in turn affects storage organization, search strategy, and retrieval properties of the stored information in the database.

In the true sense of indexing, we need to analyze a document and find the best way to represent it. This involves extraction of terms from the document. However, in the past (as is still valid), indexing was done manually by using a controlled vocabulary of terms that were believed to represent a given subject area. The manual indexers, based upon their judgment, intuition, and experience, examined a given document and tagged it with a set of predetermined terms. This corresponds to superimposing a representation structure on the documents concerned. While this may work well for a given field of interest, it precludes other possible interpretations based on different fields of interest. The proper way would be to extract terms from within a document, and this process is referred to as automatic indexing based on uncontrolled vocabulary. In doing this, the following two factors are used.

- Representation characteristics of terms and weighting schemes
- Features of natural languages

We will deal with these two points in the remainder of the section.

12.8.1 Representation Characteristics of Terms

In representing a document by a set of terms, we try to find terms that identify the document rather uniquely and/or have a high weight. The absence of such terms would render documents more similar than otherwise so that the selectivity power of the system would be reduced. By this definition, we mean to exclude those terms that appear at high frequency in all the documents. These are the terms that have low resolving power or discrimination value despite their high frequency. Yet some other very specific terms fall at the other extreme, that is, terms with a low frequency throughout the documents, but with high discrimination value, are needed to increase precision. Also, total exclusion of the terms with low resolving power may be to the detriment of the system recall. These terms are, therefore, retained but are combined into phrases to improve their representation. In the following, we will briefly survey term weighting schemes and return to these concepts later under indexing.

12.8.2 Term Weighting

Assigning weights to terms is a common practice in indexing because the purpose is to be able to choose the best representatives for documents. We can think of a term as an attribute, A, that plays the role of a representative of a document in which it appears. Depending upon the *specificity* and *exhaustivity* of the kth term in the documents (m of them) in which it appears, the value of A_k varies. That is, $a_{1k}, a_{2k}, \ldots, a_{mk}$ are defined for their respective documents based on certain weighting schemes; that is, for each attribute A_k, the value a_{ik} is assigned to document D_i, $1 \leq i \leq m$ to represent t_{ik} (or w_{ik}) in the similarity calculations such as $S(D_i, D_j)$ between the documents D_i and D_j.

As we pointed out earlier, a good term (i.e., one with a high attribute value) makes the documents it represents less similar to other documents; that is, it discriminates or distinguishes the document from the others. In that respect, term specificity reflects the level of detail of representation of a term, whereas term exhaustivity signifies the completeness of its representation. Accordingly, the higher the term specificity, the higher will be the precision at the expense of recall. Similarly, the higher the term exhaustivity, the higher will be the recall at the expense of precision. In what follows, we will briefly review some term weighting strategies each of which shows a different way of generating w_{ik} for a term.

Term frequency.   The term frequency f_i^k of the kth term in document D_i is its total number of occurrences in that document. Accordingly, F^k is used to indicate the total number of occurrences of term k in the entire collection; that is,

$$F^k = \sum_{i=1}^{m} f_i^k$$

From this, we can define $w_{ik} = f_i^k / F^k$, which indicates the weight of term k in D_i.

We can define *document frequency* F_k^d as the total number of documents that contain term k (or are represented by term k):

$$F_k^d = \sum_{i=1}^{m} f_i^d \qquad \text{where } f_i^d \text{ is } \begin{cases} 1 \text{ if term } k \in D_i \\ 0 \text{ otherwise} \end{cases}$$

We can define w_{ik} also by using F_k^d, as $w_{ik} = f_i^k / F_k^d$, which indicates the weight of term k in the entire collection.

If a term has a high frequency in a document, this indicates the importance of that term in that document. However, if the same term appears at high frequencies throughout the database, then its importance for a specific document, especially in terms of specificity, diminishes. Both measures of w_{ik} may emphasize those terms that are highly weighted in particular document collections, while being of relatively small importance in the universe of documents.

Term weighting can also be based on the communication theory that describes noise as the function of evenness of the document distribution of term k among the documents. In such an interpretation, if term k appears evenly in all the documents, the noise content will be high and signal content will be very low (signal is the surprise element). Accordingly, for the noise and signal of term k, respectively, we can define

$$N^k = \sum_{i=1}^{m} \frac{f_i^k}{F^k} \log \frac{F^k}{f_i^k}$$

$$S^k = \log F^k - N^k$$

In N^k, if $f_i^k = 1$ for all i, then N^k will be log m while S^k will be zero. However, if a term appears only in one document so that $f_i^k = F^k$, then $N^k = 0$ and $S^k = \log F^k$.

A possible weighting function using signal and noise concepts can be $w_{ik} = S^k/N^k$ or $(S^k/N^k)\, S^k$.

Because of its overemphasis on the low-frequency terms, the signal-to-noise ratio–based weighting system has been observed to be nonoptimal [Salton and McGill, 1983].

Term weighting can also be based on the variance of the distribution of term k in documents. The variance will be small for terms exhibiting even frequency distributions and for terms which occur in a few documents. When a term exhibits a skewed distribution and at least a medium-term document frequency F^k, then the variance will be large. This property can be exploited in term weighting.

Term discrimination value. The discrimination value model observes the similarity characteristics of the documents represented by a term in the document space. In this observation, the similarity of a document represented by term k is computed with each of the documents, or the centroid of the documents, in the documents space. If term k is an infrequent term between documents, then its removal will increase the similarity, whereas the removal of a frequent term will decrease the similarity. We can represent the respective differences in similarity by a discrimination value DV_k for term k. A possible weighting function can then be defined as

$$w_{ik} = \left(\frac{f_i^k}{F^k}\right) DV_k$$

To compute DV_k, we can represent the centroid, G, of the documents, as in Section 12.7.3, and then define a document space density function SD. SD

will be the sum of the similarity coefficients of all documents with the centroid G, that is

$$SD = \sum_{i=1}^{m} S(G, D_i)$$

If $0 \le S \le 1$, then $0 \le SD \le m$. SD_k will be the space density when term k is removed from all the document vectors so that the discrimination value of term DV_k will be equal to $(SD_k - SD)$. For good discriminators, DV_k will be positive so that their removal will make the space more dense, and negative otherwise (i.e., space to be less dense with $SD_k < SD$).

Finally, in the binary term representation schemes, only the existence or nonexistence of a term in a given document is considered with $f_i^k = 1$ and $f_i^k = 0$ corresponding to the existence and nonexistence of term k in document i, respectively.

12.8.3 *Features of Natural Languages*

In natural languages, especially in the studies based on the English language, *Zipf's law* [Zipf, 1949] states the observation of the human behavior of least effort. That is, in the use of a natural language, one tends to repeat certain words rather than attempting to coin new ones so that approximately 20% of the words account for 70% of the term usage. Zipf's law states that *frequency* $\times$ *rank* $\simeq$ *constant*. In this expression, rank represents the relative order of a term with respect to its frequency of use. Zipf's law can be observed from the plot of Figure 12.3 between frequency and rank [Schultz, 1968]. Based on the work of Luhn reported in this 1968 reference, a resolving power of words has been defined. Accordingly, the high- and low-frequency terms are not seen as good discriminators and the resolving power, or the discrimination capability,

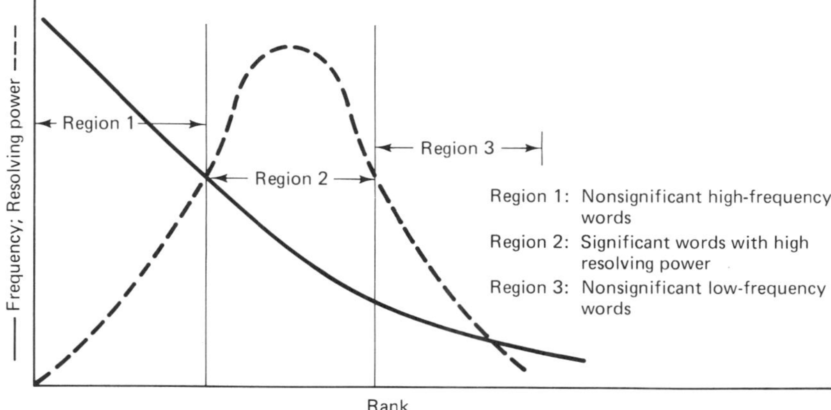

Figure 12.3   The plot of frequency and resolving power of words versus their rank.

is seen to peak at the medium-frequency words. This early observation had led to various methodologies of indexing and term weighting that we discussed in the previous sections.

12.8.4 Indexing

The interpretations of the early observations based on Figure 12.3 have resulted in the following guidelines that are frequently used in the indexing of documents.

About 300 words of the English language are in Region 1 and are referred to as the *stop* (or fluff, noise) words. The most frequent words such as (*a, above, again, and, any, before, can, every, has, he, indeed, many, once, perhaps, through, was, well, within,* etc.) are among the stop words.

To produce a realistic frequency count for various words that have the same meaning, a stemming procedure is used. In such a procedure, words are pruned of their prefixes and suffixes and combined (word coflation) in their stems. The forms such as (*-ability, -aciousnesses, -ality, -allingful, -anticism, -ater,* etc.) are suffixes. In the generation of stems, exceptional linguistic characteristics must be observed and accounted for (e.g., *absorption* → *absorb; ual* cannot be removed from equal; minimum stem length).

It has been observed that the total exclusion of low discriminators in terms of nonsignificant high- and low-frequency terms adversely affects the retrieval performance. Removal of high-frequency terms lowers recall whereas removal of low-frequency terms lowers precision. In view of this, the following basic steps can be given for document indexing:

(a) Remove the stop words from the document.
(b) Words with negative discrimination value can be combined into phrases whereas those with low nonnegative DVs can be replaced with thesaurus classes.
(c) For each of the resulting combinations (i.e., phrases or thesaurus classes) and for each of the individual words (or stems) of high resolving power, compute weights according to a chosen weighting scheme.
(d) Use the resulting words, concepts, or phrases as the keywords or terms of the documents to be indexed and represent each document by a vector consisting of term entries where the value of each entry represents the presence/absence or the weight w_{ik} of term k for document i.

A thesaurus is a term dictionary of controlled vocabulary and/or automatically generated index terms. In this dictionary, the terms are clustered into concepts, and hierarchies of concepts are constructed. One way to do this would be to use the document by term matrix of the database and compute similarities among the columns (terms) of the matrix so that clusters of terms can be formed. (Clustering will be the topic of the following section.) The uses of a thesaurus are (1) users may consult the thesaurus in selecting query terms, (2) a given query keyword may be replaced by its synonym as represented in the database (in the documents), and (3) terms with very low or close to zero discrimination values can be replaced by their respective upper hierarchy concepts or classes with an effort to increase term discrimination, as listed in step (b). As in the forming of phrases from those terms with negative DV, replacement by thesaurus class is made to increase the linkages between related documents, while at the same time, to decrease their linkages with unrelated documents. One example for a thesaurus concept is

```
INTEGRATED CIRCUIT:   SSI
                      MSI
                      LSI
                      VLSI
```

where INTEGRATED CIRCUIT is the thesaurus class or concept encompassing all the words on the right.

The example for a two-term continuous phrase is *DIE CASTING* or *DIE CAST* which may make the highly occurring words of DIE and CAST more meaningful and differentiate the documents from those that contain . . . *dies at the age of 89* . . . and . . . *finally came to the ballot to cast his vote for the primary* . . . .

12.9 CLUSTERING OF DOCUMENTS

Clustering (or classification) is an important operation in IR. We may cluster terms to build thesauruses or cluster documents for the efficiency of storage and retrieval. As indicated in van Rijsbergen [1979], closely associated documents tend to be relevant to the same request so that IR efficiency and effectiveness can benefit from the clustering of documents. Document clustering (clustering from now on) generates homogeneous groups of documents so that the documents within a group are more strongly related with each other than with those in other groups. Clustering and similarity based IR is an alternative to inverted file-based document retrieval.

The starting point in clustering is the document by term matrix where each row is a document vector whose length is the number of terms used to describe the document collection.

In a given document cluster C, we can have a varying number of documents. A cluster containing a single document is called a *singleton*. If the clustering process generates clusters with no overlap, that is, having no common documents among themselves, then the clustering process is called a *partitioning* type.

Some important considerations in clustering are

- Are the clusters stable, that is, are they invulnerable to small changes such as addition of a few documents and/or errors made in the description of documents?

- Is the structure of a cluster sensitive to the order in which the documents are initially entered to the database?
- Do the clusters overlap? Are there many clusters with very few documents in them or, on the contrary, are there a few fat clusters containing a large number of documents?
- How does clustering affect an IR system's effectiveness as well as efficiency?

The desirable answers for these questions are: We should be able to generate stable clusters that are order independent with uniform distribution of documents among clusters whose number must be optimum for system effectiveness and efficiency. For that matter, we may not be able to allow too much overlap (if any at all) between clusters considering the very large sizes of document databases.

A clustering process can be abstracted by the ordered tuple of (D, C, A), where D represents the document collection to be clustered, C clusters to be formed, and A is the association measure to group documents into clusters. There have been various strategies for A as characterized by the concepts referred to as *single link, average link, maximal complete graph or clique, stars,* and *chains*. In all of these, the similarity (or dissimilarity) coefficient is the starting point. In addition, there is the concept of a threshold indicating the minimum acceptable value of association (similarity) to qualify the documents to belong to a given cluster. We have seen various ways of computing similarities between document vector pairs in the vector space. These, among other things, used the cosine of the angle between document vectors, matching elements of vectors and their weights, the total number of matching and unmatching vector elements, and so on. From now on, we will use similarity values without specifying the way they are produced, unless otherwise stated. The following example demonstrates some of the association concepts just pointed out.

Example 12.4

Considering a set of five documents $\{D_1, D_2, D_3, D_4, D_5\}$ and the following similarity matrix:

	D_1	D_2	D_3	D_4	D_5
D_1	—	0.1	0.6	0.8	0.9
D_2	0.1	—	0.9	0.7	0.6
D_3	0.6	0.9	—	0.4	0.1
D_4	0.8	0.7	0.4	—	0.5
D_5	0.9	0.6	0.1	0.5	—

Applying a threshold of 0.5 for the similarities in the matrix, we can obtain the following clusters based on their respective association concepts:

(a) According to the resulting graph shown here, there are two cliques with three documents $\{D_1, D_4, D_5\}$ and $\{D_2, D_4, D_5\}$ and seven cliques of two documents (e.g., $\{D_1, D_3\}$ and $\{D_2, D_3\}$).

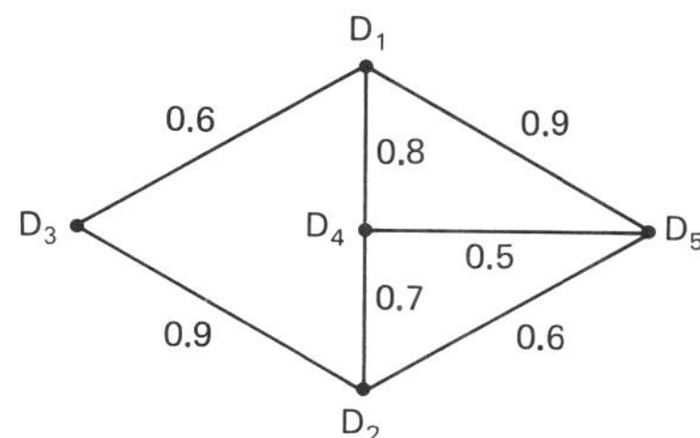

(b) One chain division with no overlap produces the clusters $\{D_1, D_3, D_2\}$, $\{D_1, D_5, D_2\}$, $\{D_1, D_4, D_2\}$, and $\{D_4, D_5\}$. Chains of smaller (e.g., $\{D_1, D_3\}$) or larger (e.g., $\{D_1, D_3, D_2, D_5\}$) segments can also be defined.

(c) In the single-link clustering, unlike a clique where all the documents must be connected to all the others in the same cluster, the members of a cluster are connected to each other by at least one link. Starting from a threshold of 0.9, then changing to 0.7, the following single-link clusters can be defined:

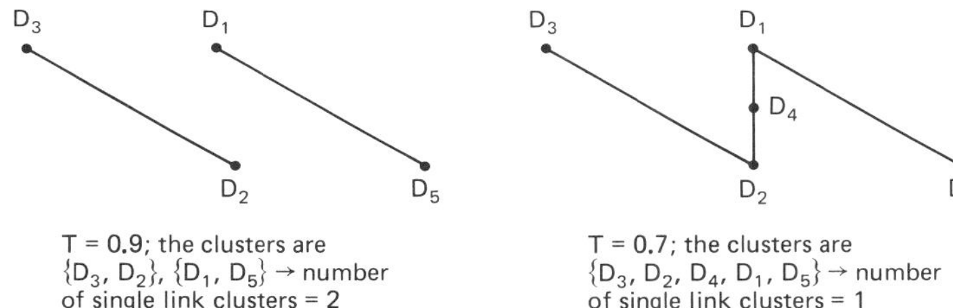

T = 0.9; the clusters are
$\{D_3, D_2\}$, $\{D_1, D_5\}$ → number
of single link clusters = 2

T = 0.7; the clusters are
$\{D_3, D_2, D_4, D_1, D_5\}$ → number
of single link clusters = 1

12.9.1 Seed-Based Clusters

Apart from clustering that is based on various forms of connected components as determined by thresholding the similarity matrix, as we have seen in the previous section, there are also seed-based clustering algorithms. In these clustering algorithms, a document is chosen as the seed (core) of a given cluster; then the subsequent documents are assigned to the clusters based on their association with the seeds. That is, a document is assigned to the cluster of the seed that is most similar to it. The following lists some seed selection strategies that have been implemented to date:

(a) Having k clusters to be generated, select the first k documents as the respective cluster seeds.

(b) Select the k seeds randomly from the entire collection.

(c) Generate the seeds randomly (i.e., generate their document vectors by a random process).

(d) Partition the database into k parts and then compute the centroid of each part to represent the seed.

(e) Compute the term document frequency (number of postings) for the terms, then choose the first k documents whose sum of term document frequencies for the terms in their document vectors is the highest. (That is, for each document, compute $sum = \Sigma_{k=1}^{n} F_k^d$ and select those documents with the first k highest sum, where as we have seen before, $F_k^d = \Sigma_{i=1}^{m} f_i^d$).

(f) Using an inverted file system, select the documents contained in the postings list as the initial cluster corresponding to a term in the index. Compute the centroid of the cluster to represent the seed. Generate k of these clusters based on some criterion (i.e., from the first k terms of the index or the first k index terms with the longest postings list).

In what follows, we will introduce a unique scheme of cluster generation due to Can and Ozkarahan [1983]. In this scheme, a new concept called the *cover coefficient* is introduced. By the use of this concept, couplings and decouplings among the documents of a collection are determined and a cluster seed power is calculated for each document. The documents having the first η_c highest seed powers are selected as the seeds. η_c is the theoretically implied number of clusters also provided by this clustering algorithm. This clustering process is a partitioning-type algorithm with no overlap among clusters.

12.9.2 A New Model of Seed-Oriented Clustering

In this section, we will cover the partitioning-type clustering algorithm (also known as the cover coefficient based clustering) we have just outlined which is detailed in Can and Ozkarahan [1983] and Can and Ozkarahan [1984]. This clustering does not depend on threshold values. A suitable threshold is hard to predict and determining it by computing similarities in the database takes a lot of time.

The starting point is the document by term matrix introduced in Section 12.7.3. This matrix describes the document collection of the database. Each row is a document vector that describes a document by the terms assigned to that document. The document vectors are produced after the indexing process. Accordingly, we will have m documents $(d_1, d_2, \ldots, d_m)$ in the collection. The document description vector for each of these documents will be n long where n is the total number of terms assigned to describe the collection. A given document description vector will have zeros at the position of terms that do not describe that document. While a zero entry indicates nonexistence of a term in a document vector, a nonzero entry can be either a 1 or a weight value depending upon whether the representation scheme is binary valued or term weighting is used. Although, for convenience, we will use the binary scheme, the methodology is also applicable to the weighted term representation.

The partitioning clustering will produce q clusters $P = \{C_1, C_2, \ldots, C_q\}$ where each C_i will be a nonempty cluster and $C_i \cap C_j = 0$ for $i \neq j$ where $1 \leq i, j \leq q$ (i.e., clusters will not have common documents). Each cluster C_i will have l_i documents, that is, $C_i = (d_{i_1}, d_{i_2} \ldots, d_{i_{l_i}})$ such that $l_i \geq 1$ and

$\Sigma_{i=1}^{q} \, l_i = m$. That is, clusters are built from the documents of the collection (m documents), and each cluster is at least a singleton (contains one document).

Each cluster will start with a seed document and be populated based on the membership of other documents as determined by an equivalence relation (i.e., a reflexive, symmetric, and transitive relationship between the cluster seed and an incoming document). We will see that a document will enter into only a single cluster with which the relationship is most equivalent.

The process starts with the document by term matrix called the D matrix which is m by n. The following is an example D matrix based on binary term representation:

$$D = \begin{bmatrix} 1 & 1 & 0 & 0 & 1 & 0 & 0 & 0 \\ 1 & 1 & 0 & 1 & 1 & 0 & 0 & 0 \\ 1 & 0 & 0 & 0 & 0 & 0 & 1 & 1 \\ 1 & 1 & 1 & 0 & 1 & 0 & 0 & 0 \\ 1 & 0 & 0 & 0 & 0 & 0 & 0 & 1 \\ 0 & 0 & 1 & 0 & 0 & 0 & 0 & 0 \\ 0 & 0 & 0 & 0 & 0 & 1 & 0 & 1 \end{bmatrix}$$

As can be observed from the matrix, the following are the two basic properties of the D matrix:

$\Sigma_{j=1}^{n} \, d_{ij} \geq 1$, i $= 1, \ldots, m$, each document is described by at least one term.

$\Sigma_{i=1}^{m} \, d_{ij} \geq 1$, j $= 1, \ldots, n$, each term describes at least one document.

The D matrix is mapped into a cover coefficient matrix, the C matrix. This cover coefficient matrix indicates the extent with which documents of the collection cover each other. If a document is alone, that is, unique in the collection, there will only be a diagonal entry for it in the C matrix, which is m by m (i.e., a document-by-document matrix). Otherwise, the sum of the off-diagonal entries of the C matrix for a document will form the coupling coefficient. The coupling coefficient is the starting point in estimating the number of clusters to be formed for the collection and in calculating the document seed power. The following summarizes the formation of the C matrix and its properties:

The two matrices S and S' can be formed and defined by their respective elements as follows:

$$s_{ij} = \frac{d_{ij}}{\sum\limits_{k=1}^{n} d_{ik}}$$

$$s'_{ij} = \frac{d_{ij}}{\sum\limits_{k=1}^{m} d_{kj}}$$

for $1 \leq i \leq m$ and $1 \leq j \leq n$.

Basically, the S and S' matrices are the normalized versions of the D matrix and obtained by dividing each entry by the total number of terms representing a document (i.e., along the rows) and by the total number of documents described by a term (i.e., along the columns), respectively. This explains the following interpretation of the matrix elements:

$$s_{ij} = \text{significance of term } j \ (t_j) \text{ for document } i$$

$$s'_{ij} = \text{significance of document } i \ (d_i) \text{ for term } j$$

The C and C' matrices are obtained as

$$C = S \times S'^{\tau} \qquad \text{and} \qquad C' = S'^{\tau} \times S$$

where τ signifies the matrix transpose operation. The C and C' matrices will be m by m and n by n, respectively. In the foregoing products of the matrices each element of the resulting matrices is obtained as follows:

For the C matrix,

$$c_{ij} = \sum_{k=1}^{n} s_{ik} \cdot s'^{\tau}_{kj} = \sum_{k=1}^{n} (\text{significance of } t_k \text{ in } d_i) \times (\text{significance of } d_i \text{ for } t_k)$$

As we indicated earlier, each c_{ij} is a cover coefficient that signifies:

- For $i \neq j$, the extent with which document d_i is covered by d_j
- For $i = j$, uniqueness of d_i (i.e., the extent with which d_i is covered by itself)

The following are the properties of the C matrix:

(a) $0 \leq c_{ij} \leq 1$, $c_{ii} > 0$: A document may or may not be covered by other documents, but certainly and always covers itself.

(b) $\sum_{j=1}^{m} c_{ij} = 1$ for all i, $1 \leq i \leq m$: Each row sum is equal to 1 and the sum of all rows gives m, the total number of documents.

(c) For all i and j, $1 \leq i, j \leq m$, $c_{ii} \geq c_{ij}$ if the D matrix is binary; otherwise c_{ii} can be less than c_{ij} in the weighted term representation of the D matrix. If d_i is alone (i.e., unique, not sharing terms with the other documents), then $c_{ij} = 0$ and $c_{ii} = 1$ or w_i (weight): a document is covered mostly by itself, other documents can, at best, match this coverage. If the document is unique, then $c_{ii} = 1$ while $c_{ij} = 0$ for $i \neq j$; that is, the terms that describe the document are not used to describe the other documents.

(d) $c_{ij} = 0$ implies $c_{ji} = 0$, and similarly, $c_{ij} > 0$ implies $c_{ji} > 0$; however generally, $c_{ij} \neq c_{ji}$ for the latter case: The coverage property is mutual among documents, however, in the case of nonzero coverage, there is no symmetry. That is, unless two documents are isomorphic, we cannot assume that they are described by the same number of identical terms.

In the following, we show the C matrix obtained from the 7-by-8 D matrix example presented earlier:

$$C = \begin{bmatrix} 0.29 & 0.29 & 0.07 & 0.29 & 0.07 & 0.00 & 0.00 \\ 0.22 & 0.47 & 0.05 & 0.22 & 0.05 & 0.00 & 0.00 \\ 0.07 & 0.07 & 0.51 & 0.07 & 0.18 & 0.00 & 0.11 \\ 0.22 & 0.22 & 0.05 & 0.34 & 0.05 & 0.13 & 0.00 \\ 0.10 & 0.10 & 0.27 & 0.10 & 0.27 & 0.00 & 0.17 \\ 0.00 & 0.00 & 0.00 & 0.50 & 0.00 & 0.50 & 0.00 \\ 0.00 & 0.00 & 0.17 & 0.00 & 0.17 & 0.00 & 0.67 \end{bmatrix}$$

The c_{ij} values in the matrix are rounded; hence, the column sums may not be exactly equal to 1.

The diagonal entries c_{ii} of the C matrix are called the decoupling (uniqueness) coefficient δ_i of d_i, $1 \leq i \leq m$. The sum of the off diagonal entries of the C matrix, ψ_i is given as

$$\psi_i = \sum_{j=1}^{m} c_{ij} = 1 - \delta_i, \qquad \text{where } i \neq j$$

ψ_i indicates the coupling coefficient of d_i with the other documents. A document that shares a lot of common terms with the other documents has a high coupling but low decoupling coefficient values. The overall coupling and decoupling coefficients of the entire collection are given by

$$\delta = \frac{\sum_{i=1}^{m} \delta_i}{m}$$

$$\psi = \frac{\sum_{i=1}^{m} \sum_{j=1}^{m} c_{ij}}{m} = 1 - \delta, \qquad \text{where } i \neq j$$

The values of δ and ψ range between 0 and 1. Looking at the C matrix, we can see that the decoupling coefficients of the documents 1 and 7 are 0.29 and 0.67, respectively. From this, the coupling coefficients for d_1 and d_7 are

$$\psi_1 = (1 - \delta_1) = 1 - 0.29 = 0.71$$

$$\psi_7 = (1 - \delta_7) = 1 - 0.67 = 0.33$$

The overall decoupling coefficient of the collection is

$$\delta = \frac{\sum_{i=1}^{7} \delta_i}{7} = 0.436$$

which gives the overall coupling coefficient ψ as $1 - \delta = 0.564$.

We can produce similar measures for the C' matrix, which is a term-by-term matrix of n by n. The C' matrix provides term clustering with the concepts of δ_i', ψ_i', δ', and ψ', which can be used for automatic thesaurus construction.

In the referenced studies, it is shown that the theoretically implied number of clusters, η_c is given by

$$\eta_c = (\text{decoupling coefficient of the collection}) \times (\text{number of documents})$$

$$= \delta \times m = \left[\sum_{i=1}^{m} \delta_i \right]$$

(Similarly, the number of term clusters, η'_c, is $\delta' \times n$.)

The average number of documents d_c within a cluster will be given by

$$d_c = \frac{m}{\delta \times m} = \frac{1}{\delta}$$

Based on the foregoing example, we obtain $\eta_c = \delta \times m = 0.436 \times 7 = 3$ and $d_c = 1/\delta = 2.3$.

As we indicated earlier, clusters are initiated by cluster seeds. Cluster seeds are in turn determined with respect to the concept called *cluster seed power* p_i of d_i. (This is a concept unique to this clustering methodology.) Each p_i is the product $\delta_i \psi_i t_i$, where t_i is the number of terms in the document description vectors (i.e., $t_i = \sum_{j=1}^{n} d_{ij}$). p_i is a metric whose δ_i contributes to the separation of clusters, ψ_i contributes to the connection among cluster members, and t_i is the normalizer. If t_i were not used, the $\delta_i \psi_i$ product may be misleadingly high for some documents with only a small number of terms.

Using the example C matrix, the cluster seed powers for the documents of the collection will be $p_1 = 0.618$ ($= 0.29 \times 0.71 \times 3$), $p_2 = 0.996$, $p_3 = 0.750$, $p_4 = 0.900$, $p_5 = 0.391$, $p_6 = 0.250$, and $p_7 = 0.444$.

In most other seed-based clustering algorithms, the selection of seeds is arbitrary resulting in dependence of clusters on the order of documents and/or nonuniform distribution of documents in clusters.

The Single-Pass Algorithm of Forming Clusters. This algorithm uses the cover coefficient concept and assigns a document d_i to the cluster seed d_{s_j} if $c_{is_j} = \max \{c_{is_1}, c_{is_2}, \ldots, c_{is_{\eta_c}}\}$, where s_j is the seed subscript. That is, if $c_{is_k} > c_{is_l}$, then between the two seeds, the document d_i would join the cluster represented by the kth seed because it is covered more by it than by the lth cluster. The following is the single-pass algorithm of cluster formation:

(a) *Determine the first η_c cluster seeds corresponding to the η_c highest cluster seed powers, $i = 1$;*

(b) **Repeat;**
   If d_i is not a cluster seed
   then;

       do;
       Find the cluster seed which maximally covers d_i, that is, $c_{is_j} = \max \{c_{is_1}, c_{is_2}, \ldots, c_{is_{\eta_c}}\}$. If there is a tie among the seeds and since there is no overlap allowed in partitioned clustering, the document d_i will be assigned to the cluster of the seed whose cluster seed power is the maximum;
       end;

$$i = i + 1;$$
Until $i > m;$

(c) *For those documents where $c_{ij} = 0$ for $i \neq j$, there will not be an assignment. Either form a ragbag cluster of the unclustered documents or find a maximal cover for each unclustered d_i among all the documents and add the document to the cluster of the covering document. This step may be repeated until the size of the cluster reaches stability.*

(d) **Stop;**

In this method of cluster generation, the estimated number of documents in cluster i, initiated by the seed d_{s_i}, is η_{ic} which is given by

$$\eta_{ic} = \frac{p_i}{\sum\limits_{k=1}^{\eta_c} p_k} \times m, \qquad \text{for } 1 \leq i \leq \eta_c$$

In the referenced study of the clustering methodology which we are discussing, a multipass version of the cluster formation algorithm has also been proposed. In that algorithm, the conventional notion of similarity is used. That is, in that algorithm, which is iterative, the documents are assigned to those clusters to which they are most similar. Similarity in the first iteration is between the incoming documents and the document description vectors of the cluster seeds. After this, a centroid is formed for each cluster and the similarity is computed, at each iteration, between the incoming documents and the centroid vectors. The algorithm terminates whenever the proportion of the stationary documents (those not changing clusters between iterations) reaches a high value such as 0.95.

In the multipass algorithm, η_{ic} cannot be computed since the cover coefficient concept is not used.

At the final stage of the seed-oriented clustering we have been discussing, we have to construct centroids for the generated clusters. Because a centroid is the representative of the documents in a cluster, it must be constructed very carefully since the effectiveness of an IR system will depend on it. This is because, in the search process of very large databases, we search the cluster centroids first until we reach a cluster or clusters that are most closely associated with our request.

We will refer to a cluster centroid as G_i where $G_i = (g_{i_1}, g_{i_2}, \ldots, g_{i_n})$ and $1 \leq i = \eta_c$. A centroid entry g_{ij} will take the value 1, depending on its state of existence rule which states that for a centroid entry to be 1, $f_j^i \delta_i' \geq f_{javg} \delta'$ must hold, otherwise g_{ij} will be zero. The following defines the criteria involved:

f_j^i is the frequency of term j within the document vectors of cluster i

f_{javg} is the average number of occurrences of term j within the clusters containing it. To compute this, we must find the document frequency (i.e., $\Sigma_{i=1}^{m} d_{ij}$)

of term j and divide it by the number of clusters whose documents contain term j in their definition vectors.

δ'_j is the diagonal entry of the C' term by term matrix $(S^\tau \times S')$ for term j. Similar to the C matrix, the δ'_j entries in the C' matrix indicate uniqueness of terms.

δ' is the overall decoupling coefficient of all the terms (i.e., sum of the diagonal entries).

The existence condition will emphasize the terms with higher uniqueness values. This emphasis can be varied by introducing a modifier constant τ into the condition; that is, $f^i_j \delta'_j \geq \tau f_{javg} \delta'$.

Example 12.5

In the demonstrations we have shown so far, we have seen that the theoretically implied number of clusters for the example is 3 ($\eta_c = 3$). Accordingly, we have to choose three cluster seeds. They are the documents two, four, and three, corresponding to the first three high-cluster seed powers of $p_2 = 0.966$, $p_4 = 0.900$, and $p_3 = 0.750$.

In forming the clusters with respect to the single-pass algorithm, we have to compare the cover coefficient values of the cluster seeds with those of the documents to be clustered:

$$\text{For } d_1: \quad c(1, 2) = 0.29,\ c(1, 4) = 0.29,\ c(1, 3) = 0.07$$

There is a tie between the seeds 2 and 4, but 2 is chosen because it has the higher cluster seed power. Therefore, document 1 will be added to the cluster of document 2, which is the seed. After repeating comparisons in the same manner for all the documents, we obtain the following clusters:

$$(2, 1),\ (4, 6),\ \text{and } (3, 5, 7)$$

In computing the centroids, we need the C' matrix. After obtaining C', we find δ'_i to be 0.33, 0.28, 0.63, 0.25, 0.28, 0.50, 0.33, and 0.44 for $i = 1$ through 8, respectively. This gives us $\delta' = \Sigma^8_{i=1} \delta'_i/8 = 0.38$. The f^i_j values are obtained from the D matrix as 2, 2, 0, 1, 2, 0, 0, 0, respectively for $j = 1$ through 8. The f_{javg} values for $j = 1$ through 8, respectively, are 5/3, 3/2, 2, 1, 3/2, 1, 1, 3. We can now form the centroid of cluster 1 by applying the existence condition to $j = 1$ through 8. These conditions are:

$$0.66 > 0.63,\ 0.56 < 0.57,\ 0 < 0.76,\ 0.25 < 0.38,$$

$$0.56 < 0.57,\ 0.0 < 0.38,\ 0.0 < 0.38,\ \text{and } 0.0 < 1.14$$

Therefore, the centroid G_1 will be $(1, 0, 0, 0, 0, 0, 0, 0)$. By using the same procedure, we obtain the other centroids as

$$G_2 = (0, 0, 1, 0, 0, 0, 0, 0)$$

$$G_3 = (1, 0, 0, 0, 0, 1, 0, 1)$$

The cover coefficient–based clustering scheme we presented here has the following advantages:

(a) It enables us to estimate the number of clusters to be generated for a collection. A quick look into the number of clusters and, therefore, the average number of documents per cluster may reveal the differences from expectations, if any, so that one may go back and revise the indexing strategy.

(b) We need to keep only the diagonal entries of the C matrix in determining the clustering seeds so that the space requirement of the algorithm is small. In cluster formation, we can calculate the entries of the C matrix one at a time and discard them after they are used.

(c) The document distribution within the clusters is rather uniform so that the cases with a few fat clusters or a lot of singletons are not encountered.

(d) Because we use the cover coefficient concept, the algorithm will be independent of the order in which documents are clustered in the clustering process. In other words, the value of the cover coefficient is not related to the order in which documents join their respective clusters. All documents will be contained in the C matrix irrespective of their order of inclusion into the matrix.

(e) The average and the worst case complexities of the algorithms (single and multipass) are determined to be $O(m^2/\log m)$, for m documents.

Some Useful Relationships and a New Matching Function.   In various experiments with the cover coefficient–based clustering methodology, some interesting relationships were observed [Can and Ozkarahan, 1985].   The observed relationships involve the following variables:

- n number of (index) terms used in the description of documents
- m total number of documents in the database
- average number of terms used to describe a document (also called *depth of indexing*, x_d)
- average number of documents described by a term (also called *term generality*, t_g)
- $t = \sum_{i=1}^{m} \sum_{j=1}^{n} d_{ij}$, which is the total number of term assignments in the document by term matrix

In the experiments, it has been observed that the number of clusters, η_c, for a collection is equal to m/t_g and n/x_d. This is reasonable because x_d and t_g are not independent quantities. Because $t_g = t/n$ and $x_d = t/m$ substituting either in $\eta_c = \dfrac{m}{t_g} = \dfrac{n}{x_d}$ will give us

$$\eta_c = \frac{m \times n}{t} = \frac{t}{x_d \times t_g}$$

As shown previously, the cover coefficient concept, or more precisely the overall decoupling coefficient, δ, for the documents (and δ' for the terms) of a collection implies the number of documents (terms) within a document (term) cluster, (i.e., $d_c(d'_c)$) as shown below:

$$d_c = 1/\delta = m/\eta_c = \frac{m}{m/t_g} = t_g$$

$$d'_c = 1/\delta' = n/\eta_c = \frac{n}{n/x_d} = x_d$$

These relationships show that the number of terms used for the description of documents, and in connection with this, depth of indexing (x_d) and term generality (t_g) are the basic determinants of the number of clusters (η_c) in document clusters and the average number of terms (d'_c) in term clusters. The relationships also indicate the effect of the total number of term assignments on the number of clusters. It is also known from information retrieval theory that the average number of documents in a document cluster is given by log m for m documents in the database. According to the relationships shown, then $d_c = t_g = \log m$, which is interesting.

The next concept that resulted from the cover coefficient–based clustering is a new matching or similarity function called the *coupling function*. In the coupling function, we compute the extent with which queries are covered by documents and the extent with which documents are covered by queries. To compute the coupling between documents of a collection and a query we start with a $(m+1) \times n$ matrix D_q which is nothing but the document D matrix augmented with the query vector as the first row. Similarly, for the cluster-based search, we start with a $(\eta_c + 1) \times n$ matrix, D_{qc}. The first row of this matrix corresponds to the query vector and the rest consists of the centroid vectors.

The amount of coverage of a particular query by document i (or the extent with which the query is covered by d_i) is found by the following formula:

$$C(q,d_i) = \sum_{j=1}^{n} s_{1j} \times s'^{\tau}_{ji} = \sum_{j=1}^{n} (\text{significance of } t_j \text{ in q}) \times (\text{significance of } d_i \text{ in } t_j)$$

Applying the definition of the S and S' matrices (see the beginning of Section 12.9.2) for the D_q matrix, we can rewrite the formula as follows:

$$C(q,d_i) = \frac{1}{|q|}\left[\sum_{j=1}^{n} q_j \times d_{ij} \times \frac{1}{COLVAL_j}\right]$$

where

$$COLVAL_j = \sum_{i=1}^{m} d_{ij} + q_j$$

In this formula, $q_j = 1$ if the query vector contains t_j, otherwise it is 0.

Conversely, the amount of coverage of d_i by the query will be:

$$C(d_i,q) = \sum_{j=1}^{n} s_{ij} \times s'^{\tau}_{j1} = \sum (\text{significance of } t_j \text{ in } d_i) \times (\text{significance of } q \text{ for } t_j)$$

Again, using the definition of the S and S' matrices, we can obtain:

$$C(d_i, q) = \frac{1}{|d_i|} \left[\sum_{j=1}^{n} d_{ij} \times q_j \times \frac{1}{COLVAL_j} \right]$$

In these formulas, $|q|$ and $|d_i|$ are defined as $\sum_{j=1}^{n} q_j$ and $\sum_{j=1}^{n} d_{ij}$, respectively.

The formulas for D_{q_c} and the documents of the selected clusters can be written very easily in a similar manner. In this case, however, we should use the centroids G_i ($i = 1, \ldots, \eta_c$) of the clusters rather than document description vectors. These formulas are also valid for the case of weighted vector descriptions involved in the computations.

According to the coupling function, the mutual coverage between a query and document i (cluster i) is defined as $C(q, d_i) + C(d_i, q)$ [for cluster i: $C(q, g_i) + C(g_i, q)$]. Generally $|q| \neq |d_i|$ ($|q| \neq |g_i|$, where $|g_i|$ is the length of the centroid vector i). Hence, in general $C(q, d_i) \neq C(d_i, q)$ and $C(q, g_i) \neq C(g_i, q)$.

We should notice that the matching function with cover coefficient gives special attention to rare terms. A rare term which appears in a very few centroids and is also used in the query will increase the mutual coupling of the query with those centroids containing the term. This is because COLVAL is small for this type of term. Similarly, the centroids with fewer terms (i.e., with smaller $|g_i|$ values) will have higher coupling with the query. This will give more selection chance to clusters that are specifically relevant for the query.

In the performance experiments conducted to evaluate the cover coefficient–based clustering, both the coupling function and the seed-based clustering using the single-pass algorithm were tested. In these experiments, it has been observed that the majority of the documents obtained in a search are concentrated in a few clusters containing a low percentage of documents of the database. In the performance experiments, the coupling function was compared with a conventional measure based on Dice's coefficient. The coupling function was found to be more effective because it takes into account the distribution of terms among the documents of a collection (note the COLVAL factor in the formula for the coupling function). On the other hand, the matching function using the conventional measure, such as the Dice's coefficient, considers only the individual document descriptions.

12.9.3 Stability and Similarity of Clustering Algorithms

A clustering algorithm is considered stable if small changes in its input lead to small changes in the clusters generated. These *input changes* can be in various forms such as distortion of a document in the process of converting it into computer-readable form; introducing a wrong term and/or dropping an important term in the indexing process; addition of new terms due to the newly added documents to the collection; and so on.

Similarity in clustering algorithms is usually used to compare different clustering algorithms.

A given measure can be used both for assessing similarity and stability. The measure itself can be based on similarity. If the clustering patterns generated by an algorithm for different inputs are similar, then this similarity can be an indication of the stability of the algorithm. On the other hand, if two clustering algorithms generate similar clustering patterns for the same input, then the clustering algorithms will be considered similar.

There are various techniques of measuring the stability of clustering algorithms [Raghavan and Ip, 1982]. We will show a brief overview of a stability measure due to [Rand, 1971] that is applicable to the partitioning-type clustering algorithms.

Rand's coefficient.   According to the Rand's metric, clusters are defined both by the documents they contain and the documents they do not contain. If a distinct document pair is assigned to the same cluster or to different clusters and if this assignment is the same in two different partitionings of the same input data, then Rand's coefficient assumes a similarity between these two clustering patterns (i.e., partitionings). That is, a pair of documents are considered to be similarly placed either if the pair is in the same cluster in two different clustering patterns or if they are in different clusters in both of these clustering patterns. The Rand's similarity measure can be summarized in a table by classifying the following pairwise combinations of documents in a partition:

Class 0: the documents are in different clusters in the partition

Class 1: the documents are in the same cluster in the partition

The following table shows the pairwise comparisons of the two partitions called P_A and P_B.

P_A/P_B	Class 1	Class 0
Class 1	a_{11}	a_{10}
Class 0	a_{01}	a_{00}

where

a_{11} the number of document pairs which appear in the same cluster in both P_A and P_B

a_{10} the number of document pairs which appear in the same cluster in P_A, but in different clusters in P_B

a_{01} reverse of a_{10}

a_{00} the number of document pairs which appear in different clusters in both P_A and P_B

Accordingly, the Rand's coefficient is given by

$$c(P_A, P_B) = \frac{a_{11} + a_{00}}{a_{11} + a_{10} + a_{01} + a_{00}}$$

The value of c varies between 0 and 1. It is zero when two partitions are not similar and 1 otherwise.

Example 12.6

Based on the 7-by-8 (document by term) D matrix and the following two sets of clusters obtained with respect to two different clustering algorithms, as cited in Can and Ozkarahan [1985], we have

(a) Cluster set 1: $C_{A_1}(1, 2)$, $C_{A_2}(4, 6)$, $C_{A_3}(3, 5, 7)$, which is the example covered earlier.

(b) Cluster set 2: $C_{B_1}(1, 2, 4)$, $C_{B_2}(3)$, $C_{B_3}(7)$, $C_{B_4}(5, 6)$, where $C_{A_i} \in P_A$ $i = 1, 2, 3$, and $C_{B_i} \in P_B$, $i = 1, 2, 3, 4$; P_A and P_B correspond to two partitions.

The similarity using the Rand's coefficient is determined as follows. Assign the document pair $<1, 2>$ to the same cluster and the document pairs $<1, 3>$, $<1, 5>$, $<1, 6>$, $<1, 7>$, $<2, 3>$, $<2, 5>$, $<2, 6>$, $<2, 7>$, $<3, 4>$, $<3, 6>$, $<4, 5>$, $<4, 7>$, $<6, 7>$ to separate clusters in both partitions. Also, assign the pairs $<3, 5>$, $<3, 7>$, $<4, 6>$, $<5, 7>$ to the same cluster in P_A and to different clusters in P_B. Then assign pairs $<1, 4>$, $<2, 4>$, $<5, 6>$ to different clusters in P_A and to the same clusters in P_B. This arrangement will lead to 14 similarities out of the total 21 pairs and yields the Rand's coefficient of $14/21 = 0.67$.

In Can and Ozkarahan [1985], it was shown that the cover coefficient–based clustering algorithm we discussed earlier demonstrated high stability under various experiments and at the same time outperformed the conventional similarity-based counterparts.

12.9.4 Clustering Hierarchy

When the number of clusters, η_c, in a system is small enough, we can afford the time to compare all the centroids with the incoming query vectors. This linear arrangement corresponds to a single-level hierarchy of clusters. If the search time is affordable, a single-level hierarchy gives the best results for precision and recall. In the case of a multilevel hierarchy, that is, when we organize clusters into a tree as will be shown, the precision-recall relationship is not straightforward. While a bottom-up search of the tree may give better results for precision, a top-down search is better for recall.

In constructing a hierarchy of clusters, we start with document clusters at the lowest level. To go up the hierarchy, we construct clusters of clusters recursively by treating centroid vectors as document vectors at each step. The following is a simple procedure for hierarchical clustering:

Repeat

1. Construct clusters by using document description vectors (η_c = number of clusters formed).
2. Obtain centroids for the clusters.
3. Construct document description vectors by copying cluster centroid vectors (hence in repeated executions, the centroids of previous steps will serve as document vectors).

Until $\eta_c = 1$ (or a small value k).

As can be seen from this algorithm, the process is bottom up, and the hierarchy goes up from the documents to the *supercentroid* as depicted in Figure 12.4. Let C represent the cluster hierarchy of l levels for the documents of the database. A node c_i of this hierarchy will have t children c_{i1}, c_{i2}, . . ., c_{it}. Accordingly, the documents contained in c_i will be

$$D_{ci} = D_{c_{i1}} \cup D_{c_{i2}} \cup ... \cup D_{c_{it}}$$

Furthermore,

$$D_{c_{ij}} \cap D_{c_{ik}} = 0 \text{ (null)}, \qquad \text{for } j \neq k$$

which leads to

$$D_{ci} \cap D_{c_{ik}} = D_{c_{ik}}$$

These properties will hold for all levels when the clustering algorithms are nonoverlapping. Based on this assumption, if T_{ci} is the set of terms used for the description of the centroid of cluster c_i, then $T_{c_{ij}} \cap T_{c_{ik}} = 0$ is not necessarily true for $j \neq k$ since a given term can also be used in the description of documents in a different cluster. Similarly,

$$T_{c_{i1}} \cup T_{c_{i2}} \cup ... \cup T_{c_{it}} = T_{ci}$$

is not necessarily true for any i where $1 \leq i \leq l$ for an l-level hierarchy because

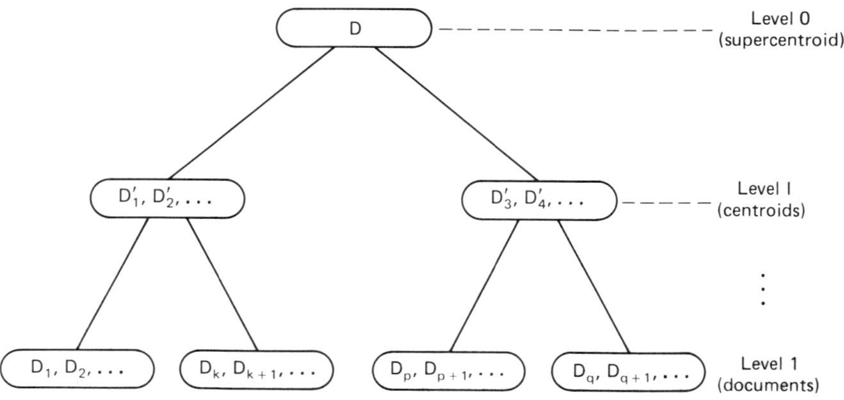

Figure 12.4   Hierarchical clustering.

we cannot assume that all documents on both sides of the relationship are isomorphic.

The hierarchical document cluster implies a partial-ordering relation. Assume that R is a generalization relation for all the documents related with node i. R will be the generalization of both the documents of the node as well as all the documents contained in the descendants of that node since the following conditions of reflexivity, antisymmetry, and transitivity will be applicable:

(a) Every node c_i is a generalization of itself by reflexivity, $c_i R c_i$.

(b) If $c_i R c_j$ and $c_j R c_i$, then this implies that $c_i = c_j$ (antisymmetry).

(c) If $c_i R c_j$ and $c_j R c_k$, then this implies that $c_i R c_k$ (transitivity).

If the database is very large, so is the η_c, clustering can take time, and this may be critical in dynamic environments where on-line service is necessary and the documents are added and/or deleted in the database. This is because most clustering algorithms are of $O(m^2)$ complexity, where m is the number of documents in the database. In such cases, we can select a random sample of documents, say, 10% of the database, and construct core clusters as suggested in Van Rijsbergen [1974, 1979]. We can then construct a hierarchical cluster tree (HCT) of these core clusters and assign the rest of the documents to this HCT. The latter process will be sublinear in that, for each of the unclustered documents, we will search the HCT (in logarithmic time), find the most similar cluster node, and assign the document to that cluster.

If we used the cover coefficient–based clustering methodology, we will have a clue in this process because we can compute the theoretically implied number of clusters, η_c, in the database, including the average number of documents in each cluster. This computation would be in $O(mn_{avg})$ time, where m and n are the number of documents and the average number of terms in the documents, respectively [Can and Ozkarahan, 1984].

We search an HCT for two purposes: (1) to construct the HCT at the beginning and when new documents are added and (2) to find the relevant clusters, hence documents, for a user query. As we will see in the following section, our search may terminate at an intermediate node, but we may need to add the document to the database. In this case, we must locate the proper leaf subcluster under that intermediate node. This can be done by locating the most similar cluster to the document vector, by comparing the latter with the cluster centroids. Another alternative can be to pick the leaf subcluster with the highest cluster seed power under the intermediate node, if we use the cover coefficient–based clustering.

12.9.5 Search of HCT

We enter an HCT with a query vector and compare it with the nodes of the HCT. Based on the value of a matching function, which can be either a similarity measure or the coupling coefficient, the decision as to which branch of the HCT to take down from the root and when to stop is made. Let us review two possible search strategies:

> *Narrow search.* At each node, the descendant that gives the highest value for the matching function is taken. The search terminates when none of the descendants of the processed node can exceed in the match function value that of the node. With this strategy, we always take a single branch out of a node.
>
> *Broad search.* From a node, descend to the children nodes that satisfy the match criterion (e.g., match function value exceeding a threshold) and search the subtrees under the parent. Stop when no child satisfies the match and output the parent. Accordingly, in this search, we may send multiple nodes from different branches of the tree to output.

Figures 12.5(a) and 12.5(b) show the narrow and broad search strategies, respectively. We arrive with a query vector $Q = q_1, q_2, \ldots, q_n$ and at each step compare it with the centroid of the HCT node being visited. In both of the examples, a binary tree is shown; however, in general, a multiway search tree (HCT) can be constructed.

As we mentioned earlier, one may use either the coupling function of the cover coefficient–based clustering or a similarity measure for the search or match function. Let us assume that, as shown in Figure 12.6, we stopped at an intermediate node in our search and that the node has three low-level subclusters whose centroid vectors are indicated, along with the query vector, Q.

To use the coupling function we construct a query-centroid matrix D_{qc} whose one row will be the query vector while the rest of the rows will be the centroids of the subclusters, at the lowest level, of the stopped node. Starting with this D_{qc} matrix, we can produce coupling values. A query would be covered by itself and the centroids of the subclusters. Those $C(q, gi)$ that exceed a threshold will identify the target clusters to be selected.

In cluster search, the final step is either to return the documents contained in the selected clusters or to conduct a further search for the documents. This search can in turn be made by either comparing the document vectors of the documents to be retrieved or by making a full text search in the documents of the selected clusters to retrieve the relevant documents.

A user's query can be in a Boolean form (i.e., using AND, OR, and NOT operations connecting predicates). In the case of NOT, there is a single-predicate or a Boolean subexpression (e.g., **NOT** *COMPUTER*, **NOT** (*COMPUTER* **AND** *SCIENCE*), respectively), whose context is negated. Accordingly, in the first example, we would be interested in the documents that do not contain the keyword *COMPUTER*. We refer to the negated query terms as the terms used in negative context. In the binary representation, a query vector containing both the terms used in the positive and negative context, for example, may look like

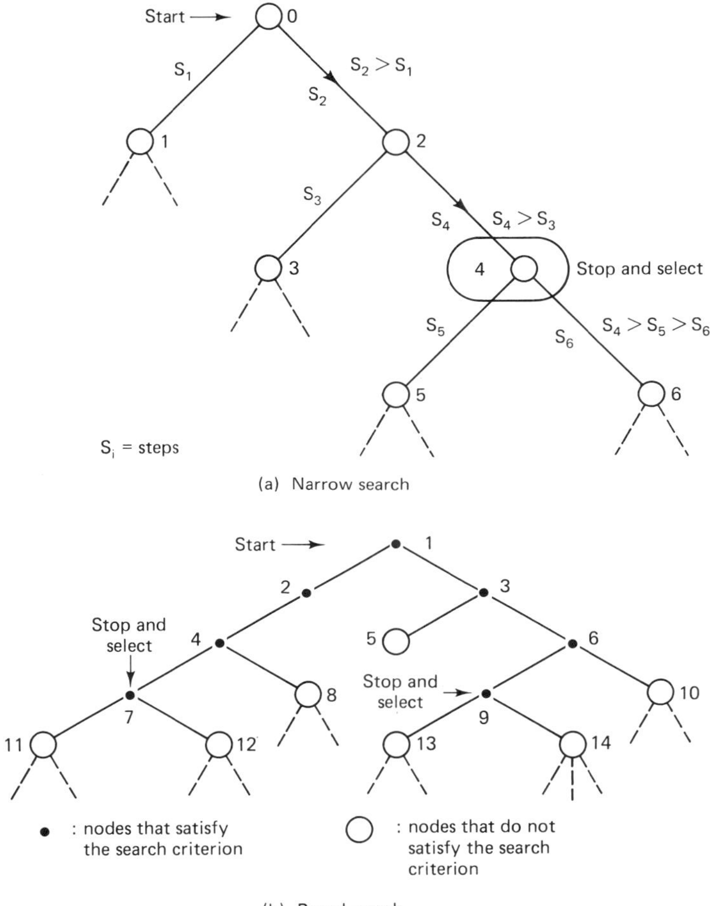

Figure 12.5   Cluster tree search.

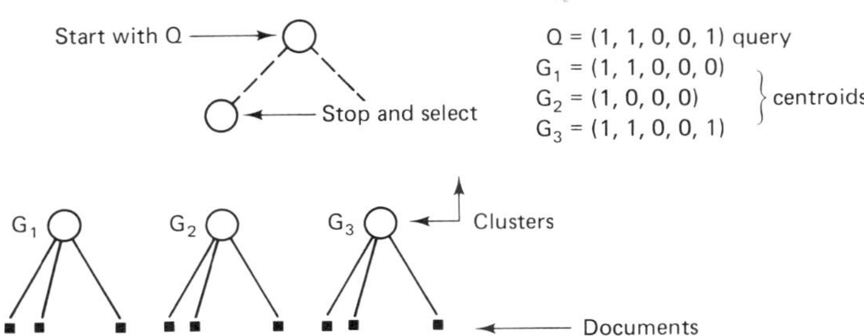

Figure 12.6   A search example.

$(1, 1, 0, -1, 1, 0, -1)$, meaning that the terms 4 and 7 are specified in the negative context.

At this point, we can show a similarity-based matching function which is presented in Ozkarahan and Can [1984]. This matching function differentiates between the positive and negative query terms as well as those terms not included in the query (i.e., zero term positions). Accordingly, we can define this matching function $SIM(Q, G)$ between a query and centroid vector as

$$SIM(Q, C) = \frac{\sum_{j=1}^{n} F_1(q_j, g_j)}{\sum_{j=1}^{n} (F_1(q_j, g_j) + F_2(q_j, g_j))}$$

where

$$F_1(q_j, g_j): \begin{cases} q_j \times g_j & \text{if } q_j > 0 \quad (1) \\ 0 & \text{if } q_j = 0 \\ abs\,(q_j) \times (|G| - g_j) & \text{if } q_j < 0 \quad (2) \end{cases}$$

$$F_2(q_j, g_j): \begin{cases} q_j \times (|G| - g_j) & \text{if } q_j > 0 \quad (3) \\ 0 & \text{if } q_j = 0 \\ abs\,(q_j) \times g_j & \text{if } q_j < 0 \quad (4) \end{cases}$$

In (1), we are saying that if a query term, q_j, position is a 1, then F_1 gives the number of documents containing that term under the centroid; g_j is the centroid entry. In (2), $|G|$ indicates the number of documents under the node; *abs* means absolute value, and F_1 gives the number of documents that do not contain the negative query term. In (3), F_2 gives the number of documents in the nodes that do not contain the query term. In (4), F_2 gives the number of documents in the nodes that contain the query term. The *SIM* function is the conditional probability of hitting a one on the centroid vector of the HCT node given that a one was given in the query vector, and hitting a zero on the centroid vector of the HCT node given that a minus one was given in the query vector.

12.10 QUERY FEEDBACK

We know that document retrieval has a nondeterministic nature. Users start with a vague knowledge of what they want and/or how the requested documents are best described to the system. It is a *feel your way as you go along* experience. Every time, the user has to make a relevance judgment as to whether things are improving toward the goal or else what should be done to *steer* them for the better. Relevance judgments can sometimes be subjective; for example, the user may become disinterested simply because he or she gets the idea of what is sought from the first few documents or some documents he or she may have already seen. For these reasons, we will be seeking a more objective view of relevance, that is, whether a retrieved piece of information meets the user need based on the values of the similarities computed.

In the iterative retrieval scenario we mentioned, in which the user at each step redirects the search by indicating which documents are relevant and which are not (or are less relevant), the query is modified at each step. This process is known as query or relevance feedback.

There are various techniques in relevance feedback for meeting the user's objectives. One may aim at high recall by adding to the query vector word phrases constructed from the high-frequency words or increase precision by including synonyms and/or concept classes from the thesaurus. Citation linkages also provide information about related topics. Such linkages are based on the reference patterns among documents and can be used in conjunction with the similarity measures in aiding the relevance decisions [Salton and McGill, 1983].

Various techniques of query modification are discussed in detail in Salton and McGill [1983]. There is also the following methodology which is suggested by Ozkarahan and Can [1984]. Let $|q_{ix}|$ denote the number of appearances of term i in a set x, where x can be one of the query (Q_s), relevant documents (RL), or nonrelevant documents (NR). If

$$|q_{iS}^P| + |q_{iRL}^P| > |q_{iNR}^P|$$

that is, if the sum of term i's used in the positive context in the query and those that appear in the relevant documents is greater than the number of positive context term i's that appear in the nonrelevant documents, then we would keep term i in the refined query, otherwise we would drop it (or reduce its weight). Also, if $|q_{iS}^N| + |q_{iNR}^N| > |q_{iRL}^N|$, that is, if the sum of term i's used in the negative context in the query and those that appear in the nonrelevant documents is greater than the number of negative context term i's that appear in the relevant documents, then we would drop term i (or reduce its weight) in the refined query.

As can be seen, relevant documents strongly affect the direction of search. Knowledge of relevant documents is more useful than the irrelevant ones. This is because relevant documents tend to be closer to one another in the document space. Document outputs are usually ranked from the most relevant (most similar) to less relevant (less similar) ones.

12.11 *RETRIEVAL EVALUATION*

Finally, we come to a point of considering how one measures the effectiveness of a given IR system. We have been mentioning the two terms, recall and precision, all along so far. Recall, precision, and fallout are the popular measures for retrieval evaluation. If we look at the popular contingency table shown in the following table, we can see that it is possible to produce different measures among the variables involved.

	RELEVANT	NONRELEVANT	TOTAL
RETRIEVED	RETRL	RETNR	C = RETRL + RETNR
NOT RETRIEVED	NRETRL	NRETNR	D = NRETRL + NRETNR
TOTAL	A = RETRL + NRETRL	B = RETNR + NRETNR	A + B + C + D

According to this table, A + B + C + D is the entire document database. *Recall* is the ability to retrieve relevant documents. It is measured as *RETRL/(RETRL + NRETRL)*. *Precision* is the ability to reject nonrelevant documents. It is measured as *RETRL/(RETRL + RETNR)*. *Fallout* measures a system's performance in rejecting nonrelevant documents. It is measured as *RETNR/(RETNR + NRETNR)*. As can be seen, recall is exhaustive whereas precision is specific. These two measures are user oriented, since a user is interested in getting as many relevant items as possible. Fallout, on the other hand, measures efficiency; hence, it is system oriented.

As can be seen from the contingency table, the knowledge of the number of relevant and nonrelevant items that are not retrieved, but are in the database, is needed. There is no way of knowing this in very large databases of real-life so one resorts to statistical sampling of large populations. In experimental systems with small databases, precounts of the quantities can be established.

In recall and precision measurements, usually a sample of k queries are run and average measures are computed, such as

$$RECALL = \frac{1}{k} \sum_{i=1}^{k} \frac{RETRL_i}{RETRL_i + NRETRL_i}$$

$$PRECISION = \frac{1}{k} \sum_{i=1}^{k} \frac{RETRL_i}{RETRL_i + RETNR_i}$$

As seen in Figure 12.7, recall and precision are in the conflicting sides of query specification, with respect to higher performance. It is therefore up to user to show a preference between systems which may sacrifice one measure for the sake of the other, if a clear distinction (i.e., superiority in both measures) is not available.

Whereas recall is the probability of retrieving a relevant item, fallout is the probability of retrieving a nonrelevant item. A good system should have high recall with low fallout.

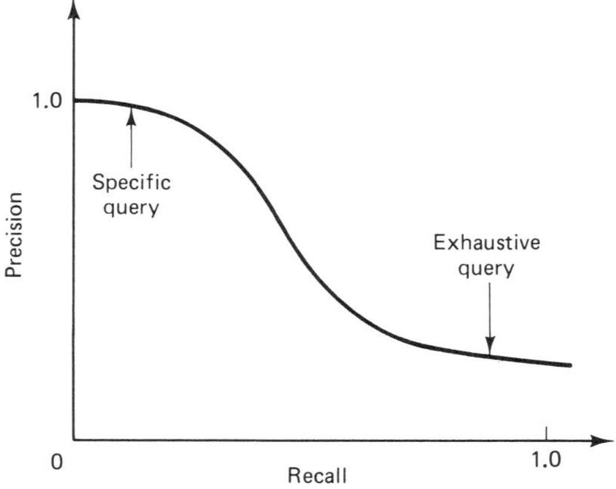

Figure 12.7 Average recall-precision curve

Example 12.7

Let us consider the HCT shown in Figure 12.8. The numbers inside the node circles indicate node numbers, and those along the sides give the total number of documents under the node indicated.

Let us follow a measurement procedure as suggested in Can [1985], which states

(a) Determine the documents and the thesaurus terms covered by a query. Also, determine the lowest-level clusters that contain at least one document that satisfies the query.
(b) For each query perform:
   (i) Create the list of selected nodes (i.e., those that satisfy the query).
   (ii) The documents related with the selected nodes will give the number of documents retrieved, and some of these will satisfy the query. Also, some of the subclusters connected to the selected nodes will contain at least one document that satisfies the query.
   (iii) Calculate recall and precision for the query.
(c) Perform an overall evaluation by using an averaging technique.

Assume that clusters 8, 10, and 12, as indicated by an asterisk in the figure, contain documents which satisfy the query and the number of relevant documents in these clusters are 5, 2, and 1, respectively. That is, $a_d = 5 + 2 + 1 = 8$ and $a_c = 3$, where a_d and a_c indicate the total number of relevant documents and clusters, respectively. Accordingly, we can denote recall and precision, by R and P, as

$$R = c/a, \qquad P = c/b$$

The quantities a_d and a_c will be fixed for a query, but b and c will change,

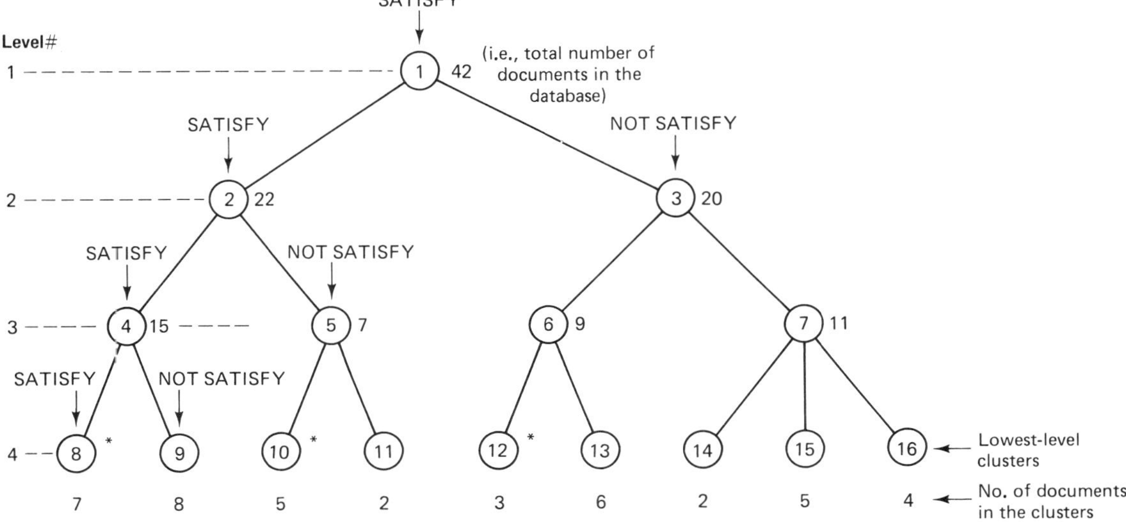

Figure 12.8 An example HCT.

depending on the HCT node selected. a equals total number of relevant documents (clusters); b equals total number retrieved; and c equals *RETL*. According to broad search, the following search steps will result:

Step 1.   Node 1 satisfies the query.

$$c_d = 8, a_d = 8, b_d = 42$$
$$c_c = 3, a_c = 3, b_c = 9$$

subscripts d, c denote documents and clusters, respectively. ($b = 9$ is the count of eligible leaf nodes and their parents up to the root.)

We can calculate recall and precision at the document (R_d, P_d) and cluster level (R_c, P_c) as

$$R_d = 8/8 = 1, P_d = 8/42 = 0.19$$
$$R_c = 3/3 = 1, P_c = 3/9 = 0.33$$

Step 2.   Node 2 satisfies the query.

$$c_d = 7, a_d = 8, b_d = 22$$
$$c_c = 2, a_c = 3, b_c = 4$$
$$R_d = 7/8 = 0.88, P_d = 7/22 = 0.32$$
$$R_c = 2/3 = 0.67, P_c = 2/4 = 0.5$$

Step 3.   Node 3 does not satisfy the query. Drop the right subtree of the HCT.

Step 4.   Node 4 satisfies the query.

$$c_d = 5, a_d = 8, b_d = 15$$
$$c_c = 1, a_c = 3, b_c = 2$$
$$R_d = 5/8 = 0.63, P_d = 5/15 = 0.33$$
$$R_c = 1/3 = 0.33, P_c = 1/2 = 0.5$$

Step 5.   Node 8 satisfies the query.

$$c_d = 5, a_d = 8, b_d = 7$$
$$c_c = 1, a_c = 3, b_c = 1$$
$$R_d = 5/8 = 0.63, P_d = 5/7 = 0.71$$
$$R_c = 1/3 = 0.33, P_c = 1/1 = 1$$

Step 6.   Node 5 does not satisfy the query.

Step 7.   Node 9 does not satisfy the query.

Node 8 is finally selected with its documents.

According to the values obtained, let us plot recall versus precision in Figures 12.9(a) and 12.9(b) for the c and d values.

In Figure 12.10, we show recall-precision versus level of the HCT. For cases in which we may have more than one node at a level, we can take the arithmetic mean. In that case, the end result will be the average of averages.

The number of observations indicates how many times a level is visited per query, whereas the number of queries shows the number of queries visiting a given level.

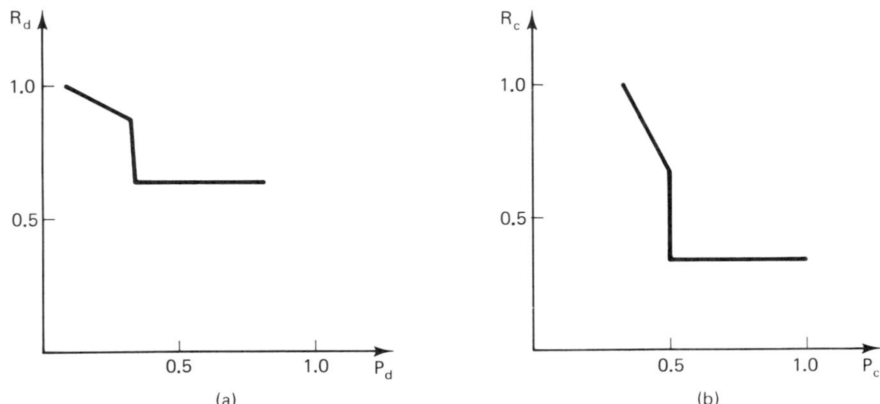

Figure 12.9   Recall versus precision plots.

We discussed earlier the effects of bottom-up and top-down HCT search on recall and precision. The plots of Figure 12.10 would be useful in that respect. In that figure, we observe the high-low–recall-precision and high-low–precision-recall values corresponding to the low and high levels of the HCT, respectively.

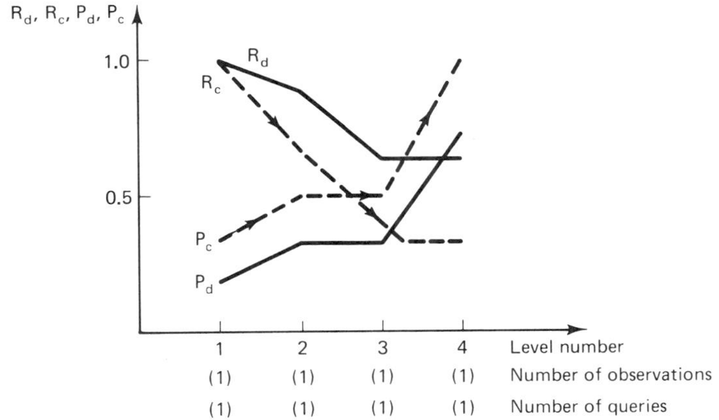

Figure 12.10   Plots of recall/precision versus HCT level.

EXERCISES

12.1. Considering the inverted file IR systems, try to model the maintenance of those systems, based on the following:

(a) The number of file operations needed when new documents are added to the database.

(b) Same as (a) when the index terms are added/deleted.

(c) Assuming various database sizes, relate (a) and (b) to the number of I/O operations, and by using storage device characteristics, translate them to response times.

12.2. If we are to support all possible context-sensitive search requests (i.e., where content and proximity are involved) by an inverted file–based system, specify what additional information should be kept in the inverted file. Would term location be sufficient?

12.3. Assuming the following inverted index:

TERMS	DOCUMENT IDS
DATABASE	1, 2, 3, 4, 5, 6, 7, 8, 9, 10
MACHINE	2, 6, 9
MODEL	1, 5, 6, 8, 10
QUERY	6, 7, 8, 9, 10

Which documents will be retrieved in response to each of the following queries? Show the set operations involved among the inverted lists.
(a) **NOT** QUERY
(b) DATABASE **AND** MACHINE **OR** (MODEL **AND** QUERY)
(c) DATABASE **NOT** (MODEL **OR** QUERY)

12.4. If the terms DATABASE, MACHINE, MODEL, and QUERY are assigned weights 3, 4, 4, and 2, respectively, in the index of Exercise 12.3, which documents will be retrieved if a retrieval threshold of 7 is assumed in each of the queries (a), (b), and (c)? What terms will the retrieved documents at least contain? *Hint: Compute the retrieval weights additively using the weights of the terms involved after the Boolean operations are carried out.*

12.5. Given the following document and query vectors:

Documents

$$D_1 = (1, 4, 0, 0, 2, 0, 0, 2)$$
$$D_2 = (5, 2, 0, 1, 1, 0, 0, 0)$$
$$D_3 = (3, 0, 0, 1, 2, 0, 2, 2)$$
$$D_4 = (0, 1, 2, 3, 2, 0, 0, 0)$$
$$D_5 = (4, 0, 0, 0, 0, 0, 0, 3)$$
$$D_6 = (1, 2, 0, 0, 3, 3, 0, 0)$$

Query

$$Q = (2, 2, 0, 1, 1, 1, 0, 1)$$

(a) Compute, for each term, the term frequency, document frequency, and term discrimination value, by assuming that the entries in the document vectors correspond to the frequencies of the associated terms in the documents. Use cosine similarity where needed.
(b) Construct a term by term similarity matrix ST where each element $st(i, j)$, for $i, j = 1, \ldots, 8$, indicates the similarity between terms i and j, where $i = j$ is included. Use Dice's coefficient.
(c) Use the cosine similarity coefficient to compute the similarities between the query and each of the document vectors. Rank the documents from most to least relevant (similar).

(d) Replace document and query vectors with their binary versions and repeat (c).

12.6. Assuming that the binary version of the document vectors you obtained in Exercise 12.5(d) constitutes your six document database, start with the 6-by-8 document by term D matrix and obtain the following:

(a) The document-by-document, that is, C, matrix

(b) Coupling and decoupling coefficients δ_i, ψ_i, δ, and ψ for each document and the collection, respectively

(c) The number of clusters, η_c, and the average number of documents per cluster, d_c

(d) Compute the cluster seed power, p_i, of the documents

12.7. Using the D matrix of Exercise 12.6, repeat (a) through (d) of that exercise for the term by term, that is, C′ matrix. (The quantities involved are the C′ matrix and δ_i', ψ_i', δ', ψ', η_c', and t_c (i.e., term clusters). Remember that in the last two quantities, $n = 8$ terms are involved, not the $m = 6$ documents.)

12.8. Using the term by term similarity matrix you computed in Exercise 12.5 (b), and assuming a threshold of 1,

(a) Find all the cliques.

(b) Find all connected components based on the single-link clustering method.

12.9. Continue with Exercise 12.6 and do the following:

(a) With the single-pass clustering algorithm, find the clusters and the estimated number of documents per cluster (i.e., η_{ic}). How do they compare with d_c?

(b) Compute the centroids of the clusters obtained in (a).

(c) Using a similarity measure repeat (a), only this time use the multipass algorithm. In doing this, use the cluster seeds determined in the single-pass algorithm. Realize that in the centroid formation, you cannot use the state of existence rule because, this time, the cluster formation will not be related with the uniqueness of terms. You should use, instead of this rule, a threshold for a centroid entry to be 1. This threshold can be $k/3$, where k is the number of documents in the cluster whose centroid is formed.

(d) Apply the Rand's coefficient to compare the clustering processes of steps (a) and (c).

12.10. Using the HCT example of Figure 12.8, do the following:

(a) Modify the example assuming that the exact right symmetry of the tree replaces the original tree. That is, drop the left subtree instead of the right one and assume that node 6 satisfies the search whereas node 7 fails. Put the asterisks on nodes 8, 12, and 14.

(b) Compute the contingency table, based on (a), both for the documents and clusters.

(c) Reproduce the curves of Figure 12.9 and Figure 12.10, using the new results.

12.11. Construct an FSA for each of the following search patterns: *DOG*, DOG, *DOG, *A?IST*, IST*, *SCHIST*, *BEST, and *BENT. Can you combine the FSAs of common substrings? Choose one FSA and construct its state table.

12.12. Using the Boyer and Moore's string search algorithm, show the comparison and shift steps involved to compare the search pattern *PAPAYA* with the text string of *BI-PARTISAN-PAPAW-OR-PAPAYA*. How many character comparisons are needed? Is the worst case complexity linear with the length of the string?

13

DOCUMENT (TEXT) RETRIEVAL COMPUTERS

Document databases that store thousands of documents are the largest collections of unformatted data. As storage costs are decreasing, computer-readable data volumes are increasing. The need for timely and accurate information is more critical than ever before and we are facing the need for more effective and efficient retrieval of information. We have seen so far that such nonnumeric tasks cannot be handled by conventional computers. In fact, the only acceptable means of implementing such databases with today's computers has always been via indirect searching of document databases based on indexing schemes and/or file inversions of limited scope. As with other forms of nonnumeric processing, the time has come to provide new architectures for the relatively neglected area of information (document) retrieval. This chapter will summarize the studies made for this purpose.

13.1 DOCUMENT DATABASES ARE LARGE AND WILL GROW

Within the past two decades, we have seen an almost 300-fold decrease in storage costs. On the other hand, the advances in computer technology are making computer reading of data easier every day. Word processors, computerized typesetting equipment, and optical readers can create computer-readable documents directly or transform old manual documents into computer form at reasonable costs.

The decreasing storage costs, improved computer facilities, and better means of data communication create the opportunity for increased storage of computer-readable data. This increase is coupled in a cause-effect cycle with the increasing need for information. The result is an information explosion that grows exponentially. The main users of this media are intelligence communities, automated libraries, newspapers, and automated offices. The volume of data is enormous and ranges from continuous flow of military and intelligence data occupying 10^{12} to 10^{15} characters of storage to specialized disciplines such as law and medicine. A legal document database storing documents such as court decisions and other legal information will be in the order of a few tens of billions characters.

13.2 CONVENTIONAL COMPUTERS ARE NO HELP

Documents must be searched entirely to accommodate unrestricted search requests. (How can we restrict intelligence inquiries?) This means that very large volumes of data must be exhaustively compared for a request pattern. Needless to say, the response must also be in real-time. These requirements imply a breakthrough in computer architecture to meet the necessary speed. We can justify this with the following arguments:

(a) First, there is no real cure in decreasing database volume. The best known data compression techniques that do not sacrifice information content can hardly offer a reduction by a factor of 2.

(b) Using the best available speed in the present-day mainframe computers, we cannot compare more than 100,000 characters per second such as the COLTS software direct search system running on IBM System 370 [Colts II, 1976]. This implies about five hours of continuous search for a database as small as 2 billion characters. New models may have improved this somewhat.

(c) Indexing alone is no cure. A 65-billion-character database, such as the U.S. Patents Office application described in Hollaar [1983a] would require 195 million characters of index space, assuming a reduction factor as low as 0.3%. Yet a new search hardware that can search data at channel speed (such hardware is novel) can search a disk of 300 megabytes in about five minutes, which is quite a way out of line for real-time processing.

13.3 INDEXING, THE ONLY WAY WE KNEW HOW

We have seen that document databases can be very large and that present computer speeds and architectures cannot provide satisfactory response times. One way out of this dilemma has been to use a different way of representing documents. Instead of storing documents in full text, indirect representation via indexing has been used extensively. In other words, documents are represented not by themselves, but with their surrogates which are substitutes constructed as indices. As we have seen in the previous chapter, document indices are prepared from terms (keywords) that best represent the documents. As can be realized, a set of terms selected from a document cannot adequately and entirely represent that document. However, this representation reduces the amount of storage required and, hence, has been used successfully in most existing, including commercial, systems. Although indexing conveys less information, it reduces the time required to locate a document besides its economy in storage. Users of indexed systems accept the one-time high cost of index creation in return for their long-standing economy in operation afterward. Besides its practicality and economy under certain conditions, indexing when carried out to the level of full text inversion loses its attractiveness. In databases where dynamism (i.e., frequent updates), along with demand for real-time operations are involved, index-based systems run into problems. Before we discuss any further details, let us review the conditions under which document inversion can and cannot be used. If the following conditions are present,

(a) The database is dedicated to a special application and queries are restricted;
(b) Full text inversion is not needed and contiguous word phrases (CWP), proximity, and partial matching are not critically required;
(c) Database size is not very large and language of the documents is uniform.
(d) Database updates need not be performed in real time.

then document inversion can be used. As consequences, however:

(1) Inversion of documents will be partial (i.e., indexing only) or incomplete (full text inversion, but on incomplete text e.g., stop words removed),
(2) Unrestricted query formulation will not be allowed.

If, however, the following apply:

(a) There is a high number of updates on the database and these updates must be done in real time,
(b) The database size is very large; it is general, with no control on its input.
(c) The database serves various users of different specialities; in other words, it is heterogeneous,
(d) Queries are unpredictable and may be complex,
(e) Queries require complex search capabilities such as context searches including unrestricted CWP, don't care (partial match), and proximity,

then full text inversion will create problems. First, the full text inversion, although it never has been implemented beyond incomplete inversion, would require up to 300% more space than the documents themselves. Even if we build such indices, we will not be able to provide the search capabilities a directly represented document database can provide. For example, imagine doing a partial match using the inverted indices. We have to do extensive OR'ing of all possible matches for the don't care part of the search pattern. Imagine further if the don't cares are variable length which will make the use of index search impossible. For the possible part, the amount of storage space required to hold all the indices created by the union (OR) operation may create problems. As can be seen, indexing shifts the problem of direct search of very large full text databases to extensive set operations such as merging and intersecting of the lists of pointers stored in indices—much less the large construction and maintenance costs of such indices.

Reassessing indexing once more, we can point out the following: indexing is, by its nature, a priori or imposed structuring of documents, especially if a controlled vocabulary of terms is used. In addition, manual indexing introduces inconsistencies since human judgment of different indexers is involved. In the case of automatic indexing, we have seen that inadequateness results when complex content-sensitive searches are required. Besides, such indices trade space for speed yet only for static applications. They run into serious problems when real-time updates are involved. For example, a database in the range of 100 megabytes will require 1000 to 2000 disk I/O accesses for adding a new document of 500 words into the database. Such an activity goes beyond real-time response limits.

As we can see, text inversion is by no means a cure for text search problems. Although all existing commercial systems presently use indexed-based inverted systems, the future systems will use direct search of documents more often despite the popularity of indexing. This does not seem to rule out indexing completely, however. As we will see in the remainder of the text, efficient and effective systems of the future will use a well-balanced synthesis of the techniques that have been proven successful.

13.4 ADVANTAGES OF FULL TEXT SEARCH

In view of the increased data acquisition facilities and the information explosion, most systems with high utility such as intelligence gathering do not afford the time to create index structures. Information flows constantly at a high rate, and it must be disseminated immediately. This implies not only the impossibility and/or impracticality of construction of indexing structures but also the need to search the incoming text streams efficiently. This, in turn, implies nothing but serial full text searching, which must be done efficiently. If we can do this mostly by hardware (something we will be doing in the rest of the chapter), then it will be cheap compared with the high cost of indexing. This cheap hardware solution for full text searching will offer the advantages of full text search, which will eliminate the disadvantages of indexing. We will be able to do efficient context-sensitive searches, including various kinds of partial matches. The high cost of index generation will be eliminated so that more applications which needed full text processing (but could not afford the high cost of indirect structures) will now be able to use it. All the limitations of a priori indexing will disappear.

It becomes apparent that if serial searching can be done efficiently in hardware, most existing commercial systems that rely on indexing will gradually drift toward full text–based systems. This is because access path free serial searching of plain text enables parallelism (i.e., parallel full text search hardware can easily be implemented).

In the remainder of the chapter, we will cover various hardware solutions to the problems of text retrieval.

13.5 INDEX LIST MERGE PROCESSORS

Hardware support of costly text processing operations has been investigated in various ways. Among the early proposals we have seen are list mergers which are aimed at maintaining index structures of the existing systems, with increased speed of their list processing. As we pointed out earlier, index structures transform the complexity of full text search to extensive set operations on inverted lists. Considering each inverted list entry to be a word of 32 bits, an average inverted list with 5000 elements for a large database, and an average query with 50 terms, we would be dealing with a total list size of 8 million bits. This bulk of data must be moved to the central processor for set processing and intermediate results must also be moved back and forth until processing is completed. Each I/O move may take about half a minute assuming lists are stored in page size (e.g., 2500 bytes) blocks and there will be a couple of these moves before inverted list Boolean processing can be finalized. This is inadequate because now we must retrieve the qualifying documents. All these will apparently be not acceptable for real-time environments. The purpose of hardware index processors is to speed up index processing at the backend of a GPC at a point closer to secondary storage. There have been some proposals for hardware solutions to index processing.

The study reported in Stellhorn [1977] proposes a backend index processor composed of a merger, coordinator, local memory, and a controller. The system gets its input from disks, carries out index processing, and sends its final result to the frontend GPC. In a given merge pass, fixed-length blocks packed with inverted lists (i.e., postings) are read from bulk storage (disk) and are fed to the merger. Two inverted list streams are processed in each pass. The merger is an even-odd merge network proposed by Batcher [1968] and demonstrated in the following example.

Example 13.1

Let us assume a relation called INDEX consisting of attributes KEYWORD and POINTER. We want to merge the inverted lists of two keywords. We will use the even-odd merge network shown in Figure 13.1. However, let us explicitly state our assumption here, which is the fact that the inverted lists are *sorted*. This is usually the way inverted lists are constructed; otherwise, we have to assume the presence of a fast sorter in our system.

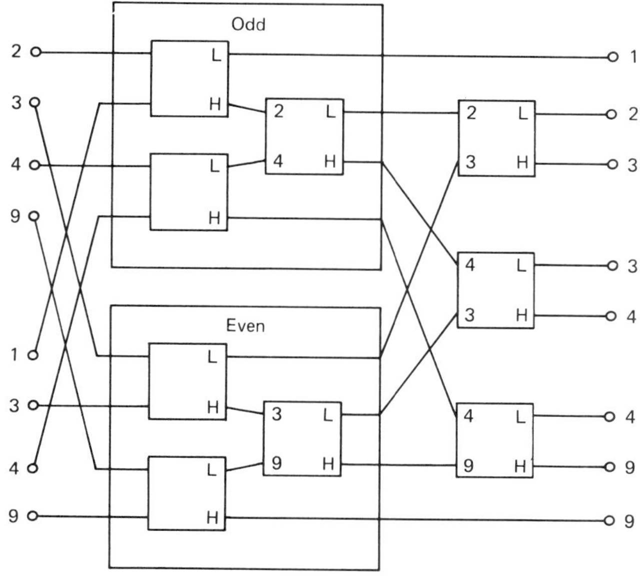

Figure 13.1 A merge example on even-odd merge network.

Suppose we want to find those documents (i.e., pointers to them) for the following two requests:

- Find those documents that contain both of the terms DATABASE and ARCHITECTURES.
- Find those documents that contain either one or both of the terms COMPUTER and PROCESSOR.

Assume that the following are the inverted lists:

```
DATABASE: 2 3 4 9   call it  L1 (list #1)
ARCHITECTURE: 1 3 4 9        L2
COMPUTER: 3 4 7 8            L3
PROCESSOR: 3 4 6 9          L4
```

Figure 13.1 shows the merging of L1 and L2, which comes out as (1, 2, 3, 3, 4, 4, 9, 9). Similarly, merging L3 and L4 will produce (3, 3, 4, 4, 6, 7, 8, 9). As can be seen, the merger splits each list into even and odd sublists with respect to their subscript (1, 2, 3, etc.). Odd sublists go to odd-merge and even sublists to even-merge. The ith output of even merge is merged with $(i+1)$th output of odd merge to produce the $2i$th and $(2i+1)$th outputs. For long lists, the process is recursive.

As we have seen in the example, the merger's output will be a merged list which may contain duplicates. In the proposed list merge architecture of Stellhorn, there is a separate subsystem called the coordinator that accepts merger output and eliminates the duplicates in it. For example, the coordinator's output for the lists merged will be $\{1, 2, 3, 3, 4, 4, 9, 9\} \rightarrow \{3, 4, 9\}$ and $\{3, 3, 4, 4, 6, 7, 8, 9\} \rightarrow \{3, 4, 6, 7, 8, 9\}$. As can be seen, the coordinator's task is not simply duplicate elimination, but at the same time Boolean processing. Accordingly, the first list is processed for conjunction and the second one for disjunction while the lists and duplicates are processed. This is because the first request requires (L1 AND L2), whereas the second request requires (L3 OR L4).

In this list processor, the local memory is used to synchronize I/O and to receive intermediate results, which may be written back to disk for further processing. In each merge pass, two blocks, one from each list, are input to the merger. The merger receiving lists of size n each, in each cycle, outputs one merged list of n elements while the other n merged elements are retained to be overlapped with the next merge. The split of the merged list of $2n$ elements is such that the top n elements in the sorted order go to the output.

According to this architecture, merging of more than two lists will require either a nested loop of pairwise merges or a network of basic mergers.

Another index merge processor is proposed by Hollaar [1978]. Instead of the parallel merger network required in the previous design, this design uses a binary tree of processors. Each processor is a node in the binary tree and is capable of executing comparisons, logic operations of AND, OR, AND NOT, and PASS, which eliminates an item from the list. All lists are input from the bottom of the tree, as in a tournament sort, and the final merged list emerges from the root. The design has also an extension which proposes a multilevel network of such mergers to provide flexible interconnectivity of subtrees to construct trees of various sizes depending on the number of lists applied at the input. Figure 13.2 shows a fragment of the basic merger.

Example 13.2

> Let us add to the previous example, using the same database, a new query that requests documents containing (DATABASE AND ARCHITECTURE) OR (COMPUTER). Let us process this on the merger shown in Figure 13.2. As can be noticed, this merger combines the role of the coordinator of the previous design with the merging function at the nodes so that there is no need for further processing for Boolean operations and duplicates. In this case, we will use three leaf nodes because we have three lists to be processed. Also, the first processors at the second and third levels from the bottom should be programmed for AND and OR merging, respectively. Each node processor performs a binary merge of lists provided from its descendants and passes its output to its immediate ancestor. As in the previous design, inputs to this merger must be sorted and the merger maintains sorted order at each node. In this example, we have three sorted lists L1, L2, and L3 that are simultaneously input at nodes 1, 2, and 3 and the merge is completed in two stages.

The index aide hardware is one step forward toward text retrieval architectures. Although index processing is done more efficiently with such merge hardware, the global architecture remains von Neumann. The von Neumann bottlenecks are still valid although somewhat deferred to larger databases with

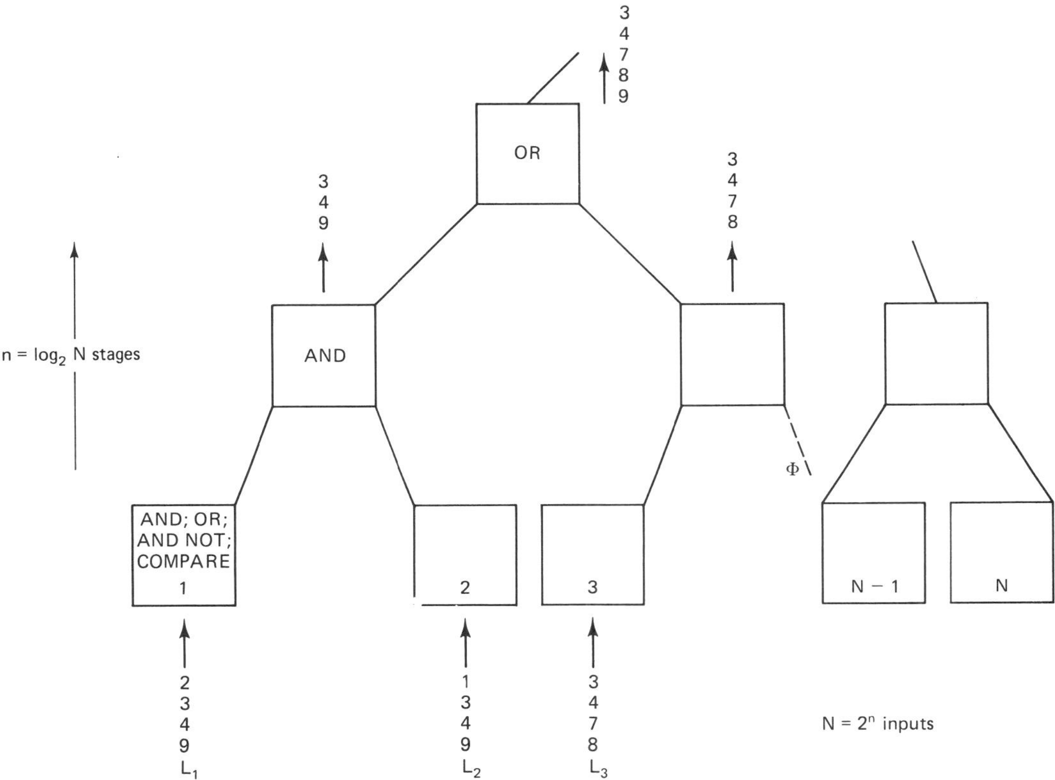

Figure 13.2   A binary tree merger.

this new hardware. No matter how efficient a specific case may utilize this hardware, the inherent problems of indexing still remain. After this partial solution, the time comes to deal with the new architectures for text retrieval which is our next topic.

13.6 DOCUMENT (TEXT) RETRIEVAL COMPUTERS

Before we start to review the developments in this area, we will first present the universal model of a document retrieval computer. This model should be conceived as a logical model and should not be mapped to a physical entity, in one-to-one manner. This is because different systems accomplish the requirements of the universal model in different ways. Figure 13.3 shows the universal model of a document retrieval computer.

According to this model, there are two main subsystems. They are the *term comparator* and *query resolver* units. The former involves full text search; the latter combines the search results with respect to the context specified in

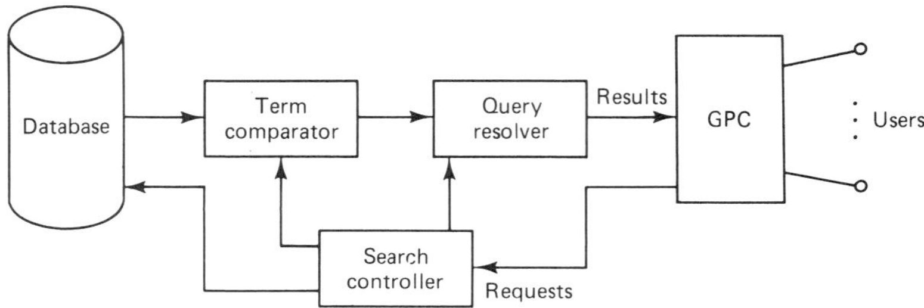

Figure 13.3   Universal model of a document retrieval computer.

user's request. For example, in Example 13.2 the request involves retrieval of (DATA **AND** ARCHITECTURE) **OR** COMPUTER. We should realize that the hardware approach to document retrieval does not use indexing (at least not in the manner and detail of the conventional systems). This implies full text processing in the term comparator. The comparator scans the entire database (more realistically, relevant parts of it) to find matches for the keywords DATABASE, ARCHITECTURE, and COMPUTER. The term comparator informs the query resolver what it found and where it happened, in other words, in which document and where exactly the keyword was. It is the query resolver's responsibility to combine and correlate these results according to the Boolean request and inform the frontend computer about the outcome. The search controller's task is similar to that of most controllers we have seen in the previous chapters. It receives orders from the GPC and drives the subsystems accordingly.

In the configuration shown in Figure 13.3, the heaviest load is on the term comparator because it deals with oceans of data. It must be fast and efficient. The majority of the studies made in the area of document retrieval computers deals with the challenge of efficient term comparator design. We will survey them in the following sections.

13.6.1 Parallel Comparators

The parallel comparators approach uses the concept of multiple search key registers we have seen in Chapter 5 in regard to content searching of secondary memory–based associative memories. The aim is to allocate a comparator for each search term in a query and perform full text search for all the query terms in parallel as data are streamed through a window buffer. The text is serially read from the bulk storage and passed through the window which has a bit parallel output bus to which search comparators are attached.

Figure 13.4(a) shows a design proposed by Stellhorn [1974]. Search comparators are loaded with search arguments, and they perform comparisons with the text in parallel. Their operation is initiated as soon as the relevant context delimiter is sensed. Whenever a comparison is successful, a match signal is sent to the query resolution unit. The ability to process context-sensitive Boolean

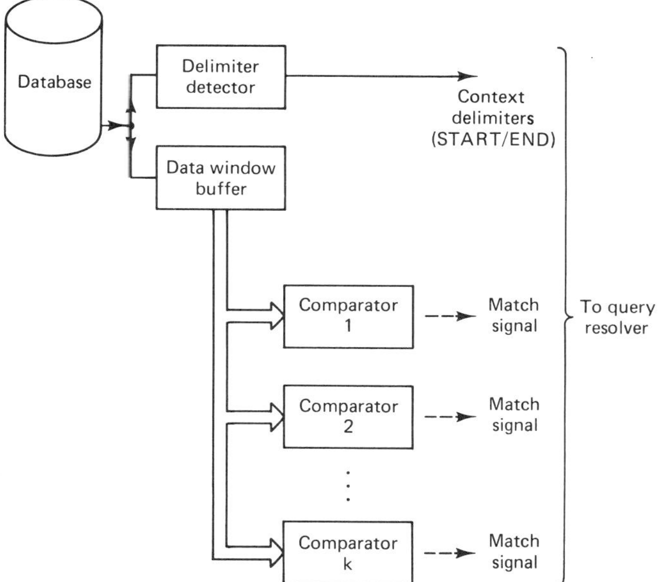

(a) Parallel comparators based term matcher

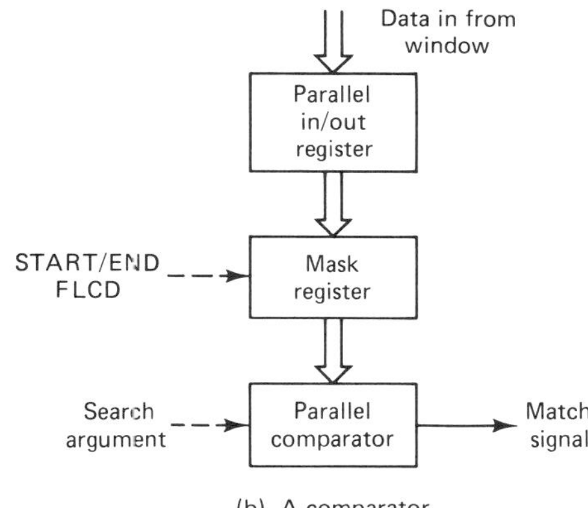

(b) A comparator

Figure 13.4 Parallel comparators. From L. A. Hollaar, "Text Retrieval Computers," *IEEE Computer*, vol. 12, no. 3, pp. 40–50, © 1979 IEEE.

queries depends upon the sophistication of the query resolver, provided that the term matcher is able to provide detailed delimiter and flag information along with term comparisons. As shown in Figure 13.4(b), if a mask register is provided in the comparator units, then it would be possible to search for fixed-length leading and trailing don't cares. This is because comparators would only be concerned with their search arguments to match and the rest would be masked out. This indirectly allows variable-length term matching within the maximum length limit equal to the length of the comparator.

Variable-length don't cares are not easy to deal with in this architecture. Also, the number and the maximum length of the comparators are fixed design parameters which may not fit well for all applications.

13.6.2 Associative Memories

We know that associative memories have parallel search capability within their structure. This virtue of associative memories is being utilized in some commercial systems such as the associative file processor (AFP) [Bird, Tu, and Worthy, 1977]. The approach here is to replace hardwired parallel comparators with an associative memory whose locations can be stored with search terms and searched while data are read off disk. Figure 13.5 shows the AFP architecture.

In AFP, search terms are held in AM, and query resolution is performed in the PDP 11 host. The bus switch connects the disk controller directly to AXP during search. The data coming off the disk are buffered and broken into individual words (terms). Word counts and document IDs are kept in AXP and reported to the host with matches. The AM of AXP is of 8196 bytes of capacity whose maximum word length is 15 characters. The AXP can deal with fixed-length don't cares but not with variable-length don't cares. Although AXP can generally keep up with disk speed, in the case of a high number of search terms, this performance degrades. ASP improves its throughput by batching various user queries into a single run.

AXP can compute a hash function on the contents of its search buffer and with the hash code partition the database on disk to cut down the search space. This is the same as the partitioning strategies we have seen earlier in database machine architectures.

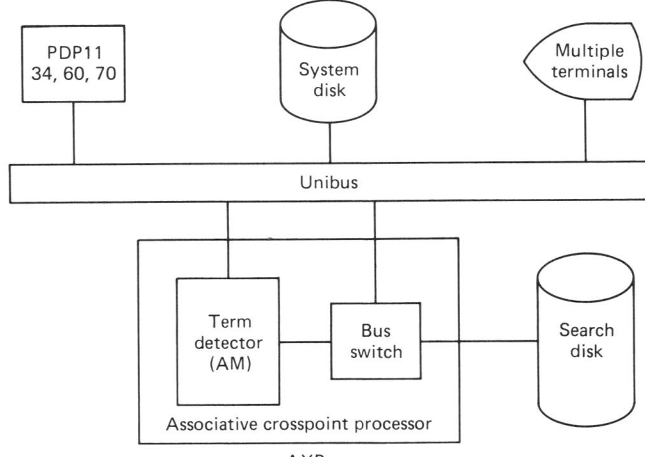

Figure 13.5 Associative file processor architecture.

13.6.3 Cellular Comparators

As opposed to the rigidity of fixed-length comparators, cellular comparators were proposed to provide dynamic reconfigurability among comparators at the character level [Mukhopadhyay, 1979; Copeland, 1978; Manuel, 1981; Mules and Warter, 1979; Foster and Kung, 1980]. According to cellular comparators, each comparator is a simple programmable unit. It can store a single character which is loaded as the search argument. It has an enable input, setup control, and match status output. A cell is shown in Figure 13.6.

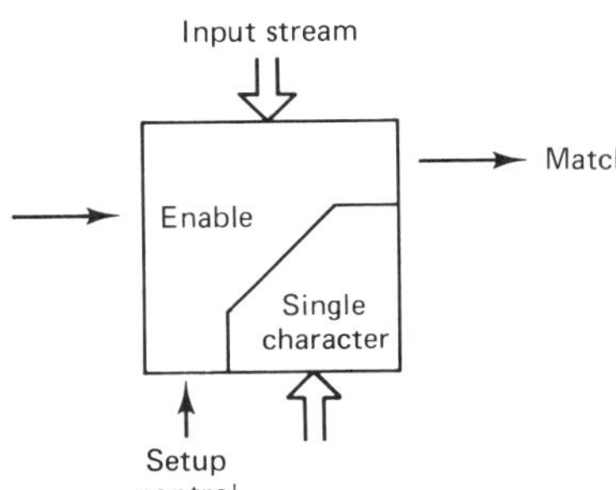

Figure 13.6   A comparison cell. From L. A. Hollaar, "Text Retrieval Computers," *IEEE Computer*, vol. 12, no. 3, pp. 40–50, © 1979 IEEE.

The cell is capable of matching the character it is programmed to recognize. A match signal is output only when both the enable and internal match signals are conjunctively present. To form a search pattern, cells must be connected in cascade. The first cell of the search pattern must be enabled externally since it is the beginning character and there is no cell on the left. If it is enabled statically throughout, then the matcher will be constantly sensitive to all substrings starting with that character (*unanchored*). If, however, the first cell is enabled dynamically at the moment of the delimiter of the relevant string, then the comparator will be restricted to search in that context (*anchored*).

In the cascaded string of cells, a cell is active and produces a match signal if its predecessor has a true (match) output and if the cell itself finds a match. Figure 13.7 shows five cascaded cells that are configured and programmed to recognize *ISSIP* and the cell operations when *MISSISSIPPI* is encountered in the data stream [Hollaar, 1979].

As can be seen in the output matrix, there are ones only in those character cells of the search pattern where the predecessor is a one. For example, looking down the first I column from the left, we see that the first cell's output is a 1 (because it is enabled) whereas output 4 is 0 because output 3 is zero. Dealing with don't cares is quite easy in this design. Fixed-length don't cares can be handled by delaying the anchor, signal and leading and trailing variable-length don't cares do not require special action. To handle embedded variable-length don't cares, we can insert a cell whose output goes true whenever its predecessor goes true and then stays true until the end of the context.

Individual term matchers constructed from cells can be combined in a circuit

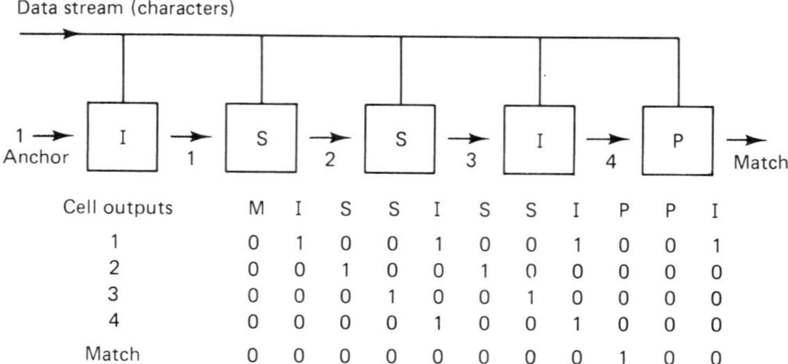

Figure 13.7   Matching of ISSIP in MISSISSIPPI with a cascaded five-cell pattern matcher. From L. A. Hollaar, "Text Retrieval Computers," *IEEE Computer*, vol. 12, no. 3, pp. 40–50, © 1979 IEEE.

to produce more complex search patterns. Figure 13.8 shows an example circuit capable of recognizing SHE, HE, or HAT. ■ indicates word delimiter. According to this circuit, trailing variable-length don't cares are allowed.

The following difficulties of cellular comparators can be foreseen in implementations:

(a) The difficulty of dynamically controlling a network of large number of cells. Both the setup time of the pattern matcher and the cost of the interconnection network may create problems.

(b) Duplicating the input stream to all the cells in the network may create driver and power limitations. For example, in Figure 13.8, we must extend the input line to all the cells shown in the circuit.

(c) Because VLSI implementation per cell will not be cost effective, several cells must be packed into silicon. This may impose certain connectivity limitations within and without chip boundaries.

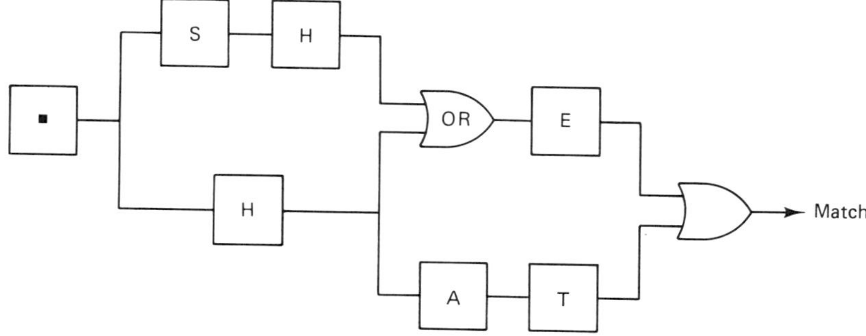

Figure 13.8   A circuit that combines cascaded cells.

In fact, the limitation we pointed out in item (c) exists as a real-life example in the GESCAN2 system, which is a commercial system [Manuel, 1981] utilizing custom LSI chips of comparator cells. Each chip contains 18 cells, and cells can be cascaded to handle more terms or stacked vertically to handle more queries. The system configuration is similar to that of ASP shown in Figure 13.4(a) except that the AXB of ASP must be substituted by a search unit shown in Figure 13.9.

The term search unit contains the cell chips. Cell chips obtain their data from the high-speed cache (of 128K bytes) which is staged in from the disk via a unibus. This results in 700,000 characters per second of search speed. Although most query processing capabilities are included in this system, proximity searches cannot be handled. Also, as can be seen from Figure 13.9, unlike ASP, the data path between the disk and the cache is via the unibus, which may create limitation in throughput.

13.6.4 Finite State Machines

The difficulty with most previous systems in dealing with embedded variable-length don't cares, including the cellular system proposed in Foster and Kung [1980], is easily solved with the FSA approach. Also, when a mismatch is encountered in the data stream, possible recurrence of a substring may be missed in systems where there is no buffer with a backtracking mechanism to try another alternative. That is, a received character may cause a default of the present sequence but commence another sequence that may include the present sequence. This can be easily handled by an FSA as shown in Figure 12.2(d) where the transition from state 5 to state 3 via S tries another match attempt for ISSIP starting with an I from state 4.

As we mentioned in the previous chapter, straightforward implementation of the FSA approach would be very inefficient. For S states and an input alphabet of N characters, a state table of size $S \times N$ words of $\log_2 S$ bits each would be necessary.

To implement an FSA machine in hardware would be straightforward if the state table can be kept in memory. All we would need are a register holding

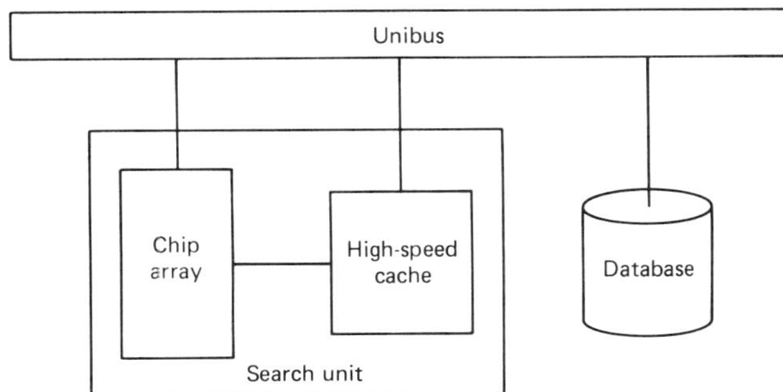

Figure 13.9   Search unit of GESCAN2.

current state and a block of memory for each state in S that would have as many entries (words) as there are characters in the input alphabet. Each word in the block would be indexable by its corresponding input character and contain the number of the next state in the transition. Therefore, as the FSA accepts each character in the input stream, a lookup is made in the current state's block for the corresponding memory word (by indexing the block with the input character) to find out the next state and bring it into the current state register. Implementing an FSA by a general-purpose microprocessor will require about three instructions to be executed per character, which would end up being four to five times slower than the data stream rate. For this reason, the FSA designs we will discuss in this chapter are implemented as higher-level architectures cast in silicon (VLSI).

We have mentioned the large memory requirement for such an approach. Considering Figure 12.2(b), we see that apart from the inputs causing transitions toward recognition of the word USA, there are 255 remaining possible input combinations, all of them represented by #, for each state forcing transition to the default state. This situation swells up the memory requirement. One solution to this is not to store default transitions per state but to imply, as a result of the mismatch to the input character received, a branch to a common location of the table that would store the default transition only once. What would remain per state block, then, are the entries causing transitions to states other than the default state. This would require an exhaustive search to be made within each block for an input character (because now we cannot index) which would fall behind the rate of data coming off disks. Figure 13.10 shows examples for various stages of this discussion. In Figure 13.10(b), we see the straightforward indexed

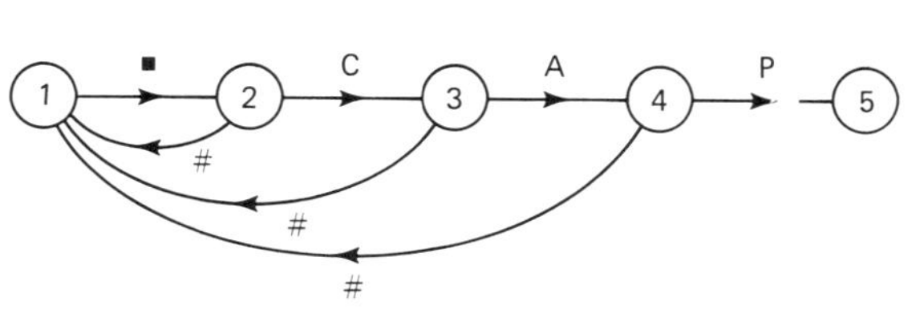

(a) FSA to recognize CAP*

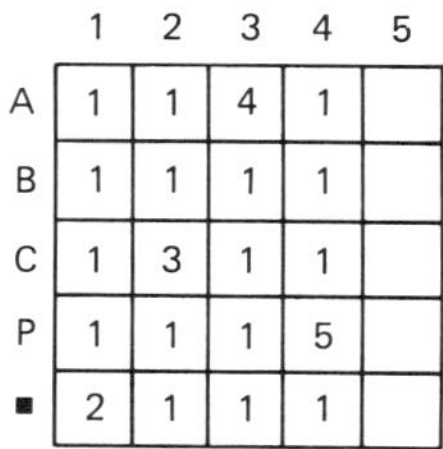

(b) Indexed state table representation

(c) Compact representation

Figure 13.10   FSA representations.

representation for the FSA of the search pattern CAP* shown in Figure 13.10(a). The simplifying assumption here is that the input alphabet consists of symbols A, B, C, P, and ■, and, therefore, we cannot see the default transitions other than a small set of 1s in the matrix. Figure 13.10(c) shows the compact representation with default implied. The difficulty with linear search in the rows cannot be shown here because there is only one entry in each row.

Bird [Hollaar and Roberts, 1978] introduced a scheme to cut down the list search in the compact representation. He divided transition states into two main groups called *index* states and *sequential* states. Index states are those having more than one nondefault transition, whereas sequential states are those that cause transition to only one state other than the implied default. The sequential states can be stored consecutively, and change of state from one to the other can be implemented in the same way of incrementing program counter during program execution, only here the address of the current state is incremented when a match occurs; otherwise, the default state is taken. In Figure 12.2(c), state 5 is an index state whereas sequences 1 through 4, 6 through 8, and 9 through 11 are blocks starting with their lowest-numbered sequential states. In the indexed state representation, state blocks, one per state, are stored in a table such that the blocks of states that can be reached from the previous state in only one transition are stored in consecutive memory locations. Each state block is made up of base and offset parts. The base contains the address of the nearest state. All other states are reached by adding onto the base the offset value corresponding to the input character. The offset entries contain zeros and ones. When a lookup is made for an input character, the offset bit is checked; if it is zero, the default state is entered; if it is one, the number of 1s in the block corresponding to previous characters (i.e., toward the base) are counted and added on the base to produce the value of the next state. Figure 13.11(a) shows an FSA representation that recognizes *CAP* and *CAN*. The corresponding Bird's memory organization is shown in Figure 13.11(b).

According to this figure, looking at the row for state 1, we see that there

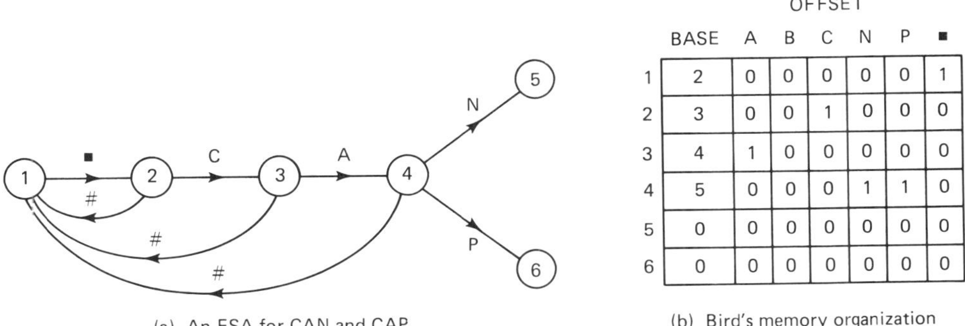

(a) An FSA for CAN and CAP   (b) Bird's memory organization

Figure 13.11   An FSA and the corresponding Bird's memory organization.

is only one transition out of that state and that is the one under column for ■. Counting the ones that precede it, we find zero and therefore $(base + 0) = 2 + 0 = 2$ (i.e., state 2 is entered). Looking at the row for state 4, we see that when the input character is P and we have a one 1 before it, the next state to go is $5 + 1 = 6$.

According to this approach by Bird, multiple sequential decisions on a succession of input characters are made in one state called the sequential state. The sequential state is represented by a block and a branch is made to the beginning of it. This reduces the number of states and, hence, simplifies the FSA table for patterns without VLDC. This is because only the identifier of the base state (beginning of block) need be stored while the rest is computed by offsets.

Although the organization shown above is relatively compact and fast, the situation worsens again when dealing with leading and embedded variable-length don't cares that make the state blocks too large. A practical note: it has been reported that [Haskin, 1980] for the CIA's SAFE system application, if queries (whose interarrival time is 4 seconds) contained 23 terms on the average totaling to 165 characters per query, the state table of the Bird's FSA would require around 800K bits.

The case with large state blocks was due to VLDCs which effectively made every state an index state. Also for 8-bit characters, sequential state blocks will be $2^8 = 256$ bits long, which is far too impractical. (The actual length is longer with other information.) The solution for this by Bird et al. [U.S. Patent Office, 1980] is to break each input code into two nibbles and provide a state for each nibble thus reducing the index word length to $2^4 = 16$ bits. (Actually, including other information, the length reduces to 37 bits.) At a multiway branch (index) state, the index state needs to look at the common nibble (the low order). If the required nibble code has a match, then the branched states look into the high-order nibble and in case of a match enter into their sequential states. For example, in Figure 13.12, we see a simplified FSA that accepts *CAT* and *DOG*. Accordingly, each character will be recognized by a two-nibble code. A word delimiter ■ has code N0N0, *C* has N0N3, and *D* has code N0N4. In this scheme,

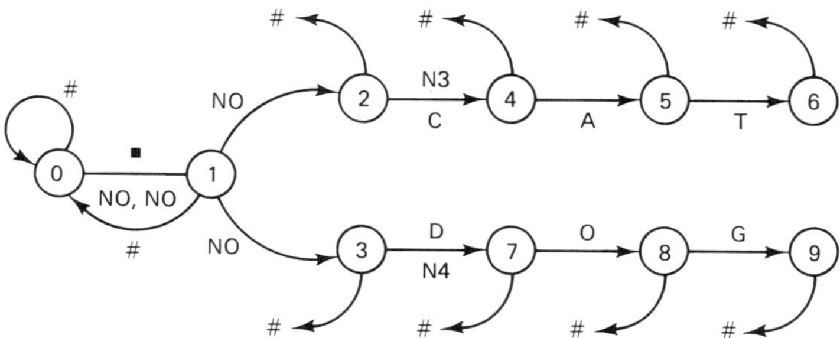

Figure 13.12 Use of nibbles for index states.

an index state is broken into two nibble states. State 1 checks the low-order nibble, and if a match for N0 is found, then states 2 and 3 are entered. With the higher-order nibble code being N3 for *C* or N4 for *D*, the corresponding sequential states of 4 or 7 are entered toward the recognition of *CAT* or *DOG*, respectively.

As a further simplification to the state table, Bird et al. introduced the *try-again index state*. To follow this, let us refer to Figure 13.13, which shows an FSA that recognizes patterns ending with *AL* and *ED* (for simplicity, nibbles are not shown). As seen in the figure, if the FSA table is to be represented directly as is, it will be large. The branching can be simplified, however, if a try-again index state concept is used. In the try-again index state, a new character is not presented to the FSA, instead the same character which resulted in the default is processed again, starting at the default state. Looking at states 2 and 3 in Figure 13.13, all branches into these states can go back to state 1, which then becomes the try-again index state. As we said, no new input is read whereas a default branch (as those marked #) would ask for new input. It has been stated that state table savings can reach as high as 40%.

Bird's FSA had one other problem. That problem is with the case where one FSA searches for patterns with initial (leading) VLDCs and another searches for patterns with trailing VLDCs. The example is the FSAs for ABC* and *DEF. However, either VLDC can give birth to the pattern sought with the other VLDC. When multiple combinations of leading and trailing VLDCs are combined into a state table, the table gets too large. The same situation occurs between leading and embedded VLDCs. The example is the FSAs for A*BC and *CBC. If the number of interacting terms is large, the number of interacting states in the combined FSA table will also increase. The solution proposed by Bird et al. was to use multiple FSAs by separating FSAs as follows:

FSA 1: senses single terms and trailing VLDCs
FSA 2: senses leading VLDCs
FSA 3: senses embedded VLDCs
FSA 4: senses contiguous word phrases

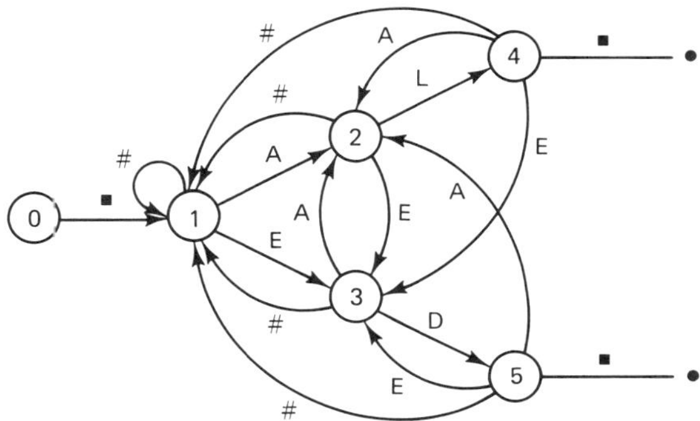

Figure 13.13   FSA for patterns ending with *AL* or *ED*.

Figure 13.14 shows the multiple FSA–based term matcher. The FSA 4 receives its input from the previous three FSAs. This reduces the number of signals sent to the query resolver. However, if the search deals with individual patterns, then the first three FSAs report directly to the query resolver.

HSTS (high-speed text search) is a system custom built by Logicon, Inc. The Logicon HSTS architecture is identical to that of ASP with two exceptions; (1) the term matcher is an FSA-based system of the type shown in Figure 13.14, and (2) the query resolver processor between the unibus and the term matcher is a separate unit outside of the PDP 11 host. The HSTS system compiles its queries into state vectors in a way similar to that of Bird's optimized FSA representation. The system provides various query capabilities including leading and embedded VLDC, which is not supported in the ASP architecture.

13.6.5 Query Resolver

The query resolver is the unit that combines individual hit results reported by the term matcher according to the context specified in user's query and reports a success to the frontend only after the hits received can build up to the satisfaction of the entire request.

The architecture of the query resolver can be a general-purpose mini- or microcomputer, the speed of which would be determined by the expected rate of hits of the application of concern. However, the pressure of data rate coming off disk is not present here since the term matcher stands in the way.

If we want keyword-based retrieval only, then query resolution is straightforward and consists of comparison of query and hit vectors. FSAs can handle a certain amount of context such as directed proximity. For resolution of Boolean

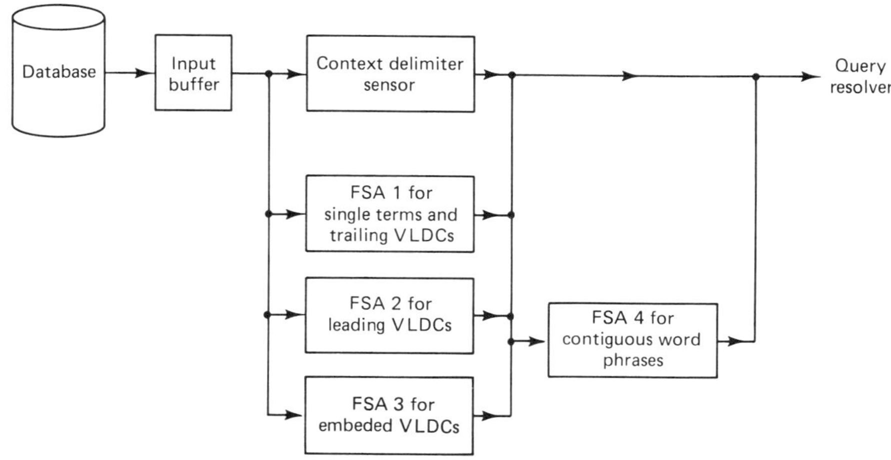

Figure 13.14 Multiple FSA–based term matcher.

queries of a context-sensitive nature, a tree-marking scheme has been proposed by Haskin [1980a] for a query resolver architecture. In the tree structure, leaves correspond to the query terms to which the term matcher sends hit signals. The intermediate nodes specify Boolean operations or context. These nodes include a count field to record the matches reported to the corresponding terms. There is a flag bit for each leaf to indicate if hits were previously reported for the term. Figure 13.15 shows a tree example from the referenced study.

The tree structure corresponds to the query below it. As can be seen, the threshold for disjunctions is 1, and for conjunctions it is 2, the latter signifying that all the leaves should report a hit to satisfy the threshold (conjunction). The threshold count field is incremented only once per term, and the flag of the leaf is set so that further hits are ignored. Once the threshold of a node is satisfied, the threshold count of its immediate parent node is incremented by one. When the root satisfies the threshold, the query is satisfied. As soon as the end delimiter of the context currently being processed by the term matcher is sensed, the query resolver is reset to zero to consider the next context in the data stream. For proximity operations, word counts must also be kept in this type of query resolver.

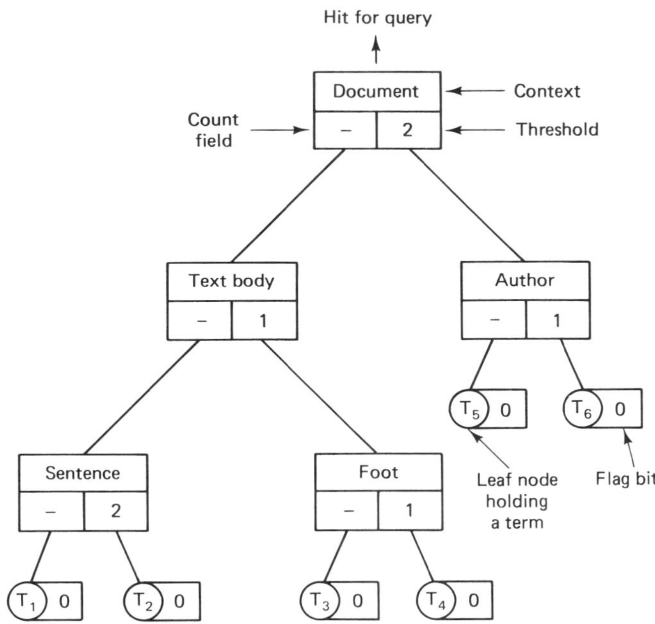

Figure 13.15   A query resolver.

13.6.6 Partitioned FSA

An alternative to the FSA approach is the nondeterministic FSA (NFSA), which is a finite state machine that can be in more than one state at a time. That is, in cases where a state has more than one transition corresponding to different input characters, NFSA enters all of the transitions by creating multiple copies of a standard FSA, and an unsuccessful match causes the current state to be terminated without transferring to a successor state. That is, the NFSA enters into an idle or default state at this point. This transitioning to multiple states is referred to as *forking*. In the case of an FSA, however, only one of the alternative branches is taken. The forking operation in NFSA requires extra hardware to schedule the FSAs, dynamically. Since an NFSA is built from a finite number of FSAs, a search process may be aborted in the middle in cases where more FSAs are required than available. Also, each replicated FSA requires duplication of state table, resulting in excessive memory requirements.

To overcome the problems encountered with NFSAs, a different type of FSA called the partitioned FSA, PFSA, which functions like NFSA, but without needing dynamic scheduling and state table duplication, has been proposed [Haskin and Hollaar, 1983; U.S. Patent Office, 1984]. In the PFSA, multiple branches are taken in the case of a fork, but for each branch only the subset of the state table which is needed for the branch is duplicated. For example, in the FSA of Figure 13.11(a), one state table may contain C, and A, whereas the others may have one table for each of N and P. Accordingly, although a single PFSA or character matcher can handle the match of CA, different character matchers are required for N and P. By forking, a character matcher can force another character matcher into a specified state.

The idea of PFSA is to partition a general FSA in such a way that the resulting PFSA must be simple. This can be done by identifying a *compatible* set of states such that during the matching of a term through a sequence of states no other transition can be forced on the PFSA by an *incompatible* state. Accordingly, the idea is to determine the maximum number of mutually incompatible states and define the number of partitions equal to this number. Let us show this principle on the example taken from the referenced study of Haskin and Hollaar.

Example 13.3

The following seven terms are given:

1. #A?ISM#
2. IST#
3. #SCHISM#
4. #BEST
5. #BENT#
6. #BUNT
7. #BUNTED#

where # represents a word delimiter (space or punctuation mark) and ? is VLDC of alphanumeric type.

Figure 13.16 shows a PFSA for these seven terms. The dashed lines draw the boundaries of partitions. Accordingly, three partitions are needed to separate the incompatible states. Each large circle in the middle corresponds to the idle state of each partition. The character inside the circle besides each start-up transition indicates the previous input character needed for the start-up while the first character outside of the idle state circle is the start-up character. In that context, @ represents an alphanumeric character, and * represents a character of any type. The small circles and labeled arcs are the standard FSA notation. If a transition causes a match of a term, the number of the term (of the seven in the example) is written preceded by a /, after the character causing the transition.

In this PFSA we see that the start-up transition, in the I_1, circle, which is created by a delimiter followed by an S that leads to state 8 is compatible with all the other states in that partition. Looking at state 12 we see that an S enters it, but the previous character is not a delimiter, it is an I. On the other hand, state

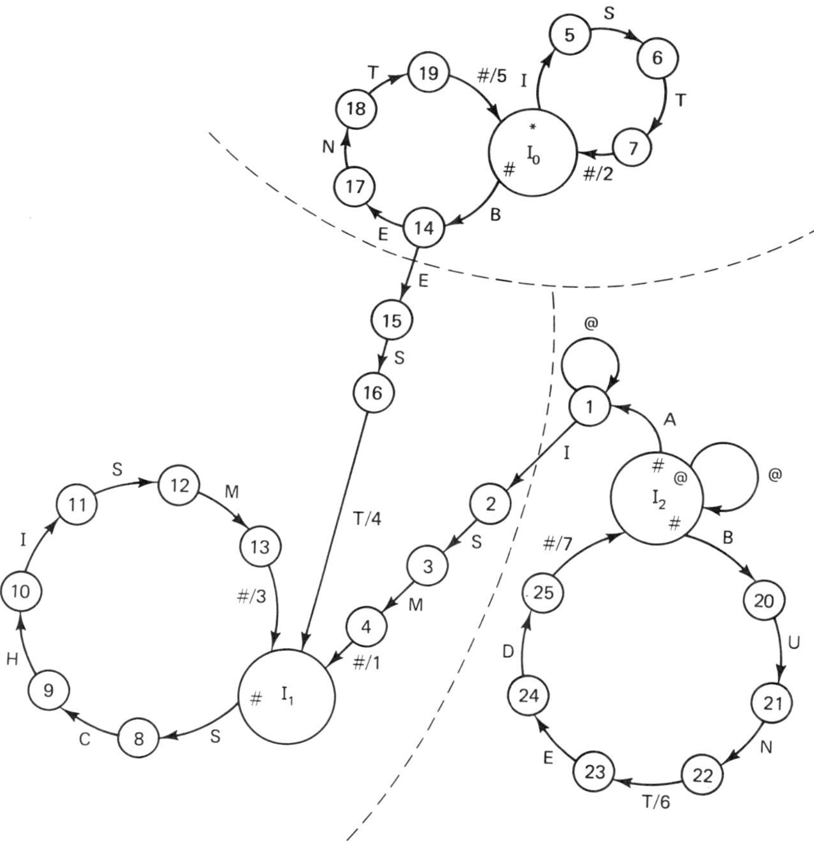

Figure 13.16 PFSA diagram for the example terms.

5 is not compatible with state 11 because state 11 is entered with the H, I sequence, whereas state 5 is entered by an I which can be preceded by any character (may include H as well). Also, the successor states 6 and 12 are incompatible because they are entered after the previous incompatible states followed by an S. Also, any two states that have the same predecessor are incompatible such as states 15 and 17. The invocation among partitions, by forking, as well as start-ups, should be unique. For example, in the partitions of I_1, the fork from I_0 into I_1 has a delimiter followed by B, E while the other invocations are a delimiter followed by an A (i.e., the fork from I_2 into I_1) and the start-up which is a delimiter followed by an S.

In the implementation of the referenced study, each partition is mapped into a character matcher. The character matcher (CM) has a structure resembling the Bird's representation; however, there are differences. Each CM has a transition table, similar to a sequential states table, a fork table, similar to an index state table, and a start-up table. While the CM can only be in transitions of single states, multiple transitions are forced by forking the neighboring CMs. A CM has two fork outputs, meaning that there cannot be a forking greater than three at a time. This limitation can be overcome by decomposing higher degree forks and cascading the decompositions. Figure 13.17(a) shows a ring of CMs and 13.17(b) shows a fork decomposition. A ring network was preferred for its simplicity and modularity in VLSI implementation. Forks between the CMs take place when a successful match in a CM triggers a fork vector from the fork table and sends it through its right and/or left (F_R and F_L) drivers. The fork vector contains the destination CMs address.

It should be noticed, however, that while in an index state there is one transition like a computed go to, in forking there can be simultaneous branch transitions. Accordingly, the PFSA of Figure 13.16 compares the input string against various partitioned patterns in parallel. The PFSA requires static scheduling and low overall memory capacity.

As indicated earlier, the number of partitions, therefore, CMs, in an application is determined by the maximum number of mutually incompatible states. Experiments have indicated that this can be estimated, at a high degree of confidence, by the following relationship

$$CMs \text{ required} = 5 + \frac{\text{no. of terms}}{16}$$

where "no. of terms" is the maximum number of terms expected in the set of queries of a given application.

The VLSI implementation of the character matcher is currently being carried out by the authors of the referenced work. A CM chip for 8-bit characters and 7 character types would require 3840 bits (256 $\times$ 15) of start-up table, 2432 bits (128 $\times$ 19) of transition table, and 256 bits (16 $\times$ 16) of fork table (i.e., a total of 6528 bits).

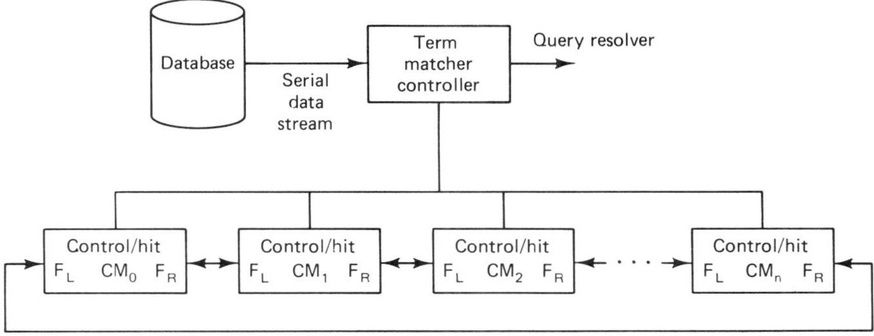

(a) A ring of character matchers

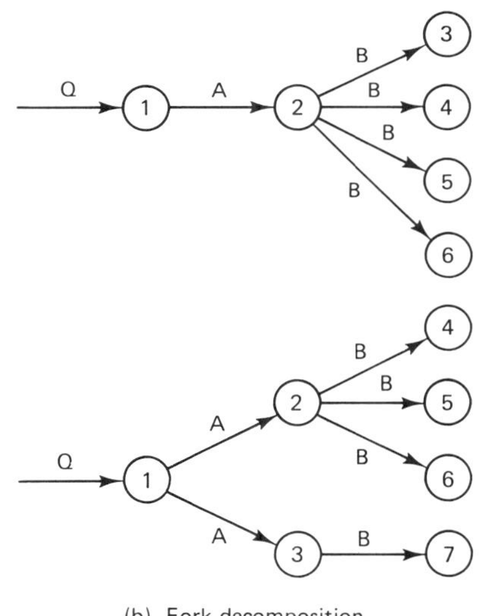

(b) Fork decomposition

Figure 13.17   PFSA implementation.

13.6.7 URSA Full Text IR System

URSA (University of Utah retrieval system architecture) is the complete full text retrieval system being built upon the PFSA implementation described earlier. URSA is an ongoing project [Hollaar, 1984] at the University of Utah, and Figure 13.18 shows a high-level logical model of the retrieval system.

URSA consists of three major functional modules. These are the user interface, indexing, and document management functional modules. The system is put together based on a message-based communications scheme among the modules. The entire system can be mapped to a distributed multiprocessor system or confined within a uniprocessor.

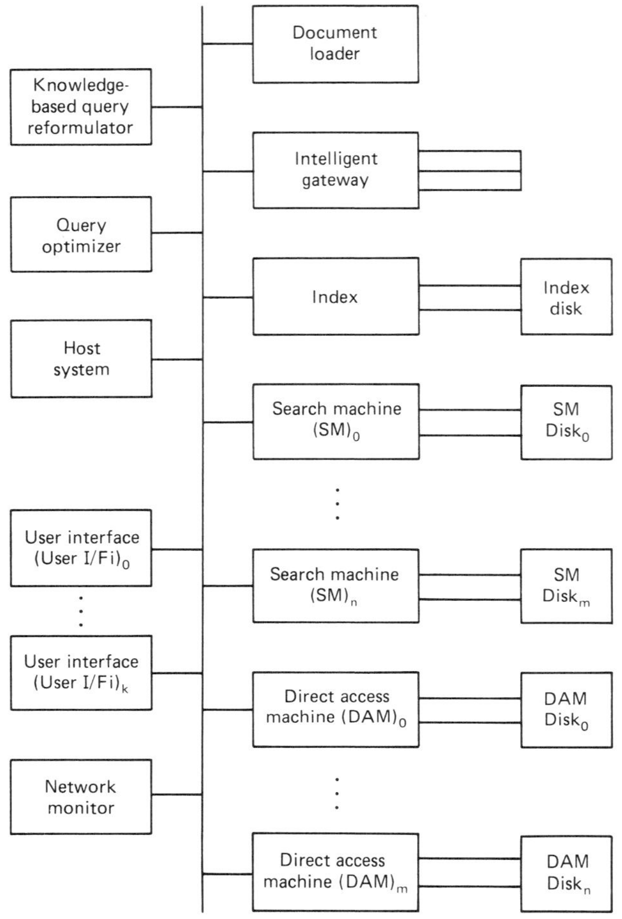

Figure 13.18 The high-level logical model of URSA.

The user interface converts the user request or query into message sequences, the index module determines the database segments to be searched for the user request, and the document management function is responsible for document storage and search. The index module may itself resolve the query by responding to the user interface with hit reports, or it may report maybe's to the document management module for final searching of the corresponding documents. In the latter case, the role of the index module is maybe filtering of documents. This situation occurs especially if the index consists of only a simple keyword directory without full text attributes so that context-sensitive queries need to be resolved by a further full text search.

Looking at the system architecture shown in Figure 13.18, we see a number of search machines and direct access machines. While the former is responsible for text search, the latter provides documents to the user interface concurrently. This parallel document search and access scheme was implemented for better performance; however, they can be combined in a minimal configuration. There is an on-line document loading facility and a network gateway to link to other document databases. The system includes connection to an external host, a network performance monitor, a query optimizer, and a knowledge-based query reformulator. The index module has its own dedicated storage unit. It is also possible to partition the index with respect to the contents of each search unit and store and run them in parallel with each partition serving a search module.

The user interface supports a window-oriented environment running on work stations. An editor process runs in each window, and all the user interface takes place through various concurrently running windows. The user query is entered, and/or selected text provided by direct access machines is screened through windows. The contents of one window can be transferred to other windows so that new queries or documents can be assembled.

The window facility simplifies the command syntax. The URSA commands include Find/Retrieve, Help, Select Database, Automatic Command Re-issue, and Display facilities. The retrieval functionality allows Boolean query formulation capability, various forms of don't care, and proximity operations.

Although currently the search modules are implemented in software, the advanced stage of the project will incorporate VLSI versions of PFSAs discussed earlier.

13.6.8 RAP.3 Text Retrieval System

Text representation. The RAP.3 architecture is augmented with text retrieval capabilities. Compared to its previous versions, RAP.3 has certain advantages in this respect. The main point is the fact that RAP.3 cells are composed of parallel subcells. Each subcell is a processing unit based on an 8086 microprocessor and contains its own RAM. The DMA hardware accesses tuples from the cell memory and places them in the RAMs of subcells for processing. In document retrieval applications, the RAP relations are structured to represent, store, and process unformatted data. The following features must be included to be able to deal with unformatted data:

(a) Literal-type domains must be represented.

(b) Literal domain length must be variable, resulting in variable-length tuples.

(c) Efficient string search primitives must be incorporated.

(d) Sentence structure and adjacency must be recognized.

(e) Operations necessary to process unformatted data must be integrated with the instruction set.

(f) Resolution capability must be built in and tied with the operations of (c) and (d).

In the document databases that exist today, full text is stored in disk sectors or page blocks. In the present RAP.3 implementation, the maximum tuple length is 1024 bytes (there is no reason for not going beyond this length). The text is represented and stored as described in the following: In the RAP.3 text relation, one long literal attribute is defined. The length of this literal attribute can be variable and as long as the tuple itself. However, normally there will be a few additional formatted attributes within the same tuple. This literal attribute is referred to as the text attribute and the text string is stored in this attribute. The entire text of a document cluster or abstracts of a given topic are made a RAP.3 text relation, and the text is stored in the text attribute of the tuple instances of the relation. The following format is used in the text attribute:

(a) Each tuple contains one or more complete sentences (i.e., a sentence is not split between tuples).

(b) The first tuple of each document starts with a blank.

(c) At least one blank should follow a punctuation mark.

(d) At the end of a sentence, an end-of-sentence (EOS) character is placed following the period. EOS must be followed with at least one blank.

(e) The last tuple of the document terminates with an end-of-document (EOD) character.

Figure 13.19 shows a RAP.3 text relation. In this relation, the texts of one or more document clusters are stored. For a very large cluster, the text relation can be horizontally split.

The RAP.3 text relation representation does not require additional overhead with the exception of a few words per tuple. They are the mark bits word and the ND_1 and ND_2 attributes. The mark bits word pays more than its price because with it the need to create new files to hold the result of intermediate steps of a query program is eliminated. The ND_1 and ND_2 attributes are two numeric attributes required by the internal workings of the RAP.3 text retrieval instructions. ND_1 stores the beginning offset, within the text attribute, of the text search operation; ND_2 specifies if all occurrences of the search pattern in the text are to be identified and, if specified, holds the total number of occurrences of the

DF	MARK BITS $t_1 \cdots t_{15}$	ND_1	ND_2	A_3	$\cdots$	LONG TEXT ATTRIBUTE A_n
						SENTENCES
						SENTENCES
						SENTENCES
	$\vdots$				$\cdots$	$\vdots$

Figure 13.19   A RAP.3 text relation.

search pattern found in the text. There will be also a primary key (e.g., A_3) and may be other formatted attributes, as required by user, besides ND_1 and ND_2 in a RAP.3 text relation.

The RAP.3 text retrieval instructions.   An important problem of text retrieval in the RAP.3 way of representing text data is to maintain text contiguity both in string searches and context resolutions. This problem is solved to a great extent by the variable-length text attribute feature of RAP.3. By this feature, the need to split a text word or sentence between tuples (referred to as overflow) and to pass overflow status and data to subsequent tuples to finalize the search has been eliminated. After this, the only remaining overflow resolution capability we need to provide is for directed and undirected proximity, fixed (i.e., <A, B>n, <A.n.B>) or variable (i.e, A . . . B). The reason for this is that these operations need not be confined within a sentence and they may span several tuples. To handle the necessary overflow resolution, the link pass operation has been defined. The following list gives the syntax of the RAP.3 text retrieval instructions:

```
1. MATCH (tc) [rel (textatr{, atrl {,atr2}}): qual] {[lit]}
2. MATCH_ZONE (tc) [rel (textatr): qual] {[lit]}{[n]}
3. MATCH_ONE (tc) [rel (textatr, atrl): qual] {[lit]}
4. MATCH_ALL (tc) [rel (textatr, atrl): qual] {[lit]}
5. MATCH_WS (tc) [rel (textatr {, atrl}): qual] {[lit]}
6. MATCH_WWC (tc) [rel (textatr {, atrl {,atr2}}): qual] {[lit]}{[n]}
7. MATCH_WSC (tc) [rel (textatr {, atrl {,atr2}}): qual] {[lit]}{[n]}
8. MATCH_WPC (tc) [rel (textatr {, atrl {,atr2}}): qual] {[lit]}{[n]}
9. LINK_PASS (tcl,tc2) [rel ({textatr,} atrl)]
```

where

t_{ci}, $1 \leq i \leq 13$, are the mark (tag) bits

rel is the text relation name

textatr, *atr*1, *atr*2 are the attributes of the relation corresponding to A_n, ND_1, ND_2 of Figure 13.19 (the difference is due to physical and logical representations—Figure 13.19 is the physical representation because the variable-length literal attribute, whose type is text, must be stored at the end of the tuple)

qual is the Boolean qualification expression

n is a positive integer

braces indicate options

lit is a literal constant representing the search pattern. The examples of search pattern are 'AA'?'BB', *'A'??'BB', *'AA'??'BB'3?'C', where * and ? correspond to VLDC and FLDC, respectively; *n*? indicates *n* repetitions of ?

The first match instruction associatively searches for the occurrences (i.e., equality) of the search pattern. Search is made in the *textatr* attributes of the tuples, and the qualifying tuple instances are t_c marked in the cells storing the document relation. The roles of atr_1 and atr_2 correspond to those of ND_1 and ND_2, which were explained earlier. If atr_1 is not specified then a search offset of zero within *textatr* is assumed.

The second match instruction performs zone searches (e.g., title, abstract, keyword, etc.). The zone code is specified by n. The specified search pattern occurrences are searched in the designated zone of the text. The third match instruction looks for only one occurrence of the search pattern, whereas the fourth instruction searches for all occurrences of it. The fifth match instruction performs the same operation as the first match, only this time the context is restricted to within sentences in all the tuples. The instructions 6, 7, and 8 perform proximity searches between two search patterns. WWC, WSC, and WPC stand for within word count, sentence count, and paragraph count respectively. The value of n can be specified explicitly within the instruction or implicitly in the atr_2 attribute. In executing this instruction, if the second search pattern is not found and the proximity specified by n extends beyond the current tuple, the current tuple is t_{14} marked (t_{c_2} in the preceding syntax). Actually, since RAP.3 is an associative/parallel device, the "current tuple" must be correctly put as "current tuples" since there may be more than one instance of the tuple in the relation marked for the occurrence of the first term. Therefore, all such tuples that cannot satisfy the execution of the proximity match instructions, in searching the second term, are t_{14} marked. To resolve this overflow situation, the *LINK_PASS* instruction is used. This instruction takes one memory scan and resets t_{14} bits and marks the t_{c_1} bits of the subsequent tuples, also passing the remaining value of the word count.

In the case of variable proximity (e.g., A . . . B) the second version of the LINK_PASS instruction, with *textatr* specified, is used. In this case if the current tuples are t_{c_2} marked and *textatr* does not contain the end of text character, then the following tuples are t_{c_1} marked and their atr_1 is set to zero.

In the case of VLDC, it is assumed that a search pattern having embedded VLDC cannot extend beyond a sentence; that is, the VLDC does not match the EOS character.

String search within tuples.   As mentioned at the beginning, each RAP.3 subcell receives a tuple in its local RAM to start the search of the text pattern within the text attribute. The string search algorithm executed within the subcell is the modified version of the Boyer-Moore algorithm covered in the previous chapter. The modification used is due to Horspool [1980]. In the algorithms of Knuth et al. and Boyer-Moore, text must be preprocessed to find the Δ_1 and Δ_2 shift values. In the modified version, Δ_2 shift is ignored (Horspool indicates that its effect is negligible and better performance can be obtained if it is ignored). The modified algorithm is

```
delta2[*]:=patlen;                  /*initialize entire array;patlen is
i:= patlen;                         search pattern length */
For j:= 1 to (patlen -1) DO          /*perform preprocessing */
   delta2[pat[j]]:=patlen - j;      /*pat is search pattern */
lastch: = pat[patlen];              /*lastch is last character */
WHILE i<=stringlen DO               /*stringlen is text string length */
   BEGIN
      ch:=string[i];               /*string is text string */
      IF ch = lastch THEN
          IF string [i - patlen + 1 . . . i] = pat THEN
              RETURN i - patlen + 1;
          i:= i + delta2[ch];
   END
RETURN 0;
```

The table called *delta2* is the same as Δ_1, with the exception that *delta2*[*lastch*] is equal to Δ_2 [*patlen*].

Although this is a software (firmware to be exact) search, it is faster than execution on a uniprocessor by a factor equal to (no. of subcells per cell) × (no. of cells storing the relation).

Query resolution.   A considerable part of query resolution in the RAP.3 system is handled during the operation of match and link pass instructions. As can be remembered, the sentence structure, VLDC, and proximity are resolved by the instructions themselves. However, to combine these basic operations into a context sensitive text retrieval request, RAP.3 programs must be written using both the DBMS and text retrieval commands. Tables 13.1 and 13.2 document the context sensitive text retrieval operations that are currently operational in the RAP.3 system.

The RAP.3 resolution programs for these operations are made into general-purpose macros with the use of a query facility called *RAPMAC*. The search operations of *match_a_or_b*, *match_a_and_b*, and *match_threshold_or* allow up to 58 search patterns in one macro (e.g., match a_1 or a_2 or, . . ., or a_{58}). Although the preceding list of operations and those given in Section 12.5.4 of the previous chapter are only the typical context-sensitive text retrieval operations, with the use of the RAP.3 instruction set any other operation can also be programmed.

13.6.9 An Integrated Fact/Document Information System

Integration of fact and document information systems, or the integration of DBMS and IR, is a recently recognized need which became a research topic in the respective communities. As technology progresses and various facilities of information systems are developed, it becomes natural to view all the related facilities as a network of interrelated subsystems. To satisfy the requests of sophisticated users some of these facilities, such as DBMS and IR, must be synthesized, not only kept together or one reduced structurally into the form of

TABLE 13.1   RAP.3 CONTEXT SENSITIVE TEXT RETRIEVAL
OPERATIONS

```
/* Macro definition for keyword search */
match_a a, text, d1, tl, qual
/* Macro definition for N number of occurrences of a term.  Find a pattern
which appears at least n times in the document. */
match_all_a a, n, text, d1, d3, t1, t2, qual
/* Macro definition for A or B */
match_or a, b, text, d1, t1, qual
/* Macro definition for A and B */
match_and a, b, text, d1, t1, t2, qual
/* Macro definition for A and NOT B */
match_a_and_not_b a, b, text, d1, t1, t2, t3, qual
/* Macro definition for A . . . B */
match_a_anywords_b a, b, text, d1, d2, t1, t2, qual
/* Macro definition for (A, B) in sentence */
match_a_and_b_in_sent a, b, text, d1, d2, t1, t2, t3, qual
/* Macro definition for B after A in sentence */
match_a_follow_b_in_sent a, b, text, d1, d2, d3, t1, t2, t3, qual
/* Macro definition for <A, B> n (n is a word count) */
match_a_nwords_b a, b, n, text, d1, d2, d3, t1, t2, t3, qual
/* Macro definition for <A, B> n (n is a sentence count) */
match_a_nsents_b a, b, n, text, d1, d2, d3, t1, t2, t3, qual
/* Macro definition for <A, B> n (n is a paragraph count) */
match_a_nparags_b a, b, n, text, d1, d2, d3, t1, t2, t3, qual
/* Macro definition for (A, B, C, . . ., M)#n */
match_threshold_or a, b, n, text, d1, d2, t1, qual
```

TABLE 13.2   THE DEFINITION OF THE MACRO PROTOTYPE ARGUMENTS

Parameter	Purpose	Type
a	search pattern A	literal
b	search pattern B	literal
n	number of pattern occurrences	integer
text	name of text relation	identifier name
d1	name of text attribute	identifier name
d2	search offset (ND1)	identifier name
d3	holds the number of pattern occurrences (ND2)	identifier name
t1	result mark bit	identifier name
t2	for internal use during search	identifier name
t3	for internal use during search	identifier name
qual	qualification expression	literal

the other. First, we know that DBMS and IR have unique features; while DBMS is deterministic, IR is not and is refined through iteration. While the former supports formatted data, the latter works with unformatted data. The best answer, then, is to synthesize DBMS and IR in a proper manner so that the advantages and capabilities of each are preserved. In what follows, a design for such integration will be presented.

Integration model: mathematical model of query processing.   The integrated information retrieval system, IS, of the RAP.3 database architecture consists of a set of subsystems and can be described by a 6-tuple

$$IS = <R, D, Q, C, E, T>$$

where R represents a set of relations that contain structured data about the database and/or document entities. The nature of interrelationships among structured entities will be described by means of a conceptual data model.

D represents the set of documents stored as unstructured entities. The relationships of these unstructured entities among themselves and/or with those of R also will be presented in the conceptual data model.

Q is a set of user queries. A given query, Q, is defined as

$$Q = \left\{ Q_T, Q_R \right\}$$

where

- Q_T is the part of the query that holds the context-sensitive document search specification.
- Q_R is the part of the query that holds search specification on the $\{R, D\}$ set operable by the DBMS instructions.
- C is a hierarchical structure of clusters for D.
- E is a mapping function, called the evaluation function, used to find the relevant documents to a query. The function is $E : Q \rightarrow 2^D$. In reality, a subset of the range of this mapping is reached through the complex operations of clustering, building hierarchies of clusters, implementing search functions for these hierarchies, and a feedback function. All these operations will be briefly discussed in the following. T represents the terms used for the description of documents.

Creation of system queries.   Figure 13.20 shows the abstract view of the integrated query processing. According to this abstract view, a query Q consists of two parts Q_T and Q_R where Q_R is the relational DBMS operable subquery and Q_T corresponds to the context-sensitive document retrieval subquery. Related with Q_T, there are a set of words, T_Q, such that

$$T_Q \cap T \subseteq T_1, T_2, ..., T_n$$

where $n = |T| \geqslant 0$.

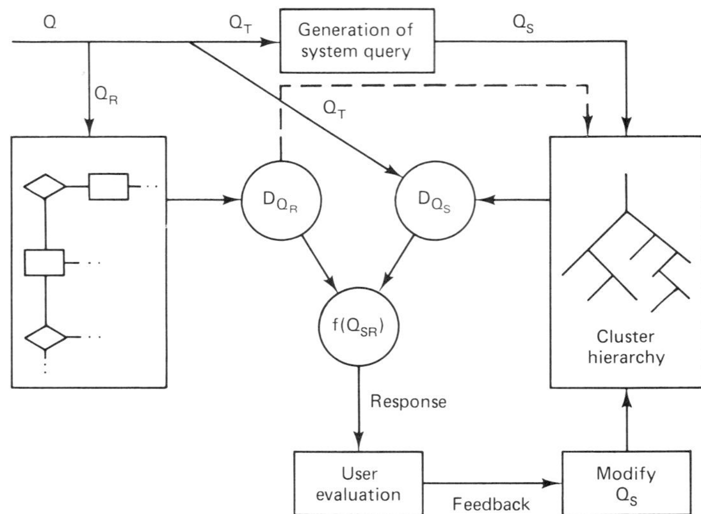

Figure 13.20   Abstract view of integrated query processing.

We cannot expect all of T_Q to appear in the filtered search query (system query) for the simple reason that not all of the words would be included in T since, as shown in the previous chapter, there are conditions for a word to be an (index) term. In Q_T, some terms will be used in the positive context, some others in the negative context, and some in both. For the reason that will be clear in what follows, Q_T, therefore, will be expressed as

$$Q_T = Q_{TP} \cup Q_{TN}$$

where Q_{TP} and Q_{TN} correspond to the parts of Q_T that deal with the terms specified in the positive and negative context, respectively, and

$$Q_{TP} \longrightarrow | \ T_{TP} = T_1, T_2, ..., T_k | \quad k \geqslant 0$$

$$Q_{TN} \longrightarrow | \ T_{TN} = T_1, T_2, ..., T_l | \quad l \geqslant 0, \qquad k, l \leqslant n \text{ and } k = l \text{ is allowed}$$

In the filtered search query for Q_T, which will be called a system query Q_S, there may be positive and negative term specifications. If a term T_i is the member of both sets; that is,

$$T_i \in T_{TP} \qquad \text{and} \qquad T_i \in T_{TN}$$

then T_i appears as a positive term in the system query. This selection is due to the fact that the information provided by the appearance of a term rather than its nonappearance is more important [Van Rijsbergen, 1979]. Therefore, a system query, Q_S, is

$$Q_S = Q_{SP} \cup Q_{SN}$$

where

$$Q_{SP} = Q_{TP}$$

$$Q_{SN} = Q_{TN} - (Q_{TN} \cap Q_{TP})$$

hence, for the respective terms,

$$|T_{SP}| = |T_{TP}|, |T_{SN}| \leq |T_{TN}| \qquad \text{and} \qquad |T_S| \leq |T_T|$$

This is reasonable since, as stated earlier, one cannot expect all the words used in a context sensitive search request to appear in the terms used for indexing.

Context-sensitive Boolean query structure.   The user query Q will be processed as follows:

(a) The query Q will be converted into a disjunctive normal form; that is,

$$Q = (Q_{11} \wedge Q_{12} \wedge \cdots \wedge Q_{1n_1}) \vee \cdots \vee (Q_{m1} \wedge Q_{m2} \wedge \cdots \wedge Q_{mn_m})$$

where each Q_{ij} $(i = 1, \ldots, m; j = 1, \ldots, n_m)$ may be a single word or a context-sensitive document retrieval operation such as *(A, B) in Sentence, A \ldots B, A.n.B, <A,B>n, A???B, A*B,* etc. Furthermore, each Q_{ij} may be either in a positive or negative context (e.g., $\neg$*(A,B) in Sentence* implies *(A,B)$_\neg$ in Sentence*).

(b) From the resulting query, generate a list of subqueries such that they will be in an ordered quadruple $<Q_R, Q_T, Q_S, Q_{SR}>$, where Q_R and Q_T are as explained before and Q_S and Q_{SR} are obtained in the following steps.

(c) The words used in Q_T will be searched in the thesaurus corresponding to the terms used in the clusters. Nonmatching words will be dropped and the query, now left with only the terms, will be a system query Q_S.

(d) Concept hierarchies, continuous word phrases, and/or citation linkages will be the possible candidates of additions to Q_S if expansion due to recall and precision will be necessary in the course of retrievals.

(e) Q_{SR}, referring to Figure 13.20, is a further retrieval operation on DQ_R and DQ_S and the answer set returned by it can be expressed as

$$f(Q_{SR}) \subseteq \Pi \, DQ_R f_{QT}(DQ_S)$$

In other words, $f(Q_{SR})$ are the data returned by a further retrieval function operating on the product of the data sets DQ_R and $f_{QT}(DQ_S)$ which correspond in turn to the data returned by Q_R and the context-sensitive operations of Q_T executed on the data set returned by the hierarchical cluster system search.

(f) Repeat Q_{SR} through the feedback loop (if necessary) until the user and/or certain performance indicators are satisfied.

In (d) through (f), $f(Q_{SR}) \subseteq D$ will be always true.

Example 13.4

Conceptual modeling and an example application.

The universe of discourse of an integrated DBMS/IR application will be defined by means of the enhanced entity/relationship (E/R) model that will allow representation of aggregates and generalizations as well as documents. In our example, an entity will correspond to a conceptualization whose representation will be in terms of formatted structures (i.e., a record type or specifically a relation) or a document whose representation will be in terms of unformatted structures. In the latter, the rectangle will be marked by an asterisk. There is a corresponding DDL for this diagrammatical notation as we have seen in Chapter 9. Figure 13.21 shows the conceptualization of the example application environment. To give an appreciation of the information conveyed by this diagram, let us list some important relationships:

(a) *AUTHOR* is a weak entity, for him or her to exist in the document database, he or she should either have written a document or be referenced by at least one document.

(b) *AUTHOR* and *DOCUMENT* entities are related through the *DOC-REF* relationship in a many to many manner. That is, an author can reference several documents and can also be referenced by several documents.

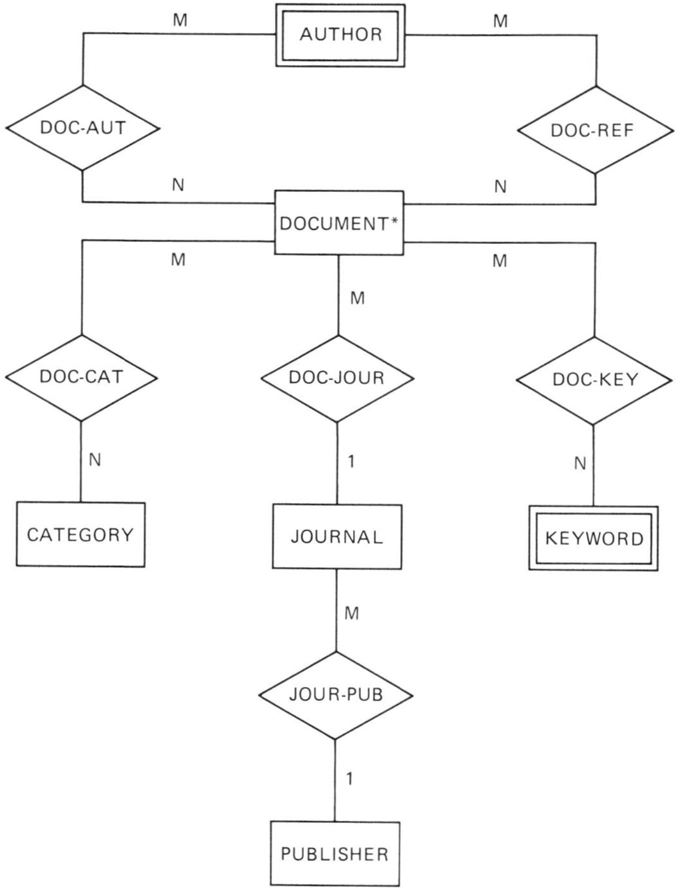

Figure 13.21 Conceptual representation of the integrated application.

(c) A specific journal is published by one publisher, yet that publisher can publish several journals.

Figure 13.22 shows the relational representation of the example application conceptualized in Figure 13.21. This relational representation conforms with the RAP.3 format specifications. According to Figure 13.22, the DOCUMENT entity is mapped into four tabular structures: DOCUMENT, CITATION, ABSTRACTS, and SUB-HEADING. The rest of the mapping is one-to-one. In the list of relations, the key attributes are in bold characters. The ABSTRACT attribute holds the full text of the corresponding document's abstract. As shown in Figure 13.19, each tuple holds one or more sentences of the corresponding document and the TUPID attribute links sentences (tuples) of one document. The unary relation DOCUMENT is added into the representation to increase the speed of database navigations (i.e., chain of mappings by semi-join). In this way, large unformatted data need not be kept in the system for the sake of the link attribute (i.e., DOCID).

DOCUMENT[**DOCID**]
CITATION[**DOCID**, TITLE, DATE, JCODE, VOLUME, PAGES, ND1, ND2]
ABSTRACT[**DOCID, TUPID**, ABSTRACT, ND1, ND2]
SUB-HEADING[**DOCID**, STITLE, ND1, ND2]
AUTHOR[**AUTID**, NAME, NPAPER]
DOC-AUT[**DOCID, AUTID**, DOCDATE]
DOC-REF[**DOCID, AUTID**, NREF]
KEYWORD[**KEYID**, KEYW, KFREQ]
DOC-KEY[**DOCID, KEYID**, WEIGHT]
CATEGORY[**CATID**, CATCODE, CFREQ]
DOC-CAT[**DOCID, CATID**]
JOURNAL[**JCODE**, JNAME, NPAGE]
DOC-JOUR[**DOCID, JCODE**]
PUBLISHER[**PUBID**, PNAME, NPUB]
JOUR-PUB[**JCODE, PUBID**]

Explanations of the abbreviated attribute names

DOCID = Document identifier, uniquely identifies a document
JCODE = Journal code
TUPID = Tuple identifier
STITLE = Subtitle
NPAPER = Number of papers written by an author
NREF = Number of times an author is referenced in a document
AUTID = Author identifier, uniquely identifies an author
DOCDATE = Date the document is published by the author
KEYW = Keyword
KFREQ = Number of times a keyword is used in the documents (keyword frequency)
CATID = Category identifier
CATCODE = Category code
PUBID = Publisher identifier
CFREQ = Number of times a category is used in the documents
NPAGE = Number of pages in a published journal
PNAME = Publisher name
NPUB = Number of journals published by the publisher of a journal
ND1, ND2 = Full text search attributes

Figure 13.22   A relational representation of the conceptual structure of Figure 13.21.

A user request such as *On the documents written by the authors who are referenced by the papers written by JOHN DOE after 1970, search for those with the phrase SEMANTIC DATA MODEL and AGGREGATION in the same sentence* would require both DBMS and IR specific operations in an interrelated sequence of processing steps. Following the notation of Figure 13.20, this user query will be denoted as Q, whereas the subsets of it dealing with DBMS and IR will be indicated by Q_R and Q_T, respectively. Q_T is the portion of the request that deals with the context-sensitive search such as the SEMANTIC DATA MODEL and AGGREGATION *in the same sentence*. While Q_T will be preserved for final processing in the work stations, a query called the system query Q_S will be derived from Q_T to initiate a search of the relevant clusters in the database. This search is carried out by the database server on the network in an effort to narrow the search space, before the full text search can be conducted.

In simple terms, a Q_S query will include those terms of Q_T that are included in the set of index terms of the collection with a possible inclusion of certain other components to increase system precision and/or recall. With Q_S, a hierarchy of clusters will be searched, and the corresponding data, DQ_S, will be returned when the cluster search is optimally terminated. The two resulting sets of data, DQ_R and DQ_S, corresponding to DBMS and IR operations, respectively, will be jointly processed by the integrated system to produce the user's response. The user, screening this response, may ask the system to repeat the operation by providing an indication of the relevant/irrelevant documents. With this information, Q_S will be modified and the previous cluster selection will be refined.

Cluster subsystem.   The clustering subsystem used in the integrated RAP.3 text retrieval system is the seed-oriented partitioning-type clustering algorithm we have seen in the previous chapter. The algorithm is based on the cover coefficient concept, and the clusters are obtained by using the single-pass algorithm. From these clusters, a cluster hierarchy is built and a combination of broad and narrow search strategies are used with the Q_S vector. The search criterion uses the matching function covered in Section 12.9.5. The cluster hierarchy is discussed in Section 12.9.4.

Query feedback.   The retrieval refinement is based on the query feedback scheme discussed in Section 12.10. The main goal of that query feedback scheme is to preserve the context-sensitive nature of the user query so that the advantages of full text search can be properly exploited.

DBMS/IR integrated retrieval with RAP.   As we have seen so far, clustering is used as an index, which provides database partitioning based on semantics. Each partition, in turn, can be made into one or more RAP relations, and horizontal relation splitting can be used if necessary. The secondary indexing facility of RAP can be used in the software emulator version to speed accesses within a partition. In the hardware implementation, where we would have the genuine associative/parallel hardware, we do not need a secondary indexing facility, because all the attributes can be accessed associatively. Before we talk about the integrated retrieval with RAP, let us first demonstrate a simple example of a keyword-based bibliographic retrieval system supported with RAP. This will be an example of using only the formatted DBMS version of RAP for text retrieval purposes. To implement a simple keyword-based retrieval system, all we have to do is to define a relation for our index or postings file. An index can be thought of as a normalized relation where each keyword value and a single-document address pair are stored as a tuple. To implement that in RAP, all we have to do is to declare a binary relation, for example, *POSTINGS* with the *KEYWORD* and *DOCADDRESS* attributes and use a *READ [POSTINGS (DOCADDRESS): KEYWORD = 'DATABASE']* instruction to retrieve document addresses of documents containing the term *DATABASE* from the *POSTINGS* relation. For merging and/or intersecting indices, we can either define an *n*'ary relation and say *READ [POST (DOCADDRESS): KEYWORD1 = 'A' & (OR) KEYWORD2 = 'B']* or, equivalently, write the following program between the two binary relations, *POST1* and *POST2*.

```
MARK(t1) [ POST1: KEYWORD = 'A']
CROSS_MARK(t2) [POST2: DOCADDRESS = POST1.DOCADDRESS]
[POST1.MKED(t1)]
READ [POST2 (DOCADDRESS): KEYWORD = 'B' & MKED (t2)]
```

The second operation is a semi-join through the matching document addresses and the *READ* combines this mapping indicated by *MKED(t2)* with those tuples containing the keyword B. The result is a chain of selection, semi-join, and output using conjunctive selection (restriction). This scheme can be extended to include the concepts of weighted Boolean retrievals and ranked output by using all the capabilities of the RAP instruction set.

At this point, we can go back to the example application presented at the beginning. Based on Figures 13.21 and 13.22 and the query statement given in Example 13.4, a possible execution sequence can be given as follows (using the relations of Figure 13.22 and with no regard to semi-join optimization):

```
1. SELECT AUTHOR with name JOHN DOE
2. SEMI-JOIN AUTHOR to DOC-AUT via AUTID
   SELECT DOC-AUT with date > 1970
3. SEMI-JOIN DOC-AUT to DOC-REF via AUTID
4. SEMI-JOIN DOC-REF to DOC-AUT via DOCID
5. SEMI-JOIN DOC-AUT to ABSTRACTS via DOCID
6. IR Search for "SEMANTIC DATA MODEL" and "AGGREGATION" within
   sentence
7. SEMI-JOIN ABSTRACTS to DOCUMENT via DOCID
8. READ DOCUMENT
```

As can be seen in this query, operations 1 through 5 and 7 and 8 are DBMS operations, and 6 is an IR operation and yet everything is linked consequentially in the execution sequence. Although operation 6 is a single item in the list, it corresponds to a set of operations implemented as a RAP macro which uses

DBMS/IR instructions. To follow these, let us refer to Figure 13.20. In this figure, Q represents the query program shown (i.e., operations 1 through 8), Q_R corresponds to DBMS operations (operations 1 through 5, 7, 8), and Q_T to *IR* operation 6. In terms of the data sets and data manipulation functions, the following correspondences can be seen:

```
DQ_R:(DOC-AUT)_R,DQ_S:(ABSTRACT)_R -subscript R indicates restriction-
f(DQ_R):step 5,  f(DQ_S): step 6,  Q_SR: step 7,  f(Q_SR) = (DOCUMENT)_R
```

The following is the actual RAP program listing corresponding to the foregoing procedure:

```
MARK (T1) [AUTHOR:NAME = "JOHN DOE"]
CROSS_MARK (T1) [DOC_AUT:AUTID = AUTHOR.AUTID][MKED (T1)]
RESET (T1) [DOC_AUT:DOCDATE <= 1970]
CROSS_MARK (T1) [DOC_REF: DOCID = DOC_AUT.DOCID][MKED (T1)]
CROSS_MARK (T2) [DOC_AUT: AUTID = DOC_REF.AUTID][MKED (T1)]
CROSS_MARK (T1) [ABSTRACTS: DOCID = DOC_AUT.DOCID][MKED(T2)]
% MATCH_A_AND_B_IN_SENT 'SEMANTIC DATA MODEL','AGGREGATION',ABSTRACTS,/
        ABSTRACT, ERDOCAT2, T1, T2, T3, MKED(T1)
        CROSS_MARK (T2) [DOCUMENT: DOCID = ABSTRACTS.DOCID][MKED (T1)]
READ [DOCUMENT (DOCID): MKED (T2)]
EOQ
```

The following is another example for the integrated query execution. This time, the execution starts with an IR operation that is then linked to DBMS instructions. The query statement precedes the query program:

```
/*      Give the DOCID of the documents which contain ENTITY and
        RELATIONSHIP within at most 5 words separation.   */
% MATCH_A_NWORDS_B 'ENTITY', 'RELATIONSHIP', '5', ABSTRACTS,   /
            ABSTRACT, ERCOCAT2, ERDOCAT3, T1, T2, T3,
CROSS_MARK (T1) [DOCUMENT: DOCID = ABSTRACTS.DOCID][MKED(T1)]
READ [DOCUMENT (DOCID): MKED(T1)]
EOQ
```

The RAP.3 integrated DBMS/IR text retrieval system claims effectiveness and efficiency due to the following factors:

(a) The RAP relational DBMS is efficient both in its software emulation and its hardware implementation. Its software implementation uses dynamic hashing for key attributes and builds inverted lists for its secondary keys. The marking or tagging concept eliminates the need to create intermediate files constantly during the execution of a query program. The semi-join operation optimizes the join performance both in centralized and distributed processing.

(b) The IR features are integrated with DBMS at the primitive level.

(c) The IR primitives are based on the efficient string search operations, and the context-sensitive full text instructions carry out query resolution to a great extent.

(d) Clustering is used as an efficient IR index in addition to the secondary key indexing of the RAP.3 DBMS.

(e) Integration of DBMS and IR at the primitive level results in minimum layers of software, which contributes to overall system efficiency.

(f) There is no need for a separate computer for query resolution and the necessary communication of term matches since all of those functions are handled in the RAP.3 system.

13.6.10 Performance Issues

In assessing performance of a given system, we must be careful in comparing systems. Some published work gives performance estimates only for a subsystem, and usually this is just for the term matcher. We can rarely find anything on the query resolver. Most of the research work covers first-order performance issues such as the overall I/O time to search the entire database given a specific term matcher hardware assuming that the rest of the unspecified system would keep pace with the backend. Yet some other systems are complete and commercially available. We must, therefore, decide upon certain variables important for our application and benchmark the available systems and construct analytical and/or simulation models for the yet to be available hardware.

To give an idea of what types of variables are involved, Table 13.3 displays a sample assessment presented in Polzer [1983]. In that table, besides certain cost items and end-user services (e.g., retrieval features), we see what features are involved in query structures (although not a complete set). We should be careful in comparing a hardware system including these features with a software system that uses inverted files (even for full text inversion) and provides only the keyword-based bibliographic retrieval. In future systems, bulk memory tech-

TABLE 13.3 FEATURE COMPARISON ESTIMATES OF SOME AVAILABLE TEXT PROCESSING SYSTEMS

	Inverted file	AFP	HSTS	GESCAN II	CAFS
Data base cost per page	$6.00	$0.03	$0.04	$0.04	$.20-.40
Creation/update					
Time per page	2 min	.25 sec	.25 sec	.25 sec	.25 sec
Timeliness	hrs-days	sec	sec	sec	sec
Database storage cost per 100MB	$18,000	$6,000	$4,500–6,000	$6,000	$30,000
Floor space per 100MB	15 ft^2	5 ft^2	3–5 ft^3	5 ft^2	15 ft^2
Search time per 100MB	11–100 sec	100–200 sec	100 sec	140 sec	25 sec

TABLE 13.3 *(continued)*

	Inverted file	AFP	HSTS	GESCAN II	CAFS
Avg. response time	10 sec	10–20 sec	10 sec	14 sec	2.5 sec
Worst case time	100 sec	400 sec	200 sec	280 sec	50 sec
Query features					
Boolean logic	yes	yes	yes	limited	yes
Nesting level	3	1	3	1	?
Fixed-length don't care	yes	yes	yes	yes	yes
Variable-length don't care (trailing, embedded, leading)	T only	no	L, E, T	L, E, T	T only
Numeric ranging	no	no	yes	no	yes
Proximity					
Word	yes	yes	yes	yes	no
Sentence	no	no	yes	no	no
Paragraph	no	no	yes	no	no
Document partitioning:					
Zones	no	no	yes	yes	no
Subzones	no	no	yes	no	no
Subdocument	no	no	yes	no	no
Weighted or approximate queries	no	no	no	yes	yes
Retrieval features					
Highlighting	yes	yes	N/A	?	N/A
Summary/abstract display	yes	no	N/A	?	N/A
Keyword in context display	yes	no	N/A	?	N/A
Computer system cost					
Host processor	$500,000–5,000,000	$140,000	$140,000	$140,000	$600,000–2,000,000
DBMS/hardware	$80,000	$50,000	$60,000	$60,000	?

From H. W. Polzer, "Document Retrieval Techniques," from presentation by Alex Nagy at the Minnowbrook Workshop on Database Machines, 1983.

N/A–Not available.

Comments: 1. All numbers are best estimates at the time of writing and should not be taken as commercial quotes and/or features.

2. Inverted file column represents a typical system, not any one version. Some systems have query features listed as "no."

3. Response time assumes moderately complex query (8 to 10 terms) resulting in 10 document hits with a uniform distribution over the database and that no previous searches are in progress.

4. Worst case times assume a 100-MB search has just started prior to submission of a user's query.

5. HSTS and CAFS currently depend on another processor for user interaction and document review. HSTS can, however, support such functions if desired.

nology will have great impact on performance at the system level. The memory technology will affect the staging strategies in the memory hierarchy. Document and term clustering techniques will be the basic partitioning tools. However, further research is needed in combining clustering with the various database machine partitioning means we discussed in the previous chapters. VLSI filters can also be used to partition the text databases.

EXERCISES

13.1. Most researchers agree that the future text retrieval systems will be a hybrid of coarse (i.e., high-level) indexing and full text systems. This indexing is needed due to the very large sizes of document databases.

Given this statement, provide a comparative assessment to the following alternatives:

(a) We can build indices based on the contents of physical storage device cells (e.g., a track, a cylinder) and provide a multilevel access path of index terms in these cells.

(b) We can first partition the database semantically and, if necessary, build secondary-level access paths in the partitions. As a subquestion, can we use document clustering as a semantic partitioning technique? If your answer is no, what alternative would you suggest?

13.2. Can we use full text search and its hardware as an effective and efficient means of automatic index creation and/or text inversion? If yes, suggest a procedure to do that.

13.3. As a further point following the previous question, can we gather the user queries over a period of time, which can be a continuous procedure for dynamic systems, and process them on the text retrieval hardware in a short amount of time (remember, we can batch queries and execute them in one pass) and create a user profile index from the results? If so, suggest a methodology considering the average number of terms of queries and batch sizes to be given to the text retrieval hardware.

13.4. Choose 10 terms from the thesaurus or keyword index of a text retrieval system with which you are familiar. Do the following with these terms:

(a) Construct an FSA for each term.

(b) Reduce the resulting FSAs in a way that will combine the individual FSAs. For example, the FSAs shown in Figure 13.14 originally added up to 29 states in total before the reduction.

(c) Draw a partitioned FSA by using the result of (b). How many partitions did you define? What is the total number of incompatible states among all the partitions? How many fork entries and start-ups do you have for each partition? Are all the invocations unique?

13.5. Given the terms *#CAT#, #CAN#, #DOG#, #DOT#* how many *CM*s are necessary for a PFSA implementation? Show a minimal partitioning.

13.6. The PFSA state diagram of Figure 13.16 uses special logic to cause a start-up transition whenever specified characters immediately follow characters of specified types. It is possible to operate the PFSA without this start-up mechanism by having the idle states of various *CM*s look for particular characters or types, and transition to a specified state when a match occurs in the idle state. However, this can dramatically increase the number of *CM*s required. For the terms in Example 13.3, show the PFSA state diagram that results if the start-up mechanism is not available.

13.7. Given the patterns *#UTAH#*, *URSA*, and *#UNIV*TY#*, indicate all incompatible states.

13.8. Using the RAP.3 text retrieval system and its query execution strategy and also the distributed database query execution methodology, do the following:

    (a) Define an office information system (OIS) that will have a remote network connection of local offices operating on local area networks. Each local area network should have several work stations (microcomputers) and a database server consisting of a RAP.3 database computer.

    (b) Define a distribution strategy of the database among the local offices. Explain how document clustering will be performed on each database server.

    (c) Based on (b), give some examples of OIS queries. After decomposing your queries, construct query execution graphs (see Chapter 10). Comment on the execution strategies, that is, data moves that the query execution monitor would perform based on your data distribution strategy. (Note: The RAP text retrieval instructions, for example, MATCH, LINK, are unary instructions. For context-sensitive text retrieval macros, you should first obtain their expansion to RAP programs.)

13.9. Using the U.S. Patent Office database example given in Hollaar [1983a], compare various hardware approaches, including index processors and available commercial systems with respect to their throughput time in carrying out the following application.

The patents database covers patents issued since 1950 and requires a storage space of 65 billion characters. Based on the applications submitted each year, a query interarrival time of 2.4 seconds is given. Using 300-megabyte disks, 220 drives will be needed to hold the database. A high-level index, with 0.3% selectivity, will narrow the database to 195 megabytes. The index itself requires 30 disk drives. With this index selectivity, you can assume one search request per disk drive during the query interarrival time. You can assume a query length of four terms which results in 10,000 postings to be processed, where each posting is 4 bytes long.

APPENDICES

The appendices that follow provide syntax and semantics of the RAP language software, ANSI/SPARC-like GDBMS, and its external schema data languages. The RAP language was covered in Chapter 3, and the GDBMS software was described in Chapter 9. The GDBMS software covers the *entire* facilities of the architecture shown in Figure 9.6.

The existing versions of the RAP language software (emulator), called SERAP (Software Emulator for RAP), are as follows:

(a) IBM mainframe versions under OS/MVS
(b) Intel microcomputer versions under ISIS-III and RMX86 (iNDS, iTPS)
(c) VAX 11/780 version under UNIX
(d) IBM PC/IX (UNIX)

While (a) is a batch compiler version, (b) and (c) are semi-interpretive and interactive. RAP can be used as a stand-alone language. Also, there are host-embedded versions of it. In (a), it can be embedded in PL/1; in (b), it can be embedded in PLM86; in (c), it can be embedded in the C language. The use of the RAP software emulator on these computers is not different from running a relational DBMS on the same. In fact, various applications using the RAP emulator have been implemented to date including the Arizona State University's RSS (Research Support Services) information system. *As stated in the preface, the author can be contacted for acquiring copies of the RAP and GDBMS software. All software is available at a charge. Along with the required version of software, the User's Guide and JCL for running the software on the related computer system will be provided. The package will also include various computer files of sample programs, syntax summary, and other related documentation.*

APPENDIX I

*RAP DBMS ASSEMBLER LANGUAGE UNIX VERSION**

This appendix describes the syntax and semantics of the RAP assembler instructions, for the Unix version of the emulator. The complete environmental information for using the emulator is provided in the User's Guide.

A1.1 EXAMPLE DATABASE

The examples given throughout this description are formulated against a simple database consisting of three relations:

```
LOCATION (FLOOR, DEPT)
SALES (DEPT, ITEM, VOLUME)
EMP (NAME, DEPT, SALARY, MANAGER)
```

Each tuple of the LOCATION relation gives the name of a department (DEPT) and the floor on which the department is located. For each department, there is exactly one tuple.

Each tuple of the SALES relation gives the volume of sales for an item sold by a department. Each tuple is uniquely identified by the department and item value pair.

Each tuple of the EMP relation gives information on an employee. It

---

* The Intel microcomputer versions of the RAP DBMS Assembler are exactly the same as the Unix version presented here. The exceptions are (1) real data type is not supported, and (2) the host language is PLM86 instead of C of the Unix version. Documentation on the Intel version can be requested from the author.

contains the employee's name, the department in which the employee works, the employee's salary, and the manager. For each employee, there is exactly one tuple. Managers are themselves employees. An employee's manager need not be working in the same department.

The user identification codes (userid) "SUXX," "YTXX," and "C.S." are assumed to exist in the database.

A1.2 INSTRUCTION FORMAT

There are minor differences among the SERAP versions. Here, we will be describing the latest version running under Unix. The general instruction format is

```
label opcode [specification qualification] [parameters]
```

label is an optional symbolic instruction address. *opcode* is a mnemonic specifying the operation to be performed. *specification* is either a relation name or a relation name followed by a list of attribute names, specifying the range of the operation. *qualification* defines the set of tuples to be involved in the operation.

A *qualification* can take one of the forms

(a) Null, implying every tuple of the relation
(b) :q1 & q2 & . . . denoting simple conjunctions
(c) :q1 | q2 | . . . denoting simple disjunctions

where each "q" is a simple qualification in one of the forms:

(a) MKED(tc), denoting combination of TRUE (or set) mark bits,
(b) UNMKED(tc), denoting combination of FALSE (or reset) mark bits,
(c) atr ~ operand, where "atr" is an attribute name, "~" is a relational operator (or comparator), and "operand" is one of
   (i) integer, signed or unsigned
   (ii) real
   (iii) literal, enclosed in either single or double quotes
   (iv) a RAP register, REGS, REGC_i, REGF_i, or REGU_i
   (v) another attribute name

The qualifications MKED(tc1,tc2) and UNMKED(tc3,tc4) are logically equivalent to MKED(tc1) & MKED(tc2) and UNMKED(tc3) & UNMKED(tc4), respectively.

A comparator can be one of =, <, ≤, >, ≥, or <>. The "<>" stands for "not equal."

A1.3 *DESCRIPTION OF INSTRUCTIONS*

Notation

In the syntax specifications, lowercase abbreviations and some special characters are used. These are explained next. Uppercase symbols and other special characters should be coded as they appear. Braces { and } enclose optional items.

Symbol	Denotes	Examples
rel	a relation name	EMP;SALES
atr	an attribute name	FLOOR;DEPT
qual	a qualification clause	
tc	any combination of mark bits	T1 T14 T03; T2T1
~	a relational operator (or comparator)	=; <
int	an integer	8; −50; 00312
lit	a literal	'ABC'; "LEVIS"
cons	a constant, integer, real, or literal	
reg	a RAP register	REGF_3; REGS
value	a RAP register or a constant	
opd	(operand) a value or an attribute name	
...	preceding construct may be repeated	

Other lowercase abbreviations (e.g., "sopr" for "set operation") are explained within the context they are used.

System-Related Instructions

```
LOCK[rel 1,rel 2,...]
```

The specified relations are locked against other users.

```
RELEASE[rel 1,rel 2,...]
```

The specified relations, locked previously by this user, are made available to other users.

```
SAVE_MARKS[rel]
```

The current mark bit settings of all tuples (briefly, marks) of the specified relation are saved in the database. If the user had previously saved marks of the relation, the previously saved marks are replaced with the current marks. In other words, a user may save only one set of marks for the tuples of a relation.

```
RESTORE_MARKS[rel]
```

The marks saved by the user for the specified relation are restored to the mark bit settings of tuples and removed from the database. If any tuples were inserted or if the key attribute values of any tuples were modified since the mark saving operation, all mark bits of those tuples are reset to 0 (or FALSE).

Example A1.1

```
LOCK[SALES,EMP]      /* Both relations locked*/
  .
  .
  .
SAVE_MARKS[SALES]
  .
  .
SAVE_MARKS[EMP]
SAVE_MARKS[SALES]    /* Replaces previous savings*/
  .
  .
RELEASE[SALES]
  .
  .
RESTORE_MARKS[EMP]   /* EMP_marks restored and*/
                     /* the saved marks removed*/
  .
  .
RELEASE[EMP]
```

Data Definition Instructions

```
RELATION[rel(prime{,ovfl})
   atr 1: type,length{,KEY}
   atr 2: type,  length{,KEY}
     .
     .                              ]{[protection]}
```

A new relation with name *rel* is defined. Relation names should be unique within a database. *prime* is an integer specifying the anticipated maximum number of tuples the relation will contain. The specified value is internally increased to a prime number and used to allocate a primary area for storing the tuples of the relation. If the optional *ovfl* is not specified, an overflow area approximately one fourth of the size of the primary area will be allocated, to handle collisions resulting from the employed hashing method. That default can be overridden by specifying an integer for *ovfl*.

atr 1, atr 2, . . . are the attribute names, which should be unique within the relation. *type* can be INTEGER, REAL, or LITERAL. *length* specifies the physical number of bytes (8 bits) to be allocated in each tuple, to the attribute. Integer attributes of lengths 1, 2, and 4 bytes and literal attributes of lengths between 1 and 256 can be specified. For real attributes, the length is 4 bytes, followed by the type, which specifies the output format (e.g., "real, 82" will print the real format as xxxxx.xx). When used, *KEY* specifies that the attribute is (part of) the primary key of the relation. At least one attribute should have the *KEY* specification. The (primary) key values of tuples are used for locating them within storage, and checked for modifications in all update operations.

protection is either PRIVATE, implying that no other users may access the relation, or a list of specifications in the form:

(a) *GRANT_READ{(usercode 1, usercode 2, . . .)}*

(b) *GRANT_UPDATE{(usercode 1, usercode 2, . . .)}*

The optional usercode list specifies the users which will be granted read or update capability. Usercodes are literals of length 2, the first two characters of the userids.

If protection is not specified, all users are granted update capability.

Example A1.2

```
/* Definition of the relations in the example database:*/

RELATION[LOCATION(20) FLOOR: INTEGER, 1
                      DEPT: LITERAL, 16, KEY]
         [GRANT_UPDATE ("YT"), GRANT_READ("C.")]
RELATION[SALES(40)    DEPT: LITERAL, 16, KEY
                      ITEM: LITERAL, 8, KEY
                      VOLUME: INTEGER, 2]
RELATION[EMP(80)      NAME: LITERAL, 8, KEY
                      DEPT: LITERAL, 16
                      SALARY: INTEGER, 4
                      COMM: REAL, 103
                      MANAGER: LITERAL, 8][GRANT_READ]
```

CREATE[rel][pathname]

The relation *rel* is populated by a set of tuples provided by the user in the external file *pathname*. The *pathname* literal should comply with the file naming rules of the underlying operating system; nevertheless, its length may not exceed 256.

If the option T is reset (T0 is specified), then the tuple file should contain a string of ASCII characters in the form:

[cons cons . . .][cons cons . . .] . . .

where each constant corresponds to an attribute value, and each constant list is a tuple instance. If the option T is set (T1 is specified), then the tuples to be inserted are assumed to be readily available in the internal logical tuple format, in the file. Option specification and the logical tuple format are described in the User's Guide. The MOVE instruction produces logical tuples that conform to the format required by the CREATE instruction executing under the T1 option.

Example A1.3

```
/*A SALES relation is created whose tuple data are
   obtained from a file called "SALES.DAT"   */

CREATE[SALES]["SALES.DAT"]
```

$$DESTROY[\text{rel 1, rel 2, ...}]$$

The specified relations are destroyed (i.e., excluded from the database). A relation cannot be destroyed by any user other than the one who had originally defined the relation. (This restriction does not apply to the database administrator.)

$$CREATE\_INDEX[\text{rel(atr)}]$$

Inverted list structures are built on the specified attribute. The structures will be maintained properly when update operations are performed on the relation *rel*.

$$DESTROY\_INDEX[\text{rel(atr)}]$$

Inverted list structures on the specified attribute are destroyed.

Example A1.4

```
CREATE_INDEX[EMP(MANAGER)]
CREATE_INDEX[EMP(DEPT)]
        .
        .
/* Faster execution of retrieval operations with qualifications
   involving the indexed attributes, can be expected */
        .
        .
DESTROY_INDEX[EMP(MANAGER)]
```

Data Manipulation Instructions

Retrieval instructions

$$MARK(tc)[\text{rel qual}]$$

Selected tuples of the relation are *tc* marked. (Tuples are selected according to the qualification *qual*.)

$$RESET(tc)[\text{rel qual}]$$

The *tc* mark bits of the selected tuples are reset. The *tc* specification has no effect on the selection process.

$$SAVE[\text{rel(atr)qual}]$$

The value of the specified attribute of the selected tuple is saved in register REGS. If there is no qualified tuple, REGS is not assigned a value. If there are two or more qualified tuples, then only the physically first tuple is selected.

Example A1.5

```
/* Find employees in the shoe department, Tl-mark the result.
   (Briefly, Tl-mark employees in the shoe department:) */

MARK(Tl)[EMP: DEPT = "SHOE"]

    .
    .
    .
/* Restrict the Tl-marked employees to those
   managed by Clark: */

RESET(Tl)[EMP: MANAGER <> 'CLARK']
```

$$GET\_FIRST[\,rel(atr\ 1,\ atr\ 2,\ \ldots\,):\ MKED(tc)]$$

The physically first *tc*-marked tuple of the specified relation is selected and its *tc* marks are reset. The values of attributes *atr 1, atr 2, . . .* are saved in the registers REGC_1, REGC_2, . . . , respectively.

This instruction is generally used for walking through a set of tuples of a relation, one at a time, whenever the set-oriented nature of the other instructions is not suitable for the processing of a particular query. Example A1.12 will show the use of GET_FIRST within loops.

$$CROSS\_MARK(tc1)[rel\ 1:\ atr\ 1 = rel\ 2.atr\ 2]\left[\left\{\begin{array}{l}ALL\\MKED(\,tc2\,)\end{array}\right\}\right]$$

The instruction performs implicit join operations, between two relations *rel 1* and *rel 2* called the target and source relations, respectively. From all or only *tc2*-marked source tuples the unique *atr 2* values are collected in a set. Then the target tuples are selected one by one, and if the *atr 1* value of a tuple is found to be a member of the set described, then that tuple is *tc1*-marked.

If *MKED(tc2)* is specified the *tc 2* marks of selected source tuples are reset. If the target and source relations are the same, then *tc 1* and *tc 2* marks should be disjoint.

In this version, only the equi-joins are allowed. Programming for the general theta-join operations is explained in Section A1.6.

Example A1.6

```
/* T3T4-mark employees working in the second floor departments: */
MARK(T3)[LOCATION: FLOOR = 2] /* 2nd floor depts */
CROSS_MARK(T3T4)[EMP: DEPT = LOCATION.DEPT][MKED(T3)]

    .
    .
    .
/* Tl-mark employees that are managers: */
CROSS_MARK(Tl)[EMP: NAME = EMP.MANAGER][ALL]
```

$$\text{CROSS\_RESET(tc 1)[rel 1: atr 1 = rel 2.atr 2]}\left[\begin{cases}\text{ALL} \\ \text{MKED}(tc2)\end{cases}\right]$$

This instruction is similar to CROSS_MARK. It is generally used to perform a further mapping into the target relation, following a mapping made previously by a MARK or CROSS_MARK. A set of *atr 2* values is formed, and *atr 1* values of all target tuples are checked for membership in that set, as before. But this time, if the *atr 1* value of a target tuple is not a member of the set, then that tuple is *tc1*-reset. The initial settings of the *tc1* marks in the target relation have no effect on the logic of the operation.

The T15 marks of target tuples may be used by SERAP, and the final settings of T15 marks of *rel 1* are undefined. *tc1* and if specified *tc2* may not include T15. If the target and source relations are the same, *tc1* and *tc2* should be disjoint.

Example A1.7

```
/* T1-mark the employees working in the second floor departments
   that sell more than 800 of any single item: */

MARK(T8)[LOCATION: FLOOR = 2]
CROSS_MARK(T1)[EMP: DEPT = LOCATION.DEPT][MKED(T8)]
   /* Employees on the 2nd floor are T1-marked */
MARK(T9)[SALES: VOLUME > 800]
CROSS_RESET(T1)[EMP: DEPT = SALES.DEPT][MKED(T9)]
   /* Only sought employees remain T1-marked */

/* The CROSS_RESET instruction above can be replaced by
   the sequence below, which produces equivalent results
   except for the final T15 settings: */

RESET(T15)[EMP]
CROSS_MARK(T15)[EMP: DEPT = SALES.DEPT][MKED(T9)]
RESET(T1)[EMP: UNMKED(T15)]
```

```
READ[rel{(atr 1, atr2, ...)}qual]
```

When using the stand-alone version of the emulator, selected tuples of *rel* are formatted and printed. If the optional attribute list is specified, then only the values of those attributes are printed, in the same order.

When using the host-embedded version, a procedure named TUPREAD (that should be provided by the user) is invoked by the emulator, once for each selected tuple. On entry to the TUPREAD procedure, the logical-tuple instance will be available in the SRTUPLE array, and the mark bits of the tuple will be available in the SRMARKS word. The optional attribute list has no effect. The user may reference values of all attributes and all mark bits, but changes made to those values are not reflected to the database.

When using the host-embedded version, the emulator procedure SRTUP-

READ can be invoked from the user-provided TUPREAD procedure, to obtain the default formatting and printing of the stand-alone version. Further information on defaulting can be found in the User's Guide.

```
READ_MARKS[rel{(atr 1, atr 2, ...)}qual]
```

This instruction is similar to READ. For the stand-alone version, the set mark bits of the selected tuples are also printed. For the host-embedded version, there is no difference between READ and READ_MARKS.

```
MOVE[rel{(atr 1, atr 2, ...)}qual]{[site-id]}
```

When using the stand-alone version of SERAP, this instruction has no effect.

When using the host-embedded version, the user-provided TUPREAD procedure is invoked by the SERAP routines, once for each selected tuple. On entry to that routine, the logical tuple instance will be available in the SRTUPLE array, the mark bits of the tuple will be available in the SRMARKS word, and a new form of the logical tuple will be available in the SRNEWTUPLE array. If the optional attribute list is not specified, the new form is the same as the original form (i.e., SRTUPLE and SRNEWTUPLE contents are identical). If an attribute list is specified, then the corresponding logical attribute values are contiguously placed in the SRNEWTUPLE array, in the order specified by the list. Logical attribute values occupy an integer number of words; integer values are contained within one word and literal values are padded on the right with spaces within the rightmost word. This logical tuple format is compatible with the form required by CREATE and INSERT executing under T1 option.

The *site-id* parameter specification is optional; if specified it is ignored.

Example A1.8

```
/* List all employee information: */
READ[EMP]

/* List all employee information for the shoe department: */
READ[EMP: DEPT = 'SHOE']

/* List the names and salaries of employees with
   salaries below 1000, in the shoe department: */
READ[EMP(NAME, SALARY): SALARY < 1000 & DEPT = "SHOE"]

/* List all employees and their managers: */
READ[EMP(NAME, MANAGER)]

/* List the names of employees on the first floor: */
MARK(T1)[LOCATION: FLOOR = 1]
CROSS_MARK(T1)[EMP: DEPT = LOCATION.DEPT][MKED(T1)]
READ[EMP(NAME): MKED(T1)]

/* List employee tuples with the mark bits: */
READ_MARKS[EMP]
```

Update instructions

```
uopr[rel(atr)qual][opd]
```

The update operation code *uopr* can be ADD, SUB, MUL, DIV, or REPLACE. *atr* value of each selected tuple is operated with the operand *opd* and the result is stored in *atr*. For the arithmetic operations, only integer attributes can be specified. Results of division are truncated. Divisions by zero are not performed.

```
INSERT[rel]{[value 1, value 2, ...]}
```

A new tuple is formed and inserted into *rel*. Under the T0 option, the value list must be specified, representing the tuple instance to be inserted. Under the T1 option, the value list is not specified; the tuple to be inserted is assumed to be in the internal logical tuple format within the SRNEWTUPLE array, which was explained while describing the CREATE and MOVE instructions. Option specification is described in the User's Guide.

```
DELETE[rel qual]
```

Selected tuples of the relation are deleted. Even if the operation results in the deletion of all tuples, the relation and any existing inverted list structures are not destroyed.

Example A1.9

```
/* Increase the salaries of employees in the shoe department by
   50 */
ADD[EMP(SALARY): DEPT = "SHOE"][50]

/* Manager Smith is replaced by Clark; update the fact: */
REPLACE[EMP(MANAGER): MANAGER = 'SMITH'][ 'CLARK']

/* Insert a new department named "FURNITURE" on to the third
   floor: */
INSERT[LOCATION][3, "FURNITURE"]
```

Set function instructions

```
sopr[rel(atr)qual]{[reg]}
```

The set operation code *sopr* can be MAX, MIN, SUM, AVERAGE, or COUNT. The specified function is computed over the integer attribute *atr* values of selected tuples, and the result is placed in *reg*. The attribute is not specified for COUNT. If *reg* is not specified, the result is placed in REGF_1.

For MAX and MIN, if there are no selected tuples, the results are undefined. For AVERAGE, the result is truncated to an integer value.

Example A1.10

```
/* Find the maximum and minimum salaries, save
   the results in REGF_1 and REGF_2, respectively: */
MAX[EMP(SALARY)]
MIN[EMP(SALARY)][REGF_2]

/* Find the average salary in the shoe department: (into
   REGF_3) */
AVERAGE[EMP(SALARY): DEPT = "SHOE"][REGF_3]

/* Find the total volume of sales in the shoe department: (into
   REGU_1) */
SUM[SALES(VOLUME): DEPT = "SHOE"][REGU_1]

/* Count the number of employees managed by Clark: (into
   REGU_4) */
COUNT[EMP: MANAGER = "CLARK"][REGU_4]

/* Count the total number of managers: (into REGU_2) */
CROSS_MARK(T2)[EMP: NAME = EMP.MANAGER][ALL]
COUNT[EMP: MKED(T2)][REGU_2]

/* Count the number of employees on the third floor: (into
   REGU_3) */
MARK(T1)[LOCATION: FLOOR = 3]
CROSS_MARK(T3)[EMP: DEPT = LOCATION.DEPT][MKED(T1)]
COUNT[EMP: MKED(T3)][REGU_3]
```

Register Manipulation Instructions

```
ropr[reg, value]
```

The register operation code *ropr* can be RADD, RSUB, RMUL, RDIV, or
RSET. The register *reg* is operated with the operand "value" in the form

```
reg <--- reg ropr value          for RADD, RSUB, RMUL, RDIV
reg <--- value                   for RSET
```

For the arithmetic operations, operands should have integer values. Note
that at the beginning of a query, the registers are not initialized and their contents
are undefined. For RDIV, result of division is truncated. Division by zero is
not performed.

```
DEC_REG[reg1, reg2, ...]
```

The specified registers are decremented by 1.

```
INC_REG[reg1, reg2, ...]
```

The specified registers are incremented by 1.

READ_REG[regl, reg2, ...]

When using the stand-alone version of the emulator, the specified registers' contents are formatted and printed.

When using the host-embedded version, a procedure named REGREAD (that should be provided by the user) is invoked, once for each register. There is one global array SRREG, with 16 elements, each of which has the union structure containing the type and values of registers. The registers REGS, REGC_1, REGC_2, . . . , REGF_1, REGF_2, . . . , REGU_1, REGU_2, . . . are referenced by indexes from 0 to 15, correspondingly. If SRREG[n].regtype is "I," then SRREG[n] contains the integer value of the register; if SRREG[n].regtype is "R," then SRREG[n] contains the real value of the register; if SRREG[n].regtype is "L," then SRREG[n] contains the literal value. The emulator uses this array for register storage; hence, any changes made to the values take effect immediately.

When using the host-embedded version, the emulator procedure SRREG-READ can be invoked from the user-provided REGREAD procedure, to obtain the default formatting and printing of the stand-alone version. Further information on defaulting can be found in the User's Guide.

Example A1.11

```
/* Set REGU_1, ..., REGU_6 to 0, -32767, 32767,
   "ADMINISTRATION", ""(blanks), and 12.34, respectively: */
RSET[ REGU_1, 0]
RSET[ REGU_2, -32767]
RSET[ REGU_3, 32767]
RSET[ REGU_4, "ADMINISTRATION"]
RSET[ REGU_5, "]
RSET[ REGU_6, 6]
RSET[ REGU_7, 12.34]


RADD[ REGU_6, -4] /* Reg. contains 2*/
RSUB[ REGU_7, 2.04] /* Reg. contains 10.3 */
RMUL[ REGU_6, 5] /* Reg. contains 10 */
RDIV[ REGU_6, 4] /* Reg. contains 2 */

/* List the minimum, average, and the maximum salaries
   of employees in the shoe and dress departments: */
MARK(Tl)[EMP: DEPT = "SHOE" | DEPT = "DRESS"]
MAX[ EMP(SALARY): MKED(Tl)]
MIN[ EMP(SALARY): MKED(Tl)][REGF_2]
AVERAGE[ EMP(SALARY): MKED(Tl)][REGF_3]
READ_REG[ REGF_1, REGF_3, REGF_2]
```

Transfer Instructions

BC label{,condition}.   BC is the abbreviation of "branch on condition." If the optional *condition* is not specified or if it yields a TRUE value, a branch is taken to the instruction at *label*; otherwise, the next instruction will be executed. The *condition* can be one of

(a) reg ~ value   An integer, real or literal comparison
(b) rel.RAIL_STAT(tc)   yielding TRUE if and only if there is at least one
                               tc-marked "rel" tuple. In the old version of RAP
                               a TEST instruction must be executed prior to BC.

BNC label{,condition}.   This instruction is similar to BC, but this time a branch to the instruction at *label* is taken only if the condition yields a FALSE value. If the optional *condition* is not specified, this instruction has no effect (i.e., it is a no-op instruction), and the label need not actually be the label of an instruction.

EOQ.   This instruction indicates the end of a query. Execution is terminated, and the user is logged off.

Example A1.12

```
/* Find the total volume of sales in each department
   on the second floor: */
MARK(T1)[LOCATION: FLOOR = 2]
CROSS_MARK(T1)[SALES: DEPT = LOCATION.DEPT][MKED(T1)]
NEXT_DEPT GET_FIRST[SALES(DEPT): MKED(T1) ] /* A dept into REGC_1 */
   SUM[SALES(VOLUME): DEPT = REGC_1] /* Result is in REGF_1 */
   READ_REG[REGC_1, REGF_1]
   RESET(T1)[SALES: DEPT = REGC_1] /* Clear processed ones */
   BC NEXT_DEPT, SALES.RAIL_STAT(T1)

/* The same query, but checking moved to the loop head: */
MARK(T1)[LOCATION: FLOOR = 2]
CROSS_MARK(T1)[SALES: DEPT = LOCATION.DEPT][MKED(T1)]
ANY_DEPT BNC NO_MORE, SALES.RAIL_STAT(T1)
   GET_FIRST[SALES(DEPT): MKED(T1)]
   SUM[SALES(VOLUME): DEPT = REGC_1]
   READ_REG[REGC_1, REGF_1]
   BC ANY_DEPT
 NO_MORE.
   .
   /* Skeleton coding, for looping 10 times: */
   RSET[REGU_1, 1]
LOOP_HEAD
   .

   .
   INC_REG[REGU_1]
   BC LOOP_HEAD, REGU_1 <= 10
```

```
    /* Skeleton for looping REGS times, decrementing REGS */
LOOP_HEAD BC LOOP_END, REGS < 1
    .
    .
    .
    DEC_REG[REGS]
    BC LOOP_HEAD
LOOP_END.
    .
```

Document Retrieval Instructions

The following present the syntax of these instructions:

```
MATCH(tc)[rel(atr 1 {, atr 2 {, atr 3}})qual]{[lit]}
MATCH_WS(tc)[rel(atr 1 {, atr 2)qual]{[lit]}
MATCH_WWC(tc)[rel(atr 1, {, atr 2}, atr 3)qual]{[lit]} {[int]}
LINK_PASS(tc 1, tc 2)[rel({atr 1,} atr 2)]
```

Chapter 13 presents a complete list of these instructions and their semantics.

Macro Instructions

The PROJECT and DIVIDE instructions described in this section perform relational algebra operations of projection and division. These operations can be programmed using a sequence of other RAP instructions or implemented as macro instructions. In this version of SERAP, these instructions are implemented directly (i.e., they are not expanded into a sequence of other instructions).

```
PROJECT(tc)[rel(atr 1, atr 2, ...)qual]
```

The specified relation is first restricted by *qual* and then projected over the specified attributes, and the result of projection is *tc* marked. T15 is used temporarily and reset at the end of projection. No resetting of previous *tc* marks takes place. T15 may not be included in *tc*. Use of T15 within *qual* is not recommended.

Example A1.13

```
    /* Find the managers in the TOY and SHOE departments;
       List the unique dept-manager pairs. */

    /* Using PROJECT: */

    PROJECT(T1)[EMP: DEPT = 'TOY' OR DEPT = 'SHOE']
    READ[EMP(DEPT, MANAGER): MKED(T1)]

    /* Not using PROJECT */
    MARK(T1 T15)[EMP: DEPT = 'TOY' OR DEPT = 'SHOE']
    NEXT GET_FIRST[EMP(DEPT, MANAGER): MKED(T15)]
       RESET(T1T15)[EMP: DEPT = REGC_1 AND MANAGER = REGC_2 AND
       MKED(T15)]
```

```
        BC NEXT, EMP.RAIL_STAT(T15)
        READ[EMP(DEPT, MANAGER): MKED(T1)]
```

```
DIVIDE(tc)[rel(atr 1, atr 2)qual 1][rel 2(atr 2)qual 2]
```

The first specification is for the dividend, and the second one is for the divisor of the division operation. The two relations are restricted by the respective qualifications, and the result of division is *tc* marked in the dividend relation *rel 1*.

The division is performed as follows: *atr 2* values of *rel 2* tuples selected by *qual 2* are collected in a set. *atr 1* and *atr 2* value pairs of *rel 1* tuples selected by *qual 1* are grouped according to *atr 1* values. Then for each group (corresponding to a single *atr 1* value), the *atr 2* values in the group are collected in another set, and if this set includes the set formed from *rel 2* (or, if the set formed from *rel 2* is a subset of this set), then a tuple of *rel 1* in that group is *tc* marked.

The result of division is readily projected over *atr 1* within *rel 1*. If projection is undesirable, the following instructions propagate the *tc* marks to proper *rel 1* tuples having the same *atr 1* values (undoing the projection):

```
CROSS_MARK(T15)[rel 1: atr 1 = rel 1.atr 1][MKED(tc)]
MARK(tc)[rel 1: MKED(T15) AND qual 1]
```

The T14 and T15 mark bits of both *rel 1* and *rel 2* are used temporarily and reset at the end of division. If *rel 1* and *rel 2* are the same relation, then T13 is also used temporarily and then reset. The *tc* specification may not include T14, T15, and if *rel 1* and *rel 2* are the same, also T13. The use of these mark bits within the qualification clauses *qual 1* and *qual 2* is not recommended.

No resetting of previous *tc* marks within *rel 1* takes place.

Example A1.14

```
        /* List the managers that manage at least one employee
           from each of the second floor departments: */
        DIVIDE(T1)[EMP(MANAGER, DEPT)][LOCATION(DEPT): FLOOR = 2]
        READ[EMP(MANAGER): MKED(T1)]
        /* List the managers, other than those working in the
           "ADMINISTRATION" department, that manage at least
           one employee from each of the second floor
           departments: */

        /* Approach-1: First restrict the managers,
                       then perform the division: */
        MARK(T2)[EMP: DEPT <> "ADMINISTRATION"]
        CROSS_MARK(T3)[EMP: MANAGER = EMP.NAME][MKED(T2)]
        DIVIDE(T1)[EMP(MANAGER, DEPT): MKED(T3)]
               [LOCATION(DEPT): FLOOR = 2]
        READ[EMP(MANAGER): MKED(T1)]
```

```
/* Approach-2: First perform the division,
                 then restrict managers in the result: */
DIVIDE(T1)[EMP(MANAGER, DEPT)][LOCATION(DEPT): FLOOR = 2]
MARK(T2)[EMP: DEPT <> "ADMINISTRATION"]
CROSS_RESET(T1)[EMP: MANAGER = EMP.NAME][MKED(T2)]
READ[EMP(MANAGER): MKED(T1)]
```

A1.4 SUMMARY OF THE RAP ASSEMBLER LANGUAGE SYNTAX

The syntax specifications in the text are slightly more abbreviated and presented in this appendix for quick reference. Lowercase symbols are descriptive; uppercase symbols and special characters should be coded as they appear. Braces that enclose a single line indicate optional specifications. Braces that enclose two or more lines indicate a choice between several specifications. Where appropriate, indexes on symbols are dropped (e.g., ''atr, atr'' is used instead of ''atr 1, atr 2''), and some symbols are reduced to more primitive ones (e.g., ''lit'' for literal is used instead of ''pathname'').

Lowercase symbols are explained next.

Symbol	Denotes
rel	a relation name
atr	an attribute name
qual	a qualification clause
tc	any combination of mark bits
~	a relational operator (or comparator)
int	an integer
lit	a literal
cons	a constant, integer, real, or literal
reg	a RAP register
value	a RAP register or a constant
opd	(operand) a value or an attribute name
...	preceding construct may be repeated
id	a usercode, literal of length 2
label	the symbolic address of an instruction
k	a positive integer (>0)

System-related instructions

```
{LOCK    }[rel, rel, ...]
{RELEASE }

{SAVE_MARKS    }[rel]
{RESTORE_MARKS }
```

Data definition instructions

```
RELATION[rel(int {, int})
    atr1:⎰INTEGER⎱,k, {, KEY}  atr2:⎰INTEGER⎱,k {, KEY}...]
         ⎱LITERAL⎰                   ⎱LITERAL⎰
    {[⎰PRIVATE                                        ⎱]}
     ⎱GRANT_READ(id,...),GRANT_UPDATE(ID,...), ···⎰
CREATE[rel][lit]
DESTROY[rel, rel, ...]

⎰CREATE_INDEX ⎱[rel(atr)]
⎱DESTROY_INDEX⎰
```

Data manipulation instructions

```
⎰MARK ⎱(tc)[rel qual]
⎱RESET⎰
SAVE[rel(atr)qual]
GET_FIRST[rel(atr, atr, ...): MKED(tc)]

⎰CROSS_MARK ⎱(tc)[rel: atr = rel.atr][⎰MKED(tc)⎱]
⎱CROSS_RESET⎰                          ⎱ALL     ⎰

⎰READ       ⎱[rel{(atr, atr, ...)}qual]
⎱READ_MARKS ⎰

MOVE[rel{(atr, atr, ...)}qual]{[cons]}

⎰ADD    ⎱
⎪SUB    ⎪
⎨MUL    ⎬[rel(atr)qual][opd]
⎪DIV    ⎪
⎩REPLACE⎭

INSERT[rel]{[value, value, ...]}
DELETE[rel qual]

⎰MAX    ⎱
⎪MIN    ⎪
⎨SUM    ⎬[rel(atr)qual]{[reg]}
⎩AVERAGE⎭

COUNT[rel qual]{[reg]}
```

Register manipulation instructions

```
⎰RADD⎱
⎪RSUB⎪
⎨RMUL⎬[reg, reg, ...]
⎪RDIV⎪
⎩RSET⎭
```

$$\left.\begin{cases} \texttt{DEC\_REG} \\ \texttt{INC\_REG} \\ \texttt{READ\_REG} \end{cases}\right\}[\texttt{reg, reg, ...}]$$

Transfer instructions

$$\begin{Bmatrix} \texttt{BC} \\ \texttt{BNC} \end{Bmatrix} \texttt{label} \left\{,\begin{Bmatrix} \texttt{reg} \sim \texttt{value} \\ \texttt{rel.RAIL\_STAT(tc)} \end{Bmatrix}\right\}$$

```
EOQ
```

Macro instructions

```
PROJECT(tc)[rel(atr, atr, ...)qual]
DIVIDE(tc)[rell(atrl, atr2)qual][rel2(atr2)qual]
```

A1.5 ABBREVIATED MNEMONICS

Abbreviated mnemonic names may be used for the opcodes of several instructions, which are listed here. These abbreviations may not be supported in subsequent versions.

Abbreviation	Opcode
RLSE	RELEASE
CRI	CREATE_INDEX
DSI	DESTROY_INDEX
GF	GET_FIRST
XM	CROSS_MARK
XR	CROSS_RESET
RM	READ_MARKS
REP	REPLACE
AVG	AVERAGE
DR	DEC_REG
IR	INC_REG
RR	READ_REG

A1.6 PROGRAMMING THETA-JOIN OPERATIONS

The relational operator (or comparator) in the cross-marking instructions is restricted to the "equal" operator, allowing only equi-joins. This restriction does not imply that user's programming capabilities are diminished; theta-joins can be programmed. The reason for restricting cross-marking operations is to force the user to employ more efficient methods for theta-join operations.

Example A1.15

```
/* Query: List all employees who earn more than any
          employee in the shoe department. */
```

```
/* Approach-1: If the CROSS_MARK instruction were not restricted: */
MARK(T1)[EMP: DEPT = "SHOE"]
CROSS_MARK(T2)[EMP: SALARY > EMP.SALARY][MKED(T1)]
READ[EMP(NAME): MKED(T2)]


/* Approach-2: Without cross marking: */
MAX[EMP(SALARY): DEPT = "SHOE"]
READ[EMP(NAME): SALARY > REGF_1]


/* If the "more" in the query is changed to "less", then
   change the ">" to "<" and "MAX" to "MIN" in the
   codings above. */


/* Query: T1-mark all employees working in the departments other
          than those located on the second floor. */


/* Approach-1: If CROSS_MARK were not restricted: */
MARK(T2)[LOCATION: FLOOR = 2]
CROSS_MARK(T1)[EMP: DEPT <> LOCATION.DEPT][MKED(T2)]


/* Approach-2: General form of coding:
MARK(T2)[LOCATION: FLOOR = 2]
CROSS_MARK(T2)[EMP: DEPT = LOCATION.DEPT][MKED(T2)]
MARK(T1)[EMP: UNMKED(T2)]


/* Approach-3: Since EMP(DEPT) is a subset of LOCATION(DEPT): */
MARK(T2)[LOCATION: FLOOR <> 2]
CROSS_MARK(T1)[EMP: DEPT = LOCATION.DEPT][MKED(T2)]
```

A1.7 NEW COMMANDS ADDED TO THE RAP LANGUAGE

The following commands whose syntaxes are listed below are added to the RAP
instruction set only in the UNIX version of the RAP software:

```
1)   keep [rel1: mked(tc1)][rel2]
2)   union [rel1: mked(tc1)][rel2: mked(tc2)][rel3]
3)   intersect [rel1: mked(tc1)][rel2: mked(tc2)][rel3]
4)   difference [rel1: mked(tc1)][rel2: mked(tc2)][rel3]
5)   join [rel1(atr1,atr2,...): mked (tc1)]
          [rel2(atr1,atr2,...): mked (tc2)][rel3(prime{,overflow})]
```

In the first command, opcode *keep*, a previously marked relation *rel1*, whose
marking is indicated by *tc1*, as a result of a selection or semi-join can be made
a permanent relation with a new assigned name *rel2*. This command helps
materializing views and making results of queries permanent relations if so desired.

In instructions 2 through 4 (the opcodes *union*, *intersect*, and *difference*)
the set operations of relational algebra are performed between two full relations
(i.e., attribute lists are not allowed). That is, full tuples of relations *rel1* and
rel2 are operated with these set operations and the result is put in *rel3*. The

operand relations need not be full-size, that is, they can be preselected and specified in their mark bits, *tc1* for *rel1* and *tc2* for *rel2*. One *important* note however, is that these operations do not have built-in projection so that user has to explicitly use the RAP PROJECT macro for *rel3* after these commands are executed.

The last command is a physical join as opposed to the traditional RAP operation of semi-join realized with the CROSS_MARK instruction. Accordingly, a new relation *rel3* is created as a result of a natural join between the two relations specified in *rel1* and *rel2*. As in the other instructions, these two relations can be preselected and specified in their mark bits *tc1* and *tc2*, respectively. User has to estimate the size of the result relation and declare it with *rel3* as in the use of the RELATION command. Finally, the attributes *atr1,atr2,...* are the join attributes of each of the relations being joined.

These additional instructions are mainly for administrative uses (i.e., DBA functions). It is suggested that user should use the regular RAP instructions rather than programming in the traditional algebra way—that is, by using set operations and physical join and assigning results to new relations.

APPENDIX II

RAP GDBMS SYSTEM AND ITS HIERARCHICAL AND NETWORK DATA LANGUAGES

In this appendix, we will present the details of the RAP's ANSI/SPARC-like GDBMS data language interfaces. The relational interface of this GDBMS is the RAP relational DBMS assembler language, which is described in Appendix I. The hierarchical and network interfaces use the set-oriented, self-iterative languages of MRI and LSL, respectively. The translators of these languages transform MRI and LSL queries into equivalent RAP code, which executes on the RAP tabular structures created at the common physical schema interface.

The experimental software for the MRI and LSL translators execute on the Intel microcomputer equipment, the VAX 11/780 UNIX system, and the IBM PC. As will be seen in the following sections, the MRI and LSL syntaxes discussed in Chapter 3 are modified to incorporate value saving and injection as well as arithmetic update capabilities.

In the following sections, we will present, for each language, the syntax descriptions, language semantics, example queries, and the error messages issued by the language translators. The appendix will conclude with a command summary of the GDBMS software and the E/R model–based conceptual schema DDL interface. Details of these were covered in Chapter 9.

A2.1 MRI TO RAP TRANSLATOR

A2.1.1 Introduction

MRI is a translator from a MRI2000-like hierarchical query language to the RAP DBMS assembler language.

The following facilities are implemented in the MRI translator:

(a) Flat selection (selecting the qualified occurrence(s) of a record type).

(b) Upward normalization (selecting an ancestor record occurrence of the qualified descendant record occurrence(s)).

(c) Downward normalization (selecting some descendant record occurrence(s) of a qualified ancestor record occurrence).

(d) Upward normalization using HAS (selecting a common ancestor record occurrence of some qualified descendant record occurrences).

(e) Twin selection using HAS (selecting the record occurrence(s) that have a common ancestor record occurrence with the qualified record occurrence(s)).

(f) Standard set (statistical) functions of COUNT, SUM, AVERAGE, MAX, and MIN that can be used both in selection and qualification of an MRI query coded using one of the facilities (a) through (e).

(g) Saving an attribute value of a record occurrence which is selected by using one of the facilities (a) through (d).

(h) Adding, subtracting, multiplying, or dividing an attribute value of the record occurrence(s), which are selected by using one of the facilities (a) through (d), with a number, saved value, or another attribute value of the same record occurrence.

(i) Replacing an attribute value of a record occurrence selected by using one of the facilities (a) through (d).

A2.1.2 MRI Railroad Diagrams*

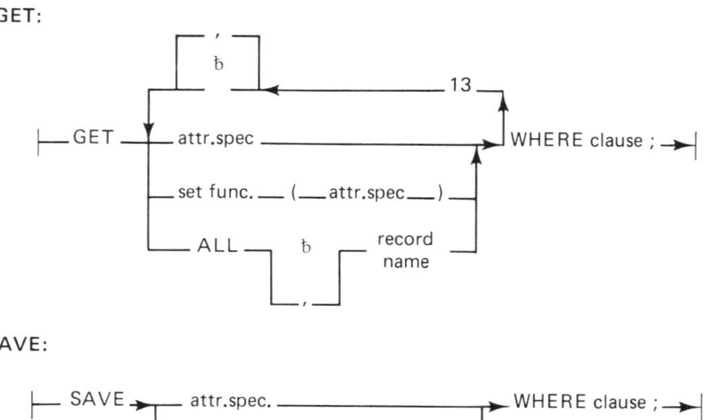

---

    * Railroad diagrams are our alternative way of describing a language syntax. In them, —| indicates the end of a diagram; → indicates the direction of source text; *n* indicates that a path can be repeated at most *n* times; parallel tracks and square brackets imply options; the order of evaluation is from left to right unless modified by the directed lines.

Update functions:

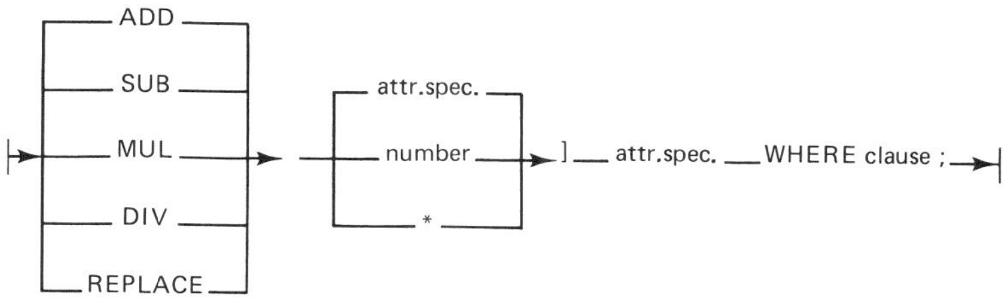

***command:**

attr.spec.:

set func.:

WHERE clause:

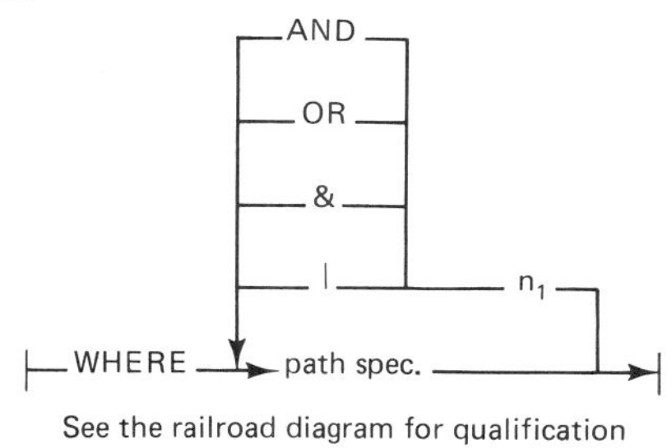

See the railroad diagram for qualification

path spec.:

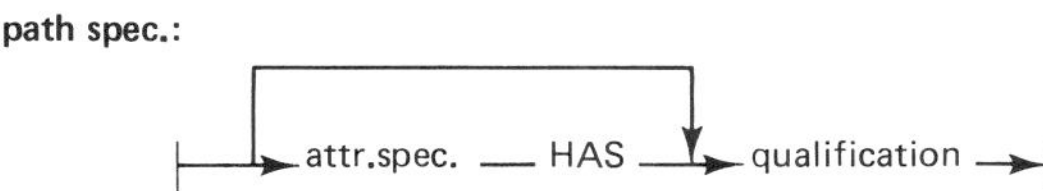

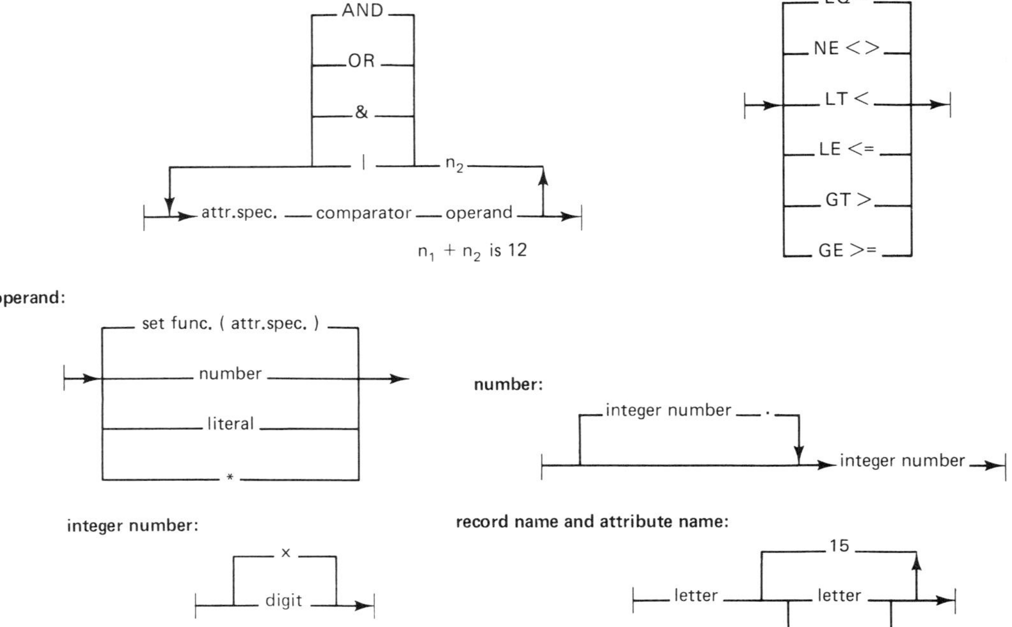

letter: any one of the letters A–Z
digit: any one of the digits 0–9
char: any one of the characters in the UNIX character set

A2.1.3 MRI Language Semantics

(a) DATABASE DEFINITION: Should be done at the conceptual data model interface.

(b) SAVE COMMAND: The MRI language is self iterative, that is, a set of values can be obtained with an *attr. spec.* However, the SAVE command can save only a single attribute value at a time, and it is the user's responsibility to ensure that a single value will be saved; otherwise, one of the values from a set of values will be randomly selected and saved.

(c) *: An attribute value saved with a SAVE command can be referred to with an "*" at the subsequent queries (see the railroad diagrams).

(d) * COMMAND: Keying an * followed by ";" causes the last saved attribute value to be retrieved.

(e) . QUALIFIER: An attribute name should be qualified with a *record_name*. whenever there is an ambiguity (i.e., whenever there is more than one record type having the same attribute name).

(f) HAS CLAUSE: The optional HAS clause allows data on one hierarchical level to be qualified on properties that data on any level below it may possess. All attributes specified in the Boolean qualification following a HAS clause must be in the same record type.

(g) STATISTICAL FUNCTIONS: As can be seen from the railroad diagrams, the functions COUNT, SUM, AVERAGE, MAX, and MIN can be used in qualifications only as operands, that is, in the form <attr. spec.> <comparator> <set func.>; hence, a qualification such as ...COUNT(EMP) GT 10 is invalid.

(h) PRECEDENCE OF OPERATORS: AND (&) and OR (|) operators have a higher precedence over the comparators = , EQ, <>, NE, >, GT, >=, GE, <, LT, <=, LE. Evaluation of simple qualifications connected with ANDs and ORs is from left to right.

(i) SEPARATORS: ʬ's and ,'s can be used as separators interchangeably.

(j) USE OF TERMINATORS: A ";" terminates an MRI query. ; can be freely used in an MRI query (not within a word, however).

A2.1.4 Example MRI Queries

The following database definition tree will be used in the examples:

Flat selection

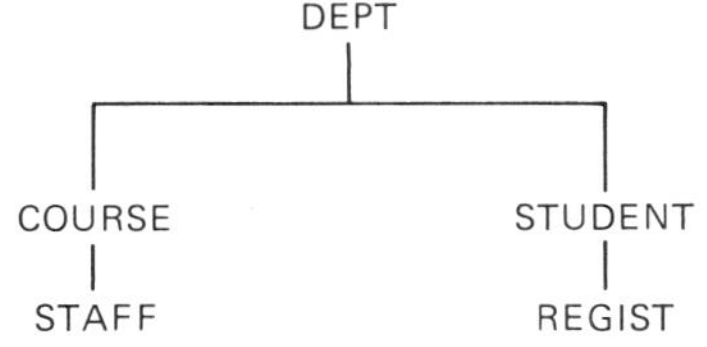


```
where

DEPT:       (DEPT_NO, DEPT_NAME)
COURSE:     (CRS_NO, CRS_NAME, YEAR, CREDIT)
STAFF:      (STF_NO, STF_NAME, SEX, BIRTHYR)
STUDENT:    (ST_NO, ST_NAME, SEX, BIRTHYR, YEAR)
REGIST:     (ST_NO, CRS_NO)
```

(a) Get the student no. and the name of all male students born in the year 1959.

```
GET ST_NO, ST_NAME WHERE
  STUDENT.SEX EQ 'M' AND STUDENT.BIRTHYR EQ 59;
```

(b) Save the total number of third-year courses.

```
SAVE COUNT(COURSE.CRS_NO) WHERE COURSE.YEAR = 3;
```

(c) Find the youngest male student and increment its YEAR field by 1.

```
ADD [1] STUDENT.YEAR WHERE STUDENT.SEX EQ 'M' AND
    STUDENT.BIRTHYR EQ MAX(STUDENT.BIRTHYR);
```

Upward normalization

(a) Get the courses offered by the female staff.

```
GET COURSE.CRS_NO, CRS_NAME, COURSE.YEAR
   WHERE STAFF.SEX EQ 'F';
```

(b) Save the department name of the staff member named 'JOHN'.

```
SAVE DEPT_NAME WHERE STF_NAME EQ 'JOHN';
```

(c) Get the number of the department that was saved in the previous query (flat selection).

```
GET DEPT_NO WHERE DEPT_NAME EQ *;
```

(d) Get the names of all students who are taking the course 'CS535.'

```
GET ST_NAME WHERE REGIST.CRS_NO EQ 'CS535';
```

(e) Get the total number of students who are taking the course 'EE101.'

```
GET COUNT(ST_NAME) WHERE REGIST.CRS_NO EQ 'EE101';
```

Downward normalization

(a) Get the names of all staff in the department whose name is saved in a previous query.

```
GET STF_NAME WHERE DEPT_NAME EQ *;
```

(b) Save the total number of staff offering third-year courses having 3 credit hours.

```
SAVE COUNT(STF_NAME) WHERE
   COURSE_YEAR EQ 3 AND CREDIT EQ 3;
```

(c) Get the names of staff who are teaching the courses that have the maximum credit.

```
GET STF_NAME WHERE CREDIT = MAX(CREDIT);
```

(d) Replace the credit of all the courses offered by the 'COMP.SC.' department with a value saved in a previous query.

```
REPLACE [*] CREDIT WHERE DEPT_NAME EQ 'COMP.SC';
```

Upward normalization using HAS

(a) Save the number of the course offered by the staff member named 'JOHN.'

```
SAVE COURSE.CRS_NO WHERE COURSE.CRS_NO HAS
STF_NAME EQ 'JOHN'.;
```

(where can also be coded as follows:

```
SAVE COURSE.CRS_NO WHERE STF_NAME EQ 'JOHN';)
```

(b) Get the name of the department offering the courses 'CS301' and the one whose number was saved in the previous query (there may not be such a department, in which case nothing is retrieved).

```
GET DEPT_NAME WHERE DEPT_NO HAS COURSE.CRS_NO EQ 'CS301'
AND DEPT_NO HAS COURSE.CRS_NO EQ *;
```

(c) Get the names of departments that have either the youngest student or the youngest staff.

```
GET DEPT_NAME WHERE DEPT_NO HAS STUDENT.BIRTHYR EQ
MAX(STUDENT.BIRTHYR) OR DEPT_NO HAS STAFF.BIRTHYR EQ
MAX(STAFF.BIRTHYR);
```

(d) Get the names of departments offering the fifth-year courses and having staff born in year 1943.

```
GET DEPT_NAME WHERE DEPT_NAME HAS COURSE.YEAR EQ 5 AND
N DEPT_NAME HAS STAFF.BIRTHYR EQ 1943;
```

(e) Increment the year of the third-year students registered to course 'CS599' by 1.

```
ADD [1] STUDENT.YEAR WHERE ST_NAME HAS STUDENT.YEAR EQ 3
AND ST_NAME HAS REGIST.CRS_NO EQ 'CS599';
```

Twin selection using HAS

(a) Get the names of students who are in the same department as the staff member 'JOHN.'

```
GET ST_NAME WHERE DEPT_NO HAS STF_NAME EQ 'JOHN';
```

We do not repeat DEPT_NO after HAS unlike the upward normalization shown previously in (b).

(b) Get the birthyear of the oldest student who is in the same department as the oldest female staff member.

```
GET MIN(STUDENT.BIRTHYR) WHERE DEPT_NO HAS STAFF.BIRTHYR
   EQ MIN(STAFF.BIRTHYR) AND STAFF.SEX EQ 'F';
```

A2.2 LSL TO RAP TRANSLATOR

A2.2.1 Introduction

LSL is a translator from the Link-and-Selector network query language to the RAP DBMS assembler language.

The following facilities are implemented in the LSL translator:

(a) Making a flat selection (selecting qualified occurrence(s) of a record type).

(b) Using the qualified record occurrence(s) of a record type and the link between two record types and selecting those occurrence(s) of another record type that meet the given qualification criterion.

(c) Saving an attribute value of a record occurrence selected by using the step (a) or (b).

(d) Updating (add, subtract, multiply, or divide) or replacing an attribute value of the record occurrence(s) selected by using the steps (a) or (b).

A2.2.2 LSL Railroad Diagrams

LSL Query:

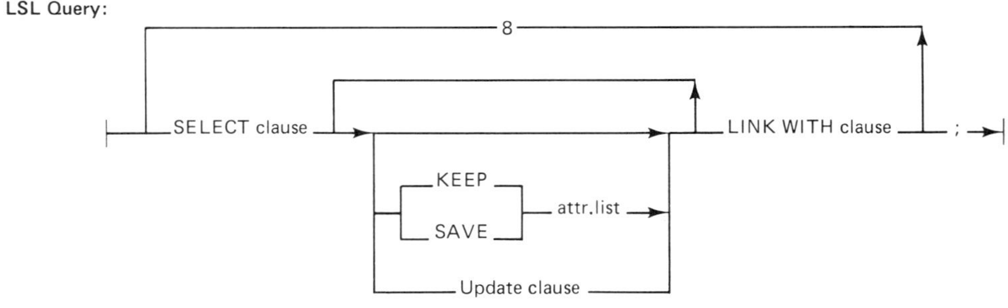

SELECT clause:

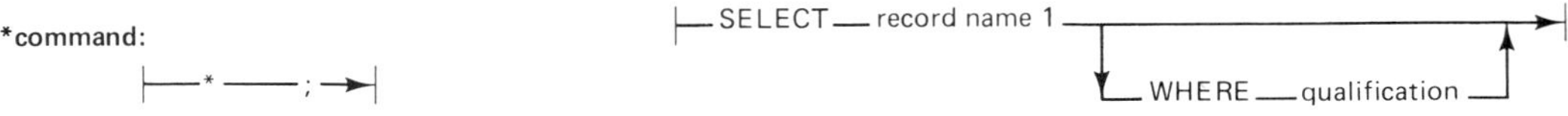

*command:

Update clause:

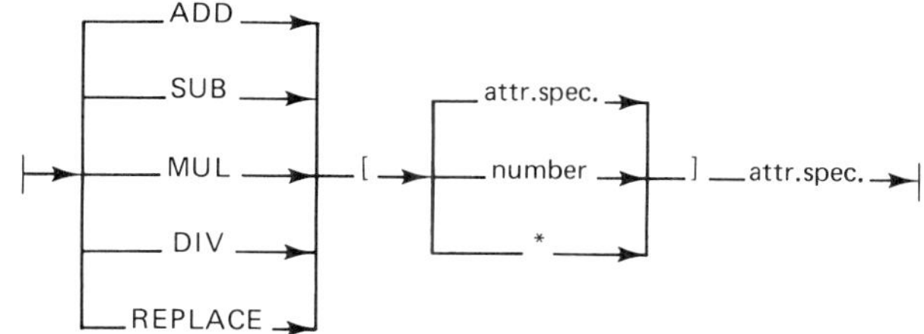

attr. list:

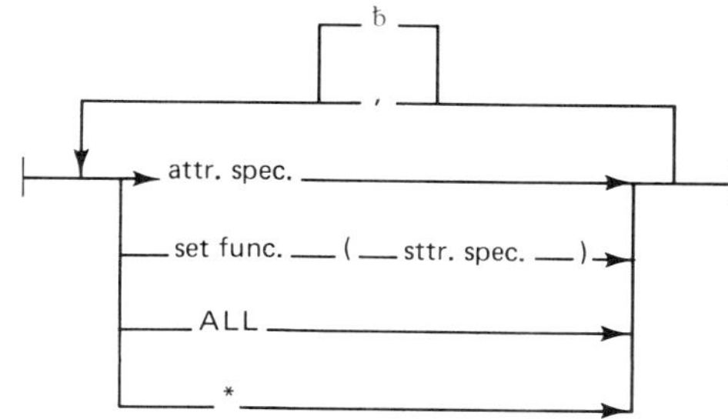

LINK WITH clause:

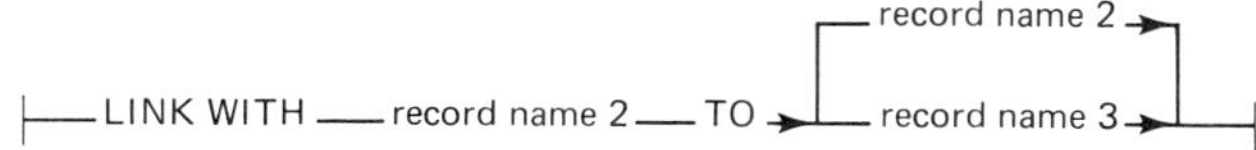

qualification:

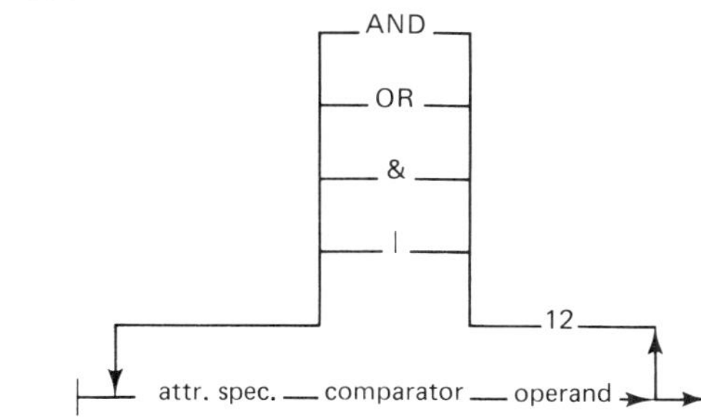

attr. spec:

operand:

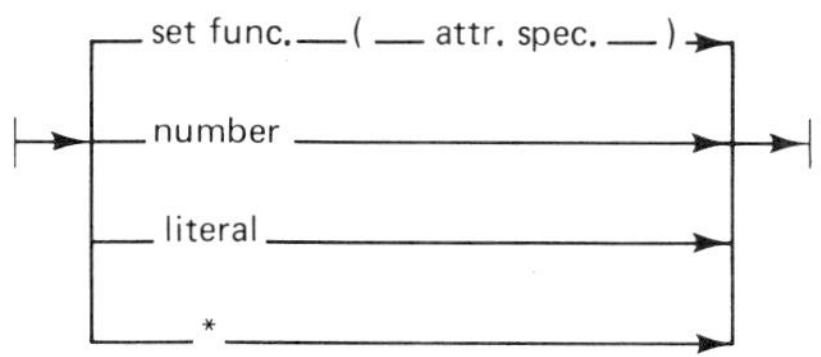

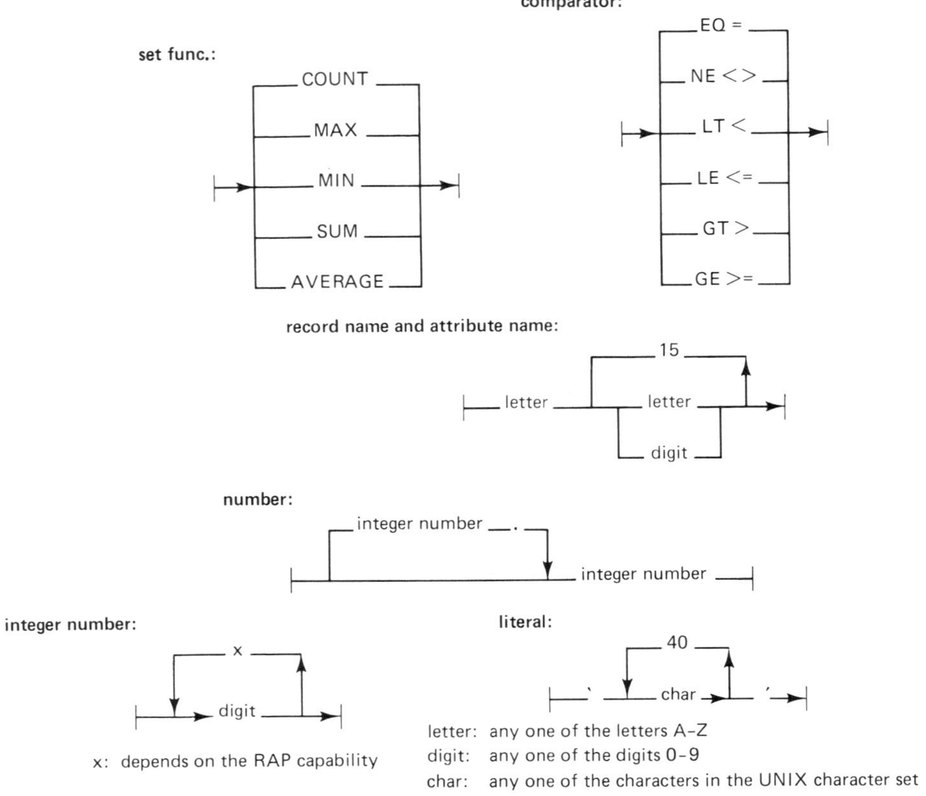

A2.2.3 LSL Language Semantics

(a) DATABASE DEFINITION: should be done at the conceptual data model interface.

(b) SAVE COMMAND: The LSL language is a nonprocedural one, that is, a set of values can be obtained with an "attr. spec." However, the SAVE command can save only a single-attribute value at a time, and it is the user's responsibility to ensure that a single value will be saved; otherwise, one of the values from a set of values will be randomly selected and saved.

(c) *: An attribute value saved with a SAVE command can be referred to with an "*" in the subsequent queries (see the railroad diagrams).

(d) * COMMAND: Keying an * followed by a ";" causes the last saved value to be retrieved.

(e) . QUALIFIER: An attribute name should be qualified with a "record name" whenever there is an ambiguity (i.e., whenever there is more than one record type having the same attribute name).

(f) STATISTICAL (SET) FUNCTIONS: As can be seen from the railroad diagrams, the functions COUNT, SUM, AVERAGE, MAX, and MIN can be used in qualifications only as operands, that is, in the form <attr. spec.> <comparator> <set func.>; hence, a qualification such as ...COUNT(EMP) GT 10 is invalid.

(g) PRECEDENCE OF OPERATORS: AND (&) and OR (|) operators have a higher precedence over the comparators = , EQ, <>, NE, >, GT, >=, GE, <, LT, <=, LE. Evaluation of simple conditions connected with ANDs and ORs takes place from left to right.

(h) LINK WITH CLAUSE: If there is no link record type between the source and target record types and the key of the source is repeated in the target record type, then the name of the target record type is used twice (record-name 2 in the related railroad diagram).

(i) USE OF TERMINATORS: A ";" terminates an LSL query. ; can be freely used in an LSL query (not within a word, however).

A2.2.4 LSL Examples

The following network database schema will be used in the examples:

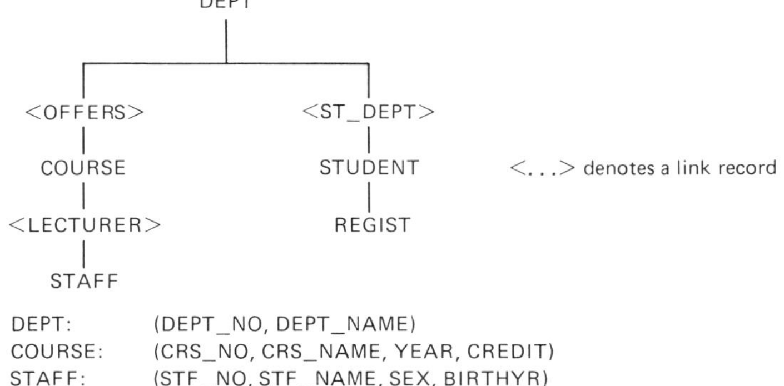

Example A2.1

Find the name of the youngest male student in the department of the instructor named "JOHN."

```
SELECT STAFF WHERE STF_NAME EQ "JOHN"
  LINK WITH LECTURER TO COURSE
  SELECT COURSE
    LINK WITH OFFERS TO DEPT
    SELECT DEPT KEEP DEPT_NAME
      LINK WITH ST_DEPT TO STUDENT
      SELECT STUDENT WHERE STUDENT.BIRTHYR
        EQ MAX(STUDENT.BIRTHYR)
        AND STUDENT.SEX EQ "M"
      KEEP ST_NAME;
```

KEEP produces output. Every record type linked with a LINK WITH should subsequently be selected regardless of the presence of a restriction (i.e., WHERE clause).

Example A2.2

Find the names of second-year students taking the third-year courses and also save and print the names of departments offering those courses.

```
SELECT COURSE WHERE COURSE.YEAR = 3
  LINK WITH OFFERS TO DEPT
  SELECT DEPT
  SAVE DEPT_NAME
  KEEP DEPT_NAME
    LINK WITH ST_DEPT TO STUDENT
    SELECT STUDENT WHERE STUDENT.YEAR EQ 2
    KEEP ST_NAME;
```

Example A2.3

Change the CRS_NO of the course CS200 to CS300.

```
SELECT COURSE WHERE COURSE.CRS_NO EQ "CS200"
SAVE COURSE.CRS_NO
REPLACE ["CS300"] COURSE.CRS_NO
  LINK WITH REGIST TO REGIST
  SELECT REGIST WHERE REGIST.CRS_NO = *
  REPLACE ["CS300"] REGIST.CRS_NO
  KEEP ALL;
```

Notes

1. SAVE is used just to demonstrate that a value saved in a query can be used later in the same query. This specific query can also be coded by deleting the SAVE command and by replacing all *'s with "CS200."

2. Note the usage of the last LINK WITH clause which uses the same record type name before and after the keyword TO. This is because there is no link record type between the COURSE and REGIST record types.

3. KEEP ALL is not required by the query; however, it is used for the documentary purpose of keeping the list of all REGIST records that are updated.

Example A2.4

Find the students taking the course "CS535" and increment their year by 1.

```
SELECT COURSE WHERE COURSE.CRS_NO EQ "CS535"
  LINK WITH REGIST TO REGIST
  SELECT REGIST
    LINK WITH STUDENT TO STUDENT
    SELECT STUDENT
    ADD [1] STUDENT.YEAR
    KEEP ST_NAME, STUDENT.YEAR;
```

A2.3 *ANSI/SPARC-LIKE GDBMS*

The following gives the list of GDBMS commands and a BNF definition of the Extended Entity/Relationship model–based conceptual schema DDL interface.

A2.3.1 *Command Summary of GDBMS*

```
|<shell command>
ASSERT triggername ON object_name : [IF condition THEN] predicate
CREATE filename
DB {APPEND/BACKUP/DELETE} relation_name [filename]
DESTORY schema_name
DISPLAY {SERAP/MRI/LSL}
DO filename
DROP viewname
DS {DELETE/INSERT/MODIFY} object_type object_name
GRANT privilege_mode ON object TO user
LIST {STRUCTURE/
      ENTITY [entity_name]/
      GENERIC [generic_name]/
      AGGREGATE [aggregate_name]/
      RELATIONSHIP [relationship_name]/
      DOCUMENT [document_name]/
      DOMAIN [domain_name]/
      AUT user [ON object_name]/
      VIEW [viewname]}
LSL [schema_name]
MRI [schema_name]
OUTPUT [OFF/filename]
REMOVE trigger_name
RENAME old_tree_name new_tree_name
REVOKE privilege_mode ON object FROM user
QUIT
SAVE schema_name [REPLACE]
SERAP
TRANSFORM {LSL/MRI}
USE schema_name
USER {Insert/Delete/Password}
VIEW view_name(atrname, ...) AS serap_code
```

Notes

1. []: optional parameters
2. {}: one of the parameters enclosed in braces and delimited by a slash.
3. Each command can be abbreviated by the first three characters including options, if any.

A2.3.2 BNF Syntax for the Data Definition Language of GDBMS

```
<domain_exp> ::= DOMAIN <domain_name> <type_exp>(<domain_size>)
                    <range_exp>
<domain_name> ::= <name>
<domain_size> ::= <integer>
                |<real>
<range_exp> ::= <lower_limit>:<upper_limit>
            |NULL
<lower_limit> ::= <integer>
                |<real>
<upper_limit> ::= <integer>
                |<real>
<type_exp> ::= LITERAL
            |INTEGER
            |REAL
<entity_exp> ::= ENTITY <entity_name>(tuple_no)(<atr_list>)
<entity_name> ::= <name>
<atr_list> ::= <atr_exp><rem_atr_list>
<atr_exp> ::= <key_exp><atr_name><domain>
<rem_atr_list> ::=,<atr_name>
                |NULL
<key_exp> ::= *
            |NULL
<atr_name> ::= <name>
<domain> ::= <domain_name>
          |NULL
<aggregate_exp> ::= AGGREGATE <agr_name>
                  |NULL
<agr_name> ::= <name>
<document_exp> ::= DOCUMENT <doc_name>(<tuple_no>)(<atr_list>)
<generic_exp> ::= GENERIC <generic_name>(<tuple_no>)
                  (<member_exp>;<atr_list>)
<member_exp> ::= <member_name><rem_member_exp>

<rem_member_exp> ::=,<member_exp>
                  |NULL
<generic_name> ::= <name>
<rel_exp> ::= RELATIONSHIP <weak_rel><rel_name>(<tuple_no>)
              (<assoc_exp>,<assoc_exp><rem_assoc_exp>
               <rel_atr_list>)
<weak_rel> ::= *
            |NULL
<role_exp> ::= / <rolename>
            |NULL
<mapping> ::= ONE
            |<many>
<many> ::= <character>
<functionality> ::= TOTAL
                  |PARTIAL
```

```
<rem_assoc_exp>  ::=,<assoc_exp>
                    |NULL
<rel_atr_list>  ::=;<atr_list>
                    |NULL
<name>  ::=  <character><rem_name>
<rem_name>  ::=  <character>
            |<digit>
            |_
<character>  ::=  a|b|c|d|e| f |g|h|i|j|k|l|m|n|o|p|q|r|s|t|u|v|w|x|y|z
<digit>  ::=  0|1|2|3|4|5|6|7|8|9|
```

REFERENCES

Aho, A. V., and Ullman, J. D. [1979]. "Universality of Data Retrieval Languages." *Proc. of ACM Symposium on Principles of Programming Languages,* pp. 110–120.

Aho, A. V., Beeri, C., and Ullman, J. D. [1979]. "The Theory of Joins in Relational Databases." *ACM Transactions on Database Systems,* Vol. 4, No. 3, pp. 297–314.

Akman, V. [1980]. "Design and Implementation of the Front-end and Controller Hardware/ Software Systems for the RAP Database Machine." M.Sc. Thesis, Department of Computer Engineering, Middle East Technical University, Ankara.

Amdahl, G. M. [1970]. "Storage and I/O Parameters and Systems Potential." *Proc. of IEEE Computer Group Conf.,* pp. 371–372.

ANSI/X3/SPARC [1975]. "Interim Report ANSI/X3/SPARC Study Group on Data Base Management Systems." *FDT,* Vol. 7, No. 2.

Apers, P. M. G., Hevner, A. R., and Yao, S. B. [1983]. "Optimization Algorithms for Distributed Queries." *IEEE Transactions on Software Engineering,* Vol. SE-9, No. 1, pp. 57–68.

Armstrong, W. W. [1974]. "Dependency Structures of Data Base Relationships." *Proc. of IFIP 1984 World Congress* (North Holland, Amsterdam), pp. 580–583.

Arora, S. K., Dumpala, S. R., and Smith, K. C. [1981]. "WCRC: An ANSI/SPARC Machine Architecture for Data Base Management." *Proc. of ACM SIGARCH Conf.,* pp. 373–387.

Astrahan, M. M., et al. [1976]. "System R: Relational Approach to Database Management." *ACM Transactions on Database Systems,* Vol. 1, No. 2, pp. 97–137.

Auer, H., et al. [1981]. "RDBM—A Relational Database Machine." *Information Systems,* Vol. 6, No. 2, pp. 91–100.

AURORA, S. K., and SMITH, K. C. [1979]. "A Language for Well-Connected Relations for Database Systems." *AICA*, Vol. 2, No. 10/13, pp. 371–380.

BABB, E. [1979]. "Implementing a Relational Database by Means of Specialized Hardware." *ACM Transactions on Database Systems*, Vol. 4, No. 1, pp. 1–29.

BABB, E. [1982]. "Joined Normal Form: A Storage Encoding for Relational Databases." *ACM Transactions on Database Systems*, Vol. 7, No. 4, pp. 588–614.

BAER, J. L. [1980]. *Computer Systems Architecture*. Rockville, Md: Computer Science Press.

BANCILHON, F., et al. [1983]. "VERSO: A Relational Backend Database Machine." In D. K. Hsiao, ed., *Advanced Database Machine Architecture*, pp. 1–18. Englewood Cliffs, N.J. Prentice-Hall, Inc.

BANERJEE, J., BAUM, R. I., and HSIAO, D. K. [1978]. "Concepts and Capabilities of a Database Computer." *ACM Transactions on Database Systems*, Vol. 3, No. 4, pp. 347–384.

BANERJEE, J., HSIAO, D. K., and KANNAN, K. [1979]. "DBC—A Database Computer for Very Large Database." *IEEE Transactions on Computers*, Vol. C28, No. 6, pp. 414–429.

BARNES, G. H., BROWN, R. M., KATO, M., KUCK, D. J., SLOTNICK, D. L., and STOKES, R. A. [1968]. "The ILLIAC IV Computer." *IEEE Transactions on Computers*, Vol. C-17, No. 8, pp. 746–757.

BATCHER, K. C. [1968]. "Sorting Networks and Their Applications." *Proc. of AFIPS Conf.*, Vol. 32, pp. 307–314.

BATCHER, K. E. [1974]. "STARAN Parallel Processor System Hardware." *Proc. of AFIPS Conf.*, Vol. 43, pp. 405–410.

BATCHER, K. E. [1977]. "STARAN Series E." *Proc. of Intl. Conf. on Parallel Processing*, pp. 140–143.

BATCHER, K. E. [1980]. "Architecture of a Massively Parallel Processor." *Proc. of Seventh Annual Symposium on Computer Architecture*, Vol. 8, No. 3, pp. 168–173.

BERG, R. O., et al. [1972]. "PEPE–An Overview of Architecture, Operation and Implementation." *Proc. of National Electronic Conf.* (IEEE, New York), pp. 312–317.

BERNSTEIN, P. A., and CHIU, D. W. [1981]. "Using Semi-joins to Solve Relational Queries." *JACM*, Vol. 28, No. 1, pp. 25–40.

BERNSTEIN, P. A., and GOODMAN, N. [1981]. "Fundamental Algorithms for Concurrency Control in Distributed Database Systems." *ACM Computing Surveys*, Vol. 13, No. 2, pp. 185–221.

BERRA, B. P., and OLIVER, E. [1979]. "The Role of Associative Array Processors in Data Base Machine Architecture." *IEEE Computer*, Vol. 12, No. 3, pp. 53–61.

BIRD, R. M., TU, J. C., and WORTHY, R. M. [1977]. "Associative/Parallel Processors for Searching Very Large Textual Data Bases." *Proc. of Intl. Workshop on Computer Architectures for Nonnumeric Processing*, pp. 8–16.

BISKUP, J., DAYAL, U., and BERNSTEIN, P. A. [1979]. "Synthesizing Independent Database Schemas." *Proc. of ACM SIGMOD*, pp. 143–152.

BITTON, D., BORAL, H., DEWITT, D., and WILKINSON, W. K. [1983]. "Parallel Algorithms for the Execution of Relational Database Operations." *ACM Transactions on Database Systems,* Vol. 8, No. 3, pp. 324–353.

BLASGEN, M. W., and ESWARAN, K. P. [1976]. "On the Evaluation of Queries in Relational Database Systems." IBM Research Report RJ1745, IBM Research, San Jose, Calif.

BLASGEN, M. W., and ESWARAN, K. P. [1977]. "Storage and Access in Relational Data Bases." *IBM Systems J.,* Vol. 16, No. 4, pp. 363–377.

BORAL, H., DEWITT, D. J., FRIEDLAND, D., JARREL, N. F., and WILKINSON, W. K. [1982]. "Implementation of the Database Machine DIRECT." *IEEE Transactions on Software Engineering,* Vol. SE-8, No. 6, pp. 533–543.

BOYCE, R. F., CHAMBERLIN, D. D., KING, W. F., and HAMMER, M. M. [1975]. "Specifying Queries as Relational Expressions: The SQUARE Data Sublanguage." *CACM,* Vol. 18, No. 11, pp. 621–628.

BOYER, R. S., and MOORE, J. S. [1977]. "A Fast String Searching Algorithm." *CACM,* Vol. 20, No. 10, pp. 762–772.

BROWNING, S. [1978]. "Hierarchically Organized Machines." In C. A. Mead and L. A. Conway, eds., *Introduction to VLSI Systems.* Reading, Mass.: Addison-Wesley.

CALINGAERT, P. [1982]. *Operating System Elements.* Englewood Cliffs, N.J.: Prentice-Hall, Inc.

CAN, F. [1985]. "A New Clustering Scheme and Its Use in an Information Retrieval System Incorporating the Support of a Database Machine," Ph.D. Thesis, Dept. of Computer Engineering, Middle East Technical University, Ankara.

CAN, F., and OZKARAHAN, E. A. [1983]. "A Clustering Scheme." *Proc. of ACM SIGIR Conf.,* pp. 115–121.

CAN, F., and OZKARAHAN, E. A. [1985]. "Similarity and Stability Analysis of the Two Partitioning Type Clustering Algorithms." *Journal of the American Society for Information Science,* Vol. 36, No. 1, pp. 3–14.

CAN, F., and OZKARAHAN, E. A. [1984]. "Two Partitioning Type Clustering Algorithms." *Journal of the American Society for Information Science,* Vol. 35, No. 5, pp. 268–276.

CANADAY, R. H., HARRISON, R. D., IVIE, L. L., RYDER, J. L., and WEHR, L. A. [1974]. "A Backend Computer for Database Management." *CACM,* Vol. 17, No. 10, pp. 575–582.

CARDENAS, A., and PIRAHESH, M. H. [1980]. "Database Communication in a Heterogeneous Data Base Management System Network." *Information Systems,* Vol. 5, pp. 55–79.

CARDENAS, A. F., ALAVIAN, F., and AVIZIENIS, A. [1983]. "Performance of Recovery Architectures in Parallel Associative Database Processors." *ACM Transactions on Database Systems,* Vol. 8, No. 3, pp. 291–323.

CHAMBERLIN, D. D., and BOYCE, R. F. [1974]. "SEQUEL: A Structured English Query Language." *Proc. of ACM SIGMOD,* pp. 249–264.

CHANG, H. [1978]. "On Bubble Memories and Relational Database." *Proc. of Intl. Conf. on Very Large Database,* pp. 207–229.

CHANG, J., and FU, K. [1981]. "Extended k-d Tree Database Organization: A Dynamic Multiattribute Clustering Method." *IEEE Transactions on Software Engineering,* Vol. SE-7, No. 3, pp. 284–290.

CHEN, P. P. [1976]. "The Entity-Relationship Model: A Basis for the Enterprise View of Data." *ACM Transaction on Database Systems,* Vol. 1, No. 1, pp. 9–36.

CHIU, D. M., and HO, Y. C. [1980]. "A Methodology for Interpreting Tree Queries into Optimal Semi-join Expressions." *Proc. of ACM SIGMOD Conf.,* pp. 169–178.

CHRISTODOULAKIS, S., and FALOUTSOS, C. [1984]. "Design Considerations for a Message File Server." *IEEE Transactions on Software Engineering,* Vol. SE-10, No. 2, pp. 201–210.

CHU, W. W., and HURLEY, P. [1982]. "Optimal Query Processing for Distributed Database Systems." *IEEE Transactions on Computers,* Vol. C-31, No. 9, pp. 835–850.

CODASYL [1971]. *CODASYL Data Base Task Group Report.* Conf. on Data System Languages, ACM, New York.

CODD, E. F. [1970]. "A Relational Model of Data for Large Shared Data Banks." *CACM,* Vol. 13, No. 6, pp. 377–387.

CODD, E. F. [1972]. "Relational Completeness of Data Base Sublanguages." in R. Rustin, ed., *Data Base Systems,* pp. 33–64. Englewood Cliffs, N.J.: Prentice-Hall, Inc.

CODD, E. F. [1979]. "Extending the Relational Model to Capture More Meaning." *ACM Transactions on Database Systems,* Vol. 4, No. 4, pp. 397–434.

COLTS II [1976]: *CRW On-line Text Search User's Manual.* Alexandria, Va.: Rosen and Wallace, Inc.

COPELAND, G. P. [1974]. "A Cellular System for Non-numeric Processing." Ph.D. Dissertation, Dept. of Electrical Engineering, University of Florida, Gainesville, Fla.

COPELAND, G. P. [1978]. "String Storage and Searching for Data Base Applications: Implementation on the INDY Backend Kernel." *Proc. of Intl. Workshop on Nonnumeric Processing,* pp. 8–17.

COPELAND, G. P., LIPOVSKI, J., and SU, S. Y. W. [1973]. "The Architecture of CASSM: A Cellular System for Non-numeric Processing." *Proc. of First Annual Symposium on Computer Architecture,* pp. 121–128.

COULOURIS, G. F., EVANS, J. M., and MITCHELL, R. W. [1972]. "Towards Context-Addressing in Data Bases." *The Computer Journal,* Vol. 15, No. 2, pp. 95–98.

CRAY RESEARCH, INC. [1977]. "CRAY-1 Computer System." Hardware Reference Manual, Minneapolis, Minn.

DATE, C. J. [1981]. *An Introduction to Database Systems,* 3rd ed. Reading, Mass.: Addison-Wesley.

DATE, C. J. [1983]. *An Introduction to Database Systems,* Vol. 2. Reading, Mass.: Addison-Wesley.

DAVIS, E. W. [1974]. "STARAN Parallel Processor System Software." *Proc. of AFIPS Conf.,* Vol. 43, pp. 17–22.

DAYAL, U., and BERNSTEIN, P. [1978]. "On the Updatability of Relational Views." *Proc. of Intl. Conf. on Very Large Databases,* pp. 368–377.

DEFIORE, C., and BERRA, P. B. [1974]. "A Quantitative Analysis of the Utilization of Associative Memories in Data Base Management." *IEEE Transactions on Computers,* Vol. C-23, No. 2, pp. 121–123.

DEWITT, D. J. [1979]. "DIRECT—A Multiprocessor Organization for Supporting Relational

Database Management Systems." *IEEE Transactions on Computers*, Vol. C-28, No. 6, pp. 395–406.

DEWITT, D. J., and HAWTHORN, P. B. [1981]. "A Performance Evaluation of Database Machine Architectures." *Proc. of Intl. Conf. on Very Large Data Bases*, pp. 199–213.

DIGBY, D. W. [1973]. "A Search Memory for Many-to-Many Comparisons." *IEEE Transactions on Computers*, Vol. C-22, No. 8, pp. 768–772.

DOGAC, A. [1980]. "Design and Implementation of a Generalized Database Management System—METUGDBMS," Ph.D. Thesis, Dept. of Computer Engineering, Middle East Technical University, Ankara.

DOGAC, A., and OZKARAHAN, E. A. [1980]. "A Generalized DBMS Implementation on a Database Machine." *Proc. of ACM SIGMOD*, pp. 133–143.

DUGAN, J. A., GREEN, R. J., and MINKER, J. [1966]. "A Study of the Utility of Associative Memory Processors." *Proc. of ACM National Conf.*, pp. 347–359.

EHRENSBERGER, M. J. [1984]. "The DBC/1012 Data Base Computer's System-Architecture, Components, and Performance." Paper presented at the *Minnowbrook Workshop on Database Machines*.

ELLIS, C. A. [1977]. "A Robust Algorithm for Updating Duplicate Databases." *Proc. of 2nd Berkeley Conf. on Distributed Data Management and Computer Networks*, pp. 146–158.

ENSLOW, P. H., JR. [1977]. "Multiprocessor Organization—A Survey." *ACM Computing Surveys*, Vol. 9, No. 1, pp. 103–129.

EPSTEIN, R., STONEBRAKER, W., and WONG, E. [1978]. "Distributed Query Processing in a Relational System." *Proc. of ACM SIGMOD Conf.*, pp. 163–180.

ESTRIN, G., and FULLER, R. [1963]. "Algorithms for Content-Addressable Memories." *Proc. of IEEE Pacific Computer Conf.*, pp. 118–130.

ESWARAN, K. P., GRAY, J. N., LORIE, R. A., and TRAIGER, I. L. [1976]. "The Notions of Consistency and Predicate Locks in a Database System." *CACM*, Vol. 19, No. 11, pp. 624–633.

FALKOFF, A. D. [1962]. "Algorithms for Parallel Search Memory." *JACM*, Vol. 9, No. 10, pp. 488–511.

FARNESWORTH, D. L., HOFFMAN, C. P., and SHUTT, J. J. [1976]. "Mass Memory Organization Study." Rome Air Development Center, Technical Report TR-76-254.

FERNANDEZ, E. B., SUMMERS, R. C., and WOOD, C. [1981]. *Database Security and Integrity*. Reading, Mass.: Addison-Wesley.

FERNSTROM, C. [1983]. "The LUCAS Associative Array Computer and Its Programming Environment." Ph.D. Dissertation, Department of Computer Engineering, University of Lund, Lund.

FLYNN, M. J. [1972]. "Some Computer Organizations and Their Effectiveness." *IEEE Transactions on Computers*, Vol. C-21, No. 9, pp. 948–960.

FOSTER, C. C. [1976]. *Content Addressable Parallel Processors*. New York: Van Nostrand Reinhold.

FOSTER, M. J., and KUNG, H. T. [1980]. "The Design of Special Purpose VLSI Chips." *IEEE Computer*, Vol. 13, No. 1, pp. 26–40.

FUND, S. [1983]. "Applications of the Amperif Data Base Machine," *Proc. of Compcon Conf.*, pp. 369–370.

GARCIA-MOLINA, H. [1979]. "Centralized Control Update Algorithms for Fully Redundant Distributed Databases." *Proc. of First Intl. Conf. on Distributed Computing Systems*, pp. 699–705.

GARDARIN, G., et al. [1983]. "SABRE: A Relational Database System for a Multimicroprocessor Machine." In D. K. Hsiao, ed., *Advanced Database Machine Architectures*, pp. 19–35. Englewood Cliffs, N.J.: Prentice-Hall, Inc.

GONZALEZ-RUBIO, R., ROHMER, J., and TERRAL, D. [1984]. "The Schuss Filter: A Processor for Nonnumerical Data Processing." *Proc. of ACM SIGARCH Conf.*, pp. 64–73.

GOSCH, J. [1982]. "Big Market Seen for Associative Memory Unit." *Electronics International*, May, pp. 92–94.

GRAY, J. [1978]. "Notes on Operating Systems." Report RJ 3120, IBM Research Center, San Jose, Calif.

GUIDE-SHARE [1970]. *Report on Data Base Management System Requirements*. Joint Guide Share Data Base Requirements Group, New York.

HASKIN, R. L. [1980a]. "Hardware for Searching Very Large Text Databases," Ph.D. Dissertation, University of Illinois, Urbana, Ill.

HASKIN, R. L. [1980b]. "Hardware for Searching Very Large Text Databases." *Proc. of Intl. Workshop on Computer Architectures for Nonnumeric Processing*, pp. 49–56.

HASKIN, R. L., and HOLLAAR, L. A. [1983]. "Operational Characteristics of a Hardware Based Pattern Matcher." *ACM Transactions on Database Systems*, Vol. 8, No. 1, pp. 15–40.

HAWTHORN, P. B., and DEWITT, D. J. [1981]. "Performance Analysis of Alternative Database Machine Architectures." *IEEE Transactions on Software Engineering*, Vol. SE-8, No. 1, pp. 61–75.

HEALY, L. D., LIPOVSKI, G. J., and DOTY, K. L. [1972]. "The Architecture of a Content Addressed Segment Sequential Storage." *Proc. of AFIPS Conf.*, Vol. 41, pp. 691–701.

HEVNER, A. R., and YAO, S. B. [1979]. "Query Processing in Distributed Database Systems." *IEEE Transactions on Software Engineering*, Vol. SE-5, No. 3, pp. 177–187.

HOLLAAR, L. A. [1979]. "Text Retrieval Computers." *IEEE Computer*, Vol. 12, No. 3, pp. 40–50.

HOLLAAR, L. A. [1983a]. "Architecture and Operation of a Large, Full-Text Information Retrieval System." In D. K. Hsiao, ed., *Advanced Database Machine Architectures*, pp. 256–299. Englewood Cliffs, N.J.: Prentice-Hall, Inc.

HOLLAAR, L. A. [1983b]. "Hardware Systems for Text Information Retrieval." *Proc. of SIGIR Conf.*, pp. 3–9.

HOLLAAR, L. A. [1984]. "The UTAH Text Retrieval Project, Status Report." *Proc. of BCS and ACM Joint Symposium on Research and Development in Information Retrieval*, pp. 123–132.

HOLLAAR, L. A., and ROBERTS, D. C. [1978]. "Current Research into Specialized Processors for Text Information Retrieval." *Proc. of Intl. Conf. on Very Large Data Bases*, pp. 270–279.

HOLLAAR, L. A. [1978]. "Specialized Merge Processor Networks for Combining Sorted Lists." *ACM Transactions on Database Systems,* Vol. 3, No. 3, pp. 272–284.

HOLLANDER, G. L. [1956]. "Quasi-Random Access Memory Systems." *Proc. of AFIPS Conf. (FJCC),* pp. 128–135.

HONG, Y. C., and SU, S. Y. W. [1981]. "Associative Hardware and Software Techniques for Integrity Control." *ACM Transactions on Database Systems,* Vol. 6, No. 3, pp. 416–439.

HORSPOOL, R. N. [1980]. "Practical Fast Searching in Strings." *Soft. Pract. and Exp.* Vol. 10, No. 6, pp. 501–506.

HSIAO, D. K., and OZSU, T. [1981]. "A Survey of Concurrency Control Mechanisms for Centralized and Distributed Databases." Technical Report, OSU-CISRC-TR-81-1, Dept. of Computer Science, Ohio State University, Columbus, Oh.

HU, T. C. [1961]. "Parallel Sequencing and Assembly Line Problems." *Operations Research,* Vol. 9, No. 6, pp. 841–848.

IBM CORPORATION [1978]. *Information Management System/Virtual Storage* publications: *General Information* (GH20-1260), *System/Application Design Guide* (SH20-9025), *Application Programming Reference Manual* (SH20-9026), *System Programming Reference Manual* (SH20-9027). IBM, White Plains, N.Y.

KAPP, D., and LEBEN, J. F. [1978]. *IMS Programming Techniques: A Guide to Using DL/1.* New York: Van Nostrand Reinhold.

KAUTZ, W. H. [1971]. "An Augmented Content-Addressed Memory Array for Implementation with Large-Scale Integration." *JACM,* January, pp. 19–33.

KEITH, M. [1983]. "The Intel Database Processor." *Proc. of Compcon Conf.,* pp. 371–373.

KERSCHBERG, L., OZKARAHAN, E. A., and PACHECO, J. E. S. [1976]. "A Synthetic English Query Language for a Relational Associative Processor." *Proc. of Intl. Conf. on Software Engineering,* pp. 505–519.

KIESSLING, W. [1983]. "Database Systems for Computers with Intelligent Subsystems Architecture, Algorithms, Optimization." Ph.D. Thesis, Institute for Informatik, Technical University of Munich, Munich.

KIESSLING, W. [1984]. "Tuneable Dynamic Filter Algorithms for High Performance Database Systems," *Proc. of Intl. Workshop on High Level Language Computer Architecture,* pp. 10–20.

KIM, W., GAJSKI, D., and KUCK, D. [1984]. "A Parallel Pipelined Relational Query Processor." *ACM Transactions on Database Systems,* Vol. 9, No. 2, pp. 214–263.

KITSUREGAWA, M., TANAKA, H., and MOTO-OKA, T. [1983]. "Application of Hash to Database Machine and Its Architecture." *New Generation Computing,* Vol. 1, No. 1, pp. 63–74.

KITSUREGAWA, M., TANAKA, H., and MOTO-OKA, T. [1984]. "Architecture and Performance of Relational Database Machine GRACE." *Proc. of Intl. Conf. on Parallel Processing.*

KLUG, A. [1978]. "Theory of Database Mappings." Ph.D. Thesis, Department of Computer Science, University of Toronto, Toronto, Ont.

KNUTH, D. E., MORRIS, J. H., and PRATT, V. R. [1977]. "Fast Pattern Matching in Strings." *SIAM J. of Computing,* Vol. 6, No. 2, pp. 323–350.

KOCAGONCU, K. [1981]. "Design and Implementation of an Operating System for the RAP.3 Database Machine." M.Sc. Thesis, Department of Computer Engineering, Ankara.

KONISHI, S. [1983]. "A New Ultra-High Density Solid State Memory: Bloch Line Memory." *IEEE Transactions on Magnetics,* Vol. MAG-19, No. 5, pp. 1838–1840.

KOWALSKI, R. A. [1979]. *Logic for Problem Solving.* New York: North Holland-Elsevier.

KRUZELA, I. [1983]. "An Associative Array Processor Supporting a Relational Algebra." Ph.D. Dissertation, Department of Computer Engineering, University of Lund, Lund.

KUCK, D. J. [1968]. "ILLIAC IV Software and Application Programming." *IEEE Transactions on Computers,* Vol. C-17, No. 8, pp. 758–770.

KUCK, D. J. [1977]. "A Survey of Parallel Machine Organization and Programming." *ACM Computing Surveys,* Vol. 9, No. 1, pp. 29–59.

KUNG, H. T., and LEHMAN, P. L. [1980]. "Systolic (VLSI) Arrays for Relational Database Operations." *Proc. of ACM SIGMOD Conf.,* pp. 105–116.

KUNIFUJI, S., and YOKOTA, H. [1982]. "PROLOG and Relational Databases for Fifth Generation Computer Systems," *Proc. of ONERA-CERT DER Informatique Conf. on Logical Bases for Databases,* Section 21.

LANGE, R. G. [1976]. "High Level Language for Associative and Parallel Computation with STARAN." *Proc. of Intl. Conf. on Parallel Processing,* pp. 170–176.

LANGEFORS, B. [1980]. "Infological Models and Information User Views." *Information Systems,* Vol. 5, pp. 17–32.

LE-VIET, C. [1983]. "The NOAH Database Machine." *Proc. of Compcon Conf.,* pp. 364–368.

LEE, C. Y., and PAUL, M. C. [1963]. "A Content Addressable Distributed Logic Memory with Applications to Information Retrieval." *Proc. of IEEE,* Vol. 51, June, pp. 924–932.

LEECH, G. [1974]. *Semantics.* Middlesex, England: Penguin Books Ltd.

LEILICH, H. O., STIEGE, G., and ZEIDLER, H. C. [1978]. "A Search Processor for Data Base Management Systems." *Proc. of Intl. Conf. on Very Large Databases,* pp. 280–287.

LIN, C. S. [1977]. "Sorting with Associative Secondary Storage Devices." *Proc. of AFIPS Conf.,* Vol. 46, pp. 691–695.

LIN, C. S., Smith, D. C. P., and SMITH, J. M. [1976]. "The Design of a Rotating Associative Memory for Relational Database Management Applications." *ACM Transactions on Database Systems,* Vol. 1, No. 1, pp. 53–65.

LOVE, H. H. [1973]. "An Efficient Associative Processor Using Bulk Storage." *Proc. of Sagamore Computer Conf. on Parallel Processing,* pp. 103–112.

LOWENTHAL, E. I. [1971]. "A Functional Approach to the Design of Storage Structure for Generalized Data Management Systems." Ph.D. Thesis, University of Texas at Austin.

MAEKAWA, M. [1981]. "Optimal Processor Interconnection Topologies." *Proc. of ACM SIGARCH Conf.,* pp. 171–185.

MAIER, D. [1983]. *The Theory of Relational Databases.* Rockville, Md.: Computer Science Press.

MANUEL, T. [1981]. "Look-up Chips Check Entire Data Base Fast." *Electronics,* Vol. 54, No. 22, pp. 42–46.

MARILL, T., and STERN, D. [1975]. "The Datacomputer—A Network Data Utility." *Proc. of AFIPS Conf.*, Vol. 44, pp. 389–395.

McGREGOR, D. R., THOMPSON, R. G., and DAWSON, W. N. [1976]. "High Performance Hardware for Database Systems." *Proc. of Intl. Conf. on Very Large Databases*, pp. 103–116.

MENON, M. J., and HSIAO, D. K. [1981]. "Design and Analysis of a Relational Join Operation for VLSI." *Proc. of Intl. Conf. on Very Large Data Bases,* pp. 44–55.

MINSKY, N. [1972]. "Rotating Storage Devices as Partially Associative Memories." *Proc. of AFIPS Conf. (FJCC),* Vol. 41, part 1, pp. 587–596.

MISSIKOFF, M., and TERRANOVA, M. [1983]. "The Architecture of a Relational Database Computer Known as DBMAC." In D. K. Hsiao, ed., *Advanced Database Machine Architectures,* pp. 87–108. Englewood Cliffs, N.J.: Prentice-Hall, Inc.

MOTO-OKA, T., and FUCHI, K. [1983]. "The Architectures in the Fifth Generation Computers." *Proc. of IFIP83 World Congress,* pp. 589–602.

MOULDER, R. [1973]. "An Implementation of a Data Management System of an Associative Processor." *Proc. of AFIPS Conf.,* Vol. 42, pp. 171–176.

MRI [1974]. "System 2000" publications: *Reference Manual; Immediate Access Feature; Procedure Language Feature (with COBOL, FORTRAN, PL/1); Report Writer Feature; Diagnostic Messages,* MRI Systems Corp., Austin, Tex.

MUKHOPADHYAY, A. [1979]. "Hardware Algorithms for Nonnumeric Computation." *IEEE Transactions on Computers,* Vol. C-28, No. 6, pp. 384–394.

MULES, D. W., and WARTER, P. J. [1979]. "A String Matcher for an Electronic File Cabinet which Allows Errors and Other Approximate Matches." Technical Report, Department of Electrical Engineering, University of Delaware, Newark, NJ.

MURASZKIEWICZ, M. [1981]. "Concepts of Sorting and Projection in a Cellular Array." *Proc. of IEEE CH1701-2,* pp. 76–79.

MYERS, G. [1983]. *Advances in Computer Architecture,* 2nd ed. New York: John Wiley & Sons.

OBERMACK, R. [1980]. "Global Deadlock Detection Algorithm." IBM Research Report RJ2845 (June).

OFLAZER, K. [1979]. "A Microprocessor Based Approach to RAP Database Machine Cell Structure: Design and Analysis." M.Sc. Thesis, Department of Computer Engineering, Middle East Technical University, Ankara.

OFLAZER, K. [1983]. "A Reconfigurable VLSI Architecture for a Database Processor." *Proc. of AFIPS Conf.,* Vol. 52, pp. 273–281.

OFLAZER, K., OZKARAHAN, E. A., and SMITH, K. C. [1980]. "RAP.3—A Multimicroprocessor Cell Architecture for the RAP Database Machine." *Proc. of Intl. Workshop on High Level Language Computer Architecture,* pp. 108–119.

OLIVER, E., and BERRA, P. B. [1980]. "RELACS—A Relational Associative Computer System." *Proc. of Intl. Workshop on Computer Architectures for Nonnumeric Processing,* pp. 106–114.

OUKSEL, M. [1983]. "Order-Preserving Dynamic Hashing Schemes for Associative Searching in Database Systems." Ph.D. Dissertation, Dept. of Electrical Engineering and Computer Science, Northwestern University, Illinois.

OUKSEL, M., and SCHEUERMANN, P. [1983]. "Storage Mappings for Multidimensional Linear Dynamic Hashing." *Proc. of ACM SIGMOD-SIGACT Symposium,* pp. 90–105.

OZKARAHAN, E. A. [1976]. "An Associative Processor for Relational Data Bases—RAP." Ph.D. Thesis, Dept. of Computer Science, University of Toronto, Toronto, Ont.

OZKARAHAN, E. A. [1983]. "Desirable Functionalities of Database Architectures." *Proc. of IFIP83 World Congress,* pp. 357–362.

OZKARAHAN, E. A. [1985]. "Evolution and Implementations of the RAP Database Machine." *New Generation Computing,* Vol. 3, No. 3. OHMSHA, LTD. and Springer-Verlag.

OZKARAHAN, E. A., and CAN, F. [1984]. "An Integrated Fact/Document Information System for Office Automation." *Information Technology: Research and Development,* Vol. 3, No. 3. London: Butterworth Scientific Publishers, Inc., pp. 142–156.

OZKARAHAN, E. A., and KAYAKUTLU, G. [1979]. "Performance Analysis of the RAP Database Machine Systems." Department of Computer Engineering, Technical Report IS-DB.9, Middle East Technical University, Ankara.

OZKARAHAN, E. A., and KERSCHBERG, L. [1982]. "A Heterogeneous Distributed Database System Architecture Incorporating Data Semantics and a Relational Database Machine Interface." Technical Report TR-82-006, Dept. of Computer Science, Arizona State University, Tempe.

OZKARAHAN, E. A., and OFLAZER, K. [1978]. "Microprocessor Based Modular Database Processors." *Proc. of Intl. Conf. on Very Large Databases,* pp. 300–311.

OZKARAHAN, E. A., and OUKSEL, M. [1985]. "Dynamic and Order Preserving Data Partitioning for Database Machines," *Proc. of Intl. Conf. on Very Large Databases.*

OZKARAHAN, E. A., and SEVCIK, K. C. [1977]. "Analysis of Architectural Features for Enhancing the Performance of a Database Machine." *ACM Transactions on Database Systems,* Vol. 2, No. 2, pp. 297–316.

OZKARAHAN, E. A., SCHUSTER, S. A., and SMITH, K. C. [1975]. "RAP—An Associative Processor for Data Base Management." *Proc. of AFIPS Conf.,* Vol. 44, pp. 379–387.

OZKARAHAN, E. A., SCHUSTER, S. A., and SEVCIK, K. C. [1977]. "Performance Evaluation of a Relational Associative Processor." *ACM Transactions on Database Systems,* Vol. 2, No. 2, pp. 175–195.

OZKARAHAN, E. A., TANSEL, A. U., and SMITH, K. C. [1982]. "Database Machine/Computer Based Distributed Databases." *Proc. of Intl. Symposium on Distributed Databases,* pp. 61–80: North Holland Publishing Co., Amsterdam.

OZSOYOGLU, M., and YU, C. T. [1980]. "On Identifying a Class of Data Base Queries that Can Be Processed Efficiently." *Proc. of Compsac Conf.,* pp. 453–461.

OZSU, T. M., and OZKARAHAN, E. A. [1980]. "SYNGLISH—A High Level Query Language for the RAP Database Machine." *Proc. of Intl. Workshop on Computer Architectures for Nonnumeric Processing,* pp. 139–150.

PARHAMI, B. [1972]. "A Highly Parallel Computing System for Information Retrieval." *Proc. of AFIPS Conf.,* Vol. 41, pp. 681–690.

PARKER, J. L. [1971]. "A Logic per Track Retrieval System." *Proc. of IFIP Conf.,* Vol. 1, pp. 711–716.

PIROTTE, A. [1978]. "High Level Database Query Languages." In H. Callaire and J. Minker, eds., *Logic and Data Bases,* pp. 409–436. New York: Plenum Press.

POLZER, H. W. [1983]. "Document Retrieval Techniques." Paper presented by Alex L. Nagy at the *Minnowbrook Workshop on Database Machines.*

RAGHAVAN, V. V., and IP, M. V. L. [1982]. "Techniques for Measuring the Stability of Clustering: A Comparative Study." Paper presented at *ACM SIGIR Conf.*

RAMAMOORTHY, C. V., and LI, H. F. [1977]. "Pipeline Architecture." *ACM Computing Surveys,* Vol. 9, No. 1, pp. 61–102.

RAND, W. M. [1971]. "Objective Criteria for the Evaluation of Clustering Methods." *Journal of the American Statistical Association,* Vol. 66, pp. 846–850.

ROSENKRATZ, D. J., STEARNS, R. E., LEWIS, P. M., II. [1978]. "System Level Concurrency Control for Distributed Database Systems." *ACM Transactions on Database Systems,* Vol. 3, No. 2, pp. 178–198.

ROTHSTEIN, J. [1976]. "On the Ultimate Limitations of Parallel Processing." *Proc. of Int. Conf. on Parallel Processing,* pp. 206–212.

RUDOLPH, J. A. [1972]. "A Production Implementation of an Associative Array Processor: STARAN." *Proc. of AFIPS Conf.,* Vol. 41, pp. 229–241.

RUSSEL, R. M. [1978]. "The CRAY-1 Computer System." *CACM,* Vol. 21, No. 1, pp. 63–72.

SADOWSKI, P. J. [1978]. "Exploiting Parallelism in a Relational Associative Processor." M.Sc. Thesis, Department of Computer Science, University of Toronto, Toronto, Ont.

SALTON, G., and MCGILL, M. J. [1983]. *Introduction to Modern Information Retrieval.* New York: McGraw-Hill.

SCHULTZ, C. K. [1968]. *H. P. Luhn: The Pioneer of Information Science—Selected Works.* London: Macmillan.

SCHUSTER, S. A., OZKARAHAN, E. A., and SMITH, K. C. [1976]. "A Virtual Memory System for a Relational Associative Processor." *Proc. of AFIPS Conf.,* pp. 855–862.

SCHUSTER, S. A., NGUYEN, H. B., OZKARAHAN, E. A., and SMITH, K. C. [1979]. "RAP.2—An Associative Processor for Databases and Its Applications." *IEEE Transactions on Computers,* Vol. C-28, No. 6, pp. 446–458.

SEEBER, R. R., and LINDQUIST, A. B. [1962]. "Associative Memory with Ordered Retrieval." *IBM Journal,* pp. 126–136.

SEKINO, A., TAKEUCHI, K., GOTO, T., and HARA, K. [1983]. "Design and Implementation of an Information Query Computer." *Proc. of Compcon Conf.,* pp. 374–377.

SHAW, D. E. [1979]. "A Hierarchical Associative Architecture for the Parallel Evaluation of Relational Algebraic Database Primitives." Dept. of Computer Science, Technical Report STAN-CS-79-778, Stanford University, Stanford, Calif.

SHOOMAN, W. [1960]. "Parallel Computing with Vertical Data." *Proc. of Eastern Jt. Computer Conf.,* pp. 111–115.

SIBLEY, E. H., and KERSCHBERG, L. [1977]. "Data Model and Data Architecture Considerations." *Proc. of AFIPS Conf.,* Vol. 46, pp. 85–96.

SIEGEL, H. J. [1979]. "Interconnection Networks for SIMD Machines." *IEEE Computer,* Vol. 12, No. 6, pp. 57–65.

SILBERSCHATZ, A., and KEDEM, Z. [1980]. "Consistency in Hierarchical Database Systems." *JACM,* Vol. 27, No. 1, pp. 72–80.

SLADE, A. E., and MCMAHON, H. O. [1956]. "A Cryotron Catalog Memory System." *Proc. of Eastern JCC*, pp. 115–119.

SLONIM, J., MACRAE, L. J., MENNIE, W. E., and DIAMOND, N. [1981]. "NDX-100, An Electronic Filing Machine for the Office of the Future." *IEEE Computer*, Vol. 14, No. 5, pp. 24–36.

SLOTNICK, D. L. [1970]. "Logic per Track Devices." *Advances in Computers*. New York: Academic Press, pp. 291–296.

SLOTNICK, D. L., BORCK, W. C., and REYNOLDS, R. C. [1962]. "The SOLOMON Computer." *FJCC, AFIPS Proc.*, Vol. 22, pp. 97–107.

SMITH, J. M., and CHANG, P. Y. [1975]. "Optimizing the Performance of a Relational Algebra Data Base Interface." *CACM*, Vol. 18, No. 10, pp. 568–579.

SMITH, J. M., and SMITH, D. C. P. [1977]. "Database Abstractions: Aggregation and Generalization." *ACM Transactions on Database Systems*, Vol. 2, No. 2, pp. 105–133.

SMITH, J. M. et al. [1981]. "Multibase—Integrating Heterogeneous Distributed Database Systems." *Proc. of AFIPS Conf.*, Vol. 50, pp. 487–499.

SONG, S. W. [1980]. "A Highly Concurrent Tree Machine for Database Applications." *Proc. of Intl. Conf. on Parallel Processing*, pp. 259–268.

SONG, S. W. [1981]. "On a High-Performance VLSI Solution to Database Problems." Ph.D. Thesis, Dept. of Computer Science, Carnegie Mellon University, Pittsburgh, Pa.

STELLHORN, W. H. [1974]. "A Processor for Direct Scanning of Text." Paper presented at *1st Intl. Workshop on Computer Architectures for Nonnumeric Processing*, Dallas.

STELLHORN, W. H. [1977]. "An Information File Processor for Information Retrieval." *IEEE Transactions on Computers*, Vol. C26, No. 12, pp. 1258–1267.

STOLFO, S. J., and SHAW, D. E. [1982]. "DADO: A Tree Structured Machine Architecture for Production Systems." *Proc. of National Conf. on Artificial Intelligence*, pp. 369–388.

STONEBRAKER, M. [1981]. "Operating System Support for Database Management." *CACM*, Vol. 24, No. 7, pp. 412–418.

STONEBRAKER, M., and WONG, E. [1974]. "Access Control in a Relational Database Management System by Query Modification." *Proc. of ACM National Conf.*, pp. 180–187.

SU, S. Y. W., and EMAM, A. [1978]. "CASDAL: CASSM's Data Language." *ACM Transactions on Database Systems*, Vol. 3, No. 1, pp. 57–91.

SU, S. Y. W., and LIPOVSKI, J. [1975]. "CASSM: A Cellular System for Very Large Databases." *Proc. of First Conf. on Very Large Databases*, pp. 456–472.

SU, S. Y. W., NGUYEN, L. H., EMAM, A., and LIPOVSKI, G. J. [1979]. "The Architectural Features and Implementation Techniques of the Multicell CASSM." *IEEE Transactions on Computers*, Vol. C-28, No. 6, pp. 430–445.

SVENSSON, B. [1983]. "LUCAS Processor Array—Design and Application." Ph.D. Dissertation, Department of Computer Engineering, University of Lund, Lund.

TANAKA, Y. [1983a]. "A Data-Stream Database Machine with Large Capacity." In D. K. Hsiao, ed., *Advanced Database Machine Architectures*, pp. 168–202. Englewood Cliffs, N.J.: Prentice-Hall, Inc.

TANAKA, Y. [1983b]. "Adaptive Segmentation Schemes for Large Relational Database Machines." *Proc. of Intl. Workshop on Database Machines,* pp. 293–318.

TANAKA, Y., NOZAKA, Y., and MASUYAMA, A. [1980]. "Pipeline Searching and Sorting Modules as Components of a Data Flow Data Base Computer." *Proc. of IFIP World Congress,* pp. 427–432.

TANSEL, A. U. [1981]. "Design and Evaluation of a Query Processing System for Distributed Database Machine Networks." Ph.D. Thesis, Dept. of Computer Engineering, Middle East Technical University, Ankara.

TEOREY, T. J., and FRY, J. P. [1982]. *Design of Database Structures.* Englewood Cliffs, N.J.: Prentice-Hall, Inc.

THOMAS, R. H. [1979]. "Solution to the Concurrency Control Problem for Multiple Copy Databases." *ACM Transactions on Database Systems,* Vol. 4, No. 2, pp. 180–209.

THURBER, K. J., and WALD, L. D. [1975]. "Associative and Parallel Processors." *ACM Computing Surveys,* Vol. 7, No. 4, pp. 215–255.

TSICHRITZIS, D. C. [1976]. "LSL: A Link and Selector Language." *Proc. of ACM SIGMOD,* pp. 123–133.

TSICHRITZIS, D., and CHRISTODOULAKIS, S. [1983]. "Message Files." *ACM Transactions on Office Information Systems,* Vol. 1, No. 1, pp. 88–98.

TSICHRITZIS, D. C., and LOCHOVSKY, F. H. [1977]. *Data Base Management Systems.* New York: Academic Press.

TSICHRITZIS, D. C., and LOCHOVSKY, F. H. [1982]. *Data Models.* Englewood Cliffs, N.J.: Prentice-Hall, Inc.

UEMURA, T., YUBA, T., KOKUBU, A., OOMOTE, R., and SUGAWARA, Y. [1980]. "Implementation of a Magnetic Bubble Database Machine." *Proc. of IFIP World Congress,* pp. 433–438.

ULLMAN, J. D. [1982]. *Principles of Database Systems,* 2nd ed. Rockville, Md.: Computer Science Press.

UNITED STATES PATENT AND TRADEMARK OFFICE [1984]. "Method and System for Matching Encoded Characters." U.S. Patent 4,450,520.

UNITED STATES PATENT AND TRADEMARK OFFICE [1980]. "Finite State Automaton with Multiple State Types." U.S. Patent 4,241,402.

UNIVERSITY OF FLORIDA [1976]. "A Collected Description of CASSM: A Context Addressed Segment Sequential Memory." Dept. of Electrical Engineering, Technical Report No. 5, Gainesville, Fla.

VAN RIJSBERGEN, C. J. [1974]. "Further Experiments with Hierarchical Clustering in Document Retrieval." *Information Storage and Retrieval,* Vol. 10, pp. 1–14.

VAN RIJSBERGEN, C. J. [1979]. *Information Retrieval,* 2nd ed. London: Butterworth Scientific Publishers.

VASSILIOU, Y., and LOCHOVSKY, F. H. [1980]. "DBMS Transaction Translation." *Proc. of IEEE Compsac Conf.,* pp. 89–96.

WEIDE, B. W. [1978]. "Statistical Methods in Algorithm Design and Analysis." Ph.D. Thesis, Department of Computer Science, Carnegie Mellon University, Pittsburgh, Pa.

WONG, E. [1977]. "Retrieving Dispersed Data from SDD-1: A System for Distributed

Databases." *Proc. of 2nd Berkeley Conf. on Distributed Data Management and Computer Networks,* pp. 217–235.

YANG, C. C., and YAO, S. S. [1966]. "A Cutpoint Cellular Associative Memory." *IEEE Transactions on Computers,* EC-15, pp. 522–528.

YAU, S. S., and FUNG, H. S. [1977]. "Associative Processor Architecture Survey." *ACM Computing Surveys,* Vol. 9, No. 1, pp. 3–28.

YU, C. T., and CHANG, C. C. [1983]. "On the Design of a Query Processing Strategy in a Distributed Database Environment." *Proc. of ACM SIGMOD Conf.,* pp. 30–39.

ZIPF, H. P. [1949]. *Human Behavior and the Principle of Least Effort.* Reading, Mass.: Addison-Wesley.

DATABASE MACHINE SOFTWARE SYSTEMS

For Hands-on Experience with

- Conceptual modeling
- ANSI/SPARC-like GDBMS
- Relational, hierarchical, and network database programming
- Context-sensitive full text retrieval
- Associative/parallel and tag-based database programming

all of which come within the following architecture:

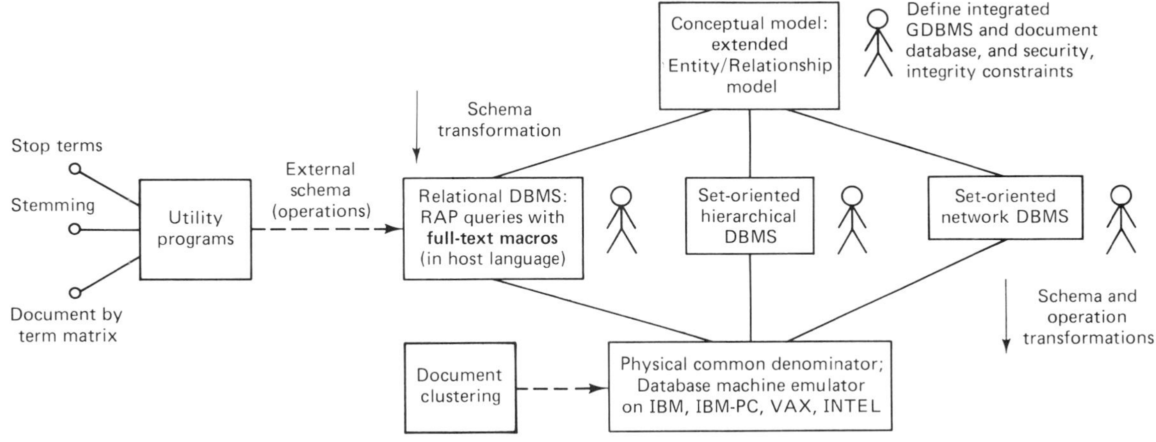

Full System

GDBMS + full text system + emulator + language translators and a host language – (VAX/UNIX)

This is the most powerful, versatile, and user friendly software. It includes an interactive GDBMS command language, for schema definition and modification, and external schema translators. It provides interactive text editing and UNIX escape facilities. A dynamic security/integrity mechanism and a powerful data dictionary system are included. In this software, RAP programs can also be imbedded in the C language. The extended Entity/Relationship model (including generalizations and aggregations) is the conceptual schema. Various administrative utilities, hierarchical user capability–granting and revoking facilities, and a limited view mechanism are included. Also, a context sensitive full text search system is integrated with this GDBMS. Interactive word stem generation and stop list exclusion utilities for external index (cluster) generation are available.

Subsets (Standalone)

- GDBMS + emulator (with MRI and LSL) – (VAX/UNIX)
- (RAP) relational DBMS + full text (with/without host language) – (UNIX)
- (RAP) relational DBMS (with MRI and LSL and/or Form Interface) – (VAX/UNIX, IBM—PC/IX, (UNIX); INTEL—ISIS-III, iNDX, iRMX86 for the form system)
- (RAP) relational DBMS with SEQUEL (IBM–OS/MVS)

The software cited is available for educational and experimental use and for production systems (in small- to medium-sized applications of up to about 50 megabytes).

A one-time usage fee is required with educational discounts. A further discount is available for those who adopt *Database Machines and Database Management* by E. Ozkarahan as the textbook for their courses. Discounted usage fees start from $316 for a configuration such as RAP Relational DBMS including MRI and LSL, or SEQUEL.

For the terms of software usage and further details, write to: Database Machine Technology, P. O. Box 5115, Scottsdale, Arizona, USA, 85261.

INDEX

S